AA

GUEST[HOUSES] FARMH[OUSES] & INNS IN EUROPE

Editor: Jeremy Kirk
Designer: Howard Aldridge
Compilers: Publications Research Unit
Maps: Cartographic Unit
Advertising: Peter Whitworth, *tel* Basingstoke 20123

Phototypeset by Vantage Photosetting Ltd, Southampton

Printed and bound by Wm Clowes Ltd, Beccles

CONTENTS

Symbols and abbreviations

The contents of this publication are believed correct at the time of printing, but the current position may be checked through the AA.

Produced by the Publications Division of the Automobile Association, Fanum House, Basingstoke, Hants RG21 2EA.

We gratefully acknowledge Featurepix, Jeremy Kirk and the Tourist Offices, Boards and Departments of the countries represented in this book for providing photographs.

© The Automobile Association 1979 ISBN 0 901088 97 8   55767

Those of us who remember motoring in Europe in the early 1960s fondly recall the days of relatively cheap petrol and a reasonably strong pound. It seemed as if you could just pop across the Channel and enjoy a really good holiday without breaking the bank.

Nowadays, what with oil crises, inflation and a wobbly pound, such holidays seem out of most people's reach. And if you don't want to go through the bother of tugging a caravan all over the place or setting up tents and things every night, how can you afford to have a motoring holiday in Europe any more?

Well, motoring in Europe was never *that* cheap – but there is no denying that today it can be very expensive indeed. This is where **Guesthouses, Farmhouses and Inns in Europe** can help. We can't do anything about petrol prices, inflation or exchange rates, but we can point you towards reasonably-priced accommodation where you can stay in comfort without hurting your pocket. Most of the establishments in this guide will cost less than £5 per night at some time in the year – many will be a good deal less – and let's face it, you would probably be paying as much per night in this country.

So whether you are planning a low-cost motor tour of Europe or just want some inexpensive places to stay en route to your destination on the Continent, **Guesthouses, Farmhouses and Inns in Europe** will be your best companion. The location of maps in the front of the book will show you where the nearest accommodation is and the lists on pages 87–217 give you details of the establishments town by town, country by country. See page 85 on how to use this guide.

In addition, this guide gives you sound, no-nonsense advice to help you plan and prepare your motoring holiday. On pages 48–64 you will find some helpful hints to keep your costs to a minimum – when and how to go, how to keep an eye on your daily expenses and petrol costs – and on pages 218–252 there's a reference section detailing just about all you need to know to prepare for and to take your holiday – the documents you need, preparing your vehicle, motoring law and so forth. On page 65 our special colour feature takes this guide into action on two back-road routes to the Riviera and to Spain which you might like to try.

So good planning and good luck – we hope you will be able to have a motoring holiday in Europe this year and that this guide will make it easier and more enjoyable.

AA # Guesthouses, Farmhouses and Inns in Europe

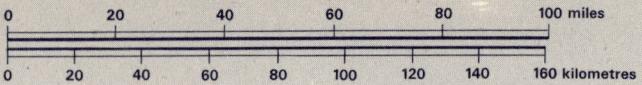

0	20	40	60	80		100 miles

0	20	40	60	80	100	120	140	160 kilometres

SCALE OF ATLAS: 33 MILES TO ONE INCH (APPROX)

Map Legend

Motorway and junction	
Toll motorway	
Motorway under construction	
Transit route (GDR)	
Single carriage motorway	
Principal route	
Main road	
Other road	
Mountain road tunnel	
Mountain pass	
Mountain railway tunnel connection	
Road snowbound during winter	
Road number	E4
Distance in kilometres	22
Frontier	
Town with gazetteer entry	Clamecy ●
Town	○
Hovercraft ferry	Ⓗ
Vehicle ferry	– – – Ⓥ OSLO
River and lake	Drava
Canal	
Mountain/Volcano	▲
Overlaps and numbers of continuing pages	10

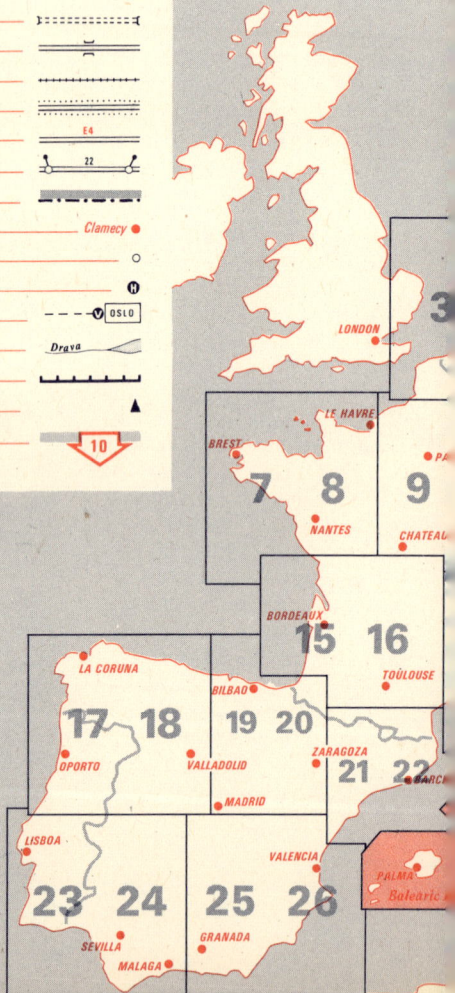

LONDON

LE HAVRE

BREST

PA

7   8   9

NANTES

CHATEAU

BORDEAUX

15   16

TOULOUSE

LA CORUNA

BILBAO

17   18   19   20

ZARAGOZA

OPORTO   VALLADOLID   21   22

BARCH

MADRID

LISBOA

VALENCIA

PALMA

23   24   25   26

Balearic I

SEVILLA

GRANADA

MALAGA

© The Automobile Association

Key to atlas pages

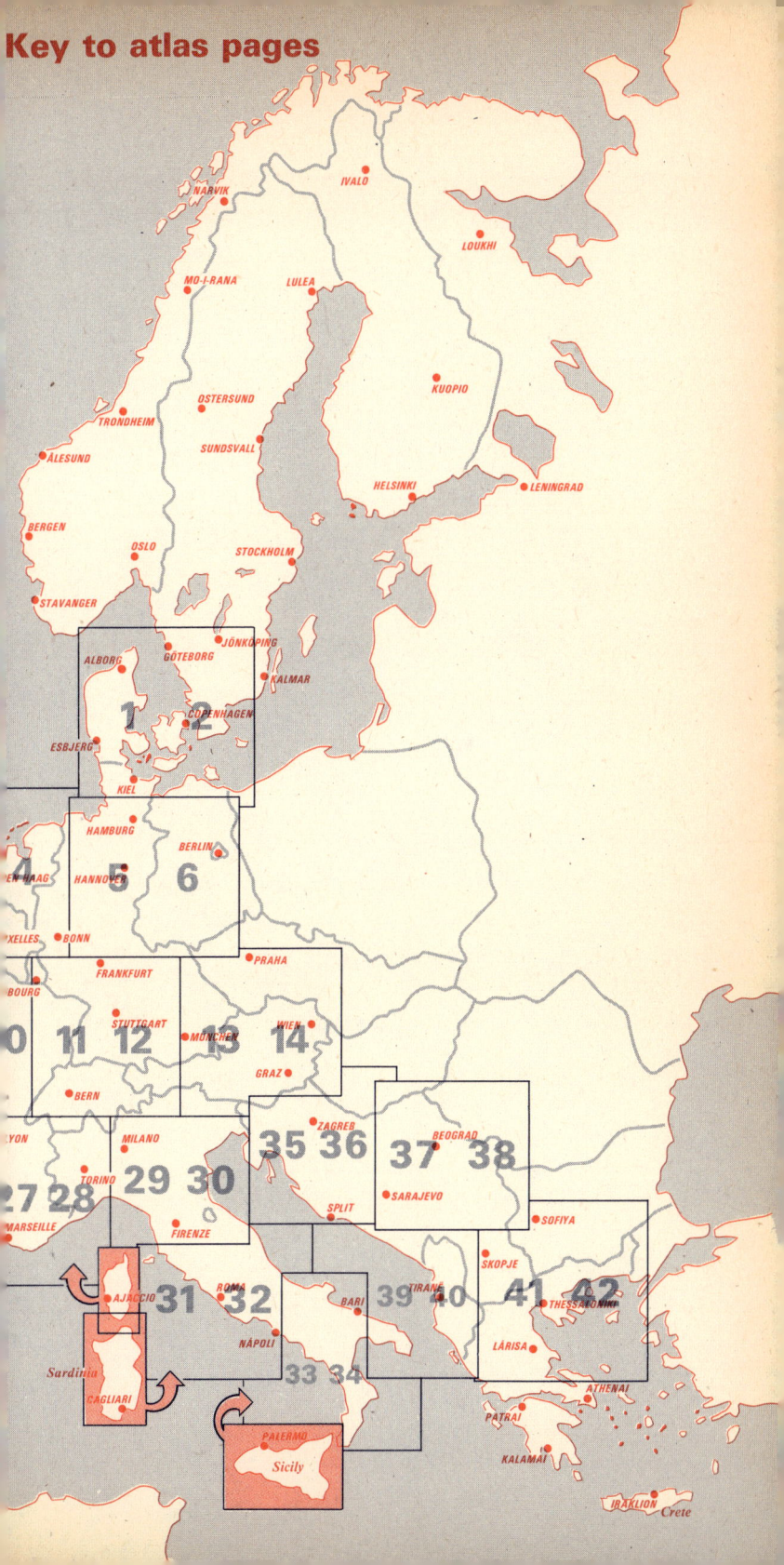

NARVIK
IVALO
LOUKHI
MO-I-RANA
LULEA
KUOPIO
OSTERSUND
TRONDHEIM
SUNDSVALL
ÅLESUND
HELSINKI
LENINGRAD
BERGEN
OSLO
STOCKHOLM
STAVANGER

1
ALBORG
GÖTEBORG
JÖNKÖPING
KALMAR
2
COPENHAGEN
ESBJERG
KIEL

5
HAMBURG
BERLIN
EN HAAG
HANNOVER
6

XELLES
BONN
BOURG
FRANKFURT
PRAHA

10
11
12
STUTTGART
13
MÜNCHEN
14
WIEN
BERN
GRAZ

LYON
MILANO
ZAGREB
35
36
37
BEOGRAD
38
27
28
TORINO
29
30
SARAJEVO
SPLIT
SOFIYA
MARSEILLE
FIRENZE
SKOPJE

AJACCIO
31
ROMA
32
BARI
39
TIRANE
40
41
42
THESSALONIKI
Sardinia
NÁPOLI
LÁRISA
CAGLIARI
33
34
ATHENAI
PATRAI
PALERMO
Sicily
KALAMAI
IRAKLION
Crete

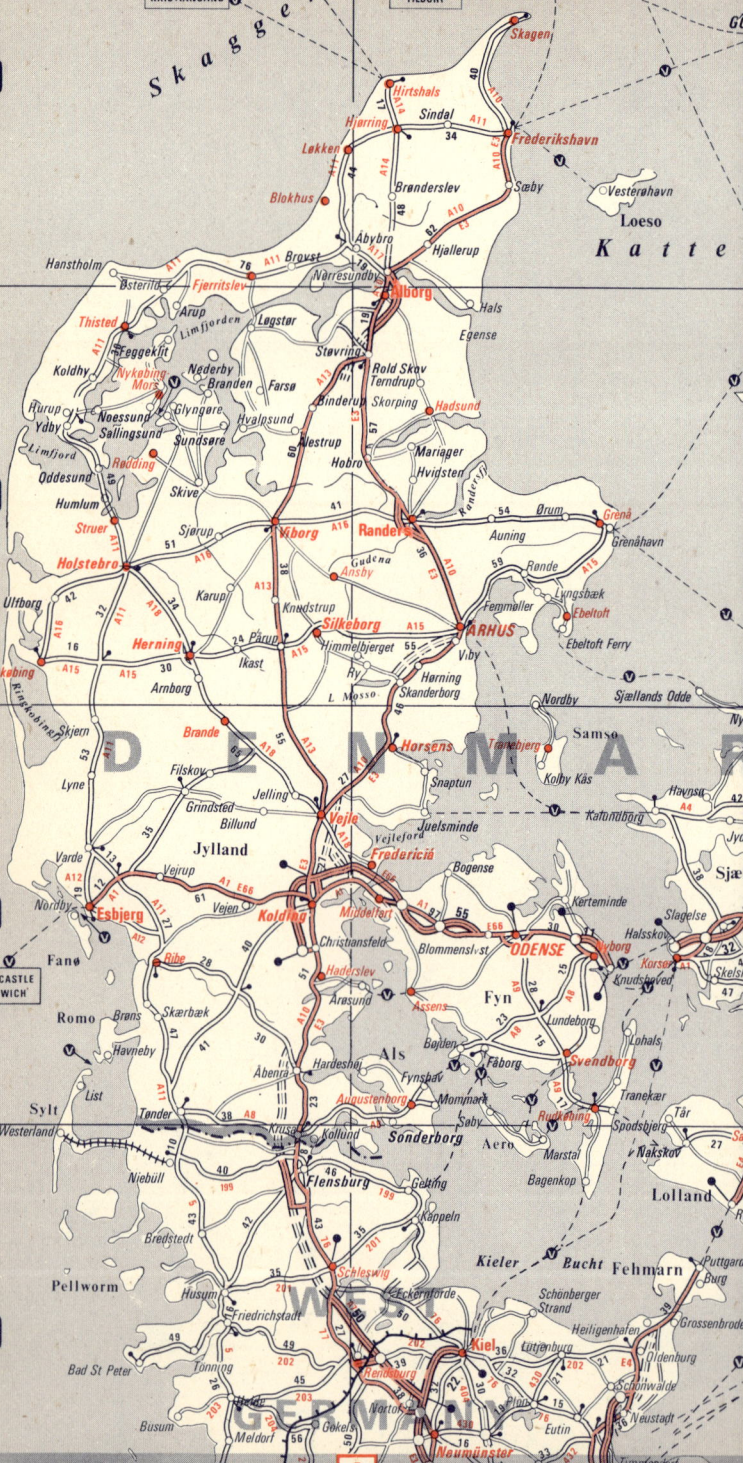

A — ARENDAL — LARVIK FREDRIKSTAD OSLO — B
Orust
Tjörn
OSLO
Kristiansand
Marstrand
HULL IMMINGHAM TILBURY
Skagen
GÖ
S k a g e r r a k
4
Hirtshals
Hjørring   Sindal
Frederikshavn
Løkken
Brønderslev
Sæby
Vesterøhavn
Blokhus
Loeso
K a t t e g
Hansholm
Åbybro
Hjallerup
Brovst
Hals
Østerild   Fjerritslev
Nørresundby
Ålborg
Egense
Thisted
Arup   Løgstør
Støvring
Feggeklit
Rold Skov
Nykøbing   Nederby   Terndrup
Koldby   Mors   Branden   Farsø   Skørping
Hadsund
Rurup   Noessund   Glyngøre   Hvalsund
Ydby   Sallingsund   Sundsøre   Nestrup
Mariager
Rødding   Hobro   Hvidsten
Limfjord   Oddesund   Skive
3
Humlum   Sjørup
Randers
Ørum   Grenå
Holstebro   Viborg   Ansby
Auning   Rønde   Grenåhavn
Ulfborg   Karup   Knudstrup
Femmøller   Ebeltoft
Herning   Silkeborg   Lyngsbæk
Ry   Himmelbjerget   ÅRHUS   Ebeltoft Ferry
Ringkøbing   Ikast   Hørning   Viby
Arnborg   L. Mosso   Skanderborg   Nordby   Sjællands Odde
Skjern   Lyne   Brande   Horsens   Samsø   Nyk
D E N M A R
Filskov   Tranebjerg
Jelling   Snaptun   Kolby Kås   Havnsu
Grindsted   Vejle   Juelsminde   Kalundborg   Jyd
Varde   Billund   Vejlefjord
Jylland   Fredericia   Bogense   Kerteminde   Slagelse   Sjæ
2   Vejrup   E66   Middelfart   ODENSE   Nyborg   Halsskov   Korsør
Nordby   Esbjerg   Vejen   Kolding   Blommenslyst   Knudshoved   Skelsk
Fanø   Christiansfeld   Fyn   Lundeborg   Lohals
NEWCASTLE HARWICH   Ribe   Haderslev   Arøsund   Bøjden   Fåborg   Svendborg   Tranekær   Tår
Romø   Brøns   Skærbæk   Als   Fynshav   Mommark   Rudkøbing   Spodsbjerg   Nakskov
Havneby   Åbenrå   Hardeshøj   Søby   Aerø   Marstal
Sylt   List   Augustenborg   Sønderborg   Bagenkop   Lolland
Westerland   Tønder   Kruså   Kollund   Gelting   Re
Niebüll   Flensburg   Kappeln   Puttgard   Burg
Bredstedt   Kieler   Bucht   Fehmarn   Grossenbrode
Pellworm   Schleswig   Schönberger Strand   Oldenburg   Neustadt
Husum   WEST   Eckernförde   Heiligenhafen   Schönwalde
1   Friedrichstadt   Kiel   Lütjenburg   Eutin
Bad St Peter   Rendsburg   Nortorf   Plön   Gnissau
Büsum   GERMANY   Eckels   Neumünster   Timmendorf
Meldorf   Timmendorf
Marne   Bad   Travemünde   Wis
Scharhorn   Itzehoe   Bramstedt   Bad Segeberg
Cuxhaven   Brunsbüttel   Lentföhrden   Lübeck   Greves
A — B

SWEDEN

Hanobukten

BALTIC SEA

EAST GERMANY (DDR)

Bornholm

COPENHAGEN

MALMÖ

Helsingör

Landskrona

Roskilde

Halmstad

Borås

Jönköping

Huskvarna

Växjö

Kristianstad

Karlshamn

Ronneby

Rostock

Stralsund

Greifswald

Rügen

Falster

Møn

NYNASHAMN HELSINKI

SLITE HELSINKI

Zatoka Pomorska

4

3

2

1

Great Yarmouth

GOTHENBURG   MIDDLESBROUGH   GOTHENBURG

HULL

Felixstowe
Harwich

Sche
DEN HA

Hook of Holland
Europoort
Briel

Ouddorp
Middelharnis
Noordgouwe
Zierikzee
Zijpe
Burgh

Domburg   Veere   Anna Jac

Middelburg   Goes

Vlissingen (Flushing)
Breskens
Schoondijke
Terneuzen
Oostburg

Zeebrugge
Knokke
Heist
Het Zoute
Blankenberge
Wenduine
De Haan

Oostende
Raversijde
Middelkerke
Westende
Nieuwpoort
Koksijde
De Panne

Brugge   Eeklo   Aalter

ANT
Beveren
St Niklaas
Lokeren

GENT
Schelde
Dendermonde

Torhout   Deurle

Roeselare   Izegem

Oudenaarde   Ninove

BRUXEL

Ramsgate

Dover
Folkestone

Dunkerque
Bergues
Diksmuide
Ieper
Kortrijk
Wevelgem
Ronse   Brakel

Sh

Blériot-Plage
Wissant
Calais
Gravelines
Ardres
Tilques
St-Omer
Cassel
Bailleul
Poperinge
Menen

Tourcoing
Roubaix
Kluisbergen
Ath
Enghien
Halle

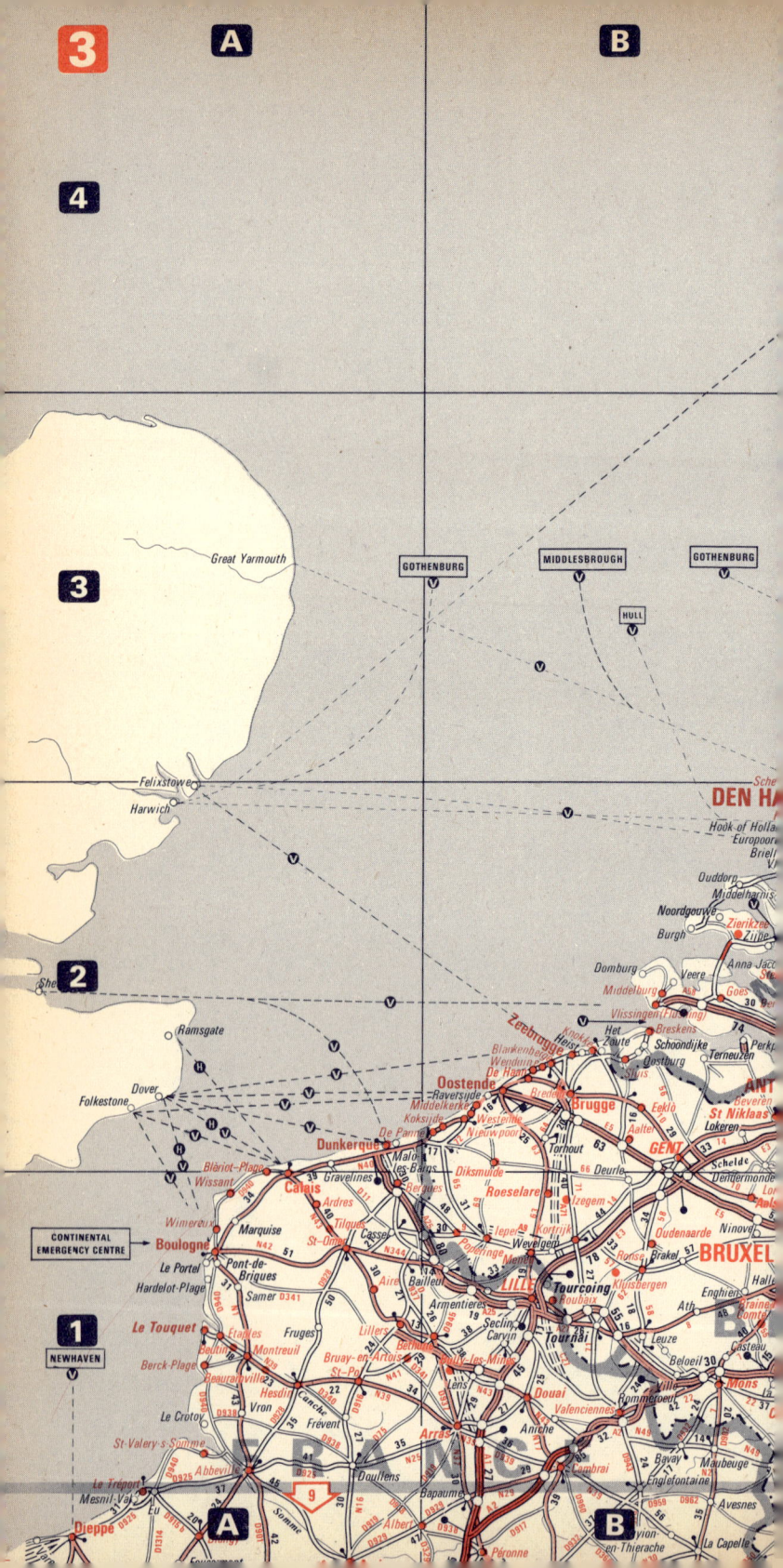

CONTINENTAL
EMERGENCY CENTRE → Boulogne

Marquise
Pont-de-Briques
Samer
Aire
Armentieres
LILLE
Tournai
Leuze
Beloeil
Casteau

Le Portel
Hardelot-Plage

Le Touquet
Etaples
Montreuil
Fruges
Lillers
Seclin
Carvin
Bruay-en-Artois
St-Pol
Bethune
Lens
Douai
Valenciennes
Mons

NEWHAVEN

Berck-Plage
Beaurainville
Hesdin
Canche
Vron
Frévent
Aniche
Bavay
Maubeuge
Englefontaine
Avesnes

Le Crotoy
Arras
Cambrai

St-Valery-s-Somme
Bapaume
Péronne
La Capelle

Le Tréport
Abbeville
Doullens
Mesnil-Val
Somme
Albert
vion-
en-Thierache

Dieppe

FRANCE

C · D · 4

KRISTIANSAND ESBJERG

BREMERHAVN HAMBURG

Nordene Langeoog
Juist Benserstel 4
Borkum Norddeich Norden
Schiermonnikoog Norddeich Ogenbargen Aurich
Ameland Uithuizen Georgsheil Emden
Terschelling Holwerd Grijpskerk Winsum Delfzijl Neermoor Hesel Logo
Vlieland Waddenzee Harlingen Groningen Nieuwe Neermoor Leer Zwis
De Koog Leeuwarden Haren Schans Winschoten Papenburg
Texel Bolsward Drachten Eelde Zuidbroek Aschendorf 401
Den Burg Sneek Paterswolde Veendam Geiten
Den Helder Staveren Heerenveen Donkerbroek Assen Lathen Rütenbrock Cloppe
De Kooy Rijs Wolvega Smilde Beilen Lastrups
Lemmer IJsselmeer Steenwijk Emmen Loningen
Alkmaar Emmeloord Eursinge Hoogeveen Apel Meppen Bersenbrüc
Enkhuizen Urk Meppel Emlichheim Lingen Bramsc
Beverwijk Hoorn Kampen Balkbrug Neuenhaus 3
Haarlem Edam Volendam Lelystad Zwolle Ommen Wierden Nordhorn 5
AMSTERDAM Zaandam FLEVOLAND Dronten Raalte Almelo Oldenzaal Rheine
Naarden Blaricum Harderwijk Nijverdal Hengelo Bentheim
Leiden Hilversum Gussum Deventer Holten Delden Enschede Gronau Glane
Alphen Loosdrecht Baarn Apeldoorn Vierhouten Lochem Münster
UTRECHT Doorn Ede Rotterdaal Warnsveld Ahaus Horstmar
Delft Wageningen Arnhem Zutphen Groenlo Winterswijk Coesfeld Dülmen Münster
ROTTERDAM Gouda Tiel Druten Nijmegen Doetinchem Katten Oding Borken Haltern Hamm
Dordrecht Gorinchem Groesbeek Kleve Bocholt Dorsten Marl Recklinghausen Herne
Etten-Leur Breda sHertogenbosch Goch Weser Gelsen Wanne Bochum DORTMUND Unna
Oisterwijk Kevelaer Geldern Oberhausen Duisburg Mülheim ESSEN Velbert Hagen Iserl
Tilburg Eindhoven Venray Arcen Venlo Kempen Moers Witten Menden
Turnhout Helmond Asten Krefeld DÜSSELDORF Wuppertal Remscheid Lüdensch
Kasterlee Mol Lommel Weert Viersen Neuss Solingen Opladen Wipperfurth
Herentals Leopoldsburg Hechtel Roermond Mönchen Rheydt Elfgen Leverkusen Bergisch Gladbach
Lier Beringen Opglabbeek Bree As Gladbach Heinsberg Grevenbroich
Aarschot Diest Zolder Sittard Geilenkirchen KÖLN Gummersbach Derschlag
Hasselt Stein Nuth Heerlen Jülich Frechen Numbre
Leuven Tienen Tongeren Maastricht Valkenburg Schwer Brühl Siegburg Waldbr
Wavre Vise Herbesthal Düren Bonn
LIEGE Calamine Zülpich Beuel Bad Hon
Namur Huy Verviers Eupen Euskirchen Schleiden Altenahr Bad Neuenahr Bad Breisig Andernach Neuwied
Gembloux Seraing Theux Spa Monschau Malmedy Adenau Maria Laach Mayen Koblenz
Gosselies Remouchamps Losheim Nürburg Kelberg
Bouvignes Dinant Ligneuville St Vith Stadtkyll Boppard
Anseremme Houyet Vielsalm Trois Ponts Prüm Daun Cochem
La Roche Marche Nadrin Manderscheid Treis Kastellaun
10 Champlon Wemperhaardt Bitburg Wittlich Zell
C Bastogne Clervaux Marnach D 11 Cochem

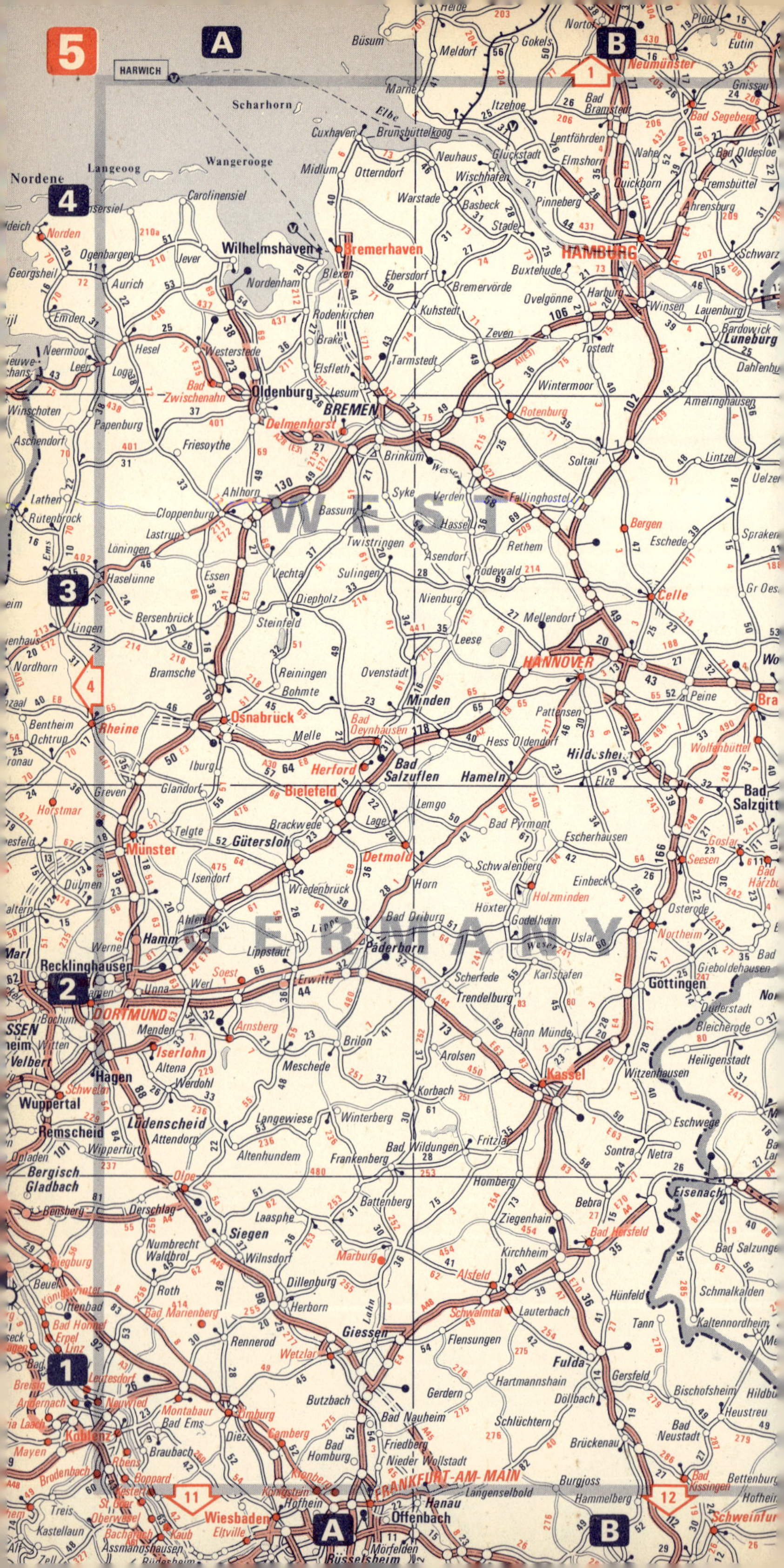

5
A
B
HARWICH
WEST GERMANY
Büsum
Scharhorn
Langeoog
Wangerooge
Nordene
Carolinensiel
Norden
Georgsheil
Ogenbargen
Aurich
Jever
Emden
Wilhelmshaven
Nordenham
Bremerhaven
Blexen
Cuxhaven
Brunsbüttelkoog
Marne
Meldorf
Gokels
Nortorf
Neumünster
Itzehoe
Bad Bramstedt
Bad Segeberg
Bad Oldesloe
Eutin
Plön
Heide
Glückstadt
Elmshorn
Lentföhrden
Nahe
Quickborn
Pinneberg
Ahrensburg
Tremsbüttel
Schwarz
HAMBURG
Harburg
Winsen
Lauenburg
Bardowick
Lüneburg
Dahlenburg
Buxtehude
Stade
Wischhafen
Neuhaus
Basbeck
Warstade
Otterndorf
Midlum
Ebersdorf
Bremervörde
Ovelgönne
Kuhstedt
Zeven
Tostedt
Rodenkirchen
Brake
Elsfleth
Tarmstedt
Wintermoor
Lesum
BREMEN
Oldenburg
Delmenhorst
Bad Zwischenahn
Westerstede
Hesel
Leer
Neermoor
Logabirum
Papenburg
Winschoten
Aschendorf
Friesoythe
Rotenburg
Soltau
Brinkum
Syke
Verden
Fallingbostel
Bassum
Ahlhorn
Cloppenburg
Lastrup
Löningen
Haselünne
Lathen
Rutenbrock
Twistringen
Sulingen
Asendorf
Hassel
Rethem
Bergen
Eschede
Celle
Amelinghausen
Lintzel
Uelzen
Sprakensehl
Vechta
Diepholz
Essen
Bersenbrück
Lingen
Nordhorn
Bentheim
Ochtrup
Rheine
Steinfeld
Bramsche
Reiningen
Bohmte
Osnabrück
Melle
Nienburg
Rodewald
Mellendorf
Leese
Ovenstädt
Minden
Bad Oeynhausen
HANNOVER
Peine
Pattensen
Hess Oldendorf
Hildesheim
Wolfenbüttel
Elze
Hameln
Bad Salzuflen
Herford
Bielefeld
Iburg
Glandorf
Greven
Horstmar
Münster
Telgte
Gütersloh
Brackwede
Lage
Lemgo
Detmold
Bad Pyrmont
Escherhausen
Einbeck
Bad Salzgitter
Goslar
Seesen
Bad Harzburg
Isendorf
Wiedenbrück
Horn
Schwalenberg
Holzminden
Höxter
Godelheim
Uslar
Northeim
Osterode
Bad Driburg
Paderborn
Lippstadt
Erwitte
Soest
Werl
Unna
Hamm
Ahlen
Werne
Dulmen
Haltern
Marl
Recklinghausen
DORTMUND
Bochum
Witten
Hagen
Iserlohn
Arnsberg
Menden
Altena
Werdohl
Schwelm
Wuppertal
Remscheid
Velbert
Opladen
Bergisch Gladbach
Lüdenscheid
Attendorn
Wipperfürth
Meschede
Brilon
Scherfede
Trendelburg
Karlshafen
Göttingen
Gieboldehausen
Duderstadt
Bleicherode
Heiligenstadt
Witzenhausen
Hann Münden
Kassel
Arolsen
Korbach
Winterberg
Langewiese
Altenhundem
Frankenberg
Bad Wildungen
Fritzlar
Eschwege
Sontra
Netra
Eisenach
Olpe
Derschlag
Bensberg
Siegburg
Siegen
Laasphe
Battenberg
Homberg
Ziegenhain
Bebra
Bad Hersfeld
Bad Salzungen
Schmalkalden
Numbrecht Waldbrol
Wilnsdorf
Dillenburg
Herborn
Marburg
Alsfeld
Kirchheim
Hünfeld
Tann
Kaltennordheim
Königswinter
Bad Honnef
Erpel
Linz
Roth
Bad Marienberg
Rennerod
Wetzlar
Giessen
Schwalmtal
Lauterbach
Flensungen
Fulda
Gersfeld
Hartmannshain
Döllbach
Bischofsheim
Butzbach
Gerdern
Schlüchtern
Brückenau
Bad Neustadt
Neuwied
Andernach
Koblenz
Mayen
Montabaur
Bad Ems
Limburg
Diez
Camberg
Bad Nauheim
Friedberg
Bad Homburg
Nieder Wollstadt
Braubach
Boppard
Rhens
Brodenbach
St. Goar
Oberwesel
Bacharach
Kaub
Treis
Kastellaun
Wiesbaden
Eltville
Königstein
Kronberg
Hofheim
FRANKFURT-AM-MAIN
Offenbach
Hanau
Langenselbold
Burgjoss
Hammelberg
Bad Kissingen
Schweinfurt
Bettenburg
Rüsselsheim
Mörfelden
Assmannshausen
Elbe
Weser
Ems
Lippe
Lahn

ROSTOCK · WISMAR · Schwerin · GÜSTROW · Neubrandenburg · SZCZECIN · MAGDEBURG · BERLIN · POTSDAM · DRESDEN · LEIPZIG · HALLE · ERFURT · GERA · ZWICKAU · KARL MARX STADT (CHEMNITZ) · Karlovy Vary (Carlsbad) · Bayreuth

E A S T   G E R M A N Y   (D D R)

C Z E C H O S L O V A K I A

A
B

4

ENGLISH   CHANNEL

Guerns

L'Erée

PLYMOUTH

CHANNEL
ISLANDS

PLYMOUTH
PORTSMOUTH

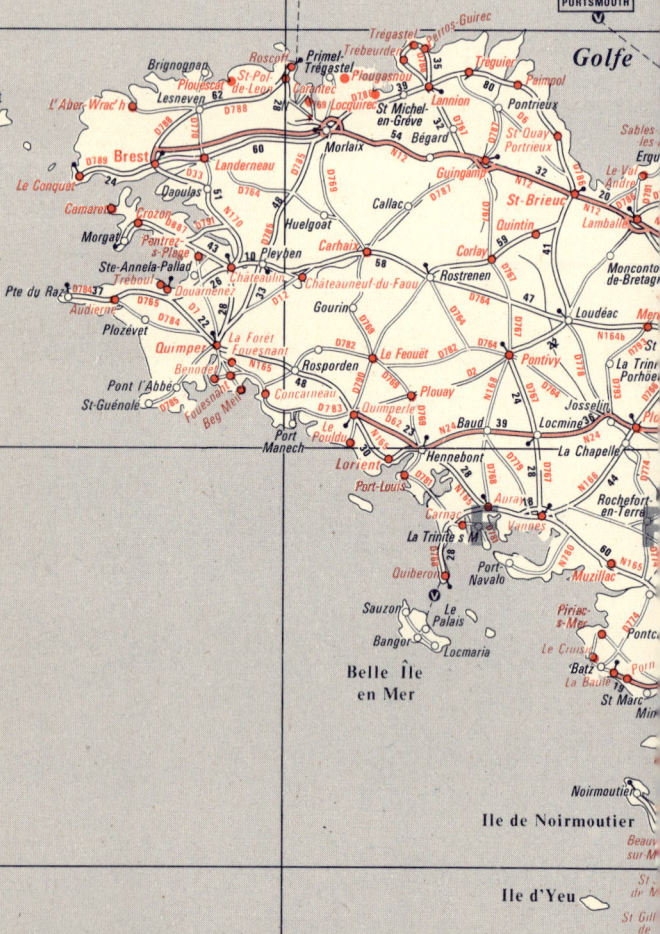

Golfe

Tregastel
Trebeurde
De105-Guirec
Roscoff
Primel
Trégastel
Treguie
Peimpol
Brignognan
Plouescat
St-Pol-
de-Leon
Carantec
Plougasnou
35
80
I d'Ouessant
L'Abor-Wrac'h
Plouescat
Lesneven
D788
Locquirec
Lannion
Pontrieux
St-Michel-
en-Grève
St-Quay
Portrieux
Sables-
les-
Erqu
Brest
D189
Landerneau
D788
54
Bégard
N12
Le Val
Andre
Le Conquet
60
Morlaix
Guingamp
St-Brieuc
20
24
Camaret
Crozon
D791
N170
D764
D769
32
D787
Lamballe
Morgat
Daoulas
Callac
D767
Quintin
N
Pontret-
s-Plage
43
Ste-Anne-la-Pallad
Trebou
Châteaulin
Huelgoat
Carhaix
58
Corlay
59
Monconto
de-Bretagne
Pte du Raz
Douarnener
D27
28
Châteauneuf-du-Faou
41
47
Loudéac
Mer
Audierne
D765
Gourin
Rostrenen
D764
D767
N164b
Plozévet
D782
D768
D764
Pontivy
La Trine
Porhöe
Quimper
La Forêt
Fouesnant
N165
Benod
Rosporden
48
Le Feouët
D768
N118
Josselin
D790
Plc
Pont l'Abbé
Concarneau
24
Locmine
St-Guénole
Fouesnant
Beg Meil
Quimperle
Plouay
D783
Baud
39
La Chapelle
Port-
Manech
Le
Pouldu
Hennebont
28
N24
Lorient
Port-Louis
Auray
Rochefort-
en-Terre
Carnac
Vannes
La Trinité s M
D780
28
Port-
Navalo
N165
Muzillac
Quiberon
Piriac-
s-Mer
Pontc
Sauzon
Le
Palais
Le Crois
Batz
Porn
Bangor
Locmaria
La Baule
St Marc
Min

2

Belle Île
en Mer

Noirmoutier

Ile de Noirmoutier

Beauv
sur M

1

Ile d'Yeu

St
dr M

St Gill
de

BAY   OF   BISCAY

A
B

WEYMOUTH
SOUTHAMPTON WEYMOUTH
SOUTHAMPTON

Alderney
Auderville
Les Pieux
Blicquebec
Carteret
Barneville Carteret
La Haye-du-Puits
Lessay
Coutainville
Montmartin-sur-Mer

Cherbourg
Maupertus
Valognes
St-Vaast-la-Hougue
Barfleur
Ste-Mère-Eglise
Carentan
Périers
St-Lô
Coutances
Villers-Bocage

Grandcamp Maisy
St-Laurent
Arromanches-s-Mer
Courseulles-s-Mer
St Aubin-sur-mer
Lion-s-Mer
Bayeux
Tilly-s-Seulles
Caen
Isigny-sur-Mer

Honfleur
Deauville
Trouville
Blonville
Villerville

LE HAVRE
Figuefleur
Tancarville
La Bouille
Pont Audemer
Bourgtheroulde
St Maclou
Pont l'Evêque
Lisieux
Brionne
Elbeu
Louvi

Varengeville
St-Valery-en-Caux
Veules-les-R
Veulettes-sur-Mer
Cany-Barville
Fécamp
Yport
Etretat
Antifer
Cauville
Harfleur
Bolbec
Yvetot
Caudebec
Duclair

LE MANS
Bernay
Orbec-en-Auge
Conches-en-Ouche
La Vieille-Lyre
Breteuil
Nonancou
Verneuil
La Ferté-Vidame
Senonches
La Loupe
La Fourche
Nogent-le-Rotrou
Chapelle-Royale
Châteaudun

St Malo
St Servan
St Briac
Dinan
Dol
Combourg
Hédé
St-Aubin-du-Cormier
Bédée
Rennes
Vitré
Laval
Château-Gontier
Segré
Candé
Châteaubriant
La Chapelle-Glain
Nozay
Blain
Bouvron
Nort
Ancenis
Varades
NANTES
Champtoceaux
Les Ponts-de-Cé
Beaupréau
Chemillé
Clisson
Cholet
Vihiers
Doué
Montaigu
Belleville-s-Vie
La Roche-sur-Yon
Chantonnay
Ste-Hermine
Luçon
Fontenay-le-Comte
Marans
Niort
Mauzé
Surgères
La Rochelle
Pallice
Châtelaillon-Plage
Ile de Ré
St-Martin-de-Ré
La Flotte
Aiguillon-s-Mer

Granville
Jullouville
St Pair
Avranches
Pontaubault
Mont-St-Michel
Pontorson
Antrain-sur-Couesnon
St-Hilaire-du-Harcouet
Fougères
Ernée
Mayenne
La Croixille
Evron
Sablé-sur-Sarthe
La Flèche
Le Lude
Baugé
Les Rosiers
Noyant
Saumur
Montreuil-Bellay
Thouars
Bressuire
La Maucarrière
Lencloître
Parthenay
Chauvigny
Lusignan
Gençay
Melle
Chaunay
Chef-Boutonne
St Jean d'Angély
Marennes
Tonnay-Boutonne

Poitiers
Fleuré
Montmorillon
Le Dorat
Bellac
Confolens
Mansle
Pressac
Charroux

Villedieu-les-Poêles
Vire
Brécey
Mortain
Domfront
La Ferté-Macé
Bagnoles-de-l'Orne
Couterne
Pré-en-Pail
Ambrières-les-Vallées
Bais
La Hutte
Alençon
Sées
Carrouges
Rânes
Nonant-le-Pin
Argentan
Le Pin-au-Haras
Gacé
Ste-Gauburge-Ste-Colombe
L'Aigle
Mortagne
Bellème
Mamers
Beaumont-s-S
Bonnétable
Conneré
Le Mans
Arnage
Ecommoy
La Flèche
Château-du-Loir
Château-la-Vallière
Neuillé-Pont-Pierre
Langeais
Tours
Bléré
Chenonceaux
Amboise
Rochecorbon
Montbazon
Azay-le-Rideau
Chinon
Ste-Maure
Loches
Descartes
Grand Pressigny
Châtellerault
La Roche-Posay
Lureuil
Le Blanc
La Trimouille
Châtillon-s-Indre

Thury-Harcourt
Aunay-sur-Odon
Clécy
Condé-s-Noireau
Flers
Fromentel
Falaise
St Pierre-s-Dives
Vimoutiers
Courteilles

Montfort
Montauban
Hédé
Fougères
Teilleul
La Tannière
Ernée
La Croixille
La Guerche-de-Bretagne
Cossé-le-Vivien
Craon
Pouancé
Derval
La Chapelle-Glain
Segré
Champigné
Le Lion-d'Angers
Angers
Seiche-sur-le-Loir
Durtal
Baugé

Cerances
Vimoutiers
Orbec-en-Auge

Pouzauges
La Roche-sur-Yon

Aigre

4
3
2
1
9
15
16
C
D

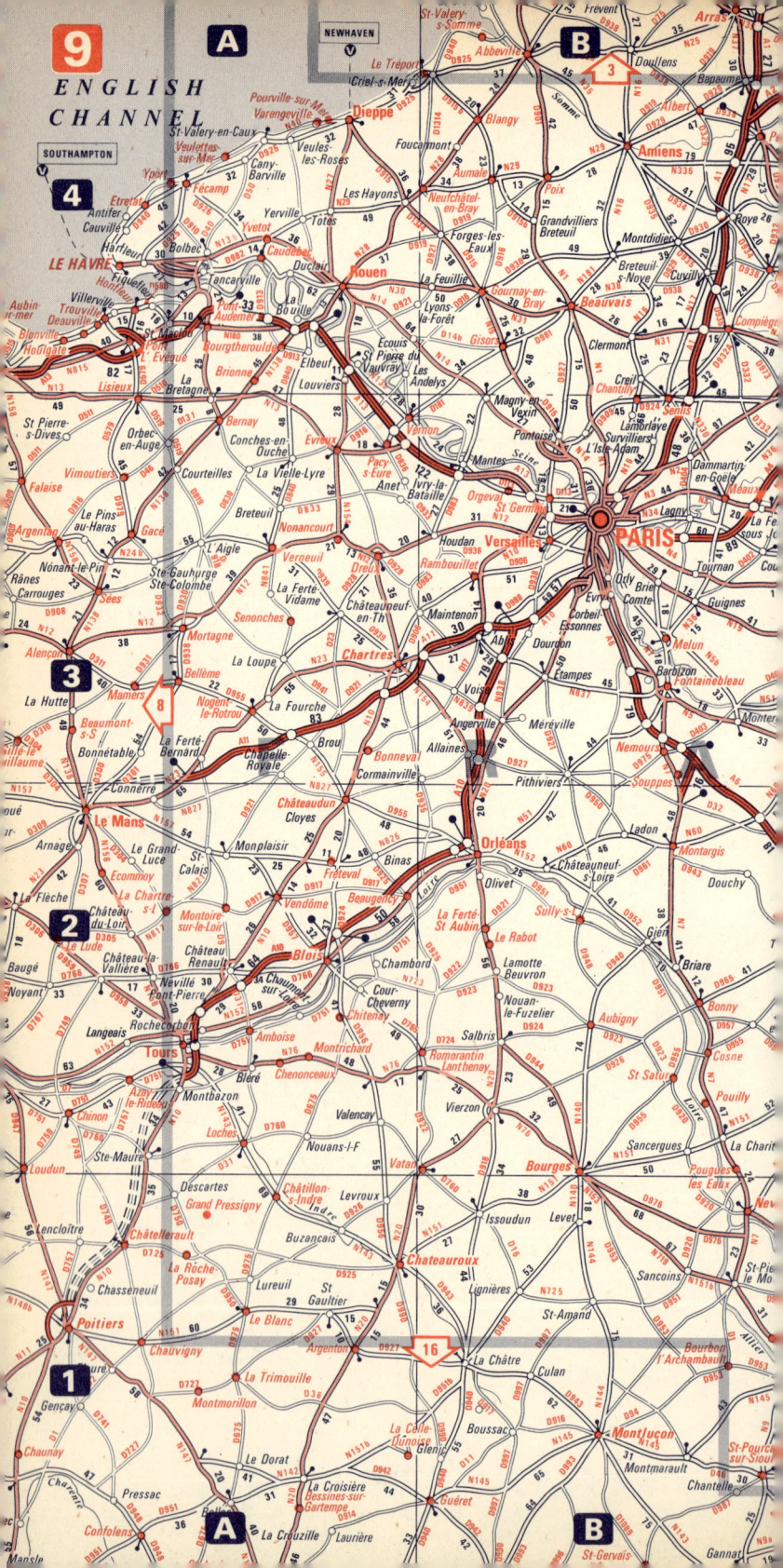

9

ENGLISH CHANNEL

NEWHAVEN

A | B

SOUTHAMPTON

4

LE HAVRE

Dieppe — Abbeville — Arras — Amiens — Beauvais

Rouen — Paris — Versailles — Chartres — Évreux

Le Mans — Tours — Orléans — Blois — Bourges

Poitiers — Châteauroux — Montluçon — Guéret

St-Valery-s-Somme · Frévent · Le Tréport · Criel-s-Mer · Doullens · Bapaume · Albert · Roye
Pourville-sur-Mer · Varengeville · Blangy · Poix · Grandvilliers · Breteuil · Montdidier · Cuvilly · Compiègne
St-Valery-en-Caux · Veulettes-sur-Mer · Veules-les-Roses · Cany-Barville · Aumale · Neufchâtel-en-Bray · Forges-les-Eaux · Gournay-en-Bray · Clermont · Creil · Chantilly · Senlis
Yport · Fécamp · Yerville · Totes · Gisors · Pontoise · L'Isle-Adam · Dammartin-en-Goële · Meaux
Étretat · Antifer · Cauville · Bolbec · Duclair · La Feuillie · Lyons-la-Forêt · Mantes · Lagny · Tournan
Harfleur · Tancarville · Pont-Audemer · La Bouille · Écouis · St-Pierre-du-Vauvray · Les Andelys · Magny-en-Vexin · St-Germain · Guignes
Villerville · Trouville · Deauville · St-Maclou · Pont-l'Évêque · Bourgtheroulde · Elbeuf · Louviers · Pacy-s-Eure · Ivry-la-Bataille · Orgeval · Corbeil · Essonnes · Melun
Blonville · Houlgate · Lisieux · La Bretagne · Brionne · Bernay · Conches-en-Ouche · Évreux · Anet · Dourdan · Étampes · Barbizon · Fontainebleau · Nemours
St-Pierre-s-Dives · Orbec-en-Auge · La Vieille-Lyre · Pontoise · Houdan · Rambouillet · Maintenon · Abis · Voise · Angerville · Méréville · Souppes
Vimoutiers · Gacé · L'Aigle · Breteuil · Nonancourt · Verneuil · Dreux · Châteauneuf-en-Th · Pithiviers · Ladon · Montargis
Falaise · Argentan · Le Pins-au-Haras · Ste-Gauburge · Ste-Colombe · Mortagne · La Ferté-Vidame · Senonches · Chartres · Bonneval · Cormainville · Orléans · Châteauneuf-s-Loire · Douchy
Nonant-le-Pin · Sées · La Loupe · Brou · Chapelle-Royale · Allaines · Olivet · Gien · Briare
Alençon · Mamers · Bellême · La Ferté-Bernard · Nogent-le-Rotrou · La Fourche · Châteaudun · Cloyes · Binas · La Ferté-St-Aubin · Le Rabot · Aubigny · Bonny · Cosne
La Hutte · Beaumont-s-S · Bonnétable · Connerré · Le Mans · Arnage · Le Grand-Lucé · St-Calais · Monplaisir · Fréteval · Beaugency · Sully-sur-Loire · St-Satur · Pouilly
La Flèche · Écommoy · La Chartre-s · Vendôme · Château-Renault · Chambord · Lamotte-Beuvron · Nouan-le-Fuzelier · Salbris
Baugé · Le Lude · Château-du-Loir · Montoire-sur-le-Loir · Blois · Cour-Cheverny · Chitenay · Romorantin · Lanthenay · Cosne
Noyant · Château-la-Vallière · Neuvillé-Pont-Pierre · Langeais · Rochecorbon · Amboise · Montrichard · Salbris · Vierzon · Bourges · La Charité
Tours · Azay-le-Rideau · Montbazon · Bléré · Chenonceaux · Valençay · Vatan · Pouges-les-Eaux
Chinon · Loches · Nouans-l-F · Sancergues · St-Pie-de-Mo
Loudun · Ste-Maure · Descartes · Châtillon-s-Indre · Levroux · Issoudun · Levet · Sancoins
Lencloître · Châtellerault · Grand Pressigny · Buzançais · Lignières · St-Amand
La Roche-Posay · Lureuil · St-Gaultier · Châteauroux · Bourbon-l'Archambault
Chassenueil · Le Blanc · Argenton · La Châtre · Culan · Montluçon
Poitiers · Chauvigny · La Trimouille · Gençay · Montmorillon · Boussac · Montmarault · St-Pourçain-sur-Sioul · Chantelle
Chaunay · Le Dorat · La Celle-Dunoise · Glénic · Gannat
Pressac · Bessines-sur-Gartempe · Guéret · St-Gervais
Confolens · La Crouzille · Laurière

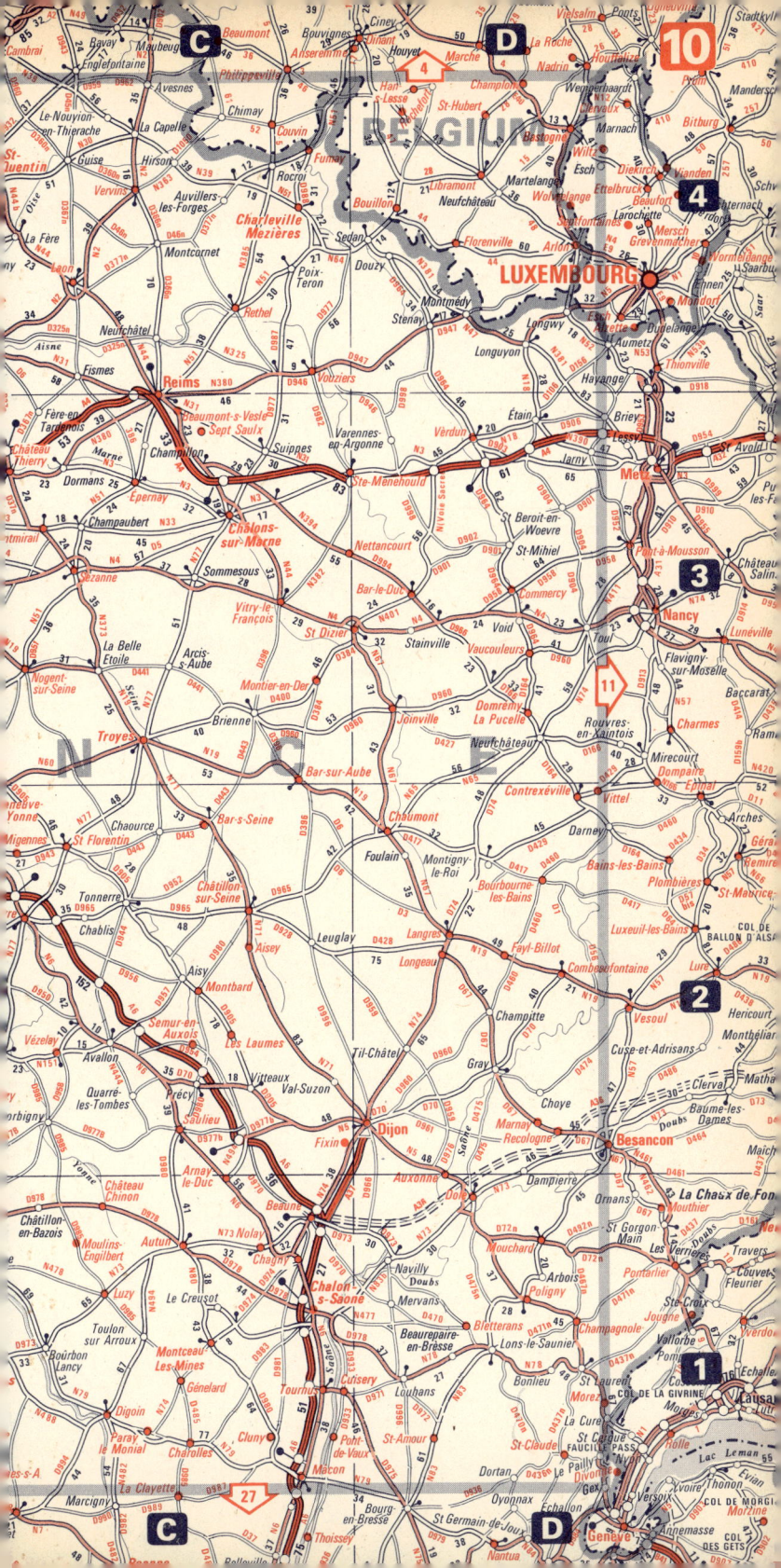

BELGIUM

LUXEMBOURG

Beaumont · Bouvignes · Ciney · Vielsalm · Pont · Stadtkyll
Cambrai · Bavay · Maubeuge · Anseremme · Dinant · Houyet · La Roche · Houffalize · Prüm
Englefontaine · Philippeville · Han · Marche · Champlon · Wemperhaardt · Mandersc
Avesnes · Lesse · St-Hubert · Bastogne · Clervaux · Bitburg
Le-Nouvion-en-Thiérache · Chimay · Libramont · Martelange · Wiltz · Diekirch · Vianden
La Capelle · Couvin · Neufchâteau · Wolwelange · Esch · Ettelbruck · Beaufort · Echternach
St-Quentin · Guise · Hirson · Fumay · Bouillon · Florenville · Arlon · Mersch · Grevenmacher · Wormeldange
Vervins · Auvillers-les-Forges · Rocroi · Sedan · Douzy · Montmédy · Longwy · Esch · Mondorf
La Fère · Montcornet · Charleville-Mézières · LUXEMBOURG · Differdange
Laon · Poix-Terron · Stenay · Longuyon · Aumetz · Thionville
Neufchâtel · Rethel · Varennes-en-Argonne · Verdun · Étain · Briey · St-Avold
Fismes · Reims · Ste-Menehould · Jarny · Metz
Fère-en-Tardenois · Beaumont-s-Vesle · Suippes · Beroit-en-Woëvre · Point-à-Mousson · Château-Salins
Château-Thierry · Sept Saulx · Champillon · St-Mihiel · Nancy
Dormans · Epernay · Châlons-sur-Marne · Nettancourt · Commercy · Toul · Lunéville
Champaubert · Sommesous · Bar-le-Duc · Void · Vaucouleurs · Flavigny-sur-Moselle · Baccarat
Sézanne · Vitry-le-François · St-Dizier · Stainville · Domrémy-La-Pucelle · Rouvres-en-Xaintois · Charmes
Troyes · Arcis-sur-Aube · Montier-en-Der · Joinville · Neufchâteau · Mirecourt · Dompaire · Epinal
Nogent-sur-Seine · Brienne · Bar-sur-Aube · Chaumont · Contrexéville · Vittel · Arches
Chaource · Bar-s-Seine · Foulain · Montigny-le-Roi · Darney · Bains-les-Bains · Plombières · St-Maurice
St-Florentin · Châtillon-sur-Seine · Bourbonne-les-Bains · Luxeuil-les-Bains · Lure
Tonnerre · Aisey · Langres · Fayl-Billot · Combeaufontaine · COL DE BALLON D'ALSA
Chablis · Montbard · Leuglay · Longeau · Champitte · Vesoul · Héricourt · Montbéliard
Vézelay · Semur-en-Auxois · Les Laumes · Til-Châtel · Gray · Cuse-et-Adrisans · Matha
Avallon · Précy · Vitteaux · Val-Suzon · Choye · Clerval · Doubs · Baume-les-Dames
Quarré-les-Tombes · Saulieu · Fixin · Dijon · Marnay · Recologne · Besançon · La Chaux-de-Fon
Château-Chinon · Arnay-le-Duc · Beaune · Auxonne · Dole · Dampierre · Ornans · Mouthier
Châtillon-en-Bazois · Moulins-Engilbert · Autun · Nolay · Mouchard · St Gorgon Main · Les Verrières · Travers
Luzy · Chagny · Navilly · Arbois · Poligny · Pontarlier · Couvet · Fleurier
Toulon-sur-Arroux · Le Creusot · Montceau-Les-Mines · Génelard · Chalon-s-Saône · Mervans · Bletterans · Lons-le-Saunier · Ste-Croix · Jougne · Vallorbe
Bourbon-Lancy · Digoin · Tournus · Cuisery · Louhans · Beaurepaire-en-Bresse · Bonlieu · St Laurent · Morez · La Cure · St Cergue
Paray-le-Monial · Charolles · Cluny · Pont-de-Vaux · St-Amour · Champagnole · FAUCILLE PASS · Nyon · Rolle
Marcigny · La Clayette · Mâcon · Bourg-en-Bresse · St Germain-de-Joux · Dortan · Divonne · Gex · Évian · Thonon
Belleville · Thoissey · Nantua · Oyonnax · Echallon · GENÈVE · Annemasse · COL DES GETS

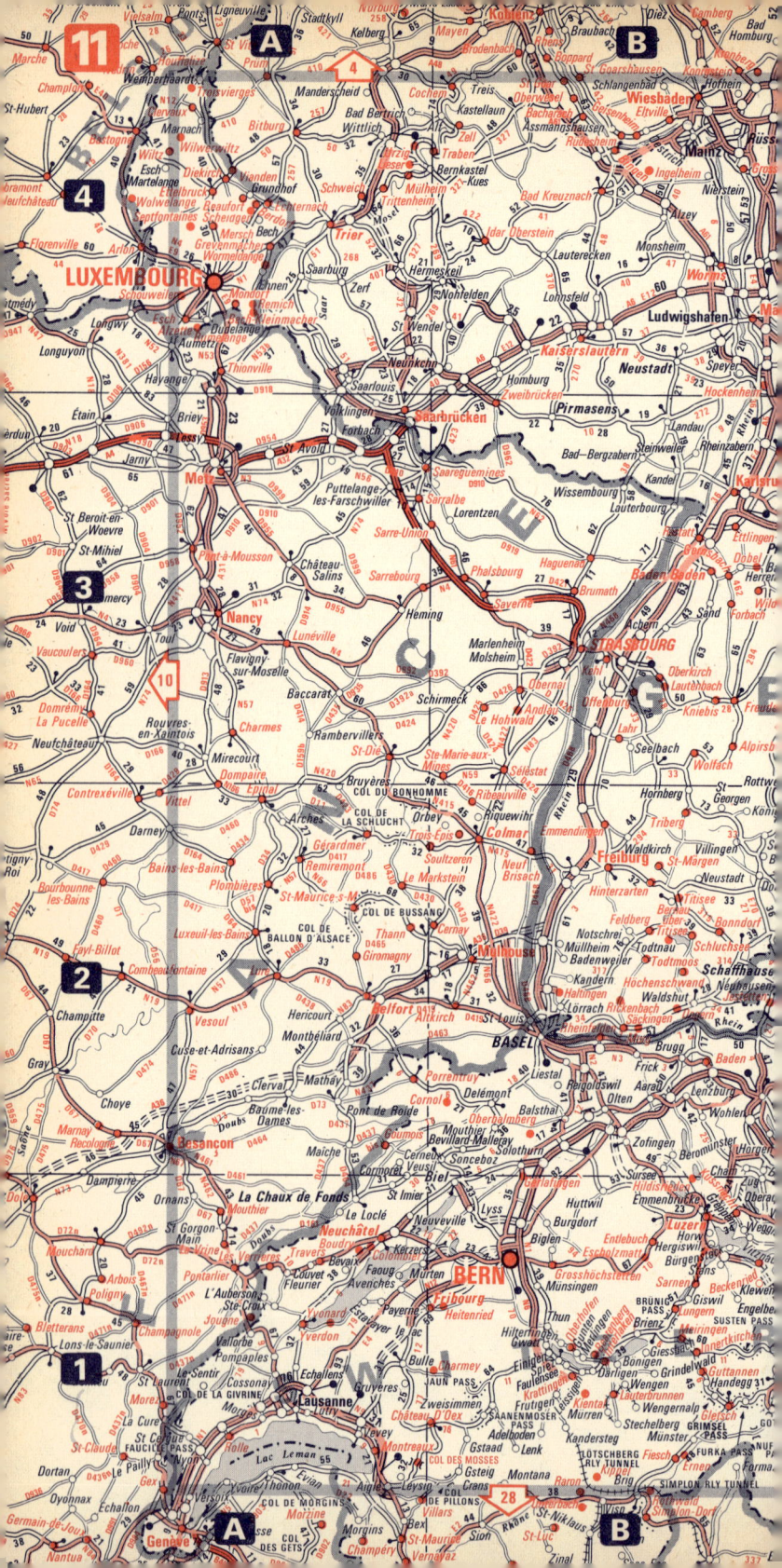

4

3

2

1

LUXEMBOURG

Trier

Koblenz
Wiesbaden
Mainz
Worms
Ludwigshafen
Neustadt
Kaiserslautern
Saarbrücken
Metz
Nancy
STRASBOURG
Colmar
Freiburg
Mulhouse
Belfort
BASEL
Besançon
Neuchâtel
BERN
Fribourg
Lausanne
Genève

RT-AM-MAIN
Langenselbold
5 Hfg

Brückenau · Neustadt · Königshofen · Coburg · Rassach · Münchberg
276 · 286 · 287 · Bettenburg · 303 · Marktzeuln · Kulmbach · Wunsiedel
Bad Kissingen · Hofheim · Lichtenfels · 54 · Bad Berneck · Marktredwitz
Schweinfurt · Ebern · Breitengüssbach · Hollfeld · Bayreuth · Kemnath · Erbendorf
Werneck · Main · Bamberg · Behringersmühle · Auerbach · Pressath · Weiden
Karlstadt · Würzburg · Kitzingen · Ebrach · 104 · Forchheim · Hersbruck · Amberg
Rohrbrunn · Marktheidenfeld · Wertheim · Ochsenfurt · Neustadt · Erlangen · Fürth · Nürnberg · Kastl · Schwandorf
Michelstadt · Tauberbischofsheim · Uffenheim · Bad Windsheim · Schwabach · Neumarkt · Burglengenfeld
Walldürn · Bad Mergentheim · Crailsheim · Ansbach · Hilpoltstein · Dasswang · Regensburg
Eberbach · Karsteinach · Rothenburg ob der Tauber · Feuchtwangen · Weissenburg · Beilngries · Kelheim · Abensberg
Bad Wimpfen · Künzelsau · Blaufelden · Schwäbisch Hall · Dinkelsbühl · Wassertrüdingen · Kindling · Eichstätt · Oberlin
Heilbronn · Gaildorf · Ellwangen · Oettingen · Nördlingen · Altmühl · Ingolstadt · Landshut
Vaihingen · Backnang · Schorndorf · Aalen · Schwäb. Gmünd · Neresheim · Donauwörth · Neuburg · Pörnbach · Mainberg
Ludwigsburg · Esslingen · Kirchheim · Geislingen · Heidenheim · Pöttmes · Pfaffenhofen · Vils
Reutlingen · Urach · Merklingen · Günzburg · Wertingen · Adelsried · Aichach · Freising · Erding · Dörfen
Sigmaringen · Riedlingen · Blaubeuren · Ulm · Zusmarshausen · Augsburg · Dachau · München
Krauchenwies · Ehingen · Vöhringen · Krumbach · Pfaffenhausen · Mindelheim · Landsberg · Fürstenfeldbruck · Grafelfing · Ebersberg
Ludwigshofen · Überlingen · Biberach · Saulgau · Memmingen · Ottobeuren · Buchloe · Starnberg · Feldafing · Wolfratshausen · Bad Aibling
Konstanz · Meersburg · Weingarten · Ravensburg · Leutkirch · Kempten · Marktoberdorf · Kaufbeuren · Peiting · Weilheim · Murnau · Bad Tölz · Gmund · Tegernsee · Bayrschzell
Kreuzlingen · Hagnau · Friedrichshafen · Isny · Wangen · Steingaden · Wildsteig · Oberammergau · Walchensee · Kochel · Fischbachau · Rottach
Romanshorn · Nonnenhorn · Langenargen · Lindau · Oberstaufen · Füssen · Hohenschwangau · Garmisch-Partenkirchen · Achen-Pass · Achenkirch · Worgl
Frauenfeld · Wil · Arbon · Rorschach · Bregenz · Dornbirn · Oberstdorf · Hindelang · Reutte · Ehrwald · Mittenwald · Leutasch · Pertisau · Jenbach · Alpbach
St. Gallen · Heiden · Appenzell · Bezau · Baad · Hochtannberg Pass · Heiterwang · Berwang · Lermoos · Seefeld · Hall in Tirol · Schwaz · Fügen · Mayrhofen
Wildhaus · Feldkirch · Frastanz · Lech · Zürs · Alberg Pass & Railway Tunnel · Imst · Telfs · Mutters · Schönberg · Steinach am Brenner · Hintertux
Buchs · Vaduz · Bludenz · St. Anton · Landeck · Arz · Umhausen · Fulpmes · Gries am Brenner
Sargans · Brand · Schruns · Langen · St. Christoph · Kauns · Ried · Ranalt · Gschnitz
Bad Ragaz · Gargellen · Partenen · Gaschurn · Serfaus · Pfunds · Brenner Pass · Campo Túres
Landquart · Bieler Höhe (Silvretta Pass) · Ischgl · Nauders · Obergurgl · Timmelsjoch (Passo del Rombo) · Vipiteno · Brunico
Chur · Klosters · Fluela Pass · Resia Pass · Sölden · S. Leonardo in Passiria · Passo di Pennes · Bressanone
Arosa · Davos · Scuol Schuls · Merano · Chiusa · Gardena Pass
Lenzerheide · Albula Railway Tunnel · Zernez · Tarasp · Ofen (Fuorn) Pass · Sta. Maria · Müstair · S. Cristina · Selva di Val Gardena · Corvara
Thusis · Bergün · Celerina · Santa Maria · Solda · Ortisei · Canazei · Pordoi Pass · Sella Pass
Tiefencastel · St. Moritz · Umbrail Pass · Bolzano · Nova · Levante Costalunga Pass · Rolle Pass
Splügen · Julier Pass · Pontresina · Börmio · Stélvio Pass · Le Palade Pass · Fonda · Mendola Pass · S. Martino di Castro
Splügen Pass & Tunnel · Maloja · Bernina Pass · Santa Caterina Valfurva · Male · Dimaro · Cavalese
San Bernardino · Biasca · Mesocco · Poschiavo · Gavia Pass · Tonale Pass · Madonna di Campiglio · Carlo Magno · Roncegno
Bellinzona · Chiavenna · Tirano · Ponte di Legno · Edolo · Aprica Pass · Dimaro · Molveno · Trento
Gravedone · Sóndrio · Tresenda · Lombardo

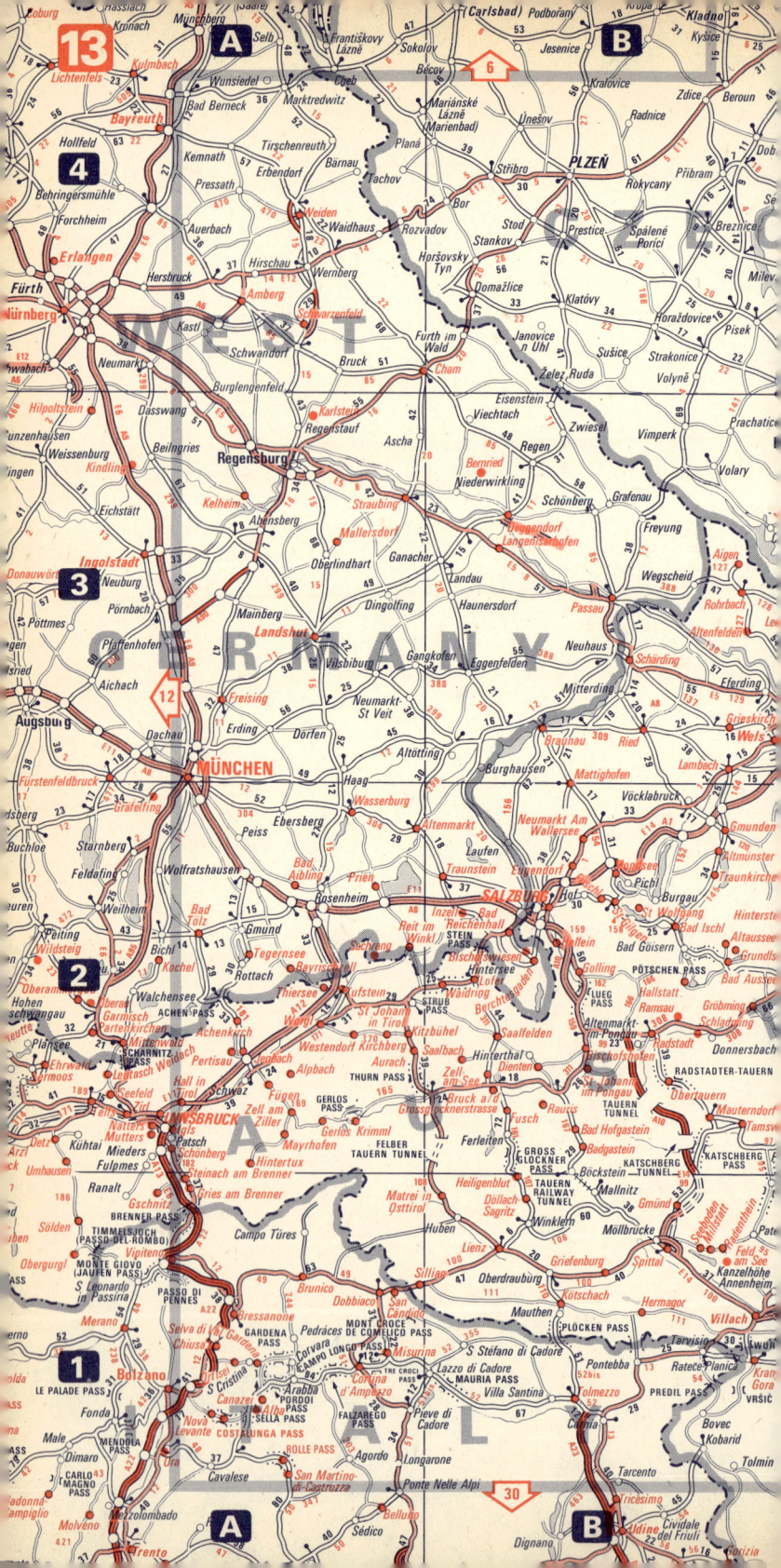

A   Selb

B   Kladno

4

3

2

1

12

WEST GERMANY

Lichtenfels · Kulmbach · Münchberg · (Carlsbad) · Podbořany · Jesenice · Kyšice
Coburg · Hasslach · Kronach · Františkovy Lázně · Sokolov · Krupa
Bayreuth · Bad Berneck · Marktredwitz · Cheb · Bečov · Kralovice · Beroun
Hollfeld · Tirschenreuth · Mariánské Lázně (Marienbad) · Únesov · Radnice · Zdice
Behringersmühle · Kemnath · Erbendorf · Bärnau · Tachov · Planá · PLZEŇ · Rokycany · Příbram
Forchheim · Pressath · Weiden · Waidhaus · Rozvadov · Stříbro · Prestice · Spálené Poříčí · Breznice
Erlangen · Auerbach · Hirschau · Wernberg · Bor · Stod · Stankov · Horšovský Týn · Sušice · Strakonice
Fürth · Hersbruck · Amberg · Schwarzenfeld · Domažlice · Klatovy · Horažďovice · Písek
Nürnberg · Kastl · Schwandorf · Bruck · Cham · Janovice n Úhl · Volyně
Schwabach · Neumarkt · Burglengenfeld · Furth im Wald · Viechtach · Zwiesel · Železná Ruda · Prachatice
Hilpoltstein · Dasswang · Beilngries · Karlstein · Regenstauf · Ascha · Regen · Vimperk · Volary
Weissenburg · Kindling · Kelheim · Abensberg · Straubing · Bernried · Schönberg · Grafenau · Aigen
Ingolstadt · Neuburg · Pörnbach · Mainberg · Oberlindhart · Ganacher · Landau · Deggendorf · Langenisarhofen · Passau · Wegscheid · Rohrbach
Donauwörth · Pottmes · Pfaffenhofen · Landshut · Vilsburg · Dingolfing · Haunersdorf · Neuhaus · Schärding · Eferding · Altenfelden
Aichach · Freising · Neumarkt-St Veit · Gangkofen · Eggenfelden · Mitterding · Grieskirchen · Wels
Augsburg · Dachau · Erding · Dörfen · Altötting · Burghausen · Braunau · Ried · St Johann · Lambach
Fürstenfeldbruck · MÜNCHEN · Haag · Wasserburg · Laufen · Traunstein · Neumarkt Am Wallersee · Vöcklabruck · Gmunden
Grafelfing · Ebersberg · Altenmarkt · Eugendorf · Attnang · Altmünster · Traunkirchen
Buchloe · Starnberg · Peiss · Bad Aibling · Prien · SALZBURG · Hof · Pichl · Burgau
Feldafing · Wolfratshausen · Rosenheim · Inzell · Reit im Winkl · Bad Reichenhall · St Wolfgang · Bad Ischl · Hinterstoder
Weilheim · Bad Tölz · Gmund · Bichl · Kochel · Tegernsee · Bayrischzell · Bischofswiesen · Hallein · Golling · Bad Goisern · Altaussee · Grundlsee
Oberammergau · Walchensee · Rottach · Thiersee · Kufstein · Lofer · Berchtesgaden · Lueg Pass · Pötschen Pass · Hallstatt · Ramsau · Gröbming · Bad Aussee
Garmisch-Partenkirchen · ACHEN PASS · Achenkirch · Wörgl · St Johann in Tirol · Kitzbühel · Saalfelden · Altenmarkt im Pongau · Radstadt · Schladming · Donnersbach
Ehrwald · Mittenwald · Weidach · Pertisau · Jenbach · Alpbach · Aurach · Saalbach · Hinterthal · Bruck a/d · Bischofshofen · RADSTADTER-TAUERN
Lermoos · CHARNITZ PASS · Seefeld · Zirl · Hall in Tirol · Schwaz · Zell am Ziller · Thurn Pass · Zell am See · St Johann im Pongau · Mauterndorf · Tamsweg
INNSBRUCK · Natters · Mutters · Igls · Patsch · Fügen · GERLOS PASS · Krimml · Grossglocknerstrasse · Rauris · Bad Hofgastein · Obertauern · Katschberg Pass
Ötz · Kühtai · Mieders · Fulpmes · Steinach am Brenner · Mayrhofen · Gerlos · FELBER TAUERN TUNNEL · Ferleiten · GROSS GLOCKNER PASS · Bad Gastein · Badgastein · KATSCHBERG TUNNEL
Umhausen · Ranalt · Gschnitz · Gries am Brenner · Hintertux · Matrei in Osttirol · Dollach · Böckstein · Mallnitz · Gmünd
Sölden · TIMMELSJOCH (PASSO-DEL-ROMBO) · BRENNER PASS · Campo Türes · Huben · Heiligenblut · TAUERN RAILWAY TUNNEL · Winklern · Möllbrücke · Spittal · Feld am See
Obergurgl · MONTE GIOVO (JAUFEN PASS) · Vipiteno · Brunico · Matrei in Osttirol · Lienz · Oberdrauburg · Griffen · Kötschach · Hermagor · Villach
S Leonardo in Passiria · PASSO DI PENNES · Bressanone · Dobbiaco · San Candido · Sillian · Mauthen · PLÖCKEN PASS · Tarvisio
Merano · Chiusa · Selva di Val Gardena · Pedraces di Comelico Pass · MONT CROCE · S Stefano di Cadore · Pontebba · Ratece Planica · Kranjska Gora
BOLZANO · Ortisei · S Cristina · Corvara · CAMPO LONGO PASS · Lazzo di Cadore · MAURIA PASS · Villa Santina · Olmezzo · VRŠIČ
LE PALADE PASS · Nova Levante · Arabba · PORDOI PASS · Cortina d'Ampezzo · Pieve di Cadore · PREDIL PASS · Bovec · Kobarid
Fondo · Canazei · COSTALUNGA PASS · FALZAREGO PASS · Agordo · Longarone · Carnia · Tolmin
Male · Dimaro · MENDOLA PASS · ROLLE PASS · San Martino di Castrozza · Ponte Nelle Alpi · Belluno · Tarcento · Tricesimo · Udine · Cividale del Friuli · Gorizia
CARLO MAGNO PASS · Mezzolombardo · Cavalese · Longarone · Dignano · Gradisca
Madonna di Campiglio · Molveno · Trento · Sédico

AUSTRIA

ITALY

A   B
6   30

CZECHOSLOVAKIA

Kolín Kutná Hora Čáslav Chrudim Vysoké Mýto Litomyšl Trebovice Mohelnice Sternberk
Olomouc Hranice
Přerov
Prostějov

Dolní Kralovice Havlíčkův Brod Žďár n Sázavou Polička Svitavy M Trebova
Vlasim Pelhřimov Jihlava Vel Meziřici Kuřim Vyškov Gottwaldov
Košetice Třešť Telč Náměšť BRNO Slavkov (Austerlitz) Napajedla Kyjov
Sobeslav Dačice Mor Budějovice Pohořelice Čejč Hodonín Veseli
Trhové Sviny Treboň Jemnice Hrušovany Mikulov Břeclav Senica

Baabs a/d Thaya Drosendorf Znojmo Laa a/d Th Poysdorf Kúty Jablonica Mestec
Retz Haugsdorf Hohenau Malacky Trnava
Weitra Gmünd Waidhofen a/d Th Hollabrunn Mistelbach Pezinok Senec
Horn Maissau Ziersdorf Ernstbrunn Angern Marchegg BRATISLAVA
Gars am Kamp Stockerau Korneuburg Hainburg a/d D Gattendorf
Zwettl Tangelois Krems Tulln Klosterneuburg WIEN Schwechat Neusiedl a S Moson

Weitra N Hrady Kaplice Dvořiště Karlstift Arbesbach Dürnstein a/d Donau Spitz Melk St Pölten Wilhelmsburg Mödling Bruck a/d Leitha
Perg Grein Ybbs a/d Donau Baden Eisenstadt
Enns Amstetten Scheibbs Hainfeld Berndorf Wiener Neustadt Sopron Nagycenk Kapuvár Csorna
Waidhofen Gutenstein Markt St Martin Oberpullendorf Lovo Beled
Weyer Göstling Annaberg Neunkirchen Köszeg Vat Sárvár Pápa
Altenmarkt Mariazell Terz Mürzzuschlag Semmering Bad Schönau Bernstein Szombathely
Hieflau Präbichl Pass Au Mönichkirchen Oberwart Körmend Vasvár Zalabér Sümeg
Eisenerz Kapfenberg Friedberg Birkfeld Hartberg Grosspetersdorf St Michael Jánoshaza
Admont Trieben Wald Kalwang Bruck an der Mur Leoben Weiz Gleisdorf Fürstenfeld Körmend Zalaegerszeg Keszthely
Mautern St Michael Peggau Feldbach Zalalövo Heviz Fenekpuszta
Knittelfeld Weisskirchen GRAZ Köflach Radkersburg Murska Sobota Lendava Nagykanizsa
St Georgen Judenburg Hirschegg Wildon Gornja Radgona Hodošan Letenye
Twimberg Deutschlandsberg Spielfeld Ljutomer Čakovec
Wolfsberg St Andrä Eibiswald Maribor Ptuj Varaždin Koprivnica
Klagenfurt Völkermarkt Dravograd Radlje ob Dravi Slovenj Gradec Slov Bistrica Dobrna Krapina Novi Marof Đurđevac
Poljana pri Prevalah Črna Na Koroškem Radmirje Celje Lasko Zabok Križevci Žabno
Kamnik Trojane Domžale Trbovlje Zidani Most Zagreb Bjelovar
LJUBLJANA Škofljica Krško Brežice Sesvete Selo Čazma

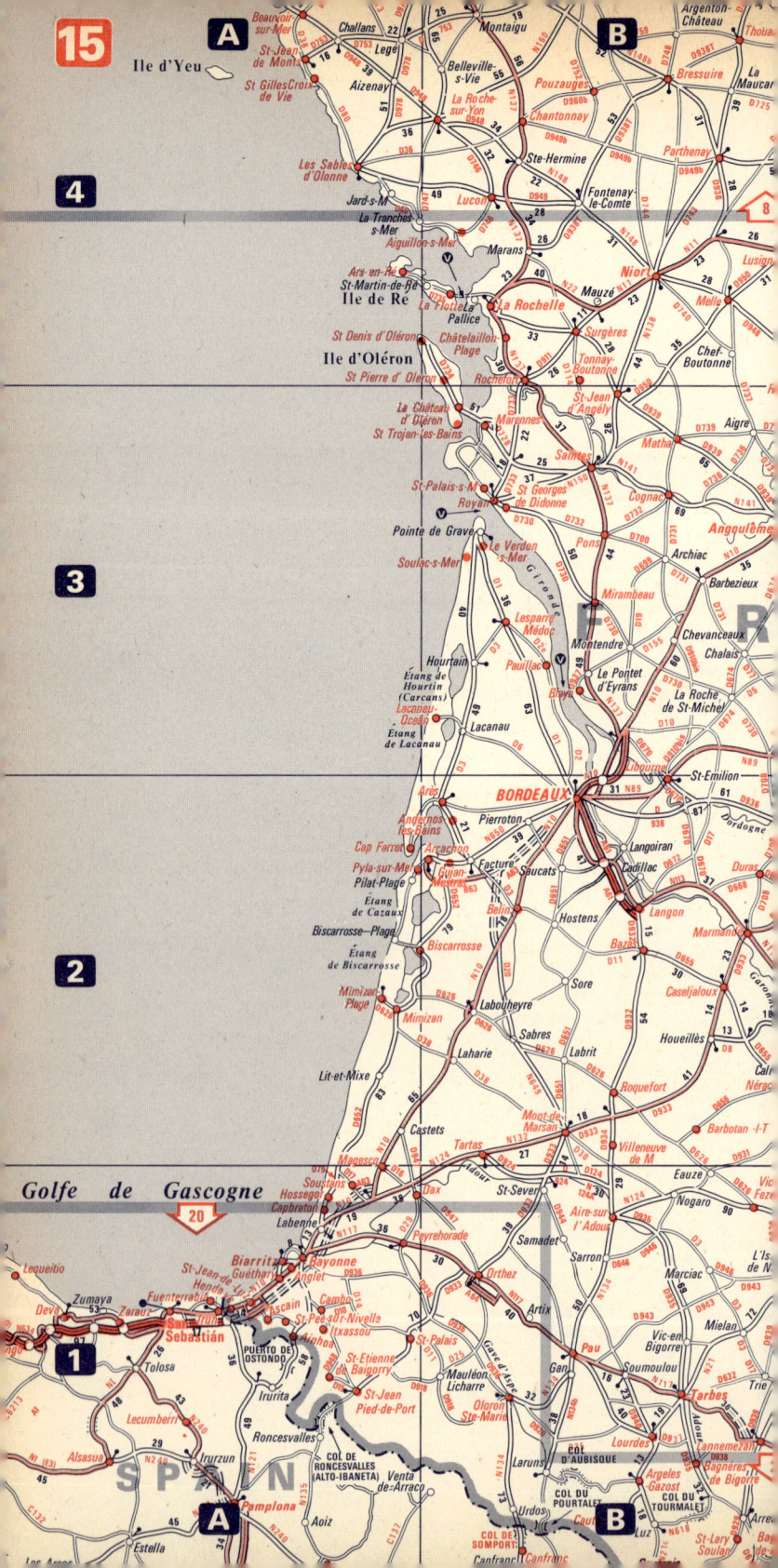

15

Ile d'Yeu

A | **B**

Beauvoir-sur-Mer
Challans · 22
Montaigu
Argenton-Château
Thouars
St-Jean-de-Monts
Legé
Belleville-s-Vie · 55
Pouzauges
Bressuire
Le Maucar
Aizenay
La Roche-sur-Yon
Chantonnay
Parthenay

4 | **8**

Les Sables-d'Olonne
Ste-Hermine
Fontenay-le-Comte
Jard-s-M
Luçon
La Tranche-s-Mer
Aiguillon-s-Mer
Marans
Niort
Lusign
Ars-en-Ré
Mauzé
Melle
St-Martin-de-Ré
Ile de Ré
La Flotte · Pallice
La Rochelle
Surgères
Chef-Boutonne
St-Denis d'Oléron
Châtelaillon-Plage
Tonnay-Boutonne
Ile d'Oléron
Rochefort
St-Jean d'Angély
Aigre
St-Pierre d'Oléron
Mathe
Le Château d'Oléron
Marennes
Saintes
Cognac
Angoulême
St-Trojan-les-Bains

3

St-Palais-s-M
St-Georges de Didonne
Royan
Pointe de Grave
Le Verdon-s-Mer
Pons
Archiac
Barbezieux
Soulac-s-Mer
Mirambeau
Chevanceaux
Chalais
Lesparre Médoc
Montendre
La Roche de St-Michel
Hourtin
Pauillac
Le Pontet d'Eyrans
Étang de Hourtin (Carcans)
Lacanau-Océan
Lacanau
Libourne
St-Émilion
Étang de Lacanau

BORDEAUX
Ares
Andernos-les-Bains
Pierroton
Dordogne
Cap Ferret
Arcachon
Langoiran
Duras
Pyla-sur-Mer
Gujan
Facture · Saucats
Cadillac
Pilat-Plage
Belin
Langon
Marmande
Étang de Cazaux
Hostens
Bazas
Biscarrosse-Plage
Biscarrosse
Caselaloux
Étang de Biscarrosse
Sore
Houeillès

2

Mimizan Plage
Labouheyre
Mimizan
Sabres
Labrit
Lit-et-Mixe
Laharie
Roquefort
Nérac
Castets
Mont-de-Marsan
Barbotan-les-T
Magescq
Tartas
Villeneuve de M
Eauze
Nogaro
Soustons
St-Sever
Hossegor
Dax
Aire-s-l'Adour
L'Is.-de F
Capbreton
St-Geours
Samadet
Labenne
Peyrehorade
Sarron
Marciac

Golfe de Gascogne

20

Biarritz
Bayonne
Anglet
Orthez
Artix
Pau
Vic-en-Bigorre
Mielan
St-Jean-de-Guéthary
Hendaye
Cambo
Tarbes
Lequeitio
Fuenterrabia
Itxassou
St-Pee-sur-Nivelle
St-Palais
Gan
Soumoulou
Zumaya
Deva
Zarauz
Ascain
St-Etienne de Baigorry
Mauléon Licharre
Lourdes
Tannemezan
Zarauz
San Sebastián
Tolosa
PUERTO DE OSTONDO
St-Jean Pied-de-Port
Oloron Ste-Marie
Argelès Gazost
Bagnères de Bigorre

1

Lecumberri
Irurita
Roncesvalles
Larun
COL D'AUBISQUE
COL DU TOURMALET
Alsasua
Irurzun
COL DE RONCESVALLES (ALTO-IBANETA)
Venta de-Arraco
COL DU PORTALET
St-Lary Soulan

SPAIN

Estella
Pamplona
Aoiz
Urdos
COL DE SOMPORT
Luz
Canfranc

A | **B**

Ste-Maure Nouans-l-F Sancergues La Charité Préf
Luçhes
C Châtillon-s-Indre Levroux Vatan **D** Bourges Pougues-Les-Eaux **16**
Descartes Grand Pressigny Issoudun Levet Nevers St-Pierre le Moûtier
Châtellerault Buzançais Chateauroux Sancoins Villeneuve-s-Allier
La Roche Posay Lureuil St Gaultier Lignières St-Amand Bourbon l'Archambault **4**
Chasseneuil Le Blanc Argenton **9** La Châtre Culan Montluçon St-Pourçain sur-Sioule
Poitiers Chauvigny La Trimouille La Celle-Dunoise Boussac Guéret Montmarault Chantelle Gannat
Fleuré Montmorillon Le Dorat La Croisière St-Bard St-Gervais d'Auvergne Combronde Riom
Pressac Bellac Bessines-sur-Gartempe Laurière Aubusson Felletin Châtelguyon Pont de Dore
Confolens St-Junien Bourganeuf Pontgibaud Royat Clermont Ferrand
Nieuil Limoges Pierre-Buffière Eymoutiers La Courtine Bourg-Lastic St Nectaire **3**
La Rochefoucauld St Mathieu La Coquille Ussel Le Mont-Dore Chambon-sur-Lac Issoire
Nontron Lanouaille Égletons Bort-les-Orgues Besse-en-C Condat Lempdes
Brantôme Savignac-les-Églises Tulle La Brioude
Périgueux Donzenac Brive Mauriac Massiac Langeac
Montignac Terrasson Cressensac Argentat Murat **27** Saugues
Le Bugue Les Eyzies Sarlat Martel Beaulieu-s-D Vic-sur-Cère St-Flour St Chely d'Apcher
Lalinde St-Cyprien Souillac Carennac Sousceyrac Aurillac **2** Mende
Siorac-en-Périgord Beynac-et-Cazenac Payrac Alvignac St Céré Montsalvy Marvejols Ste-Enimie
Villeréal Domme Gourdon Rocamadour Gramat Maurs Entraygues La Malène Le Rozier
Fumel Roque Gageac Frayssinet Figeac Conques Lot Espalion Meyrueis
Villeneuve-sur-Lot Rostassac Cabrerets Cajarc Villefranche de Rouergue Sévérac-le-Château Millau St-Jean-du-Bruel
Tournon d'Agenais Cahors Laroque-des-Arcs Baraqueville Rodez Alzon
Valence d'Agen Moissac St-Paul de Loubressac Limogne Najac Caussade Réquista St-Affrique Roquefort-s-S Lodève
Castelsarrasin Montauban Cordes Gaillac Albi St Sernin Pézenas **1**
Fleurance Grisolles Lavaur Castres Lacaune Bédarieux Béziers
Mauvezin Muret Le Vernet Revel Mazamet St Pons Lamalou les Bains Agde Valras-Plage
Auch Gimont TOULOUSE Castelnaudary Homps Lézignan-Corbières Narbonne
Boulogne s-Gesse Carbonne Carcassonne **22** Port-la-Nouvelle
St-Martory Pamiers Le Mas d'Azil Mirepoix Limoux **D** Bigeon
Col de Portet d'Aspet St Girons Foix Massat **C**

A **B**

4

ATLANTIC OCEAN

Cedeira — Ortigueira
El Ferrol del Caudillo — Vivero — Orol
Jubia
La Coruña — Puentedeume — Cabreiros — Villalba
Bayo — Betanzos — C640
Carballo — Ordenes — Baamonde — Rabade
Corcubion — Portomouro — Tambre — C544
Finisterre — Santiago de Compostela — Arzua — Mellid — Lugo
Carnota — Padron — Silleda — Guntin — Puertomarin — Sarria
Muros — Noya — La Estrada — Sotela — Chantada
Son — Oleiros — Caldas de Reyes — Lalin — Alto de Santo Domingo
Santa Eugenia — Pontevedra — Monforte de Lemos
Cambados — Puente Caldelas — Carballino — Castro Caldelas
Isla de la Toja — Redondela — Orense — Alto del Rodiciu
Sangenjo — Vigo — Mondariz-Balneario — Bibadavia — Allariz
Cangas — Porriño — La Cañiza — Celanova — Bande — Ginzo de Limia
Bayone — Tuy — Moncao — Melgaco — L. d Antela — Monterry
La Guardia — Valenca — Portela do Extremo — La Gudina
Caminha — Lindoso — Verin
Moledo do Minho — Lima — Feces de Abajo
Viana do Castelo — Pont da Barca — Reboro
Esposende — Barcelos — Loured — Venda Nova — Chaves — Pedras Salgadas
Faõ — Famalicão — Braga — Pinheiro — Baulhe — Mirandela
Vila Nova de — Guimarães — Vila Pouca de Aguiar — Murça
Póvoa de Varzim — Riba d'Ave — Felgueiras — Barca d'Alva
Vila do Conde — Caldas de Vizela — Amarante — Vila Real — Alijo
Matosinhos — OPORTO — Paredes — Regua — Torre de Moncorvo
Espinho — Castelo de Paiva — Douro — Lamego
Ovar — Oliveira de Azemers — Momenta da Beira — Figueira de Castelo Rodrigo
Béstida — Vale de Cambra — Pinhel
Murtosa — S Pedro do Sul — Trancoso — Almeida
Angeja — Albergaria a Velha — Viseu — Vila Mea — Celorico da Beira — Vilar Formoso
Aveiro — Serem — Caramulo — Vila Mea — Mangualde — Guarda
Vagos — Agueda — Tondela — Nelas — Canas de Senhorim
Mira — Curia — Luso — Seia — Manteigas
Cantanhede — Buçaco — Mondego — Oliveira de Hospital — Covilha
Figueira da Foz — Coimbra — S Martinho — Venda de Galizes — Alpedrinha
Soure — Lousã — Pampilhosa da Serra — Peramacor — Valverde del Fresno
Matos — Pombal — Fundão
S Pedro de Muel — Pontão — Figueiró dos Vinhos — Oleiros
Leiria — Sertã — Ladoeiro
Nazare — Batalha — Castelo Branco — Segura
Martinho do Porto — Aljubarrota — Fatima
Arelho — Alcobaca — Tomar — Vila Velha de Rodão — Chão-de-Codes
Obidos — Caldas da Rainha — Torres Novas

PORTUGAL

3 **2** **1**

A **B**

C D 18

BAY OF BISCAY

4

Ribadeo 26
Vegadeo Castropol Navia Canero Luarca Pravia Avilés 25
Illano La Espina N632 62 Gijón
Grandas Tineo Salas Grado El Berrón-Siero
Fonsagrada La Pola Belmonte Lugones Villaviciosa 66 Colunga
de Allande Cangas Oviedo Nava Arriondas Ribadesella 52 Llanes
de Narcea Gua Mieres Sama Pola Cangas San Vincente
Piedrafita de Laviana de Onís de la Barquera 49
Villablino Piedrafita Campo Arenas de Unquera 38
de Babia de Caso Cabrales Fuente De Potes Cabuérniga
Toreno Palacios Puerto de Osejo de Sajambre 21
del Sil Pajares PUERTO DE TARNA PUERTO DEL PONTON N62 Reinosa
La Magdalena La Pola Riaño PUERTO DE S GLORIO Cervera
de Gordón Boñar Pedrosa del Rey de Pisuerga
Bembibre La Robla Cistierna Guardo Cantoral Aguilar
Astorga León Esla Saldaña Herrera de Campóo
La Bañeza Sta Maria Mansilla de Sahagún del Pisuerga Osorno
del Páramo Las Mulas Carrión Frómista
Puebla de Castrocontrigo Villamañón Villada de los Conde
Sanabria Becilla Villalón Villarramiel
Palacios de Valderaduey Villalon de Campos Olmedilla
de Sanabria Benavente Medina Palencia de Roa
Braganza Utero de Rioseco Magaz
de Bodas PORTILLO Villalpando Quintana Peñafiel
DE SAZADÓN Tábara del Puente
Embalse Villardefrades Cuéllar 2
del Esla Muelas Zamora Valladolid 19
del-Pan Toro Duero
Tordesillas Olmedo
Bermillo Alaejos Navalmanzano
Fermoselle de Sayago Fuentesauco Medina del Campo Cantalejo
Ledesma Cañizal Turégano
Vitigudino Golpejas Madrigal de las Matabuena
Altas Torres Arévalo Segovia
Salamanca Peñaranda PUERTO DE
Ciudad de Bracamonte Adanero Villacastín NAVACERRADA
Rodrigo El Cabaco Tamames Guijuelo Ávila Navacerrada 1
Baños de Piedrahita PUERTO DE PUERTO El Molar
Villanueva Montemayor Béjar VILLATORO DE MENGA Barraco GUADARRAMA
de la Sierra Barco de Ávila Gredos PUERTO El Escorial
El Pozuelo PUERTO DE DEL PICO Navas MA
TORNAVACAS Jarandilla Candeleda Ramacastañas Sotillo de del Rey
Plasencia la Adrada Navalcarnero
PUERTO DE Villarreal C 24 Maqueda Torrejón
LOS CASTAÑOS de S Carlos C D de la Calzada

19

A SOUTHAMPTON **B**

4

BAY OF BISCAY

Golfe de Gascogne

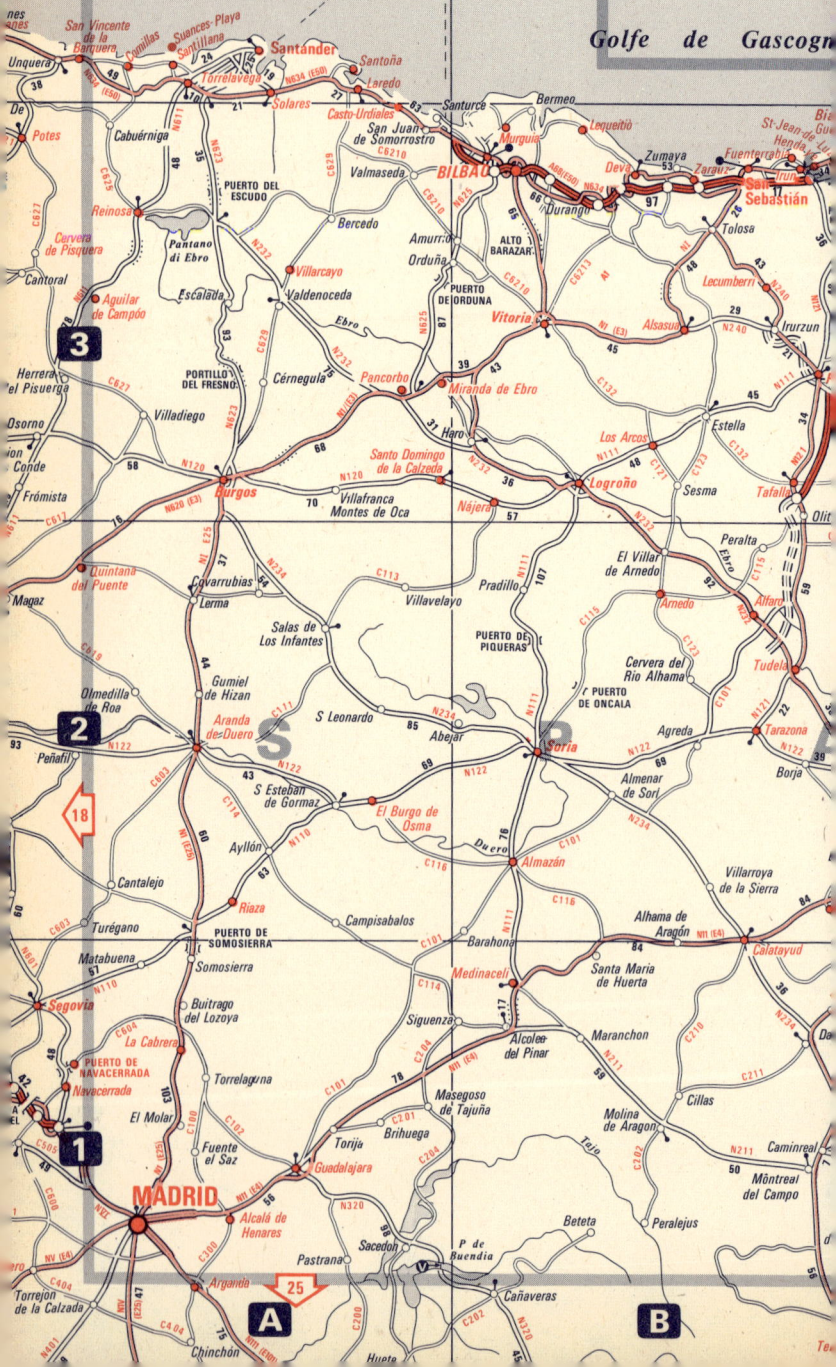

ones
San Vincente de la Barquera Comillas Suances-Playa Santillana **Santander** Santoña
Unquera Torrelavega Solares Laredo Castro-Urdiales Santurce Bermeo St-Jean-de-Luz Hendaye Fuenterrabía Bi
De Potes Cabuérniga San Juan de Somorrostro **BILBAO** Lequeitio Murguia Deva Zumaya Zaraúz Irún **San Sebastián**
Cervera de Pisuerga Reinosa PUERTO DEL ESCUDO Valmaseda Berceo Durango Tolosa
Cantoral Aguilar de Campóo Pantano di Ebro Villarcayo Amurrio ALTO BARAZAR Lecumberri Irurzun
Herrera del Pisuerga Escalada Valdenoceda PUERTO DE ORDUÑA Orduña **Vitoria** Alsasua
Dsorno Portillo del Fresno Cérnegula Pancorbo Miranda de Ebro Estella
ión Conde Villadiego Haro Santo Domingo de la Calzada Los Arcos Tafalla
Frómista **Burgos** Villafranca Montes de Oca Nájera **Logroño** Sesma Tudela
Magaz Quintana del Puente Covarrubias Lerma Villavelayo Pradillo El Villar de Arnedo Peralta Arnedo Alfaro
Olmedilla de Roa Salas de Los Infantes PUERTO DE PIQUERAS Cervera del Río Alhama PUERTO DE ONCALA Tudela
Peñafiel Gumiel de Hizan S Leonardo Abejar **Soria** Agreda Tarazona Borja
2 Aranda de Duero S Esteban de Gormaz El Burgo de Osma Almazán Villarroya de la Sierra
18 Ayllón Duero Alhama de Aragón Calatayud
Cantalejo Riaza Campisabalos Barahona Santa Maria de Huerta
Turégano PUERTO DE SOMOSIERRA Medinaceli Cillas
Matabuena Somosierra Siguenza Alcolea del Pinar Maranchon Molina de Aragón Caminreal
Segovia Buitrago del Lozoya Masegoso de Tajuña Môntreal del Campo
PUERTO DE NAVACERRADA La Cabrera Torrelaguna Brihuega Tajo Peralejus
Navacerrada El Molar Fuente el Saz Torija Beteta
1 **MADRID** **Guadalajara** Sacedon P de Buendia
Alcalá de Henares Pastrana Cañaveras
Torrejón de la Calzada Arganda **25** Huete
Chinchón

A **B**

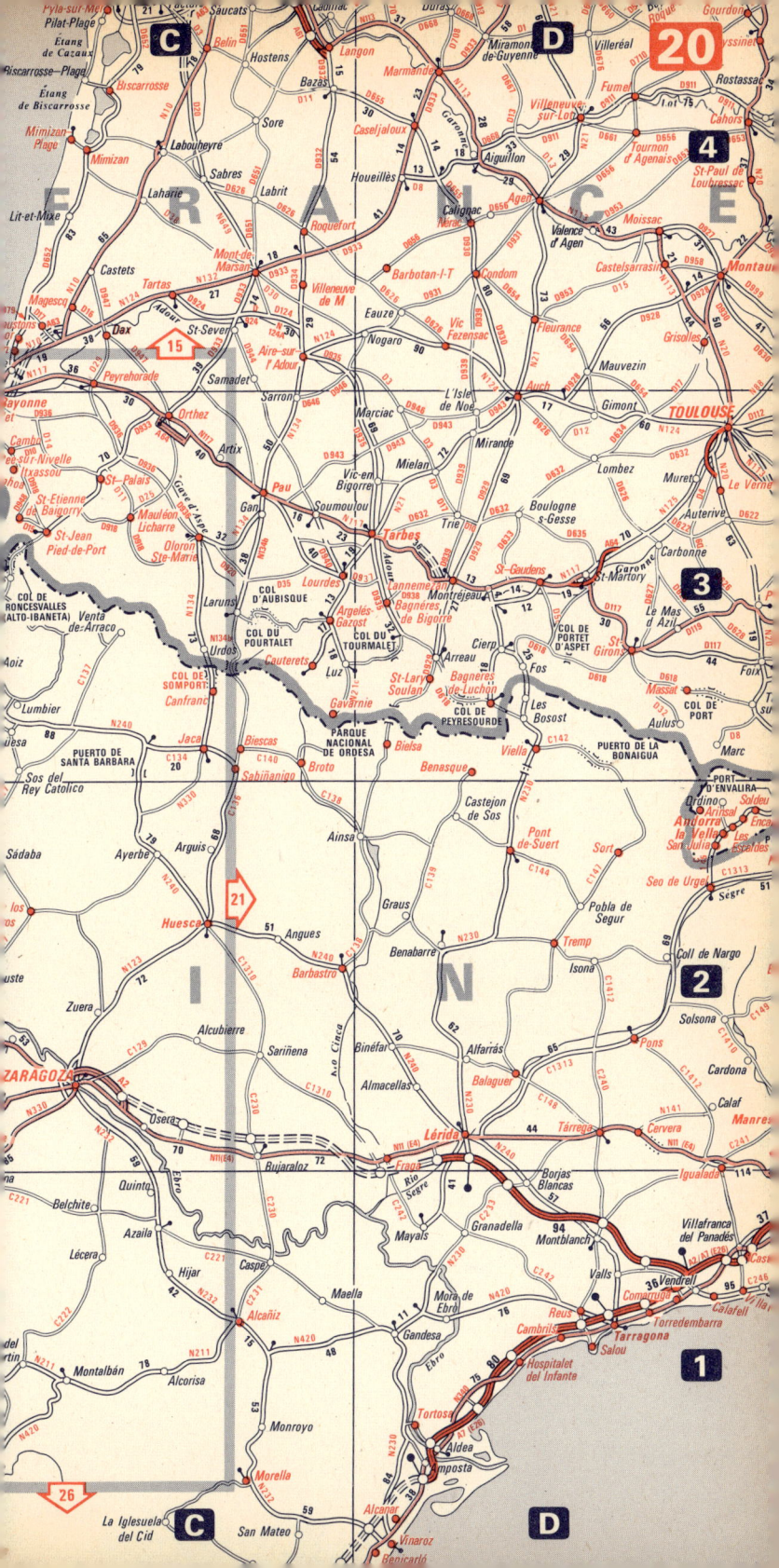

Pilat-Plage
Étang de Cazaux
Biscarrosse-Plage
Étang de Biscarrosse
Mimizan Plage
Mimizan
Lit-et-Mixe
Pyla-sur-Mer
Biscarrosse
Sore
Labouheyre
Sabres
Laharie
Labrit
Castets
Tartas
Magescq
Dax
St-Sever
Peyrehorade
Bayonne
Cambo-les-Bains
Ustaritz
St-Étienne-de-Baigorry
St-Palais
St-Jean Pied-de-Port
Mauléon Licharre
Oloron Ste-Marie
Orthez
Artix
Pau
Gan
Samadet
Sarron
Aire-sur-l'Adour
Nogaro
Eauze
Vic Fezensac
Mont-de-Marsan
Roquefort
Villeneuve de M
Barbotan-l-T
Condom
Nérac
Agen
Valence d'Agen
Moissac
Castelsarrasin
Montau
Grisolles
Fleurance
Mauvezin
Gimont
Auch
Lombez
TOULOUSE
Muret
Le Vernet
Auterive
Carbonne
St-Gaudens
Carbonne
Le Mas d'Azil
Foix
St-Martory
St-Girons
Massat
Col de Port
Marc
Aulus
Les Bosost
Viella
Benasque
Bielsa
Broto
Sabiñánigo
Biescas
Jaca
Canfranc
Col de Somport
Urdos
Cauterets
Gavarnie
Luz
Gèdre
Arreau
Fos
Cierp
Montréjeau
Lannemezan
Tarbes
Trie
Mirande
L'Isle de Noé
Marciac
Mielan
Boulogne-s-Gesse
Soumoulou
Vic-en-Bigorre
Col d'Aubisque
Laruns
Argelès-Gazost
Lourdes
Bagnères-de-Bigorre
Col du Tourmalet
St-Lary Soulan
Bagnères-de-Luchon
Col de Peyresourde
Col de Portet d'Aspet
Parque Nacional de Ordesa
Puerto de la Bonaigua
Port d'Envalira
Ordino
Andorra la Vella
San Julián
Arinsal
Soldeu
Encamp
Les Escaldes
Seo de Urgel
Segre
Coll de Nargó
Solsona
Cardona
Calaf
Manresa
Pons
Pobla de Segur
Tremp
Isona
Sort
Pont de Suert
Graus
Benabarre
Castejon de Sos
Ainsa
Arguis
Angües
Huesca
Barbastro
Alcubierre
Sariñena
Binéfar
Almacellas
Balaguer
Tárrega
Cervera
Igualada
Villafranca del Panadés
Vendrell
Calafell
Torredembarra
Comarruga
Tarragona
Salou
Cambrils
Hospitalet del Infante
Reus
Valls
Montblanch
Granadella
Mayals
Fraga
Lérida
Borjas Blancas
Bujaraloz
Osera
ZARAGOZA
Zuera
Quinto
Belchite
Azaila
Lécera
Híjar
Caspe
Alcañiz
Maella
Gandesa
Mora de Ebro
Tortosa
Aldea
Amposta
Alcañiz
Alcorisa
Montalbán
Monroyo
Morella
La Iglesuela del Cid
San Mateo
Vinaroz
Benicarló
Alcanar
Ayerbe
Sádaba
Sos del Rey Católico
Puerto de Santa Barbara
Lumbier
Aoiz
Venta de Arraco
Col de Roncesvalles (Alto-Ibañeta)

A B

Lecumberri Irurita Irún
Alsasua St-Jean Pied-de-Port Roncesvalles Licharre Mauléon Aspe Tarbes
N1 (E3) Irurzun COL DE RONCESVALLES (ALTO-IBANETA) Oloron Ste-Marie COL D'AUBISQUE Lourdes Lannemezan Montre
45 29 N240 Venta de-Arraco Laruns Argelès-Gazost Bagnères de Bigorre
Estella Pamplona Aoiz Laruns COL DU PORTALET COL DU TOURMALET COL DU SOULOR Arre
4 45 N111 Lumbier Urdos Cauterets Luz St-Lary Soulan Ba CE PEYR
Logroño Sesma Tafalla Sangüesa PUERTO DE SANTA BARBARA COL DE SOMPORT Canfranc Gavarnie PARQUE NACIONAL DE ORDESA
Peralta Olite Sos del Rey Catolico Jaca Biescas Broto Bielsa Benasque
El Villar de Arnedo Sádaba Sabiñanigo Benasque
Arnedo Tudela Ejea de los Caballeros Ayerbe Arguis Ainsa
Cervera del Rio Alhama Tudela Huesca Angues Benabarre Graus
PUERTO DE ONCALA Tarazona Tauste Zuera Barbastro
Agreda Borja Alagón Sariñena Binéfar Almacellas
Almenar de Sori La Muela ZARAGOZA Alcubierre Lérida
3 Villarroya de la Sierra Epila Osera Bujaraloz Fraga
Alhama de Aragón La Almunia de Doña Godina Cariñena Quinto Mayals
Santa Maria de Huerta Calatayud Belchite Caspe Maella Gandesa
Marachon Daroca Mainar Azaila Alcañiz Mora d'Ebro
Cillas Caminreal Vivel del Rio Martin Lécera Montalbán Hijar Tortosa
Molina de Aragon Perales del Alfambrá Alcorisa Monroyo Amposta
2 Peralejus Teruel Morella San Carlos de la Rá
Cuenca Mora de Rubielos La Iglesuela del Cid San Mateo Alcanar Vinaroz
Fuentes Torre Baja Albocácer Benicarló Peñiscola
Cañete Sta Cruz de Moya Fuentes de Ayódar Lucena del Cid Alcocéber Torreblanca
Almodóvar del Pinar Landete Oropesa del Mar Benicasim
Montilla del Palancar Chelva Segorbe Villarreal Castellón de la Plana
PUERTO DE CONTRERAS Casinos Liria Burriana
Minglanilla Utiel Turia Sagunto
1 Requena VALENCIA IBIZA PALMA
Torazona de la Mancha Villatoya El Saler
Albacete Mahora Júcar El Perelló Alcudia de Carlet Cúllera
Ayora Enguera Játiva Alcudia del Crespins

A B

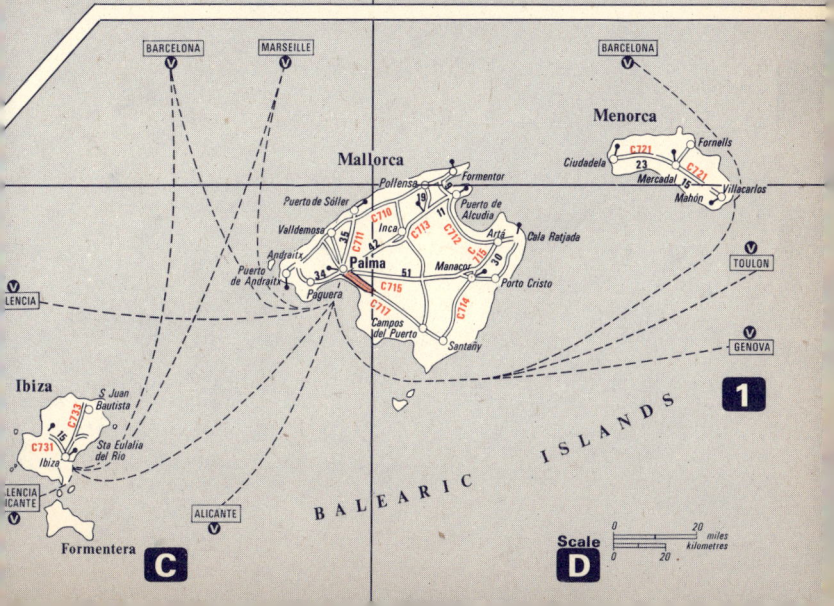

A

4

3

2

1

B

17

Nazere
S Martinho-
da Porto
Aljubarrota
Alfeizerão
Alcobaça
Foz do Arelho
Peniche
Caldas
da Rainha
Óbidos
Lourinhã
N114
Praia de
Santa Cruz
N13
Cercal
Torres
Vedras
Ericeira
N9
Carregado
Mafra
Torres
Vedras
Colares
Sintra
Rio de Mouro
Cascais
Estoril
Carcavelos
Oeiras
Costa
da Caparica
Azeitão
Sesimbra
Portinho
da Arrábida
Setúbal
Marateca

Batalha
Leiria
Fátima
Torres
Novas
Tomar
Sertã
N233
Castelo
Branco
Vila Velha
de Rodão
Chão-
de-Codes
Abrantes
Gavião
N118
Alpalhão
Crato
N119
Castelo
de Vide
Portalegre
Arronches
Alter
do Chão
Monforte
Santarém
Almeirim
Chamusca
Ponte
de Sor
Montargil
Coruche
Sorraia
Tejo
Vila Franca
de Xira
LISBOA
Montijo
Atalho
Lavre
Mora
Pavia
Estremoz
Vila
Viçosa
Elvas
Arraiolos
Montemor-
o-Novo
Évora
Redondo
Reguengos
Mourão
Villanueva
del Fresno
Alcácer
do Sal
Alcáçovas
Torrão
Portel
Grândola
Santiago do
Cacém
N121
Sines
Ferreira
do Alentejo
Érvidel
Aljustral
Beja
Serpa
Vila Verde
de Ficalho
Rosal de
la Frontera
Amareleja
Moura
Barrancos
Cortegana
Cabezas
Rubias
Cercal
Odemira
Ourique
Castro Verde
Almodôvar
Mértola
Sta Clara
a Velha
Aljezur
Alfambras
Monchique
San
Marcos da Serra
S Bartolomeu
de Messines
Cachopo
Alcoutim
Alosno
Gibraleón
Vila
do Bispo
Lagos
Portimão
Loulé
Odeleite
Barranco
do Velho
S Bráz
de Alportel
Ayamonte
Lepe
Huelva
Sagres
Praia da Salerna
Praia
da Rocha
Armação
de Pêra
Albufeira
Faro
Olhão
Tavira
Monte Gordo
Vila Real de S Antonio
Guadiana

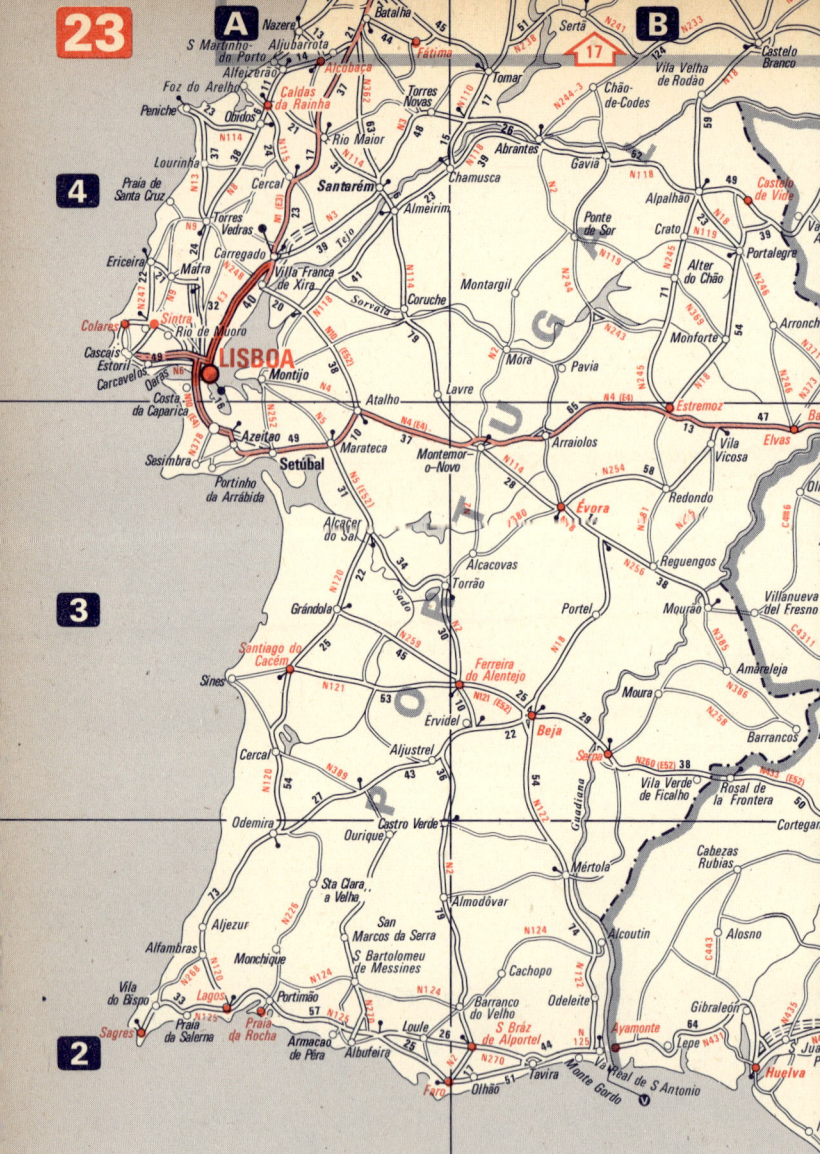

Golfo de Cadiz

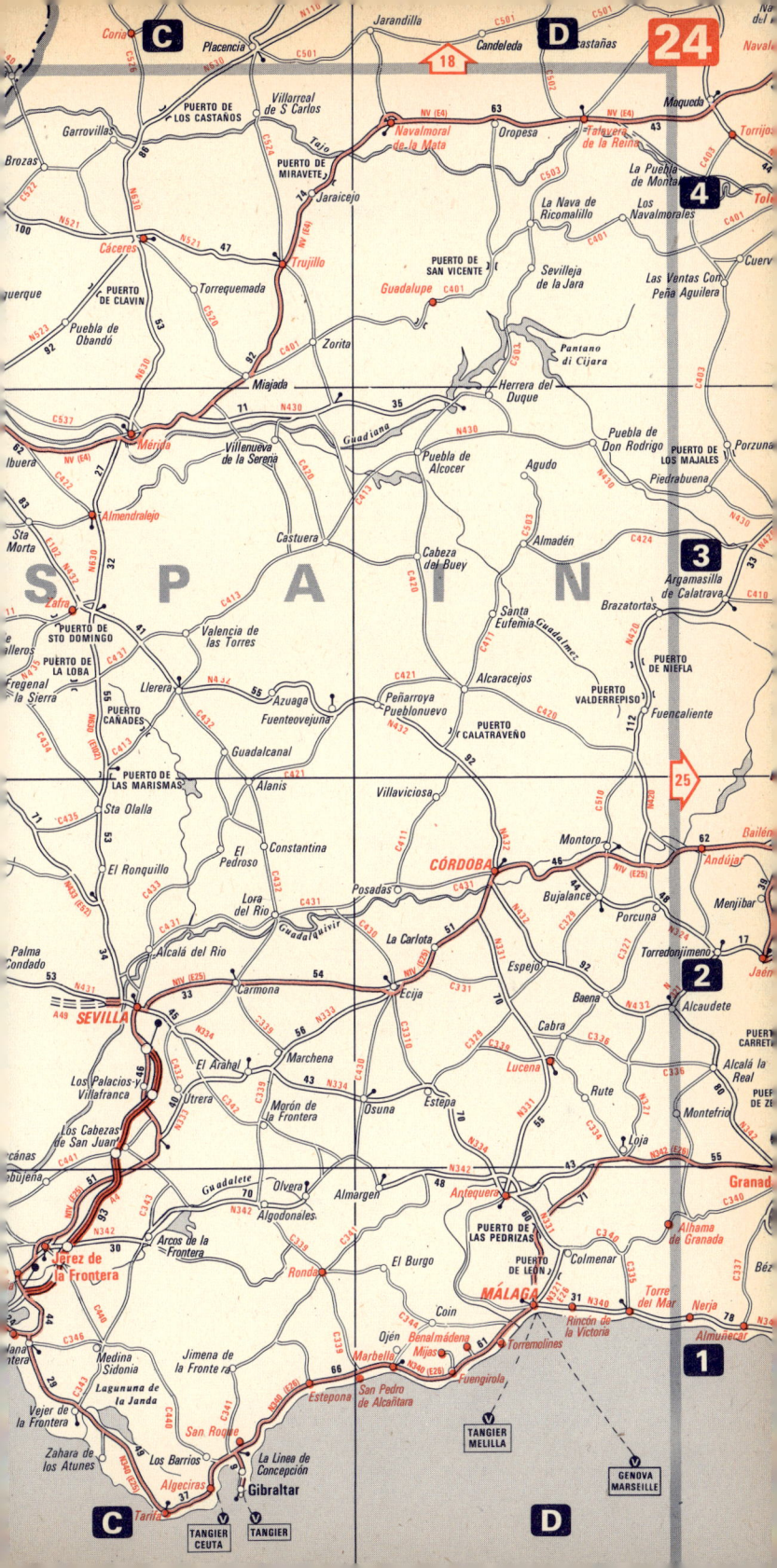

SPAIN

Coria · Plasencia · Jarandilla · Candeleda · Castañas · Navale
Villarreal de S Carlos · C501 · 18 · Moqueda
PUERTO DE LOS CASTAÑOS · Navalmoral de la Mata · Oropesa · Talavera de la Reina · Torrijo
Garrovillas · Tajo · La Puebla de Montal · 4 · Tole
Brozas · PUERTO DE MIRAVETE · Jaraicejo · La Nava de Ricomalillo · Los Navalmorales · Cuerv
Cáceres · Trujillo · PUERTO DE SAN VICENTE · Sevilleja de la Jara · Las Ventas Con Peña Aguilera
querque · Torrequemada · Guadalupe · Zorita
PUERTO DE CLAVIN · Puebla de Obandó · Miajada · Pantano di Cijara
Ibuera · Mérida · Villanueva de la Serena · Guadiana · Herrera del Duque · Puebla de Don Rodrigo · PUERTO DE LOS MAJALES · Porzuna
Sta Morta · Almendralejo · Castuera · Puebla de Alcocer · Agudo · Piedrabuena
Zafra · PUERTO DE STO DOMINGO · Valencia de las Torres · Cabeza del Buey · Almadén · Brazatortas · Argamasilla de Calatrava · 3
alleros · PUERTO DE LA LOBA · Llerrera · Azuaga · Santa Eufemia · Guadalmez · Alcaracejos · PUERTO VALDERREPISO · PUERTO DE NIEFLA
Fregenal la Sierra · PUERTO CAÑADES · Fuenteovejuna · Peñarroya Pueblonuevo · PUERTO CALATRAVEÑO · Fuencaliente
PUERTO DE LAS MARISMAS · Guadalcanal · Alanis · Villaviciosa
Sta Olalla · El Pedroso · Constantina · CÓRDOBA · Montoro · Andúja · Bailén
El Ronquillo · Lora del Rio · Posadas · Bujalance · Porcuna · Menjibar
Palma Condado · Alcalá del Rio · Guadalquivir · La Carlota · Espejo · Torredonjimeno · Jaén
SEVILLA · Carmona · Ecija · Baena · Alcaudete · 2
A49 · El Arahal · Marchena · Cabra · Alcalá la Real
Los Palacios y Villafranca · Utrera · Osuna · Estepa · Lucena · Rute · Montefrio
Los Cabezas de San Juan · Morón de la Frontera · Loja · Granad
Guadalete · Olvera · Almargen · Antequera · PUERTO DE LAS PEDRIZAS · Alhama de Granada
Arcos de la Frontera · Algodonales · El Burgo · PUERTO DE LEON · Colmenar · Torre del Mar · Nerja · Almuñécar
Jerez de la Frontera · Ronda · Coin · MÁLAGA · Rincón de la Victoria
Medina Sidonia · Jimena de la Frontera · Ojén · Benalmádena · Mijas · Torremolinos · 1
Vejer de la Frontera · Laguna de la Janda · Marbella · Fuengirola · TANGIER MELILLA
Zahara de los Atunes · San Pedro de Alcantara · Estepona · GENOVA MARSEILLE
Los Barrios · La Linea de Concepción · Gibraltar
Algeciras · Tarifa · San Roque

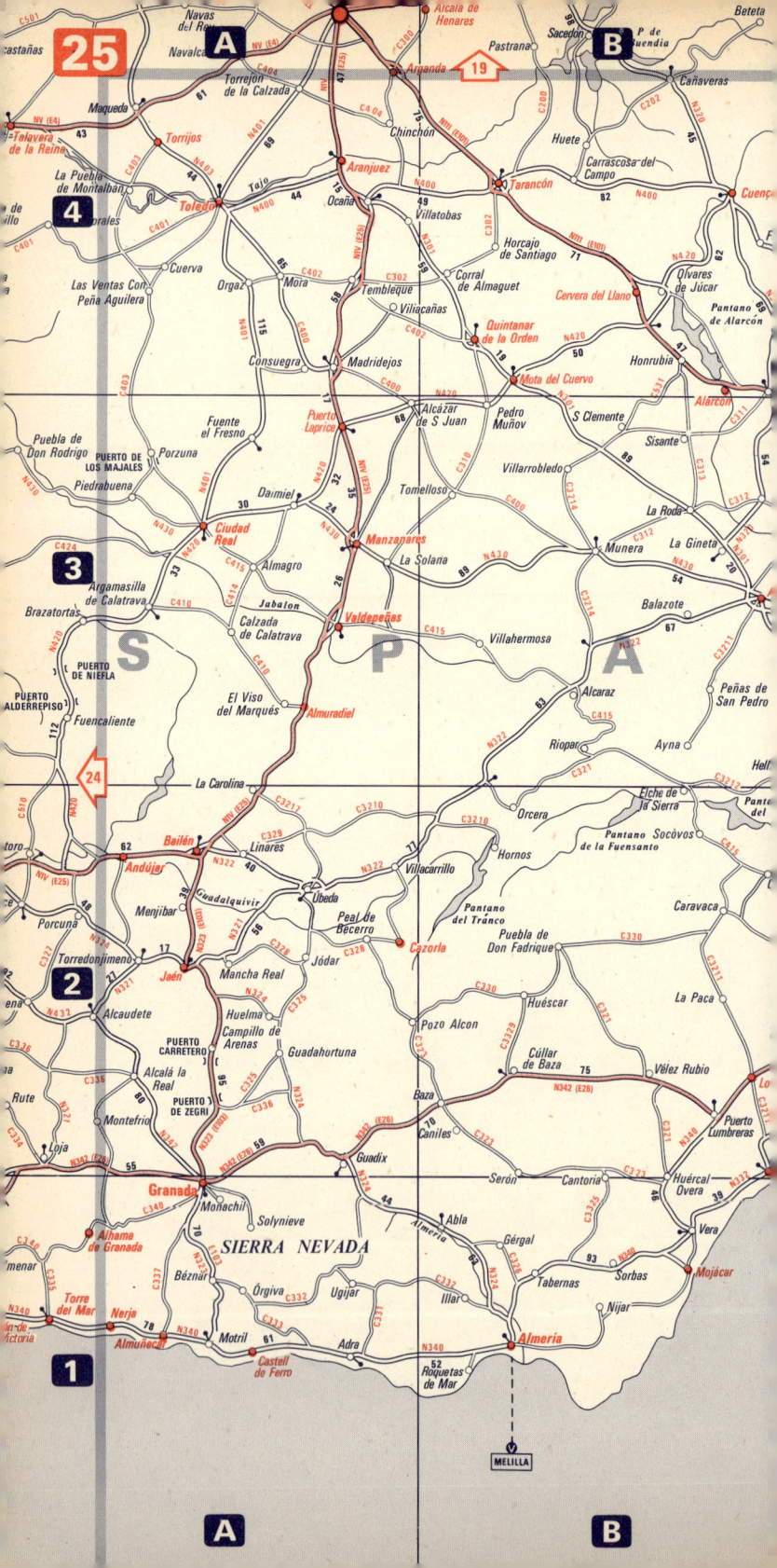

A | **B**

4 **3** **2** **1**

24 **19**

Navas del Rey
Navalca
Maqueda
Torrejón de la Calzada
Torrijos
Talavera de la Reina
La Puebla de Montalbán
Morales
Toledo
Cuerva
Las Ventas Con Peña Aguilera
Orgaz
Mora
Consuegra
Madridejos
Puerto Laprice
Alcázar de S Juan
Pedro Muñoz
S Clemente
Sisante
Villarrobledo
La Roda
La Gineta
Munera
Balazote
Peñas de San Pedro
Alcaraz
Ayna
Riopar
Orcera
Pantano Socóvos de la Fuensanto
Hornos
Villacarrillo
Pantano del Tranco
Puebla de Don Fadrique
Caravaca
La Paca
Huéscar
Vélez Rubio
Cúllar de Baza
Baza
Caniles
Serón
Cantoria
Huércal Overa
Vera
Mojácar
Puerto Lumbreras
Guadix
Abla
Gérgal
Sorbas
Níjar
Tabernas
Illar
Almería
Roquetas de Mar
MELILLA
Granada
Moñachil
Solynieve
SIERRA NEVADA
Béznar
Órgiva
Ugíjar
Adra
Motril
Castell de Ferro
Nerja
Almuñecar
Torre del Mar
Alhama de Granada
Loja
Montefrío
Alcalá la Real
PUERTO DE ZEGRI
PUERTO CARRETERO
Alcaudete
Huelma
Campillo de Arenas
Guadahortuna
Pozo Alcon
Cazorla
Jódar
Peal de Becerro
Úbeda
Mancha Real
Jaén
Torredonjimeno
Porcuna
Menjíbar
Andújar
Bailén
Linares
Guadalquivir
La Carolina
Fuencaliente
PUERTO ALDERREPISO
PUERTO DE NIEFLA
Brazatortas
Argamasilla de Calatrava
Calzada de Calatrava
El Viso del Marqués
Almuradiel
Jabalon
Almagro
Ciudad Real
Daimiel
Fuente el Fresno
Puebla de Don Rodrigo
Piedrabuena
PUERTO DE LOS MAJALES
Porzuna
Valdepeñas
La Solana
Manzanares
Tomelloso
Villahermosa
Alarcón
Honrubia
Mota del Cuervo
Quintanar de la Orden
Cervera del Llano
Olvares de Júcar
Pantano de Alarcón
Cuenca
Huete
Carrascosa del Campo
Horcajo de Santiago
Corral de Almaguet
Villacañas
Tembleque
Villatobas
Ocaña
Tarancón
Aranjuez
Chinchón
Pastrana
Sacedon
P de Buendia
Beteta
Cañaveras
Alcalá de Henares
Arganda

Perales
del Alfambra

20

La Iglesuela
del Cid

Morella
N232

San Mateo

Alcanar
San Carlos
de la Rapita

59

Viraroz

84

N230

Aldea

Teruel

N420

23

Benicarló

Mora
de Rubielos

N234

Peñiscola

4

Albocácer

N330

21

C238

A7(E26)

Torre Baja

Cañete

Sta Cruz
de Moya

110

Fuentes
de Ayódar

C232

Lucena
del Cid

Alcoceber

Oropesa del Mar

Torreblanca

Landete

C234

N330

Segorbe

C222.1

A7

Benicasim

Villarreal

Castellón
de la Plana

Chelva

C224

N234

N340

Burriana

47

Casinos

PUERTO DE
CONTRERAS

(E101)

Utiel

Turia

C224

Liria

Sagunto

71

Requena

N322

81

C3322

C234

22

N111 (E100)

VALENCIA

El Saler

PALMA

Villatoya

C3322

52

El Perelló

Júcar

Alcudia
de Carlet

N332

Cullera

IBIZA

Ayora

C322

Enguera

A7(E26)

Játiva

C3322

Alcudia de Crespins

Gandia

3

N430

74

Montealegre

Almansa

PUERTO DE
ALMANSA

N430

58

Albaida

Pego

Oliva

Ondara

Denia

Yecla

C3223

N330

C320

Villena

Alcoy

112

Jávea

Benisa

MARSEILLE

C3314

Jumilla

C313

Callosa
de Ensarriá

Moraira

Calpe

Monóvar

Elda

Jipona

N332

Altea

Benidorm

IBIZA

Pinoso

C3213

Novelda

N340

N330 S. Juan

Villajoyosa

Campello

PALMA GENOVA

Orihuela

Elche

Alicante

84

Dolores

Santa Pola

C415

Murcia

Guardamar
del Segura

2

N340 (E26)

C3319

N332

Torrevieja

57

San Javier
Santiago
de la Ribera

Cartagena

N332

La Unión

Puerto
de Mazarrón

1

M E D I T E R R A N E A N   S E A

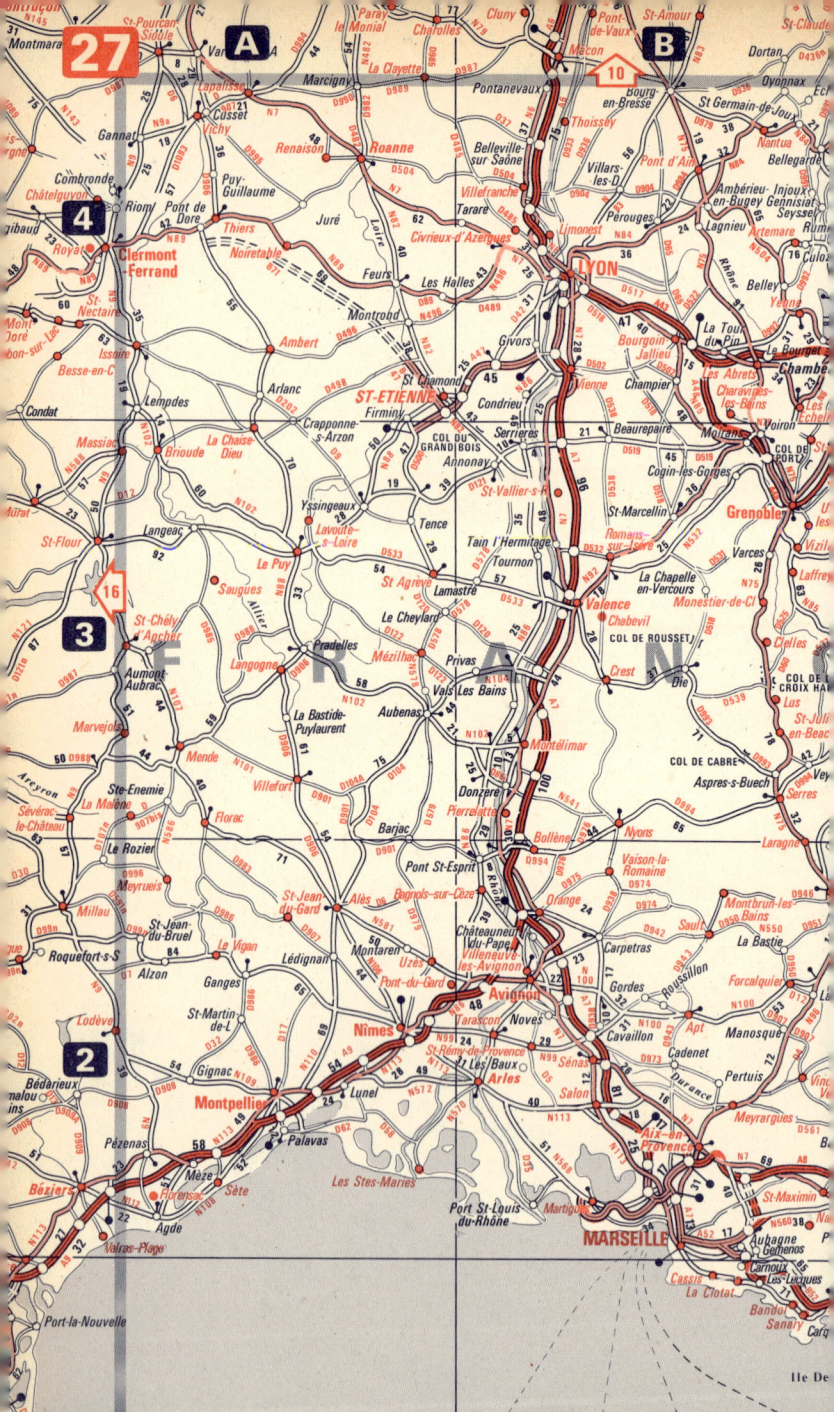

MEDITERRANEAN SEA

| A | PALMA IBIZA ALICANTE ORAN MALAGA | ALGER | B | SKIKDA ANNABA TUNIS PALERMO |

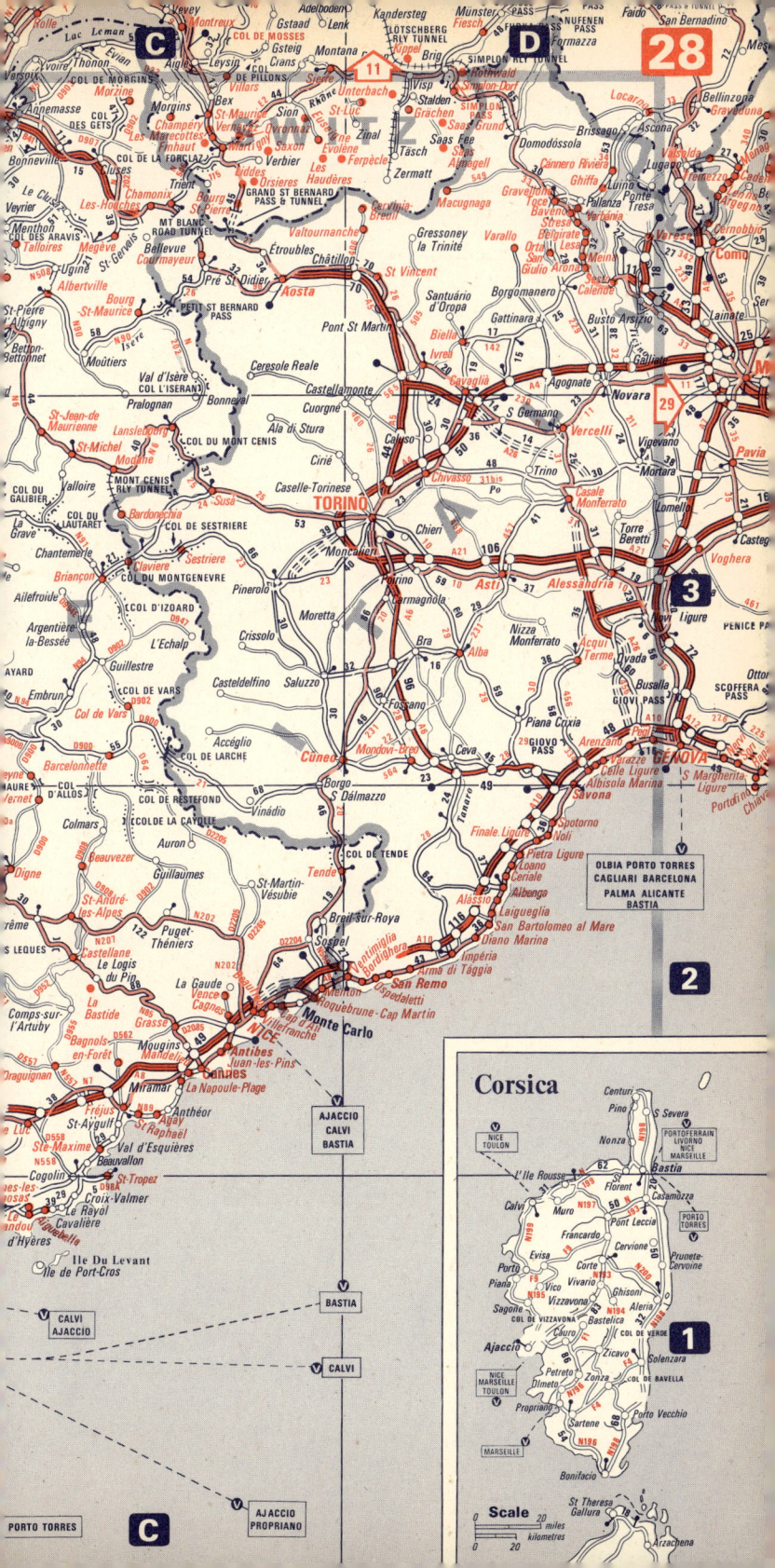

Rolle
Lac Leman
Vevey
Montreux
Gstaad Adelboden Lenk
Kandersteg
Münster PASS
Nufenen PASS
Faido
San Bernardino
COL DE MOSSES
Gsteig Montana
Brig
LÖTSCHBERG RLY TUNNEL
RAWYL PASS
SIMPLON RLY TUNNEL
Formazza
Evian
Thonon
Aigle
Leysin
Villars
Sion
Sierre
Unterbach
Visp
Stalden
Rothwald
SIMPLON PASS
Simplon-Dorf
Locarno
Bellinzona
Annemasse
Morgins
Morzine
Champéry
Bex
St-Maurice
Verbier
Grächen
Saas Fee
Saas Grund
Brissago
Ascona
Ghgiffa
Luino
COL DES GETS
Les Marecottes
Finhaut
Evolène
Täsch
Saas Almagell
Cannero Riviera
Ponte Tresa
Lugano
Bonneville
Cluses
Chamonix
Argentière
Bourg St-Maurice
Orsières
Les Haudères
Zermatt
Macugnaga
Gravedona
Varenna
Menaggio
Cadenabbia
Tremezzo
Veyrier
MT BLANC ROAD TUNNEL
Bellevue
Courmayeur
GRAND ST BERNARD PASS & TUNNEL
Cervinia-Breuil
Gressoney la Trinité
Varallo
Gravellona Toce
Baveno
Stresa
Belgirate
Lesa
Meina
Cernobbio
Como
Menthon
COL DES ARAVIS
Talloires
Megève
St-Gervais
Pré St-Didier
Étroubles
Châtillon
St Vincent
Santuário d'Oropa
Orta San Giulio Arona
Lainate
Albertville
Bourg St-Maurice
Aosta
PETIT ST BERNARD PASS
Pont St Martin
Biella
Gattinara
Borgomanero
Busto Arsizio
Gallarate
St-Pierre d'Albigny
Betton-Bettonnet
Moûtiers
Val d'Isère
COL L'ISERAN
Bonneval
Castellamonte
Ivrea
142
Cavaglià
S. Germano
Agognate
Novara
Vigevano
Pavia
St-Jean-de-Maurienne
Pralognan
Lanslebourg
Ala di Stura
Caluso
Vercelli
Mortara
Lomello
St-Michel Modane
MONT CENIS RLY TUNNEL
COL DU MONT CENIS
Ciriè
Trino
COL DU GALIBIER
Valloire
Caselle-Torinese
TORINO
Po
Chivasso
Casale Monferrato
Casteg
La Grave
Bardonecchia
Susa
Moncalieri
Chieri
Torre Beretti
Voghera
Chantemerle
Briançon
COL DU LAUTARET
Claviere
Sestriere
COL DU MONTGENEVRE
Pinerolo
Poirino
Carmagnola
Asti
Alessandria
Novi Ligure
PENICE PASS
Ailefroide
ÉCOL D'IZOARD
L'Échalp
Moretta
Bra
Alba
Nizza Monferrato
Acqui Terme
Ovada
Busalla
GIOVI PASS
SCOFFERA PASS
Ottor
Argentière la-Bessée
AYARD
Embrun
COL DE VARS
Crissolo
Saluzzo
Casteldelfino
Fossano
Ceva
Piana Crixia
Arenzano
Pegli
GÉNOVA
Barcelonnette
Vernet
Colmars
COL D'ALLOS
Accéglio
COL DE LARCHE
Vinádio
Borgo S. Dálmazzo
Cúneo
Mondovi-Breo
Tanaro
Finale Ligure
Noli
Celle Ligure
Varazze
Albisola Marina
Savona
Spotorno
S. Margherita Ligure
Portofino
Chiava
Digne
St-André-les-Alpes
ÉCOLE DE LA CAYOLLE
Auron
Guillaumes
COL DE TENDE
Tende
Pietra Ligure
Loano
Ceriale
Albenga
rême
Castellane
Le Logis du Pin
St-Martin-Vésubie
Breil-Sur-Roya
Alassio
Laigueglia
S LEQUES
La Bastide
Puget-Théniers
Sospel
San Bartolomeo al Mare
Diano Marina
Comps-sur-l'Artuby
Bagnols-en-Forêt
Grasse
La Gaude
Vence
Cagnes
Ventimiglia
Bordighera
Menton
Roquebrune-Cap Martin
Impéria
Armá di Tàggia
San Remo
Draguignan
Mougins
Mandelieu
NICE
Villefranche
Monte Carlo
Spedaletti
LUC
Fréjus
St-Aygulf
Agay
St-Raphaël
Anthéor
Antibes
Juan-les-Pins
La Napoule-Plage
CANNES
Miramar
Ste Maxime
Val d'Esquières
Beauvallon
Cogolin
St-Tropez
Croix-Valmer
Le Rayol
Cavalière
andou
d'Hyères
Ile Du Levant
Ile de Port-Cros

2

3

AJACCIO
CALVI
BASTIA

BASTIA

CALVI

CALVI
AJACCIO

AJACCIO
PROPRIANO

PORTO TORRES

Corsica

NICE
TOULON
Centuri
Pino
S. Severa
Nonza
PORTOFERRAIO
LIVORNO
NICE
MARSEILLE
Bastia
l'Ile Rousse
Casamozza
Calvi
St Florent
Muro
Francardo
Evisa
Porto
Piana
Sagone
Ajaccio
N197
Pont Leccia
Corte
Vico
Vivario
Vizzavona
COL DE VIZZAVONA
Cervione
Ghisoni
Aleria
Cauro
Bastelica
COL DE VERDE
Prunete-Cervione
PORTO TORRES
Zicavo
Solenzara
NICE
MARSEILLE
TOULON
Petreto
Olmeto
Zonza
COL DE BAVELLA
Propriano
Sartène
Porto Vecchio
MARSEILLE
N196
Bonifacio
St Theresa Gallura

Scale
0   20
miles
0   20
kilometres

Arzachena

1

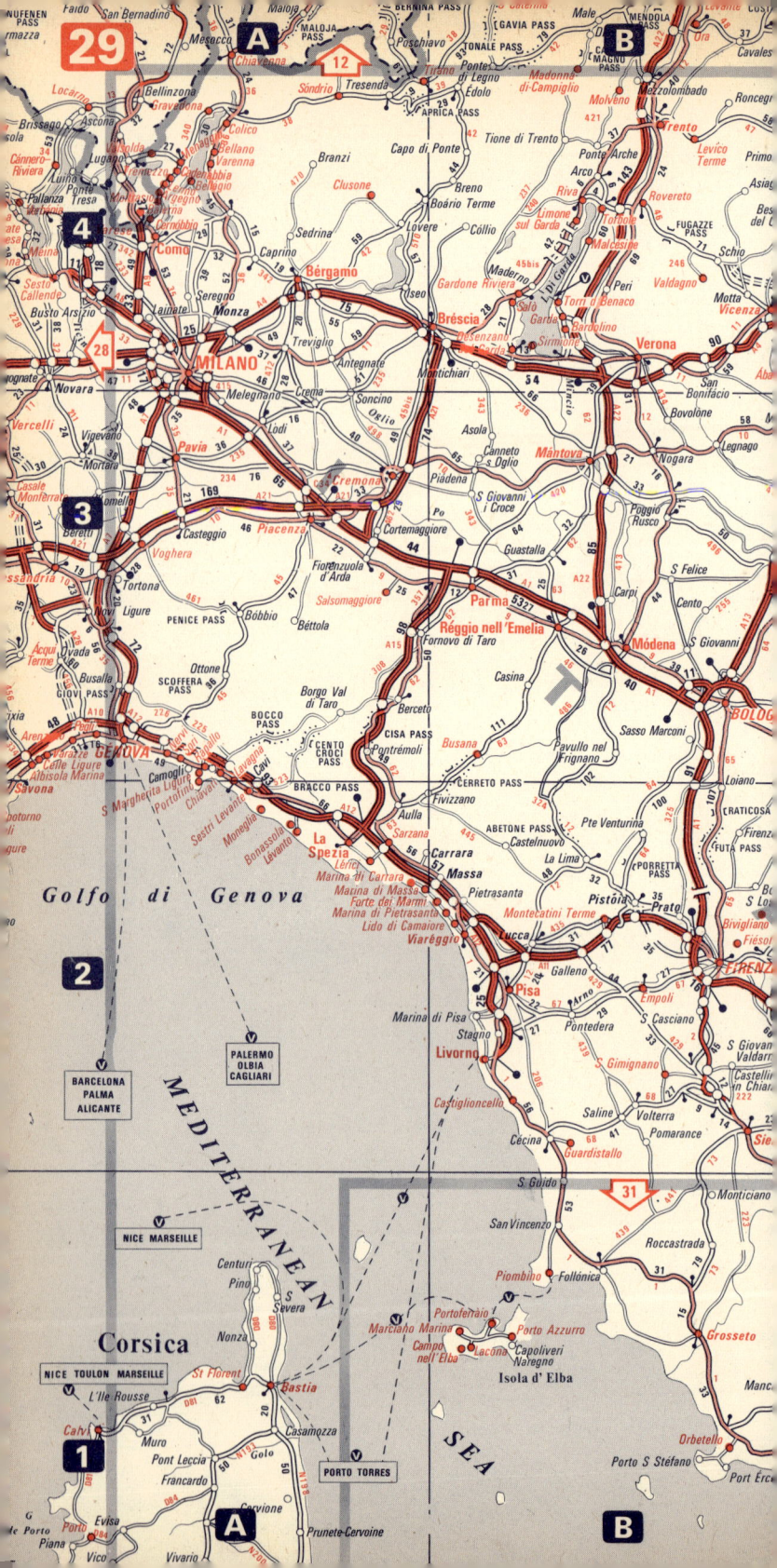

29

A

B

Nufenen Pass
Faido
San Bernardino
Mesocco
Maloja
Bernina Pass
Gavia Pass
Male
Mendola Pass
rmazza
Maloja Pass
Puschiavo
Tonale Pass
Magnum
Cavalese
12
Chiavenna
Tirano
Ponte di Legno
Edolo
Ora
Locarno
Bellinzona
Sondrio
Tresenda
Aprica Pass
Madonna di Campiglio
Molveno
Mezzolombardo
Roncegno
Brissago
Gravedona
Colico
Capo di Ponte
Tione di Trento
Ponte Arche
Trento
isola
Ascona
Menaggio
Breno
Boário Terme
Arco
Levico Terme
Primo
Cànnero Riviera
Lugano
Bellano
Varenna
Clusone
Lovere
Còllio
Riva
Torbole
Rovereto
Asiag
Pallanza
Luino
Ponte Tresa
Cadenabbia
Bellagio
Sedrina
Limone sul Garda
Maderno
Fugazze Pass
Bes
del C
Meina
Como
Caprino
Gardone Riviera
Malcésine
Peri
Valdagno
Schio
Motta
Sesto Calende
Seregno
Monza
Bérgamo
Iseo
Brèscia
Salò
Garda
Bardolino
Vicenza
Busto Arsizio
Trevíglio
Antegnate
Montichiari
Desenzano
Sirmione
Verona
Novara
Melegnano
Crema
Soncino
Oglio
San Bonifacio
Bovolone
MILANO
Pavia
Lodi
Asola
Canneto s.Oglio
Mántova
Nogara
Legnago
Vercelli
Vigévano
Mortara
Cremona
Piàdena
S.Giovanni i Croce
Poggio Rusco
Casale Monferrato
Piacenza
Cortemaggiore
Guastalla
S.Felice
Voghera
Fiorenzuola d'Arda
Parma
Carpi
Cento
Bèrceto
Tortona
Casteggio
Bóbbio
Salsomaggiore
Réggio nell'Emelia
Módena
S.Giovanni
Acqui Terme
Ottone
Borgo Val di Taro
Fornovo di Taro
Casina
Sasso Marconi
BOLOG
Busalla
Penice Pass
Pontrémoli
Busana
Pavullo nel Frignano
Loiano
GENOVA
Bracco Pass
Aulla
Cisa Pass
Abetone Pass
Pte Venturina
Porretta Pass
Savona
Camogli
Sarzana
Carrara
Pietrasanta
Pistóia
Prato
La Spezia
Massa
Montecatini Terme
Fiésole
Sestri Levante
Lérici
Marina di Carrara
Marina di Massa
Lucca
FIRENZE
S.Margherita Ligure
Bonassola
Lévanto
Forte dei Marmi
Marina di Pietrasanta
Galleno
Empoli
Golfo di Genova
Lido di Camaiore
Viaréggio
Pisa
Pontedera
S.Casciano
S.Gimignano
Marina di Pisa
Stagno
Livorno
Castelli n Chiar
Barcelona Palma Alicante
Palermo Olbia Cagliari
Castiglioncello
Saline
Volterra
Cécina
Guardistallo
Pomarance
Sie
MEDITERRANEAN
S.Guido
Monticiano
31
Nice Marseille
San Vincenzo
Roccastrada
Centuri
Pino
Piombino
Follónica
Corsica
Nonza
Nice Toulon Marseille
St Florent
L'Ile Rousse
Bastia
Portoferraio
Porto Azzurro
Marciana Marina
Grosseto
Calvi
Muro
Casamozza
Campo nell'Elba
Lacona
Capoliveri
Naregno
Isola d'Elba
1
Pont Leccia
Francardo
Golo
Porto Torres
Orbetello
Evisa
Cervione
Porto S.Stéfano
Vivario
Prunete-Corvoine
SEA
A
B

2

3

4

28

31

Agordo · Longarone · Kobarid · Tolmin · Kranj · Trojane
Martino · trozza · Ponte Nelle Alpi · Tarcento · Zelin · Idrija · Godovič · Škufljica · Litija · E94
13 · Spilimbergo · Tricesimo · Udine · Cividale del Friuli · Gorizia · Ajdovščina · Kalce · Planina · Ribnica
Belluno · Dignano · Pieris · Montalcone · Postojna · Grahovo · Lož · Kočevje
Sédico · Sacile · Pordenone · Pieris · Sezana · Lipica · E27 · Ilirska Bistrica · Rupa · Vrbno
Vittório · Veneto · Oderzo · Portogruaro · Grado · Trieste · Kozina · Delnice
Conegliano · S. Donà di Piave · Lignano Sabbiadoro · Ankaran · RIJEKA
Montebelluna · Treviso · Caorle · Lido di lésolo (Jesolo) · Piran · Portorož · Koper · Opátija · Lovran · Moščenička Draga · Crikvenica
Mogliano Veneto · Mestre · VENEZIA · Lido · 35 · Umag · Buje · Porec · Kralievica · Plomin · Porozina · Omišalj · Novi
Piove di Sacco · Chióggia · Baderna · Pazin · Krk · Silo · Rovinj · Raša · Rabac · Cres · Krk · Baška
Adige · Adria · Contarina · Vodnjan · Pula · Cres · Rab · Rab
Porto Tolle · Pompósa · Losinj · Osor · Rab · Pag
Comácchio · Porto Garibaldi · Lošinj · Lošinj · Molat
Alfonsine · Marina di Ravenna
Lugo · Ravenna
Cérvia · Cesenático · Bellária Igea Marina
Forlì · Cesena · Rimini · Riccione · Cattólica · Gabicce Mare · Pésaro · Fano
Bagno di Romagna · S. Marino · ZADAR
MANDRIOLI PASS · Urbino · Senigállia
VIAMAGGIO PASS · Fossombrone · Ancona · BRINDISI KERKIRA PATRAS PIRAEUS
Pieve S. Stéfano · Acqualagna · Iesi · Numana
Borgo Pace · Città di Castello · Scheggia · Fabriano · Villa Potenza · Civitanova Marche · KERKIRA PATRAS PIRAEUS
Sansepolcro · Gúbbio · Matélica · Macerata
Cortona · Gualdo Tadino · Tolentino · Fermo · Porto S. Giórgio
Magione · Assisi · Muccia · Amándola · San Benedetto del Tronto · Porto d'Ascoli
Perúgia · 32 · Foligno · Borgo Cerreto · Áscoli Piceno · SPLIT
Chiusi · Città della Pieve · Piedipaterno · Arquata del Tronto · Giulianova Lido
Todi · Spoleto · Téramo · Roseto degli Abruzzi
Orvieto · Amatrice · Villa Vomano · Pescara · Penne · Ortona · Marina di
Núovo · Bolsena · Térni · Piediluco · Monteréale · Antrodoco · L'Aquila · Bariciano · Chieti · Lánciano
Narni · Rieti · Cásoli
Viterbo · Vetralla · Nepi · Popoli · Celano · Sulmona · Cúpello
Veiano · Passo Corese · CARUSO PASS

ADRIATIC SEA

YUGOSLAVIA

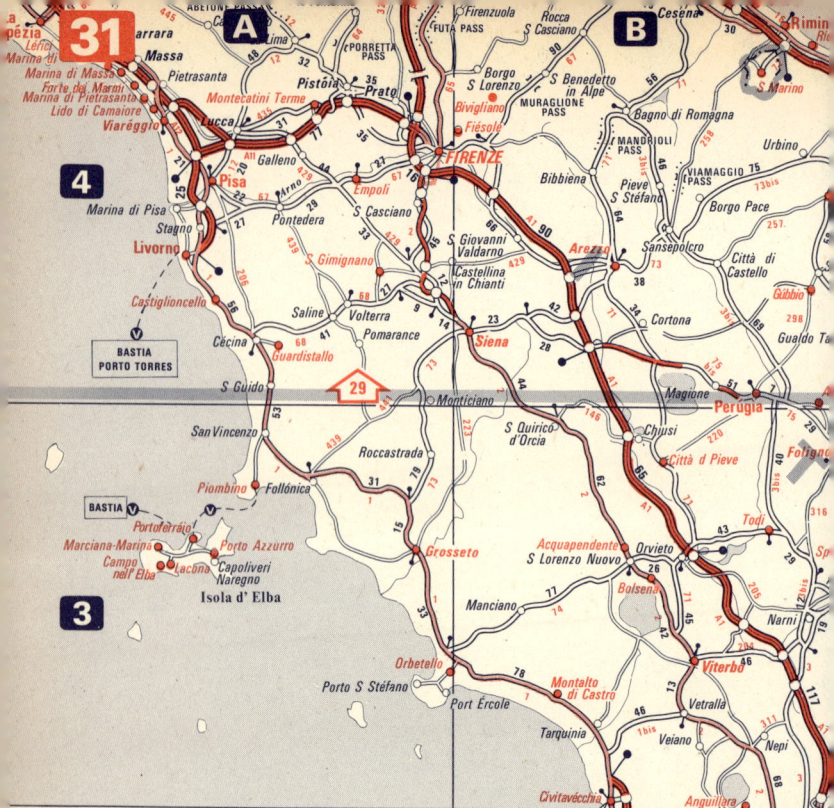

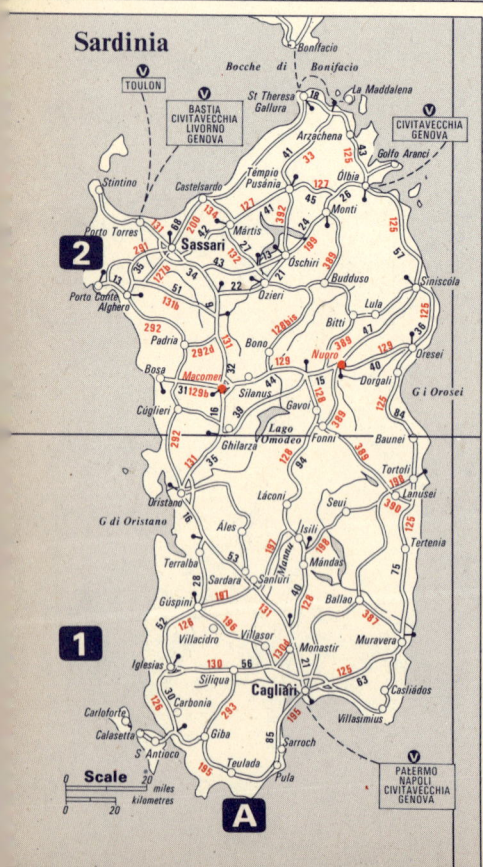

Marc...aro
Fano
18
Senigállia
...brone   38   13   Ancona
Iesi   74
18   Numana
26   Civitanova Marche
Esino   36
Villa Potenza
Macerata
Matélica   42   Tolentino   Fermo   Porto S.Giórgio
256   77   A14   148   36½
Múccia   Amándola   San Benedetto
208   80   del Tronto
Áscoli   36   Porto d'Ascoli
Borgo Cerreto   Piceno
...ediperno   356   Arquata del Tronto   Tronto   Giulianova Lido
73   Téramo   90   25   Roseto
Amatrice   156   degli Abruzzi
...luco   4   Villa   A27
Montereale   Vomano
Antrodoco   81   Penne   Pescara
25   33   L'Aquila   69   Ortona
Barisciano   Chieti   Marina San Vito
48   Lanciano   Torino di Sangro
A24   Popoli   98   Vasto
118   Celano   Cásoli   30   Térmoli
Carsoli   107   Sulmona   45   Cupello   227
94   5   Cappelle   67   CARUSO PASS   54   Montenero   Marina di Chiéuti
Avezzano   di Bisaccia   27 54   Apricena
Subiaco   76   Castiglione   138   Serracapriola   78   A14
Valmontone   411   S.Vincenzo   Roccaraso   Agnone   157   Casacalenda   San Severo
44   Nuovo   82   Pescasseroli   55   100 25   Fóggia
Frosinone   Guarcino   Alfedena   Petrella   17
Cisterna di Latina   27   Sora   14   33   Isérnia   Carpinone   Campobasso   55   Lucera
...na   156   A2   209   6   Cassino   85   25   66   Volturara   172
Priverno   Pico   20   Venafro   40   Baiano   80   Appula
Fondi   42   Liri   158   Morcone   San Marco   Giardinetto   16
Fórmia   A2   27½   Guárdia   dei Cavoti   90bis   A16
Terracina   213   Sessa   60   Sanframondi   Ascoli Satriani
San Felice   Gaeta   Aurunca   44   Caiazzo   Volturno   Ariano Irpino
Circeo   357   Capua   11   Benevento   28   Grottaminarda
San   264   Caserta   57   31   76   343   S.Andrea
Castel Volturno   33   A30   88 27   A16
NÁPOLI   268   Avellino   A30   81   164   Éboli
Pozzuoli   A3   Vesuvius   Salerno   54
Lacco Ameno   Pompei   Cava de'Tirreni   Battipáglia
Forio   Ischia   Castellammare   Vietri   20   19 56
I d'Ischia   Vico Equense   Maiori   Roccadaspide
Sorrento   Amalfi   166
Capri   Piano di   Minori
Sorrento   Paestum
I di Capri   Golfo   di   Agrópoli
Salerno   1   ...o d'Lucán

A D R I A T I C   S E A
KERKIRA   PATRAS   PIRAEUS
SPLIT
ZADAR

M E D I T E R R A N E A N   S E A
Golfo di Salerno

4
3
33
2
1

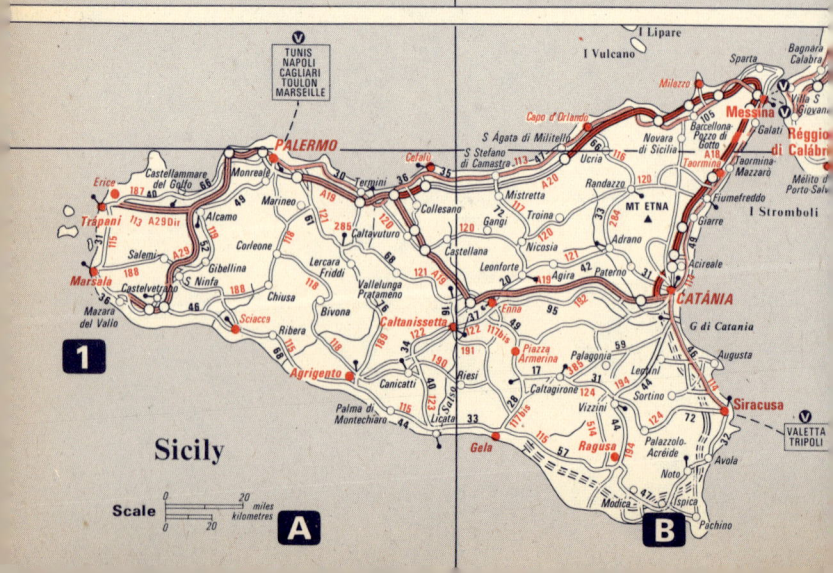

4

ADRIATIC SEA

DUBROVNIK
BAR

VENEZIA

Barletta
Trani
14
78 42
Biscéglie
Molfetta
Andria
88
Corato
BARI
35 Mola di Bari
Bitonto
Casamássima
Polignano a Mare
Castellana
Grotte
Monópoli
46
378
38
Fasano
173
Gervásio
12
Altamura
171
Gióia del Coll
Ostuni
79
San Vito dei
Normanni
Brindisi
Gravina
in Pugli
89
33
Martina Franca
Mottola
Massafra
Francavilla
Fontana
56
Mesagne
39
S. Catalau
Matera
7
Grottáglie
1
Latiano
Laterza
49
San Giorgio Iónico
Lecce
106
Migliónico
Táranto
13
Manduria
85
28 Martano
71
35
63
174
38 107
Stigliano
175
Lido di Metaponte
Galátone
17
Otranto
103
Pisticci
Máglie
16
Corleto
Missanello
103
37
Scanzano
Gallipoli
275
39
60
Senise
214
Leuca
Gagliano
del Capo
104
Noépoli
44
Golfo di Taranto
Castellúccio
Inferiore
Cerchiara
di Calábria
Trebisacce
72
38
105
Villapiàna Lido
Castrovillari
19
25
106
Sosti
65
Cariati
Rossano
46 Cetraro 69
108ter
106
Ciro Marina
Acri
58
Páole
Camigliatello
107
S Giovanni
in Fiore
107
32
71
Cosenza
Lorica
68
19
109
79 Crotone
Amantea
43
28
109
62
34
56
Nicastro
106
Tirriolo
43
36
Catanzaro
di S Eufemia
35
Maida
19d
Catanzaro Lido
Pizzo
Chiaravalle
182
Soverato
Tropea
43
Vibo
Valéntia
182
Serra
S Bruno
Marina di Badolato
41
795
51
110
Monasterace di Marina
Rosarno
37
a Táuro
A3
Taurianova
106
111
Plati
Locri
183
112
Bovalino Marina
giovanni
lábria
Brancaleone
Marina
106 74
ggio di
lábria
Mélito di Porto-Salv

39

3

2

1

C   D

A | B | GRAZ

im Pongau | Obertauern | St-Georgen | Weisskirchen | Gleisdorf
Rauris | Mauterndorf | Murau | Judenburg | Köflach | Fürstenfeld
stein | Tamsweg | Murau | PERCHAUER PASS | Hirschegg | A2 | Feldbach
GROSS | Bad Gastein | Neumarkt | Twimberg | Wilden | Feldbach
GLOCKNER PASS | KATSCHBERG PASS | Predlitz | Freisach | A2
Bockstein | KATSCHBERG PASS | Turrach | Metnitz | Wolfsberg | Deutschlandsberg | Spielfeld
TAUERN RAILWAY TUNNEL | Mallnitz | Gmünd | TURRACHER HÖHE PASS | St Andrä | Maribor
Winkeln | Möllbrücke | Patergassen | St Veit | Lavamünd | Eibiswald | Radne ob Dravo | Ptuj
Greifen | Spittal | Radenthein Feldkirchen | Völkermarkt | Dravograd | Maribor
Kötschach | Hermagor | Annenheim | Pörtsch | Klagenfurt | Slovenj Gradec | 14
Villach | Velden | Maria Wörth | Prevaljah | Na Koroskem | Slov Bistrica
PLÖCKEN PASS | Tarvisio | WURZEN PASS | Dellach | LOIBL PASSES | Crna | Dobrna | Krapina
Pontebba | Ratece Planica | WÜRZEN PASS | TUNNEL | SEEBERG PASS | Soštanj | Celje | Zabok
Tolmezzo | PREDIL PASS | Kranjska Gora | Radmirje | Lasko | Žabok
Carnia | VRŠIC PASS | Bled | Preddvor | Kamnik | Trojane | Celje | Krapina
Tarcento | Bovec | Bohinj | Kranj | Domžale | Trbovlje | Žalec | Židani Most
Tricesimo | Kobarid | Tolmin | Žirin | Litija | ZAGR
Udine | Cividale del Friuli | LJUBLJANA | Trebnje | Krško | Brežice
Gorizia | Idrija | Godovič | Škofljica | Vrhnika | N Mesto | Jastrebars
Ajdovscina | Kalce | Planina | Ribnica | Otočec | E94
Pieris | Monfalcone | Sežana | Postojna | Grahovo | Lož | Kocevje | Metlika | Semič | Črnomelj
Trieste | Lipica | Kozina | Ilirska Bistrica | Bosanci | Karlovac | Duga Resa | Tušilovic
Grado | Ankaran | Rupa | Delnice | Vrbovsko | Lesce
Lignano Pineta | Piran | Koper | RIJEKA | Bakar | Josipdol | Slunj
Caorle | Portorož | Opatija | Kraljevica | Plaški | Rakov
Umag | Poreč | Pazin | Lovran | Crikvenica | Novi | Žuta Lokva | Plitvice
Baderna | Plomin | Moščenička | Porozina | Šilo | Senj | Otočac
Rovinj | Raša | Rabac | Cres | Krk | Baška | Jurjevo | Starigrad
Vodnjan | Cres | Rab | Lun | Jablanac | Perušic
Pula | Osor | Rab | Karlobag | Gospić
Lošinj | Lošinj | Pag | Pag | Tribanj | Medak | HALANMALU PASS
Petrcane
Molat | Zadar | Novigrad
Dugi Otok | Filip Jakov
Biograd na Moru | Tijesno
Kornat

ADRIATIC SEA

Rimini | Riccione | Cattolica | Gabicce Mare | Pesaro | Fano | Fossombrone | Ancona
Iesi | Numana | Civitanova Marche
Scheggia | Fabriano | Villa Potenza | Macerata
Matélica | Tolentino | Fermo | Porto S Giórgio
Assisi | Múccia | Amándola | San Benedetto

A | B | PESCARA | KER

1 | 2 | 3 | 4

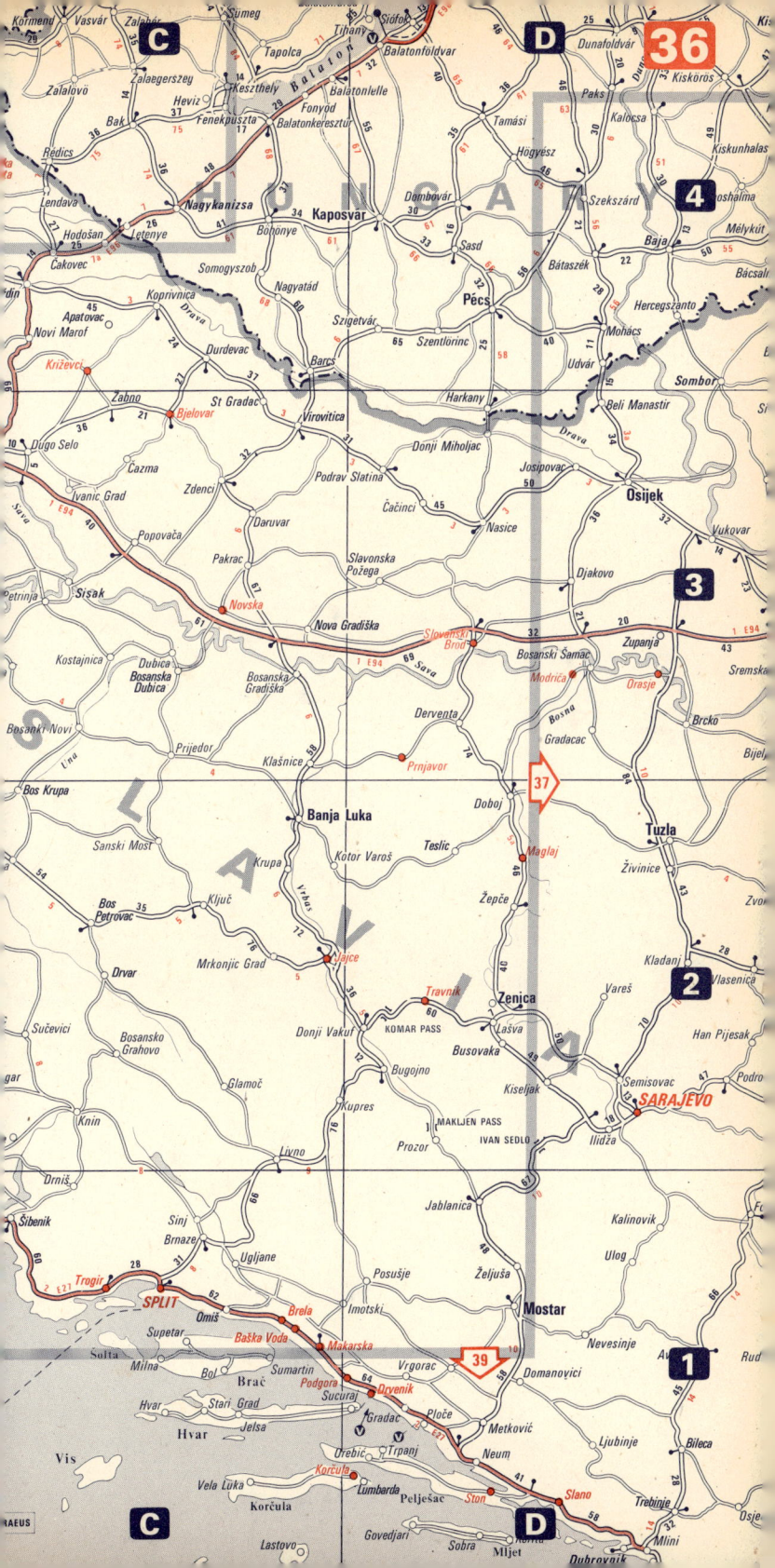

C D **36** **4** **3** **37** **2** **39** **1** C D

HUNGARY

SLAVIJA

Kormend · Vasvár · Zalaból · Sümeg · Balatonföldvár · Siófok · Dunaföldvár · Kiskörös

Tapolca · Tihany · Balatonföldvár

Zalalövö · Zalaegerszeg · Keszthely · Balatonlelle · Paks · Kalocsa

Heviz · Fonyod · Balatonkeresztúr · Tamási · Högyesz · Kiskunhalas

Bak · Fenekpuszta · Szekszárd · Boshalma · Mélykút

Zalalövö · Nagykanizsa · Kaposvár · Dombóvár · Baja · Bácsaln

Redics · Lendava · Bohonye · Somogyszob · Nagyatád · Sasd · Bátaszék · Hercegszanto · Sombor

Hodošan · Letenye · Koprivnica · Drava · Szigetvár · Pécs · Mohács · Udvár · Beli Manastir

Cakovec · Apatovac · Novi Maróf · Durdevac · Szentlörinc · Harkany

din · Kriźevci · Zabno · Bjelovar · St Gradac · Virovitica · Donji Miholjac · Josipovac · Osijek · Vukovar

Dugo Selo · Cazma · Zdenci · Podrav Slatina · Čačinci · Nasice · Djakovo · Županja

Ivanic Grad · Popovača · Daruvar · Slavonska Požega · Nova Gradiška · Slavonski Brod · Bosanski Šamac · Modrica · Orašje · Brčko · Sremska

Petrinja · Sisak · Pakrac · Novska · Derventa · Bosna · Gradacac · Bijel

Kostajnica · Dubica · Bosanska Gradiška · Klašnice · Prnjavor · Doboj · Tuzla

Bosanski Novi · Bosanska Dubica · Prijedor · Banja Luka · Teslic · Maglaj · Živinice · Zvo

Bos Krupa · Sanski Most · Kotor Varoš · Žepče · Kladanj · Vlasenica

Bos Petrovac · Ključ · Krupa · Vrbas · Vareš · Han Pijesak · Podro

Drvar · Mrkonjic Grad · Jajce · Travnik · Zenica · Lašva · Semisovac · SARAJEVO

Sučevici · Bosansko Grahovo · Donji Vakuf · Komar Pass · Busovaca · Kiseljak · Ilidža

Glamoč · Bugojno · Kupres · Makljen Pass · Ivan Sedlo

Knin · Livno · Prozor · Jablanica · Kalinovik · Ulog

Drniš · Sinj · Brnaze · Ugljane · Posušje · Željuša · Mostar · Nevesinje

Šibenik · Trogir · SPLIT · Omiš · Imotski · Domanovici · A · Rud

Supetar · Brela · Baška Voda · Makarska · Vrgorac · Drvenik

Solta · Milna · Bol · Sumartin · Podgora · Sućuraj · Ploče · Metković · Ljubinje · Bileca

Hvar · Stari Grad · Jelsa · Gradac · Neum · Trebinje

Vis · Orebić · Trpanj

Vela Luka · Korčula · Lumbarda · Peljesac · Ston · Slano · Mlini

Lastovo · Govedjari · Sobra · Mljet · Dubrovnik

PIRAEUS

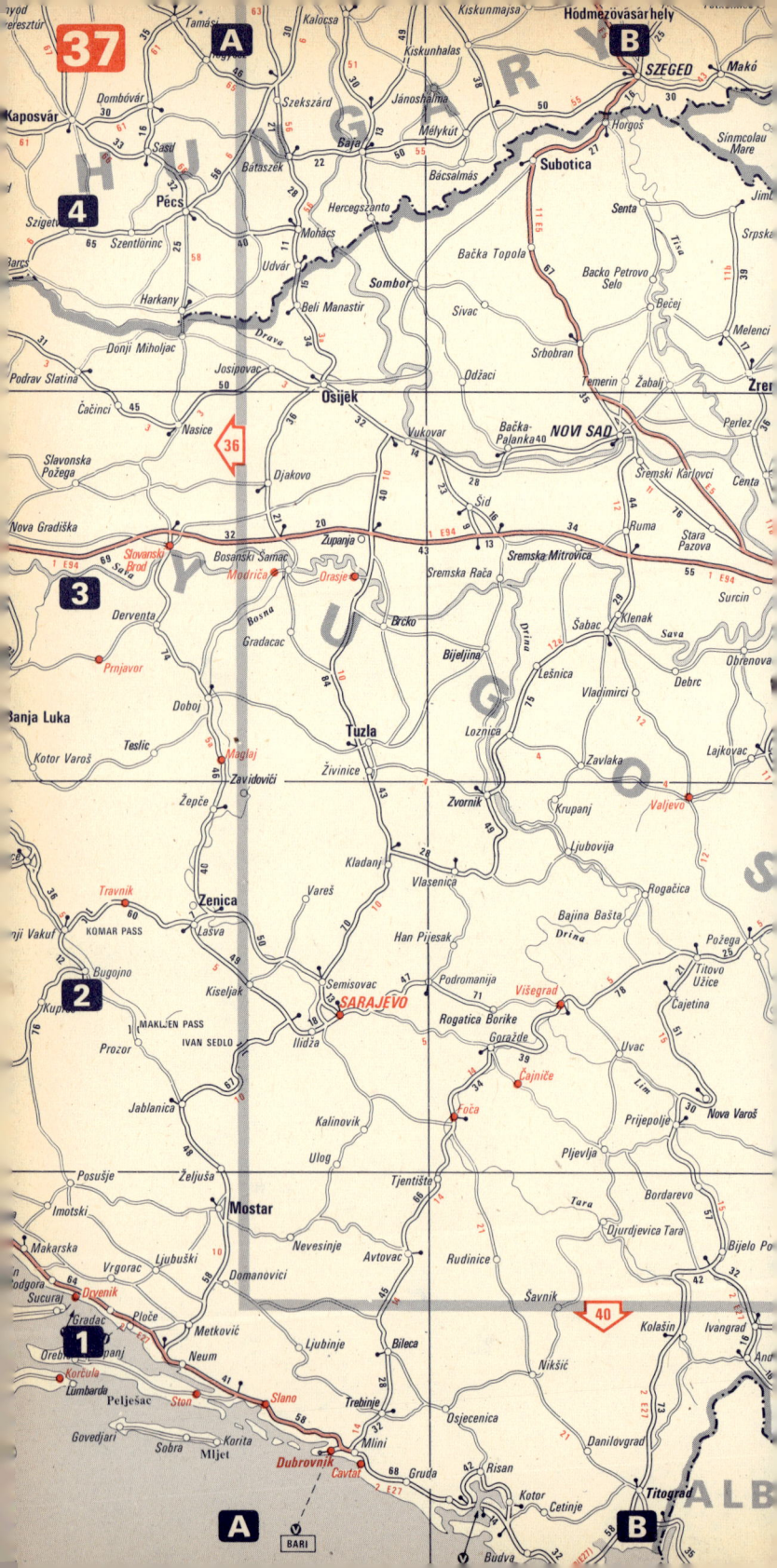

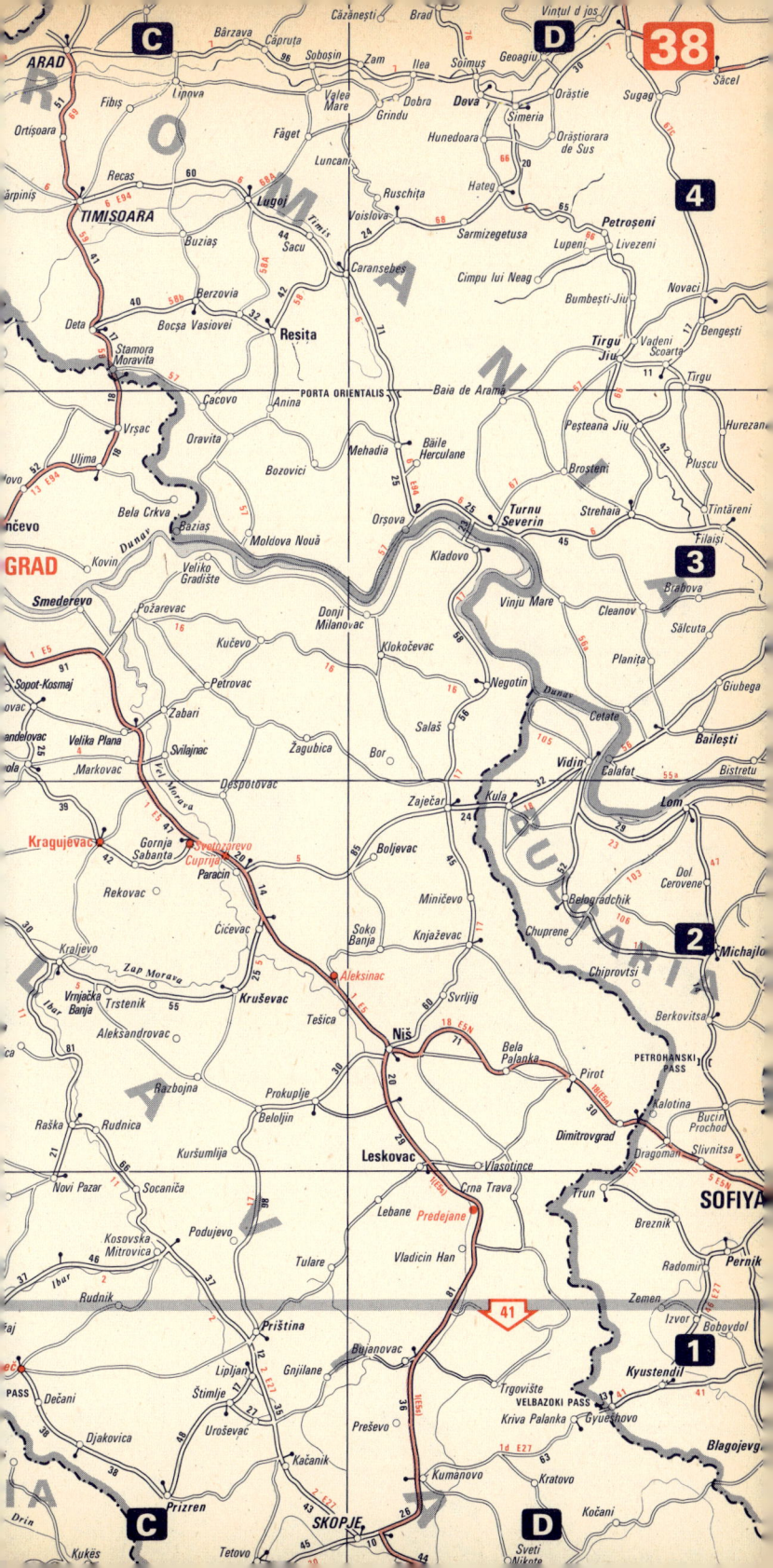

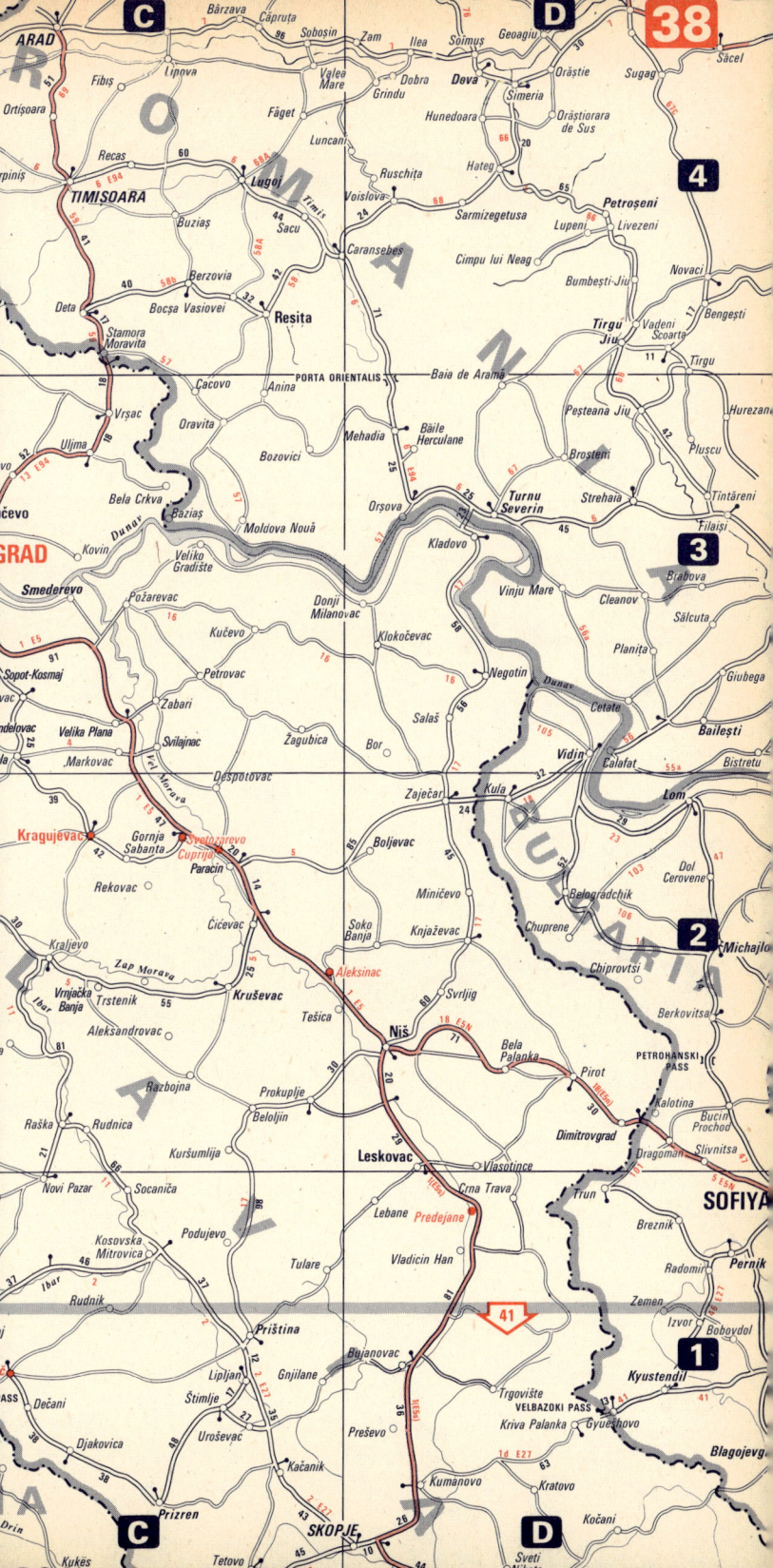

ROMANIA
BULGARIA

Căzănești
Brad
Vințul d jos
Bârzava
Căpruța
Soboșin
Zam
Ilea
Șoimuș
Geoagiu

ARAD
Fibiș
Lipova
Valea Mare
Dobra
Grindu
Deva
Orăștie
Sugag
Săcel

Ortișoara
Orăștiora de Sus

Fâget
Luncani
Hunedoara
Simeria

Recaș
Ruschița
Hateg
Petroșeni

TIMIȘOARA
Buziaș
Voislova
Sarmizegetusa
Lupeni
Livezeni

Sacu
Caransebeș
Cimpu lui Neag
Bumbești-Jiu
Novaci

Berzovia
Bengești

Deta
Bocșa Vasiovei
Resita
Vadeni Scoarta
Tirgu Jiu

Stamora Moravita
Tirgu

Cacovo
Anina
PORTA ORIENTALIS
Baia de Aramă
Hurezan

Vrșac
Oravita
Pesteana Jiu
Pluscu

Uljma
Mehadia
Băile Herculane
Broșteni

Bela Crkva
Bozovici
Orșova
Turnu Severin
Strehaia
Tintăreni

Baziaș
Moldova Nouă
Filasi

GRAD
Kovin
Veliko Gradiste
Kladovo
Vinju Mare
Cleanov
Brabova

Smederevo
Požarevac
Donji Milanovac
Planița
Sălcuta
Giubega

Sopot-Kosmaj
Kučevo
Klokočevac
Negotin
Cetata
Bailești

Petrovac
Salaš
Vidin
Calafat
Bistreti

Velika Plana
Zabari
Žagubica
Bor
Lom

Markovac
Svilajnac
Despotovac
Zaječar
Kula

Kragujevac
Gornja Sabanta
Svetozarevo
Ćuprija
Boljevac
Belogradčik
Dol Cerovene

Paraćin
Miničevo
Chuprene
Michajlo

Rekovac
Ćićevac
Soko Banja
Knjaževac
Chiprovtsi
Berkovitsa

Kraljevo
Zap Morava
Aleksinac
Svrljig

Vrnjačka Banja
Trstenik
Kruševac
Tešica
Niš
Bela Palanka
Pirot
PETROHANSKI PASS

Aleksandrovac
Razbojna
Prokuplje
Kalotina
Bucin Prochod
Slivnitsa

Raška
Rudnica
Beloljin
Dimitrovgrad
Dragoman
SOFIYA

Novi Pazar
Socanica
Leskovac
Vlasotince
Trun
Breznik

Kosovska Mitrovica
Podujevo
Crna Trava
Radomir
Pernik

Rudnik
Tulare
Lebane
Predejane
Zemen

Ibar
Priština
Vladicin Han
Izvor
Bobovdol
Kyustendil

Lipljan
Gnjilane
Bujanovac
Trgovište
VELBAZOKI PASS

PASS
Dečani
Štimlje
Preševo
Kriva Palanka
Gyueshovo

Djakovica
Uroševac
Kačanik
Kumanovo
Kratovo
Blagojevg

Prizren
SKOPJE
Kočani

Kukes
Tetovo
Sveti Nikole

A B

Sinj
Brnaze
Ugljane
Jablanica
Kalinovik
67
Posušje
Željuša
Ulog
Trogir
2 E27
28
31
66
SPLIT
62
Omiš
Supetar
Brela
Makarska
Imotski
Mostar
Ljubuški
10
Nevesinje
Avtovac

4
PESCARA

Šolta
Milna
Bol
Baška Voda
Sumartin
Vrgorac
Domanovici
65
Brač
Sućuraj
37
Podgora
64
Ploče
Hvar
Stari Grad
Jelsa
Gradac
E27
Metković
Ljubinje
Bileca
Hvar
Orebić
Trpanj
Neum
28
Vela Luka
Korčula
Lumbarda
41
Ston
Slano
58
Trebinje
Vis
Korčula
Pelj:šac
14
32
Govedjari
Korita
Mljet
Dubrovnik
Mlini
Lastovo
Sobra
68 Gruda
Lastovo
Cavtat
2 E27
ANCONA
Hercegnov

VENEZIA

3
V

San Menáio
Gargano
Vieste
A D R I A T I C
105
89
Cagnano
Varano
Apricena
54
Mattinata
Manfredonia
38
89
Zapponeta
159
56
Barletta
Trani
A14
Biscéglie
13
34
Molfetta
51
Órto
16 23
Nova Cerignola
14
78
42
BARI
triano
16
Canosa
Andria
Corato
Mola di Bari
2
Ofanto
Minervino
Bitonto
Polignano a Mare
93
97
Casamássima
Castellana
Grotte
Monópoli
Lavello
170
35
Rapolla
168
Palazzo S Gervásio
12
Altamura
Gióia del Coll
Fasano
16
175
303
57
74
97
Irsina
171
Martina Franca
Ostuni
79
San Vito dei
Normanni
S Andrea
19
72
Gravina
in Pugli
33
38
Brindisi
81
61
Tolve
97
Matera
Laterza
Massafra
172
Francavilla
Fontana
56
Mesagne
Potenza
Basento
Mottola
Grottáglie
Latiano
12
59
80
94
180
71
Miglionico
106
Taranto
San Giorgio Iónico
85
Lecce
Brienza
95
61
97
Stigliano
175
13
Manduria
174
aspide
Laurenzana
103
407
Lido di Metaponte
Galátone
166
Sala Consilina
Corleto
60
Pisticci
33
Gallipoli
allo d'Luc
Casalbuono
103
Missanello
103
Scanzano
1
200
Episcopia
104
Senise
Lagonegro
Sapri
74
104
Maratea
Castellúccio
Inferiore
Noépoli
74
Práia a Mare
Cerchiara
di Calábria
Golfo di Taranto
Trebisacce
72
Villapiàna Lido
Castrovillari
105
Circ
San Sosti
106
Marina di
A
B
65
Cariati
Rossano

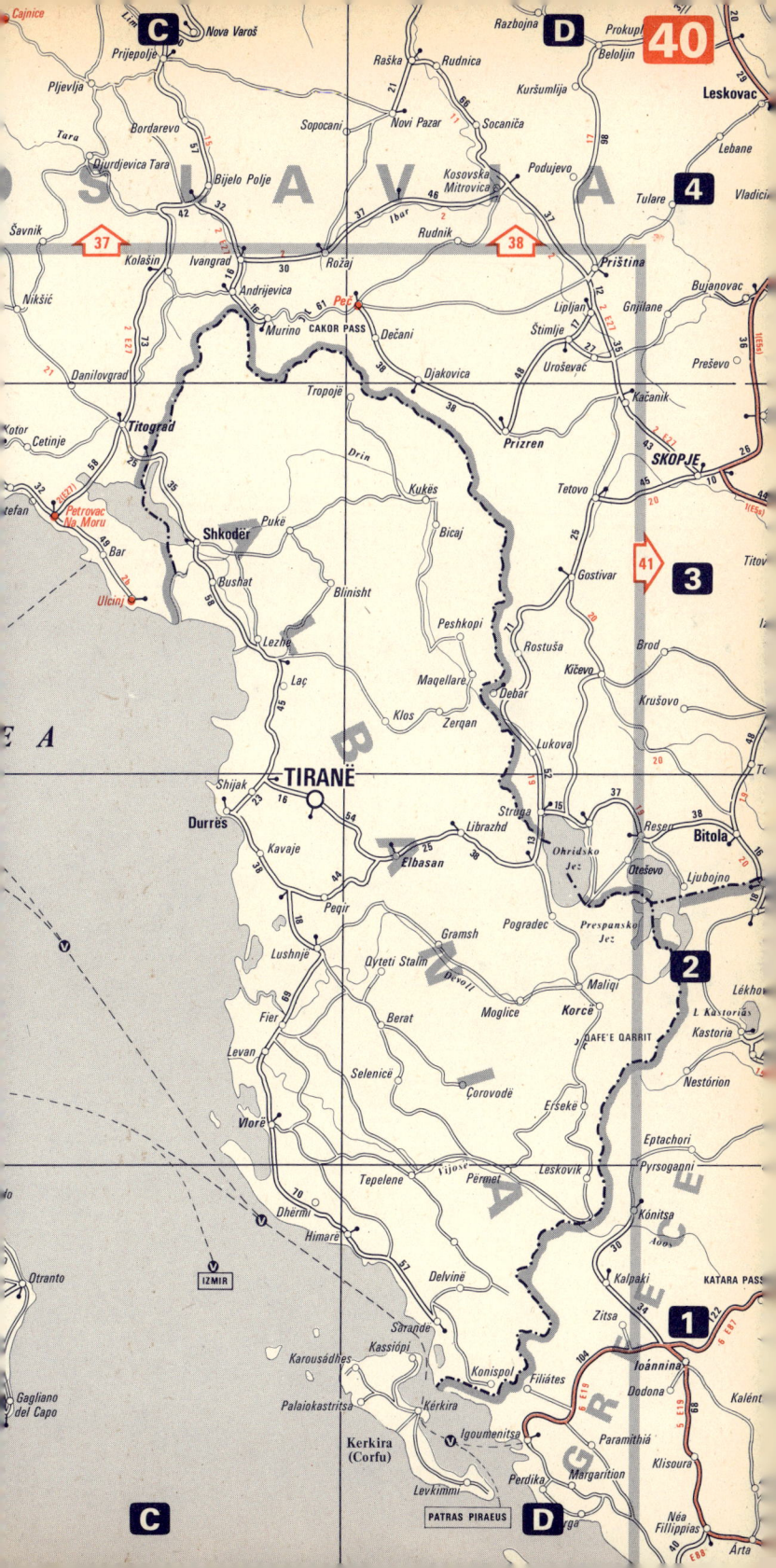

Čajnice

Nova Varoš
Razbojna · D · Prokup
Beloljin

C
Prijepolje
Pljevlja
Raška · Rudnica
Kuršumlija

LESKOVAC

Bordarevo
Sopocani · Novi Pazar · Socanica
Tara
Djurdjevica Tara
Bijelo Polje
Kosovska Mitrovica
Podujevo
Lebane

Šavnik
42 · 32
37 · Ibar · 46 · Rudnik
Tulare
Vladiči

4

37
Kolašin
Ivangrad
Andrijevica
Rožaj
38
Priština
Bujanovac
Nikšić
Murino · ČAKOR PASS
Dečani
Lipljan · Gnjilane
Preševo
Danilovgrad
Tropojë
Djakovica
Uroševac
Kačanik
Titograd
Drin
Prizren
SKOPJE
Kotor · Cetinje
Kukës
Tetovo

3 · Titov
Petrovac Na Moru
Shkodër · Puke · Bicaj
Gostivar
41
Bar
Bushat
Blinisht
Rostuša
Brod
Ulcinj
Lezhë
Peshkopi
Kičevo · Kruševo
Laç
Maqellare · Debar
Zerqan
Lukova
SEA
Klos

TIRANË
Struga · 37
Bitola
Shijak
Librazhd · Ohridsko Jez. · Resen
Durrës
Elbasan
Otešvo · Ljubojno
Kavaje
Prespansko Jez.
Peqir
Pogradec
Lushnjë
Gramsh
Maliqi
2
Fier
Qyteti Stalin · Devoll
Korçë · Lékhov
Moglice
L. Kastorias
Levan
Berat
QAFE'E QARRIT · Kastoria
Selenicë
Çorovodë
Ersekë
Nestórion
Vlorë
Eptachori
Vijose · Përmet · Leskovik
Pyrsogánni
Tepelene

Dhërmi
Kónitsa
Himarë

Kalpaki
IZMIR
Delvinë
Zitsa
1
Sarandë
Ioánnina
Kassiópi
Dodona · Kalénti
Karousádhes
Konispol · Filiátes
Otranto
Palaiokastritsa
Kérkira
Margarition
Gagliano del Capo
Kerkira (Corfu)
Igoumenitsa
Paramithiá
Klisoura
Levkímmi
Perdika
Árta
C
PATRAS PIRAEUS · D
Néa Fillippias

41
A
B
Prokuplje
Bela Palanka
PETROHANSKI PASS
Bucin Prohod
Svoge
Botevgrad
Etropole
Kalotina
Dimitrovgrad
Dragoman
Kuršumlija
Leskovac
Vlasotince
Slivnitsa
SOFIYA
Crna Trava
Trun
Elin Pelin
Lebane
Predejane
Breznik
Vakarel
Podujevo
4
Vladicin Han
Pancarevo
Iskur
Ihtiman
Tulare
Radomir
Pernik
Trekl'ano
Vranje
38
Izvor
Samokov
Priština
Bobovdol
Borovets
Lipljan
Gnjilane
Bujanovac
Kyustendil
Stanke Dimitrov
VELBAZOKI PASS
MUSALA PASS
Štimlje
Trgovište
Rilski Manastir
Yakoruda
Uroševac
Preševo
Kriva Palanka
Gyueshovo
Struma
Kocerinovo
Blagoevgrad
Kacanik
Kratovo
Razlog
Kumanovo
Simitli
Bansko
Dobrinishte
SKOPJE
Kočani
Tetovo
Sveti Nikole
Štip
Sadanski
Radoviš
Melnik
YUGOSLAVIA
Titov Veles
Gostivar
40
3
Kulata
Petrich
Izvor
Gradsko
Vardar
Strumica
Neon Petritsi
Brod
Kavadarci
Valandovo
Kičevo
Sidhirokastron
Rudopolis
Stari Dojran
Kruševo
Prilep
Aléxia
Gevgelija
Evzoni
Lukova
Topolčanj
Kilkis
Polikastron
Bitola
Gouménissa
Assiros
Struga
Ohrid
Ardhéa
Resen
Ohridsko Jez.
L. Koronia
Oteševo
Kali
Ljubojno
Niki
Yiannitsa
Gephira
THESSALONIKI
Edhessa
Axios
Áyios Prodromos
Pogradec
Flórina
L. Vegorritis
Prespansko Jez.
2
Náousa
Emvolos
Epanomi
Políyiros
Maliqi
Léhkoven
Aiyinion
Véroia
Korcë
Ptolemaís
G
R
E
Kastoria
L. Kastorias
Kalithéa
Néa Moudhania
Katerini
Árgos Orestikón
Nestórion
Neápolis
Kozáni
Sérvia
Litókhoron
Ersekë
Platamon
Eptachori
Pyrsogianni
Grevená
Stómion
Elassón
Leskovik
Vijosë
Ziakas
MELOUNAS PASS
Konitsa
Sikoúrion
Dheskáti
Ayia
Aoos
KATARA PASS
Kalpaki
Lárisa
Platikambos
Kalabáka
Métsovon
Kanália
Zitsa
Tsiótion
Portario
Trikkala
1
Ioannina
Pertoúli
Palamás
Velestínon
Vólos
Filiátes
Dodona
Kaléntzi
Sofádhes
Kardhitsa
Fársala
Paramithia
Drosopigi
Philákti
Almirós
Aspropotamos
Klisoura
Kédros
Dhomokós
Margariton
Anemorahi
Perdika
Párga
L. Xynias
Néa Filippias
Árta
Makrakomi
Lamia
Kombóti

C   Troyan   64   47   48   **D**   Yambol

Kazanlŭk   Tund-a   Nova Zagora   33

Kŭrnare   16   Karlovo   57   Tŭlovo   33   31

47   Kalofer

Koprivshtitsa   Khisar   **Stara Zagora**   Radnevo   Boljarovo

Strelca   Brezovo   Polski Gradets   Elkhovo

nagyurishte   Kaloyanovo   150   Sredets   Gálábovo   Topolovgrad

180   56   Chirpan   146   **4**

Trud   28   **Dimitrovrad**   Kharmanli   Levka   Lălapaşa

37   Popovitsa

Pazardžhik   **PLOVDIV**   5 ESN   50   33   Lyubimets   **Edirne**

Peshtera   Krichim   **Asenovgrad**   **Khaskovo**   19   2 ESN

179   45   Eylákion

Batak   196   Panickovo   57   147

Devin   52   Chepelare   Arda   **Kurdzhali**   Potonica   Ivaylovgrad   Zoni   Orestiás

157   28   Ardino   177   Momchilgrad   148   Mandrica   Dhidhimótikhon

Dospat   Ustovo   Krumovgrad

Smolyán   18   Rŭdozem   Podkova   Küplii

28   Zlatograd   154   Makaz   **3**

Skaloti   Ekhinos   Pessanis   Ipsala

Potamoi   Nestos   Komotini   18

Exochi   Paranéstion   Sápai

Káto   Stavroúpolis   **Xánthi**   Iasmos   Ávas   Ferrai

Nevrokópian   56   64   2 ESN   33

Drama   2 ESN   Pórto Lágo   Marónia   **Alexandroúpolis (Dedéagach)**

Alistáti   Dhoxáton   54   Khrisoúpolis   Enez   Hasköy

12   36

Eleftheroúpolis   **Kaválla (Cavalla)**   Keramoti   Thásos

63   2 ESN   Panagria

Kolpos Kavalla   Theologos

Thásos   Limenaria   Samothráki   **Samothráki**

Gökçe (Imroz)   Eceabot

Thrakikon   _Pelagos_   Gökçe

Ierissós   Tripiti   Pirgos   Seddülbahir

Ouranoúpolis   Dáfni   Kumkale

Nikitas   **Limnos**   **2**

Sikiá   Bozca Ada

Kólpos   Limnou (Kastron)   Moúdhros   Odun Isk.

Paliouri   Babakale

E   **C**   **E**   Mithimna

Lesvos

A E G E A N   **S E A**   Éressos

Chiliodromia   **1**

Skópelos   Skiros   Skiros   Psara   **Chios**

Linariá

Ayía Anna   Mandoúdhion   **C**   **D**

Strofiliá   Kimi

MAKE THE MOST OF YOUR MONEY

WHEN TO GO?

Most people going on holiday seek only a change – different scenery, a change of atmosphere and above all, as far as the British are concerned, reasonably reliable weather. A few may be more fortunate in pursuing specific interests such as winter sports, cultural activities or sporting events because they know precisely where and when to go. The majority, however, are really uncertain as to what they want – 'change' has different meanings for different people.

'Summer holidays' is an expression dying hard in Britain where Summer means July and August, associated with the sun. Parents, of course, are limited by school holidays, and others may have to take their holiday during the annual works shut-down. By and large, however, the British tend to take their holidays in the Summer because they know these are the best months here and assume they must be the best months overseas. Unfortunately, everybody else seems to think so (in France the whole population appears to take its holiday in August) and at peak holiday time conditions can be at their worst.

Instead of considering *climate*, it might be better to look at *seasons*. As a rough yardstick, each season we know and understand at home becomes warmer travelling south, cooler and wetter to the north and more extreme toward the east. As a finer adjustment bear in mind that it is always cooler in mountain areas, warmer inland, seas are at their warmest in middle or late Summer and that mountain lakes, served by glaciers, are very cold all the year round.

Few will deny that Spring is the loveliest season and since most tourists will motor south from Britain they can expect that season generally to be more agreeable than at home. During May and early June accommodation will be cheaper, fresher and easier to find, roads will be less crowded and touring altogether more satisfactory if you are looking for a pleasant and relaxing change. Autumn should be considered too, as September and even early October can provide a wonderful backdrop for a glorious motoring holiday.

If you finally decide on July or August, as in fact most do, you should be prepared for heavily-congested main roads, expensive and difficult-to-get accommodation, and, if you select an area roughly south of a line on Lyon, shimmering heat through the midday. These disadvantages can be mitigated by starting your daily trip early, by stopping for the lunch break between 12 and 2 and by seeking the night stop early – that is, by about 4.00pm. The peak of the tourist season is more comfortable in mountain areas with lakesides instead of seasides for relaxation – you would effect little economy but you would have greater peace of mind.

If you are seeking cultural pursuits you are lucky because weather is of secondary importance. Since, therefore, the major cities, antiquities and historical sites invariably become packed with tourists you are well advised to arrange your trip outside the peak season.

The winter sports season is anchored to social as well as sporting activities. This season is at its peak in February in central Europe and creates the same conditions as the holiday season in July and August. The high degree of organisation both natural and artificial are highly developed in Switzerland, Austria and France where resorts are fiercely expensive. Yugoslavia and Spain, although less popular, can offer robust sport and are cheaper.

HOW TO GO?

By now, of course, it is obvious that we assume you want to go by car. Not that this book can't be used if you are travelling by bicycle, train or foot – but apart from cycling or hitch-hiking, travelling by car can be the cheapest way to go, especially if costs are shared. Nonetheless there are alternatives to driving all the way which are well worth considering.

Car/sleeper services

Most holiday makers are impatient to 'get there' and those living at such a distance from the Channel port as might necessitate an overnight stop should consider the excellent car/sleeper trains run by British Rail to London, Dover and Brockenhurst (near Southampton). At first sight the fares would appear expensive but if one considers the cost of driving to the port and an overnight stop for a party there may be little in it. Also the train journey is a lot less tiring than a long drive.

Once over the Channel, European car/sleeper services run to destinations many hundreds of miles from the Channel coast and overnight one can reach a touring ground very quickly, arriving fresh and rested. Such a journey, although apparently expensive, can save car running costs and possibly the cost of two overnight stops. On p80 we compare the costs of two such journeys with the cost of driving all the way.

Pula, Yugoslavia

The crossing

The English Channel is notoriously one of the most expensive waters in the world to cross, so there is little one can do to cut costs. Normally one would assume that the shortest crossing is the most economical, but this is not always the case. It is fine if you live near Dover and want to go somewhere near Calais, but for those who live further afield the choice of crossing depends more on convenience than on cost. For example, those who live in the north may find it only marginally more expensive but a great deal less exhausting to take a ferry from a nearby North Sea port and go on a longer sea voyage.

Time is an important factor as well, both in terms of the length of voyage and when you will be embarking and disembarking. Ideally one would hope for an early crossing enabling you to make a reasonable journey in day time before your first night stop. Even so, if you were, say, to get a 9.00am ferry from Dover you probably wouldn't be able to get away on the other side until midday, giving you only half a day's driving. Then, if you had booked your first night's accommodation and there were any delays due to adverse weather or other reasons, you might be hard pushed to reach your planned destination.

So when choosing which crossing to take bear in mind the following points:

- The shortest crossing is not always the best, when you consider which is the nearest Channel port and the location of your final destination.
- Work in to your plans a degree of flexibility as delays either in the driving or in the crossing cannot be foreseen.
- Bear in mind the members of your party. Granny may not *like* getting up at 3.30 in the morning in order to catch that early boat. Or if you haven't got a very strong sea-tummy, perhaps driving 500 miles in the first day might be a little ambitious. . . .

How to find out more

Fortunately there are a great number of services to choose from and in the peak season most operators have departures round the clock. To help you choose and to help with the bookings you could do no better than seek expert advice from any AA travel agency. The experienced staff there have at hand up-to-date information on all ferry and hovercraft services to Europe and will also be pleased to advise you on motorail and other travel services. With over 40 AA travel agencies throughout the country there will be one near you.

Car hire

An alternative to taking your own car which you may not have considered is the hiring of a vehicle. Most of the large car hire firms will hire a car for international travel but they are likely to have high charges and you will still have the expense of putting the vehicle on the ferry. Alternatively you could hire through an airline or rail company. This can make the price of the car hire a good deal cheaper through inclusive terms and in the end you get your ticket abroad with a car waiting for you when you get there. The rates depend on the season, the length of stay and the number in your party. With four in the party the rates can work out much less than hiring the car at home and taking it with you but you may be restricted to driving only in the country of hire.

Probably the cheapest and most satisfactory way of hiring a car is to wait until you arrive at your destination and then seek the advice of the local tourist office as to the best local firm to approach. The advantages are that you will be dealing with principals, pay no agency commission and will see the car that you will actually drive away.

Motorcycles and scooters are not normally available for hire except in resort areas for purely local trips.

PLUGGING THE HOLE IN YOUR POCKET

– some hints to help your money go just a little further

Currency

To obtain credit for a European holiday you should first visit your private bank to get travellers' cheques and foreign currency. You will be charged for this service. This charge is likely to equal about 1% of the amount changed. When you change your travellers' cheques for local currency abroad you will pay a similar commission. Thus, merely for convenience and security, possibly 3% of your holiday money will have dripped away. No matter what you do you will lose out every time you change money, so, to make sure that such losses are kept to a minimum, give yourself the best chance by only dealing in reputable markets. Some opportunities for money changing are not necessarily dishonest but the source is a convenience for the tourist who will pay heavily. The following golden rules should be followed:

- Always use major branches of national banks or, outside banking hours, official exchange offices at main railway stations or airports.
- Always try to make exchanges during banking hours so that a proper current rate of exchange can be obtained if necessary.
- Never expect to get a reasonable deal in hotels or restaurants particularly outside banking hours. The proprietor must make sure that he does not pay to accommodate you.
- Never, but never, make exchanges with private individuals who may approach you in the street or public places.

Remember that where a bank or exchange office charges a set commission for a transaction (this is often the case, for example, when cashing a private cheque with a Eurocard) advantage can be gained by making one large transaction instead of a number of small ones. So if a number of people in the party wish to change money, it might be a good idea to appoint one as 'treasurer' who can get everybody's money at once.

The 'Penny Drip'

Having paid a premium for your currency don't let it drip away – remember the old saying about taking care of the pennies. You will soon get a pocket full of coins and the quicker you learn that some have a value of over £1 the quicker you will understand the 'drip'. It is through coins that a lot of your money will be wasted particularly when you leave because generally coins cannot be changed in another country. If you are leaving a country make sure that as much change as possible is converted into paper money – this can be done at the exchange office or filling station at the frontier. It would be wise for all the members of the party to pool their coins and settle up later. If you are leaving a country but plan to return later on your tour, keep a hold of your coins as each exchange transaction will cost you in commission.

Nürnberg, Germany

Tipping

It is difficult to generalise about tipping, but because too many fail to grasp the value of small coins it can be a great wastage. Hotels and restaurants usually present no problem because they add a stated percentage to their bill and little more is necessary save perhaps something for the porter, etc. Cafés and similar establishments where one receives a 'docket' indicating an amount due can sometimes be confusing. Often service is added but is not clear on the bill and the innocent customer tips again. Instinct will usually tell you when to tip, but the difficulty is how much. A good general rule is still 10% of the bill but when there is no value on the service think carefully before you pass over a coin.

Motorways

Motorway travelling is very fast and has advantages but it is expensive. In many European countries you pay a high toll to use most sections of motorway and of course use more petrol at higher speeds. At service stations anything you buy, including petrol, will be very much more expensive. So if you can, plan motorway travel to a minimum to have a more interesting and less expensive ride. If you do buy petrol on the motorway watch out for a self-service pump – it will be slightly cheaper.

Cafés

Most European cafés are attractive, some more so than others because their owners have taken some trouble to exploit any natural features. Much the same happens in Britain with pubs where we understand that different bars have different charges because facilities or degrees of comfort differ. European cafés have a similar system of varying the scale of charges – a quick drink at the bar, standing, is cheaper than seated at a table. If the table overlooks a lake, mountain or sea then the charges are higher. If an orchestra is playing and you sit nearby then charges are higher still. Perhaps in the evening, when you feel like relaxing in comfort watching the world go by, the charges are not so important, but during the day, quick drinks, which can run away with money anyway, can double in cost if the approach is not watched.

Evening entertainment

This can also be a battle of wits with the supplier always being an easy winner. 'Night-clubs', little more than elaborate cafés, can offer excellent shows. The well-organised ones usually offer a table reservation, some wine, dancing and the show for an inclusive charge which at first sight might seem expensive. At a lower level they offer the *promenade*, a walk around the back for considerably less, which will seem cheap. The wise tourist will take the table reservation knowing his full commitment to the house will please and all will be well. The not-so-wise tourist will take the promenade or lower charge and perhaps order soft drinks thinking he will reduce his expenses. This will not be so, for the house has heavy costs to recover and the charge for the soft drink will be very, very high.

Innsbruck, Austria

In the hotel

Drinks in the hotel bar will cost more than at the café along the road, and unopened bottles of pop or whatever as an occasional drink in the bedroom or for on the road will be cheaper from a shop in the town and a lot cheaper from supermarkets. In the hotel restaurant the best value will be in the fixed menu, being quite a bit cheaper than *à la carte*. Never try to mix the two. If you decide on the fixed menu at a set price, stick to it, otherwise your meal is likely to cost more than you bargained for.

If you are thinking of going out to another restaurant than the one in your hotel, first check that a meal is not included in the hotel price – if it is you will be charged for it whether or not you have taken it.

Souvenirs

The purchase of souvenirs is a notorious source of money wastage and this impulse buying is specially catered for. Identical mass-produced items are available all over Europe on stalls at points where tourists gather. Perhaps it is innocent to spend small amounts on such knick-knacks but value, from any point of view, is so low that it must be concluded that tourists just like wasting money. The souvenir stall at motorway service stations is probably the most expensive point for such purchases where you will pay 4 or 5 times as much as in town markets for identical merchandise.

If some object takes your eye, resist the temptation to buy because you are bound to see the same thing elsewhere for less. If you don't, the impulse will have passed and you will be better off. Probably the best way of satisfying the natural desire to take home some reminder is to allot a sum for such purchases and then to buy in established shops where you see locals shopping – a sure sign of reasonable value.

'Free' tastings

Beware of things for free such as tastings in areas perhaps famous for wines, cheeses or sweetmeats and do not blame the producers if on reflection you feel dissatisfied with any purchases you may have made. Most places which offer free tastings are quite genuine factories manufacturing for wholesale markets, but producers are also well experienced in handling the steady queue of visitors who knock at the door for a look round.

A special area is set aside and a tasting is arranged but you will then be guided to a permanent retail area where for sure you will over-buy, and certainly pay more than in local shops. There is a certain novelty and interest in visiting the factory where some internationally-famous product is made but do not lose sight of the fact that the tasting shop is part of the sales organisation where you will not be allowed to win too many points.

Excursions

Excursions can account for rather high spending but this can be reduced if you visit places as a party rather than individually. If you plan to stay in an area for a short while your first visit should be to the local tourist office to explore the possibility of reduced tourist prices for the various local attractions. Make particular enquiries about facilities available for children or elderly people if such persons are in your party because there may be special reductions for them. If you find yourself dealing with a private person operating some pleasure trip always be prepared to bargain, particularly if the operator is not too busy – *ie* if you are quoted 10 units for a ride offer 30 for four persons, etc.

PLUGGING THE HOLE IN YOUR PETROL TANK

– some tips to help with motoring economy

Once on the road, some of your biggest bills will be for petrol. The amount will vary considerably, of course, with your vehicle, its mechanical condition, the way you drive it and the country you are in. The following notes should help in getting the most for your money and the most miles per gallon.

Buying petrol abroad (see also p252)
Prices

If you haven't been motoring abroad before you may be in for a shock – petrol is cheaper in Britain than anywhere in Europe, even allowing for the various price concessions offered by some countries. Because of fluctuating exchange rates it would be misleading to give you prices in Sterling – but on page 252 you will find a chart showing prices in the countries' respective currencies.

Prices vary quite widely between countries but the ratio between them stays remarkably the same, so if you are travelling from country to country the following order of expense might prove useful. The countries are arranged in the order of the lowest price first and if you can you should buy petrol in the country with the lowest number. Thus, if you are passing from France to Spain you should try to arrive in Spain with a low tank, and in reverse you should fill up in Spain before entering France.

1	Luxembourg	7	Belgium
2	Yugoslavia*	8	Denmark
3	Italy*	9	Switzerland
4	Netherlands	10	France
5	Austria	11	Portugal
6	Spain	12	W Germany

*Tourists visiting Italy can purchase petrol coupons which can be exchanged at the pumps allowing a price reduction of about 30%. The coupons are only issued at points outside Italy and information concerning their purchase can be obtained from the Italian National Tourist Office (address on p222) or from any AA Service Centre. Without coupons Italy would be about no. 10 on the above list.

Petrol coupons are also available for Yugoslavia and can be bought at the border but the saving is not as great as in Italy.

Lake Lucerne, Switzerland

Names

'Petrol' is a term peculiar to Britain describing motor fuel but overseas it sometimes describes paraffin – so never accept fuel from a pump which delivers *petrol, petrole, petroleum, Petroleo*, etc. Fuel for your car will be described as *benzin, benzine, gasoline* or similar words except in France where it is called *essence*.

Filling stations

In most countries filling stations are open between 08.00hrs and 17.30hrs on weekdays. On Sundays they open at 10.00hrs. Petrol stations not on motorways usually close between 12.30hrs and 15.00hrs for lunch. In towns and tourist areas some will be found open during the evening while in larger towns there is at least one which operates a 24-hr service. If you intend to travel at night or anticipate an early morning start you should miss no opportunity to top up your tank. This is a wise precaution in any event because the distance between filling stations varies tremendously.

On motorways filling stations are open 24 hours a day and will be found at regular intervals but petrol is more expensive at these stations.

Self service pumps are increasing in popularity and are operated by a coin or currency note relevant to the country. At such pumps petrol is slightly cheaper. Often they are in the forecourt of filling stations alongside pumps operated by attendants.

If your homeward journey is through France you are strongly advised to ensure that you have enough fuel, or sufficient local currency to buy petrol to reach the Channel port because filling stations near the ports will not accept foreign currency nor will they serve petrol in quantities less than 5 litres. The same might also be said when approaching frontiers within certain areas of Europe.

Don't lose it!

Petrol is expensive – you are strongly advised to secure your tank with a locking petrol cap.

Octane ratings and types of petrol

Using the correct grade of petrol for your car is essential. No useful purpose is served by using petrol with a higher octane rating than the one your car requires – you will only be wasting your money. Petrol of too low an octane rating will cause 'knock' or 'pinking' – a sharp metallic noise most audible when the car is pulling hard at low speed in high gear. Persistent knock can lead to engine damage in the form of a blown cylinder head gasket, piston damage and even connecting rod failure.

The octane requirements of different types of engine, even in the same make and type of car, can vary by as much as plus or minus two octane numbers. So always follow the manufacturers' recommendations as to the correct grade of petrol to use. In general, cars should never be run on a lower grade of fuel than that specified.

In Britain we are used to the 'star' rating rather than octane numbers, so here are the equivalents:

★ ★ – 90 to 93 octane

★ ★ ★ – 94 to 96 octane

★ ★
★ ★ – 97 to 99 octane

★ ★
★ ★ ★ – over 100 octane

On page 252 you will find a table showing what octane ratings are available in the countries listed in this book. In Europe the octane ratings are usually shown at the pumps but the quality is more readily identified by the local word for petrol (*benzin, gasoline,* etc) or *normal* to describe the ordinary or lower grade and *super* to describe higher grade petrol. The lower grade will probably be equal to 2-star and the

Brussels, Belgium

higher to 4-star. Between the two you will often find *mix* or *super mix* or some other self-evident expression to describe a mixture equal to 3-star. These terms correspond to the old-style terms Regular, Mixture or Premium.

In Western Europe petrol quality compares favourably with that of Britain. International brands are usually available on main tourist routes but in remote districts familiar brand names may not be readily found.

Fuel of 100 octane or higher will be found on general sale only in Scandinavia and Benelux countries and while it would not be true to say that it is not available in other countries it may be difficult to find (as it is increasingly becoming so here). If your car requires a fuel in this higher range (100 octane or higher) and you are visiting a country where you suspect that this may not be available then it is possible that engine adjustments may be made for a satisfactory performance on a lower grade. If you are thinking of having such adjustments made you must first seek the advice of the vehicle manufacturer or an official agent.

Maintenance and tuning

Regular maintenance and correct tuning of your car are vital if maximum economy is to be achieved. This is best done by a qualified person. It is wise in any event to have the car tuned before embarking on an overseas journey, and on page 223 you will find a list of other checks you should have carried out before setting off. Remember, too, that the correct type of tyre and tyre pressure will both add to fuel economy.

59

Driving technique

Driving technique is an equally significant factor which affects fuel consumption. Whilst many of the techniques used in organised fuel economy runs using standard production cars are not practicable in everyday motoring, the following points are worth bearing in mind for the economy-conscious driver:

- Do not let the engine warm up in the drive. Start up and drive off – the engine will attain its correct and most economical running temperature sooner this way.
- Push the choke in as soon as possible after a cold start – excessive use not only increases fuel consumption considerably but causes undue engine wear.
- Avoid fast starts and rapid acceleration – a quick getaway uses 60% more fuel than smooth, steady driving.
- Do not let the engine labour in too high a gear, but change into top as soon as possible – high revs in lower gears can use up to 50% more fuel.
- Read the road ahead, planning for hold-ups and obstructions; release the accelerator early instead of braking at the last minute. Think of the accelerator as a petrol tap – the more you open it, the more fuel you use. For instance, putting your foot hard down to accelerate from 20–40 uses more petrol than cruising at 60mph.

Tahull, Spain

Wiltz, Luxembourg

Traffic and road conditions

The density of traffic, the type of road and even weather conditions are factors over which the motorist has no control but which influence economy drastically. Motorway driving uses 10–20% less fuel than a comparable journey at the same average speed on main, trunk roads. Remember, however, that your overall driving speed on a motorway will be much higher than on the main road and so the saving may not be so evident. The maximum speed on a motorway is not the one for maximum fuel economy. Remember too, that if tolls are involved you can end up paying considerably more than you anticipated and planned for.

A roof-rack, even when empty, noticeably reduces economy especially if there are headwinds. Sensible loading, *ie* giving the luggage a 'low profile', will reduce wind resistance.

Finally, the following techniques help as well to save fuel even when road and traffic conditions are not ideal:

- In heavy traffic when held up for a long time, switch off the engine. This not only saves fuel but avoids exhaust pollution. Do not, however, switch on and off at minor hold-ups.
- When stationary on a hill, do not hold the car by using the clutch; the handbrake is safer and more economical – especially on the clutch linings.
- Try to maintain a steady speed when driving uphill, but be prepared to use the gears freely to prevent the engine 'slogging'. Also, avoid restarting on severe gradients – wait till you get to the top to admire the view or take a photograph.

Self-catering accommodation

Gone are the days of cheap petrol, and few people, even using the less expensive accommodation listed in this book, can afford two or three weeks of motor touring. The purpose of **Guesthouses, Farmhouses and Inns in Europe** is to provide a list of the most reasonably-priced accommodation we can, assuming a certain standard of comfort and reliability (see *Types of accommodation covered in the guide*, p85). Unless you go camping, which after all calls for a certain amount of skill, dedication and expensive equipment, there is probably no more economical way to go touring by car in Europe.

Perhaps it is appropriate to point out that if you do intend to stay in one place for three or more nights it is normally cheaper to take *pension* terms (*ie* bed plus breakfast, lunch and dinner). Most establishments will offer such terms, but there is no reduction for meals not taken.

Many people who would like to go on a motor tour but who find 2 or 3 weeks of touring just too expensive have found a compromise in self-catering accommodation. This type of accommodation bridges the gap between straightforward camping and staying in hotels and you will find facilities in most countries. Pleasantly-situated flats, houses or villas are offered for short periods at reasonable rents which can even offer services such as a 'daily' to do the cleaning. Such a holiday does anchor you to one spot but obviously with a car there is plenty of scope for taking local excursions during the day.

What we are suggesting in this book is that if you do take a self-catering holiday, by taking a leisurely journey over a number of days to reach your destination, using this book to help you find your overnight stops, you can combine the pleasures of touring overseas with the advantages and economy of a self-catering holiday. The special feature on pages 65–83 highlights the sort of journey you might like to take.

'Summer cottages' in Denmark. Photo: Danish Tourist Board

A typical French villa in northern Brittany

What sort of accommodation is there?

Most people's idea of self-catering accommodation will be of a villa, house or flat, and indeed these probably make up the bulk of the types available. Sleeping from 2 to 10 or more, most are fully furnished including crockery but in many cases you are expected to take your own linen or pay extra to hire it locally. You will find them sited in almost any situation, town or country, but of course a house or villa in a popular resort or in a prime site by the seaside will be in much demand and accordingly more expensive.

There are a number of other types available. In some countries you can stay in holiday villages which are virtually self-contained – the accommodation units are self-catering and within the village complex are shops, restaurants, cafes and a host of recreational and sporting facilities.

If you want a more rural or isolated setting, you have a number of choices. In France, for instance, there is an organisation offering cottages and farmhouses for hire in out-of-the-way places. Or you could rent a log cabin or chalet by a lake in Scandinavia. Most countries will have self-catering accommodation of this type.

An on-site ready-erected tent gives you the economy of a camping holiday without having to buy or carry all the equipment. This one, at a site near Venice, is offered by Wigwam International in Norfolk, tel Watton 882294, who have many sites throughout Europe.

At the other end of the scale, but not necessarily the cheapest end, you could hire a ready-erected fully-equipped tent or caravan on a camping site. A number of firms in this country offer these and in effect you are going camping without all the bother of carrying a lot of equipment and setting up the tent. Some sites offer 'chalets' as well although they may be little more than wooden huts.

How can I find out more?

Many tour operators have a variety of self-catering holidays as a part of their overall tour programmes and some specialise in this sort of holiday. The AA's own tour operator, ARGOSY, for example, has a wide range of villas, apartments, tents and caravans in France, Spain and Italy as well as some apartments in Yugoslavia. In addition, the ARGOSY prices include ferry fares or air tickets.

For details of firms supplying fully-equipped tents and caravans, the AA can supply a list to its members if they apply to The Automobile Association, Hotel & Information Services Department, Fanum House, Basingstoke, Hants, RG21 2EA.

Otherwise, the people to get in touch with are the national tourist offices whose addresses and telephone numbers are on page 222. It is their job to promote tourism in their respective countries so you can be sure that they will have the most up-to-date information to hand.

Putting back roads in front

If you want to get to a
holiday destination in Europe,
going by car can still be the cheapest way
to travel, despite astronomical fuel prices abroad.
The trouble, however, with a long European journey is that
it usually involves battling with heavy traffic on major
roads or the strain of high-speed driving on motorways, not
to mention the expense of tolls. Often this means arriving
hot and bothered instead of relaxed and ready for a peaceful
holiday. And that's no way to start or finish any vacation.

A far more enjoyable way, and one which only takes a little
more time, is to go by back roads. So to find out what it's
like, we sent Lionel Clark, the AA's Route Inspector, and
Editor Jeremy Kirk on some back-road routes through France.
Their glowing report on back roads may make you think again.

We have all heard tales of people driving down to Spain in one hop. Perhaps you have done this yourself. There is certainly no harm in it, and indeed that kind of driving can be fun and challenging. But you would have to be something of an enthusiast (dare I say fanatic?) and for most people belting down Continental motorways at breakneck speeds is no way to start a holiday. Besides, a motorway is a motorway no matter what country you're in – central reservations and hard shoulders are the same the world over. Since it is impossible to get the feel of a country from a motorway you might just as well stay at home.

What are the alternatives?

If you want to get there quickly, you could go by motorail – but you would be crossing Europe overnight and wouldn't even know you were abroad. Then there are the major roads which would take a little longer, but at least you would see some of the country you're in. You would also see a lot of heavy lorries who don't want to pay motorway tolls.

Alternatively, you could go by back roads, which would take about the same time as the major roads, or perhaps a little longer, but which would take you through natural, unspoilt regions with very little traffic. You would eat and stay at authentic, local establishments rather than roadside snack-bars, meet the people and not hordes of tourists, and probably spend no more than you would have done had you gone by motorway.

What's it like?

Both Lionel and I had been motoring in Europe before, but neither of us had ever set out with the sole intention of driving on back roads only, so this was to be something of a voyage of discovery.

We wanted to try two such routes so to decide on the destinations we approached the AA's Overseas Routes Unit. They told us that the Riviera and the Costa Brava are the two areas for which they most often supply routes. Then, with their help, the Routes Planning Section set about devising two back-road routes to Nice and Barcelona, just as they would for any AA member. Nice is a good central point for most Riviera resorts and the route to Barcelona is ideal for any of the resorts on the Costa Brava or Costa del Sol. For a starting point we chose Calais quite simply because it is the nearest Channel port to Britain.

We set off, then, armed with only the AA-recommended routes, some good maps and **Guesthouses, Farmhouses and Inns in Europe** (not forgetting, of course, 5-Star Service!). What I am calling 'back roads' for the purposes of this article turned out not to be narrow, twisting country lanes, but quite wide, well-surfaced roads which, in many places, were dead straight for mile after mile. There were winding sections, of course, especially in the hilly areas, but the great joy of these roads was the ease of driving, which was truly quiet and relaxing because the traffic was so light. Admittedly it was not the high season, but we hardly saw a lorry or caravan and other cars were few and far between. We knew what we were missing, too, because on these routes there are some unavoidable stretches of main road where the traffic was much heavier. Rejoining the quiet roads again after such stretches you could almost hear the car sigh with relief.

Is it worth it?

There is no doubt in my mind that using back roads is the best way to go. It may take a little longer (for relative times and costs see p 80) but a back-roads route will take you through places whose only customers are locals and where getting better value for money can be taken for granted. All the old towns and villages you go through, the lovely countryside, the people you meet and the food you eat – we are not advocating that you take a motor tour instead of driving to your holiday destination (maybe not such a bad idea at that) but by taking these routes you will discover that there's much more to a country than endless miles of motorway.

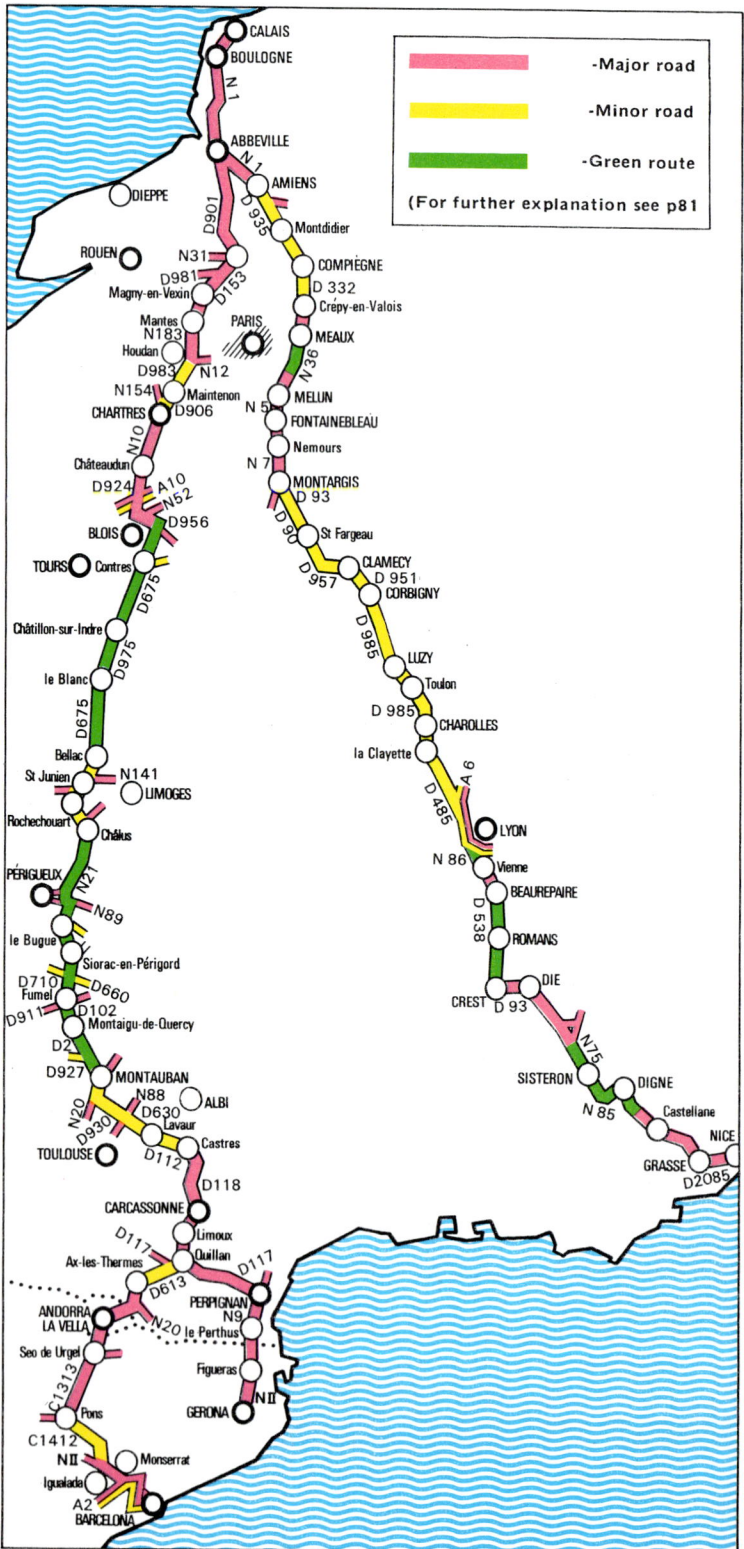

CALAIS
BOULOGNE
N 1

ABBEVILLE
N 1
AMIENS
DIEPPE
Montdidier
D 901
D 935
ROUEN
N 31
COMPIÈGNE
D 981
D 332
Magny-en-Vexin
D 153
Crépy-en-Valois
Mantes
PARIS
MEAUX
N 183
N 36
Houdan
D 983
N 12
MELUN
N 154
Maintenon
N 5
FONTAINEBLEAU
CHARTRES
D 906
Nemours
N 10
N 7
Châteaudun
MONTARGIS
D 924
A 10
D 93
N 52
BLOIS
D 956
St Fargeau
TOURS
Contres
D 90
CLAMECY
D 957
D 951
D 675
CORBIGNY
Châtillon-sur-Indre
D 985
D 975
LUZY
le Blanc
Toulon
D 675
D 985
CHAROLLES
Bellac
la Clayette
A 6
St Junien
N 141
LIMOGES
D 485
LYON
Rochechouart
Chálus
N 86
Vienne
PÉRIGUEUX
N 21
BEAUREPAIRE
N 89
le Bugue
D 538
ROMANS
Siorac-en-Périgord
D 710
D 660
DIE
Fumel
D 102
CREST
D 93
D 911
Montaigu-de-Quercy
D 2
D 927
MONTAUBAN
N 75
D 930
N 88
ALBI
SISTERON
DIGNE
N 20
D 630
Lavaur
N 85
Castellane
TOULOUSE
D 112
Castres
NICE
D 118
GRASSE
CARCASSONNE
D 2085
D 117
Limoux
Ax-les-Thermes
Quillan
D 117
D 613
PERPIGNAN
ANDORRA
N 9
LA VELLA
N 20
le Perthus
Seo de Urgel
Figueras
C 1313
N II
Pons
GERONA
C 1412
N II
Monserrat
Igualada
A 2
BARCELONA

		-Major road
		-Minor road
		-Green route

(For further explanation see p81

Imagine sitting outside a café in Beaurepaire on a balmy evening in May, sipping an ice-cold beer after the day's driving. Not tired, just relaxing. It's a quiet country town in the middle of nowhere, surrounded only by mile after mile of orchards – apricot, pear, apple and walnut. We're sitting overlooking the market square. Nothing happens. In fact you could almost imagine nothing ever happening. A torn poster on a wall flaps gently in the evening breeze. It promises a display by the Beaurepaire and District Majorettes in a few weeks' time. A major event.

A car drives past. A few minutes and a few sips later it drives down a different street in a different direction. From somewhere tantalisingly unrevealed the warm inviting smell of French cooking wafts through the square. Delicious.

Five minutes later the same car is going another way on another street. It is obviously lost. Who cares? No-one is in a hurry to do anything. And as the low evening sun changes the dim stonework and rooftops to a shimmering gold, the only break to the calm stillness is an occasional ripple of laughter coming from others within the café.

I am just drifting away into sweet reverie when Lionel accidentally knocks his glass off the table. Crash! Showers of glass across the pavement. It is as much commotion as they have seen for a week.

This is what back routes through France are all about. Places where tourists are still strangers, not sources of income. Areas with character, not an image. Towns and villages where the people in them have to live their normal daily lives.

Well, maybe it's not that idyllic *all* the way, but almost. A glance at the map on the left will show you why. If you compare our routes through

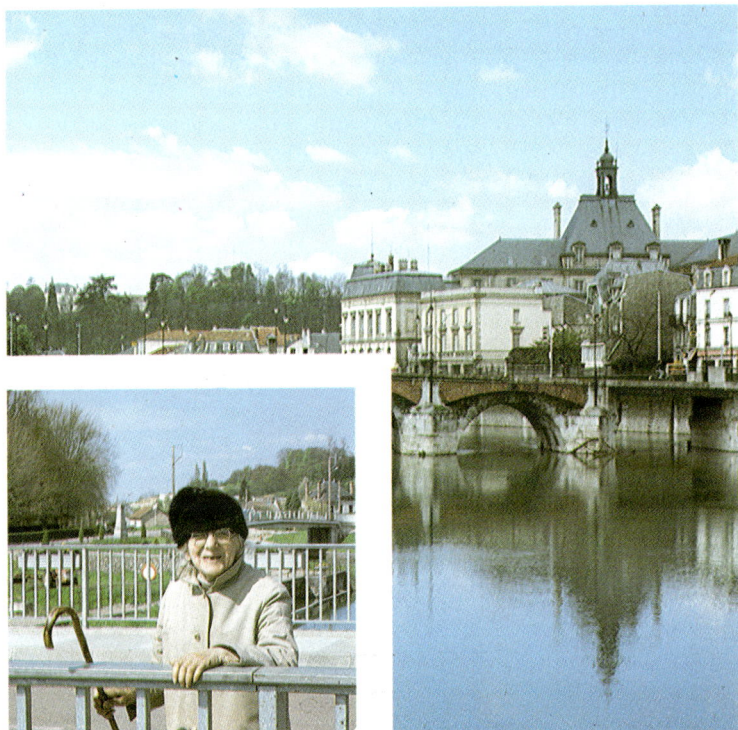

France to an equivalent route through Britain (if such a comparison is possible) it would be similar to directing someone from Dover to the north of Scotland. Such a route would take you through a good cross-section of British life and countryside – the pretty as well as the dull, the interesting as well as the ugly. But what we hope to do with a back-roads route is to avoid the dull and ugly as much as possible.

The route to Nice was 790 miles long and to Barcelona (by way of Andorra) was over 900 miles. We started at Calais, drove down to Nice, cut across to Barcelona and drove back up to Calais (noting the sign-posts in reverse) all in less than a fortnight. You'll see that the Spanish route splits at Quillan, because if you're going to the Costa Brava the best way is along the coast – but if you are heading further south or inland, it's far more interesting to go through Andorra.

On both routes we had to make four night stops – on the route to Nice we didn't get away from Calais until the afternoon, and also added half a day through sightseeing in the *Gorges du Verdon*. On the route up from Spain, on the other hand, we started in the morning and arrived back in Calais on the evening of the fifth day.

What parts of the journey were the most impressive? Naturally, crossing the Pyrenees proved probably to be the most exciting and dramatic. Everything about those tremendous craggy rocks which thrust up two or three times as high as any hill in Britain is spectacular, but the most stunning view I can remember came after we rounded a bend a little after the Col de Chioula. Suddenly the valley of the Ariège lies before you, hemmed in all round by high snow-capped mountains, and way, way, way down below, nestling in a little bowl, lies the town of Ax-les-Thermes. Utterly breathtaking.

The lower Alps, known generally as the *Basse Alpes* or *Alpes du Sud*, are not so high and dramatic as the Pyrenees but none the less impressive or beautiful. They present a lovely variety of scenery, from the stunning scrubby arid section between Digne and Barrême, where the colour of the soil and rocks range from bright sandy yellow to almost jet black, and where long-needled pines cling unbelievably to huge sheer limestone bluffs that tower frighteningly over the road – to the cool freshness of the hills round Castellane, smothered in alpine herbs, wild lavender, thyme and gorse. It was from Castellane that we took the detour round the *Gorges du Verdon*, a sort of French Cheddar Gorge – only ten times the size. To take the road right round the gorge would probably use up the better part of a day, but exploring part of the north side on the new road from La Palud took only a few hours.

*The incredible 'Grand Canyon of France', the **Gorges du Verdon**. The River Verdon has, over the eons, cut its way through solid limestone, in places over 2,000 feet deep and only a few hundred yards wide.*

Though the mountains must take first prize for impressiveness, there were a great number of other highlights which will stay planted in my memory. I was just as impressed by the great wide plains of *La Beauce* as I was by the powerful Pyrenees. All you can see for miles and miles are endless fields of wheat and corn, stretching away to the horizon, punctuated only by the occasional grain silo, water tower, isolated farmhouse or tree. I was reminded of somewhere like Kansas or Oklahoma – only there I suppose the trees would be replaced by oil wells. It's not for nothing that *La Beauce* is nicknamed *Le grenier de la France*. Perhaps the most lasting impression I have of this area is of coming over a small rise after Pierres and seeing the great twin spires and green roof of Chartres cathedral floating like a ship on the horizon of a sea of wheat.

On these routes the small things are as much joy as the dramatic scenery, for example our first taste of a quiet back road. As far as Amiens on the Nice route we were on major roads, and around Amiens the traffic was building up – but soon after the city we branched off on to the D935. Tree-lined in true French style, on a brilliantly sunny morning and with hardly another car in sight, the effect was exhilarating.

Or take the time we stopped at Rogny locks. The seven old locks on the Briare Canal were built between 1605 and 1642. I am fascinated by old canals and while taking some photographs we got chatting to a very old woman who described the locks (*'en haut, en haut, en haut'*) with much gesticulation. Some children rode past on bicycles making a lot of noise, setting off bangers, and the old woman instantly told them off. Turning back to us she explained that she used to be a school-teacher (it was obvious).

'Chartres cathedral . . . like a ship on the horizon of a sea of wheat.'

'Ah, children,' she said, 'their lives go up and up like that –' (indicating the locks) 'but me, I am old and of no use to anyone any longer, and my life, also like the locks, goes down and down.' How lyrical the French can be!

It was love at first sight with so many of the old towns and villages we went through, like Crépy-en-Valois, bustling and busy on market day, or St Fargeau, a dusty old stone village whose squat-towered chateau had the most curious tall thin skylights on top.

We stopped one day for our picnic lunch at La Clayette (pronounced 'La Claite'). The town drops down to a peaceful lake, at the end of which is a lovely chateau surrounded by a moat. All very beautiful and serene indeed. Quietly munching our quiche and bread we noticed group after group of locals coming down to the chateau and throwing bread into the moat below. So I wandered over to watch them feeding the ducks. Ducks? Never. Fish! The most enormous carp I have ever

Clamecy rises up on a hill between the Rivers Yonne and Beuvron, its old stone and timbered houses explored by wandering through winding alleyways and stone steps.

Apart from its beautiful mountain setting, Andorra can offer little more than cheap booze and fags – its duty-free attractions are enough to bring shoppers regularly from as far as Barcelona. Be prepared for snow even as late as July.

seen, the king of which was a goldfish over three feet long!

So what is it about driving through the back roads of France that is so different, that fires the imagination and refreshes the spirit? It's more than just the immense and varied countryside, more than her superb cathedrals and chateaux. It's not simply because they speak a different language and eat different (some would say better) food. And it's not solely because the French live a different sort of a lifestyle – rather it's a combination of all these things, and a number of other things besides. It is remarkable to think that only a few miles of water is all that separates us from France, yet in a subtle way it *is* so very different. The little things – the shutters on every window, the way they till the fields, the latinate sort of feelings and passions, their little idiosyncrasies – are all just symptoms of an overall difference of atmosphere and attitude.

I'm not talking about the difference in attitudes which we independent Britons feel exists throughout Europe – this is of the city and the media, a sort of Euro-thinking towards which we ourselves are inevitably steering. No, I mean the attitudes and atmosphere of the country folk, that which makes the French so different from the Spanish or the Welsh, the people from the north of France so different from those in the south, the people of the Loire valley different from the Borgognais. This is what driving through back-country France lets you discover and it is delightful.

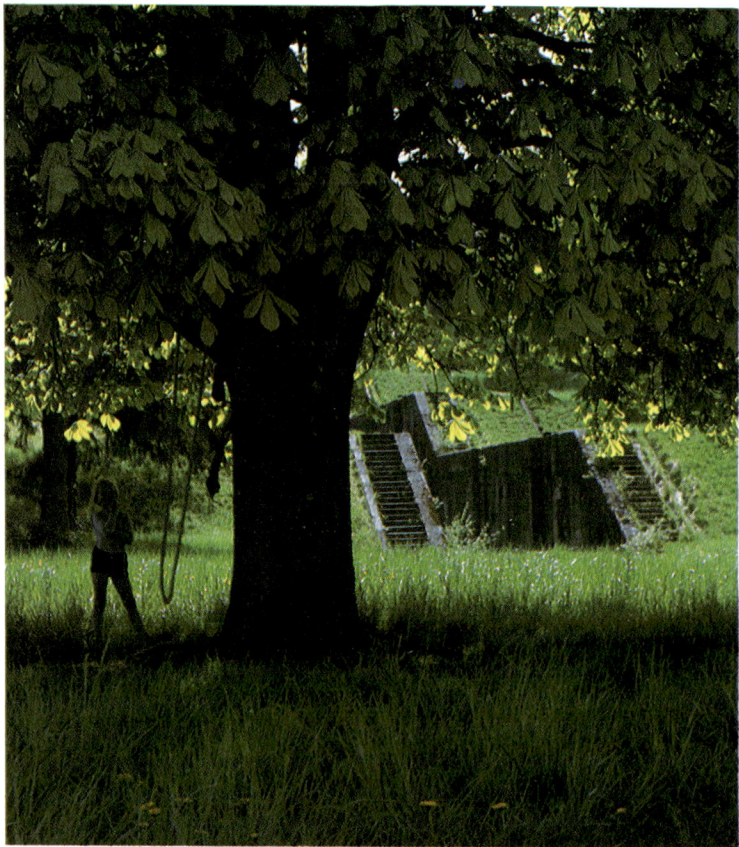

The one big problem with these routes is that they do avoid the centres of towns – no problem when you want to press on, but a great frustration when you're obviously missing so many interesting places. Ah well, you can't see everything in a few days. Of course if you want to stop for lunch, or have a few hours to spare, you can always follow the signs *Centre ville* instead of *toutes directions*. After all, are you *really* in that much of a hurry?

I am just sorry that we ourselves didn't have more time to visit and to sightsee. There are so many places where I would have liked to have stopped – to see the Palace at Fontainebleau, the Roman remains in Vienne, the old town and Cathedral in Chartres, the *Hortillonnages* at Amiens, the citadel of Sisteron, the crazy Postman's folly *Le Palais Idéal* at Hautrîves, to name but a few – but there just wasn't time.

Never mind. There's always next year – and I would hardly have known these places even existed if we had gone by motorway.

The Hotels

With only one exception, the hotels we stayed in on our journey all came from this book. The exception was in a small town on the Riviera where the two hotels listed were full. Had we telephoned ahead we could have found that out – but since it was early May and the peak season had not yet started, we were taking pot luck wherever we went. In the peak season we would have had more difficulty, when it would be advisable to phone ahead to see if the hotel you are aiming for has any room. About mid-afternoon would be a good time to do this.

The standards of the hotels did vary a little from place to place, but not much. All were clean and well run, and prices were roughly equal – usually well below the limits set in this book (see *Notes on the Gazetteer*, page 86). Naturally you wouldn't expect the frills of a Savoy or Dorchester, but we soon came to expect and appreciate the consistent standards. Every room we stayed in had a washbasin with hot and cold running water. Some hotels offered more, for example, at Beaurepaire, the **Hotel La Piscine** had a separate bathroom, with shower, bidet, sink and separate WC. In the **Hotel Central-Anzac** at Amiens there was a cubicle in the corner of the room with a sink and a shower, while the room at the **Hotel Felix** in Dunkerque had a sit-up-and-beg bath in a separate room. In most cases the bathroom and WC were on the same floor and quite near – though at the **Hotel La Dorade** in Narbonne the loo was miles away from our room!

While the general standards of the hotels were very similar, their characters differed widely. Some were quite grand-looking affairs which had obviously seen better days – as in Narbonne, where the **Hotel La Dorade**, with its superb be-statued and colonnaded façade, marble staircase and antique tile floors, seemed of a bygone age. Similarly, the **Hotel Lloret** on the Ramblas in Barcelona, was quite a grand building on one of the main streets with wrought-iron balconies and a swimming-pool-sized washbasin with most ornate taps – yet it was one of the cheapest hotels we stayed in.

On the other hand, some of the hotels had the air of being family-run businesses. At Beaurepaire, the **Hotel La Piscine** was a most unimpressive recently-built place yet we were given a good welcome from the proprietor who appeared to run the hotel with his wife and daughter. The **Hotel Central-Anzac** in Amiens was likewise unimpressive – mind you, Amiens itself didn't do much for us, being mostly industrial – but we got a friendly, if business-like,

welcome from this seemingly family-run establishment. After dinner we sat at a table in the reception area enjoying a carafe of fruity-tasting vinegar (no complaints! A half-litre cost the same as a pint of beer would in this country) with a television blaring and some of the family and staff milling around watching a soppy French film. Then, at 10 o'clock precisely, the TV was switched off, the chairs went up on the tables and the lights went out. Clearly it was time for bed!

La Boule D'Or in Clamecy was an unpretentious establishment run with an iron hand by the lady *propriétaire* who was always sending her waiter/barman/general handyman scurrying on this errand or that, just like Manuel in *Fawlty Towers*. The interesting thing about La Boule D'Or was that the dining room was a converted 13th-century chapel beautifully renovated with fine windows and lovely vaulting stone arches. At Castellane, in the Lavender Alps, the **Hotel Verdon** was a staid-looking grey building, but well furnished with a pleasant patio overlooking the Verdon River. Tired of sitting at the desk in our room writing up my notes for the day, I went down to the lively bar and at my request, the barman let me sample a number of different local alpine liqueurs. I decided I didn't want anything after all and wandered back to my room to sleep very soundly. Let me say that they were very palatable indeed.

The most well-appointed hotel of all was the **Refugi dels Isards** in Pas de la Casa, Andorra. It had the air of luxury about it and though our room had three beds crammed into it with hardly any space in between, the room had a telephone and a separate shower/WC room full of *Els Isards* towels, *Els Isards* mats, *Els Isards* bars of soap and specially-wrapped *Els Isards* glasses. Notices everywhere forbade the wearing of ski boots in the hotel. I am not sure how long this hotel will stay in our price range, though, because Pas de la Casa looks something like a gold-rush town – unpaved streets, half-finished buildings and mountain dogs (quite friendly, really) wandering unaccompanied through the streets. When the town is completed prices are bound to rise.

Generally we were well satisfied with the hotels and in fact Lionel felt that many of the hotels we stayed in were almost as good as some three-star hotels in this country. And as the AA's Route Inspector he has stayed in quite a few.

The Food

I could fill a book of this size singing my praises of French cooking – but to stop your mouths watering all over the pages I will confine myself to where and how we ate. Besides, some of the meals we had were so good that words alone could not do them justice. . . .

We found that the further away you are from established tourist centres, the cheaper and better the food. This is because the chef has to cater for locals who are experts, rather than for tourists who know no better. Find somewhere packed with locals and you are sure of a good meal.

Here is the routine for the day's eating which we adopted and found most suitable for this type of journey:

Breakfast, of course, was in the hotel and was the notorious 'Continental' breakfast of croissants, French bread, butter and jam. I was disappointed to find that croissants were not a matter of course – in some places we only got chopped-up French bread – and nowhere were the croissants hot. When you are asked 'what would you like?' it refers to drink, *ie* coffee, tea, chocolate, milk, etc.

Lunch For our midday meal we chose to have a picnic lunch. A small French loaf (we found for two a *baguette* was too much and bought instead that smaller loaf, sometimes called a *ficelle*), some ham, cheese or a piece of *quiche* each, some apples and a bottle of fruit juice (try apricot juice – very refreshing!) made an excellent and very suitable light lunch while on the road. It would be perfect for a family party, and apart from being inexpensive it seemed to suit the country.

How delicious French bread is!

Do not make the mistake we made on our first day – we tried to buy food after 12.30 and found that all the shops were shut until about 2.30 for lunch. On subsequent days we made the point of buying our picnic lunch in the morning before setting off, and this was much better.

Supper was our main meal of the day, so we ate in restaurants. Unless you are prepared to live on sandwiches and *crêpes* from cafés all the while, you will have to budget for this. But don't go rushing out to get a second mortgage, because we were surprised to find prices quite reasonable, even when compared to this country. If you wander round the town you will always be able to find the best buy as hotels and restaurants always clearly display their prices outside.

Restaurants will offer an *à la carte* menu (called *carte*) and at least one set or 'tourist' menu (simply called *menu*). When we ate *à la carte* we felt we weren't getting value for money, so on the whole we chose the *menu*, particularly as this often included service (*service compris*). Most restaurants offer two or three *menus* at varying prices to suit your pocket and your appetite. The difference between them is in the number of courses, the quality of the food, or both. A typical *menu* at the lowest end of the scale is made up of two starters, the main course, and a sweet, fruit or cheese. Coffee and wine are extra.

Don't expect the British norm of 'meat and two veg' for the main course. It usually consists only of the meat, chicken or fish you ordered by itself – though sometimes there are some *frites* (chips) or a salad to go with it. The French like to eat many small, separate courses as opposed to our liking of a plate piled high with food in one big course. So if you want some vegetables (and how well the French prepare them!) it is normal to order them as the second course, to be followed by the main course.

Wine disappointingly, was not particularly cheap, despite being in the country of origin. We had no grumbles, however, when wine was about £1 a bottle. Remember, especially in wine-growing areas, the house wine can be better than more expensive named wines.

The cost

As soon as we put prices to paper, they are out of date. By the time you read this any costs quoted will be worse than useless because of fluctuating exchange rates and rising prices. Bear in mind how dangerous it would be to budget for a holiday on last year's prices.

Having said that, however, we would like to compare the cost of taking a back-roads route with the alternatives. Comparisons of this sort are always difficult to make because of the variants involved. How many in your party? How much fuel does your car consume? How many nights will you have to stop? The only way to ensure the validity of any comparisons is to keep as many factors as possible the same, so we shall estimate what it *would* have cost us to go in the same car at the same time of year to the same destinations.

We went in May 1978 in a Ford Escort 1300 estate which averaged 33mpg while touring. As this corresponds with the AA Road Test Unit's findings for a similar car, we are using their figure of 28mpg to calculate motorway consumption. At the time petrol cost about £1.33 per gallon and the average daily expenses for two of us were: £9.47 for food, and £8.20 for hotel and breakfast. It is on these figures that the tables below are based. The costs do not include ferry or costs incurred on reaching your destination.

CALAIS–NICE	No. of days (each way)	Total Food	Total Hotels	Miles (return)	Total Petrol	Tolls (Both ways)	Fares (return)	TOTAL
By back-roads	4	£75.76	£49.20	1,580	£63.68	——	——	£188.64
By National roads	3½	£66.29	£49.20	1,550	£62.50	——	——	£177.99
By Autoroute	2½	£47.35	£32.80	1,522	£72.30	£35.73	——	£188.18
By Motorail	over-night	£15.60	——	134	£5.40	£2.68 (if Autort. used)	£241.60	£262.60 (£265.40)

CALAIS – BARCELONA	No. of days (each way)	Total Food	Total Hotels	Miles (return)	Total Petrol	Tolls (Both ways)	Fares (return)	TOTAL
By back-roads	4	£75.76	£49.20	1,868 (via Andorra)	£88.73	——	——	£213.69
				1,784 (via Gerona)	£85.35	——	——	£210.31
By National roads	4	£75.76	£49.20	1,746 (via Gerona)	£70.36	——	——	£195.32
By Autoroute	2¾	£56.82	£32.80	1,730	£82.00	£39.16	——	£210.78
By Motorail	over-night	£15.60	——	358	£14.42	(£7.20)	£213.80	£243.82 (£252.56)

Driving times are calculated assuming an average of 6 hours' driving per day.
Motorail fares are calculated for Boulogne – St Raphael (for Nice) and Boulogne – Narbonne (for Barcelona) at Tourist Return Fare (with couchettes) for 2 adults, plus a car not exceeding 14'6" at standard rate return fare. Motorail is overnight and it is assumed an evening meal will be bought.

THE ROUTES

The route directions below are, for reasons of space, as short as we can make them – but with the help of a good map you will find all you need to know to follow the routes. In the left-hand column are the mileages between the main towns which are printed in bold type. Accumulative mileages from Calais are given in brackets after the main towns.

The signposts you should follow are printed in italics, followed where appropriate by the road number. In France, however, little importance is given to road numbers and they tend to rely on town signposts instead – we print the road numbers for your reference but do not depend on them as the numbers themselves are liable to change.

The three types of road are: 'N'-roads (National roads), which are usually main routes; 'D'-roads (Departmental roads), ranging from major roads to country lanes – typically minor roads with little traffic; and Autoroutes, mainly toll-paying (but the short sections which we unavoidably have to use in these routes are toll-free).

The only other thing to watch out for are the *Itinèraires bis* or *Emeraude*, nicknamed 'green routes' because their signposts are always green. These are holiday routes which avoid heavy traffic and/or hold-ups in towns. From time to time our route joins these and it is easy to follow the green arrows – but note that our route invariably turns off these at some point and you should look out for where this happens. For example, at Fontenay-Tresigny, we leave the GREEN ROUTE SP *LYON* and continue following SP *Melun*.

Abbreviations:

SP	Signpost(s) to follow	m	mile(s)
T rt	Turn right	A	Autoroute
T lt	Turn left	D	Departmental road
fwd	forward	N	National road

Calais – Nice

CALAIS
SP *Paris, Boulogne:* N1

21 **BOULOGNE** (St Martin)
SP *Paris, Abbeville:* N1

49½ **ABBEVILLE** (70½)
SP *Amiens*: N1

29¾ **AMIENS** (100¼)
SP *Compiègne:* N35

3 Longeau. T rt D935
Continue with SP *Compiègne, Montdidier*

19½ **Montdidier**

9¼ Cuvilly. T rt N17
In 1½m t lt D935

12½ **COMPIÈGNE** (144½)
Follow SP *Centre Ville.*
From town centre follow SP *Meaux, Crépy:* D332

15 **Crépy-en-Valois**
SP *Meaux:* D332

10¾ Acy-en-Multien. T rt D18

1½ Nogeon. T lt D51 for D38
In 9½m join N330

10½ **MEAUX** (182¼)
SP *Melun* & GREEN ROUTE SP *LYON.* In 2¼m join A4
5¾m farther leave A4

8¾ Junction for Coutevroult.
Leave autoroute: N36

11 Fontenay-Trésigny
SP *Melun* (leaving GREEN ROUTE)

6½ Guignes-Rabutin
T rt N16 then lt N36

8½ (edge of) **MELUN** (217)
SP *Fontainebleau:* N5

12¼ **FONTAINEBLEAU** (229¼)
SP *Nevers:* N7

9 Junction with A6
SP *Nevers par N7, Nemours*

2 **NEMOURS** (240¼)
SP *Nevers, Montargis:* N7

20 **MONTARGIS** (260¼)
SP *Nevers:* N7. In 2m branch rt then t lt
SP *Châtillon-Coligny:* D93

13½ **CHÂTILLON-COLIGNY** (273¾)
SP *St Fargeau:* D93 then D90

19 **ST FARGEAU** (292¾)
SP *Cosne:* D18 then D2

8½ St Amand-en-Puisaye
SP *Clamecy:* D957

18 Billy-sur-Oisy
In 3m join D977

6¾ **CLAMECY** (326)
SP *Corbigny:* D951

4¾ Dornecy. T rt D985

14¼ **CORBIGNY** (345)
SP *St Honoré-les-Bains:* D985
6¼ Épiry. In 1¾m join D945
SP *Moulins-Engilbert*
5½ Aunay-en-Bazois: D985
In 4½m t lt D978
4¾ Tamnay-en-Bazois
In ½m t rt D985
7 **MOULINS-ENGILBERT** (368½)
SP *St Honoré-les-Bains:* D985
In ¾m t lt
6¾ **ST HONORÉ-LES-BAINS** (375¼)
SP *Luzy:* D985
14 **LUZY** (389¼)
SP *Toulon, Charolles:* D985
11¾ **Toulon-sur-Arroux** (401)
22 **CHAROLLES** (423)
SP *Lyon:* D985
20¼ Chauffailles. Later join D485
37¾ Civrieux-d'Azergues
In 1¾m t rt N6. 2¼ farther
join A6 SP *Lyon par Autoroute*
7¼ Junction for Ecully
Leave Autoroute
SP *Ecully:* D42
1 Ecully. SP *Brignais* & GREEN ROUTE SP *VALENCE*
8 Brignais: N86
GREEN ROUTE SP *VALENCE*
6½ Givors. SP *Vienne* & GREEN ROUTE SP *VALENCE:* N86
6½ (edge of) St Romain-en-Gal
T lt SP *Vienne* (leaving GREEN ROUTE).
Cross R Rhône
½ **VIENNE** (510¾)
SP *Beaurepaire:* D538
19 **BEAUREPAIRE D'ISÈRE** (529¾)
SP *Romans-sur-Isère:* D538
Later join GREEN ROUTE
SP *MARSEILLE*
23½ **ROMANS-SUR-ISÈRE** (553¼)
SP *Crest*, GREEN ROUTE
SP *MARSEILLE:* N92
In 2¼ t lt D538
24½ **CREST** (577¾)
SP *Die:* D93 (leaving GREEN ROUTE)
23¼ **DIE** (601)
SP *Sisteron:* D93
27¼ Col de Cabre: D993
3¼ La Beaume. In 4m t rt
SP *Sisteron:* D993b
6½ (edge of) Aspremont
T rt N75 SP *Sisteron* & GREEN ROUTE (no destination)
26¼ **SISTERON** (664¼)
SP *Nice, Digne* & GREEN ROUTE: N85
23¾ (edge of) **DIGNE** (688)
SP *Nice* & GREEN ROUTE: N85
19½ (edge of) Barrême
Fwd SP *Grasse, Nice*: N85 (leaving GREEN ROUTE)
15¼ Castellane (722¾)
40 (junction for) **GRASSE** (762¾)
Branch lt SP *Nice Direct:* D111 then D2085
16 (edge of) Cagnes-sur-Mer
SP *Nice* to join N7
8½ **NICE** (787¼)

Calais – Barcelona/Gerona

The notes on p81 apply to these routes as well. The classification of roads in Spain is similar to France, the three types being: 'A'-roads (*Autopista*) or motorways; 'N'-roads (*Carretera Nacionales*) or national roads which are major routes; and 'C'-roads (*Carretera Comarcales*) which are secondary roads. Most 'N'-roads are given numbers, but there are six radiating from Madrid which are given roman numerals, for example, the NII.

CALAIS
SP *Paris, Boulogne:* N1
21 **BOULOGNE** (St Martin)
SP *Paris, Abbeville:* N1
49½ **ABBEVILLE** (70½)
SP *Beauvais:* D901
53 **BEAUVAIS** (123½)
SP *Rouen:* N31
In 2m follow SP *Evreux* to join D981
7¼ Auneuil
In 6¼m t lt D153 SP *Mantes*
22½ Magny-en-Vexin
SP *Mantes:* N183
13½ **MANTES-LA-JOLIE** (166¾)
SP *Houdan:* N183
16¾ Maulette
T lt N12, SP *Paris*, then t rt D983, SP *Chartres*
2¾ Gambais
T rt SP *Nogent:* D983
12¼ **Nogent-le-Roi**
SP *Maintenon, Chartres*
4¾ Pierres
At end branch rt, SP *Chartres*
Later t rt D906
In 9m join N154
12 **CHARTRES** (215¼)
SP *Tours:* N10
27½ Châteaudun
SP *Blois:* D924

35 (edge of) **BLOIS** (277¾)
T lt SP *Autres Directions*
In ½m t rt GREEN ROUTE
SP *LIMOGES*. 3¾m farther
join D956

15½ Contres
SP *St Aignan* & GREEN
ROUTE: D675

11½ **St Aignan-sur-Cher**
SP *Châtillon* & GREEN
ROUTE: D675

23¾ **Châtillon-sur-Indre**
SP *Le Blanc* & GREEN ROUTE:
D975

26¾ **LE BLANC** (355¼)
SP *Bellac* & GREEN ROUTE:
D975 then D675

39¼ **BELLAC** (394½)
SP *St Junien:* N147 (leaving
GREEN ROUTE)
In 1¼m t lt D675

20¾ **St Junien**
SP *Rochechouart:* D675

7¼ **Rochechouart**
SP *Châlus:* D901

16½ CHÂLUS (439)
T rt N21 GREEN ROUTE
SP *TOULOUSE/ESPAGNE*

17¾ (edge of) Thiviers
SP *Périgueux* & GREEN
ROUTE: N21

20½ Trélissac
In 1m at traffic signals
t lt GREEN ROUTE
SP *TOULOUSE/ESPAGNE*
(Périgueux 2½m ahead).
¾m farther t lt again N89

4¾ St Laurent-sur-Manoire
In 1½m t rt D710
SP *Fumel* & GREEN ROUTE

20¾ Le Bugue
GREEN ROUTE
SP *TOULOUSE/ ESPAGNE:*
D31e then D51

5¾ Le Buisson
Join D25

4¾ Siorac-en-Périgord
T rt D710 SP *Fumel* &
GREEN ROUTE

4 (edge of) Belvès
In 7m join D660
4½m farther t rt D710

25½ (outskirts of) **FUMEL** (542¾)
T rt D911, SP GREEN ROUTE

½ Monsempron Libos
T lt D102 & cross R Lot

6½ Tournon-d'Agenais: D656
In ¾m t lt D18, SP *Montaigu* &
GREEN ROUTE

5¼ **Montaigu-de-Quercy**
SP *Montauban* & GREEN
ROUTE: D2

9½ (edge of) Lauzerte: D953
In 1m t lt D2

6¾ Durfort-Lacapelette
In 5m t lt D927

7¼ **MONTAUBAN** (578½)
SP *TOULOUSE/ESPAGNE*
to leave by N20
(end of GREEN ROUTE).
In 3m t lt D930,
SP *Lavaur, Castres*

15 Magnanac
D630

21¾ **Lavaur**
SP *Castres:* D112

24½ **CASTRES** (639¾)
SP *Carcassonne:* N112

11¾ Mazamet
SP *Carcassonne:* D118

30 **CARCASSONNE** (681½)
SP *Limoux:* D118

15¾ **LIMOUX** (697¼)
SP *Quillan, Perpignan:* D118

17¼ **QUILLAN** (714½)

To Barcelona (via Andorra):

QUILLAN (714½)
SP *Ax-les-Thermes:* D117
In 3½m t lt D59 for D613

34½ **AX-LES-THERMES** (749)
SP *Andorra, Espagna:* N20

11½ L'Hospitalet
In 4¾m t rt N20b

8¼ Pas de la Case (French Customs)

20½ **ANDORRA-LA-VELLA** (789¼)
SP *Espanya*

7¼ Spanish frontier

6 Spanish Customs

¼ Seo de Urgel
SP *Lerida:* C1313

43 Pons
SP *Barcelona, Igualada:*
C1412

33 Copóns
In 3m t lt NII, SP *Barcelona*

7½ (edge of) **Igualada**

16½ (edge of) Esparraguera

3¾ Junction with Autopista (A2)
Join A2, SP *Barcelona*
In 13¾m fwd leaving Autopista
to join NII

17¼ **BARCELONA** (923¾)

To Gerona (via coast route):

QUILLAN
SP *Perpignan:* D117

32¾ Estagel
In 12½m t rt N9

15 **PERPIGNAN** (762¼)
SP *Espagne par Le Perthus:* N9

19½ **Le Perthus** (French Customs)

2¼ La Junquera (Spanish Customs)
SP *Figueras, Gerona:* NII

10¾ (junction for) **Figueras**
SP *Barcelona, Gerona:* NII

27¼ **GERONA** (822)

GUESTHOUSES FARMHOUSES AND INNS IN EUROPE

Whilst every effort is made to exclude from our gazetteer establishments which are felt to be unsatisfactory, it should be borne in mind that it is not possible for the AA to 'vet' large numbers of widely spread establishments overseas. It is therefore of great importance that you should exercise your right to inspect any accommodation which you are offered before making any kind of payment. It is virtually impossible to obtain a refund once money has exchanged hands especially as only limited English (or none at all) is likely to be spoken at many of the smaller establishments featured in the guide, particularly those away from the main tourist areas. With this in mind, it is a good idea to provide yourself with a basic phrase book before setting out on your journey. The few words and phrases we provide on page 244 will be of some assistance but are by no means comprehensive.

If you intend to stay in one place for three or more nights it is normally cheaper to take *pension* terms (bed plus breakfast, lunch and dinner) although no reduction will be granted for any meals not taken.

TYPES OF ACCOMMODATION COVERED IN THE GUIDE

The gazetteer lists four main types of establishment, all selected on the basis that, within their respective countries, they offer accommodation of a cheaper nature. They are represented as follows:

1 AA-classified hotels are graded by stars. The AA classification system used in Europe is similar to that used in this country, although the variations in traditions and customs of hotel-keeping abroad often make identical grading difficult.

The stars indicate the type of hotel rather than the degree of merit; meals, service and hours of service should be in keeping with the classification. The requirements for classification as a one-star hotel are included in those for a two-star hotel.

★ Hotels simply furnished but clean and well kept: all bedrooms with hot and cold running water; adequate bath and lavatory facilities.

★★ Hotels offering a higher standard of accommodation: adequate bath and lavatory facilities on all floors and some private bathrooms and/or showers.

Three, four and five-star hotels, due to the nature of their accommodation and services, are in a higher price category and therefore not represented in this guide.

Classified motels, motor hotels and some purpose-built hotels are indicated by white stars (*eg*☆☆). These establishments conform to the major requirements of their star classification (as above) but their facilities are designed to cater particularly for overnight stays.

2 Inexpensive, unclassified hotels and motels are indicated by the abbreviations **H** and **M**. They are selected from information supplied by official local or national tourist offices and are not specifically recommended by the AA. They should provide bed and breakfast and many of them offer full or demi-pension terms.

3 ◆ This symbol indicates **guesthouses, pensions, inns, boarding houses and restaurants** providing overnight accommodation. Types of accommodation specific to a particular country are described in the country introductions. They are selected from the same source as category **2** and are not specifically recommended by the AA.

4 Farmhouses offering holiday accommodation are indicated by the abbreviation **FH**. Selected from the same source as category **2**, they are not specifically recommended by the AA. They offer simple, inexpensive accommodation in rural surroundings and in some cases are located within a vineyard (**V**).

NOTES ON THE GAZETTEER

The countries, the towns and the establishments in them, are listed in alphabetical order. The town is followed by the name of the region in which it is located and a map reference consisting of a number in bold (the location map number) and a square reference. The name of each establishment is followed by the address if known. This can be a street (*ie* Via V Venito), a village, possibly with a post code (*ie* Klostertal 19) or in some countries a house number only (*ie* no 72). In some cases no address is available. If you experience difficulty in locating any of these establishments, you are advised to seek assistance from the local tourist information office.

Unless otherwise stated the telephone exchange code is that of the town under which the entry is listed. These codes are quoted in the town heading wherever possible. If the exchange differs, the name will appear after the telephone symbol and before the number. Do not confuse parts of the address with the exchange.

The number of rooms has been shown to indicate the size of the establishment; where this information is not available, the number of beds is given. Accommodation in an annexe may be of a different standard from rooms in the main building; it is advisable to check the exact nature of the accommodation at the time of reservation. We have endeavoured to select establishments which open all year, however, where applicable opening dates are shown (*ie* 15 May – 30 Oct). Where no dates are shown, according to our information, the establishment is open all year.

Maps

All towns listed in the gazetteer are marked in the atlas in the front of the guide. Because maps have to be completed before final textual amendments are made, there may be individual entries unsupported by text, and in these instances the gazetteer is the more up to date.

Reservations

It is advisable, especially during July and August, to telephone ahead, whenever possible, to reserve the next night's accommodation before setting out. On arrival at your destination, it is the custom in Europe to inspect the rooms offered and to ask the price before accepting them. No embarrassment is caused by this practice and British visitors are urged to adopt it in their own interests.

Prices

Gazetteer entries have generally been selected on the basis that they offer accommodation at nightly rates of no more than £6 per person at some time during the year. The prices have been banded as follows: **A** under £5 per person per night and **B** between £5 and £6 per person per night. You are advised to check before booking as accommodation terms may change, without warning, for a variety of reasons.

Parking

A charge is often made for parking spaces, whether under cover or in the open. Before leaving your car in a street overnight, you are advised to ascertain the local regulations. Wherever you leave your car it is essential that all valuables are removed and that the vehicle is locked. Remember also to unload the roof-rack if you are carrying one.

AUSTRIA

Austria

The gazetteer which follows includes a wide range of hotels, guesthouses, pensions, inns, and farmhouses. The majority of these establishments offer accommodation for less than £6 per person per night at sometime during the year. The prices have been banded as follows: **A** under £5 per person per night and **B** between £5 and £6 per person per night. It is possible however that some may exceed these figures. If you are taking a winter sports holiday in one of the more popular resorts, you may find that the cost of accommodation will be higher than during the rest of the year. There are many more establishments in the lower price range than we have been able to list, particularly in the larger towns and main tourist areas; comprehensive lists together with information on accommodation in private houses may be obtained from local tourist authorities or from the Austrian National Tourist Office (see p 222 for address).

Abbreviations:
Nr   number
pl   platz
str   strasse

ACHENKIRCH AM ACHENSEE Tirol
(☎05246) Map**13**A2
- ♦ **Pension-Anita** ☎440 bed40 **A**
- ♦ **Gasthof-Tiroler Adler** ☎206 bed40 **A**
- ♦ **Gasthaus-Tiroler Weinhaus** ☎214 bed49 **A**
- ♦ **Gasthause-Windegg** ☎27111 bed80 Dec–Mar, May–Oct **A**

ADMONT Steiermark (☎03613) Map**14**C2
- ♦ **Putz Reinhard** ☎2601 bed30 Dec–Oct **A**
- ♦ **Zeinzinger Mafalda** ☎2188 bed16 **A**
At **Weng** 4.5km NE
- ♦ **Kretzschmar Helga** ☎2435 bed24 **B**
- ♦ **Gasthof Wengerwirt** bed18 **A**

AIGEN IM MÜHLKREIS Oberösterreich
(☎07281) Map**13**B3
- ♦ **Pension Eizelstorfer** ☎269 bed19 **A**
- FH **Lindorfer** Schlägl 19 ☎225 **B**

ALPBACH Tirol (☎05336) Map**13**A2
- ♦ **Pension-Alpbachblick** ☎273 bed21 Dec–Oct **A**
- ♦ **Gratlspitz-Fremdenheim** ☎5243 bed24 Dec–Oct **A**
- FH **Moser** 'Unterhause Nr8 ☎320 **B**

ALTAUSSEE Steiermark (☎06152)
Map**13**B2
- ♦ **Alpenverein zh Florian Berndl** ☎7202 bed30 **A**
- ♦ **Pension Kalss Heinz** ☎7189 bed12 **A**
- ♦ **Pension Wimmer Margareta** ☎7291 bed13 **A**
- ★★ **Hotel Kitzer** Hauptstr 21 ☎7227 rm21 **B**

ALTENFELDEN Oberösterreich (☎07282)
Map**13**B3
- ♦ **Gasthof Furtmueller** ☎6048 bed 14 **A**
- ♦ **Gasthof Zeller** ☎6014 bed14 **A**

ALTENMARKT Steiermark (☎03632)
Map**14**C2
- ♦ **Gasthof Weisser Adler** ☎301 bed8 **A**

ALTMÜNSTER Oberösterreich (☎07612)
Map**13**B2
- ♦ **Pension Bruderhofer** ☎8402 bed61 **A**
- ♦ **Pension Goeschlberger** ☎2863 bed25 **A**
- H **Katharinehof** ☎8118 bed46 **A**
- ♦ **Rasthaus Traunsee** ☎336 bed90 **A**
- H **Rittertal** ☎8131 bed117 **A**

AMSTETTEN Niederösterreich (☎07472)
Map**14**C3
- ♦ **Pension Alpenblick** Radingerstr Parz 1023-36 ☎37012 bed14 **A**
- ♦ **Gasthof Drei Hufeisen** Hauptplatz 39 ☎2679 bed48 **A**
- H **Guertler** Rathhausstrasse 13 ☎2765 bed60 **A**
- ♦ **Gasthof Kiermaier Guenter** Waidhofnerstrasse31 ☎2490 bed40 **A**
- ♦ **Gasthof Steinbock** Hauptplatz 47 ☎2210 bed8 **A**

ANNABERG Niederösterreich (☎02728)
Map**14**C2
- ♦ **Gasthof Alpenheim** ☎204 bed42 Dec–Oct **A**
- ♦ **Gasthof Post** ☎201 bed60 **A**
- ♦ **Gasthof zum Touristen** ☎303 bed100 **A**

ARZL IM PITZTAL Tirol (☎05412) Map**12**D2
- ♦ **Gasthof-Arzlerhof** ☎3144 bed85 Jan–Sep **A**
- FH **Krismer** 'Schlosserhof' Nr 164 ☎2862 **B**
- ♦ **Gasthof-Laerchenwald** ☎215111 bed50 **A**
- ♦ **Pension Trenkwalder** ☎3191 bed38 **A**
- ★★ **Post** ☎3111 rm62 6May–Sep **A**

AURACH Tirol (☎05356) Map**13**A/B2
- ♦ **Gasthof Andeas** ☎4437 bed28 **A**
- ♦ **Pension Erika** ☎4033 bed34 **A**
- FH **Koidl** Bachern 108 ☎4615 **B**
- ♦ **Pension Lucky** ☎4528 bed21 **A**
- ♦ **Gasthof Mesnerwirt** ☎41002 bed10 **A**
- FH **Pletzer** Wimm 91 ☎49675 **B**

AUSSEE (BAD) Steiermark (☎06152)
Map**13**B2
- ♦ **Pension Haus am Tauern** ☎2113 bed15 **A**
- ♦ **Pension Klubal** ☎2162 bed9 **A**

FH **Kühberger** 'Laimer', Sarstein 24
☎3453 **B**
- ◆ **Gasthof Staud'nwirt** ☎2427 bed50 **A**
- ◆ **Pension Stocker** ☎2484 bed15 **A**
- ◆ **Gasthof Waltl** ☎2020 bed15 **A**

BADEN BEI WIEN Niederösterreich
(☎02252) Map**14**D3
- ◆ **Pension Almschloessl** Auf der Alm 1
☎2758 bed16 **B**
- ◆ **Pension Cornelia** Poetschnergasse 5
☎37592 bed13 **B**
- ◆ **Pension Elfi** Karlsgasse 11 ☎2677
bed16 **A**
- ◆ **Pension Ferdinandshof** Rainerring
17 ☎2810 bed27 **A**
- H **Helenental** Karlsgasse 3–5 ☎3128
bed48 **B**
- ◆ **Pension Kahrer** Radetzkystrasse 43
☎41103 bed29 Apr–Oct **A**
- ◆ **Pension Margit** Muehlgasse 15
☎4376 bed35 **A**
- ◆ **Gasthof Martinek**
Jaegerhausgasse 7 ☎2186 bed35 **A**
- ◆ **Gasthof Mecl** Theresiengasse 8
☎2881 bed7 **A**
- ◆ **Pension Steinkellner** am
Schafflerhof 1 ☎4317 bed18 **A**
- ◆ **Pension Haus am Weberbergl**
Albrechtsgasse26 ☎8167 bed16 **B**

BADGASTEIN Salzburg (☎06434)
Map**13**B2
- ◆ **Pension Alpenrose** ☎2600 bed28 **A**
- ◆ **Pension Café Gamskar** ☎2042
bed10 Jan–Sep **A**
- ◆ **Pension Charlotte** ☎ 2426 bed12
Closed Nov **A**
- ◆ **Pension Haussteiner** ☎2234
bed15 **A**
- ◆ **Pension Kurhaus Echo** ☎2104
bed 26 **A**
- ◆ **Pension Landhaus Schafflinger**
☎2035 bed13 **A**

BERNDORF Niederösterreich (☎02672)
Map**14**D3
- ◆ **Gasthof Hoppel** ☎2733 bed12 **A**

BERWANG Tirol (☎05674) Map**12**D2
- ◆ **Enzian** ☎8109 bed25 **A**
- ◆ **Gasthof Rotlechhof** ☎8270 bed26 **A**

BEZAU Voralberg (☎05514) Map**12**C2
- ◆ **Gasthof Engel** ☎2203 bed15 **A**
- FH **Metzler** Kriechere 64 ☎291 bed6 **B**
- ◆ **Meusburger** ☎2412 bed26 **A**

BIRKFELD Steiermark (☎03174)
Map**14**C/D2
- ◆ **Gasthof Kirchenwirt** ☎521 bed22 **A**
- ◆ **Gasthof zur Post** ☎ 567 bed22 **A**

BISCHOFSHOFEN Salzburg (☎06462)
Map**13**B2
- ◆ **Gasthof Alte Post** ☎2307 bed26 **A**
- ◆ **Pension Feitzinger** ☎2231 bed20 **A**
- ◆ **Gasthof Karolinenhof** ☎2430
bed54 **A**
- FH **Lechner** 'Plattenhof', Kreuzberg 4
☎21472 **B**
- ◆ **Gasthof Metzgerwirt** ☎2371
bed52 **A**

FH **Rohrmoser** 'Krackbauer',
Mitterberghütten 5 ☎2202 **B**
- ★ **Hotel Tirolerwirt** Gasteinerstr 3 ☎
2776 rm8 **A**

BLUDENZ Vorarlberg (☎05552) Map**12**C2
- ◆ **Pension Bergblick** ☎29803 bed11 **A**
- H **Bludenzerhof** ☎2022 bed51 **A**
- ◆ **Rita Haus** ☎41972 bed17 **A**
- ★★ **Hotel Herzog Friedrich**
Mutterstrasse 6 ☎2703 rm18 **A**

BRAND Vorarlberg (☎05559) Map**12**C1
- ◆ **Pension Bleika** ☎267 bed20
Closed Nov **A**
- ◆ **Pension-Haus Gufer** ☎286 bed14
Jan–Sep **A**
- ◆ **Hotel-Garni Gulma** ☎246 bed27
Dec–Apr, Jun–Sep **A**
- ★ **Gasthof-Pension Zimba** ☎219 rm20
15 Dec–20Apr, 25 May–Sep **B**

BRAUNAU AM INN Oberösterreich
(☎07722) Map**13**B3
- ◆ **Central** ☎2911 bed22 **A**
- ◆ **Gasthof Alter Weinhans** ☎3396
bed10 **A**
- H **Gann** ☎3206 bed70 **A**
- ◆ **Gasthof Mayr-Breau** ☎3387 bed40 **A**
- ★★ **Hotel Post** ☎3492 rm30 **A**

BREGENZ Vorarlberg (☎05574) Map**12**C2
- ◆ **Bechter-Fremdenheim** ☎31874
bed15 **A**
- ◆ **Pension Bodensee** ☎22300 bed42 **B**
- ◆ **Falken-Fremdenheim** ☎22884
bed45 **A**
- ◆ **Gasthof Grauen Baeren** ☎22823
bed44 Mar–Nov **B**
- ◆ **Gasthaus Linde** ☎22949 bed12
Jan–Apr, May–Nov **A**
- ◆ **Merz** ☎234175 bed13 **A**
- ◆ **Gasthof Schedlberger** ☎22603
bed35 **A**

**BRUCK AN DER
GROSSGLOCKNERSTRASSE** Salzburg
(☎06545) Map**13**B2
- ◆ **Alpenheim** ☎301 bed13 **A**
- ◆ **Pension Elizabeth** ☎400 bed22 **A**
- ◆ **Pension Gassner** ☎272 bed13 **A**
- ◆ **Gasthof Glocknerhof** ☎230
bed45 **A**
- ◆ **Pension Gruber** ☎256 bed26 **A**
- ◆ **Gasthof Hirschenwirt** ☎252 bed48 **A**
- ◆ **Pension Hutter** ☎289 bed11 **A**
- ◆ **Gasthof Post** ☎215 bed46 **A**
- ◆ **Pension Wallner** ☎560 bed11 **A**
- ◆ **Gasthof Weisses Roessl** ☎253
bed50 **A**
- ◆ **Gasthof Zacherlbraeu** ☎242
bed26 **A**

BRUCK AN DER LEITHA Niederösterreich
(☎02162) Map**14**D3
- ◆ **Pension Eder** Altstadt 19 ☎2451
bed65 **A**
- ◆ **Pension Perger** Altstadt 107 ☎28124
bed24 **A**

BRUCK AN DER MUR Steiermark (☎03862)
Map**14**C2
- ◆ **Gasthof Koppelhuber** ☎51638
bed31 **A**

Austria

♦ **Gasthof Zur Waldschnepfe** ☎51474
bed5 **A**
★★ **Hotel Bayer** ☎51218 rm32 **B**
★★ **Hotel Bauer 'Zum Schwarzen Adler'**
Mittergasse 23 ☎51331 rm60 **B**

DEUTSCHLANDSBERG Steiermark
(☎03462) Map**14**C1
♦ **Gasthof Kochhansl** ☎2003 bed12 **A**
♦ **Gasthof Kollar Franz** ☎2642
bed46 **A**
♦ **Gasthof Pfeiffer Bernhard** ☎2760
bed50 Dec–Oct **A**
♦ **Wirtschafts** ☎2318 bed50 **A**

DIENTEN AM HOCHKÖNIG Salzburg
(☎06416) Map**13**B2
♦ **Gasthof Hochkoenig** ☎216 bed55 **A**

DÖLLACH-SAGRITZ Kärnten (☎04824)
Map**13**B1
♦ **Pension Haus Kahn** ☎230 bed22 **A**
♦ **Gasthof Ortner** ☎210 bed17 **A**

DORNBIRN Vorarlberg (☎05572) Map**12**C2
♦ **Hotel- Garni Andreas Hofer** ☎62711
bed40 **A**
♦ **Gasthof Dreilaenderblick** ☎639003
bed15 **A**
♦ **Pension Janner** ☎63272 bed23 **A**
♦ **Gasthof Krone** ☎62720 bed44 **A**
♦ **Gasthof Sonnblick** ☎62858 bed13 **A**
★★ **Hotel Zum Hirschen** Marktplatz 12
☎62157 rm38 **A**

DÜRNSTEIN AN DER DONAU
Niederösterreich (☎02711) Map**14**C3
♦ **Pension Fuertler Beate** ☎252 bed14
Mar–Nov **A**
♦ **Gasthof Goldener Strauss** ☎267
bed9 Feb–Dec **A**
♦ **Pension Pfeffel Leopold** ☎206
bed61 **A**

EHRWALD Tirol (☎05673) Map**12**D2
♦ **Gasthof-Pension Bayrischer Hof**
☎2365 bed32 Dec–Mar, May–Sep **A**
♦ **Pension-Daheim** ☎2350 bed30
Dec–Apr, Jun–Sep **A**
♦ **Pension-Panorama** ☎2825 bed30
Dec–Sep **B**

EISENERZ Steiermark (☎03848) Map**14**C2
♦ **Gasthof Doringer** ☎209 bed14
Closed Jul **A**
♦ **Gasthof Trofenger Volkskeller**
☎250 bed22 **A**

EISENSTADT Burgenland (☎02682)
Map**14**D2
♦ **Gasthof Haydnhof** ☎2309 bed38 **A**
H **Mayr** ☎2751 bed47 **A**
♦ **Gasthof Ohr** ☎2460 bed25 **A**
♦ **Gasthof Schueller** ☎2509 bed6
Feb–Nov **A**
★ **Eisenstadt** Sylvesterstrasse 5
☎3350 rm14 **A**

ENNS Oberösterreich (☎07223) Map**14**C3
♦ **Gasthof zum Goldenen Hirshen**
☎228 bed18 **A**
♦ **Gasthof zum Goldenen Schiff**
☎2327 bed30 **A**

ERNSTBRUNN Niederösterreich (☎02576)
Map**14**D3
♦ **Gasthof Roter Hahn** ☎217 bed21
Jul–Sep **A**

EUGENDORF Salzburg (☎06212) Map**13**B2
♦ **Gasthof Holznerwirt** ☎3205 bed34 **A**
♦ **Gasthof Neuhofen** ☎8392 bed19 **A**
♦ **Gasthof Schmid bauer** ☎28612
bed58 **A**
♦ **Gasthof zur Strass** ☎8218 bed22
Dec–Oct **A**

FELDKIRCH Vorarlberg (☎05522)
Map**12**C2
♦ **Gasthof Altdeutsche Stuben**
☎22324 bed53 **A**
H **Blenk** ☎22066 bed65 **B**
H **Buechel** ☎23306 bed93 **A**
♦ **Gasthof-Schaefle** ☎22339 bed24
Jan–Nov **B**
★★ **Hochhaus** Reichsstr 177 ☎22479
rm19 **B**

FELDKIRCHEN Kärnten (☎04276)
Map**14**C1
FH **Auernig** 'Raggonig', Leinig 9
☎29692 **B**
♦ **Gasthof Bresitz** ☎2280 bed20 **A**
♦ **Am Huegel** ☎2632 bed35 Dec–Feb,
May–Oct **A**
H **Germann Karl** ☎2287 bed64 **A**
FH **Missoni** 'Waldhof', Krahberg 3
☎29975 **B**
♦ **Gasthof Polster Josef** ☎2075
bed18 **A**
♦ **Gasthof Schinegger Erik** ☎446
bed25 Dec–Sep **A**

FRASTANZ Vorarlberg (☎05525) Map**12**C2
FH **Gassner** 'Bergerhof', Grampeluen 10
☎263953 bed10 **B**
♦ **Gasthof Kreuz** ☎22791 bed28 **A**
★★ **Stern** ☎22717 rm17 **A**

FREISTADT Oberösterreich (☎07942)
Map**14**C3
♦ **Gasthof Blauen Ochsen** ☎2218
bed19 **A**
♦ **Gasthof Goldenen Adler** ☎2112
bed51 **B**
♦ **Gasthof Goldenen Sense** ☎2297
bed26 **A**
♦ **Gasthof Wilder Mann** ☎2440
bed28 **A**
★ **Goldener Hirsch** ☎2258 rm25 **A**

FÜGEN Tirol (☎5288) Map**13**A2
♦ **Pension-Annemarie** ☎2432 bed44
Dec–Sep **A**
♦ **Gasthof-Malerhaus** ☎2278 bed34 **A**
H **Sonne** ☎2266 bed64 **B**
♦ **Gasthof-Tyrolerhof** ☎2209 bed55
Dec–Oct **A**

**FUSCH AN DER
GROSSGLOCKNERSTRASSE** Salzburg
(☎06546) Map**13**B2
♦ **Pension Danki** ☎288 bed13
Map–Sep, Dec **A**
♦ **Gasthof Edlinger** ☎465 bed26 **A**
♦ **Pension Hofer** ☎226 bed37
Dec–Sep **A**

FH **Hollaus** Nr.151 ☎281 **B**
♦ **Pension Ponyhof** ☎281 bed50 **A**
♦ **Pension Resch** ☎214 bed33 **A**
★★ **Post Hofer** ☎226 rm42 **A**
★ **Lampenhausl** ☎215 rm32
   Closed Nov–8Dec **A**

FUSCHL AM SEE Salzburg (☎06226)
Map**13**B2
♦ **Pension Fuschlerhof** ☎259 bed30 **A**
♦ **Pension Horak** ☎287 bed17 **A**
♦ **Pension Lindenhof** ☎263 bed37 **A**
♦ **Pension Rosenhof** ☎258 bed29 **A**
★★ **Seehotel Schlick** ☎237 rm50 **A**

GALTÜR Tirol (☎05443) Map**12**C1
♦ **Pension-Bergfried** ☎208 bed20
   Dec–Apr, Jun–Sep **A**
♦ **Hubertus-Fremdenheim** ☎243
   bed30 Dec–Apr, Jun–Sep **A**

GARGELLEN Vorarlberg (☎05557)
Map**12**C1
H **Marmotta** ☎6301 bed30 Dec–Apr,
   Jun–Oct **B**
♦ **Mateera Haus** ☎6387 bed24
   Dec–Sep **B**
♦ **Pension St Hubertus** ☎6217 bed25
   Dec–Oct **A**

GARS AM KAMP Niederösterreich
(☎02985) Map**14**C3
♦ **Gasthof Ehrenberger Johann**
   ☎2241 bed12 **A**
♦ **Rathauskeller** ☎2294 bed20 **A**

GASCHURN Vorarlberg (☎05558)
Map**12**C1
♦ **Pension Bergauer** ☎204 bed18
   Dec–Apr, Jun–Sep **B**
♦ **Gstrein Haus** ☎237 bed15 Dec–Apr,
   Jun–Sep **A**
♦ **Pension Sohler** ☎222 bed222 **A**

GERLOS Tirol (☎05284) Map**13**A2
♦ **Pension-Berghof** ☎227 bed34
   Dec–Apr, Jun–Sep **A**
♦ **Daxer Hildegard** ☎259 bed16
   Apr–Nov **A**
♦ **Pension-Sonnenhof** ☎228 bed32
   Dec–Apr, Jun–Sep **A**
★ **Jagerhof** ☎203 rm38 **A**

GLEISDORF Steiermark (☎03112)
Map**14**D2
♦ **Gasthof Messner** ☎3279 bed28
   Closed Jul **A**

GMÜND Kärnten (☎04764) Map**13**B1
FH **Genser** 'Nickelbauer', Treffenboden4
   ☎2006 **A**

GMÜND Niederösterreich (☎02852)
Map**14**C3
H **Fasching Konrad** Stadtplatz 15
   ☎2347 bed29 **A**
♦ **Gasthof Traxler Maria**
   Schremserstrasse 40 ☎2343 bed25 **A**

GMUNDEN Oberösterreich (☎07612)
Map**13**B2
♦ **Gasthof Bergthaler** ☎4892 bed32 **A**
♦ **Pension Egger** ☎3222 bed34 **A**
♦ **Pension Kastner** ☎25322 bed15 **A**

♦ **Gasthof Marienbruecke** ☎4011
   bed32 Apr–Sep **B**
FH **Loderbauer** 'Neuhofenbauer',
   Neuhofen 1 ☎29702 **B**
♦ **Pension Spiesberger** ☎3214
   bed30 **A**

GOLLING Salzburg (☎06244) Map**13**B2
♦ **Pension Edeltraud** ☎438 bed27
   May–Sep, Dec **A**
♦ **Gasthof Goldene Traube** ☎320
   bed5 **A**
♦ **Gasthof Hauslwirt** ☎229 bed40 **A**
FH **Köppl** 'Feichtengut', Obergau 5
   ☎558 **B**
♦ **Gasthof Pass Lueg-Hoehe** ☎280
   bed28 Dec–Jan, Mar–Oct **A**
♦ **Pension Wenger** ☎6041 bed17
   May–Oct **A**
★ **Goldener Stern** Hauptstr ☎220 rm25
   Closed Nov **A**

GRAZ Steiermark (☎03122) Map**14**C2
♦ **Gasthof Goldenen Kegel** Grabenstr
   64 ☎61482 bed24 **A**
♦ **Gaestehaus Lactan** Zinzendorfgasse
   12 ☎3369214 bed19 **A**
♦ **Gasthof Mueller Florentine** Wagner
   Birostr 8 ☎520843 bed30 **A**
H **Pressnitz Barbara** Schoenauguertel
   74 ☎73064 bed26 **A**
H **Strasser** Eggenbergerguertel 11
   ☎913977 bed56 **A**

GREIFENBURG Kärnten (☎04712)
Map**13**B1
FH **Reiter** 'Aigner', Emberg 10 ☎445 **B**

GRIES AM BRENNER Tirol (☎05274)
Map**13**A1
♦ **Alpenheim-Fremdenheim** ☎207
   bed25 **A**
♦ **Erika-Fremdenheim** ☎233 bed17 **A**
♦ **Gasthaus Waldheim** ☎300 bed15
   Closed Nov **A**

GRIESKIRCHEN Oberösterreich (☎07248)
Map**13**B3
♦ **Gasthof Schatzl** ☎2679 bed40 **A**
♦ **Gasthof Weissen Kreuz** ☎2226
   bed24 **A**

GRÖBMING Steiermark (☎03685) Map**13**B2
♦ **Gasthof Dirninger Karl** ☎2166
   bed45 Dec–Oct **A**
♦ **Pension Edelweiss** ☎2342 bed24 **A**
♦ **Pension Hoeflechner Hannelore**
   ☎2644 bed21 Dec–Oct **A**
♦ **Gasthof Moser-Loy** ☎2357 bed70 **A**
♦ **Pension Scharzenberger** ☎2225
   bed20 **A**

GRUNDLSEE Steiermark (☎06152)
Map**13**B2
♦ **Gasthof Veit** ☎8212 bed15 **A**
★ **Pension Backenstein** ☎8545 rm25 **A**

GSCHNITZ Tirol (☎05272) Map**12**D1
♦ **Pension Kirchdach** ☎23118
   bed20 **A**
FH **Pranger** Alfaierhof25 ☎23190 **B**

HALDENSEE Tirol (☎05675) Map**12**D2
★ **Rot-Flüh** ☎465 rm73
   Closed Nov–14Dec **A**

Austria

HALLEIN Salzburg (☎06245) Map **13**B2
- ◆ **Pension Anzenbach** ☎2100 bed17 **A**
- ◆ **Gasthof Auwirt** ☎2417 bed20 **A**
- ◆ **Pension Dorrerbauer** ☎2028 bed14 **A**
- ◆ **Pension Sommerauer** ☎2030 bed26 **A**
- ★ **Stern** ☎2610 rm35 **A**

HALL IN TIROL Tirol (☎05223) Map **13**A2
- ◆ **Gasthof Badl** ☎6784 bed57 **A**
- ◆ **Pension Kauth** ☎6335 bed14 **A**

HALLSTATT AM SEE Oberösterreich (☎06134) Map **13**B2
- ◆ **Gasthof Hirlatz** ☎443 bed20 Dec–Sep **A**

HARTBERG Steiermark (☎03332) Map **14**D2
- FH **Fuchs** Ziegeleigasse 30 ☎2911 **A**
- ◆ **Gasthof Klosterkeller** ☎2162 bed16 **A**

HEILIGENBLUT Kärnten (☎04824) Map **13**B1/2
- ◆ **Pension Edenbauer** ☎2294 bed15 Dec–Sep **A**
- ◆ **Pension Gletscherblick** ☎2056 bed20 **A**
- ◆ **Pension Schmidl** ☎2010 bed20 Dec–Apr, Jun–Oct **A**
- ★★ **Glocknerhof** ☎2244 rm45 18Dec–20Apr, 20May–15Oct **B**
- ★ **Rupertihaus** ☎2247 rm33 **A**

HEITERWANG Tirol (☎05674) Map **12**D2
- ◆ **Pension Alpenblick** ☎29114 bed20 **A**
- ◆ **Pension Berghof** ☎277 bed10 **A**

HERMAGOR Kärnten (☎04282) Map **13**B1
- FH **Brandner** Kreuth 1, Rattendorf ☎(04285)211 **B**
- FH **Pernul** Fritzendorf 4 ☎25542 **B**

HINTERSTODER Oberösterreich (☎07564) Map **13**B2
- ◆ **Pension Alpenrose** ☎278 bed33 **A**
- ◆ **Pension Dietlgut** ☎248 bed51 Dec–Oct **A**
- ◆ **Pension Gressenbauer** ☎359 bed25 Dec–Oct **A**
- ◆ **Gasthof Prielkreuz** ☎277 bed31 **A**
- ◆ **Pension Rohrauer** ☎207 bed13 **A**

HINTERTUX Tirol (☎05287) Map **13**A2
- ◆ **Christina-Fremdenheim** ☎22108 bed32 Dec–Sep **A**
- ◆ **Gasthof-Hintertuxerhof** ☎22106 bed30 **B**

HIRSCHEGG Steiermark (☎03145) Map **14**C2
- ◆ **Gasthof Hirscheggerhof** ☎217 bed38 **A**
- ◆ **Pension Krasser** ☎332 bed24 Dec–Mar, May–Sep **A**

HOFGASTEIN (BAD) Salzburg (☎06432) Map **13**B2
- FH **Winter** ˙Neureitgut , Gadaunern 1 ☎81273 **B**

HOHENAU Niederösterreich (☎02535) Map **14**D3
- ◆ **Gasthof Track** ☎2276 bed16 **A**

HOLLABRUNN Niederösterreich (☎02952) Map **14**D3
- H **Alte Post** Bahnstrasse 14 ☎39440 bed23 **A**
- ◆ **Gasthof Graf** Wienerstrasse 32 ☎2169 bed30 **A**

HORN Niederösterreich (☎02982) Map **14**C3
- H **Heidinger** Hauptplatz 16 ☎2398 bed60 **A**
- ◆ **Gasthof Hofbauer** Gruenberg 12 ☎222 bed18 **A**
- H **Post** Kirchenplatz 6 ☎2555 bed28 **A**

IGLS Tirol (☎05222) Map **13**A2
- ◆ **Pension-Feldheim** ☎7153 bed30 Dec–Sep **A**
- ◆ **Gasthaus Gruberhof** ☎7142 bed65 Closed Oct **A**
- ◆ **Pension Serlesblick** ☎7307 bed14 Dec–Sep **A**
- ★ **Haus Gothensitz** ☎7211 rm15 **B**
- ★ **Pension Romedihof** ☎7141 rm22 Dec–Sep **B**

IMST Tirol (☎05412) Map **12**D2
- ◆ **Gasthof Hohe Warte** ☎2414 bed33 Dec–Mar, May–Oct **A**
- ◆ **Gasthof zum Hirschen** ☎2209 bed50 **B**
- FH **Mark** Auweg 29 ☎29883 **B**

INNSBRUCK Tirol (☎05222) Map **13**A2
- ◆ **Gasthof Dollinger** Haller Strasse 7 ☎37351 bed66 **A**
- ◆ **Pension Elisabeth-Fremdenheim** Elisabethstr 2 ☎27877 bed24 **A**
- ◆ **Gasthof Goldener Winkel** Reichenauerstr 16 ☎51630 bed37 **B**
- ◆ **Heis-Fremdenheim** Dorfgasse 11 ☎36167 bed19 **A**
- ◆ **Gasthof Innbruecke** Innstr 1 ☎22416 bed40 **A**
- ◆ **Gasthof Kranebitten** Kranebitten 1 ☎22888 bed50 **A**
- ◆ **Pension Menghini** Beda-Weber-Gasse 29 ☎41243 bed36 **A**
- ◆ **Gasthaus Oelberg** Hoehenstr 52 ☎37369 bed36 Closed Oct **A**
- ◆ **Gasthaus Tirol** Pontlatzerstr 47 ☎61575 bed10 **A**
- ★★ **Pension Binder** Dr Glatzstr 20 ☎42236 rm34 **B**

ISCHGL Tirol (☎05444) Map **12**C1
- ◆ **Alpenhof-Fremdenheim** ☎261 bed28 Nov–Apr **A**
- ◆ **Gasthaus Edelweiss** ☎204 bed22 Jan–Apr, Jun–Sep **A**

ISCHL (BAD) Oberösterreich (☎06132) Map **13**B2
- ◆ **Gasthof Alpenrose** ☎3015 bed15 **A**
- ◆ **Gasthof Bachwirt** ☎3403 bed38 Dec–Sep **A**
- ◆ **Gasthof Gaestehaus Nestroystueberl** ☎3017 bed16 **A**
- ◆ **Pension Gerlinde** ☎2597 bed22 **A**

◆ **Gasthof Grabner** ☎3521 bed15
Dec–Jan, Mar–Oct **A**
◆ **Haus an der Ischl** ☎2995 bed22
Mar–Oct **A**
◆ **Gasthof Hubertushof** ☎3614 bed39
Closed Nov **A**
◆ **Pension Haus Hutflesz** ☎4230
bed9 **A**

JENBACH Tirol (☎05244) Map**13**A2
◆ **Furtner** ☎2477 bed20 **A**
◆ **Hilde-Fremdenheim** ☎3329 bed20 **A**

JUDENBURG Steiermark (☎03572)
Map**14**C2
◆ **Leitner** ☎2348 bed47 **A**
◆ **Gasthof Reichsthaler** ☎2448
bed45 **A**
◆ **Gasthof Themel** ☎2471 bed20 **A**

KAUNS Tirol (☎05472) Map**12**D1
FH **Huter** Nr31 ☎293 **A**
FH **Neururer** Platz 68 ☎312 **A**
FH **Wille** Nr 28 ☎363 **A**

KIRCHBERG Tirol (☎05357) Map**13**A2
◆ **Gasthaus Bockern** ☎2633 bed25 **A**
◆ **Eppensteiner** ☎2001 bed23
Dec–Sep **A**
◆ **Krimbacher** ☎2404 bed14 **A**

KIRCHDORF AN DER KREMS
Oberösterreich (☎07582) Map**13**B2
◆ **Pension Kremstalblick** ☎2396
bed14 **A**
◆ **Gasthof Zorn** ☎2014 bed35 **A**

KITZBÜHEL Tirol (☎05356) map**13**A/B2
◆ **Pension Foidl** ☎2189 bed30
Dec–Apr, Jun–Sep **A**
FH **Haller** 'Unterberg', Walsenbachweg
72 ☎41602 **B**
◆ **Hechenberger** ☎3134 bed26 **A**
H **Gasthof Hinterbraeu** ☎2166 bed18
Dec–Mar, Jun–Aug **A**
◆ **Gasthof Lusser** ☎2684 bed31
Nov–Mar, May–Sep **A**
◆ **Pension Maria-Hilde** ☎3130 bed18
Dec–Sep **A**
◆ **Pension Muehlbergerhof** ☎2835
bed29 Dec–Apr, Jun–Sep **A**

KLAGENFURT Kärnten (☎04222) Map**14**C1
◆ **Gasthof Geyer** Priesterhausgasse 5
☎86598 bed22 **A**
◆ **Gasthof Goldenes Roessl** Alter Platz
16 ☎83386 bed13 **A**
◆ **Gasthof Helder** St Veiterstr 130
☎41335 bed12 **A**
◆ **Pension Wachau** Wilfriedg 19
☎21717 bed20 **A**
H **Waldmannsdorferhof**
Waidmannsdorferstr 72 ☎22544
bed50 **A**
◆ **Gasthof Zentral** Lidmanskygasse 27
☎85312 bed25 **A**
◆ **Zlami** Getreideg 16 ☎83572 bed39 **A**
★ **Janach** Bahnhofstr 5 ☎85114 rm30 **A**

KLOSTERNEUBURG Niederösterreich
(☎02243) Map**14**D3
H **Buschenreiter** Wienerstr 188 ☎2385
bed68 **B**

◆ **Pension Ofner** Erzherzog
Rainergasse 4 ☎7439 bed12 **B**

KORNEUBURG Niederösterreich (☎02262)
Map**14**D3
H **Bauer** Stockerauerstr 31A ☎2322
bed60 **B**
◆ **Gasthof Sonne** Laaerstr 12 ☎2198
bed47 **A**

KÖTSCHACH-MAUTHEN Kärnten
(☎04715) Map**13**B1
◆ **Gasthof Alte Post** ☎465 bed40 **A**
◆ **Gasthof Erlenhof** ☎444 bed29 **A**
◆ **Gasthof Gailberghoehe** ☎368
bed24 Dec–Oct **A**
◆ **Pension Gailtalerhof** ☎318 bed40 **A**
◆ **Gasthof Lamprechtbauer** ☎422
bed25 **A**
◆ **Pension Marienheim** ☎632 bed23 **A**
★★ **Post** ☎221 rm32 **A**

KREMS AN DER DONAU Niederösterreich
(☎02732) Map**14**C3
H **Bruner** Obere Landstr 32 ☎2276
bed42 Feb–Dec **B**
◆ **Gasthof Goldener Engel**
Wienerstr 29 ☎2067 bed27 **A**
◆ **Karpischek** Langenloiserstr 7 ☎2192
bed27 **A**
◆ **Gasthof Unter den Linden**
Schillerstr 5 ☎2115 bed4 **A**

KRIMML Salzburg (☎06564) Map**13**A2
◆ **Pension Breitner** ☎281 bed16 **A**
◆ **Pension Frieda** ☎258 bed8
Closed Nov **A**
◆ **Pension Lachmayer** ☎247 bed16 **A**
★★ **Klockerhaus** ☎208 rm40
Closed Nov **B**

KRUMPENDORF-WÖRTHERSEE Kärnten
(☎04229) Map**14**C1
◆ **Pension Thaler** ☎591 bed18 **A**

KUFSTEIN Tirol (☎05372) Map**13**A2
◆ **Gasthaus Baerenwirt** ☎2229
bed58 **A**
◆ **Gasthof Kienbergklamm** ☎2248
bed32 **A**
H **Muenchen** ☎4775 bed40 **A**
◆ **Gasthof Tirolerhof** ☎2331 bed20 **A**
FH **Wagner** 'Bacherbauer',
Longkampfnerstr 32 ☎33965 **B**

LAMBACH Oberösterreich (☎07245)
Map**13**B3
◆ **Gasthof zum Gruenen** ☎8963
bed20 **A**
◆ **Gasthof Harrer** ☎202 bed24 **A**
◆ **Gasthof zum Weissen** ☎8868
bed28 **A**

LANDECK Tirol (☎05442) Map**12**D2
◆ **Gasthof Greif** ☎2268 bed35 **A**
◆ **Gasthof Kalfenau** ☎3620 bed50
Closed Nov **A**

LANGENLOIS Niederösterreich (☎02734)
Map**14**C3
◆ **Pension Demal** ☎2559 bed17 **A**
FH **Gruber** Mittelberg 44 ☎32242 **B**
◆ **Gasthof Post** ☎2513 bed31 **A**

Austria

LECH AM ARLBERG Vorarlberg (☎05583) Map**12**C2
- ◆ **Andrea Haus** ☎436 bed25 **B**
- ◆ **Gasthof Gotthard** ☎263 bed36 Closed May **B**
- ★ **Katharina-Haus** ☎416 bed12 Closed May **B**
- ◆ **Murmeli** ☎467 bed24 Nov–Apr, Jul–Sep **A**

LEOBEN Steiermark (☎05673) Map**14**C2
- ◆ **Krempel** ☎3202 bed85 **A**
- ◆ **Gasthof Sommersacher** ☎2655 bed30 **A**
- H **Stein** ☎3144 bed63 **A**
- H **Suedbahnhof** ☎2790 bed9 **A**

LEONFELDEN Oberösterreich (☎07213) Map**14**C3
- FH **Grasböck** Weinzierl 2 ☎341 **B**

LERMOOS Tirol (☎05673) Map**12**D2
- ◆ **Pension Alpenrose** ☎2282 bed39 Dec–Oct **A**
- ◆ **Bergheim-Fremdenheim** ☎2405 bed40 Dec–Apr **A**
- ◆ **Bergkristall-Fremdenheim** ☎2687 bed16 **A**
- ◆ **Pension Franzl** ☎2368 bed34 Dec–Mar, May–Sep **A**

LEUTASCH Tirol (☎05214) Map**12**D2
- ◆ **Helene-Fremdenheim** ☎6637 bed14 **A**
- ◆ **Leppert** ☎6584 bed14 Dec–Mar, May–Sep **A**
- ◆ **Rauth** ☎6621 bed12 **A**
- ◆ **Sabine-Fremdenheim** ☎6327 bed19 **A**

LIENZ Tirol (☎04852) Map**13**B1
- H **Gloecklturm** ☎2164 bed67 **A**
- ◆ **Gasthof Haidenhof** ☎2440 bed64 Closed Nov **A**
- FH **Tiefenbacher** 'Untertaxerhof', Schlossberg 26 ☎3639 **B**
- ★★ **Glocknerhof** Schillerstr 4 ☎2167 rm18 **A**
- ★★ **Tyrol** ☎3482 rm35 **A**

LIEZEN Steiermark (☎03612) Map**14**C2
- ◆ **Gasthof Huber** ☎2472 bed50 **A**
- ◆ **Gasthof Rolthner** ☎2365 bed28 **A**
- ◆ **Schnuderl** ☎2605 bed17 **A**
- ★★ **Karow** Bahnhofstr 4 ☎2381 rm33 **A**

LINZ Oberösterreich (☎07222) Map**14**C3
- ◆ **Gasthof Ebelsbergerhof** Weinerstr 485 ☎42125 bed42 **A**
- ◆ **Gasthof Goldenen Anker** Hofgasse 5 ☎71088 bed35 **A**
- ◆ **Pension Goldener Hirsch** Hirschgasse 9 ☎79835 bed38 **A**
- H **Hengster** Salzburgerstr 195 ☎80472 bed15 **A**
- ◆ **Gasthof Mitten in der Weld** Neusserling 9 Gde ☎28114 bed27 **A**
- ◆ **Gasthof zum Schlefen Apfelbaum** Hanuschstr 26 ☎53173 bed32 **A**
- ◆ **Gasthof Wankmuellerhof** Wankmeullerhofstr 62 ☎44147 bed42 **A**

LOFER Salzburg (☎06248) Map**13**B2
- ◆ **Gasthof Eberlwirt** ☎415 bed43 Closed Nov **A**
- ◆ **Pension Haus Eva-Maria** ☎232 bed26 Jan–Mar, May–Sep **A**
- ◆ **Gasthof Hinterhorn** ☎316 bed20 **A**
- ◆ **Pension Hirlanda** ☎220 bed17 Dec–Mar, May–Oct **A**
- ◆ **Pension Jaegerheim** ☎432 bed12 **A**
- ◆ **Pension Schopper** ☎241 bed25 Closed Nov **A**
- ◆ **Gasthof Sonnhof** ☎354 bed54 Dec–Sep **A**
- FH **Vitzthum** 'Brentnerbauer', Hallenstein 5 ☎421 **B**
- ★★ **Bräu** ☎207 rm25 May–Oct **B**
- ★★ **Post** ☎303 rm38 **B**

MAISSAU Niederösterreich (☎02958) Map**14**C3
- H **Rasthaus am Manhartsberg** ☎334 bed25 **A**

MARIA WÖRTH Kärnten (☎04273) Map**35**A4
- ◆ **Pension Riepl** ☎2094 bed16 May–Sep **A**

MARIAZELL Steiermark (☎02727) Map**14**C2
- H **Andreas Hofer** ☎2137 bed54 Closed Nov **A**
- H **Goldener Loewe** ☎2444 bed60 **A**
- ◆ **Gasthof Haas Gottfriede** ☎2874 bed9 **A**
- ◆ **Gasthof Hoehn** ☎2112 bed51 **A**
- ◆ **Marienheim** ☎2545 bed60 Closed Nov **A**
- ◆ **Pension Rechberger** ☎2553 bed13 **A**
- ◆ **Gasthof Steinacher** ☎2660 bed12 **A**
- ◆ **Pension Zechner** ☎2581 bed25 **A**

MATREI IN OSTTIROL Tirol (☎04875) Map**13**B1
- ◆ **Gasthof Hinteregger** ☎287 bed46 **A**
- ◆ **Gasthof Sonne** ☎310 bed15 **A**

MATTIGHOFEN Oberösterreich (☎07742) Map**13**B3
- ◆ **Gasthof Hofwirt** ☎420 bed19 **A**
- ◆ **Gasthof Renzl** ☎229 bed21 **A**

MAUTERN Steiermark (☎03845) Map**14**C2
- ◆ **Pension Bischof** ☎277 bed14 **A**
- ◆ **Gasthof Kuehberger Leopold** ☎286 bed21 **A**
- H **Liesintalerhof** ☎211 bed59 **A**

MAUTERNDORF Salzburg (☎06472) Map**13**B2
- FH **Messner** 'Stocker, Bergöriach 13 ☎416 **B**
- FH **Stoff** 'Maurer', Steindorf 11 ☎348 **B**

MAYRHOFEN Tirol (☎05285) Map**13**A2
- ◆ **Daringer** ☎2728 bed18 Dec–Mar, May–Sep **A**
- ◆ **Pension Eberharter** ☎2388 bed50 Closed Nov **A**
- ◆ **Gasthof Eckartauerhof** ☎2435 bed26 **A**
- ◆ **Pension Gaisberger** ☎2389 bed14 **A**

◆ **Gasthof Rose** ☎2229 bed24 A
◆ **Pension Sonnenhof** ☎2413 bed21
Closed Nov A
◆ **Pension Steiner** ☎2321 bed24
Closed Nov A
◆ **Pension Waldheim** ☎2211 bed24 A
◆ **Gasthof-Hotel Zillertal** ☎2304 bed80
Dec–Sep A

METNITZ Kärnten (☎04267) Map**14**C1/2
FH **Leitner** 'Schwegl', Oberhof 9 ☎287 **B**
FH **Reissner** 'Methwirt', Kärntn.
Lassnitz 8 ☎2917 **B**

MILLSTATT Kärnten (☎04766) Map**13**B1
H **Annenhof** ☎2031 bed34 A
◆ **Pension Haus Duermoser** ☎2681
bed18 A
◆ **Pension Haus Moser** ☎2168
bed19 A
H **Strandhotel** ☎2075 bed99 A

MISTELBACH AN DER ZAYA
Niederösterreich (☎02572) Map**14**D3
◆ **Gasthof Singer-Heindl**
Oberhoferstr 15 ☎27295 bed32 A
◆ **Gasthof Weisses Roessel**
Hafnerstr 8 ☎2431 bed23 A

MÖDLING Niederösterreich (☎02236)
Map**14**D3
H **Babenbergerhof**
Babenbergergasse 6 ☎2246 bed36 **B**
◆ **Gasthof Dracovits** Wienerstrasse 40
☎6531 bed23 Jul–May A

MONDSEE Oberösterreich (☎06224)
Map**13**B2
◆ **Pension Achleitner** ☎27653 bed15
May–Oct, Dec A
◆ **Pension Edtmeier** ☎27442 bed19 A
◆ **Pension Erlinger** ☎2281 bed16
Jun–Oct A
◆ **Gasthof Gaderer** ☎3071 bed9 A
◆ **Gasthof Gasterbauer** ☎2514 bed29
May–Oct A
H **Krone** ☎2236 bed40 A
◆ **Pension Lehrl** ☎2658 bed13 A
FH **Pöllmann** 'Kreuzinger', Hof 21
☎27292 **B**
H **Post** ☎2220 bed56 A
★ **Leitnerbräu** Marketplatz 9 ☎2219
rm17 A

MÖNICHKIRCHEN Niederösterreich
(☎02649) Map**14**D2
H **Binder** ☎235 bed44 A
◆ **Buchner** ☎204 bed32 A
◆ **Pension Hietel** ☎237 bed8 A
◆ **Gasthof Waldheim** ☎240 bed10 A

MURAU Steiermark (☎03532) Map**14**C2
◆ **Gasthof Gassenhube** ☎2318
bed22 A
H **Lercher** ☎2431 bed60 A
◆ **Gasthof Moore** ☎2477 bed23 **B**
◆ **Gasthof Neumann** ☎321 bed7 A

MÜRZZUSCHLAG Steiermark (☎03852)
Map**14**C2
H **Zum Gruenen Baum** ☎2460 bed45 **B**
◆ **Gasthof zum Weissen Roessl**
☎2125 bed19 A

MUTTERS Tirol (☎05222) Map**12**D2
◆ **Kaltenberger** ☎272504 bed13 A
H **Pension Seppl** ☎23114 bed50
Dec–Sep A
◆ **Pension Serles** ☎20486 bed29 A
★★ **Muttererhof** ☎27491 rm24
May–15Dec **B**

NATTERS Tirol (☎05222) Map**12**D2
◆ **Hornsteiner** ☎28119 bed32
Jul–15Sep A
◆ **Pension Nockspitzstüberl** ☎35362
bed15 A
★ **Eichhof** ☎266555 rm20 May–Oct A
★ **Steffi** ☎29402 rm12 15Jun–15Sep A

NAUDERS Tirol (☎05473) Map**12**D1
◆ **Schmid** ☎246 bed10 A
★ **Hochland** ☎272 rm20 Jun–Sep,
15Dec–15Apr **B**
★ **Post** ☎202 rm42 Jun–Sep,
17Dec–16Apr **B**
★ **Verzasca** ☎237 rm20 Jun–Sep,
15Dec–22Apr **B**

NEUMARKT Steiermark (☎03584)
Map**14**C2
◆ **Gasthof Knauder** ☎2403 bed23 A
◆ **Lukanz** ☎2239 bed43 May–Sep A
◆ **Pension Perner** ☎2288 bed8
Dec–Feb, Apr–Aug A
◆ **Gasthof Ressler** ☎2339 bed11 A
◆ **Pension Villa Wolf** ☎2146 bed28 A

NEUMARKT AM WALLERSEE Salzburg
(☎06216) map**13**B2
FH **Sams** 'Haldingerwirt', Sammerholz 13
☎371 A
★ **Lauterbacher** ☎456 rm15
Mar–Dec A

NEUSIEDL AM SEE Burgenland (☎02167)
Map**14**D3
H **Leiner** ☎489 bed27 A
◆ **Gaestehaus Martina** ☎582 bed32 A

OBERGURGL Tirol (☎05256) Map**12**D1
◆ **Alpenblume** ☎278 bed22 A
◆ **Broser** ☎219 bed25 A
◆ **Karl Gstrein** ☎287 bed18 A
◆ **Pillerhof** ☎284 bed10 A
◆ **Rochus** ☎257 bed8 A

OBERPULLENDORF Burgenland (☎02612)
Map**14**D2
◆ **Gasthof Domschitz** ☎2228 bed28
Closed Sep A
◆ **Pension Kraill** ☎2220 bed23 A

OBERTAUERN Salzburg (☎06466)
Map**13**B2
◆ **Gasthof Krings-Alm** ☎318 bed14
Jun–Sep A
◆ **Gasthof Petersbuehel** ☎235 bed35
Nov–Apr, Jul–Aug A
◆ **Gasthof Schulzhaus Wismayrhaus**
☎222 bed56 Nov–Apr, Jul–Sep A
◆ **Pension Weningeralm** ☎242 bed16
Dec–Apr, Jun–Sep A

OBERWART Burgenland (☎03352)
Map**14**D2
◆ **Gasthof Benkoe** ☎8293 bed12 A
FH **Halper** 'Halper', St Martin 15 ☎8807 A

Austria

OETZ Tirol (☎05252) Map**12**D2
- H **Alpenrose** ☎6208 bed90
  Closed Nov **A**
- ♦ **Marita-Fremdenheim** ☎6383
  bed19 **A**
- ♦ **Pension Pohl** ☎6275 bed28
  Dec–Sep **A**
- H **Seerose** ☎6220 bed48 **A**
- ★★ **Drei Mohren** Haupstr ☎6301 rm30 **B**

PARTENEN Vorarlberg (☎05558) Map**12**C1
- ♦ **Gasthof Partenhof** ☎319 bed35
  Closed Nov **A**
- ♦ **Gasthof Sonne** ☎308 bed60
  Dec–Apr, Jun–Oct **A**

PERTISAU AM ACHENSEE Tirol (☎05243)
Map**13**A2
- ♦ **Pension Entner** ☎5394 bed31
  Closed Nov **A**
- ♦ **Gasthof Golfvilla** ☎534203 bed20 **A**
- ♦ **Pension Klara** ☎5266 bed28
  Dec–Sep **A**
- ♦ **Pension Tirol** ☎5243 bed45 **A**

PFUNDS-STUBEN Tirol (☎05474)
Map**12**D1
- ♦ **Gasthof Dangl** ☎244 bed24 **A**
- H **Lafairserhof** ☎251 bed30 **B**
- ♦ **Gasthof Traube** ☎210 bed50 **A**

POYSDORF Niederösterreich (☎02552)
Map**14**D3
- H **Sauberer** Kleinhadersdorf ☎2625
  bed24 **A**

RAABS AN DER THAYA Neiderösterreich
(☎02846) Map**14**C3
- ♦ **Gasthof Schlossblick** ☎238 bed47
  Apr–Oct **A**
- ♦ **Pension Strohmer** ☎238 bed26 **A**
- H **Thaya** ☎202 bed45 **A**

RADENTHEIN Kärnten (☎04246) Map**13**B1
- ♦ **Gasthof Gartenrast** ☎2017 bed22 **A**
- ♦ **Gasthof Sonnenhof** ☎2135 bed18 **A**
- ♦ **Gasthof Staberhof** ☎265 bed34 **B**

RADSTADT Salzburg (☎06465) Map**13**B2
- FH **Scharfetter** 'Eggl'. Scharmberg 19
  ☎373 **B**

RAMSAU AM DACHSTEIN Steiermark
(☎03687) Map**13**B2
- H **Almfrieden** ☎2753 bed82 Dec–Mar,
  May–Oct **A**
- ♦ **Pension Berger** ☎2146 bed16 **A**
- ♦ **Pension Concordia** ☎2091 bed23
  Closed Nov **A**
- ♦ **Gasthof Fichtenheim** ☎2474
  bed37 **A**
- ♦ **Gasthof Schrempf** ☎2819 bed19
  Dec–Sep **A**

RANKWEIL Vorarlberg (☎05522) Map**12**C2
- ♦ **Burgcafe** ☎44516 bed9 **A**
- ♦ **Gasthof Gruener Baum** ☎44216
  bed27 Dec–Feb, May–Aug **A**
- ♦ **Gasthof Hoenligen** ☎44183 bed15 **A**
- H **Hoher Freschen** ☎44237 bed68
  Closed Oct **A**
- ♦ **Gasthof Mohren** ☎44275 bed36 **A**

RAURIS Salzburg (☎06544) Map**13**B2
- ♦ **Gasthof Alpenrose** ☎298 bed36 **A**
- ♦ **Pension Bergkristall** ☎234 bed20 **A**
- ♦ **Pension Moser** ☎315 bed24 **A**
- FH **Riess** Gratschberg, Wörth 16
  ☎36618 **B**
- ♦ **Gasthof Schuett** ☎403 bed32
  closed Nov **A**

RETZ Niederösterreich (☎02942)
Map**14**C/D3
- ♦ **Pension Weisser Loewe** ☎2418
  bed8 **A**

REUTTE Tirol (☎05672) Map**12**D2
- ♦ **Beck** ☎2522 bed19 **A**
- ♦ **Gasthof Rose** ☎2344 bed52 **A**
- ★ **Tirolerhof** Bahnofstr 16 ☎2557 rm40
  Apr–20Jan **B**

RIED IM INNKREIS Oberösterreich
(☎07752) Map**13**B3
- ♦ **Gasthof Auleitner** ☎2083 bed24 **A**
- ♦ **Gasthof Kellerbraue** ☎2828 bed15 **A**
- H **Merzendorfer** ☎2721 bed28 **A**
- ♦ **Gasthof Weinhaeupl** ☎2174
  bed21 **A**
- ♦ **Gasthof Zeillinger** ☎2018 bed14 **A**

ROHRBACH Oberösterreich (☎07289)
Map**13**B3
- H **Bänsch** Götzendorf 17 ☎42106 **B**
- H **Grims** Berggasse 20 ☎313 **B**
- ♦ **Hofer** Götzendorf 22 ☎42197 **B**

SAALBACH Salzburg (☎06586) Map**13**B2
- ♦ **Pension Bernhofer** ☎256 bed28 **A**
- ♦ **Pension Birkenhof** ☎336 bed25 **A**
- ♦ **Pension Gartenheim** ☎692 bed15 **A**
- ♦ **Pension Haus Hollin** ☎73524 bed4 **A**
- ♦ **Pension Kaltenegger** ☎244 bed15
  Jan–Mar, Jul–Sep **A**
- ♦ **Pension Pfleger** ☎363 bed28
  Dec–Mar, May–Oct **A**
- ♦ **Pension Salzburgerhof** ☎461
  bed25 **A**
- ♦ **Pension Steiner** ☎498 bed10
  Jan–Apr, Jun–Aug **A**

SAALFELDEN Salzburg (☎06582)
Map**13**B2
- ♦ **Gasthof Bieberglift** ☎2398 bed14 **A**
- ♦ **Pension Erlhof** ☎29552 bed25 **A**
- H **Geisler** 'Reichlbauer', Pfaffing 7
  ☎2015 **B**
- ♦ **Gasthof Hindenburg** ☎2303
  bed55 **A**
- H **Hirschbichler** 'Fritzbauer',
  Almdorf 10 ☎2351 **B**
- ♦ **Gasthof Liendlwirt** ☎2367 bed50 **A**
- ♦ **Gasthof Osterfor** ☎202 bed25
  Closed Nov **A**
- ♦ **Pension Salzmann** ☎2635 bed15 **A**
- ♦ **Pension Schmiderer** ☎2555
  bed25 **A**
- ♦ **Pension Zwickl** ☎2621 bed16 **A**
- ★★ **Dick** Bahnhofstrasse 106 ☎2215
  bed30 **B**

ST ANTON AM ARLBERG Tirol (☎05446)
Map**12**C2
- ♦ **Fallesin-Fremdenheim** ☎2517
  bed23 Desc–Apr, Jun–Sep **B**

◆ **Pension Koessler** ☎2681 bed14
Dec–Apr, Jun–Sep **A**
● **Schollberg-Fremdenheim** ☎2535
bed13 Dec–Apr, Jun–Oct **B**

ST GEORGEN OB MURAU Steiermark
(☎03537) Map**14**C2
  ◆ **Gasthof Schoegl** ☎213 bed26 **A**

ST GILGEN AM WOLFGANGSEE Salzburg
(☎06227) Map**13**B2
  ◆ **Pension am Bach** ☎324 bed21 **A**
  ◆ **Pension Falkensteiner** ☎395
   bed48 **A**
  ◆ **Pension Ferstl** ☎216 bed33
   Apr–Sep, Dec **A**
  ◆ **Pension Nistler** ☎578 bed28 **A**
  ◆ **Pension Wenghof** ☎476 bed23 **A**
★★ **Pension Alpenland** ☎330 rm17
   Jul–9 Oct **A**
  ★ **Mozartblick** ☎403 rm23 **A**

ST JOHANN AM TAUERN Steiermark
(☎03575) Map**14**C2
  FH **Stanimayer** 'Stuhlpfarrer' Nr 24
   ☎228 **B**
  FH **Wölger** 'Roanher' Nr27 ☎236 **B**

ST JOHANN IM PONGAU Salzburg
(☎06412) Map**13**B2
  ◆ **Pension Alpenblick** ☎6234 bed14
   Closed Nov **A**
  ◆ **Alpengasthof Hahnbaumalm**
   ☎6133 bed8 Closed Nov **A**
  ◆ **Gasthof Goldener Hirscht** ☎220
   bed45 **A**
  ◆ **Pension Hockkoenig blick** ☎6233
   bed18 **A**
  FH **Höller** 'Durchholz', Floitensberg 18
   ☎542 **B**
  ◆ **Gasthof Hubertwirt** ☎251 bed55
   Dec–Sep **A**
  ◆ **Pension Monika** ☎411 bed28
   Closed Oct **A**
  ◆ **Gasthof Piankenauwirt** ☎513
   bed35 **A**
  ◆ **Pension Reithof** ☎589 bed20 **A**
  ◆ **Gasthof zur Sonne** ☎443 bed18
   Dec–Sep **A**

ST JOHANN IN TIROL Tirol (☎05352)
Map**13**A2
  ◆ **Gasthaus Baer** ☎2308 bed40
   Closed Oct **A**
  FH **Erler** Hinterkaiserweg 28 ☎32334 **B**
  ◆ **Freiblick-Fremdenheim** ☎2405
   bed16 **A**
  ◆ **Hauser** ☎2106 bed16 **A**
  ◆ **Pension Johanna** ☎2789 bed24
   Dec–Sep **A**
  ◆ **Pension Kexel** ☎2447 bed18 **A**
  FH **Prem** Niederhofen 2 ☎20393 **B**
  ◆ **Pension Toni** ☎2839 bed27 **A**
  ◆ **Pension Zobler** ☎2988 bed13 **A**

ST OSWALD BEI FREISTADT
Oberösterreich (☎07945) Map**14**C3
  FH **Mayrhofer** Nr56 ☎253 **A**
  FH **Pirklbauer** Elzelsdorf 2 ☎287 **A**

ST OSWALD OB EIBISWALD Steiermark
(☎03468) Map**14**C1
  ◆ **Gasthof Fichtenhof** ☎210 bed14 **A**

◆ **Gasthof Messner** ☎216 bed18 **A**
ST PÖLTEN Niederösterreich (☎02742)
Map**14**C3
  ◆ **Pension Fuchs** Europaplatz 7 ☎2946
   bed32 **A**
  ◆ **Gasthof Langmann**
   Fuhrmanngasse 15 ☎2243 bed8
   Jul–Sep **A**

ST STEFAN OB LEOBEN Steiermark
(☎03832) Map**14**C2
  ◆ **Gasthof Eichhoebl** ☎2270 bed17 **A**
  ◆ **Gasthof Schindlbacher** ☎2321
   bed12 **A**

ST VEIT A. D. GLAN Kärnten (☎04212)
Map**14**C1
  FH **Schanrigg** 'Brandstätter'
   Unterwuhr 11 ☎(04223) 452 **B**
  ◆ **Gasthof Steirerhof** ☎2442 bed15 **A**

ST WOLFGANG AM WOLFGANGSEE
Oberösterreich (☎06138) Map**13**B2
  ◆ **Pension Almrausch** ☎267 bed40 **A**
  ◆ **Gasthof Alpenrose** ☎481 bed19 **A**
  ◆ **Gasthof Franz Josef** ☎354 bed11
   Apr–Oct **A**
  ◆ **Pension Graf** ☎279 bed24 **A**
  ◆ **Gasthof Kellerstueberl** ☎240
   bed60 **A**
  ◆ **Pension Seeheim** ☎308 bed19 **A**
  ◆ **Pension Sonnenwinkel** ☎489 bed24
   Closed Nov **A**

SALZBURG Salzburg (☎06222) Map**13**B2
  ◆ **Gasthof Alpenland**
   Klessheimerallee 69 ☎33349
   bed24 **A**
  ◆ **Pension Bergland** Rupertgasse15
   ☎72318 bed33 Closed Nov **A**
  ◆ **Gasthof Dietmann** Ignaz Harrer Str13
   ☎31364 bed62 **A**
  ◆ **Gasthof Eigenherr** Josef-von-
   Eichendorff-Str 5 ☎46326 bed36 **A**
  ◆ **Gasthof Ganshof** Ganshofstr 13
   ☎46628 bed26 **A**
  ◆ **Gasthof Jahn** Elisabethstr 31
   ☎71405 bed39 **A**
  ◆ **Gasthof Lillenhof** Siezenheimerstr
   Gp 1220/4 ☎33630 bed28 **A**
  ◆ **Gasthof Samhof** Negrelligstr 19
   ☎74622 bed42 **A**
  ◆ **Gasthof Trumerstueberl**
   Bergstrasse 6 ☎74776 bed45 **A**
  ★ **Salzburger Motel** Alpenstr 48 &
   Friedenstr 6 ☎20871 rm27
   Feb–24 Dec **B**

SCHÄRDING Oberösterreich (☎07712)
Map**13**B3
  ◆ **Pension Gugerbauer** ☎2775
   bed 70 **A**
  ◆ **Gasthof Waldgasthof Marienthal**
   ☎2692 bed33 **A**

SCHEIBBS Niederösterreich (☎07482)
Map**14**C2/3
  FH **Fenzl** Brandstatt 145 ☎2993 **B**
  ◆ **Pension Janda** Hauptstrasse 17
   ☎2256 bed36 **A**

SCHLADMING Steiermark (☎03687)
Map**13**B2
  ◆ **Pension Asinger** ☎2495 bed19 **A**

Austria

- ♦ **Gasthof Feichter** ☎2129 bed30 A
- ♦ **Pension Haus am Bach** ☎2133 bed40 A
- ♦ **Gasthof Mayer** ☎2128 bed25 A
- ♦ **Pension Mitterhofer** ☎2229 bed31 A
- FH **Perner** 'Rantlhof', Untere Klaus 7 ☎2884 B
- ♦ **Pension Plattner** ☎2323 bed17 A
- ♦ **Pension Poserhof** ☎3147 bed27 A
- ♦ **Pension Schrempf** ☎2103 bed20 A
- ♦ **Pension Tritscher** ☎2313 bed24 A
- ♦ **Gasthof Zainer** ☎26617 bed15 A

SCHÖNAU (BAD) Niederösterreich (☎02646) Map**14**D2
- ♦ **Pension Dopler** ☎2506 bed30 A
- ♦ **Pension Hofmeister** ☎2375 bed40 A

SCHÖNBERG IM STUBAITAL Tirol (☎05225) Map**12**D2
- FH **Stlexner** 'Nogl' Nr16 ☎2754 B

SCHRUNS Vorarlberg (☎05556) Map**12**C1
- ♦ **Gasthof Adele** ☎2131 bed12 A
- ♦ **Gasthof Auhof** ☎2269 bed39 Closed Nov A
- ♦ **Pension Bradlwarter** ☎2123 bed21 A
- ♦ **Pension Latons** ☎2598 bed14 A
- ♦ **Pension Moeck** ☎2515 bed21 Closed Nov A
- ♦ **Gasthaus Stlegler** ☎3180 bed16 A

SEEBODEN Kärnten (☎04762) Map**13**B1
- ♦ **Pension Haus 'Andrea'** ☎81311 bed36 A
- ♦ **Gasthof Lagger** ☎81173 bed28 A
- H **Moser** ☎81400 bed64 A
- ♦ **Pension Oase Der Ruhe** ☎81728 bed27 A
- ♦ **Gasthof Oberlerchner Seppdleter** ☎81128 bed79 A
- ♦ **Pension Seevilla** ☎81339 bed26 A
- ♦ **Pension Villa Karolina** ☎81701 bed21 Dec–Feb, Apr–Sep A

SEEFELD Tirol (☎05212) Map**12**D2
- ♦ **Antonia-Fremdenheim** ☎2214 bed21 Dec–Mar, May–Sep A
- ♦ **Antonia-Lia-Fremdenheim** ☎2988 bed21 Dec–Mar, May–Sep A
- ♦ **Eunice-Fremdenheim** ☎2240 bed13 Dec–Mar, Jun–Sep A
- ♦ **Frenes** ☎2903 bed16 Jan–Mar, May–Oct A
- ♦ **Gasthof Neuleutasch** ☎6547 bed28 B
- ♦ **Pension Sonnhof** ☎2242 bed33 Dec–Mar, Jun–Sep A

SEMMERING Niederösterreich (☎02664) Map**14**D2
- ♦ **Pension Antoinette** ☎370 bed12 A
- ♦ **Pension Daheim** ☎382 bed20 Jan–Oct A
- ♦ **Gasthof Edelweiss** ☎284 bed29 A
- ♦ **Haus Mayer** ☎251 bed11 A
- ♦ **Pension Segfried** ☎287 bed50 A
- ♦ **Gasthof Verein 'Boeck-Greissau-Werk'** ☎474 bed104 A

SERFAUS Tirol (☎05476) Map**12**D1
- ♦ **Brigitte-Fremdenheim** ☎360 bed13 Dec–May, Jul–Sep B

- ♦ **Elfriede-Fremdenheim** ☎305 bed25 Jan–Apr, Jul–Sep A

SILLIAN Tirol (☎04856) Map**13**A1
- ♦ **Pension Adelheid** ☎6286 bed37 A
- H **Atzwanger** ☎205 bed46 A

SÖLDEN Tirol (☎05254) Map**12**D1
- ♦ **Fender** ☎2371 bed20 A
- ♦ **Gstrein** ☎2394 bed16 A
- ♦ **Olympia-Fremdenheim** ☎2427 bed15 B

SPITTAL AN DER DRAU Kärnten (☎04762) Map**13**B1
- ♦ **Pension Edlinger** Mozartstr 9 ☎2948 bed12 A
- ♦ **Hoessl** Peintenstr 22 ☎2647 bed18 B
- ♦ **Gasthof Striessnig** Edlingerstr 3 bed27 A

STEINACH AM BRENNER Tirol (☎05272) Map**13**A1/2
- ♦ **Alte Schmiede-Fremdenheim** ☎6281 bed33 Dec–Sep A
- ♦ **Gasthaus Herrengschwendt** ☎6213 bed15 Dec–Apr, Jun–Sep A
- ♦ **Schafferer** ☎6317 bed16 A
- ♦ **Waldheim** ☎6358 bed25 A
- ★ **Weisses Rosel** ☎6206 rm45 15Dec–Oct B

STEYR Oberösterreich (☎07252) Map**14**C3
- ♦ **Zum Goldenen Ochsen** ☎3049 bed28 A
- ♦ **Nagl** ☎2976 bed60 A
- ♦ **Gasthof Poetzl** ☎3067 bed10 A

STOCKERAU Niederösterreich (☎02266) Map**14**D3
- H **Bauer** ☎2124 bed31 A
- ♦ **Gasthof Karl Ottille** ☎2618 bed22 A

STUBEN Vorarlberg (☎05582) Map**12**C1/2
- ♦ **Gasthof-Cafe Arlberg** ☎84519 bed57 B
- ♦ **Erna-Fremdenheim** ☎87115 bed24 B
- ♦ **Pension Rudi-Mathis** ☎84518 bed22 A
- ♦ **Pension Sonnblick Haus** ☎84598 bed14 B
- ♦ **Pension Stublgerhof** ☎87117 bed18 Dec–Sep A
- ★★ **Post** ☎84516 rm51 A

TAMSWEG Salzburg (☎06474) Map**13**B2
- FH **Gappmaier** 'Kampfbauer', Haiden 8 ☎692 A
- FH **Seitlinger** 'Lipler', Lasaberg 15 ☎6125 B

TELFS Tirol (☎05262) Map**12**D2
- ♦ **Pension Hellrigl** ☎2306 bed14 Closed Nov A
- H **Loewe** ☎2455 bed20 A
- ♦ **Gasthof Plattenhof** ☎208112 bed28 A
- H **Tirolerhof** ☎2237 bed74 A

THIERSEE Tirol (☎05376) Map**13**A2
- ♦ **Georg-Fremdenheim** ☎211 bed24 A
- ♦ **Pension Koegl** ☎250 bed35 A

♦ **Gasthaus Kraemerwirt** ☎34111
bed23 Closed Nov A
♦ **Gasthof Seerose** ☎237 bed30 A
FH **Werlberger** 'Riederbauer', Landl 34
☎33198 B

TRAUNKIRCHEN AM TRAUNSEE
Oberösterreich (☎07617) Map**13**B2
♦ **Gasthof Zum Goldenen Hirschen**
☎260 bed40 A
♦ **Gasthof Leitner** ☎219 bed90 B
♦ **Pension Reiter** ☎298 bed15 A

TRIEBEN Steiermark (☎03615) Map**14**C2
♦ **Gasthof Ebner** ☎320 bed13 A
♦ **Gasthof Klarmann** ☎2234 bed25 A

TULLN Niederösterreich (☎02272)
Map**14**D3
H **Gruber** Donaulaende 26 ☎2658
bed29 A

UMHAUSEN Tirol (☎05255) Map**12**D2
♦ **Gasthof Edelweiss** ☎229 bed28 A

VELDEN AM WÖRTHERSEE Kärnten
(☎04274) Map**14**C1
H **Annotte** ☎2087 bed46 B
♦ **Gudrun** ☎2574 bed34 A
♦ **Villa Strauss** ☎2851·bed7 A
♦ **Gasthof Zentrum** ☎3703 bed23 B

VIENNA See **WIEN**

VILLACH Kärnten (☎04242) Map**13**B1
FH **Egger** 'Prohiner', Goritschach 1
☎24680 B
♦ **Gasthof Eppinger** Klagenfurterstr 6
☎24389 bed34 A
H **Fuggerkeller** Paracelsusgasse 3
☎24808 bed40 B
♦ **Infeld** Purtschellerstr 19 ☎264465
bed15 A
♦ **Pension Klause** Mitterlingstr 1
☎24575 bed18 A
♦ **Margit** Friedenstr 7 ☎25178 bed12
May–Oct A
♦ **Pension Pinter** Kumpfallee 1
☎26034 bed28 A
♦ **Pension Pirker** Rennsteinerstr 21
☎24176 bed43 A
♦ **Gasthof Stiegenbrauer**
Kirchenplatz 5 ☎24377 bed7 A
♦ **Wolbang** Halienstr 42 ☎26877
bed8 A
★★ **Mosser** Bahnhofstr 7 ☎24115 rm30 B

WAIDHOFEN AN DER YBBS
Niederösterreich (☎07442) Map**14**C2
♦ **Pension Bruckschwaiger** Hoher
Markt 18 ☎2358 bed20 A
♦ **Gasthof Czermak** Unterer
Stadtplatz 27 ☎2303 bed16 A
♦ **Gasthof Goldener Stern** Unterer
Stadtplatz 7 ☎2533 bed16 A
♦ **Gasthof Zum Halbmond** Wienerstr 1
☎2179 bed12 A
H **Infuehr** Unterer Stadtplatz 25 ☎2137
bed54 A

WAIDRING Tirol (☎05353) Map**13**B2
FH **Danzl** Blankenhof ☎321 B
♦ **Flatscher** ☎257 bed18 A
♦ **Loisi-Fremdenheim** ☎390 bed26 B

♦ **Gasthof Steinplatte-Alpengasthof**
☎231 bed21 Jan–Mar, Jun–Sep A

WALD AM SCHOBERPASS Steiermark
Map**14**C2
♦ **Gasthof Fink** ☎228 bed20 A
♦ **Gasthof Leitner** ☎213 bed65 A
♦ **Pension Rainer** ☎250 bed12 A

WARTH Vorarlberg (☎05538) Map**12**C2
H **Gasthof Biberkopf** ☎9918 bed40
Dec–Apr, Jun–Sep A
♦ **Fritz** ☎791005 bed17 A

WEIZ Steiermark (☎03172) Map**14**C2
♦ **Gasthof Allmer** ☎2258 bed14 A
♦ **Gastof Ederer** ☎2349 bed46 A
H **Hammer** ☎2208 bed28 A

WELS Oberösterreich (☎07242) Map**13**B3
♦ **Gasthof Auerhahn** Lichteneggerstr 6
☎7516 bed23 A
♦ **Gasthof Bayrischer Hof** Dr Johann
Schauerstr 23 ☎7214 bed54 A
H **Kremsmuenstererhof** Stadtplatz 63
☎6623 bed29 A
H **Rathausstueberl** Stadtplatz 69
☎6453 bed38A
♦ **Gasthof zur Stadt Salzburg**
Schwimmschulgasse 1 ☎4496
bed12 A
♦ **Gasthof Waldschenke** Roithenstr 2
☎81640 bed11 A

WESTENDORF Tirol (☎05334) Map**13**A2
♦ **Haflingerhof-Fremdenheim** ☎6243
bed26 Dec–Sep A
♦ **Pension Klinger** ☎6262 bed55
Dec–Mar, May–Sep A
FH **Steindl** 'Zeiplhof', Nachtsöllberg 34
☎413 B
♦ **Pension Veronika** ☎6207 bed72
Dec–Mar, May–Sep B

WEIN (Vienna) (☎0222) Map**14**D3
♦ **Pension AH** 14 Muehlbergstr 18
☎9719633 bed25 A
H **Auhof** 13 Auhofstr 205 ☎825289
bed62 A
♦ **Pension Bellaria** 7 Kircheng 41
☎936381 bed43 A
H **Casino Mauer** 23 Gesslg 19
☎881228 bed26 B
♦ **Pension Edelweiss** 8 Lange G 61
☎422306 bed30 A
♦ **Pension Falstaff** 9 Muellnerg 5
☎349127 bed23 B
♦ **Pension Jaegerwald** 14 Karl
Bekehrtystr 66 ☎9410945
bed23 A
♦ **Pension Luisiana**
23 Futterknechtg 90 ☎673211
bed20 B
♦ **Pension Merlingen** 8 Zelgt 3/13
☎4219413 bed12 A
♦ **Pension Pani** 23 Erlaaer Str 37
☎671697 bed23 B
♦ **Pension Quisisana** 6 Windmuehlg 6
☎573341 bed18 A
♦ **Pension Reimer** 7 Kircheng 18
☎936162 bed30 B

Austria

♦ **Pension Stadler**
23 Hungereckstr 24B ☎675282
bed14 **A**
H **Thalia** 16 Lindauerg 2B6 ☎424513
bed47 **B**

WILDON Steiermark (☎03182) Map**14**C1
♦ **Gasthof Draxler** ☎353 bed15 **A**
♦ **Gasthof Strohmaier** ☎333 bed19 **A**

WILHELMSBURG Niederösterreich
(☎02746) Map**14**C3
♦ **Gasthof Reinberger** ☎364 bed30 **A**

WOLFSBERG Kärnten (☎04352) Map**14**C1
FH **Maler** 'Grabenthoman .
St Margarethen 17 ☎2605 **B**

WÖRGL Tirol (☎05332) Map**13**A2
♦ **Gasthaus Hauserwirt** ☎2305 bed26
Closed Nov **A**
♦ **Gasthaus Sonnblick** ☎2156
bed14 **A**

YBBS AN DER DONAU Niederösterreich
(☎07412) Map**14**C3
★★ **Weisses Rossel Royal** ☎2292
rm32 **B**
★ **Gasthof Steiner** Burgplatz 2 rm20 **A**

ZELL AM SEE Salzburg (☎06542) Map**13**B2
♦ **Pension Albert** ☎2178 bed20 **A**
♦ **Pension Albertlhof** ☎2235 bed18 **A**
♦ **Pension Bernhofer** ☎3653 bed75
Dec–Mar, May–Oct **A**
♦ **Gasthof Floriani-Stueberl** ☎3569
bed28 Dec–Sep **A**
♦ **Gasthof Lehenwirt** ☎2853 bed26 **A**

♦ **Pension Lindenthaler** ☎38624
bed21 **A**
♦ **Pension Maria** ☎2880 bed14
Dec–Sep **A**
♦ **Pension Monika** ☎3114 bed15
Dec–Mar, May–Oct **A**
★★ **Bellevue** Thumersbach ☎3104
rm50 **A**
★★ **Berner** N Gassner-Promenade 1
☎2557 rm18 **A**

ZELL AM ZILLER Tirol (☎05282) Map**13**A2
♦ **Birkenheim-Fremdenheim** ☎2447
bed28 **A**
♦ **Gasthof Neue Post** ☎2236 bed65 **A**
FH **Pfister** 'Stoffer', Rohrberg 39
☎2621 **B**
H **Tirolerhof** ☎2546 bed80 **B**
♦ **Gasthof Untermetzger** ☎2386
bed40 **A**

ZIRL Tirol (☎05228) Map**13**A2
♦ **Gasthof Hirschen** ☎2340 bed26 **A**
★★ **Goldener Lowe** Hauptplatz ☎2330
rm18 **B**
★★ **Post** Meilstr 2 ☎2207 rm27 **A**

ZWETTL Niederösterreich (☎02822)
Map**14**C3
♦ **Pension Jagerstueberl** Landstr 61
☎2453 bed13 **A**
♦ **Gasthof Miedler** Landstr 37 ☎2224
bed16 **A**
FH **Pollak** Waldhams 8 ☎2701 **A**
♦ **Gasthof Riedler** Landstr 49 ☎2373
bed14 **A**

BENELUX

BELGIUM, LUXEMBOURG AND NETHERLANDS

Benelux – Belgium

This gazetteer contains a selection of hotels and pensions. Most of these establishments will provide accommodation for £6 or less per person per night at some time during the year. The prices have been banded as follows **A** under £5 per person per night and **B** between £5 and £6 per person per night. However, these figures may vary according to their location and the time of year. Popular towns, such as Ostende, have many more less expensive establishments than it has been possible for us to list and further information, plus details of farmhouse holidays in Belgium and the Netherlands, may be obtained from local tourist authorities or from the respective National Tourist Offices in London (for addresses see p222).

The Netherlands National Reservation Centre will secure accommodation free of charge. Application may be made direct – by post, telephone or telex to: NRC Amsterdam, PO Box 3387, Hoofdpostkantor, NZ Voorburgwal, 182 Amsterdam 1001, ☎(31)20211211, telex15754. Applications for reservations can also be made to one of the local VVV Offices, which will book a room for a small charge.

Abbreviations:

av	avenue	r	rue	bd	boulevard	rte	route
pl	place, plein	str	straat				

AALST (Alost) Oost Vlaanderen (☎053) Map**3B1**
- ★ **Borse Van Amsterdam** Grote Markt 26 ☎211581 rm6 **A**

AALTER Oost Vlaanderen (☎091) Map**3B2**
- H **Capitole** Stationsstraat 95 ☎741029 rm34 **B**

AMAY Liège (☎085) Map**4C1**
- H **Trois Clochers** r de Biber 7–9 ☎311263 rm9 **A**

AMEL Liège (☎080) Map**4D1**
- H **Kreusch** Amel 115 ☎349050 rm11 **B**

ANTWERPEN (Anvers) Antwerpen (☎031) Map**4C2**
- ◆ **Cecil** Van Arteveldestraat 8 ☎327016 rm12 **A**
- H **Florida** De Keyserlei 59 ☎321443 rm38 **A**
- ◆ **Granducale** St Vincentiusstraat 4 ☎393724 15rm **A**
- H **Miro** Pelikaanstraat 34 ☎331122 rm16 **B**
- H **Résidence Rubens** Amerikalei 115 ☎383031 25rm **A**
- H **Smaragdion** Koningin Astridiaan 44 ☎316173 rm16 **A**
- ★ **Rivierenhof** Turnhoutsebaan 244, 2100 Deurne ☎242564 rm15 **B**

ARLON (Aarlen) Luxembourg (☎063) Map**10D4**
- H **Courtois** av de la Gare 45 ☎211015 rm10 **B**
- H **Cosmopolite** r de la Gare 33 ☎211191 rm8 **B**
- H **Paris** av de Luxembourg 75 ☎211292 ☎29 **A**

BASTOGNE Luxembourg (☎062) Map**10D4**
- H **Sud** r de Marche 39 ☎211114 rm13 **A**
- ★★ **Lebrun** r de Marche 8 ☎211193 rm26 **B**

BEAUMONT Hainaut (☎071) Map**3B1**
- H **Commerce** Grand Place 7 ☎588052 rm7 **A**
- H **Mouton Blanc** Grand Place 27 ☎585870 rm7 **B**

BELLEVAUX-LIGNEUVILLE (Malmédy) Liège (☎080) Map**4D1**
- H **Belle Vue** r de Ligneuville 40 ☎570064 rm12 **A**
- H **Georges** Grand'Rue, 107 ☎570003 rm15 **B**

BERINGEN Limburg (☎011) Map**4C2**
- H **Edelweiss** Steenweg op Beverlo 8 ☎422916 rm12 **A**

BEVEREN-WAAS Oost Vlaanderen (☎031) Map**3B2**
- H **Landbouwkantoor** Markt 40 ☎757026 rm6 **A**

BLANKENBERGE West Vlaanderen (☎050) Map**3B2**
- H **Aquarium** de Smet de Nayerlaan 33c ☎413713 rm24 **A**
- ◆ **Crevette** Langestraat 59 ☎412905 rm6 **A**
- ◆ **Holiday** Westraat 81 ☎411697 rm15 **B**
- H **Lion de Flandre** Kerkstraat 171 ☎411161 rm27 **A**
- H **Madonnina** Koninginlaan 73 ☎412245 rm10 **A**
- H **Miramar** Zeedijk 169 ☎412949 rm34 **A**
- H **Nismes et Tongres** de Smet de Nayerlaan 97 ☎411370 rm19 **A**
- H **Plaza** Descampsstraat 42 ☎411507 rm28 **A**
- ◆ **Univers** Elisabethstraat 4 ☎411696 rm16 **A**
- ★ **Park & Cygne** de Smet de Nayerlaan 133 ☎411811 rm29 **B**

BOOM Antwerpen (☎031) Map**4C2**
- H **Kleidal** H Spillemaeckersstr 9 ☎881954 **A**

BOUILLON Luxembourg (☎061) Map**10D4**
- H **Aux Armes de Bouillon** r de la Station 13 ☎466079 rm50 **B**
- H **Panorama** r au dessus de la Ville 25 ☎466138 rm45 **B**
- H **Semois** r du Collège 44–46 ☎466027 rm45 **A**
- ★ **Gai-Repos** r au-dessus de la Ville 4 ☎466330 rm13 **B**

BOUTERSEM Brabant (☎016) Map**4C1**
- H **Corona** Leuvensesteenweg 143 ☎733218 rm6 **A**

H **Traiteur Roger** Leuvensesteenweg
82 Roosbeek ☎733128 rm6 **A**
H **Hortensias** Leuvensesteenweg 100
☎733149 rm6 **A**

BRAINE LE COMTE Hainaut (☎067)
Map**3B1**
H **Charleroi** pl R Branquart 6 ☎552388
rm8 **A**

BREDENE West Vlaanderen (☎059)
Map**3B2**
◆ **Bastogne** Kasteellaan 17 ☎704629
rm6 **B**
H **Florida** Kapellestraat 133 ☎704644
rm9 **A**
H **Jean** Gentsestraat 24–33 ☎704663
rm28 **A**
H **Littoral** Gentstraat 19 ☎704648
rm15 **A**
◆ **Littoral** Duinenstraat 309 ☎704698
rm12 **A**
H **Marladuyne** Klemskerkestraat 4
☎709796 rm13 **B**
H **Melboom** Kapellestraat 7 ☎704677
rm18 **A**
◆ **Petra** Driftweg 95 ☎704737 rm7 **A**
◆ **St-Michel** Derbylaan 51–53
☎704456 rm11 **A**
★ **Zomerlust** Peter Benoitlaan 26
☎704640 rm20 **A**

BRUGGE (Bruges) West Vlaanderen
(☎050) Map**3B2**
H **Cosmopolite** Kuipersstraat 18
☎332096 rm29 **A**
H **Lodewijk van Maele** Maalseweg 488
St Kruis ☎355763 rm16 **B**
H **Panier d'Or** Markt 28 ☎333985
rm13 **B**
H **Rome** Zuidzandstraat 56 ☎335650
rm11 **A**
H **Sunge d'Or** 't Zand 18 ☎333109
rm19 **B**
H **Sneeuwberg** Hallestraat 2 ☎333772
rm18 **B**
H **Speelmanshuis** 't Zand 3 ☎339552
rm6 **A**
H **Spinola** Krom Genthof 1 ☎336321
rm35 **B**
At **Oostkamp** (8km S)
H **Sachs** Stationsstraat 226 ☎822472
rm9 **A**

BRUSSEL-BRUXELLES Brabant (☎02)
Map**4C1**
H **Acacias** av Fonsny, 6 Fonsnylaan
☎5381926 rm44 **B**
H **Ballon Nord** r de Brabant, 24
Brabantstraat ☎2175487 **A**
◆ **Budva** r St-Géry 27 Gérystraat
☎5119965 rm5 **B**
H **Krol** av Clémenceau 6,
Clémenceaulaan ☎5210828 rm23 **A**
H **Petit Coq** av Fonsny 4, Fonsnylaan
☎538 1421 rm18 **A**
H **Ragheno** av Fonsny 11 Fonsnylaan
☎5382221 rm22 **A**
H **Ravensteinhof** Ninoofseweg 685,
Chée de Ninove, Anderlecht
☎5226888 rm18 **A**
H **Sabot d'Or** bd d'Anvers 5,

Antwerpselaan ☎2176948 rm40 **A**
H **Touristes** r du Marché 11, Marktstraat
☎2176437 rm16 **A**
H **Yser** r d'Edimbourg 9–11,
Edinburgstraat ☎5117459 rm43 **A**

CHAMPLON Luxembourg (☎084) Map**10D4**
H **Bon Coin** r Grande 68 ☎455279
rm10 **A**
H **Bruyeres** rte de Bastogne 3 ☎455185
rm20 **A**

CHARLEROI Hainaut (☎071) Map**4C1**
H **Jacques Bertrand** Place du
Manège 22 ☎326970 rm9 **A**
H **Palais** av de l'Europe 7 ☎314715
rm10 **A**
H **Petit Bruxelles** r de Montignies 8–10
☎325494 rm7 **A**

CHAUDFONTAINE Liège (☎041) Map**4C1**
H **Bains de Perigord** av des Thermes
☎653895 rm37 **B**

COUVIN Namur (☎060) Map**10C4**
H **Gare** av de la Libération 5 ☎344103
rm7 **A**
H **Sapiniere** r Pied de la Montagne 5
☎344381 rm9 **B**

DIEST Brabant (☎013) Map**4C1**
H **Falstaff** Ed Robeynsiaan 2 ☎331634
rm8 **A**
◆ **Carine** Leuvenseweg 38, Webbekom
☎331675 rm7 **A**

DIKSMUIDE (Dixmude) West-Vlannderen
(☎051) Map**3B2**
H **Vrede** Grote Markt 35 ☎500038
rm8 **A**

DINANT Namur (☎082) Map**4C1**
H **Collegiale** r A Sax 2 ☎222372 rm14 **A**
H **Etoile** r St-Jacques 27–29 ☎222260
rm8 **A**
H **Grottes** rte de Philippeville 136
☎222282 rm8 **B**
H **Plateau** Plateau de la Citadelle
☎222834 rm11 **B**
H **Routiers** av Franchet d'Espéray 57
☎222709 rm12 **A**
★★ **Gare** r de la Station 39–41 ☎222056
rm22 **B**

EEKLO Oost-Vlaanderen (☎091) Map**3B2**
◆ **Krugerhof** Koningin Astridplein 24
☎772440 rm5 **A**
H **Rembrandt** Koningin Astridplein 2
☎772570 rm8 **B**

ELSENBORN Liège (☎080) Map**4D1**
H **Printemps** Nidrum 72 ☎446149
rm10 **A**

EUPEN Liège (☎087) Map**4D1**
H **Schmitz-Roth** Rathausplatz 13
☎552078 rm28 **B**
◆ **Zum Goldenen Ancker** Marktplatz 13
rm4 **B**

FLORENVILLE Luxembourg (☎061)
Map**10D4**
H **Central** pl Albert Ier 21 ☎311103
rm20 **A**
H **France** r des Généraux Cuvelier 26
☎311032 rm38 **B**

Benelux – Belgium

H **Franco-Belge** pl Astrid 4 ☎311054 rm13 **A**

FRAIPONT Liège (☎087) Map**4C1**
H **Concorde** r Franklin Roosevelt 252 ☎268155 rm10 **A**

GEMBLOUX Namur (☎081) Map**4C1**
H **Trois Clés** Chaussée de Wavre 1-5 ☎611617 rm16 **A**
H **Voyageurs** av de la Station 123 ☎611806 rm30 **A**

GENT (Gand) Oost-Vlaanderen (☎091) Map**3B2**
H **Alliés** Antwerpsesteenweg 1 ☎281698 rm15 **B**
♦ **Azalee-Azalea** Prinses Clementinalaan ☎225959 rm13 **A**
H **Barloria** Baarleveldstraat 2, Drongen ☎267432 rm10 **A**
♦ **Cosmopolite** Kon Astridlaan 102 ☎228591 rm11 **A**
H **Fonteyne** Gouden Leeuwplein 7 ☎254871 rm15 **B**
H **Helder** Oude Scheldestraat 17 ☎231275 rm27 **A**
H **Ijzer** Vlaanderenstraat 93 ☎259873 rm16 **A**
H **Karper** Kortrijksesteenweg 2 ☎221053 rm15 **A**
H **Lanterne** Prinses Clementinalaan 118 ☎223996 rm16 **A**
H **Maldegem** Antwerpsesteenweg 7 ☎282177 rm9 **A**

HAAN (DE) (Le Coq) West Vlaanderen (☎059) Map**3B2**
H **Bosje** Wenduineseweg 55 ☎234157 rm16 **A**
H **Brasseurs** Koninklijplein 1 ☎233413 rm28 **A**
H **Inter-nos** Leopoldlaan 12 ☎233579 rm11 **A**
H **Prince Leopold** Maria Hendrikalaan 12 ☎233880 rm10 **A**
H **Voske** Vosseslag 120 ☎233555 rm9 **B**

HAN-SUR-LESSE Namur (☎084) Map**10D4**
H **Ardennes** r des Grottes 2 ☎377220 rm38 **B**
H **Escale** r d'Hamptay 47 ☎377210 rm7 **A**

HASSELT Limburg (☎011) Map**4C1**
H **Europa** Grote Markt 14 ☎225642 rm7 **B**
H **Pax** Grote Markt 16 ☎223875 rm8 **A**
H **Rozenhof** Kempische weg 295 ☎222531 rm10 **B**
H **Warson** Bampslaan 39 ☎223664 rm8 **A**

HEIST see **KNOKKE-HEIST**

HOUFFALIZE Luxembourg (☎062) Map**4C1**
H **Vielle Auberge** r du Pont 4 ☎288139 rm7 **B**

HUY (Hoei) Liège (☎085) Map**4C1**
H **Fort** Chaussée Napoléon 4–6 ☎212403 rm22 **B**

H **Nord** pl Z Gramme 1 ☎212337 rm18 **A**
H **Renassance** r des Soeurs Grises 16–18 ☎212845 rm6 **B**

IEPER (Ypres) West Vlaanderen (☎057) Map**3B1**
H **Britannique** Grote Markt 17 ☎201115 rm14 **B**
H **Zweerd** Grote Markt 2 ☎200475 rm10 **A**

ITTRE Brabant (☎067) Map**3B1**
H **Tertre** r des Rabots 6B ☎646316 rm6 **A**

IZEGEM West Vlaanderen (☎051) Map**3B1**
H **Century** Nederweg 26 ☎301844 rm11 **A**

KASTERLEE Antwerpen (☎014) Map**4C2**
H **Bergen** Geelsebaan 74 ☎556135 rm23 **B**
H **Bergenhof** Geelsebaan 65 ☎556044 rm14 **A**
H **Den en Heuvel** Geelseweg 72 ☎556097 rm30 **B**
H **Kempenrust** Geelseweg 29 ☎556009 rm20 **B**
H **Zomerlust** Geelseweg 63 ☎556232 rm18 **A**

KLUISBERGEN Oost-Vlaanderen (☎055) Map**3B1**
H **Tyrol** Molenstraat 113 ☎388686 rm7 **A**

KNOKKE-HEIST West Vlanderen (☎050) Map**3B2**
♦ **Cambrinus** Elizabethlaan 367 ☎513120 rm6 **B**
H **Caroline** Parmentierlaan 272 ☎602930 rm14 **B**
♦ **Chapon Fin** Kustlaan 12 ☎601173 rm6 **A**
H **Coventry** Ieperstraat 19 ☎605463 rm15 **A**
H **Lac** Knokkestraat 344 ☎511100 rm15 **A**
H **Real** M Lippensplein 6 ☎601266 rm17 **A**
♦ **Regina** Leopold II, laan 9 ☎511143 rm12 **A**
H **St Tropez** Patriottenstraat 6 ☎512192 rm8 **B**
H **St Christophe** Antoine Bréartstraat 8 ☎601152 rm17 **A**
H **Square** Kinkhoorn 21 Heist ☎511237 rm32 **B**

KOBBEGEM Brabant (☎02) Map**3B1**
H **Chaumière** Gentseweg 14 ☎4526202 rm10 **A**

KOKSIJDE (Coxyde-sur-Mer) West Vlaanderen (☎058) Map**3B2**
♦ **Belvédère** Pieterslaan 1, St Idesbald ☎512712 rm8 **B**
H **Carlton** Koninklijke weg 174 ☎511012 rm15 **B**

◆ **Chalet de Bogaerde** Robert Vandammestaat 156 ☎511546 rm7 **A**

H **Fleurie** Pierre Sorellaan 21–23 ☎511017 rm22 **A**

H **Lehouck** Koninklijkebaan 122 ☎511457 rm31 **B**

H **Renommée** Koninklijkebaan 157 ☎511185 rm13 **A**

H **Sablon** Zeedijk 31 ☎511355 rm12 **B**

H **Soll Cress** Koninklijkebaan 225, St Idesbald ☎512332 rm15 **B**

H **Splendid** Zeedijk 62 ☎512087 rm25 **B**

H **Venus** Koninklijkebaan 149 ☎511370 rm12 **A**

KORTRIJK (Courtrai) West Vlaanderen (☎056) Map**3B1**

H **Continental** Stationsplein 1 ☎224593 rm16 **A**

H **Damier** Grote Markt 41 ☎221547 rm40 **B**

H **Golden River** Noordstraat 1 ☎354093 rm9 **B**

LEOPOLDSBURG Limburg (☎011) Map**4C2**

H **Apers** Stationstraat 70 ☎341249 rm10 **A**

◆ **Chemin de Fer** Stationstraat 84 ☎341399 rm 8 **A**

LEUVEN (Louvain) Brabant (☎016) Map**4C1**

◆ **Blauwputois** Tiensevest 10 ☎223152 rm6 **A**

H **Gare** Martelarenplein 15 ☎224121 rm14 **A**

H **Majestic** Bontgenotenlaan 20 ☎224365 rm14 **A**

H **Royale** Martenlarenplein 6 ☎221252 rm28 **B**

LIÈGE (Luik) Liège (☎041) Map**4C1**

H **Baviere** r des Bonnes Villes 8 ☎439921 rm17 **A**

◆ **Nations** r des Guillemins 139 ☎524434 rm10 **A**

H **Metropole** r des Guillemins 141 ☎524293 rm27 **B**

H **Monico** r Géréral Jacques 10 ☎321787 rm15 **A**

H **Monico** r Général Jacques 10 ☎321787 rm15 **A**

H **Univers** r des Guillemins 116 ☎522650 rm54 **B**

H **Venitien** r Hamal 2 ☎322317 rm15 **B**

LOMMEL Limburg (☎011) Map**4C2**

H **Lommelhof** Molsekiezel 95 ☎544604 rm36 **A**

◆ **Susamie** Kerkhovensteenweg 350 ☎341872 rm4 **B**

LONDERZEEL Brabant (☎052) Map**3B1**

◆ **St Kristoffel** Markt2 ☎309334 rm4 **A**

MALMÉDY Liège (☎080) Map**4D1**

H **Ardennes** pl de la Gare ☎777363 rm6 **A**

H **Centre** pl Albert 1er 36 ☎778008 rm8 **A**

H **Relais Sportif** av du Pont de Warche 4 ☎777530 rm7 **A**

◆ **Rochers de Falize** rte de Falize 100 ☎777213 rm6 **A**

MANDERFELD Liège (☎080) Map**4D1**

H **Ardennes** Dorf 12 ☎548055 rm7 **A**

◆ **Belle Vue** Lanzerath strasse 18 ☎548054 rm5 **A**

H **Eifelerhof** Zentrum 30 ☎548299 rm6 **A**

H **Schroder** Losheimergraben 6 ☎548059 rm8 **A**

MARCHE-EN-FAMENNE Luxembourg (☎084) Map**4C1**

H **Alfa** rte de Rochefort 11 ☎311793 rm33 **B**

H **Cygne** pl aux Foires 21 ☎311536 rm8 **A**

MECHELEN (Malines) Antwerpen (☎015) Map**4C2**

◆ **Cambrinus** Van Kerckhovenstraat 29 ☎412102 rm6 **A**

H **Drie Paardekens** Begijnenstraat 3-5 ☎202439 rm33 **B**

H **Europa** Koning Albertplein 9 ☎411070 rm9 **B**

MENEN (Menin) West-Vlaanderen (☎056) Map**3B1**

H **Flandres** Grote Markt 37 ☎51 1234 rm6 **A**

H **Paix** Rijselstraat 6 ☎511199 rm7 **A**

MIDDLEKERKE West-Vlaanderen (☎059) Map**3B2**

◆ **Bonny** Kerkstraat 21-21b ☎300015 rm24 **A**

H **Littoral** Zeedijk 129 ☎300754 rm10 **B**

◆ **Luxembourg** Gentstraat 4 ☎300155 rm8 **A**

◆ **Plaza** Leopoldlaan 45 ☎300145 rm8 **B**

◆ **Siesta** Zeedijk 123 ☎3000 96 rm8 **A**

◆ **Were Di** Desmet de Nayerlaan 19 ☎3011 88 rm14 **A**

MONS (Bergen) Hainaut (☎065) Map**3B1**

H **Bouverie** pl Léopold 13 ☎334408 rm9 **A**

H **Cloche** pl Léopold 9 ☎335365 rm18 **B**

H **Esperance** r Léopold 18 ☎331721 rm12 **A**

H **Europe** r Léopold II 7-9 ☎335710 rm22 **B**

H **Parc** r Fetis 9 ☎337381 rm11 **A**

H **Rotisserie l'Industrie** r Léopold II, 13 ☎335795 rm6 **B**

H **Terminus** pl Léopold 3 ☎335755 rm10 **A**

NAMUR (Namen) Namur (☎081) Map**4C1**

H **Charleroi** pl de la Gare 21 ☎22 3870 rm13 **A**

H **Coq d'Or** r de Fer 139 ☎220798 rm15 **A**

H **Fourquet** av Albert 1er 157-159 ☎714245 rm6 **A**

H **Poule d'Or** r J Billiart 2 ☎22 1077 rm12 **B**

NIEUWPOORT West-Vlaanderen (☎058) Map**3B2**

Benelux – Belgium

H **Beau Séjour** Albert 1 laan 98
☎233522 rm14 **A**
H **Centrale** Kaai 11 ☎233981 rm8 **A**
H **Dunes** Albert 1 Laan 101 ☎233154
rm18 **B**
H **Espérance** Albert 1 laan 77 ☎233059
rm18 **A**
H **Phare** Albert 1 laan 92 ☎233214
rm11 **B**
H **Savoy** Zeedijk 11 ☎233284 rm13 **B**
H **Tourisme** Albert 1 laan 104 ☎233051
rm12 **B**

NIJEN Anterpen (☎031) Map**4**C2
H **Nilania** Kesselsesteenweg 38
☎818841 rm8 **A**

OOSTENDE (Ostende) West-Vlaanderen
(☎059) Map**3**B2
H **Angus-Home from Home** St
Jorisstraat 1 ☎701515 rm14 **A**
H **Bécasse** Visserskaai 41 ☎701465
rm29 **A**
H **Flandria** Visserskaai 43 ☎703492
rm7 **B**
H **Georges Valcke** Langestraat 54
☎702823 rm12 **B**
H **Harwich** Boekareststraat 5 ☎704299
rm53 **A**
H **Margate** Langestraat 84 ☎707590
rm20 **A**
H **Palme** Visserskaai 37 ☎802382
rm9 **A**
H **Plymouth** Koningsstraat 29 ☎701077
rm56 **A**
★★ **Hotel Royal Midland** Zeedijk 354,
Raversyde ☎702138 rm24 **A**
★ **Hotel de Nieuwe Sportsman** de Smet
de Nayerlaan 9 ☎702384
rm10 **A**

OUDENAARDE (Audenarde) Oost-
Vlaanderen (☎055) Map**3**B1
H **Elnik** Deinzestraat 55 ☎313788
rm14 **B**
H **Pomme d'Or** Markt 62 ☎311900
rm7 **A**
H **Tijl** Stationsstraat 60–62 ☎313814
rm7 **A**
H **Zalm** Hoogstraat 4 ☎311314 rm8 **A**

PANNE (DE) (La Panne) West-Vlaanderen
(☎058) Map**3**B2
H **Commerce** Koninklijke baan 31
☎411225 rm16 **B**
◆ **Concordia-Italia** Duinkerkelaan 40
☎413241 rm8 **A**
◆ **Corbeille Royale** Zeelaan 212
☎411967 rm10 **A**
H **Filet de Sole** Nieuwpoortlaan 14
☎411680 rm16 **A**
H **Helvetia** Kerkstraat 32 ☎412482
rm13 **A**
◆ **Ideal** Sloepenlaan 9 ☎411263 rm12 **A**
◆ **Monico** Zeelaan 10 ☎411490 rm15 **A**
H **Pavillon Bleu** Meeuwenlaan 73
☎411282 rm16 **A**
◆ **Pelikaan** Kerk Straat 1 ☎412108
rm14 **A**
◆ **Phoebus** Nieuwpoortlaan 48
☎411173 rm14 **A**

PHILIPPEVILLE Namur (☎071) Map**4**C1
H **Croisee** r de France 45 ☎666231
rm12 **B**

POPERINGE West-Vlaanderen (☎057)
Map**3**B1
H **Palace** Ieperstraat 34 ☎333093
rm12 **B**
H **Pavillon** Ieperseweg 1 ☎333621
rm12 **A**

PROFONDEVILLE Namur (☎081) Map**4**C1
◆ **Pont de Lustin** Chaussée de Dinant
106 ☎411620 rm7 **A**

ROCHEFORT Namur (☎084) Map**10**D4
H **Fayette** r Jacquet 87 ☎211024
rm17 **B**

ROESELARE (Roulers) West-Vlaanderen
(☎051) Map**3**B1
H **Bourgogne** Stationplein 29 ☎200059
rm14 **B**
H **Java** Oostraat 18 ☎200007 rm13 **B**
H **Londres** Stationsplein 7 ☎201742
rm23 **A**

RONSE (Renaix) Oost-Vlaanderen (☎055)
Map**3**B1
H **Grand'Place** Grote Markt 39
☎211101 rm9 **A**
H **Postillon** Oswald Ponettestraat 47
☎214091 rm7 **A**
H **St-Sebastien** Sint-Pietersnieuwstraat
38 ☎213866 rm6 **A**
H **Savoy** Churchillplein 1 ☎213756
rm13 **B**

ST HUBERT Luxembourg (☎061) Map**10**D4
H **Abbaye** pl du Marche 18 ☎611023
rm20 **A**

ST NIKLAAS (St Nicolas) Oost Vlaanderen
(☎031) Map**3**B2
★ **Hotel Arend** O.L Vrouplaats 8
☎760126 rm10 **A**

ST VITH Liège (☎080) Map**4**D1
H **Even Knodt** Malmedystrasse 22
☎228064 rm11 **A**
H **Luxembourg** Haupstrasse 71
☎228022 rm7 **B**
H **Marquet** Haupstrasse 41 ☎228200
rm7 **A**
H **Pip Margraff** Haupstrasse 7
☎228663 rm18 **A**
H **Schulzen-Jochems**
Muhlenbachstrasse 3 ☎228109 rm6 **A**

SPA Liège (☎087) Map**4**C1
H **Bagatelle** av Reine Astrid 254
☎772717 rm6 **A**
◆ **Bij de Vlaming Roger** av Reine Astrid
☎771221 rm10 **A**
H **Chemin de Fer** pl de la Gare 25
☎771415 rm8 **A**
◆ **Cortina II** r due Marché 64 ☎773494
rm6 **A**

TIENEN Brabant (☎016) Map**4**C1
H **Cambrinus** Grote Markt 22 ☎811417
rm7 **A**
H **Castel-Pic** Grote Weg 87, Kumtich
☎812933 rm6 **B**

Belgium – Benelux

VERVIERS Liège (☎087) Map**4C1**
- H **Charlemagne** pl du Martyr 48 ☎331329 rm15 **A**
- H **Grand** r du Palais 145 ☎223177 rm28 **A**
- H **Park** r Xhavée 90 ☎330972 rm14 **A**

VIELSALM Luxembourg (☎080) Map**4C1**
- H **Myrtilles** r du Vieux Marche 1 ☎215140 rm15 **A**
- H **Relais** r de la Station 1 ☎216430 rm10 **B**
- H **Salm-Hotel** r Fosse-Roulette 1 ☎216276 rm7 **A**

WENDUINE West-Vlaanderen (☎050) Map**3B2**
- H **Boulevards** Kerkstraat 1 ☎411047 rm28 **A**
- H **Bristol** De Bruynehelling 14 ☎411344 rm6 **A**
- H **Centre** Kerkstraat 41 ☎411083 rm15 **A**
- ◆ **Churchill** Leopold II laan 8 ☎416042 rm10 **A**
- H **Commerce** Graaf Jansdyk 4 ☎411259 rm12 **B**
- H **Cosmopolite** Kerkstraat 33 ☎411417 rm23 **A**
- H **Ivan** Zeedyk 7–8 ☎411453 rm25 **A**

H Ocean Zeedijk II ☎411325 rm19 **B**
- H **Ondes** de Smet de Nayerlaan 10 ☎412137 rm26 **B**
- H **Prince Albert** Manitobahelling 2 ☎412425 rm14 **A**

WESTENDE West-Vlaanderen (☎059) Map**3B2**
- ◆ **Michel** Distellaan 15 ☎300716 rm11 **A**
- H **Noble Rose** H. Jasparlaan 181 ☎300127 rm14 **B**
- H **Splendid** Meeuwenlaan 20 ☎300032 rm17 **B**
- ◆ **Westendia** Duinenlaan 35 ☎233663 rm10 **A**

ZEEBRUGGE West-Vlaanderen (☎050) Map**3B2**
- ◆ **Jan Bart** Kerkstraat 19 ☎544327 rm5 **A**
- H **Noordzee** Kustlaan 121 ☎544235 rm17 **B**
- H **Ship** Kapitein Fryattstraat 6 ☎544068 rm8 **A**

ZOLDER Limburg (☎011) Map**4C2**
- H **Heidehoeve** Broederspad 49 ☎221746 rm11 **A**
- H **Leana** Stationsstraat 110 ☎534029 rm12 **B**

Benelux Luxembourg

BEAUFORT Map**1A4**
- H **Binsfeld** r du Bois 1 ☎86013 rm20 Mar23–Nov5, Dec21–31 **B**
- ◆ **Rustique** r du Château 55 ☎86086 rm7 Mar20–Sep **B**

BECH-KLEINMACHER Map**11A4**
- ◆ **Mosella** rte du Vin 21 ☎69124 rm6 Closed Aug25–Sep16 **B**
- ◆ **Vallée** rte du Vin 17 ☎698305 rm7 Closed Feb16–Mar2 **B**

BERDORF Map**11A4**
- ◆ **Schmitt** ☎79346 rm6 **B**

CLERVAUX Map**11A4**
- H **Commerce** r de Marnach 2 ☎91032 rm47 Closed Nov6–30 **B**

DIEKIRCH Map**11A4**
- ◆ **Aveirense** av de la Gare 33 ☎83360 rm5 Closed Aug9–14 **A**
- H **Gare** av de la Gare 73 ☎83305 rm12 Jan15–Dec20 **B**
- H **Kremer** av de la Gare 4 ☎83636 rm34 **A**

ECHTERNACH Map**11A4**
- H **Abbaye** r de la Gare 2 ☎729184 rm14 **A**
- H **Aigle Noir** r de la Gare 54 ☎72383 rm24 Mar20–Sep20 **B**
- H **Bon Accueil** r des Merciers 3 ☎72052 rm11 Apr15–Sep15 **A**
- H **Luxembourg** r de Luxembourg 36 ☎72290 rm12 **A**
- H **Petite Suisse** rue A Duchscher 56 ☎72178 rm22 Mar20–Sep **B**
- H **Prince Henri** r de la Gare 51 ☎72131 rm14 May10–Sep15 **B**

H Soleil r des Remparts 20 ☎72033 rm21 Apr–Sep **B**
- H **Wagener-Hartmann** rue de Luxembourg 29 ☎72058 rm14 **A**
At **Echternach-Lauterborn** (4km SW by E42)
- ◆ **Vieux Moulin** ☎72068 rm10 **A**

ESCH-SUR-ALZETTE Map**11A4**
- H **Astro** r de la Libération 10 ☎540712 rm30 **A**
- H **Carrefour** r Victor Hugo 1 ☎52424 rm20 **B**
- H **Parc** r X Brasseur 14 ☎549486 rm20 **B**
- H **Paris** bd Kennedy 48 ☎52488 rm16 **A**
- H **Poste** r de l'Alzette 107 ☎53504 rm17 Closed Dec25–Jan1 **A**
- ◆ **Radar** r de la Libération 29 ☎52431 rm12 Closed Aug **B**
- H **Viaduc** (n rest) bd Prince Henri 64 ☎545345 rm12 **A**

ETTELBRUCK Map**11A4**
- ◆ **Ardennes** r de Bastogne 23 ☎819406 rm11 Closed Jan **A**
- ◆ **Place du Marché** r de Bastogne ☎82244 rm8 **A**
- H **Solis** r de Bastogne 58 ☎82393 rm14 Jan3–Nov **B**

GREVENMACHER Map**11A4**
- H **Govers** Grand 'rue 15 ☎75137 rm15 **B**
- ★ **Poste** r de Treves 28 ☎75136 rm11 Apr–Sep **B**

LUXEMBOURG Map**11A4**

Benelux – Luxembourg

H **Ardennes** av de la Liberté 59
☎488582 rm13 **A**

H **Avenue** av de la Liberté 43 ☎488865
rm11 **A**

H **Baezel** r de Fort Neipperg 30
☎487255 rm15 **A**

H **Becker** r de la Station-
Dommeldarge 5 ☎431823 rm14 **A**

H **Carlton** r de Strasbourg 9 ☎484802
rm46 **A**

♦ **Delta** r Ad Fisher 76 ☎480279 rm18 **B**

♦ **Gielen Eck** rte de Thionville 208
☎484995 rm9 **B**

♦ **Place** pl Wallis 11a ☎488567 rm15 **A**

♦ **Radar** rte d'Esch 2 ☎23214 rm5
Closed Jul1–19 **A**

★★ **Graas** av de la Liberté 78 rm32 **B**

MERSCH-BERSCHBACH Map11A4

H **Bon Accueil** r de Luxembourg 34
☎32276 rm10 Jan15–Dec15 **A**

MONDORF-LES-BAINS Map11A4

H **Tibesar** av des Bains 6 ☎68087 rm10
Mar–Sep **B**

♦ **Tivoli** av des Bains 3 ☎67417 rm10

Closed Jan1–20 **B**

H **Wellenstein** r St Michel ☎68051 rm13
Mar15–Oct **B**

SEPTFONTAINES Map11A4

♦ **Vieux Moulin** Leesbach ☎30527 rm6
Closed Jan–Feb14 **B**

VIANDEN Map11A4

H **Gare** r de la Gare 3 ☎84127 rm41 **A**

H **Hof Van Holland** r de la Gare 6
☎84170 rm43 Mar–Oct **A**

H **Oranienburg** Grand 'rue 126 ☎84153
rm45 closed Jan **A**

H **Réunion** Grand 'rue 66 ☎84182 rm10
Apr–Sep **A**

H **Victor Hugo** rue Victor Hugo 1
☎84160 rm39 Mar20–Sep **B**

WILWERWILTZ Map11A4

♦ **Hengesch** ☎91415 rm5
Closed Sep **A**

WORMELDANGE Map11A4

♦ **La Toque Blanche** r Principale 87
☎76056 rm7 **A**

♦ **Weyrich** r Principale 113 ☎76308
rm6 **A**

Benelux Netherlands

AALSMEER Noord-Holland (☎02977)
Map4C3

H **Wapen van Aalsmeer't** 15 Dorpstraat
☎24321 bed21 **B**

ALKMAAR Noord-Holland (☎072) Map4C3

♦ **Houtzicht**
157–159 Kennemerstraatweg
☎110821 bed15 **A**

H **Nachtegaal de** 100 Langestraat
☎112894 bed29 **A**

H **Victory** 3 van der Boschstraat
☎118952 bed34 **B**

ALMELO Overijssel (☎05490) Map4D3

♦ **Nationaal** 69 Wierdensestraat
☎17716 bed15 **B**

AMSTERDAM Nord-Holland (☎020)
Map4C3

H **Centrum van Amsterdam't** 77
Geldersekade ☎248805 bed36
closed New Year **A**

♦ **Clemens** 39 Raadhuisstraat
☎246089 **A**

♦ **Florence** 44 van Eeghenstraat
☎793798 bed11 16Feb–4Nov **B**

♦ **Groenendael** 15 Nieuwendijk
☎244822 bed24 **A**

♦ **Groot** 137 Herengracht ☎247051
bed40 **A**

♦ **Huize Gregoire** 77 Nicolaas
Maesstraat ☎729567 bed16 **A**

♦ **Lantaerne de** 111 Leidsegracht
☎232221 bed67 **A**

♦ **Museumzicht** 22 Jan Luykenstraat
☎712954 bed25 Mar–Dec **B**

♦ **Ostade van** 123 van Ostadestraat
☎793452 bed35 **A**

♦ **Pax** 37 Raadhuisstraat ☎249735
bed22 **A**

APELDOORN Gelderland (☎055) Map4C3

H **Berg en Bos** 58 Aquamarijnstraat
☎252352 bed31 **B**

H **Central** 5 Raadhuisplein ☎212811
bed60 **B**

H **Huize Haytink** 25 Loolaan ☎213911
bed18 closed 12–30Jun **B**

ARNHEM Gelderland (☎085) Map4C2

H **Rembrandt** 1–3 Paterstraat
☎420153 bed52 **A**

BEILEN Drenthe Map4D3

H **Prakken** 63 Brinkstraat ☎302346
bed21 **B**

BERGEN ANN ZEE Noord-Holland
(☎02208) Map4C3

H **Stormvogel de** 12 Jac Kalffweg
☎2734 bed31 **B**

H **Victoria** 33 Zeeweg ☎2358 bed62 **B**

BERGEN OP ZOOM Noord-Brabant
(☎01640) Map4C2

♦ **Verpalen** 46 Wouwsestraat ☎33190
bed8 closed Xmas **A**

BEVERWIJK Noord-Holland (☎02510)
Map4C3

♦ **Parkzicht** 77 Zeestraat ☎23335
bed13 **B**

BREDA Noord-Brabant (☎076) Map4C2

♦ **Gouden Leeuw** 1 Korte Boschstraat
☎133183 bed12 **B**

H **Huis Den Deyl** 8 Marellenweg
☎653616 bed17
closed 18Dec–8Jan **B**

Netherlands – Benelux

◆ **Lion d'Or** 5 Stationsweg ☎131183 bed31 **B**

BRESKENS Zeeland (☎01172) Map**3**B2
  H **Scaldis** 3 Langeweg ☎1369 bed34 **B**

DELFT Zuid-Holland (☎015) Map**4**C2
  H **Juliana** 33 Maerten Trompstraat ☎567612 bed45 **B**

DOORN Utrecht (☎03430) Map**4**C2
  H **Driest** 6 Dorpsplein ☎2370 bed15 **B**
  H **Rodestein** 10 Sitiopark ☎2409 bed20 Mar–Oct **B**
  H **Smit** Amersfoortseweg 26 ☎2189 bed22 **B**

DRONTEN Gelderland (☎03210) Map**4**C3
  H **Galjoen** 52–56 De Rede ☎2584 bed14 **B**

EDE Gelderland (☎08380) Map**4**C2
  H **Bosrand** 28 Bosrand ☎10580 bed90 Jun–Aug **B**

EGMOND AAN ZEE Noord-Holland (☎02206) Map**4**C3
  H **Anker ten** 15 bd Ir de Vassey ☎1486 bed32 Apr–Sep **B**
  H **Atlantic** 13 Boulevard ☎1229 bed30 **B**
  H **Sunny Home** 2 Parallelweg ☎1368 bed28 **B**
  ◆ **Vassey** 3 bd Ir de Vassey ☎1573 bed37 **B**

EINDHOVEN Noord-Brabant (☎040) Map**4**C2
  ◆ **Sport** 16 Kleine Berg ☎448944 bed16 **A**

ETTEN-LEUR Noord-Brabant (☎01608) Map**4**C2
  ◆ **Hof van Holland** 41 van Bergenplein ☎12335 bed10 **A**
  H **Huis ten bosch** 2 Oude Bredaseweg ☎12340 bed26 closed 27Dec–10Jan **B**

FLUSHING see **VLISSINGEN**

GELEEN Limburg (☎04494) Map**4**C1
  ◆ **Royal** 99 Rijksweg Zuid ☎45676 bed10 **A**
  ◆ **Skol** 113 Mauritslaan ☎42766 bed17 **B**

GOES Zeeland (☎01100) Map**3**B2
  H **Terminus** 37 Fr den Hollanderlaan ☎27501 bed38 **B**

GOUDA Zuid Holland (☎01820) Map**4**C2
  H **Blauwe Kruis** 4 Westhaven ☎12677 bed24 closed 26Feb–13Mar **A**

GRONINGEN Groningen (☎050) Map**4**D4
  H **Weeva** 8 Gedempte Zuiderdiep ☎129919 bed132 Closed Xmas **B**

HAAG (DEN) (Hague, The) Zuid-Holland (☎070) Map**4**C2
  H **Bristol** 126–130 Stationsweg ☎882468 bed58 **B**
  H **Eripe** 223 Laan van Meerdervoort ☎600339 bed28 **B**
  ◆ **Forest** 37–39 Adelheidstraat ☎837379 bed14 **B**

◆ **Rondeel** 39–40 Stationsplein ☎883558 bed34 **B**
◆ **Savion** 86 Prinsestraat ☎462560 bed16 **B**
◆ **Sonnehuys** 2 Rebaanstraat ☎546170 bed55 **B**
◆ **Stationsbodega** 43–44 Stationsplein ☎882973 bed11 **A**

HAGUE (THE) see **HAAG (DEN)**

HEERLEN Limburg (☎045) Map**4**C1
  H **Kras** 16 Stationstraat ☎713231 bed60 Closed 22Dec–2Jan **B**
  H **Poort van Herte** 22 Stationstraat ☎717485 bed21 **B**
  H **Wilhelmina** 125 Molenberglaan ☎713205 bed10 **B**

HELMOND Noord-Brabant (☎04920) Map**4**C2
  H **Beugeltje** 8–10 Beugelsplein ☎22729 bed15 **B**

HILVARENBEEK Noord-Brabant (☎04255) Map**4**C2
  ◆ **Concordia** 20 Gelderstraat ☎1359 bed10 **B**
  ◆ **Toerist** 34 Diessenseweg ☎1344 bed14 **B**

HOOGERHEIDE Noord-Brabant (☎01646) Map**4**C2
  ◆ **William** 139 Raadhuissstraat ☎2520 bed13 Closed 5–26Jul **A**

HOOGEVEEN Drenthe (☎05280) Map**4**D3
  H **Beurs** 26–28 Grote Kerkstraat ☎62723 bed22 **B**
  H **Homan** 3 Stationstraat ☎62012 bed36 **B**

HOORN Noord-Holland (☎02290) Map**4**C3
  H **Petit Nord** 55 Kleine Noord ☎16059 bed55 **B**
  ◆ **Posthoorn** 25–27 Breed ☎14057 bed33 **B**

LEEUWARDEN Friesland (☎05100) Map**4**C4
  H **Pauw** 10 Stationsweg ☎23651 bed65 **B**

LOCHEM Gelderland (☎05730) Map**4**D3
  ◆ **Wapen van Lochem** 19 Nieuwstad ☎1809 bed16 **B**

LOOSDRECHT Utrecht (☎02158) Map**4**C3
  H **Nooit Gedacht** 110 Oud Loosdrechtsedijk ☎3257 bed30 16Mar–14Oct **B**

MAASTRICHT Limburg (☎043) Map**4**C1
  H **Limburgia** 5 Vrijthof ☎10665 bed22 **B**
  ◆ **Moderne** 34 Markt ☎15319 bed50 Closed 24Dec–2Jan **A**
  H **Stijns** 40 Stationstraat ☎14973 bed36 **B**
  ◆ **Wijker Central** 54 Wijker Brugstraat ☎15718 bed23 **B**

MEPPEL Drenthe (☎05220) Map**4**D3
  ◆ **Worst** 10 Steenwijkerstraatweg ☎51753 bed11 May–Sep **B**

MIDDELBURG Zeeland (☎01180) Map**3**B2
  ◆ **Overbeeke** 19 Loskade ☎13526 bed17 **B**

Benelux – Netherlands

NOORDWIJK ANN ZEE Zuid Holland
(☎01719) Map**4C**3
- H **Belvedere** 5 Beethovenweg ☎12929
  bed70 Apr–14Sep **B**
- H **Eikenloof** 26 Koepelweg ☎12501
  bed27 Closed 15Dec–15Jan **B**
- H **Golf** 120 Quarles van Uffordstr
  ☎12535 bed38 16Mar–Sep **B**
- ◆ **Mikedi Jo** 81 Quarles van Uffordstr
  ☎12460 bed22 **B**
- H **Neerlandia** 30 K W Boulevard
  ☎13458 bed13 Apr–Sep **A**
- ◆ **Renova** 208 Parallel bd ☎12987
  bed35 **A**
- ◆ **Sonnevanck** 50 Kon Astrid bd
  ☎12359 bed42 16Mar–Sep **A**
- ★ **Duinlust** 1 Koepelweg ☎12916 rm25
  Apr–Sep **A**

NUNSPEET Gelderland (☎03412) Map**4C**3
- H **Ittmann** 52 Laan ☎2441 bed90 **B**

NUTH Limburg (☎04447) Map**4C**1
- H **Hoek** 10 Stationsstraat ☎2334 bed15
  May–Sep **A**
- H **Kroon** 65 Stationsstraat ☎1401
  bed45 **B**

OISTERWIJK Noord-Brabant (☎04242)
Map**4C**2
- ◆ **Carlton** 93 Gemullenhoekenweg
  ☎2574 bed22 **A**

OLDENZAAL Overijssel (☎05410) Map**4D**3
- H **Frits Muller** 10–14 Markt ☎12093
  bed13 **B**
- H **Kroon** 17 Steenstraat ☎12402
  bed66 **B**
- H **Stege** 1 Marktstraat ☎12102 bed14 **B**

OMMEN Overijssel (☎05291) Map**4D**3
- H **Paping** 29 Stationsweg ☎1945
  bed50 **B**

OSS Noord-Brabant (☎04120) Map**4C**2
- H **Korenbeurs** 12 Heuvel ☎22103
  bed14 **B**

RAALTE Overijssel (☎05720) Map**4D**3
- H **Sallandia** 7 Grote Markt bed26 **B**

RIJSWIJK see **HAAG (DEN)**

ROTTERDAM Zuid-Holland (☎010) Map**4C**2
- ◆ **Astoria** Pleinweg 205 ☎856834
  bed20 **B**
- H **Floris** Graaf Florisstraat 68–70
  ☎259113 bed60 **A**
- H **Gunst** Brieselaan 190–192 ☎850940
  bed23 **B**
- ◆ **Huize Emma** Eendrachtsplein 1
  ☎365871 bed30 **A**
- H **Metropole** Nieuwe Binnenweg 13a
  ☎360319 bed22 Closed
  20Dec–10Jan **B**
- ◆ **Simone** Nieuwe Binnenweg 162a
  ☎362585 bed17 **B**
- ◆ **Vernon** Heemraadssingel 324
  ☎765026 bed26 **B**
- ◆ **Wapen van Charlois** Doklaan 59
  bed17 **B**

SCHEVENINGEN see **HAAG (DEN)**

SLUIS Zeeland (☎01178) Map**3B**2
- H **Hof van Brussel** Kaou 6 ☎1438
  bed14 **A**

STEENBERGEN Noord-Brabant (☎01670)
Map**4C**2
- H **Aarden** Kaaistraat 1 ☎3140 bed16 **B**
- H **Tilburg** Burg van Loonstraat 87
  ☎3550 bed20 **B**

STEIN Limburg (☎04495) Map**4C**1
- ◆ **Havenzicht** Hoogenweg 9 ☎1571
  bed18 **A**

VALKENBURG Limburg (☎04406) Map**4C**1
- H **Adler** Neerhem 13 ☎13448 bed24
  Closed Nov **B**
- ◆ **All Good** Neerhem 10 ☎13380 bed21
  16Apr–Sep **A**
- ◆ **Bleesers** Grendelplein 4 ☎12585
  bed50 16Mar–14Oct **A**
- ◆ **Curfs Couvreur** Sint Gerlachstraat 4
  ☎40208 bed38 10Apr–3Oct **B**
- H **Dwingelhof** Daalhemmerweg 22
  ☎12946 bed34 21Mar–Sep **B**
- H **Floriade** Neerhem 107 ☎13096
  bed38 Apr–14Oct **B**
- H **Gen Eikske** Raadhuisstraat 118
  ☎1305 bed23 **A**
- ◆ **Hermina** Napoleonstraat 45 ☎12490
  bed64 28Mar–Sep **B**
- H **Liberty** Walramplein 33 ☎12774
  bed48 21Mar–Sep **B**
- ◆ **Spronck** Spoorlaan 34 ☎13017
  bed31 21Apr–Oct **B**

VENLO Limburg (☎077) Map**4D**2
- H **Grolschquelle** Eindhovenseweg 3–8
  ☎13560 bed32 **B**

VLISSINGEN (Flushing) Zeeland (☎01184)
Map**3B**2
- H **Bianca** bd Evertsen 8 ☎12117 bed15
  Closed Dec **B**
- ◆ **Bos** Spuistraat 63–65 ☎13303
  bed65 **B**
- H **Cisca** Paul Krugerstraat 76–82
  ☎18006 bed34 **B**
- ◆ **Corner House** Smalle Kade 15
  ☎12110 bed20 **B**
- H **Piccard** Badhuisstraat 178 ☎12809
  bed60 **B**
- H **Royal** Badhuisstraat 1–13 ☎12401
  bed45 **B**

VOLENDAM Noord-Holland (☎02993)
Map**4C**3
- H **Spaander** Haven 15–19 ☎3595
  bed104 Closed Xmas **B**

WOERDEN Zuid-Holland (☎03480)
Map**4C**2/3
- ◆ **Rijnzicht** Utrechtsestraatweg 113
  ☎12176 bed14 **A**

ZANDVOORT Noord-Holland (☎02507)
Map**4C**3
- H **Aar** Brederodestraat 44 ☎4802
  bed55 **B**
- ◆ **Casa Blanca** Oosterparkstraat 83
  ☎4007 bed20 Apr–Sep **B**
- H **Coldall** Zandvoortselaan 18 ☎2053
  bed22 Apr–Sep **A**
- H **Esplanade** Badhuisplein 2 ☎2073
  bed35 16Mar–14Oct **A**
- H **Lammy** Hogeweg 34 ☎3466 bed35 **B**
- H **Petegem** Haarlemmerstraat 86
  ☎2076 bed15 20Mar–Sep **B**

DENMARK

Denmark

Due to the higher cost of living in Denmark this gazetteer is not as extensive as some of the others featured in the guide. Hovever, as far as possible, we have listed only hotels and pensions which offer accommodation for less than £6 per person per night at some time during the year. The prices have been banded as follows, **A** under £5 per person per night and **B** between £5 and £6 per person per night. The Accommodation Bureau, Kiosk P, Central railway Station, Copenhagen, will assist visitors in finding accommodation in hotels and private houses. The Danish Tourist Board (see p222 for address) will provide information on accommodation available at farmhouses and on the renting of summer cottages. The Danish alphabet differs from the English one in that the letters after **Z** are **AE, Ø, Å;** this must be borne in mind when using Danish reference books.

Fyn–*Funen*
Jylland–*Jutland*
Sjælland–*Zealand*

AALBORG Jylland (☎08) Map1B 3/4
  H **Missionshotellet Ansgar**
    Prinsensgade 14-16 ☎133733
    bed65 **B**
  H **Aalborg Sømandshjem**
    Nyhavnsgade 60 ☎121900 bed80 **B**

ALLINGE Bornholm (☎03) Map2D2
  ◆ **Pension Sandbogård**
    Landemaerket 3, Sandvig ☎980303
    Jun–Sep bed50 **B**

ANSBY Jylland (☎06) Map1A3
  M **Motel Ans** Østerlanggade 32
    ☎870133 bed11 **B**

ÅRHUS Jylland (☎06) Map1B3
  H **Eriksens** Banegårdsgade 6-8
    ☎136296 bed37 **B**
  H **Kraghs** Park Allé 1 ☎121127 bed25 **B**
  H **Park** Sønder Alle 3 ☎123231 bed18 **B**
  H **Århus Sømandshjem** Havnegade 20
    ☎121599 bed63 **A**

ASSENS Fyn (☎09) Map1B2
  H **Phønix** Østergade 5 ☎711018
    bed10 **B**
  H **Postgården** Strandgade 7 ☎711614
    bed14 **A**

AUGUSTENBORG Jylland (☎04) Map1B2
  H **Voigt Strand** Asserballeskov
    ☎464115 Jun–Sep 9 bed13 **A**

BLOKHUS Jylland (☎08) Map1A4
  M **Egons** Gennem Granerne 2
    ☎249193 Jun–Sep 10 bed12 **B**

BRANDE Jylland (☎07) Map **1** A2
  H **Dalgas** Storegade 2 ☎181300
    bed40 **A**

COPENHAGEN see **KØBENHAVN**

EBELTOFT Jylland (☎06) Map1B3
  H **Ebeltoft** Adelgade 44 ☎341090
    bed14 **A**

ESBJERG Jylland (☎05) Map1A2
  H **Bell-In** Skolegade 45 ☎120122
    bed60 **A**
  H **Korskroen** Skads Hovedvej 116
    ☎120059 bed23 **A**
  H **Palads** Skolegade 14 ☎123000
    bed76 **B**

FJERRITSLEV Jylland (☎08) Map1A4
  H **Grand** Vestergade 14 ☎211043
    bed25 **A**

  ◆ **Pension Lyngbjerggård** Kollerup
    Strandvej 14, Kollerup ☎211312
    Jun–Sep bed22 **A**
  H **Westpark Feriecenter** Kollerup
    ☎211800 bed80 **B**

FREDENSBORG Sjælland (☎03) Map2C3
  H **Endruplund-Country House**
    ☎280238 bed36 **A**

FREDERICIA Jylland (☎05) Map1B2
  H **Fredericia Sømandshjem** ☎920295
    bed23 **A**

FREDERIKSHAVN Jylland (☎08) Map1B4
  H **Park** Jernbanegade 7 ☎422255
    bed76 **B**
  H **Turisthotellet** Margrethevej 5
    ☎422837 bed41 **B**

GRENÅ Jylland (☎06) Map1B3
  H **Crone** Havneplads 13 ☎320157
    bed20 **A**
  M **E.K. Motel** Lillegade 47 ☎320031
    bed10 **A**
  H **Grenå Sømandshjem** Strandgade 5
    ☎321382 bed25 **A**

GUDHJEM Bornholm (☎03) Map2D2
  H **Fuglsang** Havnepladsen ☎985359
    Jun–Sep15 bed22 **B**
  ◆ **Pension Mølleglimt** Gudhjemvej III
    ☎985248 bed13 **A**

HADERSLEV Jylland (☎04) Map1A2
  H **Thomashus Kro** Hovedvej A 10
    ☎522233 bed34 **B**
  H **Årøsund Badehotel** Årøsund
    ☎584173 bed38 **A**

HADSUND Jylland (☎08) Map1B3
  H **Centralhotellet** Torvet 8 ☎571043
    bed28 **A**
  H **Øster Hurup** Kystvejen 57 ☎588014
    bed19 **A**

HELSINGØR Sjælland (☎03) Map2C3
  H **Meulenborg** Bøgebakken 5
    ☎215220 May–Sep bed50 **B**
  H **Missionshotellet** Bramstraede 5
    ☎210591 bed64 **B**
  H **Skandia** Bramstraede 1 ☎210902
    bed80 **B**

HERNING Jylland (☎07) Map1A3
  H **Arnborg Kro** Arnborg ☎149024
    bed16 **A**

H Hammerum Jernbanegade 8
Hammerum ☎116012 bed10 **B**
H Inge Marie Arnborg ☎149090
bed32 **B**

HIRTSHALS Jylland (☎08) Map1B4
H Strandlyst Tornby ☎977076
Jun–Sep 15 bed88 **A**
H Sømandshjemmet Havnegade 4
☎941944 bed20 **A**

HJØRRING Jylland (☎08) Map1B4
M Motel Nygård Strandvejen 8 Lønstrup
☎960080 May–Sep bed20 **A**
H A/S Feriebyen Skallerup Klit
Sønderlev, Skallerup ☎968211
May15–Sep15 bed32 **A**

HOLSTEBRO Jylland (☎07) Map1A3
H Højskolehotellet Skolegade 3
☎422900 bed29 **B**
H Krabbes Stationsvej 18 ☎420622
bed28 **B**

HORSENS Jylland (☎05) Map1B2
H Søvind Kro Søvind ☎659055 bed8 **B**

KØBENHAVN (Copenhagen) (☎01)
Map2C2
H Centrum Helgolandsgade 14,
DK 1653, Køben V ☎318265
bed131 **A**
H Ry Ryesgade 14, DK 2200,
København N ☎376961 bed54 **A**
H Sømandshjemmet Bethel
Nyhavn 22, DK 1051, København K
☎130370 bed63 **B**
H West Westend 11, DK 1661,
København V ☎242761 bed41 **A**

KOLDING Jylland (☎05) Map1A2
H Møllegården Dyrehavevej 198
☎520918 bed24 **B**

KORSØR Sjaelland (☎03) Map1B2
H Klubhotellet Casper Brands Plads
☎570400 bed19 **A**
H Sømandshjemmet Havnegade 12
☎570495 bed9 **A**

LØKKEN Jylland (☎08) Map1A4
H Løkkenhus Søndergade 21
☎991046 bed30 **A**
♦ Pension Sommerlyst
Damgårdsvej 15 ☎991026
Closed Dec bed62 **B**
♦ Garni Vestkysten Carl Jensens Vej 1
☎991036 May–Aug bed11 **A**

MARIBO Lolland (☎03) Map2C1
H Dana ☎881711 bed16 **A**
H Ebsens Vestergade 32 ☎881044
bed28 **B**
H Femø Kro Femø ☎915068 bed8 **B**
H Jernbanehotellet Jernbanegade 20
☎880287 bed14 **A**

MIDDELFART Jylland (☎09) Map1B2
H Kongebrogården Kongebrovej 3
☎410360 bed9 **A**

NYBORG Fyn (☎09) Map1B2
H Nyborg Adelgade 6 ☎310994
bed67 **B**

NYKØBING On the island of Mors Jylland
(☎07) Map1A3
H Centralhotellet Østergade 1
☎722550 bed13 **B**
H Det Ny Missionshotel Nygade 5
☎721155 bed29 **B**

ODENSE Fyn (☎09) Map1B2
M Ansgarhus Motel Kirkegårdsallé 17
☎128800 bed28 **B**
H Fangel Kro Fangelvej 55, Fangel
☎961011 bed29 **A**
H Kahema Dronningensgade 5
☎122821 bed21 **A**
H Ydes Hans Tausens Gade 11
☎121131 bed33 **B**

RANDERS Jylland (☎06) Map1B3
H Højskolehotellet Middelgade 6
☎428844 bed46 **B**
H Randers Sømandshjem
Østervold 42 ☎427781 bed25 **B**

RIBE Jylland (☎05) Map1A2
H Klubbens Skolegade 6 ☎420999
bed45 **A**
H Mandø Kro Mandø ☎445106 bed9 **B**
H Weis Stue Torvet 7 ☎420700 bed7 **A**

RINGKØBING Jylland (☎07) Map1A3
M Turistmotellet Herningvej 17
☎320772 bed30 **A**

RØDDING Jylland (☎04) Map1A3
H Jels Torvet 1, Jels ☎552620 bed12 **A**
H Rødding Torvet 8 ☎841404 bed31 **B**

ROSKILDE Sjaelland (☎03) Map2C2
M Skovbrynet Skovvejen 1 Kirkebjerg
☎396199 bed16 **B**

RUDKØBING Langeland (☎09) Map1B2
H Degnehaven Spodsbjergvej 277 Nr.
Longelse ☎501092 bed11 **A**
H Landevejskroen Lindelse ☎571900
bed12 **A**

SAKSKØBING Lolland (☎03) Map2C1
H Hotel du Nord Brogade 6 ☎894046
bed9 **A**
H Saxkjøbing Torvet 9 ☎894039
bed38 **A**

SILKEBORG Jylland (☎06) Map1A3
H Missionshotellet Ansgar
Drewsensvej 28–34 ☎823700
bed96 **A**
H Linå kro Linåvej 57 ☎841443
bed10 **A**
H Silkeborg Estrupsgade 21 ☎820084
bed22 **B**

SKAGEN Jylland (☎08) Map1B4
♦ Pension Strandly Øster Strandvej 35
☎441131 bed30 **A**
H Sømandshjemmet Øster Strandvej 2
☎442110 bed28 **A**

STRUER Jylland (☎07) Map1A3
H Gtand Østergade 24 ☎850400
bed58 **A**
H Humlum kro Vesterbrogade 4
☎861103 bed12 **A**

Denmark

SVENDBORG Fyn (☎09) Map1B2
- H **Royal** Toldbodvej 5 bed40 **B**
- H **Sømandshøjskolen** Overgade 6
  ☎210484 Jun27–Jul bed54 **A**
- H **Troense** Strandgade 5 Tåsinge
  ☎225412 bed64 **B**
- M **Motel Troense** Badstuen 15 Troense
  ☎225341 bed16 **B**
- H **Vindeby Kro** Vindeby, Tåsinge
  ☎225247 bed8 **A**
- H **Aerø** Brogade 1 ☎210760 bed18 **A**

THISTED Jylland (☎07) Map1A3
- H **Klitten** Nr. Vorupør ☎938108
  bed10 **A**
- H **Missionshotellet Merci**
  Frederiksgade 16 ☎925200 bed50 **A**
- H **Missionshotellet Sjørringvold**
  Sjørring ☎971009 bed14 **A**
- H **Østerild Kro** Østerild Byvej ☎997003
  bed22 **A**

TRANEBJERG Samsø (☎06) Map1B2
- H **Ballen Hotel** Åvej, Ballen ☎591799
  bed24 **B**

VEJLE Jylland (☎05) Map1A2
- H **Grejsdals** Grejsdalen ☎853004
  bed11 **B**
- M **Missionshotellet Caleb** Daemningen
  50–54 ☎823211 bed115 **B**

VIBORG Jylland (☎06) Map1A3
- H **Afholdshotellet** ☎622722 bed24 **B**
- H **Kongenshus Hotel** Daugbjerg
  ☎548125 Feb15–Dec24 bed19 **B**
- H **Missionshotellet** Sankt Mathias
  Gade 5 ☎623700 bed70 **A**

VORDINGBORG Sjaelland (☎03) Map2C2
- H **Boulevardkroen** Boulevarden 12
  ☎770129 bed18 **A**
- H **Prins Jørgen** Algade 1 ☎770027
  bed50 **B**

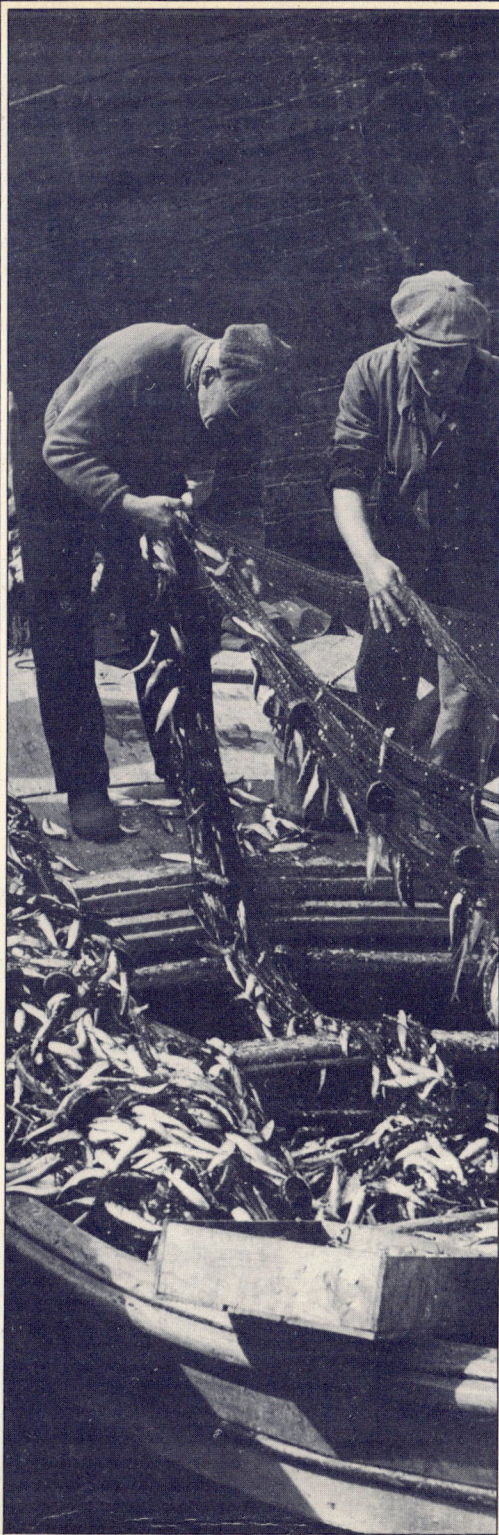

France

The gazetteer which follows contains details of hotels in most of the popular tourist areas, and also in locations along main routes, which provide accommodation for less than about £6 per person per night at some time during the year. The prices have been banded as follows **A** under £5 per person per night and **B** between £5 and £6 per person per night. It contains only a selection of the establishments available and further information, together with literature on farmhouse accommodation, can be obtained from the French Government Tourist Office in London (see p222 for address). In addition, the following organisations publish guides containing lists of inexpensive accommodation:

Logis de France: These are Government-sponsored tourist inns equivalent to the one or two star categories. They are generally located off the beaten track and offer a high standard for their type and good value for money. The *Logis de France Guide* can be purchased through bookshops.

Relais Routier: These are restaurants situated on main roads offering simple accommodation and providing a good meal at a reasonable price. The *Relais Routier Guide* can be purchased through bookshops.

Gites de France: This is furnished accommodation in rural France, often at farms, for those who prefer to cater for themselves. There are some 14,500 Gites in 4,000 villages, created with the financial support of the French Government and governed by a charter laid down by the Fédération National de Gites de France. Details are available in three booklets, entitled *North-East and North-West, South-West and South-East* from the Fédération at: 34 rue Godot-de-Mauroy, Paris 9e.

Abbreviations:

av	avenue			
bd	boulevard	Ml	Marshal, Maréchal
espl	esplanade	r	rue
fbg	faubourg	rte	route
Gl	Général	sq	square

ABBEVILLE (80) Somme (☎22) Map**3**A1
  H **France** 19 pl du Pilori ☎240042 rm77 **A**
  H **Europe** Aérodrome d'Abbeville ☎241191 rm13 **B**
  ★ **Chalet** 2 av de la Gare ☎242157 rm12 15Jan–15Dec **A**
  ★ **Conde** 14 pl de la Libération ☎240633 rm8 Closed Aug **A**

ABER-WRAC'H (L') (29) Finistère (☎76) Map**7**A3
  H **Bellevue** ☎049001 rm35 Etr–Oct **B**
  ★★ **Baie Des Anges** ☎049004 rm17 Closed Oct **B**

ABRETS (LES) (38) Isère (☎76) Map**27**B4
  ◆ **Hostellerie Abresienne** ☎320428 rm30 Closed Sep **A**
  ★ **Belle Étoile** pl de la République ☎320497 rm15 **A**

AGAY (83) Var (☎94) Map**28**C2
  H **Grand Hôtel de la Baumette** ☎440015 rm78 15May–1Oct **B**

At **Camp Long** (1km SW on N98)
  ★ **Beau Site** ☎440045 rm24 Apr–Sep **A**

AGEN (47) Lot-et-Garonne (☎58) Map**16**C2
  H **Continental** r Rabelais ☎470785 rm27 **A**
  H **Jasmin Terminus** 40 bd S-Dumon ☎663108 rm50 **A**
  H **Régina** 139 bd Carnot ☎470797 rm36 **B**
  ★★ **Perigord** pl XIV Juillet ☎661004 rm22 Feb–20Dec **A**

AIGUEBELLE (83) Var (☎94) Map**28**C1
  ★★ **Plage** ☎058074 rm52 Jun–Sep **B**

AIGUILLON-SUR-MER (85) Vendée (☎51) Map**15**B4
  ★★ **Port** 2 rue Belle Vue ☎561108 rm33 13Mar–Sep **A**

AINHOA (64) Pyrénées-Atlantiques (☎59 Map**20**C3
  H **Ur Hegian** ☎299116 rm17 **A**

AIRE SUR-L'ADOUR (40) Landes (☎58) Map**15**B1
  H **Commerce** 3 bd des Pyrénées ☎766006 rm19 **B**
  H **Platanes** 2 pl de la Liberté ☎766036 rm11 **B**

AIRE-SUR-LA-LYS (62) Pas-de-Calais (☎21) Map**3**A1
  ◆ **Hostellerie de l'Abbaye de St Andre** à Witternesse ☎390673 rm14 Closed Feb **B**
  ◆ **Hostellerie des Trois Mousquetaires** Chateau de la Redoute ☎390111 rm8 **B**
  ★ **Europ** 14 Grand pl ☎390432 rm16 **A**

AISEY-SUR-SEINE (21) Côte-d'Or (☎80) Map**10**C2
  ★ **Roy** ☎932163 rm10 15Dec–15Nov **A**

AIX-EN-PROVENCE (13) Bouches-du-Rhône (☎91) Map**27**B2
  H **Concorde** 68 bd du Roi-René ☎260395 rm39 **B**
  H **France** 63 r Esparriat ☎279015 rm27 **B**
  H **St Christophe** 2 av V-Hugo ☎260174 rm54 Closed Jan **B**
  H **St Louis** 9 r des Bretons ☎262358 rm17 **A**

★★ **Renaissance** bd de la République
(42) ☎260422 rm32 Closed Jan **A**

★★ **Rotonde** 15 av des Belges ☎262988
rm42 **B**

AIX-LES-BAINS (73) Savoie (☎79)
Map**27B4**

H **Azur** ☎350096 rm16 15Mar−30Nov **A**

H **Cécil** ☎350412 rm20 **A**

H **Savoy** ☎351333 rm22 **A**

★★ **Parc** 28 r de Chambery ☎612911
rm50 15Apr−15Oct **A**

★★ **Pavillon** pl Gare ☎351904 rm40
Apr−Sep **A**

ALBERT (80) Somme (☎22) Map**9B4**

★ **Basilique** 3/5 r Gambetta ☎750471
rm10 **A**

★ **Paix** 43 r Hugo ☎750164 rm14 **A**

ALBERTVILLE (73) Savoie (☎79) Map**28C4**

H **Berjann** ☎324788 rm11 **B**

H **Costaroche** ☎320202 rm20 **B**

H **Terminus** ☎320242 rm18 **B**

★★ **Million** ☎322515 rm30 **B**

ALBI (81) Tarn (☎63) Map**16D1**

H **George V** 29 av Ml-Joffre ☎542416
rm10 **B**

H **Modern Pujol** 22 av Col-Teyssier
☎540292 rm28 **B**

H **Parking** 31 pl F-Pelloutier ☎540907
rm15 **B**

★★ **Chiffre** 50 r Sere de Rivieres
☎540460 rm40 **A**

ALENÇON (61) Orne (☎33) Map**8D3**

H **Alentel** r de la Pyramide ☎267126
rm30 **A**

H **Industrie** 20−22 pl de Gaulle
☎262221 rm13 Closed
15Jan−15Feb **A**

H **Normandie** 20 r D-Papin ☎260112
rm18 **B**

★★ **France** 3 r Saint-Blaise ☎262636
rm31 **A**

★★ **Gare** 50 av Wilson ☎290393 rm22
3Jan−23Dec **A**

★ **Paris** 26 r D-Papin Face de la Gare
☎290164 rm18 Closed Aug **A**

ALÈS (30) Gard (☎66) Map**27A2**

H **Luxembourg** pl G-Pérl ☎521005
rm43 **A**

H **Riche** 42 pl P-Sémard ☎860033 rm20
Closed 6−20Oct **A**

ALTKIRCH (68) Haut-Rhin (☎89) Map**11B2**

H **A l'Agenau d'Or** 35 r de France
☎400102 rm21 7Jan−21Dec **B**

H **Ville de Marseille** 24 r C-de-Gaulle
☎409782 rm10 Closed Sep **A**

★ **Terrasse** ☎409802 rm20 **A**

ALVIGNAC-LES-EAUX (46) Lot (☎65)
Map**16C2**

H **Nouvel** ☎386030 rm11 Feb−Nov **B**

H **Terrasse** ☎386128 rm8 **A**

★★ **Palladium** av de Padirac ☎386023
rm27 15May−Sep **B**

AMBERT (63) Puy-de-Dôme (☎73)
Map**27A4**

H **Chaumière** ☎821494 rm13 **A**

H **Terminus** ☎820803 rm15 **A**

AMBOISE (37) Indre-et-Loire (☎47) Map**9A2**

H **Chaptal** 26 r J-Ferry ☎571446 rm8
Mar−15Nov **A**

★★ **Lion D'or** 17 Quai c-Guinot 17
☎570023 rm23 Mar−Nov **A**

★ **Bréche** 26 r J-Ferry ☎570079 rm15
Mar−Dec **A**

★ **France & Cheval Blanc** 6−7 quai C-
de Gaulle ☎570244 rm22 Mar−Nov **A**

AMÉLIE-LES-BAINS (66) Pyrénées-
Orientales (☎69) Map**22D4**

H **Grand Hotel des Thermes** ☎390100
rm82 **A**

H **Gorges** 6 pl des Thermes ☎390032
rm32 Closed Jan **A**

H **Paris** 37 av du Vallespir ☎390086
rm21 Closed Mon **A**

H **Régina** 32 au du Vallespir ☎390019
rm24 3Jan−15Nov **A**

AMIENS (80) Somme (☎22) Map**9B4**

H **Central-Anzac** 12 r A-Fatton
☎913408 rm18 **B**

★★ **Francital** 8 pl a Fiquet ☎913632
rm20 **A**

★★ **Nord-Sud** 11 r Gresset ☎915903
rm26 **B**

★ **Normandie** 1 bis r Lamartine
☎917499 rm23 **A**

★ **Paix** 8 r de la Republique ☎913921
rm26 5Jan−12Dec **A**

ANCENIS (44) Loire Atlantique (☎40)
Map**8C2**

H **Chaumière** ☎831129 rm13 Closed
10Oct−15Nov **A**

H **Voyageurs** ☎831006 rm20 **B**

ANDERNOS-LES-BAINS (33) Gironde
(☎56) Map**15B2**

H **Coulin** 3 av d'Arès ☎820435 rm11 **B**

At **Le Mauret** (1km SE)

H **Glacier** 126 bd de la République
☎820005 rm14 Apr−Sep **A**

ANGERS (49) Maine-et-Loire (☎41)
Map**8C2**

H **Mail** 8 r des Ursules ☎885622 rm21 **A**

H **St Jacques** 83 r St Jacques ☎485105
rm19 Closed Sun **B**

★★ **Boule D'or** 27 bd Carnot ☎437656
rm28 **A**

★★ **Croix de Guerre** 23 r Chateau-Gontier
☎886659 rm28 **A**

★★ **France** 8 pl de la Gare ☎884942
rm61 **A**

★★ **Univers** 16 r de la Gare ☎884358
rm45 **A**

ANGLET (64) Pyrénées-Atlantiques (☎59)
Map**20C3**

H **Chateau de Lardach** r de Hardoy
☎630635 rm25 **A**

H **Parc** 57 av de la Chambre-d'Amour
☎038261 rm26 **B**

★★ **Biarritz Golf** av Guynemer a' la
Chambre d'Amour ☎038302 rm25
Etr−Sep **A**

France

ANGOULÊME (16) Charente (☎45)
Map**15**B3
- H **Bordeaux** 236 rte de Bordeaux
  ☎950650 rm23 **A**
- H **Central** 1 r de Genève ☎950390
  rm15 **B**
- H **Lusignan** 62 av Gambetta ☎950877
  rm9 **B**
- H **Orléans** 133 av Gambetta ☎920753
  rm24 **B**
- ★ **Flore** 414 rte de Bordeaux ☎928055
  rm57 10Jan–23Dec **A**

ANNECY (74) Haute-Savoie (☎50)
Map**28**C4
- ★★ **Faisan Dor** 34 av d'Albigny ☎230246
  rm42 **B**
- ★★ **Jeanne d'Arc** 26 r Vaugelas
  ☎455337 rm42 **A**

ANTIBES (06) Alpes-Maritimes (☎93)
Map**28**C2
- H **Modern** 1 r Fourmillière ☎340305
  rm24 Closed Jan–6Feb **A**
- H **Nouvel** av du 24-Août ☎344407
  rm20 **A**
- H **Riviera** La Fontonne ☎335502
  rm15 **A**
At **Cap d'Antibes**
- ★★ **BeauSite** Boulevard de Cap
  ☎615343 rm29 Etr–Oct **A**

APT (84) Vaucluse (☎90) Map**27**B2
- H **Aptois** ☎740202 rm26 **B**
- H **Louvre** ☎742018 rm26 **B**

ARCACHON (33) Gironde (☎56) Map**15**B2
- H **Bordeaux** 39 bd Ml-Leclerc ☎830518
  rm10 **A**
- H **Pergola** 40 cours Lamarque de
  Plaisance ☎830789 rm19 **B**
- H **St Christaud** 8 allée de la Chapelle
  ☎833853 20May–20Oct **B**

ARDRES (62) Pas-de-Calais (☎21) Map**3**A1
- H **Grand Hôtel Clement** Esp Maréchal-
  Leclerc ☎354060 rm19
  Closed 21Jan–14Feb **A**
- H **Chaumière** 67 av de Rouville
  ☎354124 rm12 **A**
- H **Tilleuls** rte de Saint Omer ☎354098
  rm8 **B**
- ★★ **Relais** bd Constantin-Senlecy
  ☎354200 rm11 Feb–26Jan **A**

ARÈS (33) Gironde (☎56) **15**B2
- H **St Éloi** 11 bd de l'Aérium ☎822046
  rm12 **A**

ARGELÉS-GAZOST (66) Hautes-Pyrénées
(☎69) Map**21**B4
- H **Beau Site** 8 r de Capitaine-Digoy
  ☎970863 rm15 **A**
- H **Régina** 59 r du Ml-Foch ☎970659
  rm21 **A**
- ★ **Mon Cottage** 3 r l'Yser ☎970792
  rm21 **A**

ARGELÉS-SUR-MER (66) Pyrénées-
Orientales (☎69) Map**22**D4
- H **Clair Logis** 78 rte de Collioure
  ☎351151 rm17 **B**
- H **Lido** 50 bd de la Mer ☎360080 rm74
  10May–5Nov **B**

ARGENTAN (61) Orne (☎33) Map**8**D3
- H **Donjon** 3 r de l'Hôtel-de-Ville
  ☎670376 rm14
  Closed 15Sep–15Oct **A**
- H **France** 8 bd Carnot ☎670365 rm12
  Closed Feb **A**
- ★★ **Renaissance** av de la 2e D–B
  ☎671611 rm15 **A**

ARGENTAT (19) Corrèze (☎52) Map**16**D3
- H **Fouillard** ☎281017 rm28
  Closed Nov **B**

ARGENTON-SUR-CREUSE (36) Indre
(☎54) Map**16**C4
- ◆ **Champ-de-Foire** 48 r A-Descottes
  ☎041165 rm10 Closed 6–31Oct **A**
- ★★ **Manoir de Boisvillers** 11 r Moulin de
  Bord ☎041388 rm20 **B**
- ★ **France** 8 rue J–J Rousseau ☎040331
  rm26 **A**

ARLES (13) Bouches-du-Rhône (☎90)
Map**27**B2
- H **Diderot** pl de la Bastille ☎961030
  rm14 **A**
- H **France** pl Lamartine ☎960124
  rm15 **A**
- H **Provence** 12 r Chiavary ☎960329
  rm17 **A**
- H **Source** Pont-de-Crau ☎961232 rm16
  Mar–Oct **B**
- ★★ **Cloitre** 10 r du Cloitre ☎962950
  rm35 **A**

ARNAY-LE-DUC (21) Côte-d'Or (☎80)
Map**10**1/2
- H **Chaboud** 4 r de la Four ☎191 rm9 **A**
- ★ **Terminus** r Arquebuse ☎900033
  rm12 **A**

ARRAS (62) Pas-de-Calais (☎21) Map**3**B1
- H **Chanzy** 8 r Chanzy ☎210202 rm20 **B**
- H **Commerce** 24 r Gambetta ☎211007
  rm39 **B**
- H **Moderne** 1 bd Faidherbe ☎232957
  rm45 **A**
- ★★ **Grandes Arcades** 8 Grand Place
  ☎233089 rm22 **A**

ARTEMARE (01) Ain (☎79) Map**27**B4
- ★ **Berrard** ☎873010 rm32 **A**

ARROMANCHES-LES-BAINS (14)
Calvados (☎31) Map**8**D4
- H **Marine** quai du Canada ☎223419
  rm22 15Feb–5Nov **A**
- H **Normandie** pl du 6 Juin ☎223422
  rm19 Mar–15Nov **B**

ASCAIN (64) Pyrénées-Atlantiques (☎59)
Map**19**B3
- H **Harranederrea** ☎540023 rm10
  Jun–Sep **A**
- H **Rhune** ☎540004 rm 30
  Apr–15Sep **A**

AUBIGNY-SUR-NÈRG (18) Cher (☎36)
Map**9**B2
- H **Chaumière** 1 pl P-Lasnier ☎730401
  rm17 **B**
- ◆ **Auberge du Cheval Rouge** 6 r C-
  Lefebure ☎730548 rm4 **B**

AUBUSSON (23) Creuse (☎55) Map**16**D3
- H **Moderne** ☎661418 rm14 **A**

H **Paris** ☎661208 rm10 Jan–10Nov **B**
★ **Lion D'or** pl D'Espagne ☎661388
rm14 Feb–Dec **A**

AUCH (32) (☎62) Map**16**C1
H **Lion d'Or du Midi** 5 r Pasteur
☎050207 rm16 **B**
H **Modern** 10*bis* av de la Gare ☎050347
rm29 Closed Aug **A**
H **Paris** 38 av de la Marne ☎050123
rm22 **B**

AUDIERNE (29) Finistère (☎98) Map**7**A3
H **Plage** ☎700107 rm30 20Mar–1Nov **B**
H **Roi Gradlon** ☎700451 rm13 **B**

AUMALE (76) Seine-Maritime (☎35)
Map**9**B4
★ **Dauphin** r St-Lazare ☎934192 rm11
Closed 25Jul–10Aug, 20Dec–1Jan **A**

AUNAY-SUR-ODON (14) Calvados (☎31)
Map**8**D3
★ **St Michel** 6–8 r Caen ☎776316 rm7 **A**

AURAY (56) Morbihan (☎97) Map**7**B2
H **Gare et des Voyageurs** ☎240018
rm18 Closed Nov **A**
H **Moderne** ☎240472 rm10
Closed Nov **A**
H **Terminus** ☎240009 rm12 **A**

AURILLAC (15) Cantal (☎71) Map**16**D2
H **Commerce** ☎482390 rm17 **A**
H **Terminus** ☎480117 rm22 **A**
★★ **Grand Hôtel de Bordeaux** 2 av de la
République ☎480184 rm50 **B**

AUTUN (71) Saône-et-Loire (☎85) Map**10**C1
H **Commerce & Touring** 20 av de la
République ☎521790 rm18 **A**
H **France** 18 av de la République
☎521400 rm20 **A**
H **St-Louis et Poste** 6 r de Z'Arbalète
☎522103 rm48 10Mar–4Nov **B**

AUXERRE (89) Yonne (☎86) Map**10**C2
H **Porte de Paris** 5 r St Germain/3bd de
la Chaînette ☎520077 rm11 **A**
H **Poste** 9 r d'Orbandelle ☎521202
rm24 15Nov–15Dec **A**
H **St Nitasse** rte Chablis ☎522931
rm35 **B**
★★ **Normandie** 41 bd Vauban ☎525780
rm46 **B**

AUXONNE (21) Côte-d'Or (☎80)
Map**10**D1/2
H **Grand Cerf** 48 r A-Masson ☎363302
Closed Nov **A**

At **Villers-les-Pots** (5km NW)
★★ **Auberge du Cheval Rouge** ☎363411
rm10 **A**

AVIGNON (84) Vaucluse (☎90) Map**27**B2
H **Angleterre** 29bd Raspail ☎863431
rm32 **A**
H **Innova** 100 r J-Vernet ☎814684
rm23 **A**
H **Palais des Papes** 1 r G-Philippe
☎810866 rm25 **A**
H **Paris-Nice** 38 cours J-Jaurès
☎810888 rm15 **A**

H **St Paul** 10 r Dorée ☎812970 rm14 **A**
★★ **Angleterre** 29 Boulevard de Raspail
☎863431 rm32 **A**
★★ **Regina** 6 r de la Republique ☎864945
rm41 **B**
★ **Jaquemart** 3 r Felicien-David
☎863471 rm20 **A**

AVRANCHES (50) Manche (☎33) Map**8**C3
H **Normandie** 2 corniche St Michel
☎580133 rm16 **A**
★★ **Croix D'or** 83 r de la Constitution
☎580488 rm26 **A**
★★ **St Michel** 5 pl General Patton
☎580191 rm26 Apr–Oct **A**

AX-LES-THERMES (09) Ariège (☎61)
Map**22**C4
H **Parc** 16 av Delcassé ☎642060 rm22
20May–30Sep **A**
H **Teich** 2av Turrel et Ch-St-Roch
☎642299 rm58 **A**
H **Terminus** 31 av Delcassé ☎642055
rm28 Closed Nov **A**
★★ **Moderne** 20 av du Dr-Gomma
☎642024 rm22 Apr–30Oct **A**
★★ **Roy Rene** ☎642228 rm28
4Feb–15Oct **B**
★ **Lauzeraie** Promenade du Couloubert
☎642070 rm24 Apr–10Oct **A**

AZAY LE RIDEAU (37) Indre et Loire (☎47)
Map**8**D2
★★ **Grand Monarque** ☎433008 rm30
14Mar–Nov **A**

BAGNÈRES-DE-BIGORRE (65) Hautes-
Pyrénées (☎62) Map**21**B4
H **Fleurs d'Ajonc** 3 pl de la Piscine
☎950729 rm11 May–Sep **A**
H **Palmiers** 51 pl G-Clemenceau
☎950895 rm8 **B**
H **Petit Vosges** 17 bd Carnot ☎950831
rm8 **B**
★★ **Vignaux** 16 r de la République
☎950341 rm18 May–Oct **A**

BAGNÈRES-DE-LUCHON see **LUCHON**

BAGNOLES-DE-L'ORNE (61) Orne (☎34)
Map**8**D3
H **Beau Séjour** pl du Gl-de-Gaulle
☎370011 rm27 **B**
H **Forêt** 56 bd P-Chalvet ☎370533
rm17 **B**
H **Nancy** au R-Cousin ☎372422 rm45
26Apr–30Oct **B**
H **Terrasse** pl de la République
☎370366 rm26 Apr–Sep **B**

BAGNOLS-EN-FORÊT (83) Var Map**28**C2
H **Miresterel** ☎406049 rm7 Feb–Oct **A**
H **Provence** ☎406035 rm7 Apr–Sep **B**

BAGNOLS-SUR-CÈZE (30) Gard (☎66)
Map**27**B2
H **Ambiance** pl B-Boisson ☎895204
rm12 **A**
H **Bon Accueil** RN86 ☎895341 rm10 **A**
H **Coupole** av G-de-Gaulle ☎896106
rm14 **A**

France

BAIN DE BRETAGNE (35) Ille-et-Vilaine
(☎99) Map**8**C2
    H **Quatre-Vents** ☎477149 rm20 **B**

BAINS-LES-BAINS (88) Vosges (☎29)
Map**11**A2
    H **Commerce** 10–12 r du G-Leclerc
    ☎363365 rm30 **A**
  ★★ **Beau Site** 2 pl de la 2e-D-B ☎363174
    rm45 May–Sep **A**

BANDOL (83) Var (☎94) Map**27**B1
    H **Bel Ombra** ☎294090 rm19
    Jun–Sep **B**
  ◆ **Relais Fleuri** ☎294140 rm9
    Apr–Sep **A**
    H **Oasis** ☎294169 rm10 **A**
  ★★ **Golf** Plage de Renecros ☎294583
    rm23 Apr–Oct **B**

BANYOLS-SUR-MER (66) Pyrénées-
Orientales Map**22**D4
    H **Cap Doune** pl P-Reig ☎3833056
    rm10 14May–Sep **A**
    H **Pergola** av Fontaulé ☎383124
    rm17 **B**

BARAQUEVILLE (12) Aveyron (☎65)
Map**16**D2
    H **Agriculture** RN88 ☎690006 rm11 **A**
    H **Maurel** ☎690005 rm10 **A**

BARBEN (LE) see SALON-DE-PROVENCE

BARBOTAN-LES-THERMES (32) Gers
(☎62) Map**15**B2
    H **Dalma** ☎095228 rm29 Apr–Oct **A**
    H **Kakis** ☎095236 rm16 Apr–Oct **A**
    H **Pomme d'Or** ☎095241 rm23
    Apr–Nov **A**

BARCELONNETTE (04) Alpes-de-Hautes-
Provence (☎92) Map**28**C3
    H **Cheval Blanc** ☎810019 rm20 **A**
    H **Europe** ☎810337 rm15 **A**

BAR-LE-DUC (55) Meuse (☎28) Map**10**D3
    H **Bertrand** 19 r de l'Etoile ☎790297
    rm15 rest closed Sun **A**
    H **Gare** 2 pl de la République ☎790145
    rm10 **A**
    H **Terminus** 3 r Sébastopol ☎751599
    rm24 **A**

BARNEVILLE-CARTERET (50) Manche
(☎33) Map**8**C4

At **Barneville Plage**
  ★★ **Isles** bd Maritime ☎549076 rm36
    20Mar–15Sep **A**

At **Carteret**
    H **Angleterre** 4 r de Paris ☎548604
    rm46 25Mar–1Oct1 **A**
    H **Marine** 2 r de Paris ☎548331 rm30
    Etr–Sep **B**

BAR-SUR-AUBE (10) Aube (☎25) Map**10**C3
    H **Pomme d'Or** 79 fbg de Belfort
    ☎270993 rm30 2Jan–2Dec **B**
  ★ **Commerce** 38 r Nationale ☎270876
    rm16 **A**

BAR-SUR-SEINE (10) Aube (☎25)
Map**10**C2
    H **Commerce** pl de la République

    ☎388636 rm12 Closed Feb **A**
  ★★ **Barséquanais** 7 av General Leclerc
    ☎388275 rm24 20Jan–20Dec **A**

BASTIDE (LA) (83) Var (☎94) Map**28**C2
    H **Lachens** ☎768001 rm14 Closed
    15Nov–15Dec **A**

BAULE (LA) (44) Loire-Atlantique (☎40)
Map**7**B2
    H **Closerie** 173 av De-Lattre-de-
    Tassigny ☎602271 rm13
    15Mar–15Sep **B**
    H **Paris** 138 av des Ondines ☎603053
    rm18 **B**
    H **St-Bernard** 6 av des Evens ☎603202
    rm7 Apr–Oct **B**
    H **St-Christophe** 1 av des Alcyons
    ☎602742 rm31 **B**
    H **Ty Gwen** 25 av de la Grande-Dune
    ☎603707 rm14 Closed Oct **B**

BAYEUX (14) Calvados (☎31) Map**8**D4
    H **Gare** 26 pl de la Gare ☎921070 rm14
    Closed 1–15Sep **A**
    H **Luxembourg** 25 r des Bouchers
    ☎920004 rm25 **A**

BAYONNE (64) Pyrénées-Atlantiques (☎59)
Map**20**C3
    H **Basques** 4 r des Lisses ☎250802
    rm15 **A**
    H **Paris-Madrid** pl de la Gare ☎551398
    rm30 **A**
    H **St Esprit** 26 pl de la République
    ☎551634 rm23 **A**

BEAUGENCY (45) Loiret (☎38) Map**9**A2
  ◆ **Relais des Templiers** 68 r du Pont
    ☎445378 rm10 **B**
  ★★ **Écu de France** Pl du Martori
    ☎446760 rm26
    Closed 16Jan–14Feb **A**

BEAULIEU-SUR-DORDOGNE (19) Corrèze
(☎55) Map**16**C2
  ◆ **Ventura** ☎911273 rm18 **A**
  ★★ **Central** ☎910134 rm34 Closed Jan **A**

BEAULIEU-SUR-MER (06) Alpes-Maritimes
(☎93) Map**28**C2
    H **France** 1 montée des Orangers
    ☎010092 rm18 5Jan–5Oct **A**
    H **Marcellan** 18 av Albert-1er ☎010169
    rm20 20Jan–15Oct **A**
    H **Sélect** 1 montée des Myrtes ☎010542
    rm20 3Jan–Oct **B**

BEAUMONT SUR SARTHE (72) Sarthe
(☎43) Map**8**D3
  ★★ **Chemin de Fer** a la Gare ☎970005
    rm16 **A**

BEAUNE (21) Côte-d'Or (☎80) Map**10**C1
    H **Chateau** Challanges-Beaune
    ☎220188 rm14 **A**
    H **St Nicolas** 69 r du Faubourg-St-
    Nicolas ☎221830 rm13 Closed
    15Feb–15Mar **A**
    H **Square des Lions** bd Foch ☎220429
    rm10 **A**

BEAURAINVILLE (62) Pas-de-Calais (☎21)
Map**3**A1
  ★★ **Val de Canche** ☎903222 rm10 **A**

BEAUREPAIRE (38) Isère (☎74) Map**27**B3
    H **Piscine** ☎866450 rm10 **B**
    ★ **Fiard** 25 r de la République ☎846202
        rm21 Closed Oct **B**

BEAUVAIS (60) Oise (☎4) Map**9**B4
    H **Croix d'Or** 15 pl J-Hachette
        ☎4450751 rm15 **B**
    H **Cygne** 24 r Carnot ☎4451390 rm15
        5Jan–20Dec **B**
    H **Résidence** 24 r L-Borel ☎4483098
        rm24 **B**
    ★ **Palais** 9 r St Nicolas ☎4451258
        rm14 **B**

BEAUVEZER (04) Alpes-de-Hautes-
Provence Map**28**C2
    H **Novelty** ☎4 rm18
        Closed 19Sep–19Oct **A**

BEAUVOIR-SUR-MER (85) Vendée (☎30)
Map**7**B2
    H **Touristes** ☎687019 rm20 **B**

BEG-MEIL (29) Finistère (☎98) Map**7**A3
    ★★ **Thalamot** Le Chemin Creux
        Fouesnant ☎949738 rm33
        Etr–20Sep **A**

BELFORT (90) Territoire-de-Belfort (☎84)
Map**11**A2
    H **American** 2 r du Pont-Neuf ☎215701
        rm37 **B**
    H **Europe** 5 av Wilson ☎216389 rm48 **A**
    H **Chalet** 25 av Wilson ☎280168 rm17 **A**
    H **Lycée** 6 av Roosevelt ☎282130
        rm17 **A**
    H **Nouvel** 56 fbg de France ☎282870
        rm24 **A**

BELIN (33) Gironde (☎56) Map**15**B2
    ◆ **Hostellerie des Pins** RN10 ☎23
        rm12 **A**

BELLAC (87) Haute Vienne (☎55) Map**16**C4
    H **Terminus** ☎681040 rm12 **A**

BELLÊME (61) Orne (☎34) Map**9**A3
    H **Boule d'Or** pl du Gl-Leclerc ☎331072
        rm8 20Jan–20Dec **A**
    ★ **Relais St Louis** 1 Boulevard Bansart-
        Des-Bois ☎331221 rm9
        Feb–22Dec **A**

BÉNODET (29) Finistère (☎98) Map**7**A3
    H **Ancre de Marine** ☎910529 rm25
        Mar–Oct **B**
    ◆ **Auberge Au Bon Vieux Temps**
        ☎910141 rm14 May–15Oct **B**
    H **Trez** ☎910036 rm17 **B**
    ★★ **Ancre de Marine** 6 av L'Odet
        ☎910529 rm25 Mar–Oct **B**
    ★★ **Grand** 4 av L'Odet ☎910002 rm54
        Jun–15Sep **B**

BERCK-PLAGE (62) Pas-de-Calais (☎21)
Map**3**A1
    H **Concorde** 39 r G-Perí ☎090176
        rm16 **A**
    H **Flambée** 98 r de Rothschild ☎090487
        rm26 **A**
    H **Rusticana** 28 r de la Plage ☎091599
        rm10 Feb–20Dec **A**
    H **Valentin** 42 r A-Lambert ☎090254
        rm15 Closed Nov **A**

BERGERAC (24) Dordogne (☎53) Map**16**C2
    H **Londres** 46 r Neuve-d'Argenson
        ☎570011 rm27 **A**
    H **Terminus** Gare SNCF ☎570109
        rm20 **B**
    ★★ **Bordeaux** 38 pl Gambetta ☎571283
        rm42 Feb–30Dec **A**

BERGUES (59) Nord (☎20) Map**3**A1
    H **Commerce** Contour d'Eglise
        ☎686037 rm17 5Jan–11Dec **B**
    ★ **Tonnelier** 4 r de Mont de Piete
        ☎687005 rm10 **A**

BERNAY (27) Eure (☎32) Map**9**A3
    ★ **Angleterre Cheval Blanc** 10 r Gl-de-
        Gaulle ☎431259 rm23 Closed Feb **A**
    ★ **Lion D'or** 48 r Thiers ☎431206
        rm29 **A**

BESANÇON (25) Doubs (☎81) Map**11**A2
    H **Eden** 21 r des Boucheries ☎820578
        rm16 **A**
    H **Foch** 7 *bis* av Foch ☎803041 rm28 **A**
    H **Paris** 33 r des Granges ☎813656
        rm45 4Jan–24Dec **A**
    H **Régina** 91 Grande-Rue ☎815022
        rm22 **A**
    ★ **Gambetta** 13 r Gambetta ☎820233
        rm26 **A**

BESSE-EN-CHANDESSE (63) Puy-de-
Dôme (☎73) Map**16**D3
    H **Levant** ☎795017 rm20 Closed
        25Apr–25May & 25Sep–15Dec **A**

BESSINES-SUR-GARTEMPE (87) Haute-
Vienne (☎55) Map**16**C4
    ★★ **Vallee** N20 ☎760166 rm20 Closed
        10–27Feb & 7–23Oct **A**

BETHUNE (62) Pas de Calais (☎21)
Map**3**B1
    H **Petit Sapeur** 334 pl Clemencau
        ☎252406 rm9 Closed Aug **A**
    ★★ **Vieux Beffroi** 48 Grande-Place
        ☎251500 rm63 **A**
    ★ **Bernard Et Gare** 3 pl de la Gare
        ☎252002 rm34 **A**

BEUTIN (62) Pas-de-Calais (☎21) Map**3**A1
    H **Auberge de la Canche** Route
        National rm8 **B**

BÉZIERS (34) Hérault (☎67) Map**16**D1
    H **Clari's Hotel** 3 r V-Hugo ☎764485
        rm14 Closed Sep **A**
    H **Lux** 3 r des Petits-Champs ☎284805
        rm22 **A**
    H **Roussillon** 9 r A-de-Musset ☎764263
        rm18 **A**
    H **Unic** 41 r Guilhemon ☎284431
        rm14 **A**

BIARRITZ (64) Pyrénées-Atlantiques (☎59)
Map**20**C3
    H **Carmen** 16 av de Londres ☎230240
        rm9 **A**
    H **Comminges** 19 av Carnot ☎241046
        rm13 **A**
    H **Maritchu** 21 r Bon-Air ☎241550
        rm13 **A**
    H **Pyrénées** 30 r de Gascogne
        ☎242022 rm10 Apr–Sep **A**

France

★ **Palacito** 1 r Gambetta ☎240489
rm26 **B**

★ **Washington** 34 r Mazagran ☎241080
rm20 Apr–Sep **A**

BISCARROSSE (33) Gironde (☎56)
Map**15**A/B2

H **Gare** pl de l'Église ☎781028 rm7 **A**

H **Schuss** 26 av des Galipes ☎781190
rm10 **A**

BLAIN (44) Loire Atlantique (☎40) Map**7**C2
H **Gerbe de Blé** ☎791050 rm10 **A**

BLANC (LE) (36) Indre (☎54) Map**9**A1
H **Domaine de l'Étape** rte de Belâbre
rm14 **A**

BLANGY-SUR-BRESLE (76) Seine-
Maritime (☎35) Map**9**B4

★ **Poste** 44 r Grand ☎935020 rm14
20Jan–20Dec **A**

★ **Ville** 2 r Notre Dame ☎935157 rm6
Closed 6–27Aug **A**

BLAYE (33) Gironde (☎56) Map**15**B3
H **Toyson d'Or** 15 cours de Port
☎420041 rm12 20Jan–20Dec **B**

BLÉRIOT-PLAGE (26) Pas-de-Calais (☎21)
Map**3**A1/2

★ **Dunes** ☎345430 rm13 **A**

BLETTERANS (39) Jura (☎84) Map**10**D1
H **Cloche** 2 r L-le-Grand ☎850148
rm14 **A**

H **Jura** r d'Amond ☎850411 rm21 **A**

BLOIS (41) Loir-et-Cher (☎39) Map**9**A2
H **Chateau** 22 r Porte-Côte ☎782024
rm45 **B**

H **Médicis** 2 allée François-1er
☎780511 rm18 **B**

★ **Chevemy** ☎780670 rm10
Closed Oct **A**

★ **St. Jacques** pl Gare ☎780415 rm28
Closed 4–26Nov, 23–31Dec **A**

★ **Viennois** 5 Quai Amedee-Contant
☎741280 rm26 **A**

BLONVILLE-SUR-MER (14) Calvados
(☎31) Map**8**D4

★ **Mer** 93 av de la République ☎879323
rm20 25Mar–17Sep **A**

BOLLÈNE (84) Vaucluse (☎90) Map**27**B2
H **Bellevue** ☎301301 rm37 **A**

H **Nouvel** ☎301444 rm11 **A**

BONNEVAL (28) Eure-et-Loire (☎37)
Map**9**A3

★★ **Bois Guibert** 10 rte Nationale
☎982233 rm14 Feb–20Dec **A**

BONNY-SUR-LOIRE (45) Loiret (☎38)
Map**9**B2

◆ **Voyageurs** 1 pl de la République
☎316209 rm7 Closed Feb **A**

BORDEAUX (33) Gironde (☎56) Map**15**B2
H **Balzac** 14 r L-de-Monbadon ☎488512
rm17 **A**

H **Choiseul** 13 r Huguerie ☎527124
rm11 **A**

H **Dordogne** 4 r La Boétie ☎487668
rm17 **A**

H **Italie** 4 r des Ayres ☎484992 rm20 **A**

H **Noel** 8 r St-V-de Paul ☎916248
rm17 **A**

★★ **Bayonne** 15 Cours de L'Intendance
☎480088 rm37 **A**

BORMES-LES-MIMOSAS (83) Var (☎94)
Map**28**C1

H **Mimosas** ☎711350 rm12 **B**

★ **Belle Vue** pl Gambetta ☎711515
rm15 Closed Oct–Sep **A**

BORT-LES-ORGUES (19) Corrèze (☎55)
Map**16**D3

H **Barrage** ☎720122 rm12 **A**

H **Gare** ☎720047 rm23 **A**

H **Val** ☎720256 rm10 Feb–15Oct **B**

BOULOGNE-SUR-MER (62) Pas-de-Calais
(☎21) Map**3**A1

H **Catham** 122 quai Gambetta ☎315578
rm12 **B**

H **Jean-Bart** 20 quai Gambetta
☎316919 rm10 **A**

H **Monsigny** 13 r Monsigny ☎313270
rm12 Closed Nov **B**

H **Plage** 12 bd St-Beuve ☎314535
rm10 **A**

★★ **Alexandra** 93 r Thiers ☎313208
rm20 **A**

★★ **Lorraine** 7 pl de Lorraine ☎313478
rm21 **A**

★ **Londres** 22 pl de France ☎313563
rm20 **B**

At **Le Portel** (1km SW)

H **Place Chez Michel** 32 pl de Église
☎316191 rm11
Closed 1–21Sep **A**

★ **Beaurivage & Armada** bd Pasteur
☎315982 rm11 **A**

BOULOU (LE) Pyrénées-Orientales (☎69)
Map**22**D4

H **Grillon d'Or** 40 r de la République
☎374228 rm18 **B**

H **Pyrénées** rte d'Espagne ☎374047
rm10 **A**

BOURBON-L'ARCHAMBAULT (03) Allier
(☎70) Map**9**B1

H **Foucrier et du Commerce** ☎670193
rm14 21Jan–19Dec **A**

H **Grand Hotel Villa des Fleurs**
☎670953 rm19 **A**

BOURBONNE-LES-BAINS (52) Haute
Marne (☎25) Map**10**D2

H **Beau Séjour** 17 r d'Orfeuil ☎900034
rm57 10Apr–10Oct **A**

H **Hérard** 29–31 Grande-Rue ☎900529
rm33 **B**

BOURGES (18) Cher (☎36) Map**9**B2
H **St Jean** 23 av M-Dormoy ☎241348
rm24 **B**

★★ **Berry** 3 pl du General Leclerc
☎244358 rm21 **A**

★★ **Christina** 5 r Halle ☎705650 rm76 **A**

★★ **Poste** 22 r Mayenne ☎700806 rm34 **A**

BOURGANEUF (23) Creuse (☎55)
Map**16**C3

◆ **Tour** ☎640687 rm6 **A**

◆ **Vielle Auberge** ☎640954 rm4 **A**

France

BOURGOIN-JALLIEU (38) Isère (☎74) Map**27**B4
- H **Midi** 31 r de la République ☎933067 rm16 **B**
- H **Négociants** 22 av des Alpes ☎930204 rm12 **A**

BOURGTHEROULDE (27) Eure (☎35) Map**9**A4
- ★ **Corne d'Abondance** pl de la Mairie ☎776008 rm12 Closed Feb, Aug **A**

BOURG-ST-MAURICE (73) Savoie (☎79) Map**28**C4
- H **Bon Repos** ☎070178 rm10 Closed Nov **A**

BRANTÔME (24) Dordogne (☎53) Map**16**C3
- H **Grand Hôtel Chabrol** 58 r Gambetta ☎547015 rm30 Closed 15Nov–1Dec **A**
- ◆ **Auberge du Soir** 5 r G-Saumande ☎547186 rm8 Closed 15Jan–15Feb **A**

BRESSUIRE (79) Deux Sevres (☎49) Map**8**C1
- H **Boule d'Or** 15 p E-Zda ☎650218 rm15 Closed 1–15Aug **A**
- H **France** 5 bd Alexandre-1er ☎650047 rm18 **A**

BREST (29) Finistère (☎98) Map**7**A3
- H **Au Depart** 2 r de Siam ☎801910 rm22 **A**
- H **Comédia** 2 r d'Aiguillon ☎441123 rm15 **A**
- H **Ponant** 20 r de la Port ☎450932 rm23 **B**
- H **Sports** 4 r du Vercors ☎020165 rm8 **A**
- H **Voltaire** 37 r Voltaire ☎803764 rm19 **B**

BRIANÇON (05) Hautes-Alpes (☎92) Map**28**C3
- H **Gare** ☎210049 rm15 **A**
- H **Univers** ☎210131 rm12 **A**

BRICQUEBEC (50) Manche (☎33) map**8**C4
- ★ **Taverne Oudinet** 9 pl Ste-Anne ☎522315 rm7 **A**
- ★ **Vieux Chateau** 4 Cour du Chateau ☎522449 rm20 Closed Jan **A**

BRIGNOLES (83) Var (☎94) Map**27**B2
- H **Chateau Brignoles** ☎690688 rm39 **B**
- H **Fabre de Piffard** ☎690029 rm26 **B**
- H **Rose de Provence** ☎690989 rm10 **B**

BRIONNE (27) Eure (☎32) Map**9**A4
- ★ **Vieux Donjon** 19 r de la Soie ☎448062 rm9 Closed last 2wks Oct **A**

BRIOUDE (43) Haute-Loire (☎71) Map**27**A3
- H **Chaumine** ☎501410 rm12 **A**
- ★★ **Brivas** rte Puy ☎501049 rm30 Closed 20Nov–20Dec **A**

BRIVE-LA-GAILLARDE (19) Corrèze (☎55) Map**16**C3
- H **Gare** 65 av J-Jaurès ☎241020 rm15 **A**
- H **Terminus** av J-Jaurès ☎742114 rm49 **A**
- H **Verlhac** 63 av J-Jaurès ☎740391 rm10 **A**
- ★ **Mountauban** 6 av Edouard-Herriot ☎240038 rm21 Closed Jan **A**

BROONS (22) Côtes du Nord (☎96) Map**7**B3
- H **Cheval Breton** ☎416236 rm12 **A**

BRON see **LYON**

BRUMATH (67) Bas-Rhin (☎88) Map**11**B3
- H **Ville de Paris** 13 r du Gl-Rampont rm14 Closed 19Jun–14Jul Sun & Fri evenings **A**

BULLY-LES-MINES (62) Pas-de-Calais (☎21) Map**3**B1
- ★ **Moderne** 144 r de la Gare ☎291422 rm38 **A**

CAEN (14) Calvados (☎31) Map**8**D4
- H **Chaumine** 121 av G-Clemenceau ☎931845 rm10 **A**
- H **Coq en Pâte** 37–39 r P-Girard ☎820816 rm10 **A**
- H **Havre** 11 r du Havre ☎816627 rm17 **A**
- H **Rex** 58 pl de la Gare ☎820963 rm25 **A**
- H **Week-End** 14 quai Vendeuvre ☎813061 **A**
- ★ **St Jean** 20 r des Martyrs ☎816873 rm15 **A**

CAGNES-SUR-MER (06) Alpes-Maritimes (☎93) Map**28**C2
- ◆ **Auberge Franc-Comtoise** Grange-Rimade ☎209758 rm20 Closed 15Oct–15Nov **A**
- H **Villa Pierre** 14 r du Docteur-Mauran rm15 ☎312079 **B**

CAHORS (46) Lot (☎60) Map**16**C2
- H **Chez Jean-Pierre** 65 r d l'Université ☎354599 rm10 **A**
- H **Marine** 3 r du Pont-Neuf ☎352449 rm12 **A**
- ◆ **Paix** pl des Halles ☎350340 rm22 **A**

CALAIS (62) Pas-de-Calais (☎21) Map**3**A1
- H **Beffroi** 8 r A-Gerschel ☎344751 rm20 **A**
- H **Boulogne** 41 quai du Rhin ☎345907 rm13 **A**
- H **Cheval Noir** 27 pl Crèvecaer ☎344226 rm14 **A**
- H **Littoral** 71 r A-Briand ☎344728 rm14 **A**
- H **Windsor** 2 r du Cdt-Bonningue ☎345940 rm15 **B**
- ★★ **Bellevue** 25 pl d'Armes ☎345375 rm40 **A**
- ★★ **George-V** 36 r Royale ☎344029 rm50 15Mar–Nov **A**
- ★ **Beffroi** 10 r Andre ☎344751 rm20 **A**
- ★ **Richelieu** 17 r Richelieu ☎346160 rm15 **A**

CAMBO-LES-BAINS (64) Pyrénées-Atlantiques (☎59) Map**20**C3
- H **Assantza** av E-Rostand ☎297660 rm60 15Jun–15Sep **A**
- H **St Laurent** r des Terrasses ☎297110 rm14 Closed 15–30Nov **B**

123

France

CAJARC (46) Lot (☎65) Map**16**C2
- H **Moderne** ☎346511 rm7 **A**
- ♦ **Paix** ☎346502 rm5 **A**

CAMARET-SUR-MER (29) Finistère (☎96) Map**7**A3
- H **France** ☎279306 rm20 **B**

CAMBRAI (59) Nord (☎20) Map**3**B1
- ★★ **Mouton Blanc** 33r Alsace-Lorraine ☎813016 rm Closed Aug **A**
- ★★ **Poste** 58–60 av de la Victoire ☎813469 rm32 **B**
- ★ **France** 37 r Lille ☎813880 rm24 Closed Aug **A**

CAMP LONG see AGAY

CANCALE (35) Ille-et-Villaine (☎99) Map**8**C3
- H **Bellevue** ☎586133 rm21 Closed 25Sep–25Oct **A**
- H **Phare** ☎586024 rm7 **A**
- H **Plage** ☎586098 rm14 Etr–Oct **A**
- ★★ **Continental** au Port ☎896016 rm18 Feb–15Nov **A**

CANET PLAGE (66) Pyrénées-Orientales (☎68) Map**22**D4
- H **Font le Patio** Font de la Mer ☎803104 rm70 **A**
- H **Maricel** pl Centrale ☎803216 rm60 **B**
- H **Régina** 132 av Tixador ☎802285 rm24 26Mar–Oct **B**

CANNES (06) Alpes-Maritimes (☎93) Map**28**C2
- H **Central** 27 r des Serbes ☎991824 rm14 **A**
- H **Modern** 11 r des Serbes ☎390987 rm19 **B**
- H **Nord** 6 r J-Jaurès ☎384879 rm21 **A**
- H **St Vianny** 16 bd Carnot ☎454129 rm12 **B**
- ★★ **Roches Fleuries** 92 r G Clemenceau ☎392878 rm24 Closed 16Nov–14Dec **A**

CAP FERRET (33) Gironde (☎56) Map**15**A2
- H **Dunes** 119 av de Bordeaux ☎606181 rm13 20Mar–3Apr, May–25Oct **B**
- H **Houplinière** 1 av Bordeaux ☎606244 Feb–Oct **B**

CAPBRETON (40) Landes (☎57) Map**15**A1
- H **Béarnais** r Dargan ☎721333 rm12 **A**
- H **Centre** 17 av de la Plage rm14 Apr–10Nov **A**

CAP D'AIL (06) Alpes-Maritimes (☎93) Map**28**C2
- H **Normandy** 6 allées des Orangers ☎068120 rm18 Jan–Oct **B**

CARANTEC (29) Finistère (☎98) Map**7**B3
- H **Pors Pol** ☎670052 rm40 Etr & May–Sep **A**
- ★ **Falaise** ☎670053 rm27 May–16Sep **A**

CARCASSONNE (11) Aude (☎68) Map**16**D1
- H **Central** 27 bd J-Jaurès ☎250384 rm5 **A**

- H **Halles** 55 r A-Ramon ☎250912 rm16 **A**
- H **Voyageurs** 41 allée d'Iéna ☎250234 rm24 **A**
- ★★ **Royal** 22 bd Jean Jaures ☎251912 rm27 **A**

CARENNAC (46) Lot (☎65) Map**16**C2
- ★ **Fenelon** ☎384716 rm24 Closed Feb **A**

CARENTAN (50) Manche (☎33) Map**8**C4
- ★ **Auberge Normande** bd Verdun ☎420299 rm12 **A**

CARHAIX (29) Finistère (☎98) Map**7**B3
- H **Paradis** ☎930138 rm20 Closed 1–15Sep **A**
- ★★ **France** 14 r des Martyrs ☎930015 rm20 20Jan–20Dec **A**

CARNAC (56) Morbihan (☎97) Map**7**B2
- H **Chez Nous** pl de la Chapelle rm18 Etr & Whit–15Sep **A**

At **Carnac Plage**
- H **Ker Moor** 136d de la Plage rm12 Apr–Oct **B**
- H **Petit Navire** 5 avd'l Atlantique rm16 Etr & 30May–10Sep **A**
- ★ **Celtique** 17 av Kermaric ☎521149 rm35 Etr–15Sep **A**

CASSIS (13) Bouches-du-Rhône (☎91) Map**27**B1
- H **Commerce** ☎010910 rm15 Feb–15Dec **A**
- H **Lieutaud** ☎017537 rm32 Jan–Oct **A**

CASTELJALOUX (47) Lot-et-Garonne (☎58) Map**15**B2
- H **Cordeliers** ☎930219 rm11 **A**
- ★ **Grand Cadets de Gascogne** pl Gambetta ☎930059 rm14 Closed 1–20Nov **A**

CASTELLANE (04) Alpes-de-Hautes-Provence (☎92) Map**28**C2
- H **Levant** ☎05 rm33 15Feb–15Nov **A**
- H **Verdon** ☎22 rm18 Closed Oct **B**
- ★ **Petit Auberge** pl Marcel-Sauvaire ☎836206 rm18 15Mar–15Oct **A**

CASTELNAUDARY (11) Aude (☎68) Map**16**C1
- ★ **Fourcade** 14 r des Carmes ☎230208 rm19 16May–14Jun **A**

CASTELSARRASIN (82) Tarn-et-Garonne (☎63) Map**20**D4
- ★ **Moderne** 54 r de L'Egalite ☎043010 rm12 **A**

CASTRES (81) Tarn (☎63) Map**16**D1
- H **France** 8 r des 3-Rois ☎590489 rm20 **A**
- H **Hyppocampe** 4 r Mahuzies ☎593182 rm20 **A**
- ★★ **Grand** 11 r de la Liberation ☎590030 rm36 15Jan–15Dec **A**

CAUDEBEC-EN-CAUX (76) Seine-Maritime (☎35) Map**9**A4

★★ **Marine** 18 Quai Guilbaud ☎962011 rm34 **B**

★★ **Normandie** Quai Guilbaud ☎962511 rm11 **A**

CAUSSADE (82) Tarn-et-Garonne (☎63) Map**16**C2

★★ **Dupont** 12 r Recollets ☎021202 rm34 **A**

★★ **Lorroque** av de la Gare ☎021014 rm30 **A**

CAUTERETS (65) Hautes-Pyrénées (☎62) Map**21**B4

H **Chantilly** r de la Raillère ☎975277 rm18 **A**

H **Régent** 5 pl Ml-Foch ☎975010 rm12 **A**

H **Rotende** 38 r Richelieu ☎975268 rm22 **A**

H **Sacca** 11 bd L-Flurin ☎975002 rm23 **B**

CELLE-DUNOISE (LA) (23) Creuse (☎55) Map**16**C/D4

★ **Pascaud** ☎891066 rm13 Closed Oct **A**

CERNAY (68) Haut-Rhin (☎89) Map**11**B2

H **Belle-Vue** 10 r du Ml-Foch ☎754015 rm12 16Jan–14Dec & Closed Fri **A**

H **Trois Rois** 2 r de Thann ☎704054 rm11 Closed 14Jun–15Jul & Mon **A**

CHABEUIL (26) Drôme (☎75) Map**27**B3

H **Commerce** pl Genissieux ☎590023 rm21 Closed Oct1–20 **A**

◆ **Relais du Soleil** rte de Romans ☎590181 rm21 Closed 28Sep–28Oct **B**

CHAGNY (71) Saône-et-Loire (☎85) Map**10**C1

★ **Paris** 6 r de Beaune ☎870838 rm13 Feb–Dec **A**

CHAISE-DIEU (LA) (43) Haute-Loire (☎71) Map**27**A3

H **Centre** ☎000193 rm7 **A**

H **Lion d'Or** ☎000158 rm15 **A**

H **Vénéré** ☎000108 rm18 Mar–Oct **A**

CHALONS-SUR-MARNE (51) Marne (☎26) Map**10**C3

★★ **Angleterre** 19 pl mgr Tissier ☎682151 rm18 Closed 2Feb–3Mar **A**

★★ **Bristol** 77 av Pierre Semard ☎682463 rm24 **A**

★★ **Pot d'Etain** 18 pl République ☎680909 rm24 20Jan–20Dec **A**

At **Epine (L')** (8.5km E on N3)

★★ **Aux Armes de Champagne** ☎681043 rm40 Closed 16Jan–14Feb **B**

CHALON-SUR-SAÔNE (71) Saône-et-Loir (☎85) Map**10**C1

H **Gloriette** 27 r Gloriette ☎482335 rm18 **A**

H **Kiosque** 10 r des Jacobines ☎481224 rm25 **A**

H **Nouvel** 7 av Boucrcaut ☎480731 rm21 **A**

★★ **Europe** 11–13 r du Port Villiers ☎480386 rm21 **A**

★ **Laurentides** 30 Quai St-Cosme ☎482985 rm33 **A**

CHAMBON-SUR-LAC (63) Puy-de-Dôme (☎73) Map**16**D3

H **Beau Cottage** ☎866211 rm13 **A**

H **Pavilion Bleu** ☎886107 rm20 Jan–Oct & School hols **B**

CHAMONIX-MONT-BLANC (74) Haute-Savoie (☎50) Map**28**C4

H **Chamonix** ☎531107 rm14 **A**

H **Phalenes** ☎531225 rm15A

H **Vareppe** ☎530342 rm18 **A**

CHAMPAGNOLE (39) Jura (☎82) Map**10**D1

H **Franc-Comtois** 11 r Clemenceau ☎520495 rm10 **A**

H **Londaine** 23 r Baronne-Delort ☎520669 rm20 **A**

CHAMPTOCEAUX (49) Maine-et-Loire (☎40) Map**8**C2

★ **Côte** ☎835039 rm29 **A**

CHANTILLY (60) Oise (☎4) Map**9**B3/4

H **Au rendez-vous du Sport Hippique** pl de la Gare ☎4570005 rm18 **A**

H **Chateau** 22 r du Connétable ☎4570225 rm13 **A**

★ **Angleterre** 9 pl O-Vallon ☎4570059 rm20 5Jan–15Sep **A**

CHANTONNAY (85) Vendée (☎30) Map**8**C1

H **Petit Lundi** ☎313145 rm10 **A**

★ **Mouton** 31 r Nationale ☎943022 rm12 Closed Oct **A**

CHARAVINES (38) Isère (☎76) Map**27**B4

H **Beau Rivage** ☎066108 rm20 **A**

★★ **Hostellerie Lac Bleu** (1·5km N on D50) ☎066048 rm15 Mar–Oct **A**

CHARLEVILLE-MÉZIÈRES (08) Ardennes (☎24) Map**10**C4

H **Central** 23 av du Ml-Leclerc ☎333369 rm26 **A**

H **Lion d'Or** 28 av du Ml-Leclerc ☎572008 rm36 **A**

H **Meuse** 8 r d l'Epargne ☎333488 rm19 **A**

CHARMES (88) Vosges (☎29) Map**11**A3

H **Hôtel-de-Ville** 6 pl H-Breton ☎380309 rm10 Closed Fri **A**

CHAROLLES (71) Saône-et-Loire (☎85) Map**10**C1

H **France** 3 av de la Gare/12 pl du Champ-de-Foire rm20 15Jan–15Dec **A**

H **Midi** 3 rte de Genelard ☎241057 rm10 Closed 15–30Sep **A**

CHARTRES (28) Eure-et-Loire (☎37) Map**9**A3

H **Métropole** 1 r du Bourg-Neuf ☎215934 rm26 15Jan–15Dec **A**

H **St Jean** 6 r du Fbg-St-Jean ☎213569 rm17 **A**

★★ **Paris** 6 pl de la Gare ☎211013 rm12 Closed 1–15Feb & 19Aug–2Sep **A**

★ **Poste** 3 r du Gl-König BP152 ☎210427 rm56 **A**

France

CHARTE SUR-LE-LOIR (LA) (72) Sarthe
(☎43) Map**9**A2
- H **Cheval Blanc** ☎444001 rm32
  Closed Jan **A**
- ★★ **France** 20 pl de la République
  ☎444016 rm32 Closed Feb **A**

CHATEAUBRIANT (44) Loire-Atlantique
(☎40) Map**8**C2
- ★★ **Ferriere** ☎811012 rm15 **A**

CHÂTEAU CHINON (58) Nièvre (☎86)
Map**10**C1
- H **Oustalet** ☎851557 rm16
  Closed Sep **A**
- ★★ **Vieux Morvan** Ancienne Mairie
  ☎850501 rm23 10Jan–15Nov **A**

CHÂTEAUDUN (28) Eure-et-Loir (☎37)
Map**9**A2
- H **Rose** 12 r L-Licours ☎452183 rm8
  Closed Dec **A**
- H **Tour Eiffel** 2 bd Kellermann ☎452350
  rm16 **A**
- ★★ **Beauce** 50 r de Jallans ☎451475
  rm22 9Jan–18Dec **A**
- ★ **Trois Pastoureaux** 31 r A-Gillet
  ☎450162 rm10 Closed Mon & Feb **A**

CHÂTEAU-GONTIER (53) Mayenne (☎42)
Map**8**C2
- ★★ **Mirwault** ☎071317 rm10
  Feb–24Dec **A**
- ★ **Anglais** 10 pl Gare ☎071034 rm16 **A**

CHÂTEAULIN (29) Finistère (☎98) Map**7**A3
- H **Chrismas** ☎860124 rm20 **A**
- H **Voyageurs** ☎861126 rm10 **A**

At **Port Launay** (2·5km NE)
- ★ **Bon Accueil** rte de Brest ☎861577
  rm59 **A**

CHÂTEAUROUX (36) Indre (☎54) Map**9**A1
- H **Continental** 1 av de Verdun ☎343612
  rm24 **A**
- H **Unic-Bar** 112 bd de Cluis ☎222287
  rm7 Closed Jul **A**
- ★★ **France** 16 r V-Hugo ☎340080 rm44 **B**

CHÂTEAUNEUF-DU-FAOU (29) Finistère
(☎98) Map**7**B3
- H **Gai Logis** ☎817387 rm16 **A**
- H **Midi** ☎817550 rm15 **A**

CHÂTEAU-THIERRY (02) Aisne (☎23)
Map**10**C3
- ★★ **Ile de France** (3km N on N37)
  ☎831012 rm31 **A**
- ☆ **Girafe** pl A-Briand ☎830206 rm29 **A**

CHÂTELAILLON-PLAGE (17) Charente-
Maritime (☎46) Map**15**B4
- H **Jeanne d'Arc** 12 r G-Musset
  ☎461023 rm23 **A**
- H **Hostellerie du Sélect** 1 r Musset
  ☎461059 rm21 **B**
- ★ **Majestic** pl de St-Marsault ☎351014
  rm30 5Jan–20Dec **A**

CHATEL-GUYON (63) Puy-de-Dôme (☎73)
Map**16**D3
- H **Esplanade** ☎860984 rm11
  2May–Sep **A**

- H **Univers** ☎86027 rm37 **B**

At **St Hippolyte** (½km SW)
- H **Cantalou** ☎860467 rm19 **B**

CHÂTELLERAULT (86) (☎49) Map**8**D1
- H **Dupleix** 2 p Dupleix ☎213916 rm12 **A**
- H **Orée de la Forêt** RB10 (On S of town
  towards Poitiers) ☎212978 rm14 **A**
- ★★ **Escale** 17 av d'Argenson ☎211350
  rm32 **A**
- ★★ **Univers** 4 av G-Clemenceau
  ☎212353 rm30 Closed 2wks Dec **A**

CHÂTILLON-SUR-INDRE (36) Indre (☎54)
Map**16**C4
- ★ **Auberge de la Tour** ☎387217 rm10
  Feb–Dec15 **A**

CHÂTILLON-SUR-SEINE (21) Côte-d'Or
(☎80) Map**10**C2
- H **Montagne** 60 r Ml-de-Lattre-de-
  Tassigny ☎041061 rm12 **A**
- ★★ **Sylvia** 9 av de la Gare ☎910244
  rm20 **A**

CHAUMONT (52) Haute-Marne (☎27)
Map**10**D2
- H **Relais** la Maladière ☎030284 rm12 **A**
- H **Royal** 42 r L-Alphandery ☎030108
  rm16 **A**
- ★★ **Grand Val** rte de Langres ☎031590
  rm64 **A**

CHAUNAY (86) Vienne (☎49) Map**16**C4
- H **Commerce** RN10 ☎492502 rm10
  Closed Nov **A**

CHAUVIGNY (86) Vienne (☎49) Map**16**C4
- H **Chalet Fleuri** ☎463112 rm11 **A**
- ★ **Lion d'Or** 8 r Marche ☎463028 rm12
  Jan15–Dec15 **A**

CHENONCEAUX (37) Indre-et-Loire (☎47)
Map**9**A2
- ★★ **Bon Laboureur et Château** 75 rte
  Nationale ☎299002 rm26 **A**
- ★ **Roy** r Dr Bretonneau ☎299017 rm26
  Feb–Nov **A**

CHERBOURG (50) Manche (☎33) Map**8**C4
- H **Centre** 71 r au Blé ☎530224 rm14 **A**
- H **Grand-Balcon** 51 r du Ml-Foch
  ☎531041 rm15 **A**
- H **Moderna** 28 r de la Marine ☎530489
  rm23 **A**
- ★★ **Caligny** 41 r Ml-Foch ☎531024 rm46
  10Jan–15Dec **A**
- ★★ **Louvre** 28 r de la Paix ☎530228
  rm42 **A**
- ★ **Rennaissance** 4 r de l'Eglise
  ☎532306 rm14 **A**

CHINON (37) Indre-et-Loire (☎47) Map**8**D2
- H **France** 47 pl de l'Hôtel-de-Ville
  ☎930232 rm21 Closed 27Mar–Apr **A**
- ★ **Gargantua** 73 r Voltaire ☎930471
  rm16 Mar–5Nov **A**

CHITENAY (41) Loire-et-Cher (☎54)
Map**9**A2
- ♦ **Auberge du Centre** ☎792211 rm17
  Closed 1–15Jan **A**

CHOLET (49) Maine-et-Loire (☎41) Map**8**C2
 H **Cormier** rte de Mortagne ☎624624 rm14 **A**
 ★ **Boule d'Or** 49 r Commerce ☎620178 rm17 **A**

CIOTAT (LA) (13) Bouches-du-Rhone (☎91) Map**27**B1
 H **Belle Vue** ☎084358 rm12 **A**
 H **Gare** ☎084123 rm8 **A**
 H **Mare Nostrum** ☎086338 rm27 **B**

CIVRIEUX-D'AZERGUES (69) Rhône (☎78) Map**27**B4
 ★★ **Roseraie** ☎430178 rm12 Closed first two wks Sep **A**

CLAIRMARAIS see **ST OMER**

CLAMECY (58) Nievre (☎86) Map**10**C2
 H **Boule d'Or** 5 pl de Bethleém ☎271155 rm20 **B**
 H **Hostellerie de la Poste** 9 pl É-Zola ☎270155 rm15 20Jan–20Dec **A**

CLAYETTE (LA) (71) Saône-et-Loire (☎85) Map**10**C1
 H **Bourgogne** rte de Charolles ☎280216 rm10 **A**
 H **Post & Dolphin** 17 r Centrale ☎280245 rm15 20Jan–20Dec **A**

CLELLES (38) Isère (☎76) Map**27**B3
 ★★ **Ferrat** ☎344270 rm17 **A**

CLERMONT-FERRAND (63) Puy-de-Dôme (☎73) Map**27**A4
 H **Bristol** 6 r Ste-Rose ☎372565 rm30 **A**
 H **Excelsior** 12 r Lamartine ☎930374 rm39 **A**
 H **Minimes** 10 r des Minimes ☎933149 rm25 **A**
 H **Mirabeau** 37 av Union-Soviétique ☎914662 rm24 **A**
 H **Radio** 43 r P-Curie ☎358132 rm28 **A**

CLISSON (44) Loire-Atlantique (☎40) Map**8**C2
 ◆ **Auberge de la Cascade** ☎780241 rm10 Closed 3rd wk Jan **A**

CLUNY (71) Saône-et-Loire (☎85) Map**10**C1
 H **Commerce** 8 pl du Commerce ☎590309 rm15 Mar–Oct **A**
 H **Moderne** pont d l'Etang ☎590565 rm15 Closed 4Oct–2Dec **A**

COGNAC (16) Charente (☎45) Map**15**B3
 H **Cheval Blanc** 7 & 9 pl Bayard ☎820955 rm14 **A**
 H **Orleans** 44 r d'Angoulême ☎820136 rm42 **A**
 H **Tourist** 166 av V-Hugo ☎821042 rm8 Closed 9–30Aug **A**

COLLIOURE (66) Pyrénées-Orientales (☎69) Map**22**D4
 H **Bon Port** rte de Port-Vendres ☎380381 rm25 **B**
 H **Templiers** 12 r C-Pelletan ☎380406 rm52 **B**

COLMAR (68) Haut-Rhin (☎89) Map**11**B2
 M **Azur** 50 rte de Strasbourg ☎413215 rm17 **A**

 H **Chaumière** 74 av de la République ☎410899 rm16 **A**
 H **Soleil** 7 r St Éloi ☎414050 rm6 **A**

COMBEAUFONTAINE (70) Haute-Saône (☎84) Map**10**D2
 ★ **Balcon** rte de Paris ☎786234 rm17 23Jan–25Dec **A**

COMBOURG (35) Ille-et-Vilaine (☎99) Map**8**C3
 H **France & Châteaubriand** ☎730001 rm21 Closed Feb **A**
 H **Lac** ☎730565 rm25 **A**

COMMERCY (55) Meuse (☎28) Map**10**D3
 H **Paris** pl de la Gare ☎910136 rm11 **A**
 H **Stanislas** 13 r R-Grosdidier ☎911236 rm32 rest Closed Mon **B**

COMPIÈGNE (60) Oise (☎4) Map**9**B4
 H **France** 17 r E-Floquet ☎4400274 rm20 **A**
 H **Nord** 1 pl de la Gare ☎4400390 rm16 **A**

CONCARNEAU (29) Finistère (☎98) Map**7**A3
 H **Commerce** 15 av de la Gare ☎970088 rm29 Apr–Sep **A**
 H **Jockey** 11 av P-Guéguen ☎970028 rm14 Closed Nov **B**
 H **Sables Blancs** Plage des Sables Blancs ☎970139 rm48 18Mar–15Oct **B**
 ★★ **Grand** 1 av P-Guéguen ☎970028 rm33 May–Oct **B**

CONDOM (32) Gers (☎62) Map**15**B2
 H **Continental** 20 av Foch ☎280058 rm34 **B**
 H **Midi** 38 r Barlet ☎281502 rm21 **B**

CONFOLENS (16) Charente (☎45) Map**16**C3
 H **Mère Michelet** 19 allée de Blossac ☎840411 rm23 **A**
 H **Vienne** 4 r de la Ferrandie ☎840924 rm13 Closed 1–15Nov **A**

CONQUET (LE) (29) Finistère (☎98) Map**7**A3
 H **Bretagne** ☎890002 rm16 **A**

CONTREXÉVILLE (88) Vosges (☎29) Map**10**D2/3
 H **Souveraine** ☎080959 rm13 20May–15Sep **B**

COQUILLE (LA) (24) Dordogne (☎53) Map**16**C3
 ★ **Voyageurs** r de la République ☎558013 rm10 Apr–Oct **A**

CORDÉS (81) Tarn (☎63) Map**16**C/D2
 H **Parc** ☎560259 rm12 **A**
 H **Vieux Cordes** ☎560012 rm20 15Jan–Dec **A**

CORLAY (22) Côtes du Nord (☎96) Map**7**B3
 H **Jockey Breton** ☎294015 rm12 **A**

CORPS (38) Isère (☎76) Map**27**B3
 ★★ **Poste** pl de la Mairie ☎300003 rm40 **A**

COSNE-SUR-LOIRE (58) Nièvre (☎86) Map**9**B2

France

H **Moderne** 52 r du Commerce
☎281786 rm20 **A**

H **St Christophe** pl de la Gare ☎280201
rm15 Closed Feb **A**

★★ **Grand Cerf** 43 r St Jacques ☎280446
rm21 10Jan–12Dec **B**

COURSEULLES-SUR-MER (14) Calvados
(☎31) Map**8**D4

H **Belle Aurore** 32 r Foch ☎834623
rm14 **A**

H **Crémaillère** bd de la Plage rm20 **B**

COUTANCES (50) Manche (☎33)
map**8**C3/4

H **Grand** 1 av Albert 1er ☎450655
rm25 **A**

◆ **Relais du Viaduc** 25 av de Verdun
rm10 Closed 9Sep–10Oct **A**

★ **Moderne** bd Alsace-Lorraine
☎451377 rm17 Closed Feb **A**

CRESSENSAC (46) Lot (☎60) Map**16**C3

★ **Chez Gilles** RN20 ☎377006 rm19
Closed Feb **A**

CREST (26) Drôme (☎75) Map**27**B3

H **Champ-de-Mars** ☎751147 rm6 **A**

◆ **Auberge du Square** r du 8-Mai 1945
☎751511 rm20 **A**

CRIEL-SUR-MER (76) Seine-Maritime
(☎35) Map**9**A4

H **Hostellerie de la Vielle Ferme**
☎867218 rm36 7Feb–15Nov **A**

CROISIC (LE) (44) Loire-Atlantique (☎40)
Map**7**B2

H **Jonchères** 16 quai Port-Ciguet
☎230126 rm10 Apr–Oct **A**

H **Perthuy-du-Roy** pl Croix-de-Ville
☎230095 rm12 **A**

CROZON (29) Finistére (☎98) Map**7**A3

H **Aber** ☎811392 rm17 **A**

H **Moderne** ☎810010 rm18 **B**

CUISERY (71) Saône-et-Loire (☎85)
Map**10**C1

H **Hostellerie Bressane** ☎401163 rm9
Closed 11Feb–19Jun,
11Aug–19Dec **B**

DAX (40) Landes (☎57) Map**15**A/B1

H **Chez Calcos** 20pl Ml-Joffre rm11 **A**

H **Graciet** cours du Ml-Foch ☎740745
rm66 20Mar–26Nov **A**

H **Néhé** r de la F-Chaude ☎742646
rm26 **A**

H **Thiers** r du Taureau ☎742527 rm24
May–15Sep **A**

DEAUVILLE (14) Calvados (☎31) Map**8**D4

H **Marie-Ann** 142 av de la République
☎883532 rm22 **A**

H **Nid d'Été** 121 av de la République
☎883667 rm24 **B**

H **Patio** 178-180 av de la République
☎882507 rm11 **A**

H **Sports** 27 r Gambetta ☎882267
rm11 **A**

DIEPPE (76) Seine-Maritime (☎35) Map**9**A4

H **Plage** 20bd de Verdun ☎841828 rm33
Closed 12Nov–10Dec **B**

H **Richmond** 1r du Com-Fayolle
☎842733 rm17 **A**

DIGNE (04) Alpes-de-Hautes Provence
(☎92) Map**28**C2

H **Central** 26 bd Gassendi ☎313191
rm19 **A**

H **Tampinet** pl du Tampinet ☎313184
rm8 Closed Feb **A**

★★ **Aiglon** 1 r de Provence ☎310270
rm33 Feb–Nov **A**

★★ **Mistre** 65 bd Gassendi ☎310016
rm37 Closed 10Nov–10Dec **A**

DIGOIN (71) Saône-et-Loire (☎85)
Map**10**C1

H **Modern** 6 r de la Faïencerie ☎530580
rm12 **A**

★ **Gare** 79 av Gl de Gaulle ☎530304
rm12 Closed Dec **A**

DIJON (21) Côte-d'Or (☎80) Map**10**D2

H **Ducs** 5r Lamonnoye ☎326945
rm58 **A**

H **Jacquemart** 32 r Verrerie ☎324496
rm33 **A**

H **Lycée** 28 r du Lycée ☎321864 rm18 **A**

H **Monge** 20 r Monge ☎305541 rm23 **A**

H **St-Michel** 92 r Vannerie ☎322837
rm44 **A**

H **Hostellerie du Sauvage** 64 r Monge
☎413121 rm24 **A**

DINAN (22) Côtes-du-Nord (☎96) Map**8**C3

H **Consigne** 41r Carnot ☎390012
rm12 **A**

H **Printanier** L'Aublette Quévert
☎390757 rm10 **A**

DINARD (35) Ille-et-Vilaine (☎99) Map**8**C3

H **Arrivée** 5 pl de Gare ☎461305 rm12 **A**

H **Balmoral** 26 r Ml-Leclerc. ☎461697
rm33 **B**

H **Prievré** 1 pl du Gl de Gaulle ☎461374
rm6 **A**

H **Terminus** 11 pl de la Gare ☎461065
rm22 **A**

★★ **Bains** 38av George V, ☎461371
rm40 **A**

DIVONNE-LES-BAINS (01) Ain (☎50)
Map**10**D1

H **Divona** 3 r de Genève ☎5000091
rm21 **A**

H **Provençal** 9 r de Genève ☎500187
rm18 **A**

DOL DE BRETAGNE (35) Ille-et-Villaine
(☎99) Map**8**C3

★★ **Bretange** 17 pl Chateaubriand
☎480203 rm30 Closed Xmas **A**

★ **Bresche Arthur** bd Deminiac
☎480144 rm25 **A**

DOLE (39) Jura (☎82) Map**10**D1

H **Abréal** 3r de Crissey ☎720225
rm10 **A**

H **Logis Comtois** 290 av de Genève
☎722448 rm 13 **A**

H **Petit Parc** pl de la Gare ☎721382 rm19 **A**

DOMFRONT (61) Orne (☎4) Map**8**C/D3
  H **Donjon** 26r des Fossés Plisson ☎386455 rm11 Apr–25Sep **A**
  ★ **France** r Mont St-Michel ☎385144 rm22 **A**

DOMPAIRE (88) Vosges (☎29) Map**11**A2/3
  ★★ **Commerce** pl Maréchal Leclerc ☎365028 rm11 **B**

DOMRÉMY-LA-PUCELLE (88) Vosges (☎29) Map**10**D3
  ★ **Basilique** av Bois-Chenu (1.5km S by D53) ☎940781 rm28 **A**
  ★ **Pucelle** ☎940460 rm12 Jan–Oct **A**

DOUAI (59) Nord (☎20) Map**3**B1
  H **Paris** 52 pl d'Armes ☎889563 rm24 **A**
  H **Terrasse** 8 r Terrasse St-Pierre ☎887004 rm20 **A**
  ★ **Grand Cerf** 46 r St-Jacques ☎887960 rm36 **A**

DOUARNENEZ (29) Finistère (☎98) Map**7**A3
  H **Hirondelle d'Or** 29 r Croas ar Talud ☎921689 rm10 **A**
  H **Sporting** 7 r J-jaurès ☎920559 rm16 **A**

DRAGUIGNAN (83) Var (☎94) Map**28**C2
  H **Postillon** ☎680014 rm36 **A**
  H **Théâtre** ☎681576 rm10 **A**

DREUX (28) Eure (☎37) Map**9**A3
  ♦ **Colmar** 117 r du Bois-sabot ☎461864 rm23 **B**

DUNKERQUE (Dunkirk) (59) Nord (☎20) Map**3**A2
  H **Félix** 17 pl de la Gare rm24 **A**
  H **Métropole** 28 r Thiers rm17 **B**
  H **Tigre** 8 r Clemenceau rm28 **B**
  ★ **Moderne** 2 r Gambetta ☎668024 rm20 Closed 16Aug–7Sep **A**

DURAS (47) Lot-et-Garonne (☎58) Map**15**B2
  ♦ **Auberge du Chateau** pl J-Bousquet ☎937058 rm10 **A**

DURTAL (45) Maine-et-Loire (☎41) Map**8**D2
  H **Boule d'Or** ☎801020 rm8 Closed Mon **B**

ÉCHELLES (LES) (73) Savoie (☎79) Map**27**B4
  H **Centre** ☎366014 rm15 **A**

At **St Christophe La Grotte** (4km E on D520⁰)
  ♦ **Auberge St Christophe** ☎366030 rm10 Feb–Dec **A**

ECOMMOY (72) Sarthe (☎43) Map**8**D2
  ★ **Commerce** 19 pl Republique ☎271034 rm13 15Jan–15Dec **A**

ENTRAYGUES-SUR-TRUYÈRE (12) Aveyron (☎65) Map**16**D2
  H **Deux Vallées** 7 av Pont-de-Truyère rm12 **A**
  ★ **Truyère** ☎445110 rm21 Mar–Nov **A**

ÉPERNAY (51) Marne (☎26) Map**10**C3
  H **Chapon Fin** 2 pl Thiers ☎514003 rm12 **B**
  H **Progès** 6 r des Berceaux ☎512207 rm15 **A**
  H **Terrasse** 7 quai de Marne ☎513112 rm7 Closed Jan **A**
  ★ **Europe** 18 r Porte Lucas ☎518028 **A**

ÉPINAL (88) Vosges (☎29) Map**11**A2
  H **Commerce** 13–15 pl des Vosges ☎822134 rm16 **A**
  ★★ **Vosges et Terminus** pl de la Gare ☎823578 rm48 **A**
  ★ **Azur** 54 Quai des Bons Enfants ☎822915 rm20 **A**

ÉTRETAT (76) Seine-Maritime (☎35) Map**8**D4
  H **Angleterre** 35 av George-V ☎270134 rm20 **A**
  H **Welcome** 10 av de Verdun ☎270089 rm10 **A**

ÉVREUX (27) Eure (☎32) Map**9**A3
  H **Biche** 9 r Joséphine ☎390254 rm26 **A**
  H **Centre** 6 pl Clemenceau ☎393277 rm8 **A**
  ★★ **Normandy** 37 pl Dupont de L'Eure ☎331440 rm25 **B**
  ★★ **L'Orme** 13 r Lombards ☎393412 rm20 **B**

EYMOUTIERS (87) Haute-Vienne (☎55) Map**16**C3
  H **St-Psalmet** ☎691006 rm24 **B**

EYZIES-DE-TAYAC (LES) (24) Dordogne (☎53) Map**16**C2
  H **Centre** ☎069713 rm19 Closed 2Jan–15Feb **A**
  ★ **France** ☎069723 rm16 Mar–Oct **A**

EZE-BORD-DE-MER (06) Alpes Maritimes (☎93) Map**28**C2
  ★★ **Bananaraie** ☎015139 rm32 May–Sep10 **A**
  ★★ **Cap Roux** ☎015123 rm36 Mar–Sep **B**

FALAISE (14)Calvados (☎31) Map**8**D3
  ★★ **Normandie** 4 r Amiral Courbet ☎901826 rm30 **A**
  ★★ **Poste** 38 r Georges-Clemenceau ☎901314 rm22 **A**
  ★ **Belle Eppe** 1 r Gambetta ☎900529 rm12 Closed 16Aug–9Sep **A**

FAOUËT (Le) (56) Morbihan Map**7**B3
  ★ **Croix d'or** pl Bellanger ☎230733 rm16 **A**

FAVERGES (74) Haute-Savoie (☎50) Map**28**C4
  H **Alpes** ☎445005 rm18 **A**

At **Doussard** (7km NW by N508)
  ★★ **Marceau** Marceau-Dessus ☎443011 rm28 Feb–Nov **A**

FAYL-BILLOT (52) Haute Marine (☎27) Map**10**D2
  ♦ **Cheval Blanc** pl de la Barre ☎846144 rm9 **A**

France

FÉCAMP (76) Seine-Maritime (☎35)
Map**9**A4
- H **Canchy & Chariot d'Or** 10 pl Thiers
☎280028 rm23 **A**
- H **Moderne de la Gare** 3 av Gambetta
☎280404 rm15 **A**

FELLETIN (25) Creuse (☎55) Map**16**D3
- ◆ **Barbichet** ☎664022 rm11 **A**
- ◆ **Gare** ☎664104 rm15 **A**

FERTÉ-ST-AUBIN (LA) (45) Loiret (☎38)
Map**9**B2
- ★★ **Perron** 9 r de Gl-Leclerc ☎915336
rm33 **A**

FIGEAC (46) Lot (☎60) Map**16**D2
- H **Croix Blanche** ☎341366 rm10 **A**
- H **Promenade** ☎341466 rm10 **A**
- H **Terminus St Jacques** ☎340043
rm12 **A**

FIXIN (21) Côte d'Or (☎80) Map**10**C2
- H **Chez Jeannette** ☎343108 rm11
Closed early Jan **A**

FLERS (61) Orne (☎34) Map**8**D3
- H **Bretagne** 42 pl P-Duhalde ☎650185
rm13 **A**
- H **Normandie** 44 pl P-Duhalde
☎652338 rm8 **A**
- H **Oasis** 3 *bis* r de Paris/Pl C-de Gaulle
rm29 **B**

FLEURANCE (32) Gers (☎62) Map**16**C1
- H **Capelli** 43 r R-Trémoulet ☎061188
rm32 **A**
- H **Relais** 6 av des Pyrénées ☎062110
rm28 **A**

FLORAC (48) Lozère (☎66) Map**27**A3
- ★ **Gorges du Tarn** ☎450063 rm31
Etr–Sep **A**
- ★ **Parc** ☎450305 rm50 15Mar–Nov **A**

FLOTTE (LA) see **RÉ (ILE DE)**

FONTAINEBLEAU (77) Seine-et-Marne
(☎1) Map**9**B3
- ★★ **Londres** 1 pl du General de Gaulle
☎4222021 rm22 Closed Feb **B**
- ★ **Foret** av President Roosevelt
☎4223926 rm30 **A**

FONT ROMEU (66) Pyrénées-Orientales
(☎68) Map**22**C4
- H **Ermitage** RN618 ☎300002 rm32
Closed Oct & Nov **B**
- H **Villa St Paul** r Calvet ☎300992 rm25
15Feb–20Apr, 15May–15Nov **B**
- ★★ **Pyrenees** ☎300149 Jan–Apr,
Jun–Sep rm42 **B**

FORCALQUIER (04) Alpes de Haute-
Provence Map**27**B2
- H **Lavandes** ☎750029 rm15
Closed 5–31 Jan **A**
- H **Hostellerie des Quatre Reines**
☎750029 rm8 Closed Nov **A**

FORÊT-FOUESNANT (LA) (29) Finistère
(☎98) Map**7**A3
- H **Port** ☎560219 rm17 **A**
- ★ **Beauséjour** ☎560208 rm30
Apr–Sep **A**

- ★ **Esperance** ☎560135 rm30 (A18)
15Mar–25Sep **A**

FOUESNANT (29) Finistère (☎98) Map**7**A3
- ◆ **Auberge du Bon Cidre** ☎560016
rm33 **B**
- H **Orée du Bois** ☎560026 rm15 **B**

At **Pointe de Mousterlin** (6km SW by D145 &
D134)
- ★★ **Pointe Mousterlin** ☎560412
25May–20Sep rm48 **A**

FOUGÈRES (35) Ille-et-Vilaine (☎99)
Map**8**C3
- H **Bretagne** ☎993168 rm19 **A**
- ★★ **Voyageurs** 10 pl Gambetta ☎990890
rm38 Closed 6–31 Dec **A**
- ★ **Moderne** 15 r Tribunal ☎990024
rm26 **A**

FRAYSSINET (46) Lot (☎60) Map**16**C2
- ★ **La Bonne Auberge** ☎310002 rm10
Feb–11Nov **A**

FRÉJUS (83) Var (☎94) Map**28**C2
- H **Bellevue** ☎954158 rm13 **A**
- H **Nouvel** ☎953386 rm10 **A**

FRÉTEVAL (41) Loir-et-Cher (☎39) Map**9**A2
- ★ **Chalet du Loir** ☎826499 rm9
Feb–Oct **A**

FUMAY Ardennes (☎24) Map**10**C4
- H **Lion** pl de la Gare ☎369027 rm10
Closed Wed **A**
- ★★ **Roches** 28 av J-Jaurès ☎369072
rm36 Closed Feb **A**

FUMEL (47) Lot-et-Garonne (☎58)
Map**16**C2
- H **Réserve** 41 av Gambetta ☎711034
rm7 **A**

At **Condat** (2km E via D911)
- H **Rescrue** av Gambetta ☎Condat 3
rm7 **B**

GACÉ (61) Orne (☎34) Map**8**D3
- H **Hostellerie Les Champs** N138
☎355145 rm24
Closed 15Jan–16Feb **B**
- ★ **Etoile d'Or** 60 Grande Rue ☎355003
rm12 **A**

GAILLAC (81) Tarn (☎63) Map**16**C1
- H **Occitan** pl de la Gare/41 av G-
Clemenceau ☎571152 rm12 **A**
- H **Parc** sq du Parc ☎570207 rm10 **A**

GAN see **PAU**

GAP (05) Hautes-Alpes (☎92) Map**28**C3
- H **Beausoleil** pl de la République
☎511040 rm12 **A**
- H **Méridional** 1 av de Provence
☎510074 rm26 **A**
- ★★ **Fons Regina** ☎510253 rm21
Closed Oct **A**
- ★ **Poyo** pl Frederic-Euziere ☎510413
rm17 **B**

GAVARNIE (65) Haute-Pyrénées (☎62)
Map**21**B4
- H **Astazou** ☎974807 rm14
Closed 1Nov–24Dec **A**

France

H **Taillon** ☎974820 rm20
Closed 1Nov–20Dec **A**

GÉNELARD (71) Saône-et-Loire (☎85)
Map**10**C1
   H **Commerce** r Nationale ☎792087
   rm7 **A**
   H **Gare** r de la Gare ☎792058 rm18
   Closed Jan **A**

GENNES Maine-et-Loire (☎41) Map**8**D2
   ★★ **Naulets d'Anjou** ☎518188 rm15
   Mar–Oct **B**
   ★ **Hostellerie de la Loire** ☎518103
   rm11 Closed 4Jan–9Feb **A**

GERARDMER (88) Vosges (☎29) Map**11**A2
   H **Croisette** 2 bd de Colmar rm32 **A**
   H **Roméo** 57 bd Keisch ☎630090 rm17
   Closed 1Oct–15Nov **A**
   ★★ **Parc** av de la Ville de Vichy ☎630243
   rm38 (A14) Etr–15Oct & Xmas **A**
   ★ **L'Echo de Ramberchamp** ☎630227
   rm17 Closed 11Nov–19Dec **A**

GIROMAGNY (90) Territoire-de-Belfort
(☎84) Map**11**A2
   H **Sapinière** 56 r du Tilleul ☎293288
   rm7 **A**

GISORS (76) Seine Maritime (☎35) Map**9**B4
   H **Moderne** pl de la gare ☎552351 rm23
   7Jan–15Jul & 7Aug–20Dec **A**
   H **Paris-Dieppe** 15 r de Dieppe
   ☎551117 rm2 **A**

GLUGES see **MARTEL**

GOUMOIS (25) Doubs (☎81) Map**11**A2
   ◆ **Auberge Le Moulin du Plain**
   ☎444199 rm17 15Feb–15Nov **A**

GOURDON (46) Lot (☎93) Map**16**C2
   ◆ **Auberge du Plain Joly** ☎572474
   rm8 **A**

GOURNAY-EN-BRAY (76) Seine Maritime
(☎35) Map**9**B4
   H **Normandie** 21 pl Nationale ☎900108
   rm15 **A**

GRAMAT (46) Lot (☎60) Map**16**C2
   H **Europe** ☎387168 rm10 **A**
   ◆ **Quercy** ☎387268 rm15 **A**
   ◆ **Auberge Le Roulage** ☎387169 rm8
   Closed 15Jan–15Feb **A**
   ★ **Lion d'or** pl République ☎387318
   rm18 15Jan–15Nov **A**

GRANDCAMP-MAISY (14) Calvados (☎31)
Map**8**C4
   H **Grandcopaise** 84 r A-Briand
   ☎226344 rm10 Jan–Nov **A**

GRAND-PRESSIGNY (LE) Indre-et-Loire
(☎47) Map**9**A1
   ★ **Espérance** ☎949012 rm10
   Closed Jan **A**

GRANVILLE (50) Manche (☎33) Map**8**C3
   H **Bains** 19 r G-Clemenceau
   ☎501731 **A**
   H **Pirate** pl du Cours Jonville
   ☎500171 **A**
   H **Terminus** 5 pl P-Sémard ☎500205 **A**
   ★ **Gourmets** r G-Clemenceau ☎501987
   rm20 **A**

GRASSE (06) Alpes-Maritimes (☎93)
Map**28**C2
   H **Aigle** 33 bd du Jeu-de-Ballon
   ☎360324 rm20 **A**
   H **Mon Repos** Terrasse Tressemannes
   ☎361067 rm13 **A**
   H **Napoléon** 6 av Thiers ☎360587
   rm16 **A**

GRENOBLE (38) Isère (☎76) Map**27**B3
   H **Beau Soleil** 9 r des Bons Enfants
   ☎442940 rm23 **A**
   H **Montfleury** 6 r E-Delacroix ☎420659
   rm11 **B**
   H **Lux** 6 r Crépu ☎444189 rm27 **B**
   H **Victoria** 17 r Thiers ☎440636 rm25 **B**
   ★★ **Alpazur** 64 av Alsace-Lorraine
   ☎444280 rm30 **A**
   ★★ **Paris-Nice** 61 bd J-Vallier ☎963618
   rm29 **A**

GRISOLLES (82) Tarn-et-Garonne (☎63)
Map**16**C1
   ★★ **Relais des Garrigues** ☎303159 rm27
   25Jan–Nov & Xmas **B**

GUÉRET (23) Creuse (☎55) Map**16**D4
   H **Bon Coin** 35 pl Bonnyaud ☎520282
   rm12 **A**
   H **Globe** pl du Marché ☎520200 rm11 **A**
   ★★ **St François** 31 pl Bonnyaud ☎524976
   rm30 **A**

GUÉTHARY (64) Pyrénées-Atlantiques
(☎59) Map**20**C3
   ★★ **Juzan** ☎265009 rm28 Jun–Sep **A**
   ★★ **Marienia** ☎265104 rm14 Jun–Sep **A**

GUINGAMP (22) Côtes du Nord (☎96)
Map**7**B3
   H **Escale** ☎437219 rm16 **A**
   H **France** ☎437616 rm20 **A**

GUJAN-MESTRAS (33) Gironde (☎56)
Map**15**B2
   H **Pyrénées** 83 cours de la République
   ☎660246 rm9 Closed Nov **A**

HAGUENAU (67) Bas-Rhin (☎88) Map**11**B3
   H **Étoile** 46 rte de Marienthal ☎938925
   rm11 16Jan–23Dec Closed Mon **A**
   H **Kaiserhof** 119 Grand-Rue ☎934981
   rm11 9Feb–29May & 14Jun–23Jan
   Closed Tue **A**

HAVRE (LE) (76) Seine-Maritime (☎35)
Map**8**D4
   H **Atlantic** 14 r F-Arago ☎480873
   rm13 **A**
   H **Bauza** 15 r G-Braque ☎422727
   rm18 **B**
   H **France** 85 r L-Brindeau ☎429873
   rm17 **A**
   H **Paris** 81 quai George-V ☎428218
   rm16 **A**
   ★★ **Ile de France** 104 r Anatole France
   ☎424929 rm17 **A**
   ★★ **Monaco** 16 r de Paris ☎422101 rm11
   Closed Feb **A**
   ★ **Petit Vatel** 86 r L-Brindeau ☎428510
   rm28 **A**

HAYE-DU-PUITS (LA) (50) Manche (☎33)
Map**8**C4

131

France

H **Croix Blanche** 2 r du Docteur-Gallegari ☎460122 rm12 **A**
★ **Gare** ☎460422 rm11 10Jan–8Feb **A**

HENDAYE (64) Pyrénées-Atlantiques (☎59) Map**19**B3

H **Irrintzina** 6& 8 bd Gl-Leclerc ☎267455 rm21 13May–1Oct **A**
H **Sud-Américan** r d'Othaz ☎267598 rm11 11Apr–Sep **A**

At **Hendaye-Plage** (½km N)

H **Ondaraitz** 59 bd Leclerc ☎267073 rm26 Feb–Sep **B**
H **Valencia** 29 bd de la Mer ☎267725 rm20 **B**

HESDIN (62) Pas de Calais (☎71) Map**3**A1

H **Flandres** 22 r d'Arras ☎068021 rm18 **A**

At **Marconne** (2km S on N28)

H **3 Fontaines** rte d'Abbeville ☎068165 rm10 **A**

HOHWALD (LE) (67) Bas-Rhin (☎88) Map**11**B3

♦ **Pension Hazemann** ☎083060 rm8 **A**

HONFLEUR (14) Calvados (☎31) Map**8**D4

H **Belvédère** 36 rte E-Renouf ☎890813 rm10 **B**
H **Hostellerie Lechat** pl Ste-Catherine ☎890813 rm26 Closed 20Nov–17Dec **B**

HOSSEGOR (40) Landes (☎57) Map**15**A1

H **Côte d'Argent** av du Touring Club ☎720182 rm13 **A**
H **Plage** Grande-Plage ☎720012 rm26 Apr–15Sep **A**
H **Pomme de Pin** av de la Grande-Dune rm12 Feb–20Sep **A**

HOUCHES (LES) (74) Haute-Savoie (☎50) Map**28**C4

H **Mont Blanc** ☎544002 rm19 Closed 20Apr–15Jun & 15Sep–20Dec **A**
★★ **Piste Bleue** rte Les Chavants ☎544066 rm25 15Dec–Etr & 15Jun–20Sep **A**

HOULGATE (14) Calvados (☎31) Map**8**D4

H **Chemin de Fer** pl de la Gare ☎910847 rm16 **B**
H **Plage** 99–101 r des Bains ☎910909 rm10 **A**

ISIGNY-SUR-MER (14) Calvados (☎31) Map**8**C4

★★ **France** 17 r Demagny ☎220033 rm20 Feb–Nov **A**

ISSOIRE (63) Puy-de-Dôme (☎73) Map**27**A4

H **Terminus** ☎892234 rm15 **A**
★★ **Pariou** 18 bd Kennedy ☎892211 rm29 **A**

ITXASSOU (64) Pyrénées-Atlantiques (☎59) Map**20**C3

H **Fronton** ☎257510 rm13 Apr–Sep **A**
H **Txistulari** ☎257509 rm16 **A**

JOINVILLE (52) Haute-Marne (☎27) Map**10**D3

★★ **Grand Pont** r á Briand ☎960986 rm27 (A16) **A**

★ **Poste** pl Greve ☎961263 rm12 Closed 16Jan–14Feb **A**
★ **Soleil d'Or** 9 r des Capucin ☎961566 rm12 **A**

JOUGNE (25) Doubs (☎81) Map**11**A1

H **Europe** ☎891155 rm11 Closed 15Sep–15Dec **A**
H **Suchet** ☎891038 rm16 **B**
★ **Deux Saisons** ☎891386 rm21 15Jun–20Sep & 15Dec–25Apr **A**

JUAN-LES-PINS (06) Alpes-Maritimes (☎93) Map**28**C2

H **Casino** av Gallice ☎610084 rm17 **A**
H **Central** av Docteur-Dautheville ☎610943 rm25 **A**
★★ **Emeraude** av Saramartel ☎610967 rm20 Etr–Oct **A**
★★ **Noailles** av Georges-Gallice ☎611170 rm22 Jun–Sep **A**
★ **Midi** 93 bd Poincare ☎613516 rm18 Jan–Oct **A**

JULLOUVILLE (50) Manche (☎33) Map**8**C3

H **Grand Pins** Route départementale ☎618163 rm17 Mar–Sep **A**

LA Each place name beginning with La is listed under the name which follows it.

LACANAU-OCÉAN (33) Gironde (☎56) Map**15**B3

H **Étoile d'Argent** pl E-Faugères ☎602107 rm23 **A**

At **Le Moutchic** (5.5km E by D6)

H **Moutchico** ☎600005 rm10 Feb–Sep **A**

LACAUNE (81) Tarn (☎63) Map**16**D1

H **Fusies** 2 r République ☎507203 rm70 20Jan–20Dec **A**
H **Glacier** 4 pl de la Vierge ☎507328 rm22 **A**

LAFFREY (38) Isère (☎76) Map**27**B3

★★ **Grand Lac** ☎681290 rm20 **A**

LALINDE (24) Dordogne (☎53) Map**16**C2

H **Château** 1 r de Verdun ☎610182 rm10 Apr–Oct **A**
★★ **Residence** 3 r Prof Testut ☎610181 rm11 Etr–Oct **A**

LAMBALLE (22) Côtes-su-Nord (☎96) Map**7**B3

★★ **Angleterre** bd Jobert ☎310016 rm35 (A13) **A**
★ **Tour d'Argent** 2 r de Dr Lavergue ☎310137 rm15 **A**

LANDERNEAU (29) Finistère (☎98) Map**7**A3

H **Raould** ☎850079 rm22 **A**

LANGOGNE (48) Lozère (☎66) Map**27**A3

H **Gaillard** rte de Puy ☎330005 rm21 Feb–15Sep **A**
H **Luxembourg** pl de la Gare ☎330011 rm12 **A**

LANGON (33) Gironde (☎56) Map**15**B2

H **Chantilly** 24 r-Pasteur ☎631195 rm16 **A**
H **Midi Modern** 3 pl du Gl-de-Gaulle ☎630665 rm14 **B**

LANGRES (52) Haute-Marne (☎27)
Map**10**D2
- ★★ **Europe** 23 r Diderot ☎851088 rm28
  Closed Oct **A**
- ★★ **Lion d'Or** rte de Vesoul ☎850330
  rm17 Closed Feb **B**
- ★ **Cheval Blanc** ☎850700 rm20
  Mar–Dec **A**

LANNEMEZAN (65) Hautes-Pyrénées
(☎62) Map**15**B1
- H **Gare** 269 av de la Gare ☎980010
  rm50 **A**
- H **Hostellerie du Pont d'Espagne** r du
  8-Mai-1945 ☎980152 rm10 **A**

LANNION (22) Côtes du Nord (☎96)
Map**7**B3
- H **Arrivée** ☎370067 rm12 **A**
- H **Terminus** ☎370367 rm16 **B**

LANSLEBOURG (73) Savoie (☎79)
Map**28**C3
- H **Vieille Poste** ☎052257 rm17 **A**
- ★★ **L'Etoile des Neiges** ☎050041 rm20
  15Jun–15Sep & 15Dec–15Apr **B**
- ★ **Relais de Deux Cols** 73 Val Cenis 73
  ☎052341 rm20 May–Sep **A**

LAON (02) Aisne (☎23) Map**10**C4
- H **Trois Provinces** 2 av Carnot
  ☎230611 rm12 **A**
- ★★ **Angleterre** 10 bd Lyon ☎230462
  rm30 **B**
- ★ **Banniere de France** 11 r de Franklin
  Roosevelt ☎232144 rm18
  10Jan–20Dec **A**

LA PALISSE (03) Allier (☎70) Map**27**A4
- ★ **Galland** 20 pl de la République
  ☎990721 rm12 **A**

LARAGNE (05) Hautes-Alpes (☎92)
Map**27**B2/3
- ★ **Terrasses** av Provence ☎650854
  rm17 May–Oct **A**

LARCENAC-ST-VINCENT see **LAVOUTE-
SUR-LOIRE**

LAUMES (LES) (21) Côte-d'Or (☎80)
Map**10**C2
- ★★ **Gare** ☎960046 rm26 **A**

LAVAL (53) Mayenne (☎43) Map**8**C3
- H **Gerbe de Blé** 83 r V-Boissel ☎531410
  rm12 Closed Mon & Aug **A**
- H **Poste** 19 r du Vieux-St-Louis
  ☎531957 rm22 Closed Wed **A**
- H **St-Pierre** 95 av R-Buron ☎530610
  rm14 Closed Sat in season **A**
- H **Voyageurs** 70 r Magenta ☎531511
  rm10 5Jan–30Jun & 20Jul–20Dec **A**

LAVANDOU (LE) (83) Var (☎94) Map**28**C1
- H **Neptune** ☎710101 rm35 **A**
- H **St Clair** ☎710024 rm11 Etr–15Oct **A**
- ★ **Petite Boheme** av Franklin Roosevelt
  ☎711030 rm16 Whitsun–Sep **A**

LAVAUR (81) Tarn (☎63) Map**16**C1
- H **Central** 7 A-Lorraine ☎580416
  rm14 **A**

LAVOUTE-SUR-LOIRE (43) Haute Loire
(☎71) Map**27**A3

At **Larcenac St Vincent** (3km N on D103)
- ★ **Relais** ☎085109 rm10 **A**

LE Each place name beginning with Le is
listed under the name which follows it.

LES Each place name beginning with Les is
listed under the name which follows it.

LESPARRE-MEDOC (33) Gironde (☎56)
Map**15**B3
- H **Paris** 16 cours du Gl-de-Gaulle
  ☎410022 rm10 **A**

LESSAY (50) Manche (☎33) Map**8**C4
- H **Normandie** 3 pl St Cloud ☎464111
  rm10 **A**
- ★ **Abbaye** pl St Cloud ☎464388 rm12 **A**

LIBOURNE (33) Gironde (☎56) Map**15**B2/3
- H **Moulin Blanc** 132 av G-Clemenceau
  ☎510666 rm8 **A**
- H **Parc** 109 av Gallieni ☎511842 rm12 **A**

LILLE (59) Nord (☎20) Map**3**B1
- H **Bourse** 23 r Lepelletier ☎554101
  rm24 **B**
- H **Chopin** 4 r de Tournai ☎553450
  rm31 **A**
- H **Liberty** 10 r B-Monnoyer ☎573116
  rm18 **A**
- H **Paris-Nord** 16 r du Molinel ☎552520
  rm35 **A**
- H **Regina** 139 bd de la Liberté ☎574895
  rm14 **A**

LILLERS (62) Pas-de-Calais Map**3**A1
- ★ **Commerce** 50 pl de la Gare ☎022077
  rm10 Closed Aug **A**

LIMOGES (87) Haute-Vienne (☎55)
Map**16**C3
- H **Barbès** 37 r A-Barbès ☎773172
  rm18 **A**
- H **Familia** 18 r du Gl-du-Bessal
  ☎775140 rm18 **A**
- H **Paris** 5 cours Vergniaud ☎773982
  rm33 **A**
- ◆ **Toulouse** 22 av G-Dumas ☎325913
  rm12 **A**

LIMONEST (69) Rhône (☎78) Map**27**B4
- H **Platane** 36 Grande-Rue ☎351210
  rm14 **A**
- H **Puy-d'Or** RN6 ☎351220 rm8
  Closed Nov **A**

LION-SUR-MER (14) Calvados (☎31)
Map**8**D4
- H **Moderne** 3 bd P-Doumer ☎972048
  rm14 Apr–Sep **B**
- H **Plage** r É-Belin ☎972166 rm4
  30May–10Sep **A**

LISIEUX (14) Calvados (☎31) Map**8**D4
- H **Condorcet** 26 r Condorcet ☎620002
  rm21 **A**
- H **Ouest** 34 r de la Gare ☎310143
  rm28 **A**
- H **Paix** 11 r Lecouturier ☎620413
  rm22 **A**

LOCHES (37) Indre-et-Loire (☎47) Map**9**A2
- H **Palais** 2-4 pl de Verdun ☎590116
  rm12 15Jan–15Dec **A**
- ★★ **Barbe Bleue** Bridore ☎947269 rm12
  Closed mid Feb–Mar **A**

France

★ **France** 6r Picois ☎590032 rm23
Closed 16Nov–14Dec **A**

LOCQUIREC (29) Finistère (☎98) Map**7**B3
H **Armorique** ☎674006 rm60
Apr–20Dec **B**

LODÈVE (34) Hérault (☎67) Map**27** A2
★★ **Croix Blanche** ☎441087 rm32
Apr–Nov **A**
★ **Nord** 18 bd de la Liberté ☎441008
rm21 Closed Nov **A**

LONGEAU (52) Haute Marne (☎25)
Map**10**D2
H **Escale** ☎844259 rm13 Feb–Oct **B**

LORIENT (56) Morbihan (☎97) Map**7**B2/3
H **Arvor** 104 r L-Carnot ☎210755
rm20 **A**
H **Lion d'Orient** 99 r L-Roche ☎643114
rm11 **B**
H **Royal** 8*bis* r Turenne ☎210764
rm15 **A**
H **Trois Poussins** 40 r de Verdun
☎644829 rm13 Closed Jun & Jul **A**

LOUDUN (86) Vienne (☎49) Map**8**D2
H **Hostellerie de la Rove d'Or** 1 av
d'Anjou ☎220123 rm15 **B**
H **Jockey Bar** 60 r Porte-de-Chinon
☎221296 rm10 **A**

LOURDES (65) Hautes-Pyrénées (☎62)
Map**15**B1
H **Albret** 21 pl du Champ-Commun
☎941179 rm25 **B**
H **Aquitaine** 1 r des Pyrénées ☎942031
rm25 **A**
H **Béarn** 23 av de la Gare ☎942540
rm12 **A**
H **Café de la Gare** 24 av de la Gare
☎942510 rm20 **A**
H **Lorus** 7 av A-Marqui ☎942508
rm22 **A**
H **Nevers** 13 av Maransin ☎942605
rm39 **A**

LUC (LE) (83) Var (☎94) Map**28**C2
★ **Hostellerie du Parc** 1 r Jean-Jaures
☎735001 rm10 **A**

LUCHON (31) Haute-Garonne (☎61)
Map**21**B4
H **Bon Accueil** 1 pl du Ml-Joffre
☎790220 rm38 **A**
H **Marcel** 32 allée d'Étigny ☎790136
rm18 **A**
H **Petit Auberge** 15 r Lamartine
☎790288 rm31 **A**
★★ **Bains** 75 Allées d'Étigny ☎790058
rm52 Closed 21Oct–19Dec **B**

LUCON (85) Vendée (☎30) Map**8**C1
★ **Croissant** 1 pl des Acacias ☎561115
rm40 Closed Oct **A**

LUNÉVILLE (54) Meurthe-et-Moselle (☎28)
Map**11**A3
H **Central & des Vosges** 6 r Carnot
☎730050 rm45 Restaurant
Closed Mon **A**
H **Rivolet** 25 r Carnot ☎731020 rm13 **A**

LURE (70) Haute-Saône (☎84) Map**11**A2
H **Commerce** 40 r de la Gare ☎301263
rm16 **A**
H **Pomme d'Or** 75 av de la République
☎300531 rm10 **A**

LUSIGNAN (86) Vienne (☎49) Map**15**B4
H **Laurier Vert** 12 av de Poitiers
☎433091 rm12 Closed Tue **A**
♦ **Promenades** 19 rte de Poitiers
☎433135 rm10 **A**

LUS-LA-CROIX-HAUTE (26) Drôme (☎75)
Map**27**B3
H **Pervenches** ☎585032 rm10 **A**
★ **Touring** off N75 ☎585001 rm17
Apr–Oct **A**

LUXEUIL-LES-BAINS (70) Haute-Saône
(☎84) Map**11**A2
H **Ermitage** 21 r M-Donjon ☎401564
rm26 **A**
H **France** r du Parc ☎401390 rm19 **B**
★★ **Beau Site** 18 r Thermes ☎401467
rm44 **A**

LUZY (58) Nièvre (☎86) Map**10**C1
H **Centre** 26 r République ☎300155
rm11 **A**
H **Gare** 3 av de la Gare ☎300403 rm8 **A**

LYON (69) Rhône (☎78) Map**27**B4
See also Limonest
The number in brackets following the address
is the arrondissement number
H **Angleterre** 22 pl Carnot (2) ☎375548
rm85 **A**
H **Atlantic** 13 cours de Verdun (2)
☎370707 rm30 **B**
H **Celtic** 5 pl St-Paul (5) ☎280112
rm39 **B**
H **Lafayette** 13 r F-Garcin (3) ☎604459
rm24 **A**
H **National** 15 cours de Verdun (2)
☎375349 rm30 **A**
H **Pasteur** 17 r-Pasteur (7) ☎722808
rm16 **A**
H **St Étienne** 22 r Jarente (2) ☎370192
rm18 **A**
H **Stella** 127 r Vendôme (6) ☎245389
rm17 **A**
H **Veubecour** 28 r Vaubecour (2)
☎374491 rm17 **A**

At **Bron** (7km SE on N6 Grenoble rd)
♦ **Relais d L'Aviation** 314 av F-
Roosevelt ☎260810 rm22 **A**

At **St-Fons** (5km S on N7 Vienne rd)
H **Moderne** 2 r M-Berthetot ☎250155
rm2 **A**

At **Tassin-La-Demi-Lune** (3km W on N7
Roanne rd)
H **Levant** 64 av C-de-Gaulle ☎341424
rm14 **A**

MACHEVAZ see **SEVRIER**

MÂCON (71) Saône-et-Loire (☎85)
Map**10**C1
H **Relais Fleuri** 29 r des Minimes
☎383602 rm20 **A**
H **Savoie** 87 r Rambuteau ☎384222
rm20 **A**

France

★★ **Geneve** 1 r Bigonnet ☎381810
rm61 **A**

★ **Charollais** 71 r Rambuteau ☎383623
rm12 **A**

MAGESCQ Landes (☎58) Map**15**A1/2
★★ **Relais de la Poste** ☎577025 rm16
Closed 20Oct–12Nov **B**

MALÈNE (LA) (48) Lozère (☎66) Map**27**A3
H **Embarcadère** ☎475103 rm14
Mar26–Sep30 **A**

MAMERS (72) Sarthe (☎43) Map**8**D3
★ **Croix Blanche** 2 r Dalliu ☎976263
rm7 **A**

MANDELIEU (06) Alpes-Maritimes (☎93)
Map**28**C2
H **Bagatelle** ☎479169 rm15 **A**
★ **Pavillion des Sports** ☎479086 rm11
Closed Nov–Dec19 **B**

MANS (LE) (72) Sarthe (☎43) Map**8**D2
H **Commerce** 41 bd de la Gare
☎852160 rm30 **A**
H **Galaxie** 39 bd de la Gare ☎850320
rm38 **A**
H **Pommeraie** rte de l'Éventail ☎843832
rm35 **A**
★★ **Central** 5 bd Rene Levasseur
☎240893 rm50 **B**

MARENNES (17) Charente-Maritime (☎46)
Map**15**B3
◆ **France** 8 & 10 r de la République
☎850037 rm7 **A**

MARKSTEIN (LE) (68) Haut-Rhin (☎89)
Map**11**A2
★ **Bellevue** ☎826182 rm16 **A**

MARMANDE (47) Lot-et-Garonne (☎58)
Map**15**B2
H **Lion d'Or** 1 r de la République
☎642190 rm19 **A**
H **Paris** 5 bd Meyneil ☎642250 rm16 **A**

MARSEILLE (13) Bouches-du-Rhône (☎91)
Map**27**B2
The number in brackets following the address
is the arrondissement number
H **Européen** 115–117 r Paradis (6)
☎377720 rm43 **B**
H **Fortia** 32 r Fortia (1) ☎333375 rm11 **A**
H **Glaris** 1 pl des Marseillaises (1)
☎391907 rm15 **A**
H **Méridional** 6 r Glandevès (1)
☎332747 rm23 **A**
H **Nady** 157 cours Lieutaud (6)
☎487021 rm19 **A**
H **Sablier** 72 av de Mazargues (8)
☎778185 rm15 **A**

MARNAY (70) Haute Saone (☎84) Map**10**D2
H **Commerce** 64 Grande-Rue ☎0–25
rm13 Closed 20Sep–20Oct **A**

MARTEL (46) Lot (☎60) Map**16**C2
H **Turenne** ☎373030 rm12
15Feb–15Dec **B**

At **Gluges** (5km SE on N681)
★★ **Falaises** ☎373359 rm17
Feb–15Dec **A**

MARTIGUES (13) Bouches-du-Rhône (☎91)
Map**27**B2
H **Lido** ☎070032 rm19 **B**
H **Provencal** ☎804916 rm18 **A**

MARVEJTOLS (48) Lozère (☎66) Map**16**D2
H **Gare** ☎321058 rm30 **A**
★ **Paix** 2 av de Brazza ☎321017 rm27 **B**

MASSAT (09) Ariège (☎61) Map**22**C4
★★ **Hostellerie Trois Seigneurs**
av de St Girons ☎669589 rm25 (A20)
Mar–Oct **A**

MASSIAC (15) Cantal (☎71) Map**16**D3
H **Mairie** ☎230251 rm27
Closed 14Nov–16Dec **B**
★★ **Poste** av de Clermont Ferrand (N9)
☎230201 rm37 15Mar–10Nov **A**

MATHA (17) Charente-Maritime (☎46)
Map**15**B3
H **Modern** pl Sanson ☎335011 rm13 **A**

MAULÉON-LICHARRE (64) Pyrénées
Atlantiques (☎59) Map**20**C3
★★ **Bidegain** 13 r de la Navarre ☎281605
rm30 15Jan–15Dec **A**

MAURIAC (15) Cantal (☎71) Map**16**D3
H **Central** ☎680190 rm26 **A**
H **Écu de France** ☎680075 rm26 **A**
H **Voyageurs & Bonne Auberge**
☎680101 rm20 **A**

MAURS (15) Cantal (☎71) Map**16**D2
H **Périgord** ☎490425 rm20 **B**
H **Plaisance** ☎490247 rm10 **A**

MEAUX (77) Seine-et-Marne (☎1) Map**9**B3
★★ **Sirene** 34 Gl-Leclerc ☎4340780
rm16 **A**

MEGÈVE (74) Haute-Savoie (☎50)
Map**28**C4
H **Croix de Savoie** ☎210590 rm12 **A**
H **Marmotte** ☎212449 rm20 **A**
H **Sévigné** ☎212309 rm7 **A**

MELLE (79) Deux-Sèvres (☎48) Map**15**B4
H **Central** 5 pl R-Groussard ☎270111
rm14 Closed 16Sep–3Oct **A**
H **Voyageurs** 12 av Cdt-Bernier
☎270053 rm12
Closed 15Aug–5Sep **A**

MELUN (77) Seine-et-Marne (☎1) Map**9**B3
H **Bruxelles** 19 r R-Pouteau ☎4371849
rm23 **A**
H **Commerce** 16 r Carnot ☎4370122
rm16 **B**

MENDE (48) Lozère (☎66) Map**27**A3
H **Gévaudan** r Aigues-Basses ☎651474
rm10 **A**
H **Pont-Roupt** av du 11-Novembre
☎650143 rm19
Closed 10Jan–20Feb **A**
★★ **France** 9 bd L-Arnault ☎650004
rm28 **A**

MENTON (06) Alpes-Maritimes (☎93)
Map**28**C2
H **Céline-Rose** 57 av de Sospel
☎357469 rm36 **A**

135

France

H **Edward's** 7–9 av Riviéra ☎357479 rm28 **A**

H **Résidence Menton** 6 r P-Morillot ☎358310 rm11 **A**

H **New York** av K-Mansfield ☎357869 rm17 **A**

★★ **Londres** ☎357462 rm26 Jan–15Oct **A**

★★ **Rives d'Azur** Prom Ml–Joffre ☎357209 rm36 **A**

MERDRIGNAC (22) Côtes du Nord (☎96) Map**7**B3

H **Madeleine** ☎284078 rm13 **A**

METZ (57) Moselle (☎87) Map**11**A3

H **Bristol** 7 r Lafayette ☎622748 rm64 **A**

H **Centre** 14 r Dupont-des-Loges ☎751057 rm15 **A**

H **Café de Paris** 67 pl St-Louis ☎755067 rm10 **A**

H **Terminus** 13 r Lafayette ☎682415 rm43 **A**

MEYRARGUES (13) Bouches-du-Rhône (☎91) Map**27**B2

H **Cigale** ☎575012 rm19 **A**

MEYRUEIS (48) Lozère (☎66) Map**27**A2

H **Terrasse** ☎456024 rm15 Apr–Oct **A**

MÉZILHAC (07) Ardèche (☎75) Map**27**A3

H **Cévennes** ☎1 rm22 2Jan–16Dec **A**

MIGENNES (89) Yonne (☎86) Map**10**C2

H **Escale & de la Gare** pl E-Laporte ☎802099 rm12 **A**

★★ **Paris** 57 av J-Jaurès ☎802322 rm10 **A**

MILLAU (12) Aveyron (☎65) Map**16**D2

H **Commerce** 8 pl du Mandarous ☎600056 rm11 **A**

H **Terminus** 18 r A-Merle ☎600136 rm23 **A**

★★ **Moderne** 11 av J-Jaurès ☎600123 rm45 15Mar–Sep **A**

★ **Causses** 26 av J-Jaurès ☎600319 rm24 **A**

MIMIZAN-PLAGE (40) Landes (☎58) Map**15**A2

On the North Beach

H **Forêt** 39 av M-Martin ☎090906 rm17 **A**

H **France** 18 av de la Côte-de-Argent ☎090901 rm17 19Mar–15Oct **A**

On the South Beach

H **Parc** 6 r de Papeterie ☎091074 rm15 **B**

MIRAMBEAU (17) Charente-Maritime (☎46) Map**15**B3

★ **Union** Rue-Principale ☎496164 rm14 (A2) **A**

MIREPOIX (09) Ariège (☎61) Map**22**C4

★ **Commerce** Cours du Docteur-Chabaud ☎681029 rm32 Closed 1–20Oct **A**

MODANE (73) Savoie (☎79) Map**28**C3

H **France** ☎052346 rm15 **A**

H **Maurienne** ☎050302 rm19 **A**

MOISSAC (82) Tarn-et-Garonne (☎63) Map**16**C2

H **Hôtel-Restaurant Bon Accueil** 1 av M-Cugnat ☎040504 rm8 Closed 15Oct–15Nov **A**

H **Terminus** l av de Gascogne ☎040209 rm20 **A**

★ **Pont Napoleon** ☎040155 rm20 Closed Nov–15Dec **A**

MONESTIER-DE-CLERMONT (38) Isère (☎76) Map**27**B3

H **Gare** ☎340087 rm10 **A**

H **Modern** ☎340735 rm23 Closed 1Nov–20Dec **A**

MONTARGIS (45) Loiret (☎38) Map**9**B2

H **Central** 2 r Gudin ☎850307 rm16 **A**

H **Cheval Blanc** 22 r J-Jaurès ☎852265 rm14 **A**

H **Bon Gîte** 21 bd Chinchon ☎853101 rm31 **B**

MONTAUBAN (82) Tarn-et-Garonne (☎63) Map**16**C2

★★ **Midi** 12 r Notre-Dame ☎631723 rm62 **A**

★ **Languedoc** fbg Toulousain 98 ☎633215 rm14 **A**

★ **Orsay** Face Gare ☎630057 rm30 Closed 1–20Jun **A**

MONTBARD (21) Côte-d'Or (☎80) Map**10**C2

H **Côte d'Or** 26 r Carnot ☎920177 rm18 **A**

MONTBRUN-LES-BAINS (26) Drôme (☎75) Map**27**B2

H **Voyageurs** ☎34 rm8 **A**

MONTCEAU-LES-MINES (71) Saône-et-Loire (☎85) Map**10**C1

H **Epoque** 4 r Blanqui ☎090946 rm9 **A**

H **Nord** 13 r du 11-Novembre 1918 rm12 **A**

MONT-DE-MARSAN (40) Landes (☎58) Map**15**B2

H **Midou** 12 Porte-Campet ☎752426 rm10 **A**

H **Sablar** pl J-Jaurès ☎752111 rm68 **B**

MONT-DORE (LE) (63) Puy-de-Dôme (☎73) Map**16**D3

H **Mouflons** ☎210290 rm20 **A**

H **Ventadour** ☎210044 rm23 **A**

At Pied du Sancy (4km S on N683)

★★ **Puy Ferrand** ☎210258 rm43 Closed Oct–14Dec **A**

MONTÉLIMAR (26) Drôme (☎75) Map**27**B3

H **Cévennol** 6 av du Teil ☎012831 rm11 **A**

H **Expo-Route** rte de Valence ☎081375 rm14 **A**

H **St-Gaucher** 20 r St-Gaucher ☎018820 rm10 **B**

H **Tricastin** 3 r A-Ducatez ☎013208 rm10 **A**

MONTFORT-SUR-MEU (35) Ille-et-Vilaine (☎99) Map**8**C3

◆ **Relais de la Cane** ☎090007 rm16 Closed 15–30Aug **A**

MONTIER-EN-DER (52) Haute Marne (☎25) Map**10**C3

◆ **Auberge de Puisie** 22 pl de l'Hotel-de-Ville ☎042318 **A**

MONTIGNAC (24) Dordogne (☎53) Map**16**C3

  ★ **Soleil d'Or** 16 r IV-Septembre ☎518022 rm24 Closed 26Nov–26Dec **A**

MONTLUÇON (03) Allier (☎70) Map**16**D4

  H **Écu** ☎050288 rm21 **A**

  H **Gare** ☎005008 rm25 **A**

  H **Idéal** ☎050977 rm11 **B**

MONTMARTIN-SUR-MER (50) Manche (☎33) Map**8**C3

  H **Hotellerie du Bon Vieux Temps** ☎475444 rm21 **A**

MONTMIRAIL (51) Marne (☎26) Map**10**C3

  ★ **Vert Galant** 2 pl Vert-Galant ☎422017 rm14 Closed Feb **A**

MONTMORILLON (86) Vienne (☎49) Map**16**C4

  H **Berry** 34 bd Gambetta ☎911224 rm16 **A**

  H **Palais** 6 pl Ml-Leclerc ☎910954 rm14 **A**

MONTOIRE-SUR-LE-LOIR (41) Loir-et-Cher (☎39) Map**9**A2

  ★★ **Cheval Rouge** pl Ml-Foch ☎870705 rm17 Closed Feb **A**

MONTPELLIER (34) Hérault (☎67) Map**27**A2

  H **Edouard VII** 10 r A-Olivier ☎584213 rm47 **A**

  H **Fauvettes** 8 r Bonnard ☎631760 rm17 **A**

  H **Littoral** r A-France ☎922810 rm8 **A**

  H **Nova** 8 r Richelieu ☎725756 rm16 **A**

  H **Relais** 6 r Baudin ☎584080 rm16 **B**

MONTREUIL-SUR-MER (62) Pas-de-Calais (☎21) Map**3**A1

  ★ **Chez Edouard** 7–9 rde Change ☎061033 rm10 Closed Oct **A**

MONTRICHARD (41) Loir-et-Cher (☎39) Map**9**A2

  H **Gare** 20 av de la Gare ☎320436 rm9 **A**

  ★★ **Tête-Noir** rte de Tours ☎320555 rm42 Closed Jan **A**

MONT-ST-MICHEL (LE) (50) Manche (☎33) Map**8**C3

  H **Confiance** Grand-Rue ☎601407 rm18 15Jan–15Nov **A**

  H **Mouton Blanc** ☎601408 rm20 Closed 5Jan–5Feb **A**

  H **Vieille Auberge** ☎601434 rm4 **A**

  ★★ **Mère Poulard** ☎601401 rm28 Etr–Sep **A**

MONTSALVY (15) Cantal (☎71) Map**16**D2

  ◆ **Auberge Fleurie** ☎492002 rm17 Restaurant closed 15–30Nov **A**

  H **Nord** ☎492003 rm28 **A**

MOREZ (39) Jura (☎82) Map**10**D1

  ★★ **Central Modern** 106 r de la République ☎330307 rm52 **A**

MORTAGNE-AU-PERCHE (61) Orne (☎34) Map**9**A3

  H **Grand-Cerf** 25 r St-Croix ☎250488 rm15 Closed Feb **A**

  H **Voyageurs** 48 fbg St Eloi rm10 **A**

  ★★ **Tribunal** pl Palais ☎250477 rm14 Closed Jan **A**

MORTAIN (50) Manche (☎33) Map**8**C3

  H **Cheval Blanc** 14 av de l'Abbaye-Blanche (N of town on D577 Vire rd) ☎590060 rm16 **A**

  H **Poste** l pl des Arcades ☎590005 rm27 10Feb–20Dec **A**

  ★ **Cascades** 16 r du Bassin ☎590003 rm14 Feb–Oct **A**

MORZINE (74) Haute Savoie (☎50) Map**28**C4

  ★★ **Dahu** ☎791112 rm26 18Dec–15Apr & Jul–Aug **B**

MOUCHARD (39) Jura (☎82) Map**10**D1

  H **Promenade** quartier Bel-Air ☎41 rm10 **A**

MOULINS (03) Allier (☎70) Map**9**B1

  H **Allier** ☎443230 rm30 **A**

  H **Danguin & Terminus** ☎443212 rm37 **A**

  H **Français** ☎443219 rm19 **A**

MOULINS-ENGILBERT (58) Nièvre (☎86) Map**10**C1

  H **Bon Laboureur** pl Boucaumont ☎842055 rm20 **A**

  H **Parisien** r G-Blin ☎842144 rm8 **A**

MOUTHIER (25) Doubs (☎81) Map**11**A1

  ★ **Cascade** ☎621900 rm16 20Dec–3Nov **A**

MULHOUSE (68) Haut-Rhin (☎89) Map**11**B2

  H **Bâle** 19 passage Central ☎461987 rm30 **B**

  H **Musée** 3 r d l'Est ☎454741 rm40 **B**

  H **Paix** 7 r de Mittelback ☎454417 rm12 **A**

  H **Schcenberg** 14 r Schcenberg ☎441941 rm11 **A**

  H **Touring** 10 r du Moulin ☎453284 rm30 **A**

MURAT (15) Cantal (☎71) Map**16**D3

  H **Bredons** ☎200566 rm15 **A**

  H **Croix Blanche** ☎200102 rm15 **B**

MUZILLAC (56) Morbihan (☎97) Map**7**B2

  H **Genêts d'Or** ☎266076 rm10 **A**

  H **Pen Mur** ☎266134 rm13 20Mar–3Nov **A**

NAJAC (12) Aveyron (☎65) Map**16**C2

  ★★ **Miguel** ☎457080 rm31 Mar–Oct & 16Nov–15Feb **A**

  ★ **Belle Rive** ☎457420 rm34 (A4) 15Mar–Oct **A**

NANCY (54) Meurthe-et-Moselle (☎28) Map**11**A3

  H **Académie** 7 r des Michottes ☎245860 rm28 **A**

  H **Lycée** 15 r de la Visitation ☎526471 rm26 **A**

France

H **St Georges** 7 *ter* r du Tapis Vert
☎242295 rm27 **B**

★★ **Albert 1 er/Astoria** r Armee Patton
☎403124 rm140 **B**

★ **Americain** 61 r Pierre Semard rm51 **B**

★ **Poincare** 81 r Raymond-Poincare
☎402599 rm25 **A**

NANS-LES-PINS (83) Var (☎94) Map**27**B2
H **Nans & Ste-Baume** ☎789062 rm16 **A**

NANTES (44) Loire-Atlantique (☎40)
Map**8**C2

H **Atlantique** 9 r de Lattre-de-Tassigny
☎719441 rm20 **A**

H **Grand Monarque** 36 r Ml-Joffre
☎740240 rm 28 **A**

H **Maison Rouge** 5*bis* rte de Clisson
☎756241 rm 24 **B**

H **Strasbourg** 16 r de Strasbourg
☎475447 rm16 **A**

H **Tiercé** 11 r Fourcroy ☎714961 rm18 **A**

NANTUA Ain (☎74) Map**27** B4

H **Commerce** 65 r Docteur-Mercier
☎765195 rm10 **A**

★★ **Lac** 15 av de la Gare ☎765012 rm18
Closed Nov–Dec15 **B**

★★ **Lyon** 19 r Docteur-Mercier ☎765043
rm18 Closed Oct **A**

NAPOULE-PLAGE (LA) (06) Alpes-
Maritimes (☎93) Map**28**C2

H **Corniche d'Or** pl de la Fontaine
☎389251 rm12
Closed 15Oct–20Dec **B**

H **Petit Savoy** bd H-Clews ☎389508
rm10 **A**

NARBONNE (11) Aude (☎64) Map**22**D4

H **Alsace** 2 av Carnot ☎320186 rm20 **A**

H **France** 6 r Rossini ☎320975 rm 15 **A**

H **Paris** 2 r Lion d'Or ☎320868 rm34 **A**

★★ **Dorade** 44r J-Jaurès ☎326595
rm44 **A**

★ **Lion d'Or** 39 av Pierre Semard
☎320692 rm25 Closed Feb **A**

NEMOURS (77) Seine-et-Marne (☎1)
Map**9**B3

★★ **Écu de France** 3 r de Paris ☎4281154
rm28 **A**

★ **Roches** av d'Ormesson ☎4280143
rm17 (A6) Closed Oct

★ **St Pierre** 10 av Carnot ☎4280157
rm25 Closed 16Jan–14Feb **A**

NÉRAC (47) Lot-et-Garonne (☎58)
Map**15**B2

H **Albret** 40–42 allées d'Albret
☎650147 rm11 **A**

H **Commerce** 4 pl du Gl-Leclerc
☎650063 rm11 **A**

NETTANCOURT (55) Meuse (☎28)
Map**10**C/D3

◆ **Cloche d'Or** ☎701318 rm15 **A**

NEUF-BRISACH (68) Haut-Rhin (☎89)
Map**11**B2

H **France** 17 r de Bâle ☎725606 rm15
Closed Wed in high season **A**

NEUFCHÂTEL-EN-BRAY (76) Seine-
Maritime (☎35) Map**9**B4

H **Lion d'Or** 17 pl Notre-Dam ☎930001
rm22 Closed Jan **A**

NEVERS (58) Nièvre (☎86) Map**9**B1

H **Clèves** 8 r St-Didier ☎611587
rm15 **A**

H **Morvan** 28 r de Mouësse ☎611416
rm19 **A**

H **Thermidor** 14 r C-Tillier ☎571547
rm16 **A**

★ **Sainte-Marie** r Petit-Mouesse 25
☎611002 rm17 (A9) Closed
16Jan–Feb **A**

NICE (06) Alpes-Maritimes (☎93) Map**28**C2

H **Choiseul** 29 av Thiers ☎889681
rm48 **A**

H **Forum** 12 bd Gambetta ☎889309
rm40 **A**

H **Midland** 41 r Lamartine ☎851321
rm50 **A**

H **Panorama** 38 r Ségurane ☎552936
rm9 **A**

H **Sportsman** 4 r Barberis ☎892718
rm40 **A**

H **Villa Rose** 43 av Bellevue ☎844593
rm12 **A**

H **Wilson** 39 r Hôtel-des-Postes
☎854779 rm16 **A**

NÎMES (30) Gard (☎66) Map**27**A2

H **Amphithéâtre** 4 r des Arènes
☎672851 6Jan–20Dec **A**

H **Milan** 17 av Feuchères ☎672990
rm32 **A**

H **Royal** 3 bd A-Daudet ☎672836
rm32 **A**

H **Voyageurs** 4 r Roussy ☎674652
rm20 **A**

NIORT (79) Deux Sèvres (☎48) Map**15**B4

H **Bordeaux** 117 r de la Gare ☎240074
rm13 **A**

H **Paris** 12 av de Paris ☎240245 rm38 **A**

H **St-Jean** 21 av St-Jean ☎240690
rm12 **A**

NOGENT-LE-ROTROU (28) Eure-et-Loir
(☎37) Map**9**A3

◆ **Chêne Daré** 23 r Giroust ☎520080
rm20 **A**

★★ **Dauphin** 39 r Villette-Gate ☎521730
rm26 Closed 26Jan–Feb **A**

NOGENT-SUR-SEINE (10) Aube (☎25)
Map**10**C3

H **Beau-Rivage** 20 r Villiers-aux-Choux
☎258422 rm7 Closed 26Jan–3Mar **B**

H **Deux Ponts** 7 r des Ponts ☎258740
rm12 **A**

NOIRÉTABLE (42) Loire (☎77) Map**27**A4

H **Rendez-Vous des Chasseurs**
rte d l'Hermitage ☎247251 rm11 **A**

NOLAY (21) Côte-d'Or (☎80) Map**10**C1

◆ **Auberge de la Cloche d'Or** 79 r de la
République ☎217077 rm8 **A**

★ **Ste-Marie** 36 r de la République
☎217319 rm13 Closed 3Jan–1Feb **A**

NONANCOURT (27) Eure (☎32) Map**9**A3

H **France** 87 r Grande ☎581218 rm11
4Jan–3Dec **A**

France

H **Rendez-Vous des Pêcheurs** 117 av
V-Hugo rm10 **A**

NOYON (60) Oise (☎4) Map**9**B4
H **Bon Pêcheur** 109 r d'Orroire
☎4440413 rm15 **A**
★ **St Eloi** 81 bd Carnot ☎4440149
rm25 **A**

NYONS Drôme (☎75) Map**27**B3
H **Alpes** 7 r des Déportés ☎260564
rm5 **A**
H **Monnier** av H-Rochier ☎260900
rm20 **B**
H **Provence** av H-Rochier ☎260005
rm7 **A**
★★ **Colombet** pl de la Liberation
☎260366 rm32
Closed 26Oct–9Dec **A**

OBERNAI (67) Bas-Rhin (☎88) Map**11**B3
H **Cloche** 90 r du Gl-Gouraud ☎955289
rm11 Closed Feb & Thurs **A**
H **France** 42 r de Sélestat rm10 **A**

OLÉRON (ILE DE) (17) Charente Maritime
(☎46) Map**15**B3/4
At *Chateau d'Oléron* (Le)
H **Mail** bd Thiers ☎476140 rm15
Mar–Sep **B**
At *St Denis d'Oléron*
H **Ormeau** 1 r de la Libération ☎478672
rm28 Etr–Sep **B**
H **Tamaris** plage de St-Denis ☎478604
rm16 **A**
At *St Pierre d'Oléron*
H **Olympia** 4 pl D-Rochereau ☎470035
rm13 Apr–Sep **A**
H **Square** 4 pl Gambetta ☎470205
rm9 **A**
At *Trojan-les-Bains*
H **Paix** 23 r de la République ☎474136
rm14 **A**
◆ **Panier Fleuri** av de la Gare ☎474023
rm11 **A**

OLIVET see **ORLÉANS**

OLORON-STE-MARIE (64) Pyrénées-
Atlantiques (☎59) Map**20**C3
H **Eskualduna** av S-Carnot ☎390325
rm7 **A**
H **Poste** 11 pl de la Résistance
☎391811 rm18 **A**
H **Terminus** pl de la Gare ☎390172
rm14 **A**

ORANGE (84) Vaucluse (☎90) Map**27**B2
H **Milan** ☎341331 rm9 **A**
H **Père Tranquille** ☎340923 rm12
Closed Jun **A**
H **St-Florent** ☎341853 rm16
2Jan–23Dec **A**

ORGEVAL (78) Yvelines (☎1) Map**9**B3
★★ **Moulin d'Orgeval** ☎9759574 rm13
Feb–20Dec **B**

ORLÉANS (45) Loiret (☎38) Map**9**B2
H **Blois** 1 av de Paris ☎626161 rm20 **A**
H **Central** 6 r d'Avignon ☎879300
rm20 **B**
H **Moderne** 37 r de la République
☎871094 rm38 **A**

H **Sonis** 46 *bis* bd Châteaudun
☎877236 rm16 **A**
H **Trévise** 7 r Croix-de-Malte ☎626906
rm17 **A**
At **Olivet** (5km S off N20)
◆ **Auberge des 4 Saisons** 351 r de la
Reine-Blanche ☎661430 rm14 **A**
H **Château de Bel-Air** 501 r Hème
☎635653 rm10 **A**
At **St Jean-le-Blanc** (1.5km S on D951)
H **Marjane** 121 rte de Sandillon
☎663513 rm17 **A**
At **Semoy** (3.5km NE on D101)
H **Forêt** 106 av Gallouedec ☎864134
rm12 Closed 15Aug–16Sep **A**

ORTHEZ (64) Pyrénées Atlantiques (☎59)
Map**20**C3
H **Béarn** 8 pl St-Pierre ☎691041 rm12 **A**
H **Voyageurs** rte de Bordeaux ☎690229
rm10 **A**

PACY-SUR-EURE (27) Eure (☎32) Map**9**A3
H **Espérance** 39 r Isambard ☎360122
rm9 **A**
★★ **L'Etape** r Isambard ☎361277 rm10 **A**

PAIMPOL (22) Côtes-du-Nord (☎96)
Map**7**B3
H **Chalutiers** ☎208215 rm21
Closed 15Sep–Nov **B**
H **Goëlo** ☎208274 rm32 **A**
H **Marne** ☎208216 Closed Nov **A**

PAMIERS (09) Areège (☎61) Map**16**C1
H **Paix** 4 pl A-Tournier ☎671271 rm 15 **A**
H **Terminus** 21 pl P-Sémard ☎670059
rm13 **A**

PARAY-LE-MONIAL (71) Saône-et-Loire
(☎85) Map**10**C1
H **Aux Vendanges de Bourgogne** 5 r
D-Papin ☎810512 rm15 Closed Feb **A**
H **Nord** 45 av de la Gare ☎810512 rm16
24Jan–25Dec **A**

PARIS (75) (☎1) Map**9**B3
Districts covered by each *arrondissement*
follow the *arrondissement* heading.
1st Arrondissement Opéra, Palais-Royal,
Halles, Bourse
H **Lux** 12 r du Roule ☎2330071 rm24 **A**
H **Nantes** 55 r St-Roch ☎0738565
rm19 **B**

2nd Arrondissement Opéra, Palais-Royal,
Halles, Bourse
H **Caire** 46 r du Caire ☎5080585 rm29 **B**
H **Gramont** 22 r Gramont ☎7428022
rm32 **B**

3rd Arrondissement Bastille, République,
Hotel de Ville
H **Grand Hôtel des Arts & Mértrers**
4 r Borda ☎8877389 rm34 **B**
H **Ste Élisabeth** 10 r Ste-Élizabeth
☎2720166 rm 20 **A**

4th Arrondissement Bastille, République,
Hôtel de Ville
H **Sully** 48 r St. Antoine ☎2784932
rm22 **B**
H **Unic** 11 r du Temple ☎2727222
rm38 **B**

France

5th Arrondissement Quartier Latin, Luxembourg Jardin des Plantes

H **Gay-Lussac** 29 r G-Lussac ☏0332396 rm37 **B**

H **Grand Oriental** 2 r d'Arras ☏0333812 rm32 **B**

H **St-Christophe** 27 r Lacépède ☏3318154 rm39 **B**

6th Arrondissement Quartier Latin, Luxembourg, Jardin des Plantes

H **Kenmore** 37 bd du Montparnasse ☏5482057 rm28 **B**

H **Novelty** 10 r Dupuytren ☏0338972 rm24 **B**

7th Arrondissement Faubourg-St-Germain, Invadides, École Militaire

H **Comète** 15 r de la Comète ☏7050853 rm29 **A**

H **Paix** 19 r du Gros-Caillou ☏5555004 rm23 **A**

H **Pretty** 8 r Amélie ☏7054621 rm 57 **B**

8th Arrondissement Champs-Élysées, St. Lazare, Madeleine

H **Bellevue** 46 r Pasquier ☏3875068 rm51 **A**

H **Edimbourg** 8 r d'Edimbourg ☏5222164 rm24 **A**

★★ **Elysee** 12 r Saussaies ☏2652925 rm31 **B**

★★ **Europe** 15 r Constantinople ☏5228080 rm49 Closed Aug **A**

★ **Brescia** 16 r d'Edimbourg ☏5221431 **A**

9th Arrondissement Opéra, Gare du Nord, Gare d'l'Est, Grands Boulevards

H **Avenir** 39 bd Rochechouart ☏8782137 rm43 **A**

H **Austin's** 26 r d'Amsterdam ☏8744871 rm30 **A**

H **Canada** 27 r de Navarin ☏8787528 rm26 **A**

H **Geoffroy-Marie** 12 r G-Marie ☏8744041 rm37 **B**

H **Parme** 61 r de Chichy ☏8744041 rm 37 **A**

H **Plata** 14 r G-Marie ☏7703733 rm33 **A**

H **Vintimille** 5 r de Vintimille ☏8749320 rm35 **B**

★ **Haffon** 25 r Buffault ☏8784991 rm47 **B**

10th Arrondissement Opéra, Gare du Nord, Gare d'l'Est, Grands Boulevards

H **Albany** 4 r L-Sampaix ☏2082009 rm34 **A**

H **Deux-Hémisphères** 30 r L-Sampaix ☏2081974 rm44 **A**

H **Lafayette** 198 r Lafayette ☏6074479 rm22 **A**

H **Moris** 13 r R-Boulanger ☏6079208 rm40 **A**

H **Verdun** 5 r St-Laurent ☏6077093 rm52 **A**

11th Arrondissement Bastille, République, Hôtel de Ville

H **Camélia** 6 av P-Auguste ☏3736750 rm30 **A**

H **Daval** 21 r Daval ☏7005123 rm21 **A**

H **Garden** 1 r du Gl-Blaise ☏7005793 rm52 **A**

12th Arrondissement Bastille, Gare de Lyon, Place d'Italie, Bois de Vincennes

H **Daumesnil** 95 r C-Decaen ☏3076066 rm 35 **A**

H **Nouvel** 9 r de Austerlitz ☏3074466 rm 28 **B**

H **St-Bernard** 44 r St-Bernard ☏3719997 rm 36 **A**

13th Arrondissement Bastille, Gare de Lyon, Place d'Italie, Bois Vincennes

H **Ariane** 102 av de Choisy ☏5873480 rm36 **A**

H **Place des Alps** 2 pl des Alpes ☏5351414 rm42 **A**

★ **Arts** 8 r Coypel ☏3312230 rm42 **A**

14th Arrondissement Vaugirard, Grenelle, Gare Montparnasse, Denfert-Rocherau

H **Parc Montsouris** 4 r du Parc Montsouris ☏5890972 rm34 **A**

H **Plaisance** 53 r de Gergovie ☏5421139 rm36 **A**

H **St-Lô** 4 r d'Odessa ☏3267042 rm42 **A**

15th Arrondissement Vaugirard, Gare Montparnasse, Grenelle, Denfert-Rocherau

H **Joigny** 8 r St-Charles ☏5793335 rm54 **B**

H **Principal** 7 r du Gl-Beuret ☏8282932 rm43 **A**

16th Arrondissement Passy, Auteil, Bois de Boulogne, Chaillot, Porte Maillot

H **Cimarosa** 79 r Lauriston ☏7272838 rm38 **B**

17th Arrondissement Clichy, Ternes, Wagram

H **Moncey** 5 r Lécluse ☏5222559 rm38 **B**

H **Niel** 11 r S-Leroy ☏2299927 rm37 **B**

18th Arrondissement Montmartre, La Villette, Belleville

H **Paradis** 11 pl E-Goudot ☏2557479 rm74 **B**

H **Torcy's** 58 r de Torcy ☏6078313 rm33 **B**

19th Arrondissement Montmatre, La Villette, Belleville

H **Laumière** 4 r Petit ☏2061077 rm54 **B**

20th Arrondissement Montmatre, La Villette, Belleville

H **Printania** 150 r d'Avron ☏3438023 rm67 **B**

H **Unic** 6 r Dupont-de-l'Eure ☏6369310 rm36 **B**

PARTHENAY (79) Deux Sevres (☏49) Map8D1

H **Commerce** 30 bd E-Quinet ☏640155 rm11 **A**

H **Grand** 85 bd Meilleraye ☏640016 rm26 **A**

H **Meilleraye** 93 *bis* bd de Meilleraye ☏640328 rm8 **A**

PAU (64) Pyrénées-Atlantiques (☏59) Map15B1

H **Corona** 71 au Gl-Leclerc ☎274040 rm17 **B**

H **Supervie** 1 r Nogué ☎278769 rm10 **A**

H **Terminus** Gare SNCF ☎270975 rm10 **A**

★★ **Roncevaux** 25 r Louis Barthou ☎270844 rm44 **A**

★ **Central** r Leon Daran 15 ☎277275 rm27 **A**

At **Gan** (7m S on N134)

★ **Hostide l'Horizon** ☎687272 rm17 **A**

PAUILLAC (33) Gironde Map**15**B3

H **France & d'Angleterre** 4 quai A-Pichon ☎590120 rm13 **A**

H **Sport La Coquille** 18 quai L-Perrier ☎590752 rm17 Closed 24Sep–1Oct **A**

PÉRIERS (50) Manche (☎33) Map**8**C4

H **Poste** 5 r de la Gare ☎466401 rm10 **A**

PERIGUEUX (24) Dordogne (☎53) Map**16**C3

H **Arènes** 21 r du Gymnase ☎534985 rm19 **A**

H **Fénelon** 10 cours Fénelon ☎532152 rm34 **A**

H **Midi** 18 r D-Papin ☎534106 rm13 **A**

H **Régina** 14 r D-Papin ☎534809 rm38 **B**

PÉRONNE Somme (☎22) Map**9**B4

★★ **St Claude** pl L Daudre ☎841175 rm30 Closed Jan **A**

★ **Remparts** r Beay bois 23 ☎840122 rm16 Closed 8–27Aug **A**

PERPIGNAN (66) Pyrénées-Orientales (☎69) Map**22**D4

H **Avenir** 11 r de l'Avenir ☎342030 rm20 **A**

H **Express** 3 av Gl-de-Gaulle ☎348905 rm21 **A**

H **Trianon** 16 r Horloge ☎513828 rm14 **A**

★★ **Baleares** 20 av Gl-Guillot ☎850493 rm48 **A**

★★ **Christina** 50 cours de Lassus rm35 **A**

PERROS-GUIREC (22) Côtes-du-Nord (☎96) Map**7**B3

H **France** 14 r Rouzig ☎352027 rm31 May–15Sep **A**

H **Gulf-Stream** 26 r des 7 Iles ☎352186 rm14 **A**

H **Plage** 30 bd Clemenceau ☎352289 rm12 **A**

At **Ploumanac'h** (6km W on D788)

H **Parc** ☎352488 rm12 30Mar–Sep **A**

H **Pen-ar-Guer** ☎352327 rm31 Apr–15Sep **A**

H **Oratoire** Plage St-Guirec ☎352597 rm10 **B**

PENTREZ-PLAGE (29) Finistère (☎98) Map**7**A3

H **Mer** ☎815203 rm23 Jun–15Sep **A**

PEYREHORADE (40) Landes (☎57) Map**20**C4

H **Bon Accueil** rte de Pau ☎730360 rm17 Closed 20Oct–20Nov **A**

H **Mimi** r N-Truquez ☎730006 rm16 Closed 1–15May & 1–15Oct **A**

PHALSBOURG (57) Moselle (☎87) Map**11**B3

H **Erckmann-Chatrian** 14 pl d'Armes ☎071102 rm18 Closed Nov **A**

PIED-DU-SANCY see **MONT DORE (LE)**

PIERRE-BUFFIÈRE (87) Haute Vienne (☎55) Map**16**C3

♦ **Gare** ☎006008 rm8 **A**

★ **Providence** r Nationale ☎006016 rm12 **A**

PIERRELATTE Drôme (☎75) Map**27**B3

H **Azur** 7 av De-Lattre-de-Tassigny ☎040374 rm26 **A**

H **Blaches** RN7 ☎040721 rm15 **A**

★★ **Tom** 5 av Gl-de-Gaulle ☎040035 rm12 Closed Nov **A**

PILATE-PLAGE see **PYLA-SUR-MER**

PIRIAC SUR MER (44) Loire Atlantique (☎40) Map**7**B2

★ **Plage & du Port** Quai de Verdun ☎235009 rm24 **A**

PLOERMEL (56) Morbihan (☎97) Map**7**B3

H **Commerce** ☎740532 rm20 Feb–Dec **A**

PLOMBIÈRES-LES-BAINS (88) Vosges (☎29) Map**11**A2

H **Alsace** 34 r Liétard ☎660005 rm60 May–25Sep **A**

H **Bellevue** 10–12 av Gl-de-Gaulle ☎660002 rm26 Apr–Oct **A**

H **Strasbourgeous** pl Beaumarchais ☎660070 rm15 **A**

PLOUESCAT (29) Finistère (☎98) Map**7**A3

H **Azou** ☎696016 rm15 Closed Nov **B**

H **Baie du Kernic** ☎696341 rm15 Closed Nov **B**

PLOUGASNOU (29) Finistère (☎98) Map**7**B3

H **Grand Hotel de Primel** ☎673501 rm40 Closed July & Aug **A**

H **Roc Velen** ☎673306 rm10 **A**

PLOUMANAC'H see **PERROS-GUIREC**

POITIERS (86) Vienne (☎49) Map**8**D1

H **Alsace-Lorraine** 2bis r Alsace-Lorraine ☎412583 rm14 **A**

H **Lion d'Or** 28 fbg du Pont Neuf ☎411302 rm12 Closed Aug **A**

H **Régina** 149 bd Grand-Cerf ☎410339 rm26 **A**

H **Terminus** 3 bd de Pont-Achard ☎410288 rm19 **B**

♦ **Trois Piliers** 37 r Carnot ☎413212 rm28 **A**

POIX-DE-PICARDIE (80) Somme (☎22) Map**9**B4

★ **Cardinal** pl République ☎900771 rm23 Closed 2wks Feb **A**

★ **Poste** pl de la République ☎900033 rm19 Closed last 2wks Jan **A**

POLIGNY (39) Jura (☎82) Map**10**D1

★★ **Paris** r Travot 7 ☎371387 rm27 Mar–Oct **A**

France

★★ Vallee Heureuse ☎371213
rm9 (A1) **A**

PONS (17) Charente-Maritime (☎46)
Map**15**B3
★★ Pontoise r Gambetta ☎940099 rm17
20Jan–20Dec **B**

PONT-À-MOUSSON (54) Meurthe-et-
Moselle (☎28) Map**11**A3
★ Européen 158 av Metz ☎810759
rm28 **A**
★ Poste 42 r Victor Hugo ☎810116
rm24 **A**

PONTARLIER (25) Doubs (☎81) Map**11**A1
H France 8 r de la Gare ☎390520
rm13 **A**
H Morteau 26 r J-d'Arc ☎391483
rm16 **A**
★★ Bon Gite 12 r Salins ☎390872 rm22
Closed Mar **A**
★★ Poste 55 r de la République ☎391812
rm55 Closed 16Oct–14Dec **A**
★★ Terrasse 1 r de la République
☎390515 rm32 Closed May **A**

PONTAUBAULT (50) Manche (☎33)
Map**8**C3
★ 13 Assiettes N176 ☎581403 rm36
Mar–Nov **A**

PONT-AUDEMER (27) Eure (☎32) Map**9**A4
H Agriculture 84 r de la République
☎410123 rm9 **A**
★★ Vieux Puits 6 r Notre Dame du Pre
☎410148 rm8 15Jan–15Dec **A**
★ Risle 16 Quai Rheblanc ☎411457
rm18 **A**

PONT D'AIN (01) Ain (☎74) Map**27**B4
H Pont 25 r B-Savarin ☎390547 rm15 **A**
★★ Allies ☎390009 ☎18 **B**

PONT-DU-GARD (30) Gard (☎66) Map**27**A2
H Pont-du-Gard ☎870110 rm11
Mar–Oct **B**

PONT DE VAUX (01) Ain (☎85) Map**10**C1
H Commerce 5 pl Joubert ☎373056
rm7 **A**
★ Reconnaissance 9 pl Joubert
☎373055 rm12 **A**

PONT L'ÉVÊQUE (14) Calvados (☎31)
Map**9**A4
H Lion d'Or pl du Calvaire ☎640038
rm16 **A**

PONTIVY (56) Morbihan (☎97) Map**7**B3
H Friedland ☎252711 rm12 **A**
H Robic ☎251180 rm29 **A**
H Voyageurs ☎250935 rm10 **A**

PONTORSON (50) Manche (☎33) Map**8**C3
H Normandy 82 r St-Michel ☎601115
rm10 **A**
♦ Relais Clemenceau 40 bd
Clemenceau rm16 **A**

PORNIC (44) Loire-Atlantique (☎40)
Map**7**B2
H Hostellerie Ourida 43 r de Verdun
☎820083 rm10 **B**
♦ Relais St-Gilles r F-de-Mun ☎820225
rm21 Closed Jul–12Sep **A**

PORNICHET (44) Loire-Atlantique (☎40)
Map**7**B2
H Charmettes 7 av Flornoy ☎610430
rm32 Jul–12Sep **A**
H Normandy 120 av du Mazy ☎610308
rm26 Apr–Sep **A**
★ Sud-Bretagne 42 bd de la République
rm35 15Mar–15Oct **B**

PORTEL (LE) see **BOULOGNE**

PORT-LOUIS (56) Morbihan (☎97) Map**7**B2
H Belle-Vue ☎654603 rm27
Closed Jul–12Sep **A**
H Commerce ☎654605 rm34 **A**

PORT-LA-NOUVELLE (11) Aude (☎64)
Map**22**D4
H Rascasse av de la Mer ☎332289
rm36 **A**
H St-Michel 13 r Riquet ☎332151
rm32 **B**

PORT-VENDRES (66) Pyrénées-Orientales
(☎69) Map**22**D4
H Albères r C-Pelletan ☎380077 rm19
Apr–Sep **A**
H Castellane pl J-Jaurès ☎380062
rm21 **B**
★★ Résidence rte de Banyuls ☎380068
rm21 (A4) Feb–Oct **B**

POUGUES-LES-EAUX (58) Nièvre (☎86)
Map**9**B2
H Central 62 rte de Paris ☎688500
rm13 Closed 15Nov–15Dec **A**

POUILLY-SUR-LOIRE (58) Nièvre (☎86)
Map**9**B2
H Écu de France 64 r W-Rousseau
☎391097 rm10 **A**

POULDU (LE) (29) Finistère (☎98) Map**7**B3
★★ Castel Treaz ☎969111 rm28
Jun–12Sep **B**
★ Quatres Chemins ☎969044 rm35
Jun–12Sep **A**

POUZAUGES (85) Vendée (☎30) Map**8**C1
★★ Bruyere r Docteur-Barhanneau
☎571346 rm30 **B**

PRADES (66) Pyrénées-Orientales (☎68)
Map**22** D4
H Glycines 81 route-nationale
☎050707 rm18 **A**

PUY (LE) (43) Haute-Loire (☎71) Map**27**A3
H Régional ☎093774 rm11 **A**
H Verveine ☎093539 rm28 **A**
★★ Bristol av MI-Foch ☎091338 rm35
(A20) 15Jan–15Nov **A**
★ Verveine 6 pl Cadelade ☎020077
rm28 **B**

PYLA-SUR-MER (33) Gironde (☎56)
Map**15**A2
H Etche Ona 193 bd de l'Océan
☎227218 rm15 **A**
H Maloune av du Figurer ☎225391
rm12 Feb–11Oct **A**
★★ Beau Rivage 10 bd de L'Ocean
☎225241 rm16 (A4) Jun–15Sep **B**

At **Pilate-Plage** (2.5km S on D112)
H Tkiti Etchea ☎227115 rm26
Jun–Sep **B**

QUIBERON (56) Morbihan (☎97) Map**7**B2
  H **Cornouaille** 47 av Janvier ☎305841
    rm21 **A**
  H **Paris** 8 bd de Beaumont ☎308626
    rm20 **A**
  H **Relais** 59 av Janvier ☎306192 rm12 **A**

QUILLAN (11) Aude (☎64) Map**22**D4
  ★ **Cartier** 31 bd Ch-de-Gaulle ☎200514
    rm30 **A**

QUIMPER (29) Finistère (☎98) Map**7**A3
  H **Amorique** 2 r de Concarneau
    ☎900144 rm12 **A**
  H **Terminus** 15 av de la Gare ☎900063
    rm25 **A**
  ★★ **Celtic** 13 r de Douarnenez ☎950297
    rm33 **A**
  ★★ **Gradlon** 30 r Brest ☎950439 rm25
    16Jan–16Dec **A**
  ★★ **Tour d'Auvergne** 11–13 r des
    Reguaires ☎950870 rm45 (A2) **A**

QUIMPERLÉ (29) Finistère (☎98) Map**7**B3
  H **Europe** ☎960002 rm25 **A**
  H **Moderne** ☎960132 rm15 **A**
  H **Robin** ☎960035 rm10
    Closed 15Oct–15Nov **A**

RABOT (LE) Loir-et-Cher (☎39) Map**9**B2
  ☆ **Motel Bruyeres** RN20 ☎080570
    rm38 **B**

RAMBOUILLET Yvelines (☎1) Map**9**B3
  ★ **St Charles** 1 r Groussay ☎4830634
    rm14 (A2) Closed 1–15Jul **A**

RÉ (ILE DE) (17) Charente-Maritime (☎46)
Map**15**B4

At *Ars-en-Ré*
  H **Clocher** 6 pl Camot ☎094120 rm22
    20Jan–20Dec **A**
  H **Sénéchal** 4 r Gambetta ☎094042
    rm14 Closed Oct **A**

At *Flotte (La)*
  H **Hippocampe** 4 r Château-des-
    Mauléons ☎096068 rm17 **A**

RECOLOGNE Doubs (☎81) Map**10**D2
  ★ **Escale** ☎863213 rm15 (A4)
    Etr–Oct **A**

REIMS (51) Marne (☎26) Map**10**C3/4
  H **Alsace** 6 r du Gl-Sarrail ☎474408
    rm22 **A**
  H **Cours-Langlet** 53 cours Langlet
    ☎471389 rm12 **A**
  H **Jeanne-d'Arc** 26 r J-d'Arc ☎402962
    rm12 **A**
  H **St Nicaise** 6 pl St-Nicaise ☎403048
    rm12 **A**
  ★★ **Europa** 8 bd Joffre ☎473329 rm32
    6Jan–23Dec **A**
  ★★ **Univers** 41 bd Foch ☎475271 rm44 **A**

REMIREMONT (88) Vosges (☎29) Map**11**A2
  H **Magdelaine** 38 fbg d'Alsace
    ☎622922 rm7 **A**

RENAISON (42) Loire (☎77) Map**27**A4
  H **Central** pl du Il-Novembre ☎044017
    rm7 **A**
  ★ **Jaques Coeur** rte Vichy ☎044005
    rm10 **A**

RENNES (35) Ille-et-Vilaine (☎99) Map**8**C3
  H **Astrid** 32 av Barthou ☎308238
    rm30 **B**
  H **Cornouaille** 47 av Janvier ☎305841
    rm21 **A**
  H **Léon** 15 r de Léon ☎305528 rm10 **A**
  H **Méridional** 8 r D-des-Loges ☎303821
    rm20 **A**
  H **Voltaire** 109 bd Voltaire ☎303447
    rm32 **A**
  ★ **Angleterre** 19 r Ml-Joffre ☎307766
    rm28 **A**

REQUISTA (12) Averon (☎65) Map**16**D2
  H **Bru** 4 pl des A.C. ☎172 rm20 **A**

RETHEL Ardennes (☎24) Map**10**C4
  ★★ **Moderne** pl Gare ☎390454 rm25 **B**

REVEL (31) Haute-Garonne (☎61)
Map**16**C1
  H **Centre** pl Centrale ☎835315 rm18 **A**

RIBEAUVILLÉ (68) Haut-Rhin (☎89)
Map**11**B2
  H **Cheval Blanc** 122 Grand 'Rue
    ☎736138 rm12 Closed Mon & Jan **A**
  H **Ville de Nancy** 7 Grand 'Rue
    ☎736057 rm24 2Mar–14Dec
    Closed Wed & Thur **A**

RIBÉRAC (43) Dordogne (☎53) Map**16**C3
  H **Chêne-Vert** 42 r Couleau ☎950555
    rm10 **A**
  H **France** 3 r M-Dufraisse ☎900061
    rm19 Feb–15Dec **A**

ROANNE (42) Loire (☎77) Map**27**A4
  H **France** 19 r A-Roche ☎712117
    rm44 **A**
  H **Paix** 29 av Gambetta ☎712433
    rm15 **A**
  H **Splendid** 5 r de Cadore ☎713787
    rm15 **A**

ROCAMADOUR (46) Lot (☎60) Map**16**C2
  H **Belvédère** ☎386325 rm12
    3Mar–2Nov **A**
  H **Voyageurs** ☎386319 rm12
    Closed Nov **A**
  ★★ **Beau Site & Notre Dame** r R-le-Preux
    ☎386308 rm61 (A10) Apr–Oct **A**
  ★ **Lion d'Or** Porte Figuier ☎386204
    Etr–15Oct rm25 (A7) **A**

ROCHEFORT -SUR-MER (17) Charente-
Maritime (☎46) Map**15**B4
  H **Grand Bacha** 53 av C-de-Gaulle
    ☎993711 rm37 **B**
  H **Lafayette** 10 av Lafayette ☎990331
    rm23 **A**
  ♦ **Routiers** av C-Fuller ☎990785 rm7
    Closed Sun **A**

ROCHELLE (LA) (17) Charente-Maritime
(☎46) Map**15**B4
  H **Français** 37 av R-Poincaré ☎340038
    rm10 **A**
  H **Perrio** 1 cours de la Commanderie
    ☎410003 rm11 **A**
  H **Savary** 2 r A-Lorraine ☎348344
    rm21 **B**
  ★ **Trianon et Plage** 6 r de la Monnaie
    rm18 Closed Feb **A**

France

ROCHE-POSAY (LA) (86) Vienne (☎49)
Map**9**A1
- H **Amicis** 53 av des Fontaines ☎862020 rm31 **A**
- H **Europe** 19 av des Fontaines ☎862151 rm30 15Apr–1Oct **A**

RODEZ (12) Aveyron (☎65) Map**16**D2
- H **Avenir** 40 r St-Gyrice ☎681164 rm12 **A**
- ★★ **Grand Hotel Broussey** 1 av V-Hugo ☎681871 rm78 **A**
- ★ **Poste** 2 r Béteillo ☎680147 rm25 **A**

ROMORANTIN-LANTHENAY Loir-et-Cher (☎39) Map**9**B2
- ★ **Orleans** pl du Gl-de-Gaulle ☎760165 rm10 **A**

ROQUEBRUNE-CAP-MARTIN (06) Alpes-Maritimes (☎93) Map**28**C2
- H **Reine d'Azur** 29 promenade du Cap Martin ☎357684 rm17 Feb–Oct **A**
- ★ **Westminster** av L-Laurens 14 ☎350068 rm30 (A4) Feb–Sep **A**

ROQUEFORT (40) Landes (☎58) Map**15**B2
- H **Colombier** ☎585057 rm19 **A**
- H **Commerce** r Thiers ☎585013 rm15 22Oct–14Nov **A**

ROQUE-GAGEAC (LA) (24) Dordogne (☎53) Map**16**C2
- ★★ **Gardette** ☎295158 rm16 (A4) Etr–11Nov **A**
- ★ **Belle Étoile** ☎295144 rm15 15Mar–15Oct **A**

ROSCOFF (29) Finistère (☎98) Map**7**B3
- H **Bains** ☎697012 rm70 10Apr–Sep **A**
- H **Bellevue** ☎697175 rm23 15May–25Sep **A**
- H **Plage** ☎697026 rm28 14Apr–Sep **A**
- ★ **Bains** 25 pl L-Duthiers ☎697012 rm60 (A30) Etr–Oct **A**

ROSIERS SUR LOIRE (LES) (49) Maine-et-Loire (☎41) Map**8**D2
- ★★ **Jeanne de Laval** pl Église ☎518012 rm15 Closed 11Nov–24Dec **B**

ROUBAIX (59) Nord (☎20) Map**3**B1
- H **Coq Hardi** 1 pl de la Gare ☎708286 rm38 **A**
- H **Gare** 4 pl de la Gare ☎708416 rm24 Closed 12–31Aug **A**

ROUEN (76) Seine-Maritime (☎35) Map**9**A4
- H **St-Christophe** 53 r d'Amiens ☎701081 rm18 **A**
- ★★ **Cardinal** 1 pl Cathedral ☎702442 rm20 Closed Feb **A**
- ★★ **Nord** 91 r Gros-Horloge ☎704141 rm60 **A**
- ★★ **Paris** 12-14 r de la Champmesle ☎700926 rm22 **A**
- ★★ **Viking** 21 quai du Havre ☎703495 rm37 **A**
- ★ **Vielle Tour** 42 pl Haute Vielle Tour ☎700327 rm23 **A**

ROYAN (17) Charente-Maritime (☎46) Map**15**B3
- H **Plazza** 17 r Font-de-Cherves ☎053427 rm11 **A**
- H **Ralleye** 44 bd Albert-1er ☎050238 rm12 **A**
- H **Snack du Casino** 62 Front de la Mer ☎052002 rm8 **B**
- ★★ **Grand Hotel de Pontaillac** 195 av de Pontaillac ☎380044 rm55 Jun–15Sep **A**

ROYAT (63) Puy-de-Dôme (☎73) Map**16**D3
- H **Cottage** ☎358253 rm33 7Apr–Sep **A**
- H **Pépinière** ☎358119 rm17 Mar20–Oct1 **A**

RUFFEC (16) Charente (☎45) Map**15**B4
- H **Toque-Blanche** 16 r du Ml-Leclerc ☎310016 rm18 **A**

ROCHE-SUR-YON (LA) (85) Vendée (☎30) Map**8**C1
- H **Gallet** 75 bd Leclerc ☎370231 rm21 **A**
- H **St-Jean** 6-7 r Chanzy ☎371207 rm24 2Jan–21Dec **A**

ROMANS (26) Drôme (☎75) Map**27**B3
- H **Magdeleine** 31 av P-Sémard ☎023353 rm16 **B**
- H **Ors** quartier des Ors ☎022624 rm24 **A**
- H **Valence** ☎023501 rm14 **A**

SABLÉ-SUR-SARTHE (72) Sarthe (☎43) Map**8**D2
- H **Bretagne** ☎950215 rm7 Closed Fri & 10Sep–2Oct **A**

SABLES-D'OLONNE (LES) (85) Vendée (☎30) Map**8**C1
- H **Becs Fins** 84 av A-Garabet ☎321596 rm12 Closed Mon **A**
- H **Embruns** 46 r du Docteur-Canteteau ☎322599 rm20 **A**
- H **Théâtre** 20 bd F-Roosevelt ☎320092 rm21 15Mar–Sep **A**
- ★★ **Residence** 36 Prom Clemenceau ☎320666 rm35 **B**

SABLES-D'OR-LES-PINS (22) Côtes-du-Nord (☎96) Map**7**B3
- ★★ **Ajoncs d'Or** ☎414212 rm75 (A45) Etr & 15May–25Sep **A**
- ★★ **Dunes d'Armor** ☎414206 rm65(A18) Jun–Sep **A**
- ★★ **Voile d'Or** r des Acacias ☎414249 rm16 Mar–15Nov **B**

ST-AFFRIQUE (12) Aveyron (☎65) Map**16**D1
- ★★ **Moderne** av A-Pezet ☎990137 rm37(A11) **A**

ST-AGRÉVE (07) Ardèche (☎75) Map**27**A3
- H **Cévennes** 10 pl de la République ☎301022 rm10 **A**
- H **Faurie** 36 av des Cévennes ☎301160 rm16 15May–15Sep **A**

ST-AMOUR (39) Jura (☎82) Map**10**D1
- ★ **Alliance** ☎251003 rm16 Apr–9Oct **B**
- ★ **Commerce** pl Chevalerie ☎251206 rm22 **A**

ST-ANDRÉ-LES-ALPES (04) Alpes-de-Haute-Provence (☎92) Map**28**C2
- H **Grand** ☎50 rm24 Apr–Sep **A**
- H **Monge** ☎399111 rm16 15Mar–1Oct **A**
- H **Pidanoux** ☎14 rm17 Closed Jan **A**

ST-AUBAN see **CHÂTEAU-ARNOUX**

ST-AUBIN-SUR-MER (14) Calvados (☎31)
Map**8**D4
    H **Normandie** 126 r Pasteur ☎973017
    rm10 15Mar–20Sep **A**

ST BRIAC (35) Ille et Villaine (☎99) Map**8**C3
    H **Houle** ☎463217 rm20 Etr–25Sep **A**

ST-BRIEUC (22) Côtes-du-Nord (☎96)
Map**7**B3
    H **Arrivée** 35 r de la Gare ☎333615
    rm12 **A**
    H **Beau Soleil** 55 r du Docteur-Rahuel
    ☎332468 rm15 **A**
    H **Parc** 8 r J-Mermoz ☎335102 rm10 **A**

ST-CAST (22) Côtes-du-Nord (☎96)
Map**8**C3
    H **Dunes** ☎410031 rm27 Feb–Sep **A**
    H **Pins** ☎410781 rm32 **B**
    H **Marine** ☎410021 rm20 **A**

ST-CÉRÉ (46) Lot (☎60) Map**16**C2
    H **Parc** ☎381729 rm20 **A**

ST CHELY-D'APCHER (48) Lozère (☎66)
Map**16**D2
    ★ **Lion d'Or** 132 r T-Roussel ☎310014
    rm30 Feb–Dec **A**

ST-CLAUDE-SUR-BIENNE (39) Jura (☎82)
Map**11**A1
    H **Poyat** 7 r La-Poyat ☎451053 rm11 **A**
    H **Pont de Rochefort** ☎450213 rm10 **A**

ST-CYPRIEN (24) Dordogne (☎53)
Map**16**C2
    H **Terrasse** pl du Champ-de-Foire
    ☎292169 rm16
    Closed 15Nov–15Dec **A**

ST-DIÉ (88) Vosges (☎29) Map**11**A3
    H **Hôtel Restaurant de l'Est** 1 r de la
    Gare ☎561045 rm14 Closed Sun **A**
    H **Terminus** 15 r Gambetta ☎561751
    rm18 **A**
    ★ **Nouvel** 10 r Gambetta ☎562221
    rm32 **A**

ST-DIZIER (52) Haute-Marne (☎27)
Map**10**C/D3
    H **Agriculture** pl de la Liberté ☎050140
    rm12 **A**
    H **Gare & Voyageurs** 32 av de Verdun
    ☎050125 rm20 5Jan–20Dec **A**
    H **Picardy** 15 av de Verdon ☎050912
    rm12 **A**

ST ÉTIENNE (42) Loire (☎77) Map**27**A4
    H **Anjou** 33 r D-Rochereau ☎323436
    rm12 **A**
    H **Europe** 63 r de la République
    ☎322152 rm29 **A**
    H **Univers** 3 r L-Nautin ☎329871 rm19 **A**
    H **Voyageurs** 2 r du Gris-de-Lin
    ☎322095 rm26 **A**

ST-ÉTIENNE-DE-BAIGORRY (64)
Pyrénées-Atlantiques (☎59) Map**20**C3
    H **Izarra** RN648 ☎374177 rm19
    Jan–10Nov **A**
    H **Manechenia** ☎374168 rm11
    Mar–15Nov **A**

ST-FLORENTIN (89) Yonne (☎86) Map**10**C2
    ★ **Est** 7 r Faub St Martin ☎351035
    rm29(A6) Jan–Nov **A**

ST-FLOUR (15) Cantal (☎71) Map**16**D2
    H **Commerce** ☎5601031 rm37 **A**
    H **Roches** ☎600970 rm30 **A**
    ★★ **Voyageurs** 25 r College ☎601551
    rm40 May–Sep **B**

ST FONS see **LYON**

ST-GAUDENS (31) Haute-Garonne (☎61)
Map**16**C1
    H **Esplanade** 7 pl du Mas-St-Pierre/33
    bd Beptmale ☎891590 rm12 **A**
    ★★ **Ferrière & France** 1 r Gl- Leclerc
    ☎891457 rm18 **A**

ST-GEORGES-DE-DIDONNE (17)
Charente-Maritime (☎46) Map**15**B3
    H **Central** 7 r du Gl-de-Gaulle ☎050724
    rm25 **A**
    H **Floréal** 10 allée du Repos ☎050812
    rm31 Apr–Sep **A**
    ★ **Bellevue** ☎050742 rm19(A5)
    Mar–Sep **A**

ST-GERMAIN-EN-LAYE (78) Yvelines (☎1)
Map**9**B3
    H **Grand Cerf** 64 r de Poissy ☎9630237
    rm17 **A**
    H **Papillon Bleu** 19 pl Guynemer
    ☎9630864 rm13 **A**

ST-GERVAIS-D'AUVERGNE (63) Puy-de-
Dôme (☎73) Map**16**D3
    H **Castel** ☎857042 rm26 Feb–Dec **A**
    H **Place** ☎857204 rm6 **A**

ST-GILLES-CROIX-DE-VIE (85) Vendée
(☎30) Map**7**B1
    ★ **Embruns** 16 bd de la Mer ☎551140
    rm23 **A**

ST-GIRONS (09) Ariège (☎61) Map**22**C4
    H **Madrid** 68 rte de Villefranche
    ☎660232 rm24 **A**
    H **Mirouze** 19 av Galliéni ☎661277
    rm25 **A**

ST-HILAIRE-DU-HARCOUET (50) Manche
Map**8**C3
    H **Cygne** 67 r W-Rousseau ☎491184
    rm35 **A**
    ★ **Lion d'Or** 120 r Avranches ☎491082
    rm20 **A**

ST JEAN D'ANGÉLY (17) Charente Maritime
(☎46) Map**15**B3
    H **Chalet** 66 av A-Briand ☎320108
    rm19 **A**
    H **Paix** 5 av Gl-de-Gaulle ☎320093
    rm15 **A**

ST-JEAN-DE-LUZ (64) Pyrénées-
Atlantiques (☎59) Map**19**B3
    H **Verdun** 13 av de Verdun ☎260255
    rm14 **A**
    ★★ **Paris** 1 bd Passicot ☎260062
    Mar–15Dec **A**
    ★★ **Plage** 33 r Garat ☎260646 rm24
    Etr–mid Oct **B**
    ★ **Ciboure** rte d'Espagne, Cibourne
    ☎260057 rm22 **A**

France

ST JEAN DE MAURIENNE (73) Savoie
(☎79) Map**28**C3
- ★★ **St Georges** 344 r République
  ☎640105 rm24 **A**

ST-JEAN-DE-MONTS (85) Vendée (☎30)
Map**7**B1
- H **Pinède** 181 av Valentin ☎586444
  rm10 Closed Wed **A**

ST JEAN-DU-GARD (30) Gard (☎66)
Map**27**A2
- H **Corniche-des-Cévennes** ☎853038
  rm16 Closed Nov **A**
- H **Moderne** 103 Grande'Rue ☎853034
  rm25 Closed 21Jan–1Apr **A**

ST JEAN-LE-BLANC see **ORLÉANS**

ST-JEAN-LE-THOMAS (50) Manche (☎33)
Map**8**C3
- ★★ **Bains** Face Poste ☎488420 rm30(A8)
  15Mar–15Oct **A**

ST-JEAN-PIED-DE-PORT (64) Pyrénées-
Atlantiques (☎59) Map**20**C3
- H **Navarre** pl Floquet ☎370167 rm8
  Jun–Sep **A**
- H **Ramuntcho** 1 r de France ☎370391
  rm15 15May–Oct **B**

ST-JULIEN-EN-BEAUCHÊNE (05) Hautes-
Alpes (☎92) Map**27**B3
- ★★ **St Bermond-Gauthier** RN75 rm21 **A**

ST-JULIEN-EN-GENEVOIS (74) Haute-
Savoie (☎50) Map**28**C4
- ★ **Savoyarde** rte de Lyon ☎492579
  rm10 **A**

ST-JUNIEN (87) Haute-Vienne (☎55)
Map**16**C3
- H **Cheverny** ☎021530 rm8 **A**
- H **Lion d'Or** ☎023184 rm20 **A**
- H **Modern** ☎021782 rm18 **A**

ST-LARY-SOULAN (65) Hautes-Pyrénées
(☎62) Map**21**B4
- H **Pons Le Dahu** ☎984366 rm31 **A**

ST-LÔ (50) Manche (☎33) Map**8**C4
- ★★ **Terminus** 3 av Briovere ☎571471
  rm15 **A**
- ★★ **Univers** l av Briovere ☎571153
  rm25 **A**
- ★ **Armoric** 15 r de la Marne ☎571747
  rm21 5Jan–26Dec **A**
- ★ **Cremaillere** pl de la Prefecture
  ☎571468 rm12 Closed Jan **A**
- ★ **Gare** pl de la Gare ☎571515 rm18
  Closed 16Jan–14Feb **A**

ST-LUNAIRE (35) Ille-et-Vilaine (☎99)
Map**8**C3
- H **Longchamp** ☎463036 rm59
  Etr–Sep **A**
- H **Richemond** ☎463028 rm32
  Apr–Sep **A**

ST MALO (35) Ille-et-Vilaine (☎99) Map**8**C3
- H **Armor-Hôtel** 8 r R-Schumann
  ☎560075 rm10 **A**
- H **Marguerite** 2 r St-Benoit ☎408703
  rm12 **B**
- H **Parlesien** 8 r A-Magon ☎562104
  rm16 **A**

- ★ **Celtic** 25 Chaussée du Sillon ☎560948
  rm15 15May–15Sep **A**
- ★ **Noguette** 9 r de la Fosse ☎408357
  rm13 **A**

ST-MAURICE-SUR-MOSELLE (88) Vosges
(☎29) Map**11**A2
- H **France** 26 r de la Gare ☎615242 rm15
  Closed Mon **A**
- H **Vallée Vosgienne** 18 r de la Goutte-
  du-Rieux ☎615218 **A**
- ★ **Bon Sejour** ☎615233 rm16 **A**

ST-MAXIMIN-LA-STE-BAUME (83) Var
(☎94) Map**27**B2
- ★ **Chez Nous** 3 bd J-Jaurès ☎780257
  rm7 15Jan–3Dec **A**

ST-MICHEL-DE-MAURIENNE (73) Savoie
(☎79) Map**28**C3
- H **Galibier** ☎196 rm22 **A**
- ★★ **Savoy** r Gl Ferrié 25 rm24
  Closed 19Jun–10Jul **A**

ST NAZAIRE Loire-Atlantique (☎40)
Map**7**B2
- H **Courbet** 63 av de la République
  ☎225176 rm28 **A**
- H **Guérandais** 40 r A-de-Mun ☎225479
  rm10 **A**
- H **Renaissance** 49 r R-Salengro
  ☎224137 rm18 **A**
- ★★ **Dauphin** 33 r J-Javrès ☎225685
  rm22 **A**

ST OMER (62) Pas de Calais (☎21) Map**3**A1
- H **Bretagne** 2 pl du Vainquai ☎382578
  rm37 **B**
- H **Comte de Luxembourg** 32 r du
  Comte de Luxembourg ☎381009
  rm18 **B**
- H **Grand Hotel du Commerce**
  3 r Aldegonde ☎380822 **A**

At **Clairmarais** (4·5km NE by D209)
- H **Grand St Bernard** ☎380927 rm12 **B**

ST PALAIS (64) Pyrénées Atlantiques (☎59)
Map**20**C3
- H **Gare** ☎387325 rm15 **A**
- H **Midi** r du Jeu-de-Paume ☎387064
  rm10 Closed 5–25Oct **A**

ST-PALAIS-SUR-MER (17) Charente-
Maritime (☎46) Map**15**B3
- H **Falaises** à la Grande-Côte
  ☎222049 rm11 Etr–Sep **A**
- H **Océan** A la Grande Côte ☎026825
  rm10 Etr–Sep **A**
- H **Régina** 25 pl de la Océan ☎026062
  rm10 **A**

ST-PAUL-DE-LOUBRESSAC (46) Lot
Map**16**C2
- ★ **Relais de la Madeleine** ☎319808
  rm20 10Jan–10Dec **A**

ST-PÉE-SUR-NIVELLE (64) Pyrénées-
Atlantique (☎59) Map**20**C3
- H **Etchegarray** ☎541038 rm15 **A**
- H **Nivelle** ☎541027 rm39 **A**

ST-PIERRE-DE-CHARTREUSE (38) Isère
(☎76) Map**27**B3

★★ **Beau Site** ☎086134 rm34 **A**

ST-POL-DE-LÉON (29) Finistère (☎98)
Map**7**A/B3
 H **Cheval Blanc** ☎690100 rm15 **A**
 H **Voyageurs** ☎690021 rm28 **A**

ST POL SUR TERNOISE Pas-de-Calais
(☎21) Map**3**A1
 ★ **Lion d'Or** 74 r Hesdin ☎031044
  rm16 (A5) **A**

ST-POURCAIN-SUR-SIOULE (03) Allier
(☎70) Map**9**B1
 ★ **Chene Vert** 35 bd L-Rollin ☎454065
  rm35 (A15) Closed 3Jan–9Feb **A**
 ★ **Deux Ponts** Ilot de Tivoli ☎454114
  rm27 Closed Dec **A**

ST-QUAY-PORTRIEUX (22) Côtes-du-Nord
(☎96) Map**7**B3
 ★★ **Bretagne** 36 quai de la Republique
  ☎704091 rm15 **A**
 ★ **Gerbot d'Avoine** 2 bd Littoral
  ☎704009 rm26 Closed 3wks Oct **A**
 ★ **Plage** ☎704004 rm25 Etr–Sep **A**

ST-QUENTIN (02) Aisne (☎23) Map**10**C4
 H **Départ** pl du Monument-aux-Morts
  ☎623169 rm16 **A**
 H **Paris** 22 quai Gayant ☎622848
  rm20 **A**
 H **St-Jacques** 14 r St-Jacques
  ☎623173 rm30 **A**
 ★★ **Paix & Albert** pl de Huit Octobre
  ☎627762 rm64 **A**

ST-RAPHAËL (83) Var (☎94) Map**28**C2
 H **Astoria** ☎954279 rm14 **A**
 H **Bel Azur** ☎951408 rm14 **B**
 H **Sélect** ☎950622 rm 19 **A**
 H **Touring** ☎950172 rm24 **A**

ST-RÉMY-DE-PROVENCE (13) Bouches-
du-Rhône (☎90) Map**27**B2
 H **Arts La Palette** ☎920850 rm19
  Closed 20Jan–28Feb **A**
 H **Provence de St-Rémy** ☎920627
  rm27 15Mar–28Feb **A**

ST-SATUR (18) Cher (☎36) Map**9**B2
 ★★ **Laurier** r du Commerce ☎541720
  rm10 Closed Feb **A**

ST-SERNIN-SUR-RANCE (12) Aveyron
(☎65) Map**16**D1
 ★★ **France** ☎996026 rm25 **A**

ST-TROPEZ (83) Var (☎94) Map**28**C1/2
 H **Bonne Ensignure** ☎970692 rm 9 **A**
 H **Méditerranée** ☎970044 rm13 Closed
  10Jan–1Mar & 31Oct–15Dec **B**
 H **Subcontinental** ☎970002 rm26
  Mar–Oct **B**

ST-VALERY-SUR-SOMME (80) Somme
(☎22) Map**3**A1
 H **Colonne de Bronze** 43 quai du
  Romeral ☎275007 rm19 **A**
 H **Port & des Bains** l quai Blavet
  ☎275009 rm14 **A**

ST-VALLIER (26) Drome (☎75) Map**27**B3
At **Sarras** (2km W on N86)

★★ **Vivarais** av de Viverais ☎230188
 rm10 Closed Feb **A**

STE-MARIE-AUX-MINES (68) Haut-Rhin
(☎89) Map**11**B3
 H **Commerce** 86 r Wilson ☎588081
  rm10 Closed Wed **A**

STE-MAXIME-SUR-MER (83) Var (☎94)
Map**28**C2
 H **Castellamar** ☎961997 rm10
  Apr–Sep **A**
 H **Pourquoi-Pas** ☎961299 rm10
  Closed Nov **B**
 H **Preconil** ☎960173 rm13 **A**

STE-MENEHOULD (51) Marne (☎26)
Map**10**C/D3
 H **Cheval Rouge** 1 & 3 r Chanzy
  ☎608104 rm19 15Feb–Dec **A**
 H **St Nicolas** 36 r Chanzy ☎608059
  rm18 Closed 1–16Feb & 1–16Sep **A**

SAINTES (17) Charente-Maritime (☎46)
Map**15**B3
 H **Olympia** 33 r D-Rochereau ☎930879
  rm12 **A**
 H **Parc des Sports** 51 rte de Rochefort
  ☎930804 rm16 **A**
 ★★ **Terminus** esp de la Gare ☎930162
  rm37 **A**
 ★ **Messageries** r des Messageries
  ☎936499 rm37 **A**

SAINTES-MARIES-DE-LA-MER (LES) (13)
Bouches-du-Rhône (☎90) Map**27**A2
 H **Castellet** ☎978347 rm16 Mar–Dec **B**
 H **Grill** ☎978235 rm8 Mar–Oct **A**

SALON-DE-PROVENCE (13) Bouches-du-
Rhône (☎90) Map**27**B2
 H **Provence** ☎562704 rm15 **A**
 H **Régina** ☎562892 rm18 **A**
At **La Barben** (8km E on N572)
 ★ **Touloubre** ☎551685 rm14 **A**

SANARY-SUR-MER (83) Var (☎94)
Map**27**B1
 H **Beauséjour** ☎740079 rm16 **A**
 H **Chardon** ☎740044 rm21 Mar–Oct **A**
 H **Plage & des Voyageurs** ☎740103
  rm10 **A**
 ★★ **Tour** quai Gl-de-Gaulle ☎741010
  rm25 15Jan–15Nov **A**

SARLAT (24) Dordogne (☎53) Map**16**C2
 H **Verperie** ☎590020 rm10
  Closed 10–30Oct **B**
 ★ **Lion d'Or** 48 av Gambetta ☎590083
  rm26 **A**

SARRALBE (57) Moselle (☎87) Map**11**A3
 H **Sutter** 2 r J-Burger ☎028114 rm12
  3Jan–24Dec **A**

SARRAS see **ST-VALLIER**

SARREBOURG (57) Moselle (☎87)
Map**11**A3
 H **Mathis** 7 r Gambetta ☎032167 rm11
  Closed 6–31Aug **A**
 H **St-Hubert** 8 pl de la Gare ☎031062
  rm10 **A**

SARREGUEMINES (57) Moselle (☎87)
Map**11**A3

France

H **2 Étoiles** 4 r des Généraux-Crémer ☎984632 rm18 **A**

H **Terminus** 7 av de la Gare ☎985546 rm60 **A**

SARRE-UNION (67) Bas-Rhin (☎88) Map**11**A/B3

H **Cheval Noir** 16 r de Phalsbourg rm15 Closed Mon & 1–22Sep **A**

H **Klein** 42 r du Ml-Foch ☎001182 rm6 Closed Sun & 6–23Aug **A**

SAUGES (43) Haute-Loire (☎71) Map**27**A3

H **France** ☎778354 rm22 **A**

H **Terrasse** ☎778310 rm17 Closed 5Oct–2Nov **A**

SAULIEU (21) Côte-d'Or (☎80) Map**10**C2

H **Lion d'Or** 7 r Courtépée ☎641633 rm12 Closed 4Jan–4Feb **A**

H **Renaissance** 7 r Grillot ☎640872 rm13 **A/B**

SAULT-DE-VAUCLUSE (84) Vaucluse (☎90) Map**27**B2

H **Louvre** ☎640001 rm30 **A**

SAUMUR (49) Maine-et-Loire (☎41) Map**8**D2

H **Central** 23 r Daillé ☎510578 rm42 **A**

H **Terminus** 15 av D-d'Angers ☎503101 rm21 **A**

★★ **Roi Rene** 94 av Gl-de-Gaulle ☎504530 rm40 Mar–15Nov **A**

SAVERNE (67) Bas-Rhin (☎88) Map**11**B3

H **Marne** 5 r du Griffon ☎911918 rm20 Closed Wed & Feb **A**

H **National** 2 Grand 'Rue ☎911454 rm30 Closed Fri & Sep **A**

★ **Boeuf Noir** 22 Grand'Rue ☎911053 rm20 **A**

★ **Chez Jean** 3 r de la Gare ☎911019 rm22 **A**

ST-PONS-DE-THOMIÈRES (34) Hérault (☎67) Map**16**D1

H **Pastré** Grand Rue ☎970054 rm20 23Jan–16Dec **A**

SOUMOULOU (64) Pyrénées-Atlantiques (☎59) Map**15**B1

H **Béarn** ☎336009 rm13 **A**

SÉES Orne (☎34) Map**8**D3

★ **Cheval Blanc** 1 pl St-Pierre ☎278048 rm9 **A**

SEGRÉ (49) Maine-et-Loire (☎41) Map**8**C2

H **Corvette** ☎921946 rm10 Closed 15Jan–15Feb **A**

H **Gare** ☎921552 rm21 15Jan–20Dec **A**

SÉLESTAT (67) Bas-Rhin (☎88) Map**11** B3

♦ **Buffet de la Gare** pl de la Gare ☎920852 rm14 **A**

H **Schutzenberger** 48 r Poincaré ☎921269 rm11 Closed Mon **A**

SEMOY see ORLÉANS

SEMUR-EN-AUXOIS (21) Côte-d'Or (☎80) Map**10**C2

H **Commerce** 19 r de la Liberté ☎970018 rm13 **A**

★ **Cote d'or** 3 pl G. Gaveau ☎970313 rm15 Closed 11–31Dec & Feb **A**

SÉNAS (13) Bouches-du-Rhône (☎90) Map**27**B2

★ **Luberon** RN7 ☎572010 rm7 Closed 16Oct–Nov **A**

SENLIS (60) Oise (☎4) Map**9**B3

H **Point du Jour** 1 r de la République ☎4530122 rm10 Closed 15Jan–16Feb **A**

H **Hostellerie de la Port Bellon** 51 r Bellon ☎4530305 15Jan–15Dec **B**

H **St-Éloi** fbg St-Martin ☎4530293 rm17 Closed Sun **A**

SENONCHES (28) Eure-et-Loir (☎37) Map**9**A3

★ **Foret** pl Champ de Foire ☎377850 rm14 4Mar–Oct **A**

SENS (89) Yonne (☎86) Map**10**C3

H **Gare** 3–5 pl de la Gare ☎651277 rm18 Closed 15Feb–15Mar **A**

H **St-Pregts** 89 r Gl-de-Gaulle ☎651963 rm17 Closed 15Jan–15Feb **A**

SEPT-SAULX Marne (☎26) Map**10**C3

★★ **Cheval Blanc** ☎616027 rm25 (A2) Closed 16Jan–14Feb **A**

SERRES (05) Hautes-Alpes (☎92) Map**27**B3

H **Nord** ☎25 rm17 Closed 15Jan–15Feb **B**

★ **Alpes** av Grenoble ☎670018 rm18 **A**

SÈTE (34) Hérault (☎67) Map**27**A2

H **Grand Hôtel de Paris** 2 r F-Mishal ☎742424 rm58 **A**

H **Hippocampe** 3 r Longuyon ☎741006 rm9 **A**

H **Mistral** 19 quai Rhin-et-Danube ☎743328 **A**

H **National** r du Pont-de-l'Hérault ☎741724 rm20 **A**

SÉVÉRAC-LE-CHÂTEAU (12) Aveyron (☎65) Map**16**D2

H **Causses** r A-Briand ☎466015 rm8 **A**

H **Moderne Hôtel Terminus** ☎20 rm25 Closed Sep **A**

SEYNE-LES-ALPES (04) Alpes-de-Hautes-Provence (☎92) Map**28**C3

H **Chalet-de-Maures** ☎350404 rm10 **A**

H **Chaumière** ☎350048 rm10 **A**

SEZANNE (51) Marne (☎26) Map**10**C3

★★ **Croix d'Or** 53 r Notre Dame ☎420127 m13 **A**

SILLÉ LE GUILLAUME (72) Sarthe (☎43) Map**8**D3

H **Bretagne** ☎201010 rm14 **A**

SIORAC-EN-PÉRIGORD (24) Dordogne (☎53) Map**16**C2

H **Escale** pl de Siorac ☎296023 rm17 **A**

♦ **Auberge de la Petite Reine** ☎296042 rm18 Apr–Sep **A**

SISTERON (04) Alpes-de-Hautes-Provence (☎92) Map**27**B2

H **Poste** ☎027 rm18 **A**

H **Rocher** ☎611256 rm30 Apr–Sep **A**

SOISSONS (02) Aisne (☎23) Map**10**C4

H **Marine** 2 r de St-Quentin ☎533194 rm18 **A**

H **Nord** 6 r de Belleu ☎531255 rm12 **A**
★ **Rallye** 10 bd de Strasbourg ☎530047 rm12 **B**

SOUILLAC (46) Lot (☎60) Map**16**C2
◆ **Vieille Auberge** ☎377943 rm10 **A**
★★ **Ambassadeurs** 12 av Gl-de Gaulle ☎377836 rm24 Closed Oct **A**
★★ **Grand** pl Verninac ☎377830 rm17 May–Sep **B**
★★ **Perigord** av de Paris rm50 (A20) May–Oct **A**

SOULAC SUR MER (33) Gironde (☎56) Map**15**B3
H **France** 24 r de la Plage ☎598021 rm20 Apr–15Sep **A**
H **Michelet** 1 r Baguenard ☎598418 rm10 Apr–15Sep **A**
H **Progrès** 4 r Brémontier ☎598072 rm24 30May–1Oct **A**

SOULTZEREN (68) Haut-Rhin (☎89) Map**11**B2
H **Belle-Vue** 4 rte de la Schlucht ☎773187 rm10 Closed Wed (high season) & 14Nov–16Dec **A**
H **Ville de Gérardmer** 83 r Principale ☎773157 rm18 Closed Tue & Nov **A**

SOUPPES (77) Seine-et-Marne (☎1) Map**9**B3
★ **Mouton** av Gl-heclerc 72 ☎4297008 rm12 **A**

SOUSCEYRAC (46) Lot (☎60) Map**16**D2
★ **Au Dejeuner de Sousceyrac** ☎380256 rm11 (A4) Etr–Dec **A**

SOUSTONS (40) Landes (☎58) Map**15**A1
H **Lac** 63 av Galleben ☎480880 rm11 **A/B**
H **Hostellerie du Marensin** pl Sterling ☎480516 rm16 **A**

STRASBOURG (67) Bas-Rhin (☎88) Map**11**B3
H **Astoria** 7a r de Rosheim ☎321722 rm28 **A**
H **Central** 10 pl du Marché-aux-Cochons-de-Lait ☎320305 rm27 **A**
H **Gutenberg** 31 r des Serruriers ☎321715 rm50 **A**
H **Reech** 26 r de Rosheim ☎321860 rm23 **A**
H **Victoria** 7–9 r du Maire-Kuss ☎321306 rm37 **A**
★★ **Vendôme** 9 pl de la Gare ☎324523 rm39 **A**

SULLY-SUR-LOIRE (45) Loiret (☎38) Map**9**B2
★★ **Poste** 11 r Faubourg St Germain ☎352622 rm30 (A10) Closed Feb–Apr **A**

SURGÈRES (17) Charente-Maritime (☎46) Map**15**B4
H **Croix Blanche** 124 r A-de-Puyravault ☎070252 rm8 **A**
◆ **Devise** (At Les Ances 6.5km SW on D911 Rochefort rd) ☎070569 rm15 **A**

TALLOIRES (74) Haute-Savoie (☎50) Map**28**C4
H **Bartavelle** ☎447043 rm 10 15May–20Sep **A**
H **Villa Tranquille** ☎447043 rm19 15May–15Sep **A**

TARASCON-SUR-ARIÈGE (09) Ariège (☎61) Map**22**C4
H **Confort** 3 quai A-Sylvestre ☎646190 rm14 20Jan–19Dec **A**
★★ **Poste** 16 r V-Pilhes ☎646041 rm30 Etr–Nov **A**

TARASCON-SUR-RHÔNE (13) Bouches-du-Rhône (☎91) Map**27**B2
★★ **Terminus** ☎911895 rm27 15Feb–15Nov **A**
★ **Provençal** 12 cours A-Briand ☎911141 rm22 **A**

TARBES (65) Hautes-Pyrénées (☎62) Map**15**B1
H **Bayonnais** 62 r V-Hugo ☎930552 rm12 **A**
H **Fontaine** 2 r J-Pellet ☎933795 rm10 **A**
H **Marne** 4 av de la Marne ☎930364 rm20 **A**

TARTAS (40) Landes (☎58) Map**15**B2
H **Paix** pl A-Briand ☎734636 rm10 **A**

TASSIN-LA-DEMI-LUNE see **LYON**

TENDE (06) Alpes-Maritimes (☎93) Map**28**C2
H **Bogreau** 19 av du 16-Septembre ☎046078 rm10 **A**
H **Centre** 12 pl de la République ☎046219 rm13 **A**

THANN (68) Haut-Rhin (☎89) Map**11**A2
H **France** 22 r du Gl-de-Gaulle ☎370293 rm10 Closed Sat **A**
★ **Parc** 23 r Kléber ☎371098 rm21 Closed Nov **A**

THIERS (63) Puy-de-Dôme (☎73) Map**27**A4
H **Nord** ☎800201 rm10 **A**
★ **Centre** 10 r Traversière ☎801912 rm12 **A**

THIONVILLE (57) Moselle (☎87) Map**11**A4
H **Central** 1 r du Four-Banal ☎591693 rm24 **A**
H **Industrie** 56 rte de Metz ☎884590 rm12 **A**
H **Relais** 40 r du Ml-Joffre ☎591004 rm10 **A**

THOISSEY (01) Ain (☎74) Map**27**B4
★ **Beau Rivage** av Port ☎040166 rm10 Mar–Oct **A**

THOUARS (79) Deux-Sèvres (☎48) Map**8**D1/2
★ **Cheval Blanc** 53 r Tremoile ☎660021 rm38 **A**

THURY-HARCOURT (14) Calvados (☎31) Map**8**D3
H **Normandy** 7 r de Condé ☎797095 rm15 Apr–Sep **A**

France

TILLY-SUR-SEULLES (14) Calvados (☎31)
Map**8**D4
- H **Jeanne-d'Arc** 2 r de Bayeaux
  ☎238013 15Jan–15Dec **A**

TONNAY-BOUTONNE (17) Charente-
Maritime Map**15**B4
- ★ **Beau Rivage** r du Passage ☎332001
  rm7 **A**

TOULON (83) Var (☎94) Map**27**B1
- H **Europe** 7 *bis* r de Chabanne
  ☎923744 rm30 **A**
- H **Lux** 52 r J-Jaurès ☎929746 rm24 **A**
- H **Paris** 1 r Corneille ☎923640 rm25 **A**
- H **Strasbourg** 10 r Leblond ☎928478
  rm19 **A**

TOULOUSE (31) Haute-Garonne (☎61)
Map**16**C1
- H **Capoul** 13 pl Wilson ☎215187
  rm110 **A**
- H **Héliot** 3 r Héliot ☎624766 rm14 **A**
- H **Lutetia** 33 r Maynard ☎625157
  rm16 **A**
- H **Pays d'Oc** 53 r Riquet ☎623376
  rm21 **A**
- H **Severin** 69 r Bayard ☎627139
  rm15 **A**

TOUQUET-PARIS-PLAGE (LE) (62) Pas-
de-Calais (☎21) Map**3**A1
- ★★ **Windsor** 7 r St-Georges ☎050544
  rm28 **A**
- ★ **Chalet** 15 r de la Paix ☎051299 rm16
  Mar–Sep **A**
- ★ **Robert's** 66 r de Londres ☎051198
  rm14 Apr–Sep **A**

TOURNON D'AGENAIS (47) Lot-et-Garonne
(☎58) Map**16**C2
- H **Midi** pl de l'Hotel-de-Ville ☎Tournon 8
  rm9 Closed Sep1 – 15 **A**
- H **Voyageurs** ☎707128 rm8 **A**

TOURNUS (71) Saône-et-Loire (☎85)
Map**10**C1
- ★★ **Gare** 4 ar Gambetta ☎511056 rm15 **A**
- ★ **Terrasses** 18 av du 23-Janvier
  ☎510174 rm12 **A**

TOURS (37) Indre-et-Loire (☎47) Map**9**A2
- H **Cyrano** 17 r V-Hugo ☎615287 rm11 **A**
- H **Idéal** 11 r de la Scellerie ☎056262
  rm12 **A**
- H **Orléans** 2 r E-Vaillant ☎053458
  rm20 **A**
- H **Rabelais** 24 pl Rabelais ☎613164
  rm16 **A**
- ★★ **Cygne** 6 r du Cygne, 6 ☎052325
  rm20 **B**
- ★ **Foch** 20 r Ml Foch ☎057059 rm15 **B**

TRÉBEURDEN (22) Côtes-du-Nord (☎96)
Map**7**B3
- H **Écume de Mer** ☎355060 rm38
  Apr–20Sep **A**
- H **Potinière** ☎355043 rm14 Etr–Sep **A**

TRÉBOUL (29) Finistère (☎98) Map**7**A3
- H **Grand Hôtel de la Plage & des
  Sables Blancs** ☎920079 rm100
  Etr–Oct10 **B**

TREGASTEL-PLAGE (22) Côtes-du-Nord
(☎96) Map**7**B3

- H **Caboteur** ☎388833 rm16
  15Mar–15Oct **A**
- ♦ **Auberge de la Vieille Église**
  ☎388831 rm12 **A**
- ★ **Beau Sejour** ☎388802 rm23
  15Mar–15Oct **A**

TRÉGUIER (22) Côtes-du-Nord (☎96)
Map**7**B3
- H **Estuaire** ☎203025 rm15 **A**

TRIMOUILLE (La) 86 Vienne (☎49)
Map**16**C4
- ★ **Paix** pl Église et de la Mairie ☎916050
  rm20 Closed 26Jan–19Feb **A**

TROIS-ÉPIS (68) Haut-Rhin (☎89) Map**11**B2
- H **Croix d'Or** ☎498355 rm12
  Closed Wed & 9Jan–7Feb **A**
- H **Mon Repos** ☎498315 rm7
  Closed Mon & Nov **A**

TROUVILLE (14) Calvados (☎31) Map**8**D4
- H **Carmen** 24 r Carnot ☎883543 rm17
  Feb–Sep **A**
- H **Florian** r de la Plage ☎881740 rm11 **A**
- H **Paix** 4 pl F-Moureaux ☎883515
  rm29 **A**

TROYES (10) Aube (☎25) Map**10**C3
- H **Cirque** 5*bis* r de Preize ☎431192
  rm21 **A**
- H **Marigny** 3 r Charbonnet ☎433287
  rm15 **A**
- H **Nevers** 46 r R-Salengro ☎723203
  rm14 **A**
- ★★ **Paris** 56 r Salengro ☎433713 rm30
  10Jan–22Dec **A**

TULLE (19) Corrèze (☎55) Map**16**C3
- H **Bon Accueil** 8–10 r du Canton
  ☎267057 rm17 **A**
- H **Terminus** 13 av W-Churchill
  ☎266342 rm12 **A**
- ★★ **Toque Blanche** 29 r J-Jaurès/ pl
  Brigouleix ☎267541 rm11 **A**

URIAGE-LES-BAINS (38) Isère (☎76)
Map**27**B3
- ★★ **Alpes** Grand Allee ☎891028 rm42
  May–Sep **A**
- ★★ **Manoir** ☎891088 rm19 **A**

USSEL (19) Correze (☎55) Map**16**D3
- H **Grand Hôtel Mabru** ☎721009 rm23 **A**
- H **Midi** ☎721799 rm10 **A**
- H **Teillard** ☎721254 rm25 **A**

UZERCHE (19) Corrèze (☎55) Map**16**C3
- ★★ **Amboise** ☎731008 rm20 **A**
- ★★ **Teyssier** r Pont-Turgot ☎731005
  rm25 Closed 11Jan–Feb **A**

UZÈS (30) Gard (☎66) Map**27**A2
- H **Taverne** 4 r Sigalon ☎221310 rm8 **A**
- H **Terminus** 4 bd des Alliés ☎221266
  rm15 **A**

VAISON-LA-ROMAINE (84) Vaucluse
(☎90) Map**27**B2
- H **Orient** ☎360011 rm10
  Closed 15Nov–15Dec **A**
- H **Théâtre Romain** ☎360587 rm23
  15Feb–Sep **A**

★★ **Beffroi** r de l'Eveche
☎360471 rm20 (A10)
Closed 11Jan–9Feb & 1–16Dec **A**

VAL-ANDRE (LE) (22) Côtes-du-Nord (☎96)
Map**7**B3
  H **Mer** ☎722044 rm20 15Feb–15Sep **B**
  H **Régina** ☎722059 rm28
    Etr & 30May–15Sep **A**
  ★ **Bains** pl Gl-de-Gaulle ☎722011 rm26
    20Mar–20Sep **A**

VALENCE-SUR-RHÔNE (26) Drôme (☎75)
Map**27**B3
  H **Chaumont** 79 av S-Carnot ☎431012
    rm11 **A**
  H **Lyon** 23 av P-Sémard ☎440063
    rm47 **A**
  H **Siècle** 22 r Pasteur ☎440353 rm11 **A**

VALENCIENNES (59) Nord (☎20) Map**3**B1
  H **Beaujolais** 1–3 r D-la-Tour ☎462393
    rm33 **A**
  H **Coupole** 25 r Tholozé ☎463712
    rm38 **A**
  H **Grand Hôtel Terminus** 43 av du
    Sénateur-Girard ☎462224 rm30 **A**

VALOGNES (50) Manche (☎33) Map**8**C4
  H **Agriculture** 16 r L-Delisle ☎400021
    rm36 **A**
  ★ **Louvre** 28 r Religieuses ☎400007
    rm20 Closed Dec **A**

VALRAS-PLAGE (34) Hérault (☎67)
Map**16**D1
  H **Chalet** Front de la Mer ☎930030 rm10
    Jun–20Sep **A**
  H **Provençale** 15 av Gl-de Gaulle
    ☎930035 rm18 20Mar–Oct **A**

VANNES (56) Morbihan (☎97) Map**7**B2
  H **Verdun** 10 av Verdun ☎662123
    rm10 **A**
  ★ **Image Ste-Anne** 8 pl de la Libération
    ☎632736 rm31 Closed 16–31Oct **A**
  ★ **Marée Bleue** 8 pl B-R-Hakeim
    ☎662429 rm16 **A**
  ★ **Relais Nantais** 38 r A-Briand
    ☎661585 rm14 **A**

VARENGEVILLE-SUR-MER (76) Seine-
Maritime (☎35) Map**9**A4
  H **Terrasse** ☎851254 rm28 **A**

VARENNES-SUR-ALLIER (03) Allier (☎70)
Map**9**B1
  ♦ **Auberge du Coq Hardi** N7 ☎450612
    rm10 **A**
  H **Nouvel** ☎450006 rm16 **A**

VARS (Col de) (05) Hautes-Alpes (☎92)
Map**28**C3
  H **Paneyron** ☎455004 rm11
    Apr & 10Jun–20Sep **A**
  H **Vieille Auberge** ☎455319 rm10
    Closed 30Apr–15Jun **A**

VARZY (58) Nièvre (☎86) Map**10**C2
  H **Gare** av de la Charité ☎294416 rm7 **A**
  H **Poste** fbg de Marcy ☎294189 rm10 **A**

VATAN (36) Indre (☎54) Map**9**B2
  ♦ **Promenade & Chez Philippe**

14 r de la République ☎497044
20May–Dec **A**

VAUCOULEURS (55) Meuse (☎28)
Map**10**D3
  H **Jeanne-d'Arc** pl d'Armes ☎894156
    rm19 Closed Nov, also
    restaurant Mon in winter **A**
  H **Poste** 12 av Maginot ☎894001 rm10
    restaurant closed Mon in summer **A**

VENCE (06) Alpes-Maritimes (☎93)
Map**28**C2
  H **Closerie des Genets** 4 impasse M-
    Maurel ☎583325 rm10 Closed Nov **A**
  H **Coq Hardi** rte de Cagnes ☎581127
    rm12 Feb–Dec **A**

VENDÔME (41) Loir-et-Cher (☎39) Map**9**A2
  H **Château** 28 pl du Château ☎772098
    rm15 15Oct–15Nov **A**
  H **Moderne** 8 bd Tremault ☎772115
    rm16 15Jan–15Dec **A**
  ★ **Vendôme** 15 fbg Chartrain ☎770288
    rm20 **A**

VERDON SUR MER (LE) (33) Gironde (☎56)
Map**15**B3
  H **Parc** 9 bd Lahens ☎596008 rm27 **A**
  H **Terrasses** 64 cours de la République
    ☎596201 rm17 **A**

VERDUN (55) Meuse (☎28) Map**10**D3
  H **Beauséjour** av de la Metz ☎860770
    rm8 Feb–24Dec **A**
  H **Parc** 45 r des Minimes ☎860122
    rm38 **A**
  H **Paris** 21 r des Minimes ☎860870
    rm20 **A**

VERNET (LE) (04) Alpes-de-Haute-
Provence Map**28**C2
  H **Auzet** ☎350501 rm32 Jan–Sep **A**

VERNET (LE) (31) Haute-Garonne (☎61)
Map**16**C1
  ★ **Platanes** N20 ☎085013 rm23 **A**

VERNET-LES-BAINS (66) Pyrénées-
Orientales (☎69) Map**22**D4
  H **Deux Lions** 18 av-Clemenceau
    ☎055542 rm14 Apr–Sep **A**
  H **Moderne** 9 av des Thermes ☎055217
    rm50 Mar–Sep **A**

VERNEUIL-SUR-AVRE (27) Eure (☎32)
Map**9**A3
  H **Normandie** pl A-Briand ☎321305 rm9
    Closed 15Jan–15Feb **A**
  H **Saumon** 89 pl se la Madeleine rm14
    Closed Feb **A**

VERNON (27) Eure (☎32) Map**9**A3
  H **Roussel** 12 r du Soleil ☎512332 rm13
    Closed Aug **A**
  H **Strasbourg** 6 p d'Evreaux ☎512312
    rm25 **A**

VERSAILLES (78) Yvelines (☎1) Map**9**B3
  H **Eden** 2 r P-de-Dangeau ☎9506806
    rm23 **B**
  H **Palais** 6 pl Lyautey ☎9503929 rm23 **A**
  ♦ **Residence du Berry** 14 r d'Anjou
    ☎9500180 rm39 **A**
  ★ **Cheval Rouge** 18 r A-Chernier
    ☎9500303 rm41 10Jan–20Dec **A**

France

VERVINS (02) Aisne (☎23) Map**10**C4
★★ **Tour du Roy** ☎980011 rm15
Closed 16Jan–14Feb **B**

VESOUL (70) Haute-Saône (☎84) Map**11**A2
H **Europe** 6 pl de la Gare ☎753393
rm40 **A**
H **Point Central** 6–8 r des Casernes
☎751995 rm14 **A**
H **Vendanges de Bourgogne**
49 bd C-de-Gaulle ☎751209 rm13
Closed 4–26Oct **A**

VEULETTES-SUR-MER (76) Seine-
Maritime (☎35) Map**9**A4
H **Clos Normand** r de Creenock
☎975176 Whit & Jul–15Sep **A**
H **Frégates** av de la Mer ☎975122
rm10 **A**

VÉZELAY (89) Yonne (☎86) Map**10**C2
H **Cheval Blanc** pl du Champ-de-Foire
☎332212 rm22 15Mar–15Sep **A**
H **Relais du Morvan** pl du Champ-de-
Foire ☎332533 rm10 **A**

VIC-FEZENSAC (32) Gers Map**15**B1
H **Artagnan** 3 cours Delon ☎063137
rm10 **A**

VICHY (03) Allier (☎70) Map**27**A4
H **Beau Souvenir** 11*bis* r Desbrest
☎982870 rm21 **A**
H **Cygne** 4–6 r Dacher ☎982103
rm26 **A**
H **Gramont** 21 av de Gramont ☎985181
rm10 **A**
H **Leopold III** 14 r Bardiaux ☎983464
rm32 **A**

VIC-SUR-CÈRE (15) Cantal (☎71) Map**16**D2
H **Grand Hôtel Vialette** ☎475022 rm57
Closed Nov **A**
H **Relais** ☎475009 rm11 **A**

VIENNE (38) Isère (☎74) Map**27**B4
H **Dauphiné** 15 r Boson ☎850540 rm17
Closed 27Sep–27Oct **A**
H **Gare** 37 cours de Briller ☎851748
rm19 Closed Nov **A**
H **St-Maurice** pl St-Maurice ☎850848
rm15 **A**

VIGAN (LE) (30) Gard (☎66) Map**27**A2
H **Commerce** 28 r des Barris ☎910328
rm14 30Sep–25Oct **A**
H **Voyageurs** r sous le Quai ☎910034
rm19 Feb–Dec **A**

VILLARS-COTTERÊTS (02) Aisne (☎23)
Map**9**B3/4
H **Parc** 26 pl A-Briand ☎960051 rm13 **A**
H **Ralleye** 67 r A-Dumas ☎960767 rm7
Closed Aug **A**

VILLÉDIEU LES POÊLES (50) Manche
(☎33) Map**8** C3
H **Paris** 1 bd du Ml-Leclerc ☎610066
rm15 **A**
H **St-Pierre & St Michel** 12 pl de la
République ☎610011 rm25 **A**

VILLEFORT (48) Lozère (☎66) Map**27**A3
H **Balme** pl du Portalet ☎336014 rm23
Feb–Oct **A**

VILLEFRANCHE DE ROUERGUE (12)
Averyon (☎65) Map**16**D2
H **Farrou** rte de Figeac (D122n)
☎451811 rm13 **A**
H **Univers** 2 pl de la République
☎451663 rm26 **A**

VILLEFRANCHE-SUR-MER (06) Alpes-
Maritimes (☎93) Map**28**C2
H **Darse** port de Plaisance ☎807252
rm22 15Jan–Sep **A**
H **Riviéra** 2 av S-Carnot ☎807243 rm35
Closed 15Nov–15Dec **A**
★ **Coq-Hardi** bd Corne d'Or ☎807106
rm11 Closed Nov **A**

VILLEFRANCHE-SUR-SAÔNE (69) Rhône
(☎74) Map**27**B4
H **Bourgogne** 91 r de Stalingrad
☎650642 rm22 **A**
H **Sirène** RN7 ☎653913 rm8 **A**
★ **Écu de France** 35 r d'Anse ☎683448
rm28 **A**

VILLENEUVE-DE-MAR SAN (40) Landes
(☎57) Map**15**B2
★ **Europe** ☎582008 rm26 **B**

VILLENEUVE-LÈS-AVIGNON (30) Gard
(☎90) Map**27**B2
H **Coya** Impasse du Rhône ☎822861
rm23 **A**
H **Florence** 40 av Gl-Leclerc ☎826723
rm8 15Jan–15Dec **A**

VILLENUEVE-SUR-ALLIER (03)
Allier(☎70) Map**9**B1
H **Grillon** ☎433039 rm8 **A**
H **Tour d'Argent** ☎433016 rm8 **A**

VILLENEUVE-SUR-LOT (47) Lot-et-
Garonne (☎58) Map**16**C2
H **Allées** 42 bd de la Marine ☎700129
rm23 **A**
H **Tortoni** 3 bd G-Leygues ☎700402
rm10 **A**

VILLENEUVE-SUR-YONNE (89) Yonne
(☎86) Map**10**C2
★ **Boursine** ☎871426 rm8 Closed Oct **A**
★ **Dauphin** r Carnot 14 ☎871855 rm9 **A**

VILLERS-LES-POTS see **AUXONNE**

VIMOUTIERS (61) Orne (☎34) Map**8**D3
H **Couronne** 9 r du 8-Mai ☎390304
rm15 Closed Feb **A**
H **Soleil d'Or** 16 pl de Mackau ☎390715
rm18 16Jan–20Dec **A**

VINON-SUR-VERDON (83) Var (☎94)
Map**27**B2
H **Colombier** ☎788111 rm14 **A**
H **Relais des Gorges** ☎788024 rm13 **A**

VIRE (14) Calvados (☎31) Map**8**C3
H **France** 4-6 r d'Aignaux ☎680035
rm10 **A**
H **Voyageurs** 47 au de la Gare
☎680116 rm16 **A**
★★ **Cheval Blanc** pl du 6 Juin ☎680021
rm22 Feb–Dec **B**

France

VITRÉ (35) Ille-et-Vilaine (☎99) Map**8**C3
    H **Dugvesclin** ☎750296 rm10 **A**
    ★ **Chêne Vert** 2 pl de la Gare ☎750058
    rm22 Closed 23Sep–Oct **A**

VITRY-LE-FRANÇOIS (51) Marne (☎26)
Map**10**C3
    ★ **Bon Séjour** rte de St Dizier ☎740236
    rm28(A19) Closed Jan **A**
    ★ **L'Étoile** ☎741256 rm22 (A3) **A**

VITTEL (88) Vosges (☎29) Map**11**A2
    H **Bellevue** 10 av de Châtillon ☎080798
    rm47 15Jan–30Nov **A**
    H **Oiseaux** r de Sugène ☎080627
    rm10 **A**

VIZILLE (38) Isère (☎76) Map**27** B3
    ★ **Parc** 5 av A-Briand ☎680301 rm25 **A**

VOUZIERS (08) Ardennes (☎24) Map**10**C4
    H **Relais des Ardennes** 22 r Gambetta
    ☎308018 rm 8 15Feb–15Dec **A**
    H **Deux Ponts** 12 r de l'Aisne ☎308292
    rm13 **B**
  ★★ **Rennes** 12 r Chanzy ☎308403
    rm23 **A**

WIMEREUX (62) Pas-de-Calais (☎21)
Map**3**A1
    H **Arts** 143 r Carnot ☎324313 rm12 **A**
    ★ **Centre** 78 r Carnot ☎324108 rm18
    Closed 1–19Jan **A**

WISSANT (62) Pas-de-Calais Map**3**A1
    H **Bellevue** r P-Crampel ☎359107 rm30
    Apr–Sep **A**
    ★ **Normandy** ☎359011 rm33
    Mar–Oct **B**

YENNE (73) Savoie Map**27**B4
    ★ **Logis Savoyard** pl C-Dullin ☎367038
    rm13 **A**

YPORT (76) Seine-Maritime (☎35) Map**9**A4
    H **Sirène** 7 bd A-Dumont ☎273187
    rm10 **A**

YVETOT (76) Seine-Maritime (☎35) Map**9**A4
    H **Chemin de Fer** pl de la Gare
    ☎951033 rm11 Closed Aug **A**
    H **Havre** pl des Belges ☎951677 rm26
    15Jan–15Dec **B**

GERMANY

Germany

This gazetteer contains a selection of hotels, guesthouses, inns, pensions and farmhouses. Also included is accommodation in farmhouses attached to vineyards, indicated by the symbol (**V**). The prices have been banded as follows: **A** under £5 per person per night, and **B** between £5 and £6 per person per night at sometime during the year. More detailed information, including accommodation in private houses, can be obtained from the German National Tourist Office (see p222 for address).

NB: *In Berlin, Hamburg, Hannover and München the number immediately following the establishment name is the postal district number.*

Abbreviations
Pl   Platz
Str   Strasse

AACHEN Nordrhein-Westfalen (☎0241) Map**4**D1
- ◆ **Ejjene Klenkes** Heinrichsallee 46 ☎508273 bed22 **B**

AHRWEILER Rhineland-Pfalz (☎02641) Map**4**D1
- ★ **Stern** Marktpl 9 ☎34738 rm15 15Jan–15Dec **B**

AIBLING (BAD) Bayern (☎08061) Map**13**A2
- H **Parkhotel Ludwigsbad** Rosenheimer Str 18–20 ☎2011 bed100 **B**

ALPIRSBACH Baden-Württemberg (☎07444) Map**11**B3
- ◆ **Grüner Baum** Aischbachstr 105 ☎2955 bed12 **A**
- ◆ **Schwanen** Marktstr 5 ☎2205 bed16 **A**

At **Ehlenbogen** (4km N on B294)
- ★ **Adler** ☎2215 bed40 **B**

ALSFELD Hessen (☎06631) Map**5**B1
- H **Erholung** Grünberger Str 26 ☎2023 bed24 **A**
- ◆ **Klingelhöffer** Hersfeld Str 47–48 ☎2073 bed50 **A**
- H **Krone** Schellenstr 2 ☎884/85 bed45 **A**

ALTENMARKT-AN-DER ALZ Bayern (☎08621) Map**13**A2
- FH **F. Marotzke** Muhlstr 4 ☎2206 rm4 **A**

AMBERG Bayern (☎09621) Map**13**A4
- H **Bahnhof** Battieriegasse 2 ☎12178 bed60 **A**
- ◆ **Brunner** Battieriegasse 3 ☎23944 bed70 **B**
- ★ **Goldenes Lamm** Rathaus Str 6 ☎12153 rm24 **A**

ANDERNACH Rheinland-Pfalz (☎02632) Map**4**D1
- ◆ **Andernacher Hof** Breite Str 83 ☎43175 bed60 **A**
- H **Romer** Hochstr 93 ☎42209 rm37 **A**
- H **Stadion** Stadionstr 10 ☎43878 bed28 **A**
- ★ **Anker** Konrad Adenauer Allee 21 ☎42907 rm32 **B**
- ★ **Rhein** an der Rheinpromenade ☎42240 rm25 **B**

ARNSBERG Nordrhein-Westfalen (☎02931) Map**5**A2
- ◆ **Bahnhofshotel** 2 Clemens-August-Str 110 ☎10818 bed18 **B**
- H **Krone** Al Neheim, Johannesstr 62 ☎(02932) 24231 bed48 **A**
- H **Post** Bruchhausstr 29 ☎(02932) 31396 bed65 **A**
- ◆ **Haus Tanneck** Sundener Str 25 ☎10457 bed38 **A**

ASCHAFFENBURG Bayern (☎06021) Map**12**C4
- ◆ **Central** Steingasse 5 ☎23392 bed33 **B**
- ◆ **Pape** Wurzburger Str 16 ☎22673 bed20 **A**

BACHARACH Rheinland-Pfalz (☎06743) Map**11**B4
- H **Gelber Hof** Blucherstr 26 ☎1340 bed34 **B**
- (**V**)FH **Hermesdorf** Blücherstr 60 ☎1294 rm10 **A**
- H **Krone** Langstr 7 ☎1573 bed16 Apr–Oct **A**
- ◆ **Pension Im Malerwinkel** Blucherstr 34–41 ☎1239 rm20 **A**
- H **Park** ☎1422 bed40 **B**
- H **Post** Oberstr 38 ☎1277 bed32 **B**
- ★★ **Altkonischer Hof** Bluderstr 2 ☎1339 rm20 Apr–Oct **B**
- ★★ **Engelsburg** ☎243 rm14 May–Oct **B**

BAD Each placename beginning with Bad is listed under the name that follows it.

BADEN-BADEN Baden-Württemberg (☎07221) Map**11**B3
- ◆ **Greiner** Lichtentaler Allee 88 ☎71135 bed54 **A**
- ◆ **Schweizer Hof** R-Schuman-Platz 73 ☎24231 bed36 **B**
- H **Tanneck** Werderstr 14 ☎23035 bed30 **B**
- ★ **Bischoff** Romer pl 2 ☎22378 rm21 Feb–15Nov **B**
- ★ **Romerhof** Sofienstr 25 ☎23415 rm27 Feb–15Dec **B**

BAMBERG Bayern (☎0951) Map**12**D4
- ◆ **Gasthof Weierich** Lugbank 5 ☎57404 bed45 **B**
- H **Hospiz** Promenadestr 3 ☎26624 bed58 **A**

BAYREUTH Bayern (☎0921) Map**12**D4
- H **Kolpinghaus** Kolpingstr 5 ☎22270 bed22 **A**
- H **Reichsadler** Bahnhofstr 23 ☎24094 bed54 **B**

155

Germany

BAYRISCHZELL Bayern (☎08023)
Map**13**A2
- ◆ **Alpengasthof Feuriger Tatzlwurm**
  ☎(08034) 574 bed30 **A**

BERCHTESGADEN Bayern (☎08652)
Map**13**B2
- ◆ **Lochstein** Am Lockstein 1 ☎2122
  bed14 **A**
- ◆ **Tauernhof** Untersteinerstr 101
  ☎2680 bed65 **B**
- H **Waltzmann** Franziskanerpl 2 ☎2055
  bed60 **A**
- ◆ **Weinerwald** Maximilianstr 17 ☎2068
  bed19 **A**

BERGEN Niedersachsen (☎05051) Map**5**B3
- ★ **Kohlman** Lubenstr 6 ☎2012 rm15 **A**

BERGHEIM Nordrhein-Westfalen (☎02271)
Map**4**D1
- H **Alte Post** Hauptstr 9 ☎7729 rm6 **A**
- H **Krone** Hauptstr 78 ☎7727 rm7 **B**

BERLIN (☎030) Map**6**D3
- ◆ **Alter Westen** 30 Genthiner Str 30 K
  ☎246808 bed15 **A**
- ◆ **Bamberg** 30 Bambergerstr 58
  ☎2117877 bed14 **A**
- ◆ **Brandenburg** 31 Brandenburgische
  Str 18 ☎878905 bed24 **B**
- ◆ **Pension Peters** Kantstr 146
  ☎3122278 bed11 **B**
- H **Steiner am Kurfurstendamm** 31
  Albrecht-Achilles-Str 58bed 44 **A**
- ◆ **Terminus** 15 Fasanenstr 48
  ☎8814909 bed22 **A**
- ◆ **Hotelpension Wittelsbach** 31
  Wittelsbacheistr 22 ☎876345 bed40 **B**
- ★★ **Sachsenhof** Motzstr 7 ☎2162074
  rm61 **A**
- ★ **Charlottenburger Hof**
  Stuttgarter Pl 14 ☎3244819 rm34 **B**

BERNAU-ÜBER-TITISEE Baden-
Württemberg (☎07675) Map**11**B2
- H **Schwanen** ☎348 rm12 **B**
- H **Stöckerwald** ☎408 rm13 **B**

BERNRIED Bayern (☎09905) Map**13**B3
- FH **F. Greinwald** Hapberg 3 ☎1095
  rm3 **A**

BIBERACH AN DER RISS Baden-
Württemberg (☎07351) Map**12**C2
- H **Bahnhotel Keller** Bahnhofstr 26
  ☎6574 bed24 **A**

BIELEFELD Nordrhein-Westfalen (☎0521)
Map**5**A2
- H **Bielefelder Hof** am Bahnhof 3
  ☎66055 bed75 **B**
- H **Brede** Gadderbaumerstr 5 ☎62434
  bed20 **B**
- H **Oerkenkrug** Vilsendorfer Str 97
  bed17 **A**

BINGEN Rheinland-Pfalz (☎06721)
Map**11**B4
- H **Engelbert** Rheinkai 9 ☎14715
  bed24 **A**
- H **Krone** 1 Rheinkai 19–20 ☎17016
  bed47 **A**
- H **Krupp** Koblenz-Olper-Str 165 ☎2335
  bed24 **A**

- H **Rheinhotel Starkenburger Hof**
  Rheinkai 1–2 ☎14341 bed50 **B**
- H **Römerhof** am Rupertsberg 10
  ☎32248 bed42 **A**
- H **Roten Ochsen** Hauptstr 63 ☎2348
  bed38 **A**
- ◆ **Sayntal** im Sayntal 55 ☎7472
  bed15 **A**
- ◆ **Gasthof am Schlossberg**
  1 Schlossbergstr 23 ☎14659 **A**
- H **Traube** Bachstr 22 ☎2609 bed12 **A**
- ◆ **Vater Rhein** Kirchpl 2 ☎2621 bed10 **A**

BISCHOFSWIESEN Bayern (☎08652)
Map**13**B2
- FH **M. Aschauer** Kampenweg 6 ☎7412
  rm4 **A**
- FH **F. Brandner** Reitweg 10 rm3 **A**

BITBURG Rheinland-Pfalz (☎06561)
Map**11**A4
- H **Plein** Karenweg 2 ☎3175 bed24 **A**

BLANKENHEIM Nordrhein-Westfalen
(☎02449) Map**4**D1
- ★★ **Schlossblick** Nonnenbacher Weg
  2–4 ☎238 rm29 **B**

BONNDORF Baden-Württemberg (☎07703)
Map**11**B2
- H **Bonndorfer Hof** Bahnhofstr 2 ☎7118
  bed19 **B**
- H **Steinasäge** ☎584 bed14 **A**
- ★★ **Schwarzwald-Hotel** Rothausstr 7
  ☎421 rm67 **B**

BOPPARD Rheinland-Pfalz (☎06742)
Map**5**A1
- H **Hollingshauser** Rheinallee 52
  May–Oct bed6 **A**
- H **Lindenhof** Burgstr 4 ☎5011 bed15
  Mar–Oct **A**
- H **Römer** Eltzerhofstr 21 ☎2586 bed25
  (May–Oct) **A**
- ◆ **Weller** Ritter-Schwalbach-Str 1
  ☎2436 bed30 **A**
- ★★ **Gunther** Rheinallee 40 ☎2335 rm20
  15Jan–Nov **B**
- ★★ **Spiegel** Rheinallee 34 ☎2971 rm32 **B**
- ★ **Hunsruckerhof** Steinstr 26 ☎2433
  rm26 **A**

BRAUNSCHWEIG (Brunswick)
Niedersachsen (☎0531) Map**5**B3
- H **Aquarius** Br-Buchhorst,
  Ebertallee 44g ☎71957 bed54 **B**
- ◆ **Gästehaus am Kohlmarkt**
  Kohlmarkt 2 ☎41766 bed40 **A**
- H **Stadthalle** Leonhardstr 21 ☎73068
  bed36 **B**
- H **Thüringer Hof** Sophienstr 1 ☎81222
  bed40 **A**
- ◆ **Wollmarkt** Wollmarkt 9–12 ☎46139
  bed48 **B**

BREISIG (BAD) Rheinland-Pfalz (☎02633)
Map**4**D1
- H **Anker** Rheinufer 12–13 ☎9329
  bed28 Apr–Oct **A**
- H **Mathilde** Waldstr 5–7 ☎9360 bed33
  Feb–Nov **B**
- H **Mühie** am Rheinufer ☎9142 bed58 **B**
- H **Quellenhof zum Fritze Will**

A-Mertes-Str 23 ☎9479 bed29 **B**
- ◆ **Traube** Eulengasse 14, ☎9325 bed13 **A**
- ★ **Vater & Sohn** Zehnerstr 78 ☎9148 rm8 **B**
- ★ **Rheineck** Brunnerstr 8 ☎9180 rm31 **B**

BREMERHAVEN Bremen (☎0471) Map**5**A4
- H **Borse** B-Lehe Lange Str 34 ☎88041 bed62 **B**
- H **Columbus-Logenhaus** Lange Str 145–147 ☎51666 bed45 **B**
- ◆ **Landhaus** Weserstr 2 ☎73758 bed18 **A**
- H **Metropol** Potsdamer Str 45 ☎52392 **B**

BRODENBACH Rheinland-Pfalz (☎02605) Map**5**A1
- ★★ **Post** Dorfstr 35 rm30 Apr–Oct **A**

BRUCHSAL Baden-Württemberg (☎07251) Map**11**B3
- ◆ **Goldenen Lamm** Kubelmarkt 8 ☎2058 bed20 **A**
- H **Ratskeller** Kaiserstr 68 ☎15111 bed31 **A**
- ★★ **Friedrichshof** Bahnhofpl 7 ☎2692 rm40 **A**

BRÜHL Nordrhein-Westfalen (☎02232) Map**4**D1
- ◆ **Balsen** Romerstr 363 ☎27422 bed8 **B**
- H **Kurfurst** Kölnstr 40 ☎42239 bed21 **A**
- ◆ **Rheinischer Hof** Euskirchner Str 123 ☎31368 bed26 **A**

CAMBERG Hessen (☎06434) Map**5**A1
- H **Guttenberger Hof** Guttenberg Pl 1 ☎7297 bed20 **A**
- H **Pohl** Parkstr 5a ☎6243 bed15 **A**

CELLE Niedersachsen (☎05141) Map**5**B3
- H **Blühende Schiffahrt** Fritzenwiese 39 ☎22761 bed25 **B**
- H **Goldenen Lamm** Mauernstr 29 ☎25413 bed15 **B**
- H **Post** Grosse Pl 12 ☎22183 bed12 **B**
- H **Treppenspeichern** An der Lake 2 ☎(05086) 498 bed22 **B**

CHAM Bayern (☎09971) Map**13**A/B4
- ★★ **Randsberger Hof** Randsbergerhofstr 15 ☎1916 rm65 **B**

COBURG Bayern (☎09561) Map**6**C1
- H **Haus Blankenburg** Rosenauer Str 30 ☎9874 bed65 **B**
- H **Goldene Anker** Rosengasse 14 ☎95027 bed90 **B**

COCHEM Rheinland-Pfalz (☎02671) Map**11**B4
- ◆ **Brigitte** an der Moselstrasse ☎3081 bed17 **A**
- H **Hafen** Zehnthausstr ☎490 bed24 **B**
- H **Karl Noss** Moselpromenade 17 ☎3612 bed50 **B**
- ◆ **Löhnerz** Sehler Anlagen 29 ☎7127 bed20 **A**
- ◆ **Mondial** Moselpromenade 27 ☎7462 bed35 **A**
- H **Panorama** Klostergartenstr 44 ☎630 bed40 **B**
- H **Thul** Brauslaystr 27 ☎7134 bed40 **B**
- ◆ **Winnenburg** Endertstr 141 ☎527 bed16 **A**

CELBE see **MARBURG AN DER LAHN**

CREGLINGEN Baden-Württemberg (☎07933) Map**12**C4
- ◆ **Jägerstüble** Hauptstr 7 ☎7293 bed20 **A**
- ★★ **Krone** Hauptstr 12 ☎558 rm25 **A**

DAUN Rheinland-Pfalz (☎06592) Map**4**D1
- H **Elfelperte** Reifenbergstr 1 ☎548 bed34 **B**
- H **Heines** Leopoldstr 15 ☎2180 bed20 **A**
- H **Liesertal** (near tennis courts) ☎553 bed49 **A**
- H **Müller** D-Gemünden ☎2506 bed24 **A**

DEGGENDORF Bayern (☎0991) Map**13**B3
- H **Drei Mohren** Luitpoldstr 2 ☎5777 bed50 **B**

DELMENHORST Niedersachsen (☎04221) Map**5**A3
- H **Burggrafen** Brauenkamperstr 28 ☎82546 bed14 **A**
- H **Thomsen** Bremer Str 186 ☎70098 bed103 **B**
- ★★ **Central** Bahnhofstr 16 ☎19019 rm34 **A**
- ☆☆ **Motel Annenriede** Annenheide Damm 129 ☎62392 rm50 **B**

DETMOLD Nordrhein-Westfalen (☎05231) Map**5**A2
- H **Kanne** 14 Berlebeck, Paderborner Str 155 ☎47212 bed40 **A**
- H **Berghotel Schweizerhof** Denkmalstr 100 ☎47466 bed22 **B**
- ★ **Friedrichshöne** Paderborner Str 6 ☎47053 rm14 **B**

DINKELSBÜHL Bayern (☎09851) Map**12**C3
- ◆ **Gasthof Dinkelbauer** Feuchtwanger Str 4 ☎574 bed18 **A**
- H **Weisses Ross** Steingasse 12 ☎2274 bed26 **A**
- ★★ **Goldene Rose** Marktpl 4 ☎2276 rm18 10Mar–10Nov **B**

DOBEL Baden-Württemberg (☎07083) Map**11**B3
- ◆ **Rossie** JP–Hebel Str 7 ☎2353 bed40 **A**
- ★★ **Funk** Hauptstr 32 ☎2077 rm30 20Dec–2Nov **B**

DOGERN Baden-Württemberg Map**11**B2
- H **Bahnhof** ☎3677 rm9 **A**
- H **Rheinblick** ☎3646 rm4 **A**

DONAUWÖRTH Bayern (☎0906) Map**12**D3
- ★★ **Traube** Kapellstr 14 ☎3142 rm33 **A**

DORMAGEN Nordrhein-Westfalen (☎02106) Map**4**D2
- H **Knechtstedener Hof** Knechtstedener Str 13 ☎49873 bed5 **A**
- H **Vater Rhein** Oberstr 4, Sturzelberg ☎47330 rm11 **B**

DORTMUND Nordrhein-Westfalen (☎0231) Map**5**A2
- M **Autohof** Koln-Berliner Str 39–43 ☎443636 bed16 **B**
- H **Bender** Burgtor 7 ☎527121 bed44 **B**
- H **Florianblick** Wittbräucker Str 465

Germany

☎462449 bed21 **B**
H **Stiftshof** Stiftstr 5 ☎526320 bed12 **B**

DÜREN Nordrhein-Westfalen (☎02421)
Map**4**D1

  H **Allen Post** J-Schregel Str 36 ☎15508
    bed105 **B**
  H **Monopol** Annapl 3 ☎13444 bed18 **B**
  H **Ring-Hotel-Düren** Euskirchener Str
  ★ **Nachtwächter** Kolner Landstr 12
    ☎74031 bed40 **B**

DÜSSELDORF Nordrhein-Westfalen
(☎0211) Map**4**D2

  H **Rheinischer Hof** Am Poth 2a
    ☎283081 rm20 **B**
  H **Schumann** Bonner Str 15 ☎791602
    bed25 **B**

EBRACH Bayern (☎09553) Map**12**D4

  ★★ **Krone Post** Hauptstr 1 ☎2310
    rm50 **A**

EHLENBOGEN see **ALPIRSBACH**

ELTVILLE AM RHEIN Hessen (☎06123)
Map**11**B4

  H **Glockenhof** Marktstr 3, ☎61141
    bed14 **A**
  H **Krug** Hauptstr 34 ☎(06723) 2812
    bed12 **A**
  H **Muller** Rheingauer Str 5 ☎2494
    bed21 **B**
  ♦ **Post** Rheingauer Str 46 ☎2231
    bed29 **A**
  H **Rheingauer Hof** Rheingauerstr 21
    ☎2283 bed15 **A**
  H **Weinhaus Ress** Haupstr 19
    ☎(06723) 3013 bed43 **B**
  ★ **Rosenhof** am Marktpl ☎3360 rm6 **B**

EMMENDINGEN Baden-Württemberg
(☎07641) Map**11**B2

  H **Windenreuter Hof** 7831
    Windenreuter ☎7692 bed18 **B**
  ★★ **Park** Markgrafenstr 9 ☎8639 rm35 **B**

EMMERICH Nordrhein-Westfalen (☎02822)
Map**4**D2

  H **Berliner Hof** Zevenaarer Str 3 ☎563
    rm6 **B**
  H **Reyers** Eltener Str 414 ☎70450
    rm8 **A**
  H **Wanders** Markt 2, ☎2220 rm11 **B**

ERLANGEN Bayern (☎09131) Map**12**D4

  ♦ **Einkehr** Dorfstr 14 ☎43833 bed15 **A**
  ★ **Rasthaus am Heusteg** Heusteg 13
    ☎41225 rm18 **B**

ERPEL Rheinland-Pfalz Map**4**D1

  ♦ **Koch** Bergstr 22 ☎2702 bed15 **A**
  H **Traube** Marktgasse 13 ☎2551
    bed38 **A**

ETTLINGEN Baden-Württemberg (☎07243)
Map**11**B3

  ★ **Rebstock** Leopoldstr 13 ☎12281
    rm11 **A**

FELDBERG IM SCHWARZWALD Baden-
Württemberg (☎07676) Map**11**B2

  ♦ **Auerhahn** ☎330 bed20 **A**
  H **Haus zum Löwen** Falkauer Str 1

☎(07655) 358 bed29 **A**
♦ **Seehof Windgfallweiher**
  ☎(07655) 255 bed20 **A**

FORBACH Baden-Württemberg (☎07228)
Map**11**B3

  H **Felner Schnabel** Hundseckstr 24
    ☎272 bed20 **A**
  ♦ **Haus Hermann** Biberach 1
    ☎(07220) 219 bed9 **A**

FRANKFURT AM MAIN Hessen (☎0611)
Map**11**B4

  ♦ **Aida** Schäffergasse 22 ☎281693
    bed18 **B**
  H **Central** Gutleustr 95–97 ☎233014
    bed120 **B**
  ♦ **Ebel** 1 Taunusstr 26 ☎252736
    bed55 **B**
  H **Goldener Stern** Karlsruher Str 8
    ☎233309 bed36 **A**
  ♦ **Martha** 1 Elefantengasse 1 ☎287494
    bed18 **B**
  H **Vera** Mainzer Landstr 118 ☎745023
    bed37 **B**

FREIBURG IM BREISGAU Baden-
Württemberg (☎0761) Map**11**B2

  H **Barbara** Poststr 4 ☎26060 bed30 **B**
  H **City** Wasserstr 2 ☎31766 bed100 **B**
  ♦ **Heidenhof** Elässer Str 7 ☎83348
    bed18 **A**
  H **Schiff** Basler Landstr 37 ☎43378
    bed50 **A**
  ♦ **Schützen** Schützenallee 12, ☎72021
    bed20 **A**
  H **Weinstube Schwarzwalder Hof**
    Herrenstr 43 ☎32386 bed42 **B**
  ★★ **Roten Bären** Oberlinden 12, ☎35121
    rm24 **B**

FREISING Bayern (☎08161) Map**13**A3

  H **Gred** Bahnhofstr 8 ☎5528 bed45 **B**
  ★★ **Bayerischer Hof** Untere Hauptstr 3
    ☎3125 rm70 **B**

FREUDENSTADT Baden-Wurttemberg
(☎07441) Map**11**B3

  ♦ **Berghof** Hardsteige 20 ☎82637
    bed65 **A**
  ♦ **Ege** Hartranfstr 11 ☎4117 bed20 **A**
  ♦ **Engel** Lossburger Str 6 ☎2578
    bed30 **A**
  ♦ **Herrenfeld** Landhausstr 55 ☎3304
    bed13 **A**
  ♦ **Rebstock** Marktplatz 63 ☎2158
    bed25 **A**
  ♦ **Rose** Marktplatz 20 ☎2181 bed30 **B**
  ♦ **Schauinsland** Hartranfstr 56 ☎2488
    bed10 **B**
  ♦ **Schönblick** Wolperwiesenweg 4
    ☎2843 bed9 **B**
  ★★ **Drei-Konig** M-Luther Str 3 ☎3333
    rm19 **B**
  ★ **See** Forststr 17 ☎2688 rm10 **A**

FÜRSTENFELDBRÜCK Bayern (☎08141)
Map**12**D3

  ★ **Post** Hauptstr 7 ☎2474 rm45
    Closed Xmas **B**

GARMISCH-PARTENKIRCHEN Bayern
(☎08821) Map**12**D2

Germany

H **Leiner** Wildenauer Str 20 ☎50034
bed74 **B**

H **Olympiahaus** K & M Neuner Platz 1
☎2281 bed14 **B**

★★ **Drei Mohren** Mohrenpl 7 ☎58088
bed60 18Dec–30Oct **B**

GEISENHEIM Hessen (☎06722) Map**11**B4

◆ **Fischer** Winkeler Str 72 ☎8136
bed7 **A**

H **Germania** Bischof-Blum-Platz ☎8198
rm12 **A**

◆ **Henn** Behlstr 14 ☎8206 bed21 **A**

H **Post** Rudesheimer Str 35 ☎8188
bed30 **B**

GERNSBACH Baden-Württemberg
(☎07224) Map**11**B3

◆ **Gruner Baum** G-Reichental, Susser
Winkel 1 ☎3438 bed21 **A**

H **Höhenhotel** Kurhaus ☎1044 bed17 **A**

H **Kurpark** Kelterbergstr 2 ☎2220
bed22 **B**

H **Stern-Hirsch** Hofstätte 3–5 ☎2264
bed36 **B**

★ **Ratsstuben** Hauptstr 34 rm12
15Nov–15Oct **A**

GODESBERG (BAD) Nordrhein-Westfalen
(☎02229) Map**4**D1

◆ **Nussbaum** Bürgerstr 4 ☎362009
bed12 **A**

★ **Sonnenhang** Mainzerstr 275
☎346820 rm11 **A**

GÖPPINGEN Baden-Württemberg
(☎07161) Map**12**C3

H **Goldenes Rad** Poststr 37 ☎72526
bed25 **B**

◆ **Hasen** Eislinger Str 30 ☎812246
bed17 **A**

H **Stern** Eislinger Str 15 ☎812213
bed19 **A**

★★ **Hohenstaufen** Obere Freihofstr 64
☎73484 rm53 (A12) **A**

★ **Apostelhotel** Markstr 7 ☎73462
rm28 7Jan–23Dec **B**

GOSLAR Niedersachsen (☎05321) Map**5**B2

◆ **Epping** Bergdorfstr 14 ☎21312
bed14 **A**

H **Goldener Stern** Bäringer Str 6
☎23390 bed28 **B**

◆ **Henne** 1 Braunsberger Str 8 ☎81749
bed11 **A**

H **Landhaus Harzblick** Vor dem
Nordhees 2–2A ☎84433 bed24 **A**

◆ **Haus Niedersachsen**
Wiesenstr 11–12 ☎(05325)2336
bed20 **B**

H **Niedersachsischer Hof**
Klubgartenstr 1–2 ☎23301 bed120 **B**

H **Parkhotel Weissleder** am
Bocksberg 1–3 ☎(05325)2342
bed65 **B**

GRAFELFING Bayern (☎089) Map**12**D2

★★ **Würmtaler** Rottenbucherstr 55
☎851281 rm60 (A4) **B**

GROSS GERAU Hessen (☎06152)
Map**11**B4

H **Wiesengrund** ☎4243 bed8 **A**

★ **Adler** Frankfurter Str 11 ☎2286
rm60 **A**

HALTINGEN Baden-Württemberg (☎07621)
Map**11**B2

★ **Rebstock** Grosse Grasse 30 ☎62257
rm14 **B**

HAMBURG Hamburg (☎040) Map**5**B4

H **Austria** 4 Talstr 4 ☎313161 bed60 **A**

H **Brückner** Adenauerallee 811
☎245284 bed10 **A**

◆ **Buchner** 1 Repoldstr 50 ☎244240
bed10 **A**

H **Clausen** 76 Armgartstr 14 ☎2209238
bed18 **B**

H **Grindel** Grindelallee 32 ☎451281
bed16 **A**

H **Johannsen** Colonnaden 43 ☎346822
bed20 **B**

H **Paulienhof** 4 Paulienstr 12
☎4300223 bed20 **A**

H **Schaub** Erikastr 37 ☎4603430
bed23 **B**

H **Stein** 4 Reeperbahn 75 ☎314253
bed70 **B**

H **Zentral** 90 Julius-Ludowieg-Str 4
☎778241 bed23 **B**

HANNOVER Niedersachsen (☎0511)
Map**5**B3

H **Hannover** Jaachimstr 1, ☎326705
bed59 **A**

◆ **Knuth** 1 Marienstr 7, ☎17577
bed14 **B**

◆ **Sniehotta** 1 Dieterichsstr 2, ☎3244
bed12 **A**

H **Union** Maschstr 15, ☎882424
bed90 **B**

HARZBURG (BAD) Niedersachsen
(☎05322) Map**5**B2

H **Berghotel der Silberborn** Am
Silberborn 1 ☎51006 bed25 **A**

H **Jagdhof** Hindenburgring 12a ☎7091
bed106 **B**

◆ **Kupferborn** Bismarckstr 65 ☎3231
bed23 **A**

◆ **Parkblick** Am Stadtpark 6, ☎1498
bed25 **B**

◆ **Tannenhof** Nordhauser Str 6 ☎2872
bed24 **B**

HECHINGEN Baden-Württemberg
(☎07471) Map**12**C3

At **Stein**

◆ **Lamm** ☎4290 **B**

HEIDELBERG Baden-Württemberg
(☎06221) Map**11**B4

H **Central** Kaiserstr 75 ☎20672 bed76 **A**

◆ **Eisenbahn** Odenwaldstr 66 ☎71172
bed36 **B**

H **Grimminger** Heinrich-Fuchs-Str 1
☎30938 bed54 **B**

H **Humbert** Schlierbacher Landstr 15,
☎802133 bed20 **A**

H **Königstuhl** Konigstuhl 2, ☎21607
bed23 **B**

H **Neu Heidelberg** Kranichweg 15,
☎75110 bed40 **B**

♦ **Pfalzgrafen** Kettengasse 21 ☎20489 bed55 **B**

HEIDENHEIM AN DER BRENZ Baden-Württemberg (☎07321) Map**12**C3
- ♦ **Grüner Baum** Sankt Poltener Str 1 ☎20004 bed24 **A**
- ♦ **Schönblick** Sauerbruchstr 4 ☎41000 bed14 **A**

HELMSTEDT Niedersachsen (☎05351) Map**6**C3
- ★★ **Petzold** Schöninger Str 1 ☎6001 rm28 **B**

HERFORD Nordrhein-Westfalen (☎05221) Map**5**A3
- H **Hausa** Brüderstr 40, ☎56124 bed27 **B**
- H **Stadt Köln** Bugelstr 6 ☎3198 bed12 **B**

HERRENBERG Baden-Württemberg (☎07032) Map**12**C3
- H **Brauereigasthof Hasen** Hasenplatz 6, ☎5210 bed25 **A**
- H **Neumann** Reinhold-Schick-Pl 2 ☎5139 bed13 **B**
- H **Schloss Sindlingen** Schloss Sindlingen ☎5434 bed20 **B**
- ★ **Neue Post** Wilhelmstr 48 ☎5156 rm7 10Jan–23Dec **A**

HERSFELD (BAD) Hessen (☎06621) Map**5**B1
- H **Deutsches Haus** Breinstr 1 ☎4671 bed25 **A**
- ♦ **Herzog** Alsfelder Str 50 ☎5691 bed13 **A**
- H **Sander** am Bahnhof ☎4802 bed80 **A**
- H **Schönewolf** Brückenmüllerstr 5 ☎4740 bed35 **A**
- H **Wenzel** Nachtigallenstr 3, Am Kureck ☎72017 bed43 **B**
- H **Wildes Wässerchen** Meisebacher Str 31, ☎5055 bed46 **A**

HILPOLTSTEIN Bayern (☎09174) Map**12**D3
- ★ **Post** Markstr 8 ☎20716 **A**

HINTERZARTEN Baden-Württemberg (☎07652) Map**11**B2
- H **Imbery** Rathausstr 14, ☎318 bed23 **B**
- ♦ **Ketterer** Windeckweg 26 ☎260 bed18 **A**

HOCKENHEIM Baden-Württemberg (☎06205) Map**11**B4
- ♦ **Adler** Neulussheim, Hockenheimer Str 2 ☎31180 bed30 **A**

HÖCHENSCHWAND Baden-Württemberg (☎07672) Map**11**B2
- H **Alpenblick-Gasthof** St-Georg-Str 9 ☎2055 bed48 **B**
- H **Bergfrieden** ☎418 rm22 **A**
- H **Fernblick** ☎354 bed60 **A**
- ♦ **Hanni** ☎830 rm2 **A**

HOLZMINDEN Niedersachsen (☎05531) Map**5**B2
- ♦ **Tannenhof** Himbeerbusch 23 ☎2116 bed20 **A**

HONNEF AM RHEIN (BAD) Nordrhein-Westfalen (☎02224) Map**4**D1

H **Ziepchen** Drachenfelsstr 23 ☎2398 bed30 **B**

HORSTMAR Nordrhein-Westfalen (☎02558) Map**4**D2
- ★ **Crins** ☎7370 rm10 **A**

IBACH see **TODTMOOS**

IDAR-OBERSTEIN Rheinland-Pfalz (☎06781) Map**11**B4
- H **Handelshof** Tiefensteiner Str 235 ☎31011 bed26 **A**
- H **Keller** Hauptstr 354 ☎22138 bed14 **A**
- H **Pfälzer Hof** Wasenstr 90 ☎22164 bed14 **A**

INGELHEIM Rheinland-Pfalz (☎06132) Map**11**B4
- H **Erholung** Bahnhofstr 16 ☎7063 bed20 **B**
- ♦ **Jägerstube** Bahnhofstr 1, ☎75610 bed11 **A**
- H **Multatuli** Mainzer Str 255 ☎2259 bed16 **A**
- ♦ **Park** Binger Str 17 ☎3066 bed22 **A**

INGOLSTADT Bayern (☎0841) Map**12**D3
- ★★ **Rappensberger** Harderstr 3 ☎2307 rm93 **B**
- ★ **Adler** Theresienstr 22 ☎2707 rm50 15Jan–24Dec **B**
- ★ **Auwaldsee Motel** ☎68484 rm12 15Mar–30Oct **A**

INZELL Bayern (☎08665) Map**13**B2
- FH **L. Weibhauser** Sterr 15 ☎600 rm8 **A**

ISERLOHN Nordrhein-Westfalen (☎02371) Map**5**A2
- H **Buchenwäldchen** Westfalenstr 49 ☎60361 bed20 **B**

ISNY Baden-Württemberg (☎07562) Map**12**C2
- ★★ **Hohe Linde** Lindauerstr 75 ☎2401 rm30 15Nov–Sep **B**

JESTETTEN Baden-Württemberg (☎07745) Map**11**B2
- H **Löwen** ☎7301 rm12 **A**
- H **Salmen** ☎7345 rm5 **A**

KAISERLAUTERN Rheinland-Pfalz (☎0631) Map**11**B4
- H **Barbarossa-Hof** Eselsfürth 10 ☎42402 bed33 **A**
- H **Lautertal** Mühlstr 31–33 ☎72772 bed33 **B**
- H **Seoul** Schulstr 1a ☎60490 bed21 **A**
- H **Zepp** Pariser Str 4–6 ☎73660 bed80 **A**

KARLSRUHE Baden-Württemberg (☎0721) Map**11**B3
- H **Anker** Lameystr 36 ☎557337 bed60 **B**
- ♦ **Central** Hirschstr 81 ☎813957 bed31 **B**
- H **Elite** Sachsenstr 17 ☎817363 bed45 **B**
- H **Weinstube Fässle** Lameystr 12 ☎554433 bed45 **B**
- ♦ **Zoo** 1 Ettlinger Str 33 ☎33678 bed17 **A**

KARLSTEIN Bayern Map**13**A3
  FH **G. Leitner** Nonn 59 ☎8052 rm12 **A**
  FH **F. Streibel** Nonn 65 ☎8810 rm4 **A**

KASSEL Hessen (☎0561) Map**5**B2
  H **Berghof** Ihringshaüser Str 204
    ☎811438 bed33 **A**
  H **Central & Gaststätte Kurassier**
    Erzburger Str 40 ☎12501 bed50 **B**
  ◆ **Hamburger Hof** W-Hilpert Str 18
    ☎16002 bed10 **A**
  H **Nürnberger Hof** Erzberger Str 7
    ☎15243 bed42 **B**
  H **Rathauschänke** Wilhelmsstr 29
    ☎13768 bed19 **B**
  H **Schönfelder Hof** Frankfurter Str 191
    ☎24306 bed25 **A**
  H **Wald & Strandhotel Graue Katze**
    Fuldatalstr 362 ☎811315 bed10 **A**
  H **Walhotel Schaferberg**
    Wilhelmstaler Str
    ☎(05673)7971 **B**

KEHL Baden-Württermberg (☎07851)
Map**11**B3
  H **Barbarossa** Hauptstr 120 ☎5542
    bed45 **A**
  H **Bierkeller** Bierkellerstr 16 ☎2273
    bed42 **A**
  H **Rebstock** Haupstr 183 ☎2470
    bed59 **A**

KELHEIM Bayern (☎09441) Map**13**A3
  ◆ **Stockhammer** am Oberen Zweck 2
    ☎3254 bed20 **A**
  ◆ **Weisses Lamm** Ludwigstr 12 ☎9825
    bed48 **A**
  ★★ **Ehrnthaller** Donaustr 22 ☎3333
    rm71 **B**

KEVELAER Nordrhein-Westfalen (☎02832)
Map**4**D2
  H **Burgerhaus** Hauptstr 46 ☎2209
    rm5 **A**
  H **Rheinischer Hof** Basilikastr 6 ☎2152
    rm6 **A**

KIEL Schleswig-Holstein (☎0431) Map**1**B1
  ◆ **Dietrichsdorfer Hof** 14 Heikendorfer
    Weg 54 ☎26108 bed41 **B**
  H **Muhls** Lange Reihe 5 ☎95155
    bed25 **B**
  ◆ **Schweriner Hof** Konigsweg 13
    ☎61416 bed48 **A**
  H **Seestern** Hamburger chaussee 13
    ☎(04347)3325 bed60 **A**
  ◆ **Ziemssen** 14 Passader Str 6
    ☎722715 bed18 **B**

KINDING Bayern (☎08467) Map**12**D3
  FH **W Reitzer** Beilgrieser Str ☎256 rm2 **A**

KISSINGEN (BAD) Bayern (☎0971)
Map**5**B1
  H **Bartenstein** Kurhausstr 14 ☎2124
    bed23 **B**
  H **Deutsches Haus** Obere Markstr 12
    ☎4479 bed20 **B**
  H **Hanseat** Salinenstr 27 ☎4345
    bed34 **B**
  ◆ **Kurheim Asta** Pfaffstr 9 ☎4511
    bed34 **A**

  H **Kurheim Dösch** Maxstr 4–5 ☎2306
    bed75 **A**
  ◆ **Kurheim Villa Heinigarten** Pfaffstr 7
    ☎4511 bed40 **A**

KNIEBIS Baden-Württemberg (☎07442)
Map**11**B3
  ◆ **Schwarzwald** Rippoldsauer Str 53
    ☎3292 bed35 **A**

KOBLENZ (Coblenz) Rheinland-Pfalz
(☎0261) Map**5**A1
  ◆ **Daheim** Scheckendorfstr 26 ☎37842
    bed8 **A**
  H **Kornpforte** Kornpfortstr 11 bed30 **B**
  ◆ **National** Roonstr 47 ☎14194
    bed35 **B**
  H **Park-Hotel** 1 Pfarrer-Krauss-Str 140
    ☎68880 bed18 **A**
  H **Petershof** Schlachthofstr 76–78
    bed22 **B**
  H **Romerbrunnen** Florinsmarkt 2a,
    ☎33750 bed42 **B**
  H **Servatius** Laubach Str 14 ☎33656
    bed20 **A**
  H **Wikinux-Dorf** Jesuitengasse 6,
    ☎31860 bed25 **B**
  ◆ **Wild** am Löwentor 14 ☎41551
    bed11 **A**

KOCHEL AM SEE Bayern (☎08851)
Map**12**D2
  H **Grauer Bär** Mittenwalder Str 82–86
    ☎217 bed46 **A**

KÖLN (Cologne) Nordrhein-Westfalen
(☎0221) Map**4**D1
  H **Bauernschänke** 60, Longerischer
    Hauptstr 2 ☎5991737 bed40 **B**
  ◆ **Berg** Brandenburger Str 6 ☎121124
    bed30 **B**
  ◆ **Central** an den Dominikauern 3
    ☎235222 bed60 **B**
  H **Deymanns** Venloer Str 15 ☎515597
    bed38 **A**
  M **Nord** Christinastr 4, Nippes ☎721212
    bed13 **B**
  ◆ **Park** Stadtwaldgürtel 6 ☎402374
    bed43 **A**
  H **Schmidt** Elisenstr 16 ☎211706
    bed25 **A**
  H **Schmitze Lang** Severinstr 62
    ☎316129 bed6 **B**
  ◆ **Theis** Venloer Str 334 ☎515712
    bed40 **B**
  H **Verteiler** 51 Am Verteiler
    Kreis/Banner Str ☎382869 bed75 **B**

KÖNIGSTEIN IM TAUNUS Hessen
(☎06174) Map**5**A1
  ★★ **Parkhotel Bender** Frankfurterstr 1
    ☎7105 rm40**B**

KÖNIGSWINTER Nordrhein-Westfalen
Map**4**D1
  H **Anker** I am Rheinufer 102, ☎21627
    bed18 **A**
  H **Bergischer Hof** Drachenfelsstr 33
    ☎22276 bed28 **B**
  H **Haus Germania** Hauptstr 519–523
    ☎22004 bed44 **A**
  ◆ **Gertrudenhof** Kantering 36 ☎21460
    bed27 **A**

Germany

◆ **Glocke** Hauptstr 411 ☎21440 bed16 **A**

H **Loreley** Rheinallee 12 ☎23039 bed92 **A**

H **Rebstock** Bergstr 6 ☎22810 bed12 **A**

◆ **Rheinhotel Immenhof** 1 Rheinallee 6 ☎21436 bed12 **A**

H **Weinhaus Metternich** Hauptstr 345 ☎21170 bed20 **A**

★ **Siebengebirge** 1 Hauptstr 342 ☎21359 rm8 Feb–15Dec **B**

KONSTANZ (Constance) Baden-Württemberg (☎7531) Map**12**C2

H **Barbarossa** Obermarkt 8–12 ☎22021 bed100 **B**

◆ **Blauer Bock** Hussenstr 36 ☎22741 bed23 **A**

H **Germania** Konradigasse 2 ☎23735 bed21 **A**

H **Goldener Adler** Furstenbergstr 70 ☎77128 bed45 **A**

◆ **Ingeburg** Bodaustr 8 ☎22841 bed26 **B**

◆ **Linde** Radolfzeller Str 27 ☎77036 bed25 **A**

◆ **Rösch** Hussenstr 44 ☎22440 bed17 **A**

H **Weinstube Dischinger** Untere Laube 49 ☎23255 bed7 **B**

◆ **Weisentäler Hof** Zogelmannstr 5 ☎23385 bed18 **A**

KREFELD Nordrhein-Westfalen (☎02151) Map**4**D2

H **Epping** Neusser Str 43 ☎34763 bed14 **A**

◆ **Haus Faensen** 1 Krüllsdyk 25–27 ☎754312 rm15 **A**

H **Lindenecke** Lindenstr 159 ☎770720 bed21 **B**

KREUZNACH (BAD) Rheinland-Pfalz (☎0671) Map**11**B4

H **Fessner** Steingasse 6 ☎28497 bed16 **B**

H **Gruner Baum** Kreuznacher Str 33 ☎33906 bed40 **A**

H **Siebe** Kornmarkt 1 ☎32288 bed24 **B**

KRONBERG/TAUNUS Hessen (☎06173) Map**5**A1

H **Schützenhof** Friedrich-Ebert-Str 1 ☎4968 bed15 **B**

KULMBACH Bayern (☎09221) Map**6**C1

◆ **Adler** Dorfberg 7 ☎1476 bed24 **A**

◆ **Kronprinz** Fischergasse 4–6 ☎5151 bed24 **B**

◆ **Rohrleinshof** Trebgast-Eichholz 6 ☎(09227) 5033 bed20 **B**

LAHR Baden-Württemberg (☎07821) Map**11**B3

◆ **Adler** Hauptstr 18 ☎7035 bed20 **A**

◆ **Dammenmühle** ☎22290 bed16 **A**

H **Gruner Baum** L. Bergheini ☎22282 bed40 **A**

H **Löwen** Obertortstr 5 ☎23022 bed47 **A**

H **Sonne-Post** Marktpl 1 ☎22080 bed65 **A**

★ **Schulz** Alte Bahnhofstr 6 ☎22674 rm22 **A**

LANDSHUT Bayern (☎80871) Map**13**A3

H **Park-Café** Papiererstr 36 ☎69339 bed50 **A**

LANGENISARHOFEN Bayern (☎09938) Map**13**B3

★ **Buhmann** ☎277 rm25 15Jan–23Dec **A**

LAUTENBACH Baden-Württemberg (☎07802 Map**11**B3

★ **Sternen** Hauptstr 47 ☎3538 rm40 Closed Nov **B**

LEIPHEIM Bayern (☎08221) Map**12**C3

H **Hirsch** Ulmer Str 1 ☎7757 bed40 **A**

LEONBERG Baden-Württemberg (☎07152) Map**12**C3

H **Glemseck** ☎43134 bed25 **B**

LEUBSDORF Rheinland-Pfalz Map**4**D1

◆ **Hellenthal** Hauptstr 11 ☎2531 bed6 **A**

◆ **Pitt-Jupp** Hauptstr 26 ☎2527 bed10 **A**

◆ **Traube** Hauptstr 2 ☎2270 bed15 **A**

LEUTESDORF Rheinland-Pfalz (☎02631) Map**4**D1

H **Kurtrieischer Hof** Rheinstr ☎72772 bed19 **A**

LICHTENFELS Bayern (☎09571) Map**6**C1

H **Preussischer Hof** Bamburger Str 30 ☎2188 bed44 **A**

LIESER Rheinland-Pfalz (☎06531) Map**11**A4

★★ **Mehn** Moselstr 2 ☎3011 rm25 15Jan–15Dec **B**

LIMBURG AN DER LAHN Hessen (☎06431) Map**5**A1

★ **Huss** Bahnhofspl 3 ☎6638 rm38 **B**

LINDAU IM BODENSEE Bayern (☎08382) Map**12**C2

◆ **Engel** Schafgasse 4 ☎5240 bed16 **A**

◆ **Goldenes Lamm** Schafgasse 3 ☎5732 bed75 **B**

◆ **Haus Inselblick** Hasenweidweg 31 ☎5779 bed30 **A**

◆ **Peterhof** Schafgasse 10 ☎5700 bed50 **A**

◆ **Tannheim** Bregenzer Str 16 ☎3736 bed11 **A**

◆ **Toscana** Aschacher Ufer ☎3131 bed28 **A**

◆ **Ziegler** Bodenseestr 32 ☎5410 bed22 **A**

★★ **Kellner** Alwindstr ☎5686 rm12 mid Apr–Sep **B**

LINDENFELS Hessen (☎06255) Map**12**C4

◆ **Forsthotel Seidenbuch** Buchen Str ☎756 bed35 **A**

◆ **Hechler** Burgstr 26 ☎592 bed25 **A**

H **Kuhler Grund** Nibelungenstr 111 ☎546 bed26 **B**

LINZ Rheinland-Pfalz (☎02644) Map**4**D1

H **Burgklause** Burgpl 11 ☎2468 bed10 **A**

H **Gut Fruhscheid** am Roniger Weg ☎2757 bed30 **B**

MALLERSDORF Bayern (☎08772)
Map**13A3**
  ★ **Ohne Sorge** Hofmark 5 ☎272 rm8 **A**

MANNHEIM Baden-Württemberg (☎0621)
Map**11B4**
  H **Basler Hof** 1 Tattersallstr 27 ☎28816
    bed80 **B**
  H **Bergsträsser Hof** Käfertaler Str 5
    ☎332589 bed19 **A**
  ◆ **Goldener Gans** 1 Tattersallstr 19
    ☎22353 bed36 **B**
  ◆ **Lamm** Breisacher Str 2 ☎475127
    bed16 **A**
  ◆ **Löwen** Hauptstr 159 ☎472035
    bed65 **B**
  ◆ **Park** Mannheimer Str 35 ☎738016
    bed 32 **B**

MARBURG AN DER LAHN Hessen
(☎06421) Map**5A1**
  ◆ **Burgruine Frauenburg** Cappleistr 10
    ☎(06424) 1379 bed25 **A**
  H **Drei Kronen** Kasseler Str 90 ☎83524
    bed25 **A**
  H **Fasanerie** zur Fasanerié 15 ☎7039
    bed40 **B**
  ◆ **Kreutz** Bahnhofstr 14 ☎65644
    bed30 **B**
  ★★ **Orthwein** Colbe ☎82594 rm24 **A**

MARIA LAACH Rheinland-Pfalz (☎02652)
Map**4D1**
  ★★ **See-Hotel** ☎251 rm77 **B**

MARIENBERG (BAD) Rheinland-Pfalz
(☎02661) Map**5A1**
  H **Hubertus-Klause** Europastr 2 ☎3625
    bed20 **A**

MARKTHEIDENFELD Bayern (☎09391)
Map**12C4**
  ◆ **Mainblick** Mainkai 11 ☎2373 bed40 **A**
  ★ **Anker** Obertorstr 6-8 ☎3420 rm30 **B**
  ★ **Schöne Aussicht** Bruickenstr 8
    ☎3455 rm45 **B**

MARKTOBERDOR Bayern (☎08342)
Map**12D2**
  ★ **Sepp** Bahnhofstr 13 ☎2414 rm55 **B**

MAYEN Rheinland-Pfalz (☎02651) Map**4D1**
  ◆ **Dicken baum** Burresheimer Str 1
    ☎2672 bed30 **A**
  ◆ **Traube** Bäckeistr 3&6 ☎2456
    bed50 **A**

MEERSBURG Baden-Württemberg
(☎07532) Map**12C2**
  ◆ **Schiff** Bismarckpl 5 ☎6025 bed70 **B**
  H **Sentenhart** Stefan Lochner Str17
    ☎6427 bed16 **A**
  ★ **Bären** Marktpl 11 ☎6044 rm15
    Mar – 15Nov **B**

MEMMINGEN Bayern (☎08331) Map**12C2**
  ◆ **Weisses Lamm** ☎2102 bed26 **A**
  H **Weisses Ross** Kalchstr 16
    Salzstr 12 – 14 ☎2020 **B**

MERGENTHEIM (BAD) Baden-Württemberg
(☎07931) Map**12C4**
  H **Brauereigaststätte Herbsthausen**
    Alte Kaiser Str 28 ☎(07932) 286
    bed14 **A**

◆ **Chiemgau** Michlingstr 43 ☎3209
    bed32 **A**
◆ **Reichshof** Hörterichstr 10 ☎7394
    bed27 **B**

MITTENWALD Bayern (☎08823) Map**12D2**
  ★★ **Post** Obermarkt 9 ☎1094 rm95 **B**
  ★ **Jagdhaus Drachenburg** Elmaurweg
    20 ☎1249 rm14
    Closed 21Oct – 19Dec **B**
  ★ **Zerhoch** H-Barth-Weg 7 ☎1508 rm19
    Closed 4Nov – 14Dec **B**

At **Wallgau** (9km N on B11)
  FH **F Achner** ☎(08825) 424 rm3 **A**
  FH **W Neuner** ☎(08825) 231 rm4 **A**

MONSCHAU Nordhein-Westfalen (☎02472)
Map**4D1**
  H **Hirsch** Monschauer Str 7 ☎2283
    bed60 **A**
  ★★ **Horchem** Monschauer Str 7 ☎2283
    bed60 **A**

MONTABAUR Rheinland-Pfalz (☎02602)
Map**5A1**
  H **Kalb** Grosser Market 9 ☎3401
    bed30 **A**
  H **Spielmann's Hotel Waldesruhe**
    Gelbachtal ☎3510 bed28 **B**
  ★ **Post** Bahnhofstr 30 ☎3361 bed36
    10Jan – 20Dec **B**
  ★ **Schlemmer** Kirtchstr 18 ☎5022 rm25
    10Jan – 20Dec **B**

MÜLHEIM AN DER MOSEL Rheinland-Pfalz
(☎06534) Map**11A4**
  ★★ **Moselhaus Selzer** Moselstr 7 rm15
    15Mar – 15Nov **A**

MÜNCHEN (Munich) Bayern (☎0811)
Map**13A3**
  ◆ **Anchora** 2 Landwehr Str 32c
    ☎592078 bed40 **A**
  ◆ **Augsburg** Schillerstr 18, ☎597673
    bed40 **B**
  ◆ **Aurora** 60 Limesstr 68a ☎877273
    bed32 **B**
  ◆ **Grünwald** 60 Altostr 38 ☎875226
    bed60 **A**
  ◆ **Herta** H-Sachs-Str 2 ☎265877
    bed21 **A**
  H **Köberl** 60 Bodenseestr 222 ☎876488
    bed50 **B**
  ◆ **Lämmle** 21 Friedenheimerstr 137
    ☎571529 bed50 **B**
  ◆ **Toskana** 2 Schwanthalerstr 42
    ☎531970 bed16 **B**
  ◆ **Viet-Nam** 5 Utzschneideistr 14
    ☎242430 bed35 **A**
  ◆ **Weigand** Lucile Grahn Str 39
    ☎473752 bed17 **B**

MÜNSTER Nordrhein-Westfalen (☎0251)
Map**5A2**
  H **Pension Haus Lorenz** Kapitän-
    Lorenz-Ufer 18 ☎1841 bed36 **A**
  H **Schloss Hotel Reichsgräfin von**
    Sickingen Triftstr 8
    Schlossgartenstr 31 ☎2207 bed20 **A**

NAGOLD Baden-Württemberg (☎07452)
Map**11B3**
  ★★ **Post** Bahnhofstr 2 ☎4048 rm42 **B**

Germany

NECKARGEMÜND Baden-Württemberg
(☎06223) Map**12**C4
- ◆ **Hirsch** Hauptstr 62 ☎2202 bed35 **A**
- ◆ **Rössel** Heidelberger Str 15 ☎2665 bed20 **B**

NECKARSTEINACH Hessen (☎06229)
Map**12**C4
- ◆ **Steinachperle** Schönauer Str 43 ☎548 bed10 **A**

NERESHEIM Baden-Wüttemberg (☎07326)
Map**12**C3
- ◆ **Krone** Hauptstr 13 ☎218 bed18 **A**

NEUMUNSTER Schleswig-Holstein
(☎04321) Map**1**B1
- ★★ **Wappenklause** Gasstr 12 ☎45071 rm22 **A**

NEUSTADT AN DER AISCH Bayern
(☎09161) Map**12**D4
- H **Aischtal-Hotel** Ostendstr 29 ☎2766 bed22 **B**
- ◆ **Roter Adler** Riedfelder Ortsstr 34–38 ☎2319 bed28 **A**
- ★★ **Römerhof** R-Wagner-Str 1 ☎2498 rm38 **A**

NEUWIED Rheinland-Pfalz (☎802261)
Map**5**A1
- H **Viktoria** Augustastr 37 ☎23766 bed27 **A**

NORDEN Niedersachsen (☎04931)
Map**4**D4
- ★ **Deutsches Haus** Neuer Weg 26 ☎4271 rm45 15Jan–31Dec **B**

NÖRDLINGEN Bayern (☎08931) Map**12**D3
- H **Alte Post** Hallgasse 2–4 ☎4275 bed18 **B**
- H **Biergarten** Schützenhof Kaiserweise 2 ☎3940 **B**
- H **Goldenen Lamm** Schaffelesmarkt 3 ☎4206 bed22 **B**
- H **Goldenes Rad** Lopsinger Str 8 ☎4311 bed15 **A**
- H **Ring** Burgermeister-Reiger-Str 14 ☎4028 bed46 **B**

NORTHEIM Niedersachsen (☎05551)
Map**5**B2
- H **Deutsche Eiche** Bahnhofstr 16 ☎293 bed40 **A**
- H **Deutsches Haus** am Münster 27 ☎3682 bed50 **A**
- H **Goldener Löwe** Breite Str 38 ☎3610 bed14 **A**
- H **Leineturm** ☎3368 bed50 **A**

NÜRBURG Rheinland-Pfalz (☎02691)
Map**4**D1

At **Nurburgring** 1 km SW
- ★★ **Sport Hotel Tribune** ☎2035 rm48 **A**

NÜRNBERG (Nuremberg) Bayern (☎0911)
Map**12**D4
- ◆ **Frankenhof** Luitpoldstr 8 ☎225633 bed28 **A**
- ◆ **Kein** Peuntgasse 10 ☎225940 bed17 **B**

- ◆ **Kronfleischküche** Kaiserstr 22 ☎227845 bed26 **B**
- ◆ **Meistersingerhalle** Kirchenstr 27 ☎467811 bed 12 **A**
- ★★ **Kaiserhof** Konigstr 39 ☎203686 rm66 **B**

OBERAMMERGAU Bayern (☎08822)
Map**12**D2
- H **Ambronia** Ettaler Str 5 ☎532 bed40 **B**
- H **Turmwirt** Ettaler Str 2 ☎4946 bed40 **B**
- H **Wittelsbach** Dorfstr 21 ☎4546 bed100 **A**
- H **Wolf** Dorfstr 1 ☎4731 bed60 **B**

OBERAU Bayern (☎08824) Map**12**D2
- FH M **Deisenberger** Mühlberg 1 ☎472 rm4 **A**

OBERKIRCH Baden-Württemberg
(☎07802) Map**11**B3
- ★★ **Obere Linde** Hauptstr 25–27 ☎3038 rm34 **B**

OBERSPAY see RHENS

OBERWESEL Rheinland-Pfalz (☎06744)
Map**11**B4
- (V)FH **Rupert Schmid** Hardtweg 3 ☎391 rm2 **A**
- H **Weiler** Marktpl 4 ☎310 bed20 **A**
- ★ **Goldener Pfropfenzieher** ☎207 rm30 **B**

OCHSENFURT Bayern (☎09331) Map**12**C4
- ★ **Baren** Hauptstr 74 ☎2282 bed29 Closed 25Jul–26Aug **B**

OEYNHAUSEN (BAD) Nordrhein-Westfalen
(☎05731) Map**5**A3
- ◆ **Parkblick** Ostkorso 6 ☎28328 bed54 **A**
- H **Rehmer Eck** 1 Mindener Str 115 ☎29773 bed24 **A**
- H **Westfäldischer Hof** Herforder Str 16 ☎22910 bed26 **B**
- ◆ **Wiehen** Jager pl 10 ☎(05734) 529 bed17 **A**

OFFENBURG Baden-Württemberg (☎0781)
Map**11**B3
- H **Drei Könige** Klosterstr 9 ☎24390 bed60 **B**
- ◆ **Engel** Hauptstr 58 ☎22255 bed30 **A**
- ◆ **Rheinischer Hof** Hauptstr 52 ☎24275 bed20 **A**
- ◆ **Schwarzwaldblick** Weinstr 81 ☎32488 bed40 **B**
- ◆ **Union** Hauptstr 19 ☎24478 bed65 **B**
- ★ **Glattfelder** Ortenberg ☎31219 rm16 Closed Oct–14Nov **A**

OLPE Nordrhein Westfalen (☎02761)
Map**5**A1
- ★★ **Tillman** Kolnerst 15 ☎5252 rm20 **B**

OSNABRÜCK Niedersachsen (☎0541)
Map**5**A3
- H **Aquarium** Breiter Gang 5 ☎28329 bed19 **B**
- H **Himmelreich** zum Himmelreich 11 ☎51700 bed42 **B**

Germany

H **Klute** Lotter Str 30 ☎45001 bed24 **B**
H **Park Hotel Osnabrück** am Heger
Holz ☎46083 bed 180 **A**

PASSAU Bayern (☎0851) Map**13**B3
H **Abrahamhof** Innstr 167 ☎6788
bed46 **A**
◆ **Deutscher Kaiser** Bahnhofstr 30
☎6405 bed25 **A**
H **Dreiflusse-Stadion** Danziger Str 40-
42 ☎51018 bed75 **A**
H **Pell** 16 Steinbachstr 60 ☎81501
bed59 **A**
◆ **Rittsteig** Alte Poststr 58 ☎8458
bed61 **A**
◆ **Sager** Vilshofener Str 40 ☎54258
bed60 **A**
H **Schwarzer Ochse** Ludwigstr 22
☎2119 bed115 **B**
H **Weinerwald** Grosse Klingergasse 17
☎4480 bed45 **A**

PATERSBERG see **ST-GOARSHAUSEN**

PRIEN AM CHIEMSEE Bayern (☎08051)
Map**13**A2
H **Seehotel Feldhutter** Seestr 101
☎4321 bed50 **B**

PRÜM Rheinland-Pfalz (☎06551) Map**4**D1
H **Kolner Hof** Tiergartenstr 20-22
☎2503 bed21 **A**
H **Post** Hauptstr 41 ☎3101 bed20 **A**
H **Wenzelbach** Kreuzerweg 30 ☎2727
bed19 **A**
★ **Gabauer** Hahnpl 6 ☎2346 rm8
16Oct–24Sep **A**

RASTATT Baden-Wurttemberg (☎07222)
Map**11**B3
★★ **Blume** Kaiserstr 38 ☎32222 rm34 **B**
★★ **Schwert** Herrenstr 3A ☎35984
rm22 **B**

REICHENHALL (BAD) Bayern (☎08651)
Map**13**B2
H **Alpenhotel Fuchs** Nonn 74 ☎3919
bed60 **B**
◆ **Brauerei Gasthof Bürgerbräu**
Waaggrasse 2 ☎2411 bed55 **B**
H **Pfleger** Wisbacher Str 6 ☎2497
bed34 **B**

REIT IM WINKL Bayern (☎08640) Map**13**A2
H **Gaststatte Zur Post** Kirchpl 7 ☎8914
bed70 **B**

REMAGEN Rheinland-Pfalz (☎02642)
Map**4**D1
H **Fahrhaus** Rheinallee 23 ☎24410
bed30 **A**
H **Rhein-Ahr** Quellenstr 67-69 ☎22612
bed30 **B**
★ **Fassbender** Marktstr 78 ☎23472
rm17 **A**

RENDSBURG Schleswig-Holstein (☎04331)
Map**1**B1
H **Deutsches Haus** Materialhofstr 1
☎22216 bed18 **A**
H **Schutzenheim** ☎88041 bed18 **A**

REUTLINGEN Baden-Württemberg
(☎07121) Map**12**C3
H **Garni** Kurtz Weinstube

Rappenhaldestr 11 ☎37214 bed16 **B**
H **Germania** Unter den Linden 20
☎35062 bed20 **B**

RHEINE Nordrhein-Westfalen (☎02531)
Map**5**A3
H **Blömer** Tiefe Str 32 ☎2913 bed50 **B**
H **Freye** Emmstr 1 ☎2069 bed22 **B**
H **Gastätte Thomann** auf dem Thie 15
☎3043 bed12 **B**

RHENS Rheinland-Pfalz (☎02628) Map**5**A1
H **Konigstuhl** am Rhein 1 ☎2244
bed24 **B**
H **Winzerhaus** Bahnhofstr 4 ☎2272
bed14 **A**

At **Oberspay** (4km S on B9)
◆ **Lorscheid** Hauptstr 39 ☎41521
bed8 **A**
H **Waldesruh** am Kurgarten 12 ☎42102
bed26 **B**

RICKENBACH Baden-Württemberg
(☎07765) Map**11**B2
H **Drei Konig** ☎243 rm4 **A**
H **Frieden** ☎229 rm9 **A**

RIEDLINGDEN Baden-Württemberg
(☎07371) Map**12**C2
H **Mohren** Marktpl 7 ☎7320 bed55 **A**
H **Ochsen** Marktpl 9 ☎7203 bed15 **A**

ROTENBURG Niedersachsen (☎04241)
Map**5**B3
H **Burgerhöf** am Galenburg 2 ☎5274
bed23 **B**
H **Müller** unter den Eichen 1
☎(04268) 521 bed13 **B**
★ **Deutsches Haus** Grosse Str 51
☎3300 rm10 **B**

ROTHENBURG OB DER TAUBER Bayern
(☎09861) Map**12**C4
◆ **Butz** Kapellenpl 4 ☎2201 bed28 **A**
◆ **Fränkische Vesperklause**
Georgengasse 2 ☎3494 bed24 **B**
H **Goldenen Lamm** Markt 2 ☎3488
bed45 **B**
H **Goldenes Fass** Ansbacher Str 39
☎3431 bed80 **B**
★★ **Glocke** Plönlein 1 ☎3025 rm35 **B**
★★ **Reichs-Kuchenmeister** Kirchpl 8
☎3406 rm35 **B**
★★ **Tilman Riemanschneider**
Georgengasse 11 ☎4606 rm50 **B**

RÜDESHEIM Hessen (☎06722) Map**11**B4
◆ **Pension Panorama** Sudetenstr 3
☎2897 bed22 **A**

SAARBRÜCKEN Saarland (☎0681)
Map**11**A3
★★ **Wein** Gutenbergstr 29 ☎55088
rm27 **B**

SÄCKINGEN Baden-Württemberg
(☎07761) Map**11**B2
◆ **Krone & Münsterkeller** Münster pl 18
☎7365 bed12 **A**
◆ **Stiftsmuhle** ☎2074 rm20 **A**
H **Traube** ☎2069 rm11 **A**

Germany

H **Trompeter** ☎2356 rm3 **A**
♦ **Tröndle** ☎2349 rm15 **A**

ST GOAR Rheinland-Pfalz (☎06741)
Map**11**B4
    H **Germania** Heerstr 207 ☎210 bed19 **A**
    ★★ **Hauser** Heerstr 160 ☎333 rm15
      15Feb–15Dec **B**
    ★ **Schneider am Markt** Heerstr 158
      ☎289 rm17 15Mar–Jan **B**

ST-GOARSHAUSEN Rheinland-Pfalz
(☎06771) Map**11**B4
    H **Berghotel auf der Loreley** auf der
      Loreley ☎676 bed32 **B**
    H **Colonius** Bahnhofstr 147–148 ☎604
      bed60 **B**
    ♦ **Herrmannsmühle** Forstbachstr 2
      ☎7317 bed15 **A**
    H **Krone am Markt** Markt pl 101 ☎7513
      bed32 **A**
    H **Pohl's Rheinhotel Adler**
      Rheinstr 125 ☎613 bed100 **B**
    H **Winzerhaus** Wellmicher Str 199
      ☎614 bed80 **A**

At Patersberg (1km E)
    H **Agira–kur-Bad** Kosmotel Loreley
      ☎505 bed65 **A**
    H **Berghof Teufelstein** Herschelberg 5
      ☎425 bed14 **A**

ST-MÄRGEN Baden-Württemberg
(☎07669) Map**11**B2
    ♦ **Kranz** Südhang 20 ☎311 bed15 **A**
    ★★ **Hirschen** Felberg Str 9 ☎201
      20Dec–15Nov rm40 **B**

SACHRANG Bayern Map**13**A2
    FH **J Danner** Aschach 2 ☎228 bed4 **A**

SAULGAU Baden-Württemberg (☎07581)
Map**12**C2
    ♦ **Adler** Hauptstr 41 ☎7330 bed20 **A**
    H **Bären** Hauptstr 93 ☎8778 bed32 **A**

SCHACKENFORD see **SEGEBERG (BAD)**

SCHLESWIG Schleswig-Holstein (☎04621)
Map**1**A1
    H **Goldener Stern** Gottorfstr 7 ☎32256
      bed24 **B**
    H **Hohenzollern** Moltkestr 41 ☎24919
      bed30 **B**
    H **Skandia** Lollfuss 89 ☎24190 bed50 **A**
    H **Waldhotel am Schloss Gottdorf** An
      der Stampfmühle 1 ☎23288 bed20 **B**

SCHLUCHSEE Baden-Württemberg
(☎07656) Map**11**B2
    H **Blasiwälder Hof** Eisenbreche 3
      ☎276 bed35 **A**
    ★ **Schiff** Kirchpl ☎252 rm34
      15Dec–Nov **A**

SCHRIESHEIM Baden-Württemberg
(☎06203) Map**11**B4
    ★★ **Luisenhohe** Eichenweg ☎65617
      rm28 **B**

SCHWÄBISCH HALL Baden-Württemberg
(☎0791) Map**12**C3
    ♦ **Dreikonig** Neue Str 25 ☎7473
      bed20 **B**
    ♦ **Krone** Schmiedsgasse 1 ☎2021
      bed20 **A**

♦ **Rossle** Marktpl 10 ☎51607 bed11 **A**
H **Scholl** Klosterstr 3–4 ☎6795 bed30 **B**

SCHWALMTAL-HERGERSDORF
Nordrhein-Westfalen (☎02163) Map**5**B1
    H **Luttelforst Mühle** Lullelforst 175
      ☎45277 rm10 **B**
    H **Haus Waldnpoler Heide** Steeg 11
      ☎4134 rm6 **A**

SCHWARZENFELD Bayern (☎09435)
Map**13**A4
    ♦ **Flora** Floraweg 3 ☎344 bed14 **A**

SCHWEICH Rheinland-Pfalz (☎06502)
Map**11**A4
(V)FH Josef Schiff Schaumbach ☎2787
    rm6 **A**
(V)FH Willi Schmitt Corneliusstr 67 ☎2171
    rm4 **A**

SCHWEINFURT Bayern (☎09721)
Map**12**C4
    ♦ **Grafen Zeppelin** Cramerstr 7
      ☎22173 bed17 **A**
    H **Parkhotel** am Jagersbrunnen 6a
      ☎1277 bed50 **B**
    H **Ross** Postplatz 9 ☎1571 bed100 **B**

SCHWELM Nordrhein-Westfalen (☎02125)
Map**4**D2
    ★★ **Prinz Van Preussen** Altmarkt 8
      ☎13444 rm17 **A**

SEESEN Niedersachsen (☎05381) Map**5**B2
    H **Post** Poststr 1 ☎201 bed53 **B**
    ♦ **Seesener Hof** Petersilienstr 7 ☎3644
      bed15 **A**
    ★★ **Goldener Löwe** Jacobsonstr 20
      ☎1202 rm25 **B**

SEGEBERG (BAD) Schleswig-Holstein
(☎04551) Map**5**B4
    ★★ **B404 and Hotel Stefanie** Schnellstr
      B404-Kiel ☎3600 bed35 **A**

SIEGBURG Nordhein-Westfalen (☎0224)
Map**4**D1
    H **Weissen Ross** Bonner Str 11
      ☎62252 bed25 **A**

SIGMARINGEN Baden-Württemberg
(☎07571) Map**12**C2
    ♦ **Gmeiner Weinstube** Jose Finenstr 13
      ☎13006 bed20 **B**

SINDELFINGEN Baden-Württemberg
(☎07031) Map**12**C3
    H **Eichholz** Wolfstr 25 ☎84509 bed50 **A**
    ♦ **Roaf** Nagoldstr 15 ☎82370 bed13 **B**
    ♦ **Stern** Bahnhofstr 15 ☎84781 bed12 **B**
    ♦ **Wiesengrund** Tubinger Allee 48
      ☎874106 bed22 **B**

SOEST Nordrhein-Westfalen (☎02921)
Map**5**A2
    H **Haus zur Börde** Nöttenstr 1 ☎3544
      bed14 **A**
    ♦ **Pilgrim Haus** Jakobistr 75 ☎3265
      bed22 **B**

SONSBECK Nordrhein-Westfalen (☎02838)
Map**4**D2
    H **Budapest** Xanteuer Str 163 rm10 **B**

STRAUBING Bayern (☎09421) Map**13**A3

Germany

★★ **Wittelsbach** Stadtgraben 25 ☎5017 rm42 **B**

STUTTGART Baden-Württemberg (☎0711) Map**12**C3
◆ **Erika** Rotestr 67A ☎634800 bed60 **A**
H **Geroksruhe** 1 Pischekstr 70 ☎240104 bed40 **B**
H **Krämers Burgerstuben** Gablonberger Hauptstr 4 ☎465481 bed15 **B**
H **Marktplatz** Markt pl 22 ☎244344 bed100 **A**
H **Sautter** Johannesstr 28 ☎616033 bed80 **B**

At **Bad Cannstatt**
H **Perglas** Kreuznacherstr 6 ☎565507 bed9 **B**

At **Feuerbach**
◆ **Freizeitheim** 30 Triebweg 140 ☎8851432 **B**

At **Rohr**
◆ **Wolf** Herschelstr 30 ☎741942 bed12 **A**

TEGERNSEE Bayern (☎08022) Map**13**A2
H **Bayern** Neureuthstr 23 ☎4605 bed146 **A**
H **Leeberghof** Ellinger Str10 ☎4476 bed24 **B**
H **Seehotel Atte Post** Seestr 3 ☎4561 bed90 **B**

TITISEE Baden-Wurttemberg (☎07651) Map**11**B2
H **Bären** Neustädter Str 35 ☎8223 bed85 **A**
H **Jägerhaus** Post pl 1-2 ☎5055 bed40 **B**
◆ **Schwarzwaldgasthaus Seebachstüble** Seebachstr 43 ☎8231 bed25 **A**
◆ **Seerose** Seestr 21 ☎8274 bed37 **A**
H **Sonneneck** Parkstr 2 ☎8246 bed56 **B**

TODIMOOS Baden-Württemberg (☎07674) Map**11**B2
◆ **Haus an der Wehra** Hohwehrweg 3 ☎237 bed16 **A**
◆ **Kurhotel Simon** Salesiaweg 2 ☎402 bed36 **B**
★★ **Lowen** Hauptstr ☎505 bed35 Closed 15 Nov–20Dec **B**

At **Ibach** (8km E off the St Blaisen rd)
H **Adler** ☎358 rm8 **A**
H **St Hubertus** ☎2340 rm11 **A**

TÖLZ (BAD) Bayern (☎08041) Map**13**A2
◆ **Pichler** Angerstr 23 ☎9672 bed20 **B**
★ **Gaissacher Haus** zuf Umgehungsstr ☎9583 Closed Nov rm29 **A**

TRABEN-TRARBACH Rheinland-Pfalz (☎06541) Map**11**B4
(V)FH H **Boor** Stadtteil Wolf Uferstr 10 ☎6130 rm4 **A**
H **Central** Bahnstr 43 ☎6238 bed50 **B**
★★ **Clauss-Feist** am Moselufer ☎6431 rm24 Mar–Oct **B**

TRAUNSTEIN Bayern (☎0861) Map**13**B2
◆ **Härtl** Leonrodstr 4a ☎4938 bed50 **A**

TRIBERG Baden-Württemberg (☎07722) Map**11**B2
H **Adler** Hauptstr 52 ☎4574 bed35 **B**
H **Baren** Hauptstr 10 ☎4493 bed60 **A**
H **Römischer Kaiser** 2 Sommerauerstr 35 ☎4418 bed 45 **A**

TRIER Rheinland-Pfalz (☎0651) Map**11**A4
H **Christophel** an der Porta Nigra ☎74041 bed26 **A**
H **Deutscher Hof** Sudallee 25 ☎73320 bed160 **B**
H **Fassbenders Central** Sichelstr 32 ☎74077 bed60 **A**
H **Hostert** Saarstr 1 ☎75328 bed25 **B**
H **Karlsmühle** im Muhlengrund 1 ☎52035 bed60 **A**
H **Post** Ruwerer Str18 ☎5100 bed33 **A**
H **Weinhaus Weis** Eitelbacherstr 4 ☎52016 bed75 **B**
◆ **Wienerhof** Bahnhofstr 25 ☎78547 bed26 **A**
H **Zender** Ehranger Str 207 ☎66111 bed24 **A**

TRITTENHEIM Rheinland-Pfalz (☎06507) Map**11**A4
(V)FH **August Britz-Bollig** Moselweinstr 321 ☎5396 rm4 **A**
(V)FH **Ernst Clüsserath** Moselweinstr 337 ☎2607 rm4 **A**
(V)FH **Victor Eifel** Moselweinstr III ☎2256 rm5 **A**
★ **Moselperle** Moselweinstr 67 ☎2221 rm13 10Jan–15Dec **A**

TÜBINGEN Baden-Württemberg (☎07122) Map**12**C3
H **Bad** beim Freibad ☎34095 bed54 **B**

TUTTLINGEN Baden-Württemberg (☎07461) Map**12**C2
H **Bundesbahnhotel & Gaststätten** am Hauptbahnhof 1 ☎72074 bed27 **A**
H **Schlack** Bahnhofstr 53, 57 & 59 ☎72091 bed44 **B**
★ **Ritter** Konigstr 12 ☎8855 rm18 **A**

ÜBERLINGEN Baden-Württemberg (☎07551) Map**12**C2
◆ **Bürgerbräu** Aufkilcher Str 20 ☎63407 bed22 **A**
H **Heidenhöhlen** Goldbach 3-5 ☎63360 bed40 **B**
H **Kur & Parkhotel St Leonard** Obere St-Leonard-Str 83 ☎61041 bed84 **B**
◆ **Löwen** Riedbachstr 21 ☎61600 bed28 **A**
◆ **Waldhorn** Lippertsreuter Str 27 ☎4423 bed24 **A**
H **Weinstube Schäpfte** Kessenringstr 14 ☎63494 bed20 **B**
◆ **Zähringer Hof** Münsterstr 36–38 ☎3665 bed50 **B**
★★ **Bad** Christopstr 2 ☎61055 rm60 **B**

UFFENHEIM Bayern (☎09842) Map**12**C4
★ **Traube** am Marktpl 3 ☎8288 rm17 Closed Nov **A**

ÜRZIG (Mosel) Rheinland-Pfalz (☎06532) Map**11**A4

Germany

(V)FH **Hermann Josef Schmitz** Moselufer 7
📞2459 rm3 **A**
★ **Rotschwanzchen** 📞2183 rm10 **B**

VAIHINGER AN DER ENZ Baden-
Württemberg (📞07042) Map**12**C3
★ **Post** Franckstr 23 📞4071 rm29
Closed 21Dec–9 Jan **B**

WALLGAUL see **MITTENWALD**

WASSERBURG AM INN Bayern (📞08071)
Map**13**A2
H **Lipprandt** Hauptstr 26-30 📞5383
bed37 **A**
H **Schloss Wasserburg** Hauptstr 5
📞5692 bed21 **B**
★★ **Fletzinger** Fletzingergasse 1 📞3876
rm31 9Jan–16Dec **A**

WEIDEN IN DER OBERPFALZ Bayern
(📞0961) Map**13**A4
H **Holltaler Hof** Oberhöll 2 📞42901
bed38 **B**
★ **Schmid** Obere Bachgasse 8 📞42231
rm18 **A**

WERTHEIM Baden-Württemberg (📞09342)
Map**12**C4
♦ **Hofgarten** Untere Heeg 1 📞6426
bed20 16 **A**
♦ **Klosterhof** Hauptstr 1 📞7316
bed16 **A**
H **Lindenhof** Lindenstr41 📞1353
bed30 **B**

WERTINGEN Bayern (📞08272) Map**12**D3
★ **Gasthof zum Hirsch** Schulstr 7
📞2083 rm28 **A**

WESEL Nordrhein-Westfalen (📞0281)
Map**4**D2
H **Blumenthal** Schermbecker Landstr
11 📞5704 rm8 **B**
H **Wacht am Rhein** Rheinallee Buderich
📞302 rm13 **B**

WETZLAR Hessen (06441) Map**5**A1
♦ **Dern** Kirschenwäldchen 8 📞24175
bed18 **B**
♦ **Kessel** Ed-Kaiser-Str 2 📞42811
bed20 **B**
H **Mayerle** Kirchstr 1 📞32197 bed22 **A**
★★ **Eulerhaus** Buderuspl 1 📞43549
rm31 **B**

WIESBADEN Hessen (📞06121) Map**11**B4
♦ **Eilermann** Martinstr 14 📞301004
bed30 **A**
♦ **Krüger** Parkstr 24 📞373300 bed13 **B**
♦ **Petri** Taunusstr 43 📞521508 bed18 **B**
H **Stadtmitte** Neugasse 9 📞300800
bed55 **B**
★ **Kohler** Konig Adolf Str 6 📞540804 **B**

WILDBAD IM SCHWARZWALD Baden-
Württemberg (📞07081) Map**11**B3
H **Bechtle** Wilhelmstr 14 📞8160
bed25 **B**
H **Goldener Stern** Wilhelmstr 2 📞3414
bed30 **B**
♦ **Kiessling** Bätznerstr 28-32 📞624
bed50 **A**
H **Kleinenzhof** 📞3435 bed30 **A**
H **Lichtenstein** Tannenbergstr 7 📞8494
bed16 **A**

H **Sonnenhof** Bismarckstr 23 📞481
bed40 **B**

WILDSTEIG Bayern Map**12**D2
FH **M Oswald** Unterbauern 5 📞370 rm4 **A**

WIMPFEN (BAD) Baden-Württemberg
(📞07063) Map**12**C3
H **Blauer Turm** Burgviertel 5-7 📞225
bed44 **B**
♦ **Traube** Hauptstr 1 📞266 bed17 **B**

WOLFACH Baden-Württemberg (📞07834)
Map**11**B3
♦ **Talblick** W Halbmeil 📞6676 bed12 **A**
★★ **Krone** Alter Markepl 33 📞350 rm23 **B**
★ **Hecht** Hauptstr 51 📞538 rm20 **A**

WOLFENBÜTTEL Niedersachsen
(📞05331) Map**5**B3
♦ **Kersten** Rosenmüllerstr 8 📞1467
bed20 **A**
H **Kronprinz** Bahnhofstr 12 📞1265
bed20 **B**
♦ **Schimmel** Kornmarkt 8 📞2331
bed25 **A**
★ **Stadt Schenke** Gr Kirchstr 9 📞2359
rm26 **A**

WORMS Rheinland-Pfalz (📞06241)
Map**11**B4
♦ **Grünen Baum** 24 Gaugasse 9
📞25569 bed20 **A**
H **Lortze-Eck** Schlossergasse 10–12
📞4561 bed13 **A**
♦ **Malepartus** Luisenstr 1 📞6122
bed30 **A**

WÜRZBURG Bayern (📞0931) Map**12**C4
H **Erholung** Petrinistr 19 📞21977
bed23 **A**
H **Fischzucht** J-Echter-Str 15 📞705288
bed50 **A**
♦ **Klein-Nizza-Park** F-Ebert-Ring 20
📞72893 bed20 **B**
H **Meesenburg** Pleicherforstr 8 📞53304
bed30 **A**
H **Ochsen** J-Promenade 1 📞53546
bed100 **B**
H **Urlaub** Bronnbachergasse 4 📞54813
bed30 **A**

ZELL AN DER MOSEL Rheinland-Pfalz
(📞06542) Map**11**B4
(V)FH **Elli Pellio** Winzerstr 9 📞4862 rm2 **A**
★ **Marienburg** 📞2382 rm11
Mar–15Nov **B**

ZUSMARSHAUSEN Bayern (📞08291)
Map**12**D3
★★ **Post** 📞302 rm30 **A**

ZWEIBRÜCKEN Rheinland-Pfalz (📞06332)
Map**11**B3
H **Erika** Rosengartenstr 5 📞2882
bed29 **B**
H **Löhle** Poststr 22 Wallstr 54 📞2812
bed40 **B**
★★ **Rosen** Von-Rosen-Str 2 📞2837
rm42 **B**

ZWISCHENAHN (BAD) Niedersachsen
(📞04403) Map**5**A4
★ **Ferien Motel** am Schlart 📞2005
rm31 **B**

ITALY
AND SAN MARINO

Italy

The gazetteer which follows contains details of hotels and pensions located in popular tourist areas and along throughroutes. We have, in the main, limited our selection to establishments offering overnight accommodation for less than £6 per person at sometime during the year. The prices have been banded as follows: **A** under £5 per person per night, and **B** between £5 and £6 per person per night. Generally speaking, the north of Italy is more expensive than the south and the nature of the accommodation is likely to vary accordingly. Further information on this type of accommodation may be obtained through the Italian State Tourist Department (ENIT) in London who classify and agree prices for all the establishments we have listed. Details of farmhouse accommodation, in selected areas, may also be obtained from the same source (see p222 for address).

Abbreviations:
pza   piazza

ÁBANO TERME Padova Map**30**C4
- H **Aurora** via Pietro d'Abano 13 ☎669081 rm114 **B**
- H **Firenze** via V-Flacco 74 ☎669242 rm66 21Nov–10Jan **A**
- H **Risorta** viale delle Terme 58 ☎669258 rm49 15Mar–Nov **A**
- H **Villa Piave** viale delle Terme 60 ☎669666 rm100 Apr–Nov **B**

ACQUALAGNA Pesaro e Urbino Map**30**C2
- H **Leon d'Oro** ☎79164 rm12 **A**

ACQUAPENDENTE Viterbo (☎0763) Map**31**B3
- H **Aquila d'Oro** ☎74175 rm17 **A**
- ★★ **Milano** via Cassia 29 ☎74110 rm20 **A**
- ★ **Roma** Viale del Fiore 13 ☎74016 rm26 **A**

ÁCQUI TERME Alessandria (☎0144) Map**28**D3
- H **Ariston** pza Matteotti 13 ☎2996 rm35 **A**
- H **Mignon** via Monte verde 34 ☎2594 rm29 **A**
- H **Pineta** strada della Salita 1 ☎50688 rm100 Apr–Oct **A**
- H **Regina** viale Donati ☎2114 rm105 Jun–Sep **A**
- H **San Marco** via Ghione 5 ☎2456 rm22 **A**

AGRIGENTO see **SICILIA (Sicily)**

ALÁSSIO Savona (☎0182) Map**28**D2
- ★★ **Bellevue** via A Vespucci 38A ☎42013 rm30 15Mar–15Oct **A**
- ★★ **Mare** Via Boselli 1 ☎40635 rm47 **B**
- ★★ **Villa Charlotta** via Adelasia 11 ☎40463 rm17 **A**
- ★ **Bel Sit** via D. Boselli 28 ☎40395 rm48 Apr–Oct **A**

ALBA Cuneo (☎0173) Map**28**D3
- H **Gallo d'Oro** ☎43972 rm15 **A**
- H **Langhe** ☎43923 rm9 **A**
- H **Piemonte** ☎43967 rm8 **A**
- H **Vecchio Elefante** ☎43918 rm5 **A**
- ★★ **Savona** pza Savona ☎2381 rm110 **A**

ALBA Trento (☎0462) Map**13**A1
- H **Alba** ☎61326 rm28 **A**
- H **Aurora** ☎61261 rm33 **A**

ALBENGA Savona (☎0182) Map**28**D2
- H **Italia** ☎50405 rm14 **B**
- H **Torino** ☎50844 rm15 **B**

ALBISOLA MARINA Savona (☎019) Map**28**D3
- H **Astoria** ☎41770 rm30 **B**
- H **Europa** ☎41679 rm20 **B**
- H **Splendor** ☎41796 rm11 15Mar–Oct **B**

ALLASSÁNDRIA Alessándria (☎0131) Map**28**D3
- H **Bolognese** via Marengo 136 ☎54696 rm8 **A**
- H **Londra** corso F-Cavallotti 51 ☎51721 rm30 **A**
- H **Napoleon** Marengo ☎61333 rm8 **A**
- H **Parigi** via Alessandro III 6 ☎51656 rm30 **A**
- H **Royal** corso C-Marx 18 ☎32284 rm24 **B**
- H **Venezia** via Carlo Caniggia 23 ☎2393 rm36 **A**
- ★★ **Europa** via Palestro ☎2219 rm34 **B**

AMALFI Salerno (☎089) Map**33**B3
- H **Bussola** ☎871131 rm52 **A**
- H **Lidomare** ☎871332 rm13 **B**
- ★★ **Bellevue** ☎871846 rm23 **B**
- ★★ **Marina Riviera** via F-Gioia 22 ☎871104 rm10 **A**

At **Minori** (3km E)
- ★★ **Caporal** ☎877408 rm27 **A**
- ★★ **Santa Lucia** Via Nationale 44 ☎877142 rm35 **A**

ANCONA Ancona (☎071) Map**30**D2
- H **Excelsior** via San Martino 43 ☎28298 rm22 **A**
- H **Gino** via Flaminia 4 ☎23073 rm59 **A**
- H **Rosa** pza F. Ili Rosselli 3 ☎23254 rm40 **A**

ÁNZIO Roma Map**31**B2
- H **Banzai** ☎9846143 rm52 Apr–Sep **A**
- H **La Bussola** ☎9845625 rm27 **A**
- H **Capriccio** ☎9846106 rm20 **A**
- H **Esperia e Parco** ☎9846063 rm35 **A**
- H **Golfo** ☎9846141 rm49 **A**
- H **Lido Garda** ☎9845389 rm32 May–Sep **A**

AOSTA Aosta (☎0165) Map**28**C4
- H **Excelsior** via Chambery 150 ☎41461 rm14 **A**
- H **Gran Paradiso** via Archibugio 14 ☎40654 rm39 **A**
- H **Joli** via della Valli Valdostane 11 ☎35747 rm22 **A**
- H **Mignon** viale Gran San Bernardo 7

🏠40980 rm22 **A**
- H **Turin** via Torino 14 ☎44593 rm51 **B**
- ★★ **Rayon de Soleil** (2km N SS27)
  ☎2247 rm32 15Mar–Oct **A**

ARENZANO Genova (☎010) Map**28**D3
- H **Ena** ☎917379 rm15 **B**
- H **Miramare** ☎917325 rm45 Mar–Oct **B**
- ★★ **Roma** ☎9127314 rm45 Etr–Sep **B**
- ★ **Europa** ☎9127384 rm15
  15Mar–Sep **A**

AREZZO Arezzo (☎0575) Map**30**C2
- H **Africa** via Adigrat 1 ☎32491 rm10 **A**
- H **Eturia** via Spinello 33 ☎27611 rm28 **A**
- H **Graverini** via G Monaco 49 ☎21881
  rm60 **A**

ARGEGNO Como (☎031) Map**29**A4
- H **Argegno** ☎821455 rm14 **A**
- H **Barchetta** ☎821105 rm9 **A**
- ★ **Belvedere** ☎821116 rm17
  15Mar–20Oct **A**

ARMA DI TÁGGIA Imperia (☎0184)
Map**28**D2
- H **Eden** ☎43000 bed32 **B**
- H **Roma** ☎43076 bed23 **B**
- H **Sappla** ☎43108 bed45 **B**
- ★★ **Umbra** via Degli Archi 2 ☎812240
  rm27 **A**

ARONA Novara (☎0322) Map**28**D4
- H **Antares** ☎3438 rm51 **A**
- H **Atlantic** ☎46521 rm82 **A**
- H **Cristallo** ☎2310 rm14 **A**
- H **La Rocca** ☎3637 rm68 **A**
- H **Splendor** ☎3316 rm15 **A**

ASCOLI PICENO Ascoli Piceno (☎0736)
Map**32**C3
- H **Castelli** via Tibaldeschi 5 ☎63825
  rm41 **A**
- H **Piceno** via Minnuccia 10 ☎52553
  rm40 **A**
- H **Selene** ☎81382 rm10 **A**

ASSISI Perugia (☎075) Map**31**B4
- H **Asces** ☎812420 rm11 **A**
- H **Berti** ☎813466 rm10 **A**
- H **Italia** ☎812625 rm13 **A**
- H **Minerva** ☎812416 rm28 **A**
- H **Roma** ☎812390 rm29 **A**

ASTI Asti (☎0141) Map**28**D3
- H **Cavour** pza Marconi 3 ☎50222
  rm15 **A**
- H **Lis** via Fratelli Rosselli 10 ☎55051
  rm27 **A**
- H **Rainero** via Cavour 85 ☎32566
  rm36 **A**
- H **Reale** pza Alfieri 6 ☎50240 rm27 **A**

AVELLINO Avellino (☎0825) Map**33**B3
- H **Cesare** via Tagliaments 2 ☎35815
  rm22 **A**
- H **Patria** pza Garibaldi 14 ☎36065
  rm25 **A**

BARDOLINO Verona (☎045) Map**29**B4
- H **Bologna** ☎623003 rm20 **A**
- H **Lac** Santa Cristina ☎623025 rm83
  Mar–Oct **A**
- H **Nettuno** ☎623323 rm67 Mar–Oct **A**
- H **Speranza** ☎623355 rm12 **A**

BARDONÉCCHIA Torino (☎0122)
Map**28**C3
- H **Bardonecchia** ☎9845 rm25 **A**
- H **Bucaneve** ☎9892 rm12 **A**
- H **Genzianella** ☎9897 rm26 **A**
- H **Sommeiller** ☎99582 rm44 **A**
- H **Stella Alpina** ☎99007 10 **A**
- H **Tabor** ☎9857 rm15 **A**

BARI Bari (☎080) Map**13**C4
- H **Adria** via Luigi Zuppetta 10 ☎339043
  rm38 **A**
- H **Costa** via Crisanzio 12 ☎210006
  rm23 **A**
- H **Roma** pza Roma 45 ☎224190 rm49 **A**
- ★★ **Grand Moderno** via Crisanzio 60
  ☎213313 rm51 **A**

BARLETTA Bari (☎0883) Map**34**C4
- H **Artu** ☎31721 rm34 **A**
- H **Savola** ☎31046 rm19 **A**

BAVENO Novara (☎0323) Map**28**D4
- H **Ankara Touring** ☎23048 rm95 **A**
- H **Beau Rivage** ☎2534 rm8 Apr–Oct **A**
- H **Florida** Frazione Loita ☎24824
  rm27 **A**
- H **Lido Palace** ☎2573 rm71
  May–Sep **A**
- H **Nazionale San Gottardo** ☎24529
  rm23 **A**
- H **Rigoli** ☎2756 rm28 **A**

BELGIRATE Novara (☎0322) Map**28**D4
- H **Pellegrino** ☎7491 rm10 **A**
- H **Terrazza** ☎7493 rm17 **A**

BELLÁGIO Como (☎031) Map**29**A4
- H **Barchetta** ☎950271 rm9 **A**
- H **Florence** ☎950342 rm49
  15Apr–Sep **A**
- H **Valsecchi** ☎950175 rm5
  15Feb–15Nov **A**
- ★★ **Firenze** pza Mazzini ☎950342 rm47
  Apr–Oct **B**

BELLANO Como (☎0341) Map**29**A4
- H **All'Orrido** ☎821203 rm19 **A**
- H **Cavallion Bianco** ☎821101 rm12 **A**

BELLÁRIA IGEA MARINA Forli (☎0541)
Map**30**C2
At Bellaria
- H **Adriatico** via Adriatico 38 ☎44125
  rm21 May–Sep **A**
- H **Principe** viale G-Pascoli 1 ☎44279
  rm34 May–Sep **A**
- ★ **Levante** via C-Colombo 1 ☎44223
  rm32 May–Sep **A**

At Igea Marina
- H **Doge** via Tibullo 66 ☎630100 rm41
  Jun–Sep **A**
- H **Edelweiss** viale Pinzon 232 ☎630187
  rm21 May–Sep **A**
- H **Onafri** viale Ennio 21 ☎630046 rm37
  May–Sep **A**

BELLUNO Belluno (☎0437) Map**30**C4
- H **Centrale** via Loreto 2A ☎23349
  rm22 **A**
- H **Sole** pza Marconi 11 ☎25146 rm24 **A**

BENEVENTO Benevento (☎0824)
Map**33**B3/4

Italy

H **President** via Perasso 1 ☎21000 rm76 **A**

H **Italiano** viale Pricipe di Napoli 137 ☎21564 **A**

BÉRGAMO Bérgamo (☎035) Map**29**A4

H **Commercio** viale T Tasso 88 ☎243626 rm32 **A**

H **Piemontese** pza G-Marconi 11 ☎242629 rm57 **A**

H **Sole** via B-Colleoni 1 ☎218238 rm10 **A**

BIELLA Vercelli (☎015) Map**28**D4

H **Coggiola** via Cottolengo 5 ☎28181 rm38 **A**

H **Colibri** via V-Cerrutis 5 ☎20944 rm25 **B**

H **Commercio** via B-Bona 15 ☎22669 rm27 **A**

H **Michelangelo** pza Adua 5 ☎21270 rm15 **A**

H **Principe** via Gramsci 4 ☎28631 rm47 **A**

BIVIGLIANO Firenze (☎055) Map**29**B2

★★ **Giotto Park** ☎406608 rm38 Mar–Oct **B**

BOLOGNA Bologna (☎051) Map**29**B3

H **Maggiore** via Emilia Ponente 62 ☎381634 rm50 **B**

H **Nettuno** via Galleria 65 ☎274769 rm38 **B**

H **Palace** via Montegrappa 9 ☎278954 rm97 **A**

H **Touring** via Mattuniani 1 ☎584305 rm41 **A**

BOLSENA Viterbo (☎0761) Map**31**B3

H **Eden** ☎98015 rm10 **A**

H **Loriana** ☎98104 rm7 **A**

H **Moderno** ☎98079 rm19 **A**

H **Naidi** ☎98017 rm25 **A**

H **Nazionale** ☎98006 rm11 **A**

BOLZANO/BOZEN Bolzano (☎0471) Map**12**D1

H **Adria** via Perathoner 17 ☎25735 rm26 **A**

H **Chris** via Mendel 100 ☎33122 rm22 **B**

H **Herzog** pza del Grano 2 ☎26267 rm20 **A**

H **Vajolet** pza Verdi 14 ☎27325 rm28 **A**

★★ **Figl** pza Grano 9 ☎21412 rm25 **B**

BONASSOLA La Spezia (☎0187) Map**29**A2

H **Belvedere** ☎813622 rm31 **B**

★★ **Lungomare** ☎813632 rm44 May–Sep **A**

BORCA see **MACUGNAGA**

BORDIGHERA Imperia (☎0184) Map**28**D2

H **Helios** via G-Biamonte 23 ☎21677 rm30 **B**

H **Rosalia** via V-Emanuele 429 ☎21366 rm32 **B**

◆ **Soetje** via Gioberti 26 ☎21573 rm12 **B**

◆ **Tina** via Regina Margherita 62 ☎22850 rm14 **D**

◆ **Villa S'Agnese** via Romano 119 ☎21559 rm17 15Dec–Oct **B**

★★ **Excelsior** via Gl-Biamonti 30 ☎261488 rm43 18Dec–Oct **A**

★★ **Villa Elisa** via Romana 70 ☎261313 rm35 20Dec–10Oct **A**

BÓRMIO Sondrio (☎0342) Map**12**D1

H **Alù** ☎902307 rm21 **A**

H **Derby** ☎901278 rm24 Dec–Apr & 15Jun–15Sep **A**

H **Everest** ☎901291 rm27 Dec–Apr & Jun–Sep **B**

H **Terminus** ☎901691 rm20 **A**

★★ **Posta** via Roma 66 ☎901106 rm55 Dec–20Apr & 20Jun–20Sep **B**

BRÉSCIA Bréscia (☎030) Map**29**B4

H **Ambasciatori** via Crocifissa di Rosa 92 ☎308461 rm69 **B**

H **Ascot** via Luigi Apollonio 72 ☎294191 rm65 **A**

H **Cristallo** viale Stazione 12A ☎293237 rm20 **A**

H **Montini** via Moretto 51 ☎49141 rm20 **A**

H **Solferino** via Solferino 1 ☎46300 rm15 **A**

BREUIL see **CERVÍNIA-BREUIL**

BRESSANONE/BRIXEN Bolzano (☎0472) Map**13**A1

H **Albero Verde** ☎22218 rm37 **A**

H **Aquila d'Oro** ☎22250 rm19 **A**

H **Heiseler** ☎22163 rm16 **A**

H **Orso Grigio** ☎22472 rm16 **A**

BRINDISI Brindisì (☎0831) Map**39**B2

H **Barsotti** via Cavour 1 ☎31998 rm60 **A**

H **Corso** corso Roma 83 ☎24128 rm44 **A**

H **Regina** via Cavour 5 ☎22122 rm42 **A**

H **Torino** Largo Palumbo 6 ☎22587 rm14 **A**

BRUNICO/BRUNECK Bolzano (☎0474) Map**13**A1

H **Bologna** ☎85917 rm25 **B**

H **Blitzburg** ☎85723 rm19 **A**

H **Corso** ☎85434 rm17 **A**

At **Riscone/Reischach** (3km SE)

H **Petrus** ☎84263 rm27 Closed May & 15Oct–Nov **A**

H **Reischacherhof** ☎85009 rm25 **A**

BUSANA Reggio nell'Emilia Map**29**B3

H **Ventasso** ☎890137 rm25 **A**

CADENÁBBIA Como (☎0344) Map**29**A4

H **Britannia Excelsior** ☎40413 rm143 20Mar–Oct **A**

H **Riviera** ☎40422 rm18 15Apr–15Oct **A**

★ **Beau-Rivage** via Regina 87 ☎40426 rm20 Apr–Oct **A**

CAMAIORE (LIDO DI) Lucca (☎0584) Map**29**B2

H **Berna** viale Pistelli 1 ☎64223 rm28 May–Sep **A**

H **Bixio** viale Colombo 395 ☎64558 rm18 **A**

H **Mariotti** viale C Colombo 147 ☎64170 rm34 **A**

H **Riva Mare** via G Pascoli 12 ☎64967
rm18 15Jan–15Sep & Dec–10Jan **A**

H **Tony** viale Carducci 7 ☎64736
rm24 **B**

CAMPOBASSO Campobasso (☎0874)
Map**33**B4

    H **Eden** via Colle delle Api 91 ☎62663 **A**

    H **Italia** via Ferrari 69 ☎65398 rm15 **A**

    H **Miramonti** via Colle delle Api ☎62724
rm21 **A**

    H **Roxy** pza Savoia 7 ☎91741 rm41 **A**

    H **Tricolore** via San Giovanni in
Golfo 112 ☎62787 rm10 **A**

CAMPO NELL'ELBA see **ELBA (ISOLA D')**

CANAZEI Trento (☎0462) Map**13**A1

    H **Alla Rosa** ☎61107 rm40 **A**

    H **Bellavista** Pecol ☎61165 rm46
Closed 19Jun & Nov–19Dec **A**

    H **Diana** ☎61477 rm28
Closed 21Apr–19Jun & 1–20Dec **A**

    H **Tyrol** ☎61156 rm36
20Dec–20Apr & 15Jun–Sep **A**

  ★★ **Croce Bianca** ☎61111
rm30 26Dec–15Apr & 15Jun–Oct **B**

CÁNNERO RIVIERA Novara (☎0323)
Map**28**D4

    H **Franco** ☎78095 rm11 **A**

    H **Milano** ☎78021 rm28 Mar–Oct15 **A**

    H **Miralago** ☎78282 rm11 **A**

  ★★ **Cannero** Lungo Lago ☎78046
15Mar–Oct **B**

CÁORLE Venezia (☎0421) Map**30**C4

    H **Caorle** ☎81231 rm45 May–Sep **A**

    H **Florida** ☎81103 rm50
15May–15Sep **B**

    H **Monaco** ☎81504 rm68
10May–Sep **A**

  ★★ **Parigi** ☎81430 rm56 15May–Sep **A**

CAPRI (ISOLA DI) Napoli (☎081) Map**32**D1

    H **Canasta** ☎8370561 rm16
13Mar–Sep **A**

    H **Floridiana** ☎8370101 rm36 **B**

    H **Residenza** ☎8370142 rm81 **A**

    H **Splendid** ☎8370187 rm23
15Mar–15Oct **A**

CARRARA (MARINA DI) Massa-Carrara
(☎0585) Map**29**A2

    H **Maestrale** viale Marinella ☎58551
rm52 May–Sep **A**

    H **Miramare** viale C. Colombo 23
☎56092 rm39 Jun–Sep **A**

  ◆ **Pineta** viale C. Colombo 119 *bis*
☎59701 rm7 May–Sep **A**

  ★★ **Mediterraneo** via Genova 2 *bis*
☎57397 rm50 **A**

CASALE MONFERRATO Alessandria
(☎0142) Map**28**D3

    H **Botte d'Oro** ☎2310 rm29 **A**

    H **Dell'Angels** ☎2065 rm17 **A**

    H **Leon d'Oro** ☎4356 rm35 **A**

    H **Milano** ☎2007 rm33 **A**

    H **Paradiso** ☎2543 rm9 **A**

    H **Principe** ☎2019 rm30 **A**

CASERTA Caserta (☎0823) Map**33**A3

    H **Centrale** via Roma 170 ☎21892
rm41 **A**

    H **Eden** via G-Verdi 26 ☎25417 rm12 **A**

    H **Vittoria** via Cesare Battisti 44
☎22068 rm22 **A**

CASSINO Frosinone (☎0776) Map**32**C2

    H **Alba** via G de Blasio 71 ☎21873
rm26 **A**

    H **Cannone** via E de Nicola 103 ☎21177
rm13 **A**

    H **Excelsior** corso Repubblica 1
☎21300 rm30 **A**

    H **Pace** via Abruzzi 8 ☎22288 rm39 **A**

    H **Pavone** via Ausonia 14 ☎21944
rm11 **A**

    H **Silvia Park** via Ausonia 47 ☎21975
rm50 **A**

CASTELLANA GROTTE Bari (☎080)
Map**39**B2

    H **Autostella Aci** ☎735495 rm6 **A**

    H **Vittoria** ☎735008 rm10 **B**

CASTIGLIONCELLO Livorno (☎0586)
Map**29**B2

    H **Genova** ☎752129 rm11 **A**

    H **Park** ☎752229 rm12 **A**

  ★★ **Guerrini** via Roma12 ☎752047
rm29 **A**

CASTROVILLARI Cosenza (☎0981)
Map**34**C2

    H **Dolcedorme** ☎21131 rm19 **A**

    H **Tarsia** ☎21518 rm9 **A**

CATÁNIA see **SICILIA (Sicily)**

CATANZARO Catanzaro (☎0961) Map**34**C2

    H **Diana** Discesa pza Nuova 11 ☎29813
rm43 **A**

    H **Serravalle** via ALberghi 8 ☎21663
rm25 **A**

    H **Splendore** via Damiano Assanti 7
☎29414 rm12 **A**

CATTÓLICA Forli (☎0541) Map**30**C2

    H **Cristina** via Bologna 45 ☎961071
rm41 May–Sep **A**

    H **Savoia** viale G-Carducci 38 ☎961174
rm72 May–Sep **A**

    H **Turismo** viale Fiume 34 ☎961285
rm22 May–Sep **A**

  ★★ **Maxim** via Facchini 7 ☎962137 rm55
30May–19Sep **A**

  ★★ **Senior** viale del Prete ☎963443 rm46
May–Sep **A**

  ★ **Bellariva** via Fiume 10 ☎961609
rm24 5May–20Sep **A**

CAVA DE' TIRRENI Salerno (☎089)
Map**33**B3

    H **Vincenzo** ☎842679 rm8 **A**

  ★★ **Victoria** Corso Mazzini 4 ☎841064
rm42 **A**

CAVAGLIÀ Vercelli (☎0161) Map**28**D4

  ★★ **Prateria** ☎96115 rm32 Mar–Nov **B**

CAVI see **LAVAGNA**

CELLE LIGURE Savona (☎019) Map**28**D3

    H **Colombo** via Monte Tabor 37
☎990043 rm31 **B**

    H **Lazaro** via Pozzuolo 5 ☎990044
rm21 **B**

    H **Pescetto** via Poggi 4 ☎990003
rm30 **B**

Italy

CERIALE Savona (℡0182) Map**28**D2
- H **Cavallino Blanco** ℡90692 rm12 **B**
- H **Miramare** ℡90006 rm18 **B**
- H **Moresco** ℡90175 rm40 **B**
- H **Zephir** ℡90031 rm25 **B**
- ★★ **Torelli** Lungomare ℡90040 rm80 Jan–15Oct **B**

CERNÓBBIO Como (℡031) Map**29**A4
- H **Centrale** ℡511212 rm15 **A**
- H **Miralago** ℡510125 rm32 Apr–Oct **A**
- ★ **Asnigo** pza San Stefano ℡510062 rm22 Apr–Oct **A**

CÉRVIA Ravenna (℡0544) Map**30**C3
- H **Cervetta** viale dei Mille 2 ℡72014 rm9 **A**
- H **San Carlo** Lungomare G-Deledda 78 ℡71251 rm26 May–Sep **A**
- ★★ **Buenos Aires** Lungomare G-Deledda 130 ℡71948 rm58 Apr–Sep **B**

At **Milano Marittima** (3km N)
- H **Amigos** XIII Traversa 13 ℡992295 rm30 May–Sep **A**
- H **Flamingo** viale Matteotti 170 ℡991066 rm42 May–Sep **A**

CERVÍNIA-BREUIL Aosta (℡0166) Map**28**D4
- H **Edelweiss** ℡94078 rm41 **A**
- H **Europa** ℡94660 rm41 Nov–Apr & Jul–Sep **A**
- H **Jumeaux** ℡94044 rm29 Nov–Apr & Jul–Sep **A**
- H **Lac Bleu** ℡94103 rm20 **A**
- H **Rosà** ℡94022 rm72 **A**
- H **Serenella** ℡94041 rm13 **A**
- ★★ **Valdotain** Lago Bleu ℡948776 rm30 Dec–May & Jul–Sep **B**

CESENÁTICO Forli (℡0547) Map**30**C2
- H **Baltic** via del Fortino 1 ℡82585 rm27 May–Sep **A**
- H **Lido** viale G-Carducci 49 ℡80048 rm58 Jun–Sep **A**
- H **Week-End** viale dei Mille 99 ℡80173 rm30 Jun–Sep **A**

At **Valverde** (1km SE)
- H **Bruna** via Melozzo da Forli ℡86423 rm24 Jun–Sep **A**
- H **Garden** viale G-Carducci 292 ℡86045 rm48 May–Sep **A**

At **Villamarina** (2km SE)
- H **Sport** via Pitagora 5 ℡86247 15May–20Sep **A**
- H **Stacchini** via Euclide 15 ℡86080 rm15 Jun–Sep **A**

At **Zadina Pineta** (3km NW)
- H **Kiss** via dei Pini ℡83012 rm20 Jun–Sep **A**
- H **Zadina** via dei Pini 40 ℡81050 rm50 May–Oct **A**

CHIÁVARI Genova (℡0185) Map**29**A2/3
- H **Castagnola** ℡307119 rm74 **B**
- H **Monterosa** ℡300321 rm76 **B**
- ★★ **Mignon** via A-Saliette 7 ℡309420 rm32 **A**
- ★★ **Tigullio Rocks** via Aurelia 61 ℡318193 **A**

CHIAVENNA Sondrio (℡0343) Map**12**C1
- H **Crimea** ℡32240 rm16 **A**
- H **Elvezia** ℡32165 rm23 **A**
- H **Flora** ℡32254 rm19 **A**

CHIÓGGIA Venezia (℡041) Map**30**C3
- H **Bella Venezia** ℡400500 rm16 **A**

At **Sottomarina** (1km E)
- H **Capinera** ℡400961 rm50 15May–20Sep **B**
- H **Montecarlo** ℡403638 rm26 15May–Sep **A**
- H **Stella d'Italia** ℡400600 rm31 **A**

CHIUSA/KLAUSEN Bolzano (℡0472) Map**13**A1
- H **Sylvanerhof** ℡47557 rm17 **B**
- H **Corona** ℡47516 rm24 **A**
- H **Goldener Engel** ℡47592 rm15 **A**
- ★ **Posta** ℡47514 rm61 **A**

CHIVASSO Torino (℡011) Map**28**D3
- H **Centauro** ℡9102169 rm12 **A**
- H **Europa** ℡9101181 rm32 **B**
- H **Moro** ℡9102191 rm39 **A**
- H **Scudo di Francia** ℡9102170 rm15 **A**

CITTÀ DELLE PIEVE Perugia (℡0578) Map**31**B3
- H **Vannucci** ℡28063 rm13 **A**

CIVITAVÉCCHIA Roma (℡0766) Map**31**B3
- M **Cacciatore** ℡22219 rm8 **A**
- H **Mediterraneo-Suisse** ℡23156 rm68 **A**
- H **Medusa** ℡24327 rm9 **A**
- M **Palamite** ℡23657 rm7 **A**
- H **Traghetto** ℡25920 rm22 **A**

CLAVIERE Torino (℡0122) Map**28**C3
- H **Grande Albergo Claviere** ℡8802 rm30 **A**
- H **Passero Pellegrino** ℡8802 rm27 **A**
- H **Roma** ℡8812 rm36 **A**
- H **Savoia** ℡8803 rm24 **A**
- H **Torino** ℡8886 rm14 **A**

CLUSONE Bergamo Map**29**A4
- H **Erica** ℡21667 rm22 **A**
- H **Terminus** ℡21151 rm23 **A**

CÓLICO Como (℡0341) Map**29**A4
- H **Aurora** San Giorgio ℡940323 rm23 **A**
- H **Continental** ℡940217 rm22 **A**
- ★★ **Isola Bella** via Nazionale 6 ℡940101 rm44 **A**
- ★ **Risi** pza Cavour 1 ℡940123 rm50 **B**

COMO Como (℡031) Map**29** A4
- H **Continental** via Innocenzo XI 15 ℡273343 rm65 **A**
- H **Minerva** pza Grimoldi 8 ℡266482 rm25 **A**
- H **Politeama** viale Cavallotti 1 ℡271205 rm12 **A**
- H **Posta** via Garibaldi 2 ℡266012 rm19 **A**
- H **Terminus** Lungo Lario Trieste 14 ℡267042 rm32 **A**
- ★★ **San Gottardo** pza Volta ℡263531 rm55 **B**

CORTINA D'AMPEZZO Belluno (℡0436) Map**13**A1

H **Bellevue** corso Italia 195 ☎3271 rm67 Apr–Sep & 20Dec–15Mar **A**

H **Corona** via C-Battisti 10 ☎3251 rm46 20Jun–15Sep & 20Dec–Mar **A**

H **Olimpia** Largo della Poste 37 ☎3256 rm46 Jun–Sep & Dec–Mar **A**

★★ **Pioner** Carbonin Di Dobbiaco ☎72240 rm85 15Dec–Oct **A**

COSENZA Cosenza (☎0984) Map**34**C2

H **Alexander** via Monte San Michele 3 ☎26939 rm46 **A**

H **Bologna** corso Telesio 208 ☎26196 rm18 **A**

H **Mondial** via Molinella 24E ☎22558 rm46 **A**

COSTALUNGA (Passo di) Trento (☎0471) **13**A1

★★ **Savoy Tamion** Carezza al Lago ☎616824 **B**

COURMAYEUR Aosta (☎0165) Map**28**C4

H **Berthod** via Puchoz ☎82286 rm17 **A**

H **Edelweiss** via Marconi ☎82325 rm29 **A**

H **Montanina** strada Regionale ☎82284 rm21 **A**

H **Sciattolo** via Monte Bianco 48 ☎82274 rm15 **A**

H **Petit Meublè** strada Margherita 17 pr82426 rm10 **A**

H **Svizzero** strada Nazionale ☎82035 rm30 **A**

CREMONA Cremona (☎0372) Map**29**A3

H **Astorio** via Bordigallo 19 ☎30260 rm27 **A**

H **Este** viale Po 131 ☎32220 rm24 **A**

H **Ideale** corso Garibaldi 275 ☎22738 rm14 **A**

CROTONE Catanzaro (☎0962) Map**34**C2

H **Cerviani** Sannella ☎26296 rm17 **A**

H **Italia** ☎23910 rm20 **A**

H **Reale** ☎26850 rm19 **A**

CÚNEO Cuneo (☎0171) Map**28**C/D3

H **Cervino** via Meucci 36 ☎67647 rm13 **A**

H **Ciriegia** corso Nizza 11 ☎2703 rm14 **A**

H **Fiamma** corso Giolitti 30 ☎68051 rm51 **A**

H **Smeraldo** corso Nizza 27 ☎3451 rm18 **A**

H **Torrismondi** via M Coppino 33 ☎61939 rm25 **A**

DESENZANO DEL GARDA Brescia (☎030) Map**29**B4

H **Astoria** ☎9142308 rm32 30Mar–Oct **A**

H **Benaco** ☎9141710 rm23 Mar–Oct **A**

H **Desenzano** ☎9141500 rm20 Apr–Sep **A**

H **Nazionale** ☎9141501 rm 32 **A**

★★ **Eden** Lungolago Cesare Battisti 27 ☎9141416 rm18 **A**

DIANO MARINA Imperia (☎0183) Map**28**D2

H **Airone** via Milano 32 ☎44782 rm13 Jan–Oct **B**

H **Bala Bianca** pza Mazzini 5 ☎45167 rm64 **B**

H **Delfina** via G-Ardoino 107 ☎45564 rm17 **B**

H **Helios** via la Fiorita 9 ☎45755 rm24 **B**

H **Raffy** via G-Ardoino 134 ☎46172 rm46 **B**

DOBBIACO/TOBLACH Bolzano (☎0474) Map**13**A1

H **Cristallo** ☎72138 rm27 Closed 11Apr–29May & 21Sep–16Dec **B**

H **Oberhammer** ☎72195 rm24 **A**

H **Union** ☎72146 rm54 **A**

ELBA (ISOLA D') Livorno (☎0565) Map**31**A3

At Campo nell'Elba

♦ **Fine** ☎987017 rm11 **A**

At Lacona

H **Alfio** ☎964052 rm24 Apr–Sep **A**

H **Della Lacona** ☎964050 rm210 Apr–Sep **A**

At Marciana Marina

H **Gabbiano Azzurro** ☎99226 rm39 **B**

H **Imperia** ☎99082 rm21 **A**

At Porto Azzurro

H **Arrighi** ☎95315 rm18 **A**

H **Plaza** ☎95010 rm25 **A**

H **Rocco** ☎95127 rm27 **A**

★ **Belmare** ☎95012 rm25 **A**

At Portoferráio

H **Emy** ☎92370 rm12 **A**

H **Falconetta** ☎92130 rm16 15Mar–15Oct **A**

H **Massimo** ☎92766 rm67 **B**

H **Nobel** ☎93217 rm21 **A**

H **Touring** ☎93815 rm25 **B**

ÉMPOLI Firenze (☎0571) Map**29**B2

H **Plaza** ☎74751 rm22 **A**

H **Posta** ☎74279 rm11 **A**

H **Sole** ☎73779 rm12 **A**

★★ **Tazza D'Oro** via del Papa 46 ☎72129 rm51 **B**

ENNA see **SICILIA (Sicily)**

ERICE see **SICILIA (Sicily)**

FANO Pesaro & Urbino (☎0721) Map**30**C2

H **Corallo** ☎878200 rm20 **A**

H **Siri** ☎83767 rm15 **A**

H **Vittoria** ☎82231 rm27 Jun–Sep **A**

★★ **Astoria** Viale Cairoli ☎82474 rm42 May–Sep **A**

★★ **Excelsior** Lungomare Simonetti 17 ☎82558 rm30 15Jun–10Sep **A**

FASANO DEL GARDA see **GARDONE RIVIERA**

FERRARA Ferrara (☎0532) Map**30**C3

H **Carlton** via Garibaldi 93 ☎33141 rm85 **A**

H **Ferrara** pza della Repubblica 4 ☎33015 rm66 **A**

M **Nord-Ovest** viale Po 52 ☎36385 rm38 **A**

H **Touring** viale Cavour 11 ☎26096 rm36 **A**

FIESOLE Firenze (☎055) Map**29**B2

Italy

H **Villa Bonelli** ☎59513 rm23 **A**

FINALE LIGURE Savona (☎019) Map**28**D2
    H **Giardino** via T-Pertica 49 ☎63475 rm22 Apr–Oct **B**
    H **Vecchie Mura** via delle Mura ☎62155 rm13 **B**

At **Varigotti** (5km E)
    ★★ **Nazionale** via Aurelia 183 ☎698012 rm26 15May–Sep **A**

FIRENZE (Florence) Firenze (☎055) Map**29**B2
    H **Firenze** pza Donati 4 ☎214203 rm48 **A**
    H **Lido** via del Ghirlandaio 1 ☎687887 rm12 **A**
    H **Paris** via dei Banchi 2 ☎263690 rm60 **A**
    H **Santa Croce** via Bentaccordi 3 ☎260370 rm10 **A**
    H **Stazione** via dei Bianchi 3 ☎283133 rm14 **A**
    H **Sul Ponte** via Senese 315 ☎2049056 rm8 **A**
    H **Varsavia** via Panzani 5 ☎215615 rm9 **A**
    ★ **Losanna** via V-Alfieri 9 ☎587516 rm9 **A**

FÓGGIA Fóggia Map**33**B4
    H **Asti** via Monfalcone 1 ☎23327 rm94 **A**
    H **Bologna** via Monfalcone 53 ☎21341 rm20 **A**
    H **Roma** pza Giordano 17 & 18 ☎21749 rm38 **A**
    H **Valleverde** via Monfalcone 68 ☎72110 rm24 **A**

FOLIGNO Perugia (☎0742) Map**31**B3
    H **Belvedere** ☎53990 rm14 **A**
    H **Italia** ☎50412 rm29 **A**
    H **Posta** ☎50526 rm39 **A**
    H **Roma** ☎50472 rm22 **A**

FONDI Latina (☎0773) Map**32**C2
    H **Appia** ☎51243 rm10 **A**
    H **Bella Roma** ☎51001 rm14 **A**
    H **Fiori** ☎51161 rm13 **A**
    H **Principe** ☎51729 rm22 **A**

FORLÌ Forlì (☎0543) Map**30**C2
    H **Astoria** pza Ordelaffi 4 ☎26220 rm37 **A**
    H **Masini** corso Garibaldi 28 ☎28072 rm42 **A**
    H **Vittorino** bia Baratti 4 ☎24393 rm21 **A**

At **Ronco** (4km SE)
    H **Galliano** ☎780068 rm19 **A**

FÓRMIA Latina (☎0771) Map**32**C2
    H **Ariston** ☎22170 rm56 **A**
    H **Bajamar** ☎28063 rm27 **A**
    H **Caposele** ☎21925 rm45 **A**
    H **Grand** ☎21020 rm33 **A**
    H **Paradiso** ☎21955 rm22 **A**
    H **Romantic** ☎22000 rm40 **A**

FORTE DEI MARMI Lucca (☎0584) Map**29**B2
    H **California Park** via Colombo 32 ☎82222 rm41 Apr–Sep **B**

H **Goya** viale Carducci 69 ☎81741 rm55 May–Sep **A**
H **Olimpia** via Marco Polo 4 ☎81046 rm28 Apr–Sep **A**
★★ **Adams Villa Maria** Lungomare 110 ☎80901 rm44 Jun–Sep **B**

FREGENE Roma (☎06) Map**31**B2
    ★★ **Fiorita** (Pensione) via Castellammare 86 ☎6460435 **A**

FROSINONE Frosinone (☎0775) Map**32**C2
    H **Astor** via Casilina Nord ☎853222 rm52 **A**
    H **Cesari** via Licinio Refice 235 ☎81581 rm60 **B**
    H **Nikla** pza Madonna della Neve ☎850752 rm30 **A**
    H **Palombella** via Maria 234 ☎851706 rm34 **A**
    H **Sora Giulia** pza Madonna della Neve 21 ☎850001 rm97 **A**
    ★★ **Palace-Hasser** via Brighindi 1 ☎852747 rm60 **B**

GABICCE MARE Pesaro & Urbino (☎0541) Map**30**C2
    H **Atlantic** via Panoramica ☎962254 rm52 May–Sep **A**
    H **Star** via Redipuglia 6 ☎961297 rm30 May–Sep **A**
    ★★ **Club de Bona** via Panoramica 33 ☎962622 rm50 30Apr–Sep **B**

GAETA Latina (☎0771) Map**32**C2
    H **Flamingo** ☎41738 rm51 **A**
    H **Mirasole** Serapo ☎40073 rm136 **A**
    H **Sabbia d'Oro** Serapo ☎40909 rm34 **A**
    H **Serapo** Serapo ☎40092 rm72 **A**
    H **Viola** ☎40414 rm26 **A**

GALLÍPOLI Lecce (☎0833) Map**34**D3
    H **Cristina** ☎473871 rm27 **A**
    H **Rivabella** ☎476969 rm36 **A**

GARDA Verona (☎045) Map**29**B4
    H **Bisesti** ☎624227 rm90 10Mar–Oct **B**
    H **Continental** ☎624398 rm56 **A**
    H **Eden** ☎624482 rm19 **A**
    ★★ **Tre Corone** via Lungolago 44 ☎264033 rm25 Mar–20Oct **A**

GARDONE RIVIERA Brescia (☎0365) Map**29**B4
    H **Fiordaliso** ☎20158 rm8 **A**
    H **Giardino** ☎21010 rm17 **A**
    H **Savoy** ☎21451 rm97 15Apr–Oct **A**
    ★★ **Bellevue** via Zanardelli 44 ☎20235 rm34 Apr–10Oct **A**

At **Fasano del Garda** (2km NE)
    H **Paradiso** ☎20269 rm36 Apr–Sep **A**
    H **Riccio** ☎21987 rm19 Apr–Sep **A**

GELA see SICILIA (Sicily)

GÉNOVA (Genoa) Génova (☎010) Map**29**A3
    H **Cristallo** vico San Pancrazio 9 ☎297979 rm27 **B**
    H **Rex** via de Gasperi 9 ☎317131 rm10 **B**
    H **Virginia** vico dello Scalo 1 ☎265820 rm24 **B**

At **San Pier d'Arena** (5km W)
    H **Stella** ☎459004 rm13 **B**

GENZANO DI ROMA Roma (☎06)
Map**31**B/C2
    H **Belvedere** ☎9396009 rm16 A
  ★★ **Villa Robinia** viale Frattelli Rosselli 19
    ☎9396409 rm30 A

GHIFFA Novara (☎0323) Map**28**D4
  ★★ **Ghiffa** via Belvedere 66 ☎59285 rm26
    Apr–Sep A

GIÓIA TÁURO Reggio di Calabria (☎0966)
Map**34**C1
    H **Centrale** ☎51010 rm23 A
    H **Commercio** ☎52085 rm15 A
    H **Mediterraneo** ☎51854 rm54 A

GIULIANOVA LIDO Teramo (☎085)
Map**32**C3
    H **Algeri** ☎862935 rm60 A
    H **Atlantic** ☎863029 rm38
    10May–10Oct A
    H **Promenade** ☎862338 rm50
    15May–Sep A
    H **Residence Palace** ☎862920 rm34
    May–Sep A
    H **Ritz** ☎863470 rm40 Apr–Oct A
    H **Riviera** ☎863490 rm18 A

GORÍZIA Gorízia (☎0481) Map**30**D4
    H **Posta** via Garibaldi 7 ☎2668 rm41 A
    H **Silvano** corso Italia 231 ☎83839
    rm10 A

GRADO Gorizia (☎0431) Map**30**D4
    H **Capri** via A-Vespucci 1 ☎80091 rm27
    May–Sep A
    H **Helvetia** viale Kennedy 15 ☎80598
    rm38 May–Sep A
    H **Hilde** via Parini 4 ☎80919 rm23 A
  ★★ **Hungaria** via Carducci 13 ☎80183
    rm47 May–Sep A

GRAVEDONA Como (☎0344) Map**29**A4
    H **Italia** ☎85294 rm17 A
   ★ **Turismo** ☎85227 rm14 Mar–Nov A

GRAVELLONA TOCE Novara (☎0323)
Map**28**D4
    H **Diana** ☎84137 rm7 A
    H **Sant'Antonio** ☎84080 rm9 A
    H **Sempione** ☎84050 rm18 A
   ★ **Helios** ☎84096 rm19 A

GRIGNANO see **TRIESTE**

GROSSETO Grosseto (☎0564) Map**31**A3
    H **Bastiani** via Manin 11 ☎20047
    rm71 A
    H **Nalesso** via Senese 35 ☎412441
    rm24 A
    H **Ombrone** via Mattesotti 71 ☎22585
    rm11 A

GUARDISTALLO Pisa (☎0586) Map**29**B2
  ★★ **Villa Elena** ☎655035 rm30 (A10) B

GUBBIO Perugia Map**30**C2
    H **Gattapone** via Ansidei 6 ☎924089
    rm13 A
    H **Oderisi** via Mazzatinti 2 ☎922547
    rm16 A
    H **San Marco** ☎922516 rm30 A
    H **Tre Ceri** via Benamati 6/8 ☎922104
    rm12 A

IÉSOLO (Jesolo) (LIDO DI) Venezia
(☎0421) Map**30**C4
    H **Carlton** via Altinate 118 ☎90485
    rm63 May–Sep A
    H **Galles** via Verdi ☎92666 rm46
    May–Sep A
    H **Nettuno** via A-Bafile 737 ☎92803
    rm74 May–Sep A
  ★★ **Regina** via Bafile 115 ☎90383 rm50
    May–Sep A

At **Pineta** (6km E)
  ★★ **Danmark** via Oriente 170 ☎961013
    rm58 May–Sep A

IMPÉRIA Impéria (☎0183) Map**28**D2
    H **Corallo** corso Garibaldi 29 ☎79480
    rm36 B
    H **Miramare** viale Matteotti 24 ☎25559
    rm14 B
    H **Robina** via Pirinoli 14 ☎79720 rm58 B

INTRA see **VERBÁNIA**

ISÉRNIA Isérnia Map**32**D2
    H **Emma** valgianese ☎26386 rm19 A
    H **Europa** ☎2126 rm30 A
    H **Ragno d'Oro** pza della Repubblica 22
    ☎2280 rm31 A
    H **Sayonara** via G-Berta ☎2592 rm31 A
    H **Tequila** Contrada S hazzaro
    ☎265174 rm69 A

IVREA Torino (☎0125) Map**28**D4
    H **Dora e Scudo di Francia** ☎422328
    rm41 A
    H **Moro** ☎40170 rm33 A
    H **Aquila Antica** ☎423309 rm27 A
  ★★ **Eden** Corso Massimo d'Azeglio 67
    ☎49190 rm36 B

JESOLO see **IÉSOLO**

LACCO AMENO see **ISCHIA (ISOLA D')**

LACONIA see **ELBA (ISOLA D')**

LAGONEGRO Potenza (☎0973) Map**33**B3
    H **Autostello Aci** ☎21154 rm21 A
    H **Immacolata** ☎21241 rm10 A

LAIGUÉGLIA Savona (☎0182) Map**28**D2
  ★★ **Mariolina** via Concezione 15 ☎49024
    rm22 A
  ★★ **Windsor** pza 25 Aprile 7 ☎49000
    rm50 20Apr–25Oct B

LAVAGNA Genova (☎0185) Map**29**A2/3
    H **Miramare** ☎309825 rm35 Jun–Sep B
    H **Santa Lucia** ☎309943 rm17 B
  ★★ **Tigullio** via Matteotti 3 ☎307623
    rm42 15Mar–15Nov A

At **Cavi** (3km SE)
   ★ **Scogliera** ☎390072 rm22
    25May–Sep A

LECCE Lecce (☎0832) Map**39**B1
    H **Patria-Touring** pza G-Riccardi 13
    ☎29431 rm60 A
    H **Risorgimento** rm57 A
    H **Savoia** via Ussano 5 ☎24568 rm10 A

LENNO Como (☎0344) Map**29**A4

Italy

H **Roma** ☎55137 rm25 15Mar–Sep**A**
★★ **San Giorgio** ☎40415 rm30
Apr–15Oct**A**

LÉRICI La Spezia (☎0187) Map**29**A2
H **Florita** Carbognano ☎967479 rm12 **B**
H **Italia** pza Garibaldi 1 ☎967108
rm16 **A**

LESA Novara (☎0322) Map**28**D4
H **Lago Maggiore** ☎7259 rm5 **A**
H **Manzoi** ☎7486 rm10 **A**
H **Margherita** ☎7392 rm10 **A**
★★ **Giardino** ☎7283 rm40 **A**

LÉVANTO La Spezia (☎0187) Map**29**A2
H **Dora** ☎808168 rm36 **B**
H **Europa** ☎808126 rm20 Mar–Oct **B**
H **Mare** ☎808253 rm22 **B**
★ **Garden** Corso Italia 6 ☎808173 rm15
Apr–Sep **A**

LEVICO TERME Trento (☎0461) Map**29**B4
H **Alietti-Miralago** ☎71359 rm27 **A**
H **Cristallo** ☎71427 rm30 Jun–Sep **A**
H **England** Campiello ☎72024 rm31 **A**
H **Royalty** ☎71437 rm41
15May–15Sep **A**

LIDO DI IÉSOLO (Jesolo) see **IÉSOLO
(LIDO DI)**

LIGNANO PINETA see **LIGNANO
SABBIADORA**

LIGNANO RIVIERA see **LIGNANO
SABBIADORA**

LIGNANO SABBIADORO Udine (☎0431)
Map**30**C4
H **Cavallino Bianco** viale dei Platani 88
☎71509 rm34 **A**
H **Italia** viale Italia 7 ☎71185 rm107 **A**
H **Luna** Lungomare Trieste ☎71490
rm57 May–Sep **A**
H **Nettuno** ☎71333 rm32 **A**

At **Lignano Pineta** (5km SW)
H **Continental** viale delle Palme 45
☎72207 rm40 May–Sep **B**
H **Erica** Arco del Grecale 21–23
☎72123 rm38 15May–Sep **A**

At **Lignano Riviera** (7km SW)
H **Meridianus** viale della Musica 7
☎72412 rm90 May–Sep **A**
H **Smeraldo** viale della Musica ☎72240
rm51 15May–15Sep **A**

LIMONE SUL GARDO Brescia (☎0365)
Map**29**B4
H **Berna** ☎94047 rm52 **A**
H **Castel** ☎94025 rm46 Jan–Oct **A**
H **Roxy Park** ☎94040 rm48 May–Sep **A**
H **Royal** ☎94122 rm72 **A**
H **Splendid** ☎94031 rm62
15Mar–15Oct **A**

LIVORNA (Leghorn) Livorno (☎0586)
Map**29**B2
H **Cabour** via Adua 10 ☎23604 rm11 **A**
H **Italia** corso Mazzini 120 ☎29020
rm11 **A**
H **Milano** via degli Asilia 48 ☎22271
rm18 **A**

LOANO Savona (☎019) Map**28**D2
H **Colibri** via Aurelia 12 ☎668315
rm16 **B**
H **Miramare** corso Roma 2 ☎668071
rm33 **B**
H **Savoia** via N-Sauro 1 ☎668301
rm40 **B**

MACUGNAGA Novara (☎0324) Map**28**D4

At **Borca**
H **Alpi** ☎65135 rm14 **A**

At **Pecetto**
H **Edelweiss** ☎65124 rm24 **A**
H **Nuovo Pecetto** ☎65025 rm20 **A**
★★ **Lagger** ☎65139 rm21 **A**

At **Staffa**
H **Anza** ☎65008 rm43 **A**
H **Girasole** ☎65052 rm16 **A**
H **Glacier** ☎65051 rm18 **A**
H **Macugnaga** ☎65005 rm14 **A**

MADONNA DI CAMPÍGLIO Trento (☎0465)
Map**29**B4
H **Diana** ☎41104 rm27 **A**
H **Excelsior Ferrari** ☎41007 rm41
Aug–10Sep & Dec–15Apr **A**
H **Ideal** ☎41016 rm37
Jul, Aug & Dec–Mar **A**
H **Montanara** ☎41105 rm10 **A**
H **St Raphael** ☎41570 rm30
Jun–Sep & Dec–Apr **A**

MAEN see **VALTOURNANCHE**

MAIORI Salerno (☎089) Map**33**B3
H **Garden** ☎877555 rm78 **A**
H **Mare** ☎877225 rm30 **A**
H **San Pietro** ☎877220 rm 32
17Mar–Sep **A**

MALCÉSINE Verona (☎045) Map**29**B4
H **Augusta** ☎600300 rm14
20Mar–20Oct **A**
H **Capri** ☎600385 rm21 Mar–Oct **A**
H **Goethe** ☎600092 rm12 **B**
H **San Marco** ☎600115 rm14 **A**

MÁNTOVA Mántova (☎0376) Map**29**B3
H **Europa** via S-Bettinelli 5 ☎22767
rm16 **A**
H **Ferrata** via Oberdan 23 ☎25298
rm15 **A**
H **Moderno** pza Don E Leoni 25 ☎22329
rm16 **A**

MARATEA Potenza (☎0973) Map**33**B2/3
◆ **Quisisana** ☎76582 rm10 **A**

MARCIANA MARINA see **ELBA (ISOLA D')**

MARINA DI CARRARA see **CARRARA
(MARINA DI)**

MARINA DI MASSA see **MASSA (MARINA
DI)**

MARINA DI PIETRASANTA see
PIETRASANTA (MARINA DI)
MARINA SAN VITO Chieti Map**32**D3
M **River** ☎61396 rm10 **A**

MARSALA see **SICILIA (Sicily)**

Italy

MASSA (MARINA DI) Massa Carrara
(☎0585) Map**29**A2
- H **Milano** pza Betti 24 ☎20076 rm23
  May–Sep **A**
- H **Rex** via G-Rossini 14 ☎20177 rm38
  Apr–Sep **A**
- H **Scandinavia** via Zolezzi 4 ☎20295
  rm37 **A**

MATERA Matera (☎0835) Map**34**C3
- H **Italia** via Ridola 5 ☎21195 rm31 **A**
- H **President** via Roma 13 ☎24075
  rm76 **A**

MAZZARÒ see **TAORMINA** under **SICILIA**
(Sicily)

MÉINA Novara (☎0322) Map**28**D4
- H **Bel Sit** ☎6483 rm12 **A**
- H **Verbano** ☎6229 rm27 **A**
- H **Victoria Palace** ☎6470 rm75 **A**

MENÁGGIO Como (☎0344) Map**29**A4
- H **Flora** ☎32866 rm10 18Mar–10Oct **A**
- ★★ **Loveno** via N-Sauro 5 ☎32110
  rm14 (A5) 15Mar–30Oct **A**

At **Nobiallo** (1kmN)
- ★★ **Miralago** ☎32363 rm28
  30Mar–30Oct **A**

MERANO/MERAN Bolzano (☎0473)
Map**12**D1
- H **Cremona** pza Steinach 19 ☎22159
  rm33 **A**
- H **Nido** via Gilm 6 ☎26880 rm 42
  15Mar–Oct **A**
- ★★ **Adria** via Glim 2 ☎26183 rm51 (A9)
  Mar–Oct **B**
- ★★ **Irma** via Belvedere 7 ☎30124
  rm62 (A2) 24Feb–Oct **B**
- ★★ **Regina** via cavour 101 ☎33432 rm75
  15Mar–Oct **B**

MESSINA see **SICILIA (Sicily)**

MESTRE Venezia (☎041) Map**30**C4
- ★★ **Aurora** pza G-Bruno 15 ☎989832
  rm33 **B**

MILANO (Milan) Milano (☎02) Map**29**A4
- H **Adler** via Ricordi 10 ☎221441 rm20 **B**
- H **Bassano** via Bassano del Grappa 28
  ☎287607 rm20 **A**
- H **Campion** viale Berenganò 3
  ☎462363 rm19 **B**
- H **Emilia** via Ponte Seveso 38 ☎600158
  rm28 **B**
- H **Garden** via Rutilia 6 ☎560838 rm20 **A**
- H **Kent** via F-Corridoni 2-7 ☎705173
  rm18 **A**
- H **Union** via Lazzaro Papi 18 ☎585890
  rm32 **A**
- ★★ **Terminus** viale Vittorio Veneto 32
  ☎664917 rm65 **A**

MILANO MARITTIMA see **CÉRVIA**

MINORI see **AMALFI**

MISURINA Belluno (☎0436) Map**13**A1
- ★★ **Sorapiss** ☎8209 rm24 (A6)
  12Dec–Mar & 15May–Sep **A**

MÓDENA Módena (☎059) Map**29**B3
- H **Libertà** via Blasia 10 ☎222365
  rm37 **A**

- H **Milano** corso Vittorio Emanuele 68
  ☎223011 rm62 **A**

MOLTRÁSIO Como (☎031) Map**29**A4
- H **Posta** ☎290444 rm14 **A**
- ★★ **Caramazza** ☎290050 rm20
  Apr–20Oct **A**

MOLVENO Trento (☎0461) Map**29**B4
- H **Gloria** ☎58962 rm30 **B**
- H **Lac** ☎58965 rm37 **A**
- H **Miralago** ☎58935 rm34 **A**
- H **Villanova** ☎58938 rm23 **A**
- ★★ **Miralago** ☎58935 rm52
  Dec–Mar & May–Sep **A**
- ★ **Cina Tosa** via Scuole 3 ☎586928
  rm32 Jun–20Sep **A**

MONDOVÌ-BREO Cúneo (☎0174)
Map**28**D3
- H **Genova** ☎43522 rm32 **A**
- H **Nuovo Torrismondi** ☎2702 rm37 **A**
- H **Park** ☎43550 rm55 **B**

MONÉGLIA Genova (☎0185) Map**29**A2
- H **Moneglia** ☎49314 rm36 **B**
- H **Paradiso** ☎49223 rm33
  15Mar–Sep **B**

MONFALCONE Gorizia (☎0481) Map**30**D4
- H **Adriaco** via Bagni 187 ☎74277
  rm16 **A**
- H **Carlina** via 1 Maggio 29 ☎40130
  rm34 **A**

MONTALTO DI CASTRO Viterbo (☎0766)
Map**31**B3
- H **Montebello** ☎89014 rm11 **A**
- H **Vulci** ☎89065 rm22 **A**

MONTECATINI TERME Pistoia (☎0572)
Map**29**B2
- H **Centrale** pza del Popolo 20 ☎70151
  rm46 **A**
- H **Columbia** Corso Roma 19 ☎70661
  rm60 Apr–Oct **B**
- ★★ **Lido Palace Risorgimento**
  via IV – Novembre14 ☎70731 rm56
  Apr–Oct **A**

MÚCCIA Macerata (☎0737) Map**32**C4
- H **Cacciatore** ☎43121 rm10 **A**

NAPOLI (Naples) Napoli (☎081) Map**32**D2
- H **Ambassador's Palace** via Medina 70
  ☎312031 rm278 **B**
- H **Cavour** pza Garibaldi 32 ☎337488
  rm92 **A**
- H **Grilli** via Galileo Ferraris 40 ☎514344
  rm198 **A**
- H **Guiren** via Bologna 114 ☎336030
  rm23 **A**
- H **Prati** via C-Rosaroli 4 ☎518898
  rm45 **A**
- H **Rex** via Palepoli 12 ☎416102 rm35 **A**

NERVI Genova (☎010) Map**29**A3
- H **Garden** via Marco Sala 10 ☎378597
  rm17 **B**
- H **Milanese** via Aurelia 5 ☎379636
  rm24 **B**
- H **Riposo** via Capolungo 44 ☎378677
  rm16 **B**

At **Sant' Ilaria Ligure** (2km E)
- H **Belvedere** ☎378285 rm10 **B**

Italy

NOBIALLO see **MENÁGGIO**

NOLI Savona (☎019) Map**28**D2
- H **Diana** ☎748975 rm25 Dec–Sep **B**
- H **Italia** ☎748971 rm10 **B**

NOVA LEVANTE WELSCHNOFEN Bolzano (☎0471) Map**13**A1
- H **Centrale** ☎613164 rm19 **A**
- H **Croce d'Oro** ☎613120 rm22 **A**
- H **Panorama** ☎613232 rm18 Closed 16Apr–14May & 16Oct–19Dec **A**
- H **Sonne** ☎613163 rm 31 **A**

NUMANA Ancona (☎071) Map**32**C4
- H **Morelli** ☎936227 rm10 **A**
- H **Villa Sirena** ☎936420 rm22 **A**

ORA/AUER Bolzano (☎0471) Map**13**A1
- H **Heide** ☎80019 rm41 **A**
- H **Wasserfal** ☎80150 rm15 15Mar–Oct **A**
- ★★ **Elefant** via Nazionale ☎80129 rm32 **A**

ORBETELLO Grosseto (☎0564) Map**31**A3
- H **Laguna** ☎867570 rm8 **A**
- H **Piccolo Parigi** ☎867233 rm15 **A**
- H **Touring** ☎867151 rm14 **A**

ORTA SAN GIULIO Novara (☎322) Map**28**D4
- H **Bussola** ☎90198 rm17 **B**
- H **Conca d'Oro** Ortello ☎90252 rm6 **A**
- H **Leon d'Oro** ☎90254 rm16 **A**
- H **Orta** ☎90253 rm33 15Mar–15Oct **A**

ORTISEI/ST ULRICH Bolzano (☎0471) Map**13**A1
- H **Angelo** ☎76336 rm40 Closed Nov **A**
- H **Hell** ☎76785 rm24 10Jun–Sep & 15Dec–10Apr **B**
- H **Rainell** ☎76145 rm28 **A**

OSPEDALETTI Imperial (☎0184) Map**28**D2
- H **Italia** ☎59045 rm11 **B**
- H **Pins** ☎59301 rm14 **B**

PÁDOVA (Padua) Pádova (☎049) Map**30**C4
- H **Autostrada** via San Marco 5 ☎34247 rm13 **A**
- H **Firenze** via GB Belzoni 172 ☎650830 rm30 **A**
- H **Igea** via Ospedale Civile 87 ☎36214 rm43 **B**
- H **Vienna** Bia Beato Pellegrino 106 ☎28489 rm25 **A**

PAESTUM Salerno (☎0828) Map**33**B3
- H **Esplanade** ☎843203 rm30 20Mar–Oct **A**
- ★★ **Calypso** Zona Pineta ☎811031 rm40 (A10) **B**

PALERMO see **SICILIA (Sicily)**

PALLANZA see **VERBÁNIA**

PAQUIER see **VALTOURNANCHE**

PARMA Parma (☎0521) Map**29**B3
- H **Bristol** via Garibaldi 73 ☎22683 rm33 **A**
- H **Touring** via Gramsci 11 ☎36588 rm13 **A**
- ★★ **Milano** viale Ponte Bottego 9 ☎35877 rm47 **A**

PAVIA Pavia (☎0382) Map**29**A3
- H **Excelsior** pza Stazione 25 ☎28596 **A**
- H **Moderna** viale Vittoria Emanuelle 11, 45 ☎26819 rm39 **A**

PECETTO see **MACUGNAGA**

PEGLI Genova (☎010) Map**28**D3
- H **Colombo** ☎480176 rm13 **B**
- H **Puppo** ☎480017 rm15 **B**

PERGUSA see **ENNA** under **SICILIA (Sicily)**

PERÚGIA Perúgia (☎075) Map**31**B3
- H **Bonazzi** via Bonazzi 45 ☎23355 rm12 **A**
- H **Centrale** via Balbo 4 ☎61431 rm18 **A**
- H **Eden** via C Caporali 9 ☎28102 rm15 **A**
- H **Etruria** via della Luna 21 ☎23730 rm10 **A**
- H **Italia** via Boncambi 8 ☎61114 rm39 **A**
- H **Signa** via del Grillo 9 ☎61080 rm23 **A**

PÉSARO Pesaro & Úrbino (☎0721) Map**30**C2
- H **Due Palme** viale Trieste 52 ☎31355 rm30 May–Sep **A**
- H **Liana** viale Trieste 102 ☎68330 rm21 May–Sep **A**
- H **Losanna** viale Dante 39 ☎33681 rm40 May–Sep **A**
- H **Olympia** viale Trieste 96 ☎30325 rm34 **A**
- H **Regina** pza Matteotti 15 ☎30275 rm9 **A**
- ★★ **Atlantic** Viale Trieste 365 ☎61911 rm40 10May–Sep **A**

PESCARA Pescara (☎085) Map**32**C3
- H **Adria** via Firenze 141 ☎21246 rm27 **A**
- H **Astoria** ☎27074 rm64 **A**
- H **Bellariva** viale Riviera 213 ☎70641 rm40 **A**
- H **Holiday** Lungomare C Colombo 104 ☎60913 rm51 **A**
- H **Pescara** pza duca d'Aosta 33 ☎23797 rm31 **A**
- H **Salus** Lungomare Matteotti 13 ☎374196 rm22 **A**
- H **Valle Verde** corso Vittorio Emanuele 301 ☎23211 rm16 **A**

PESCASSÉROLI L'Aquila (☎0863) Map**32**C2
- H **Bamby** ☎91319 rm37 **A**
- H **Conca** ☎91562 rm12 **A**

PIACENZA Piacenza (☎0523) Map**29**A3
- H **Astra** via R-Boselli 19 ☎70364 rm10 **A**
- H **Nazionale** via Genova 35 ☎20387 rm74 **A**
- H **Piacenza** via Buffalari 4 ☎27777 rm19 **A**
- ☆☆ **K2** via Emilia Parmense 133 ☎25381 rm45 **A**

PIANO DI SORRENTO Napoli (☎081) Map**33**A3
- H **Cappuccini** ☎8786152 rm20 **A**

PIAZZA ARMERINA see **SICILIA (Sicily)**

PIETRA LIGURE Savona (☎019) Map**28**D2

H **Continental** ☎647346 rm38 **B**

H **Cristal** ☎645226 rm31 **B**

H **Minerva** ☎647189 rm91 Mar–Oct **B**

PIETRASANTA (MARINA DI) Lucca
(☎0584) Map**29**B2

 H **Bresciani** viale Versilia 132/134
  Motrone ☎20180 rm21 **A**

 H **Orione** viale G Carducci 29 Fiumetto
  rm20 Apr–Oct **A**

 H **Ritz** via Dalmazia 13 Focette ☎20517
  15May–Sep **B**

 ★★ **Esplanade** viale Roma 235, Tonfano
  ☎21151 rm33 **B**

PIOMBINO Livorno (☎0565) Map**31**A3

 H **Ariston** ☎34390 rm27 **A**

 H **Aurora** ☎30548 rm33 **A**

 H **Joli** ☎33263 rm20 **A**

 ★★ **Centrale** pza G-Verdi 2 ☎32581
  rm38 **A**

PISA Pisa (☎050) Map**29**B2

 H **Capitol** via E. Fermi 13 ☎49597
  rm15 **A**

 H **Fenice** via Catalani 8 ☎25131 rm30 **A**

 H **Pisa** via Manzoni 22 ☎44551 rm16 **A**

 H **Roma** via Bonanno 111 ☎22698
  rm27 **A**

 ☆☆ **California** via Aurelia ☎890726
  rm74 **B**

 ★★ **Kinzica** pza Arcivescovado ☎22300
  rm33 **B**

PORDENONE Pordenone (☎0434)
Map**30**C4

 H **Minerva** pza XX Settembre 5 ☎26066
  rm48 **A**

 H **Residence** via Montereale 27
  ☎35160 rm30 **A**

 H **Santin** via delle Grazie 9 ☎22443
  rm97 **B**

PORTO AZZURRO see **ELBA (ISOLA D')**

PORTOFERRÁIO see **ELBA (ISOLA D')**

PORTOFINA Genova (☎0185) Map**29**A2/3

 ♦ **Pension Clipper** ☎69037 rm5 **B**

PORTO SAN GIÓRGIO Ascoli Piceno
(☎0734) Map**32**C4

 H **Pini** via N-Sauro 104 ☎48211 rm36
  Apr–Oct **A**

 H **Victoria** via Vittoria 190 ☎4233
  rm34 **A**

 ★ **Terrazza** via Andrea Costa ☎4244
  rm36 **A**

POSITANO Salerno (☎089) Map**33**A3

 H **Santa Caterina** ☎875019 rm19 **A**

 H **Vittoria** ☎875049 rm16
  15Mar–15Sep **A**

 ★★ **Maresca** ☎875140 rm19
  15Mar–15Nov **A**

 ★★ **Margherita** via G-Marconi 31
  ☎875188 rm14 15Mar–30Oct **A**

POTENZA Potenza (☎0971) Map**33**B3

 H **San Michele** via IV Novembre 46
  ☎24852 rm30 **A**

 H **Tourist** via Vescovada 4 ☎21437
  rm99 **A**

 H **Vittoria** via Pretoria 228 ☎23462
  rm19 **A**

POZZUOLI Napoli (☎081) Map**32**D1

 H **American** ☎7605209 rm46 **B**

 H **Hideaway** ☎7606333 rm45 **B**

PRÁIA A MARE Cosenza (☎09285)
Map**33**B2

 H **Garden** ☎72382 rm41 **A**

 H **Germania** ☎72016 rm62 **A**

 H **Mondial** ☎72214 rm66 **A**

PRAIANO Salerno (☎089) Map**33**A/B3

 H **Perla** ☎874052 rm13 **A**

 ★★ **Grand Tritone** ☎874005 rm77
  Apr–20Oct **B**

RAGUSA see **SICILIA** (Sicily)

RAPALLO Genova (☎0185) Map**29**A3

 H **Lucciola** via al Carmelo 1-A ☎51416
  rm25 **B**

 H **Rosa Blanca** via Cairoli 7 ☎50390
  rm17 **B**

 H **Vittoria** via San Filippo Nero ☎54838
  rm40 **B**

 ★ **Bandoni** via Marsala 24 ☎50423
  rm18 **A**

RAVELLO Salerno (☎089) Map**33**B3

 H **Bardi** ☎857255 rm16 **A**

 ★★ **Parsifal** pza Fontana ☎857144 rm19
  Apr–30Oct **A**

RAVENNA Ravenna (☎0544) Map**30**C3

 H **Argentario** via di Roma 45 ☎22555
  rm30 **B**

 H **Diana** via G-Rossi 49 ☎39164
  rm23 **A**

 H **Italia** viale Pallavicini 4 ☎35610
  rm39 **A**

 ☆ **Romea** via Romea 1 ☎61247 rm39 **B**

REGGIO DI CALABRIA Reggio di Calabria
(☎0965) Map**34**C1

 H **Continental** via Florio 10 ☎24990
  rm36 **A**

 H **Delfins** via Gebbione a Mare ☎90658
  rm45 **A**

 H **Eremo** via Eremo Botte ☎22433
  rm23 **A**

 H **Metropol** via Palamolla 43 ☎99443
  rm11 **A**

RÉGGIO NELL'EMILIA Reggio Nell'Emilia
(☎0522) Map**29**B3

 H **Brasile** via Roma 37 ☎31231 rm22 **A**

 H **Cairoli** pza XXV Aprile 2 ☎32207
  rm17 **A**

 H **San Marco** pza Marconi 1 ☎35364
  rm50 **A**

 H **Sporting** via G-Rinaldi ☎73974
  rm14 **A**

RICCIONE Forli (☎0541) Map**30**C2

 H **Admiral** viale G-d'Annunzio 90
  ☎41836 rm36 May–Sep **A**

 H **Boemia** via Gramsci 87 ☎602055
  rm60 May–Oct **A**

 H **Corona** viale G-d' Annunzio 107
  ☎41125 rm33 May–Sep **A**

 H **Desiré** via C-Battisti 33 ☎41461 rm31
  15May–25Sep **A**

 H **Roma** via Milano 17 ☎43202 rm31
  May–Sep **A**

Italy

RÍMINI Forlì (☎0541) Map**30**C2
- H **Aquila** viale Alfieri 18 ☎81296 rm58 20May–20Sep **A**
- H **Bridge** viale Regina Elena 117 ☎81077 rm20 May–Sep **A**
- H **Lloyd** via Santa Maria al Mare 8 ☎25736 rm24 **A**
- ★★ **Alpen** viale Regina Elena 203 ☎80662 rm60 May–Sep **A**

RISCONE/REISCHACH see **BRUNICO/BRUNECK**

RIVA DEL GARDA Trento (☎0464) Map**29**B4
- H **Astoria** viale Trento 9 ☎52659 rm96 **A**
- H **Giardino Verdi** ☎52516 rm43 **A**
- H **Liberty** viale Carducci 3 ☎53581 rm34 **A**

At **Varone** (2 km N)
- H **Alberello** ☎52566 rm24 **A**
- H **Varone** ☎52357 rm18 **A**

ROCCARASO L'Aquila (☎0864) Map**32**C2
- H **Conca d'Oro** ☎62131 rm33 20Dec–10Apr & 20May–10Sep **A**
- H **Edelweiss** ☎62132 rm55 **B**
- H **Iris** ☎62194 rm40 **A**
- H **Julia** ☎62136 rm31 20Dec–20Apr & 20Jun–20Sep **A**
- H **Suisse** ☎62139 rm50 **A**
- H **Valentino** ☎62400 rm35 **A**

ROLLE (Passo di) Trento (☎0439) Map**13**A1
- ★ **Passo di Rolle** ☎68216 rm22 **A**

ROMA (Rome) Roma (☎06) Map**31**B2
- H **Astor** via Tevere 5-d ☎851224 rm27 **A**
- H **Cesari** via Pietra 89-A ☎6792386 rm51 **A**
- H **Gemini** via Guido Mazzoni 24 ☎4270176 rm48 **A**
- H **Lugano** via Tritone 132 ☎460733 rm31 **A**
- H **Nuova Italia** via Como 1 ☎850051 rm70 **A**
- H **Siracusa** via Marsala 50 ☎4957838 rm100 **A**
- H **Villa Delle Rose** via Vicenza 5 ☎4951788 rm29 **A**
- ★★ **Ariston** via Turati 16 ☎7310341 rm110 **B**
- ★★ **Nordland** via Alciato 14 ☎231841 rm120 **A**
- ★ **Margutta** via Laurina 34 ☎6798440 rm25 **A**

RONCO see **FORLÍ**

ROVERETO Trento (☎0464) Map**29**B4
- H **Ancore** via delle Scuole 16 ☎33707 rm20 **A**
- H **Rovereto** corso Rosmini 82 ☎35222 rm51 **A**
- H **Villa Cristina** via Abetone 48 ☎23482 rm14 **A**

ROVIGO Rovigo Map**30**C3
- H **Cristallo** viale Porta Adige 1 ☎30701 rm42 **A**
- H **Granatiere** corso del Popolo 235 ☎22301 rm34 **A**

- ★★ **Bologna** viale R-Margherita 6 ☎22406 rm14 **A**

SACRO–MONTE see **VARALLO**

ST VINCENT Aosta (☎0166) Map**28**D4
- H **Alba** pza Zerbion 22 ☎2654 rm10 **A**
- H **Bijou** pza V-Veneto 3 ☎2770 rm28 **A**
- H **Delle Rose** viale IV Novembre ☎2237 rm21 **A**
- H **Grange** strada Cillian 11 ☎2652 rm17 **A**
- H **Haiti** via E-Chanoux 19 ☎2114 rm24 **A**
- H **Leon d'Oro** via E-Chanoux 26 ☎2202 rm49 **A**
- H **Posta** via E-Chanoux 2 ☎2250 rm39 **A**
- H **Riviera** via Farnet 3 ☎2557 rm17 **A**

SALERNO Salerno (☎089) Map**33**B3
- H **Elea** via Trento 98 ☎353583 rm32 **A**
- H **Garibaldi** via Torriore 54 ☎350061 rm22 **A**
- H **Suisse** via G.B. Amendola 62 ☎356330 rm14 **A**
- H **Vittoria** Lungomare Trieste 190 ☎220045 rm11 **A**

SALÒ Brescia (☎0365) Map**29**B4
- H **Benaco** ☎20308 rm18 **B**
- H **Laurin** ☎22022 rm40 **A**
- H **Vigna** ☎20516 rm22 **A**

SALSOMAGGIORE TERME Parma (☎0524) Map**29**A3
- H **Donelli** ☎52260 rm19 Apr–Sep **A**
- H **Plaza** ☎52121 rm37 Mar–Nov **A**
- H **Tabiano** ☎52158 rm36 Apr–Nov **A**

SAN BARTOLOMEO AL MARE Imperia (☎0183) Map**28**D2
- H **Adrimer** ☎400869 rm34 **B**
- H **Stella Maris** ☎44233 rm43 Apr–Sep **B**
- ★ **Mayola** ☎400739 rm80 May–10Oct **A**

SAN BENEDETTO DEL TRONTO Ascoli Piceno (☎0735) Map**32**C3
- H **Garden** via Buozzi 8 ☎60246 rm54 **A**
- H **Marconi** via Maffei 114 ☎81857 rm40 Jun–20Sep **A**
- H **Progresso** via Trieste 40 ☎2828 rm24 **A**
- H **Sabbiadoro** Lungomare Marconi ☎80911 rm63 25May–15Sep **A**

SAN CANDIDO/INNICHEN Bolzano (☎0474) Map**13**A1
- H **Bellevue** ☎73146 rm14 **A**
- H **Olympia** ☎73105 rm20 **A**

SAN GIMIGNANO Siena (☎0577) Map**29**B2
- H **Leon Bianco** ☎941294 rm20 **A**
- H **Pescille** ☎940186 rm14 **A**
- ★★ **Cisterna** pza della Cisterna 23 ☎940328 rm42 **B**

SAN MAMETE see **VALSOLDA**

SAN MARINO follows Italy

SAN MARTINO DI CASTROZZA Trento (☎0439) Map**13**A1
- H **Alpino** via Passo Rolle 26 ☎68193 rm22 **A**
- H **Bel Sito** via Dolomiti ☎68195 rm22 **A**
- ★ **Belvedere** ☎68000 rm30

Italy

25Jun–3Sep & 20Dec–10Apr **B**

SAN PIER D'ARENA see **GÉNOVA (Geno)**

SAN REMO Imperia (✆1084) Map**28**D2
- H **Joli Site** via Solaro 55 ✆60797 rm20 **B**
- M **Lugano** via Aurelia ✆52381 rm19 **B**
- H **Pláza** via Roma 6 ✆84326 rm47 **B**
- ★★ **King** corso Cavallotti 92 ✆56054 rm26 **B**
- ★★ **Morandi** corso Matuzia 25 ✆85275 rm32 **B**

SANTA CATERINA VALFURVA Sondrio (✆0342) Map**12**D1
- H **Capanna** ✆935562 rm27 Dec–Apr & 15Jun–15Sep **A**
- H **Compagnoni** ✆901856 rm28 Jun–Sep & 5Dec–Apr **A**
- H **Sobretta** ✆902593 rm31 25Jun–15Sep & Dec–2May **A**

SANTA MARGHERITA LIGURE Genova (✆0185) Map**29**A3
- H **Florina** pza Mazzini 26 ✆87517 rm55 **B**
- H **Terminus** pza Nobili 4 ✆86121 rm24 20Dec–Sep **B**
- ★★ **Villa Anita** viale Minerva ✆86543 rm20 (A5) **B**

SANT'ILARIO LIGURE see **NERVI**

SAPRI Salerno (✆0973) Map**33**B3
- H **Santa Caterina** ✆31109 rm24 **A**
- H **Vittoria** ✆31001 rm45 **A**
- ★★ **Tirreno** corso Italia ✆31157 rm58 **A**

SARZANA La Spezia (✆0187) Map**29**A2
- H **Laurina** ✆60173 rm20 **A**
- H **Portanova** ✆62357 rm19 **A**

SAVONA Savona (✆019) Map**28**D2/3
- H **Acqui** via Paleocapa 22 ✆20887 rm32 **B**
- H **Italia** pza del Popolo 2 ✆21040 rm42 **B**

SCIACCA see **SICILIA (Sicily)**

SELVA DI VAL GARDENA/ WOLKENSTEIN IN GRÖDEN Bolzano (✆0471) Map**13**A1
- H **Alpenroyal** ✆75178 rm31 **A**
- H **Condor** ✆75055 rm26 Dec–15Apr & Jun–Sep **A**
- H **Posta al Cervo** ✆75174 rm30 **A**

SENIGÁLLIA Ancona (✆071) Map**30**D2
- H **Eleonora** ✆62483 rm38 **A**
- H **Europa** ✆63800 rm60 May — Sep **A**
- H **Gabbiano** ✆63597 rm45 May–Sep **A**

SESSA AURUNCA Caserta (✆0823) Map**32**C2
- H **Sinuessa** S. S. Doniziana km14 ✆978655 rm51 **A**

SESTO CALENDE Varese (✆0331) Map**28**D4
- H **Cervo** ✆230821 rm29 **A**
- H **Milord** ✆256591 rm16 **A**

SESTRIERE Torino (✆0122) Map**28**C3
- H **Belvedere** ✆7091 rm37 **A**

- H **Miramonti** ✆7048 rm36 **B**
- H **Savoy Edelweiss** ✆7040 rm30 Jul–15Apr **A**
- H **Torre** ✆7123 rm148 19Dec–17Apr **B**

SESTRI LEVANTE Genova (✆0185) Map**29**A2
- H **Bono** via Olive Stanghe 24 ✆41285 rm22 **B**
- H **Celeste** Lungomare Decalzo 14 ✆41166 rm22 10Mar–Sep **B**
- H **Elisabetta** via Novara 7 ✆41128 rm39 Dec–Sep **B**
- ★ **Daria** via Rimenbranze 46 ✆41139 rm23 **A**

SICILIA (Sicily) Map**33**Inset
Agrigento Agrigento (✆0922)
- H **Belvedere** via San Vito 20 ✆20051 rm35 **A**
- H **Colleverde** via dei Templi, Bonamorone ✆29555 rm27 **A**
- H **Paris** via Imera 57 ✆26024 rm15 **A**

Caltanissetta Caltanissetta (✆0934)
- H **Diprima** via Kennedy 16 ✆26088 rm106 **A**
- H **Europa** via B-Gaetani 5 ✆21051 rm27 **A**

Capo D'Orlando Messina (✆0941)
- H **Bristol** ✆91390 rm75 **A**
- H **Faro** ✆91484 rm30 **A**
- H **Tartaruga** San Gregorio ✆91657 rm38 **A**

Catánia Catania (✆095)
- H **Aesculapius** via P Caifanni 5 ✆336021 rm24 **A**
- H **Bristol** via S Maria del Rosario 9 ✆278540 rm67 **B**
- H **Italia** via Etnea 310 ✆317833 rm46 **B**
- H **Moderno** via Alessi 9 ✆226250 rm47 **A**
- H **Roma** viale Libertà 63 ✆271833 rm10 **A**

Cefalù Palermo (✆0921)
- H **Artù** ✆21450 rm22 **A**
- H **Astro** ✆21639 rm35 **A**
- H **Terminus** ✆21034 rm14 **A**

Enna Enna (✆0935)
- H **Belvedere** pza Francesco Crispi 2 ✆21020 rm62 **A**
- H **Enna** via Sant' Agata 43 ✆21882 rm18 **A**

At *Pergusa* (10km S)
- H **Pergola** ✆36017 rm16 **A**
- H **Serena** ✆36113 rm28 **A**

Erice Trapani (✆0923)
- ◆ **Pension Edelweiss** ✆29553 rm16 **A**
- H **Pineta** ✆29130 rm21 **A**

Gela Caltanissetta (✆0933)
- M **Gela** SS N 117 *bis* Central Sicula km92 ✆933030 rm91 **A**
- H **Mediterraneo** ✆930721 rm72 **A**

Marsala Trapani (✆0923)
- H **Stella d'Italia** ✆953003 rm42 **A**

Messina Messina (✆090)
- H **Belvedere** viale S Martino 146 ✆2939933 rm25 **A**

H **Europa** Pistunina ☎781601 rm115 A
H **Milano** via dei Verdi 65 ☎772078
rm28 A
H **San Rizzo** Colle San Rizzo ☎41164
rm10 A
H **Venezia** pza Cairoli 4 ☎718076
rm76 A

Milazzo Messina (☎090)
H **Diana** ☎921382 rm24 A
H **Flora** ☎921882 rm23 A
H **Rosa** ☎921922 rm11 A

Palermo Palermo (☎091)
H **Bristol** via Maqueda 437 ☎589247
rm13 A
H **Centrale** corso Vittorio Emanuele 327
☎588409 rm117 A
H **Metropol** via Turrisi Colonna 4
☎588608 rm44 A
H **Olimpia** pza Cassa di Risparmio 18
☎230276 rm15 A
H **Regina** corso Vittorio Emanuele 316
☎231997 rm45 A
H **Sausele** via Vincenzo Errante 12
☎237524 rm40 A

Piazza Armerina Enna (☎0935)
H **Gangi** ☎81614 rm19 A
H **Selene** ☎82776 rm42 A

Ragusa Ragusa (☎0932)
H **Montreal** via San Giuseppe 10
☎21026 rm27 A
H **Tivoli** via Gabriele d'Annunzio 60
☎21885 rm39 A

Sciacca Agrigento (☎0925)
H **Garden** ☎21203 rm58 A

Siracusa (Syracuse) Siracusa (☎0931)
H **Bellavista** via Diodoro Sicula 4
☎36912 rm49 A
H **Grand** viale Mazzini 12 ☎65101
rm47 A
H **Neapolis** via Carlo Forlanini 14
☎31853 rm21 A
H **Riviera** via Eucleida 9 ☎68240
rm15 A

Taormina Messina (☎0942)
H **Continental** via Dionisio Primo
☎23805 rm43 A
H **Garden** via Costantino Patricio 1
☎25120 rm14 A
H **Residence** Salita Dente 4 ☎23463
rm28 A
H **Sirius** via Guardiola Vecchia ☎23477
rm37 B
H **Victoria** corso Umberto 81 ☎23372
rm19 A

At *Mazzarò* (5.5km E)
H **Baia Azzurra** ☎23249 rm49 A
H **Isolabella** Isolabella ☎24289 rm42
Apr–Oct B
♦ **Raneri** ☎23962 rm15 A

Trápani Trápani (☎0923)
H **Moderno** via Serraino Vulpitta 4
☎21247 A
H **Sole** pza Umberto 1 , 3 ☎22035
rm34 A
H **Vittoria** pza Vittorio Emanuele
☎27244 rm58 A

SIENA Siena (☎0577) Map**29**B2
H **Bernini** via della Sapienza 15
☎289047 rm9 A
H **Garden** via Custoza 2 ☎47056
rm29 A
H **Italia** viale Cavour 67 ☎41177 rm77 A
H **Perla** via delle Terme 25 ☎47144
rm9 A
H **Vico Alto** via delle Regioni 26
☎48571 rm44 A

SIRACUSA (Syracuse) see **SICILIA (Sicily)**

SIRMIONE Brescia (☎030) Map**29**B4
H **Eden** ☎916127 rm29 15Mar–Oct A
H **Grifone** ☎916014 rm17 15Mar–Oct B
H **Olvi** ☎916110 rm59 A
★★ **Lac** via Colombare 54 ☎916026
rm35 (A7) Mar–Oct A

SOLDA/SULDEN Bolzano (☎0473)
Map**12**D1
H **Alpenhof** ☎75414 rm33
Jul–20Sep & 20Dec–20Apr B
H **Eller** ☎75421 rm49
3Jun–Sep & 26Nov–8Apr B
H **Gampen** ☎75423 rm26 B

SÓNDRIO Sóndrio (☎0342) Map**29**A4
H **Cristallo** Largo Codorna 72 ☎23005
rm18 A
H **Europa** Lungomallero Cadorna 5
☎23341 rm43 A
H **Stazione** pza Bertacchi ☎22020
rm41 A

SORA Frosinone (☎0776) Map**32**C2
H **Autostello Aci** ☎81138 rm14 A
M **Mattei** ☎81050 rm34 A
H **Michelangelo** ☎82100 rm36 A
H **Rea** ☎81080 rm17 A
M **Valentino** ☎81071 rm56 A

SORI Genova (☎0185) Map**29**A3
♦ **Pension Milano** ☎700674 rm9 B

SORRENTO Napoli (☎081) Map**33**A3
H **Atlantic** via Capo 76 ☎8783444
rm44 A
H **Bristol** via Capo 22 ☎8781436 rm87
Mar–Oct A
H **Central** corso Italia 254 ☎8781646
rm54 A
H **Metropole** via Nastro Verde 2
☎8782123 rm39 Mar–Oct A
H **Vesuvio** corso Italia ☎8781804 rm37
Mar–Oct A

SOTTOMARINA see **CHIÓGGIA**

SPÉZIA (LA) La Spézia (☎0187) Map**29**A2
H **Astra** via G-Costantini 48 ☎511105
rm12 B
H **Diana** via C-Colombo 30 ☎25120
rm18 B
H **Mary** via Fiume 177 ☎37270 rm22 B

SPOLETO Perugia (☎0743) Map**31**B3
H **Del Duchi** ☎23105 rm50 B
H **Clarici Commercio** ☎24206 rm18 A
H **Lello Caro** ☎22219 rm42 A
H **Manni** ☎24135 rm19 A

SPOTORNO Savona (☎019) Map**28**D2
H **Corallo** via Aurelia ☎745582 rm30
Jan–Oct B

Italy

H **Miramare** via Aurelia ☎745116 rm30 B
H **Pineta** via Serra 22 ☎745412 rm30 May–Sep B
★ **Villa Teresina** via Imperia ☎745160 rm26 (A4) Apr–Sep A

STAFFA see **MACUGNAGA**

STÉLVIO (Passo dello) Sondrio (☎0473) Map**12**D1
H **Perego** ☎901094 rm58 Jun–Oct B
H **Pirovano IV** ☎901891 rm69 Jun–Oct B

STRESA Novara (☎0323) Map**28**D4
H **Boston** ☎30533 rm33 25Mar–30Sep A
H **Della Torre** ☎31175 rm34 A
H **Savoia** ☎30548 rm40 A
H **Villa Pineta** ☎30335 rm15 Apr–15Oct A
★★ **Italia & Svizzera** Lungolago ☎30540 rm34 A
★★ **Lido La Perla Nera** pza Stazione Funivia ☎30384 rm27 15Mar–15Oct A
★★ **Royal** via Nazionale del Sempione ☎30471 rm43 Etr–Sep A
★ **Flora** via Nazionale del Sempione 30 ☎30524 rm21 Apr–Sep A

SULMANO L'Aquila Map**32**C3
H **Artu** ☎52758 rm23 A
H **Italia** ☎52308 rm28 A
H **Risorgimento** ☎51351 rm11 A
H **Traffico** ☎51221 rm20 A

SUNA see **VERBÁNIA**

SUSÀ Torino (☎0122) Map**28**C3
H **Meana** ☎2490 rm39 A
H **Parco** ☎31027 rm8 A
H **Sole** ☎82474 rm13 A
H **Stazione** ☎2477 rm17 A
★★ **Napoleon** ☎2704 rm45 B

TAORMINA see **SICILIA (Sicily)**

TÁRANTO Táranto (☎099) Map**39**B1
H **Bologna** via Margherita 4 ☎26700 rm52 A
H **Edelweiss** viale Virgilio 111 ☎331823 rm18 A
H **Plaza** via d'Aquino 46 ☎91925 rm112 A
H **Sorrentino** pza Fontana 7 ☎47456 rm16 A

TERNI Terni (☎0744) Map**31**B3
H **Brenta** viale Brenta 12 ☎404193 rm22 A
H **Roma** corso Tacito 5 ☎406117 rm15 A
H **Teatro** corso Vecchio 124 ☎56073 rm9 A
M **Tiffany** via Narni ☎812501 rm36 A

TERRACINA Latina (☎0733) Map**32**C2
H **Meson Feliz** Lido d'Ulisse ☎71408 rm14 A
H **Riva Gaia** ☎730166 rm60 A
H **River** via Mediana ☎71575 rm94 A
H **Torino** ☎727023 rm26 A
H **Torre del Sole** via Mediana ☎71671 rm120 Apr–15Sep A

TIRANO Sondrio (☎0342) Map**29**A/B4
H **Corona** ☎701266 rm36 A
H **Tirano** ☎701497 rm48 A
★ **Posta & Stelvio** via Lungo Adda IV Novembre 1 ☎702555 rm36 Dec–Oct A

TODI Perugia (☎075) Map**31**B3
H **Cavour** ☎882417 rm21 A
H **Zodiaco** ☎882625 rm29 A

TOLMEZZO Udine (☎0433) Map**13**B1
H **Coop-Ca** ☎2572 rm30 A
H **Nuova Italia** ☎2092 rm15 A

TÓRBOLE Trento (☎0464) Map**29**B4
H **Elisabetta** ☎55176 rm34 Apr–10Oct A
H **Paradiso** ☎55126 rm28 Apr–10Oct A

TORINO (Turin) Torino (☎011) Map**28**D3
H **Antico Distretto** corso Valdocco 10 ☎545453 rm25 A
H **Cairo** via la Loggia 2 ☎352003 rm38 A
H **Canelli** via San Dalmazzo 7 ☎546078 rm33 A
H **Derby** corso Palestrol ☎545840 rm17 A
H **Eden** via Donizetti 22 ☎659545 rm26 A
H **Piemontese** via Berthollet 21 ☎651101 rm29 B
H **Regina** via Arsenale 34 ☎543822 rm31 A
H **Scoiattolo** Cavoretto, via XXV Aprile 186 ☎67472 rm19 A
H **Universo** corso Peschiera 166 ☎336480 rm33 B
H **Verna e Guarene** via Nizza II ☎659358 rm29 A

TORRI DEL BENACO Verona (☎045) Map**29**B4
H **Baia dei Pini** ☎626215 rm7 A
H **Eden** Canevani ☎626188 rm22 A

TRANI Bari (☎0883) Map**34**C4
H **Capirro** ☎46912 rm14 A
H **Trani** ☎42340 rm51 B

TREMEZZO Como (☎0344) Map**29**A4
H **Azalea** ☎40424 rm10 B
H **Villa Marie** ☎40427 rm15 Jun–Aug A

TRENTO Trento (☎0461) Map**29**B4
H **America** via Torre Verde 50 ☎83010 rm30 A
H **Bologna** via Belenzani 76 ☎21197 rm23 A
H **Roma** via Malpaga 9 ☎23881 rm62 A
★★ **Venezia** pza Duomo 45 ☎26335 rm50 A

TREVISO Treviso (☎0422) Map**30**C4
H **Carlton** Largo Altinia 15 ☎46988 rm96 A
H **Giustiniani** pza Giustiniani 9 ☎43787 rm23 A
H **Vittoria** via San Nicolò 3 ☎52285 rm15 A

TRICÉSIMO Udine (☎0432) Map**30**C4
H **Diana** ☎851136 rm23 A
H **Stella d'Oro** ☎851262 rm12 A

Italy

TRIESTE Trieste (☎040) Map**30**D4
- H **Adria** Capo di pza 1 ☎65944 rm48 **A**
- H **Brioni** via Ginnastica 2 ☎795169 rm23 **A**
- H **Istria** via R-Tirreus 5 ☎795244 rm29 **B**
- H **Roma** via C-Ghega 7 ☎37761 rm42 **A**
- ★ **Citta di Parenzo** via Degli Artisti 8 ☎30119 rm43 **A**

At **Grignano** (7km NW)
- H **Mignon** ☎224130 rm13 **A**

ÚDINE Udine (☎0432) Map**30**C4
- H **Apollo** via Paparotti 11 ☎207706 rm40 **A**
- H **Commercio** via Aquileria 200 ☎204386 rm26 **A**
- H **Ramandolo** via Forni di Sotto 28 ☎40994 rm37 **A**

VALDAGNO Vicenza (☎0445) Map**29**B4
- H **Marietto** ☎41295 rm12 **A**
- H **Roma** ☎42173 rm13 **A**

VALSOLDA Como (☎0344) Map**29**A4
- ♦ **Ombretta** Oria ☎68275 rm12 15Mar–Oct **A**

At **San Mamete**
- ★★ **Stella D'Italia** ☎68139 rm38 10Apr–10Oct **A**

VALTOURNANCHE Aosta (☎0166) Map**28**D4
At **Maen**
- H **Sans Soucis** ☎92105 rm18 **A**
At **Montaz**
- H **Millefiori** ☎92 114 rm11 **A**
At **Paquier**
- H **Bich** ☎92148 rm37 **A**
- H **Etoile de Neige** Evette ☎92081 rm18 **A**
- H **Meynet** ☎92075 rm18 **A**
- H **Punta Margherita** ☎92087 rm17 **A**

VALVERDE see **CESENÁTICO**

VARALLO Vercilli (☎0163) Map**28**D4
- H **Italia** ☎51106 rm29 **A**
- H **Monte Rosa** Sebrey ☎51100 rm21 **A**
At **Sacro-Monte**
- H **Casa del Pellegrino** ☎51656 rm20 **A**

VARAZZE Savona (☎019) Map**28**D3
- H **Iris** via Corosu 4 ☎97778 rm29 **B**
- H **Palme** via San Domenico 9 ☎97243 rm60 **B**
- ★★ **Delfino** via Colombo 48 ☎97073 rm39 (A14) **A**

VARENNA Como (☎0341) Map**29**A4
- H **Sole** ☎83206 rm10 **A**
- H **Victoria** ☎830102 rm32 **A**
- ★★ **Olivedo** ☎830115 rm29 (A4) 15Dec–5Nov **A**

VARESE Varese (☎0332) Map**29**A4
- H **Acquario** via Giusti 7 ☎240525 rm41 **A**
- H **Bologna** via Broggi 7 ☎234362 rm12 **A**
- H **Italia** via Belforte 114 ☎239095 rm18 **A**

VARIGOTTI see **FINALE LIGURE**

VARONE see **RIVA DEL GARDA**

VASTO Chieti (☎0873) Map**33**B4
- H **Nuova Italia** ☎2168 rm23 **A**
- H **Panoramic** ☎2152 rm47 **A**
- H **San Marco** ☎3952 rm24 Apr–Sep **A**
- M **Total** Raccordo Auto stradale Vasto Nord ☎3669 rm38 **A**

VENÉZIA (Venice) Venézia (☎041) Map**30**C4
No road communications in city. Vehicles may be left in garages in piazzale Roma at end of causeway from mainland or at open parking places on the mainland approaches. Garages will not accept advance bookings. Transport to hotels by water-bus, etc, for which there are fixed charges for fares and porterage. Hotel rooms overlooking the Grand Canal normally have a surcharge.
- H **Austria & de la Ville** Cannaregio 227 rm70 **A**
- H **Belsito** San Marco 2157 ☎23365 rm33 **A**
- H **Casanova** San Marco 1284 ☎706855 rm37 **B**
- H **Terminus** Lista di Spagna 116 ☎715095 rm65 **A**
- ★★ **Antico Panada** c larga San Marco 656 ☎709088 rm47 **B**

VENTIMÍGLIA Imperia (☎0184) Map**28**D2
- H **Lido** ☎31473 rm12 Apr–Sep **B**
- H **Torino** ☎31173 rm29 **B**
- ★★ **Posta** via Cavour 56 ☎351218 rm21 20Dec–10Nov **A**

VERBÁNIA Novara (☎0323) Map**28**D4
At **Intra**
- H **Ancora** ☎42580 rm26 **A**
- H **Intra** ☎44004 rm37 Mar–Nov **A**
- H **Miralgo** ☎44080 rm41 **B**
At **Pallanza**
- H **Astor** ☎42161 rm65 Apr–Oct **A**
- H **Castagnola** ☎51121 rm109 15Jun–15Sep **A**
- H **Italia** ☎503206 rm14 **A**
- H **Metropole** ☎42125 rm50 **A**
- ★★ **Belvedere** pza IV Novembre 10 ☎503202 rm58 (A35) Etr–Oct **B**
- ★★ **San Gottardo** viale Delle magnolie ☎42119 rm40 15Mar–Sep **A**
At **Suna**
- ★★ **Pesce d'Oro** ☎502330 rm24 May–Sep **A**

VERCELLI Vercelli (☎0161) Map**28**D3
- H **Brusasca** corso Magenta 71 ☎66010 rm24 **A**
- H **Dell Auto** corso Novara 65 ☎53268 rm14 **A**
- H **Europa** via Santorre Santarosa 16 ☎66847 rm22 **B**
- H **R12** via Galileo Ferraris 90 ☎64742 rm27 **A**
- H **Savoia** viale Garibaldi 14 ☎65047 rm38 **A**
- H **Sport** corso Matteotti 31 ☎2459 rm25 **A**

VERONA Verona (☎045) Map**29**B4
- H **Aurora** via Pellicciai 2 ☎594717 rm22 **A**
- H **Doge** via C-Abba 12B ☎912491 rm16 **A**

Italy

H **Mazzanti** via Mazzanti 6 ☎26813 rm21 A
H **Sabrina** via Scalzi 5 ☎32200 rm23 A
H **Valverde** via Valverde 91 ☎33611 rm20 A
★★ **Capuleti** via del Pontiere 26 ☎32970 rm36 A
★★ **Italia** via G-Mameli 54 rm50 10Jan–25Dec A

VIARÉGGIO Lucca (☎0584) Map**29**B2
H **Belmare** viale G Carducci ☎42712 rm45 A
H **Bristol** viale Manin 14 ☎46441 rm37 A
H **Miramare** via Carducci 27 ☎48441 rm33 A

VICENZA Vicenza (☎0444) Map**29**B4
H **Cristina** corso San Felice 32 ☎34280 rm24 A
H **Elen** viale Camisano 28 ☎500463 rm21 A
H **Palladio** via Oratorio dei Servi 25 ☎21072 rm24 A
★★ **Jolly Stazione** viale Milano 92 ☎22209 rm74 B

VICO EQUENSE Napoli (☎081) Map**33**B3
H **Mary** ☎8798120 rm44 A
H **Sporting** ☎8798505 rm43 Apr–Oct A
★★ **Oriente** ☎8798143 rm53 A

VIESTE Foggia (☎0884) Map**34**C4
H **Falcone** ☎78251 rm54 B
H **Lido** Carmine ☎78609 rm15 A
H **Riviera** ☎78495 rm25 A

VILLAMARINA see **CESENÁTICO**

VIPITENO/STERZING Bolzano (☎0472) Map**12**D1
H **Fugger** ☎65329 rm26 B
H **Sole** ☎65404 rm19 A
H **Wipptalerhof** ☎65428 rm11 A

VITERBO Viterbo (☎0761) Map**31**B3
H **Olimpia** viale Trieste 94 ☎32829 rm17 Mar–15Oct A
H **Terme Salus** strada Toscanese ☎31739 rm76 A
H **Tuculca** Cassia Sud ☎220650 rm15 B
H **Tuscia** via Cairoli 41 ☎34943 rm48 A
★★ **Leon D'Oro** via della Cava 36 ☎31012 rm48 A

VOGHERA Pavia (☎0383) Map**29**A3
H **Corona** ☎49247 rm14 A
H **Rallye** ☎36178 rm16 A

ZADINA PINETA see **CESENÁTICO**

San Marino (Republic of)

SAN MARINO (☎0541) Map**30**C2
H **Joli San Marino** via Federico d'Urbino 233 ☎991009 rm24 Closed Nov & Dec A
H **Quercia Antica** via Cellabella ☎991257 rm27 A
★ **Tre Penne** via Giovanni de Simone della Penne ☎992437 rm12 10Mar–Nov A

PORTUGAL

Portugal

This gazetteer contains details of hotels and pensions, approved by the office of the Secretary of State for Information and Tourism, which, in most cases, offer accommodation for less than £6 per person per night at some time during the year. The prices have been banded as follows: **A** under £5 per person per night, and **B** between £5 and £6 per person per night. It includes a number of tourist inns known as *pousadas* and *estalagems*. *Pousadas* are Government-owned but privately run. They have been specially built or converted and are often located in the more remote touring areas where there is a lack of other hotels. Visitors may not usually stay more than five nights. *Estalagems* are small, well-equipped wayside inns (although there are some in towns) which are privately-owned and run. Details of farmhouse accommodation are not available.

Abbreviations:
av   avenida
Capt   Captain

Cdt   Commandant
espl   esplanade

ALBERGARIA-A-VELHA Aveiro (☎0034) Map**17**A2
  M **Alameda** N1 2km S ☎52402 rm18 **A**
  H **Pousada de Santo António** N1 5kmS ☎52230 rm12 **B**

ALCOBAÇA Leiria (☎0044) Map**23**A4
  H **Mosteiro** av Frei Estêvão Martins 58-A ☎42183 rm12 **A**

ALPEDRINHA Castelo Branco Map**17**B1
  ★ **Estalagem São Jorge** ☎57154 rm11 Closed Oct **A**

AMARANTE Porto (☎0025) Map**17**B2
  ★ **Silva** Rua Cândido dos Reis 53 ☎43110 rm22 **A**

AVEIRO Aveiro (☎0034) Map**17**A2
  H **Imperial** Rua Dr Nascimento Leitão ☎22141 rm49 **A**
  H **Afonso V** Rua Dr Manu I das Neves ☎25191 rm36 **A**
  ★★ **Arcada** r Viana do Castelo 4 ☎23001 rm55 **A**

At **Cacia**
  H **Albergaria de Cacia de João Padeiro** ☎91306 rm27 **A**

At **Praia da Barra**
  H **Barra** ☎25144 rm64 **B**

BEJA Beja (☎0079) Map**23**B3
  H **Cristina** Rua de Mértola 71 ☎23035 rm31 **A**
  H **Santa Bárbara** Rua de Mértola 56 ☎22028 rm26 **A**

BRAGA Braga (☎0023) Map**17**A2
  H **João XXI** Av João XXI-849 ☎22146 rm28 **A**

BRAGANÇA Bragança Map**18**C2
  H **Bragança** Praça 1 st de Maio ☎22578 rm42 **A**
  H **Albergaria Santa Isabel** Rua Alexandre Herculano 67 ☎22427 rm14 **A**

CACIA see **AVIERO**

CALDAS DE RAINHA Leiria (☎0012) Map**23**A4
  ★ **Central** Largo do Dr J-Barbosa 22 ☎22078 rm40 **A**

CALDAS DE VIZELA Braga (☎0023) Map**17**A/B2
  H **Sul Americano** Rua Dr Abílio Torres ☎48237 rm64 **A**

CASTELO DE VIDE Portalegre (☎0045) Map**23**B4
  H **Albergaria Jardim** Rua Sequeira Sameiro 6 ☎91217 rm19 **A**
  H **Casa do Parque** av da Aramenha 37 ☎91250 rm24 **A**

COIMBRA Coimbra (☎0039) Map**17**A1
  H **Almedina** Av Fernão de Magalhães 203 ☎29161 rm28 **A**
  H **Domus** Rua Adelino Veiga 62 ☎28584 rm15 **A**
  H **Kanimambo** Av Fernão de Magalhães 484 ☎27151 rm45 **A**

COLARES Sintra Map**23**A4
  ★ **Estalagem do Conde** Quinta do Conde ☎2991652 rm11 **A**

CURIA Aveiro (☎0031) Map**17**A1
  H **Das Termas** ☎52185 rm39 **B**
  H **Lourenço** ☎52214 rm42 **A**
  H **Santos** ☎52413 rm44 **A**

ELVAS Portalegre Map**23**B3
  ★ **Pousada de Santa Luzia** (outside the walls of Elvas on the main road from Borba to Badajoz) ☎22194 rm11 **B**

ESPOSENDE Braga (☎0023) Map**17**A2
  ★★ **Suave Mar** av E-Duarte Pacheco ☎89445 rm46 **A**

ESTREMOZ Évora Map**23**B3
  H **Carvalho** Largo da República 27 ☎22712 rm12 **A**

ÉVORA Evora (☎0069) Map**23**B3
  H **Riviera** Rua 5 de Outubro 49 ☎23304 rm12 **A**
  H **Santa Clara** Travessa da Milheira 19 ☎24141 rm22 **A**

FAO Braga (☎0023) Map**17**A2
  H **Estal do Parque do Rio** ☎89521 rm30 **B**

FARO Faro (☎0089) Map**23**A/B2
  H **Marim** Rua Gonçalo Barreto 1 ☎24063 rm29 **A**

Portugal

★★ **Albacor** Rua Brites de Almeida 25 ☎22093 rm38 **A**

FÁTIMA Santarém (☎0049) Map**17**A1
- H **Casa das Irmãs Dominicanas** Rua Francisco Marto 50 ☎97117 rm57 **A**
- H **Zeca** Rua Jacinta Marto ☎97262 rm12 **A**
- H **Jorguel** ☎97303 **A**
- H **Dávi** Estrada de Leiria ☎97278 rm14 **A**
- ★★ **Estalagem Os Três Pastorinhos** Cova da Iria ☎97629 rm92 **A**

FERREIRA DO ALENTEJO Beja (☎0079) Map**23**B3
- H **Santo António** Estrada N2 ☎72320 rm11 **A**

FIGUEIRA DA FOZ Coimbra (☎0033) Map**17**A1
- H **Rio-Mar** Travessa Nova 4 ☎23053 rm24 **A**

GUARDA Guarda Map**17**B1
- ★★ **Filipe** Rua V-da Gama 9 ☎22659 rm32 **A**

LAGOS Faro (☎0082) Map**23**A2
- ★★ **Marazul** Rua 25 de Abril 13 ☎62181 rm17 **A**

LAMEGO Viseu (☎0095) Map**17**B2

On **N2** (1.5km S)
- H **Parque** no Santuário de Na. Sra. dos Remédios ☎62105 **A**

LEIRIA Leiria (☎0044) Map**17**A1
- H **São Francisco** Rua São Francisco 26 ☎25142 rm18 **A**

LISBOA (Lisbon) Lisboa Map**23**A4
- H **Roma** Av de Roma 33 ☎767761 rm265 **B**
- H **Dom Carlos** av Duque de Loulé 121 ☎539071 rm73 **B**
- H **Rex e Rest. Cozinha d'El Rey** Rua Castilho 169 ☎682161 rm70 **B**
- H **Eduardo VIII** av Fontes Pereira de Melo 5 ☎530141 rm100 **B**
- H **York House** Rua das Janelas Verdes 32 ☎662435 rm60 **B**
- H **Do Reno** av Duque d'Ávila 195 ☎548181 rm53 **A**
- H **Capitol** Rua Eça de Queiroz 24 ☎536811 rm58 **A**

★★ **Borges** Rua Garrett 108 ☎361951 rm105 **B**
★★ **Jorge V** Rua Mouzinho da Silveira 3 ☎562525 rm49 **B**
★★ **Miraparque** av Sidonio Pais 12 ☎578070 rm100 **A**

LUSO Aveiro (☎0031) Map**17**A1
- H **Serra** Rua Costa Simões ☎93276 rm44 **A**

MACEDO DE CAVALEIROS Bragança Map**17**B2
- H **Monte Mel** Praça Agostinho Valente 26 ☎78 rm12 **A**

MANGUALDE Viseu (☎0032) Map**17**B1
- H **Onda** Estrada N 16 ☎62478 rm15 **A**

MANTEIGAS Guarda (☎0059) Map**17**B1
13km N on the Gouveia road
- H **Pousada de São Lourenço** ☎47150 11rm **B**

OLIVEIRA DO HOSPITAL c Coimbra (☎0037) Map**17**B1
- ★★ **Pousada Santa Barbara** ☎52252 rm18 **B**

PRAIA DA BARRA see AVIERO

PRAIA DA ROCHA Faro (☎0082) Map**23**A2
- ★★ **Estalagem São José** ☎24037 rm25 **A**

SAGRES Faro (☎0082) Map**23**A2
- ★★ **Pousada do Infante** Ponta da Atalaia ☎64222 rm15 **B**

SANTIAGO DO CACÉM Setúbal (☎0017) Map**23**A3
- ★ **Pousada de Sao Tiago** ☎22459 rm4 **B**

SÃO BRÁS DE ALPORTEL Faro Map**23**B2
- ★ **Pousada de Sao Bras** (in the Serra do Caldeirão on the main road 5km N) ☎42305 rm16 **B**

SERPA Beja (☎0079) Map**23**B3
- ★★ **Pousada de São Gens** ☎52327 rm18 **B**

VALENÇA Viano do Castelo (☎0021) Map**17**A3
- ★★ **Pousda de São Teotónia** ☎22252 rm16 **B**

VILA DO CONDE Porto (☎0022) Map**17**A2
- ★★ **Estalagem do Brasão** Rua J M de Melo ☎64016 rm24 **A**

SPAIN AND ANDORRA

Spain

This gazetteer contains a selection of hotels and pensions which have been approved and classified by the government. In most cases they should offer accommodation for less than £6 per person per night at sometime during the year. The prices have been banded as follows: **A** under £5 per person per night, and **B** between £5 and £6 per person per night. You will find that hotels away from coastal resorts tend to be old fashioned as far as architecture and plumbing are concerned. Although there are a great many establishments offering very cheap accommodation we have not listed those which charge less than £1.50. There are state-owned hotels (*paradores*), inns (*albergues*) and small establishments offering adequate shelter in mountain areas (*refugios*). Some of these stipulate maximum length of stay – in some cases one night only. Details of farmhouses accommodation are not available but further information on hotels and pensions can be obtained from the Spanish National Tourist Office in London. (see p222 for address).

Abbreviations:
av	avenida
c	Calle
Cdt	Commandant
ctra	Carretera
GI	Generalissimo
pl	plaza
ps	paseo

AGUILAR DE CAMPÓO Palencia (☎988) Map**19**A3
- H **Comercio** pl de España 14 ☎122780 rm10 **A**
- H **Portico de Castilla** av José Antonio ☎122225 rm25 **A**
- H **Valentín** av Generalisimo 21 ☎122125 rm47 **B**

AGUILAS Murcia (☎968) Map**25**B2
- H **Calarreona** ctra de Vera ☎750 rm44 **A**
- H **Madrid** pl de Robles Vives 5 ☎410500 rm33 **A**

ALERCÓN Cuenca (☎966) Map**25**B4
- ♦ **Luansa** cta Madrid-Valencia ☎331356 rm7 **A**

ALBACETE Albacete (☎967) Map**25**B3
- H **Albacete** Carcelen 4 ☎213588 rm40 **A**
- H **Albar** Asaac Peral 3 ☎214484 rm51 **A**
- H **Belín** Serrano Alcazar 49 ☎222049 rm9 **A**
- H **Madrid** av Pío XII 3 ☎213281 rm53 **A**

ALCALÁ DE HENARES Madrid (☎91) Map**19**A1
- H **Bari** ctra Madrid-Barcelona ☎8881450 rm53 **A**

ALCANAR Tarragona (☎977) Map**21**B2
- H **Atlantis** ctra Vinaroz – Venta Nueva ☎64 rm24 **A**
- H **Maricel** ctra Vinaroz – Venta Nueva ☎56 rm5 Jun–Sep **A**
- H **Montecarlo** ctra Vinaroz – Venta Nueva ☎737049 rm17 **A**
- ★★ **Biarritz** ☎737025 rm24 Jun–Sep **A**

ALCAÑIZ Teruel (☎974) Map**21**B2
- H **Aragón** Alejandro 4 ☎80 rm28 **A**
- H **Guadalope** pl de España 2 ☎130750 rm14 **A**
- H **Senante** ctra de Zaragoza ☎130550 rm29 **A**

ALCOCÉBER Castellón (☎964) Map**21**B2
- H **Alcocebre** Camino Ribamas ☎410255 rm88 Jul–Aug **A**

ALCOY Alicante (☎965) Map**26**C3
- H **San Jorge** San Juan de Ribera 11 rm86 **A**
- H **Font Roja** Partida Monte Carrascal ☎331048 rm32 Apr–Oct **A**

ALCUDIA DE Carlet Velencia (☎96) Map**26**C3
- H **Casa Galbis** av Antonio Almela 15 ☎2541093 rm14 **A**

ALFARO Logoño (☎941) Map**19**B2
- H **Palacios** ctra de Zaragoza ☎180100 rm86 **B**

ALGECIRAS Cádiz (☎956) Map**24**C1
- H **Anglo Hispano** av Villanueva 7 ☎671590 rm26 **A**
- H **Bahía** playa el Rinconcillo ☎661370 rm 52 **A**
- H **Estrecho** av Virgen del Carmen 15 ☎672690 rm20 **A**
- H **Marina Victoria** av Cañonero Dato 7 ☎673996 rm92 **A**
- ★★ **Alarde** Alfonso XI – 4 rm68 **B**

ALHAMA DE GRANADA Granada (☎958) Map**24**D1
- H **Balneario Alhama de Granada** Zona del Balneario ☎1 rm85 10Jun–10Oct **A**

ALICANTE Alicante (☎965) Map**26**C2
- H **Alamo** San Fernando 56 ☎218355 rm48 **A**
- H **Alfonso el Sabio** Alfonso el Sabio 22 ☎203144 rm86 **A**
- H **Argelia** San Francisco 13 ☎212176 rm29 **A**
- H **Bahía** Pravia 14 ☎206522 rm22 **A**
- H **Benacantil** San Telmo 7 ☎207422 rm47 **A**
- H **Cristina** Angel Lozano 6 ☎707938 rm37 **A**
- H **Marhuenda** Navas 32 ☎204644 rm33 **A**
- H **Marítimo** San Fernando 42 ☎224941 rm33 **A**
- H **Navas** Las Navas 26 ☎204011 rm40 **A**
- H **Reycar** Pintor Lorenzo Casenova 31 ☎221646 rm116 **A**

Spain

ALMANSA Albacete (☎967) Map**26**C3
  H **Rosales** ctra de Circumvalación
  ☏340750 rm36 **A**
  H **Velencia** calvo Sotelo 140 ☏340550
  rm32 **A**

ALMAZÁN Soria Map**19**B2
  H **Antonio** av de Soria 13 ☏110 rm29 **A**

ALMENDRALEJO Badajoz (☎924)
Map**24**C3
  H **Salamanca** Méndez Nuñez 18
  ☏661150 rm25 **A**

ALMERÍA Almería (☎951) Map**25**B1
  H **Embajador** Calzada de Castro 14
  ☏221508 rm67 **A**
  H **Fatima** San Leonardo 22 ☏233512
  rm52 **A**
  H **Guerry** Generalisimo 51 ☏234422
  rm43 **A**
  H **Nixar** A Vico 28 ☏237255 rm27 **A**
  H **Sevilla** Gl Saliquet 23 ☏230799
  rm37 **A**
  H **Torreluz** pl de Flores 6 ☏234799
  rm24 **A**

ALMUÑÉCAR Granada (☎958) Map**25**A1
  H **Angeles** av Costa del Sol 1 ☏630012
  rm18 **A**
  H **Goya** av Gl Galindo ☏630550 rm14
  Apr–Oct **A**
  H **Mediterráneo** J Antonio 1 ☏630662
  rm28 **A**
  H **Puente** ctra de Málaga ☏630065
  rm25 **A**

ALMUNIA DE DOÑA GODINA (LA)
Zaragoza (☎976) Map**21**A3
  H **Donã Godina** av Generalísimo 22
  ☏600269 rm8 **A**
  ★ **Patio** Generalísimo 6 ☏600608
  rm11 **A**

ALMURADIEL Ciudad Real (☎926)
Map**25**A3
  H **Cazador** ctra Madrid Cádiz ☏339075
  rm26 **A**

ALSASUA Navarra (☎948) Map**19**B3
  H **Hostería Ulayar** ctra Madrid Irún
  ☏560075 rm9 Mar–Nov **A**
  H **Leku Ona** ctra Madrid Irún ☏560275
  rm7 Mar–Dec **A**
  ★★ **Alaska** ctra Madrid-Irun (7km) 402
  ☏560100 rm30 Mar–Oct **A**

ALTEA Alicante (☎965) Map**26**D2
  H **Altaya** Generalísimo 113 ☏840800
  rm23 **A**
  H **San Miguel** Generalísimo 67
  ☏840400 rm24 **A**
  H **Solymar** av del Puerto 17 ☏840250
  rm17 **A**
  H **Trovador** Partida Cap Negret
  ☏841275 rm14 **A**

ANDORRA follows Spain

ANDÚJAR Jaén (☎953) Map**25**A2
  H **Del Val** c IV Madrid-Cadiz ☏500950
  rm79 **A**
  H **Don Pedro** Capitán Cortes 5
  ☏501866 rm33 **A**

  H **Quijote** Santo Domingo 1 ☏500500
  rm33 **A**
  H **Soto** ctra Madrid-Cadiz ☏501127
  rm40 **A**

ANTEQUERA Málaga (☎952) Map**24**D1
  H **Reyes** Tercia 4 ☏841028 rm18 **A**
  H **Vega** ctra Nacional 331 ☏841846
  rm37 **A**

ARANDA DE DUERO Burgos (☎947)
Map**19**A2
  H **Aranda** San Francisco 15 ☏501600
  rm48 **A**
  H **Hostería de Castilla** ctra Nal Madrid
  Irún ☏310 rm 31 Mar–Nov **A**
  H **Tres Condes** Pol Res Parcela 4
  ☏502400 rm35 **A**
  H **Ulloa** pl de Santa Maria 7 ☏502038
  rm24 **A**

ARANJUEZ Madrid (☎91) Map**24**A4
  H **Delicias** ctra de Madrid 2 ☏8941340
  rm20 **A**
  H **Infantas** c de las Infantas 4
  ☏8911341 rm42 **A**
  H **Mercedes** ctra Madrid Cádiz
  ☏8910440 rm37 **A**
  H **Príncipe** av del Príncipe 11
  ☏8910075 rm11 **A**
  H **Salmantina** Gobernación 13
  ☏8910246 rm13 **A**

ARCOS (LOS) Navarra (☎948) Map**19**B3
  H **Ezequiel** Gl Mola ☏640296 rm13 **A**
  H **Monaco** pl del Coso 22 ☏640000
  rm20 **A**

ARENAS DE CABRALES Oviedo Map**18**D4
  ★ **Naranjo de Bulnes** ☏845024 rm8
  Apr–Sep **A**

ARENYS DE MAR Barcelona (☎93)
Map**22**D3
  H **Carlos I** Rial Canalias ☏3920383
  rm100 May–Oct **A**
  H **Nereida** J Antonio 79 ☏3921140
  rm24 **A**
  H **Titus** ctra de Francia ☏3930000
  rm44 **A**
  ★★ **Floris** Playa Cassá 80–82 ☏7920384
  rm32 **A**

ARÉVALO Ávilla (☎918) Map**18**D1/2
  H **Fray Juan Gil** av E Romero ☏800
  rm36 **A**

ARNEDO Logroño (☎941) Map**19**B2
  H **Victoria** Gl Franco 113 ☏380100
  rm48 **B**
  H **Virrey** Gl Franco 27 ☏380150 rm36 **A**

ÁVILA Ávila (☎918) Map**18**D1
  H **Continental** pl de la Catedral 4
  ☏211502 rm54 **A**
  H **Encinar** av del 18 de Julio ☏220212
  rm20 **A**
  H **Jardín** San Segundo 38 ☏211074
  rm26 **A**
  H **Rastro** pl del Rastro 4 ☏211219
  rm17 **A**
  H **Santa Teresa** ctra Avila-Villalba
  ☏220211 rm15 **A**
  ★★ **Cuatro Postes** ☏212944 rm36 **A**

Spain

★★ **Reina Isabel** av J-Antonio 17
☎220200 rm44 **A**

AVILÉS Oviedo (☎985) Map**18**C4
H **San Félix** av de Lugo 48 ☎565146
rm18 **A**

AYAMONTE Huelva (☎955) Map**23**B2
H **Marqués de Ayamonte** Gl Mola 14
☎320125 rm31 **A**

BADAJOZ Badajoz (☎924) Map**23**B2
H **Conde Duque** Muñoz Torrero 29
☎224641 rm35 **A**
H **Montecristo** Afligidos 4 ☎221340
rm16 **A**
H **Río** av de Elvas ☎225125 rm90 **B**

BADALONA Barcelona (☎93) Map**22**D3
H **Betulo** pl Obispo Irurita 6 ☎3893002
rm24 Jun–Oct **A**
H **Miramar** Santa Madrona 60
☎3805541 rm42 **A**

BAGUR Gerona (☎972) Map**22**D3
H **Bagur** de Comay Ros 8 ☎622207
rm35 Mar–Oct **A**
H **Bonaigua** pl de Fornells ☎622050
rm47 Apr–Oct **B**
H **Casa Gran** Ventura Sabater 3
☎312138 rm14 Jun–Sep **A**
H **Plaja** Calvo Sotelo 4 ☎622197 rm19 **A**
★★ **Riera** Playa de sa Riera ☎623000
rm44 Mar–Dec **A**

BAILÉN Jaén (☎953) Map**25**A2
H **Sur** c Radial IV Madrid Cádiz ☎158
rm17 **A**
H **Valencia Al-Andalus** ctra Madrid-
Cadiz ☎345 rm44 Jun–Sep **A**
H **Zodiaco** ctra Nat IV ☎1051 rm52 **B**

BALAGUER Lérida (☎973) Map**22**C3
H **Mirador del Segre** GL Vives 3
☎445750 rm33 **A**
H **Solanes** Gl la Llave ☎445002
rm12 **A**
H **Urgel** Urgel 31 ☎445348 rm23 **A**

BARBASTRO Huesca (☎974) Map**21**B3
H **Rey Sancho Ramírez** ctra Tarragona
S Sebastián ☎310050 rm78 **B**
H **San Ramón** San Ramon 34 ☎310250
rm23 **A**

BARCELONA Barcelona (☎93) Map**22**C3
H **Apolo** Ramblas 33 ☎3015700 rm93 **A**
H **Cortés** Santa Ana 25 ☎2211106
rm53 **A**
H **España** San Pablo 9 & 11 ☎3181758
rm84 **A**
H **Flor Park** Ramblas 57 ☎2218566
rm18 **A**
H **Lleo** Pelayo 24 ☎3181312 rm43 **A**
H **Lloret** rambla Canaletas 125
☎3173366 rm53 **A**
H **Moderno** Hospital 11 ☎3014154
rm69 **A**
H **Park** av Marqués de Argentera 11
rm95 **A**
H **Rialto** Fernando 42 ☎3185212
rm53 **A**

H **San Agustín** pl de San Agustin 3
☎3181658 rm73 **A**
H **Villa de Madrid** pl Villa de Madrid 3
☎3174910 rm27 **A**

BAYONA Pontevedra Map**17**A3
H **Anunciada** Elduayén 16 ☎4 rm20
Apr–Sep **A**
H **Bayona** Conde 36 ☎127 rm33
Jun–Sep **A**
H **Rompeolas** L Calleja ☎80 rm25
Jun–Sep **A**

BÉJAR Salamanca (☎923) Map**18**C1
H **Blázquez Sánchez** Travesía Santa
Ana 6 ☎402400 rm33 **A**
H **Colón** Colón 42 ☎26809 rm54 **B**
H **Comercio** Puerta de Avila 5 ☎400304
rm13 **A**

BENALMÁDENA Malaga (☎952) Map**24**D1
H **Arenas** ctra de Cádiz ☎441539
rm104 May–Oct **A**
H **Bali** ctra de la Telefonica ☎441940
rm202 **A**
H **Balmoral** ctra de Cádiz-Malaga
☎441738 rm210 **A**
H **Palmasol** av del Mar ☎441480
rm244 **A**
H **Rubens** ctra Nacional 340 Cádiz-
Malaga rm106 **A**
H **San Fermín** Vizcondesa de
Portacarrero ☎442040 Apr–Oct **A**
H **Roca** ctra Cádiz-Málago ☎441740
rm71 **A**
H **Van Dyck** Finca Mena rm192
Apr–Sep **A**

BENASQUE Huesca (☎974) Map**21**B4
H **Aneto** c Anciles 2 ☎42 rm38
Jul–Oct **A**
H **Baños de Benasque** ☎43 rm41
Jul–Sep **A**
H **Benasque** c Anciles 3 ☎8 rm56 **A**
H **Pilar,** ctra de Francia ☎323 rm31 **A**
H **Valero** ctra Anciles ☎42 rm78
20Jun–Sept **A**

BENICASIM Castellón (☎964) Map**22**1B1
H **Benicasim** Bayer 46 ☎300558
rm87 **A**
H **Bonaire** Paseo Maritimo ☎300800
rm79 Apr–20Oct **B**
H **Felipe II** Cristóbal Colón ☎300547
rm41 Jun–Sep **A**
H **Miami** Partida Masía Frailes
☎300050 rm44 Apr–Sep **A**
H **Montornes** Partida Parreta ☎300953
rm11 **A**
H **Plaza** 18 de Julio 47 ☎300072 rm7 **A**
H **Tres Carbelas** av F.Salvador
☎300649 rm39 Apr–Oct **A**
H **Vista Alegre** av Barcelona (Las Villas)
☎300400 rm68 **A**

BENIDORM Alicante (☎965) Map**26**D2
H **Alemeda** av del Generalisimo 36
☎855650 rm68 5Apr–5Oct **A**
H **Brisa** Playa de Levante ☎855400
rm70 **A**
H **Didac** vía E. Ortuño ☎851549
rm100 **A**
H **Fenicia** Prolongacion del Mercado 1
☎851146 rm279 Apr–Oct **A**

H **Haway** Viena ☎850400 rm230
Apr–Oct **A**

H **Presidente** av de Filipinas ☎853950
rm228 **A**

H **Riudor** av del Mediterraneo ☎852608
rm168 **A**

H **Royal** vía E Ortuño ☎853500 rm88
Apr–Oct **A**

H **Tanit** av Almendros 1 ☎853612 rm83
Apr–Oct **A**

H **Tropicana Gardens** Sierra Dorada
☎851175 rm251 **A**

BERRON-SIERO (EL) Oviedo (☎985)
Map**18**D4

H **Samoa** ctra Santander – Oviedo
☎741154 rm40 **B**

BIELSA Huesca Map**21**B4

H **Bielsa** Medio ☎7 rm15 **A**

H **Valle de Pineta** Los Cuervos ☎40
rm21 Mar–15Oct **A**

BIESCAS Huesca (☎974) Map**21**B4

H **Casa Ruba** Esperanza 18 ☎485001
rm33 **A**

H **Giral** av Zaragoza ☎485005 rm16 **A**

H **Rambla** La Rambla de San Pedro 7
☎485177 rm28 **A**

BILBAO Vizcayo (☎944) Map**19**B3

H **Arana** Bidebarrieta 2 ☎4156411
rm66 **A**

H **Cantabrico** Miravilla 8 ☎4152811
rm51 **B**

H **España** Ribera 2 ☎212050 rm35 **A**

H **Excelsior** Hurtado de Amezaga 6
☎4153000 rm64 **A**

H **Gurea** Bidebarrieta 14 ☎4163299
rm21 **A**

H **Maroño** Correo 21 ☎4160011 rm49 **A**

H **San Mames** L Briñas 15 ☎4417900
rm36 **A**

H **Zabalburu** P Martinez Artula 8
☎4437100 rm27 **A**

BLANES Gerona (☎972) Map**22**D3

H **Boix Mar** av Villa de Madrid ☎330928
rm170 May–Oct **A**

H **Cónsul Park** av Villa de Madrid
☎331547 rm225 **A**

H **Lyons Magestic** Villa Marot ☎330393
rm121 Apr–Sep **A**

H **Ruiz** Flechas Azules 45 ☎330300
rm59 May–Sep **A**

H **San Antonio** Paseo Maritimo 63
☎331150 rm156 May–Sep **A**

H **Stella Maris** av de Madrid ☎330092
rm44 May–Sep **A**

BURGO DE OSMA (EL) Soria (☎975)
Map**19**A2

H **Perdiz** Universidad 33 ☎340309
rm18 **A**

H **Virrey Palafox** Travesía de Acosta
☎340222 rm22 **A**

BURGOS Burgos (☎947) Map**19**A3

H **Asubio** Carmen ☎203445 rm30 **B**

H **Avila** Almirante Bonifaz 13 ☎205543
rm65 **A**

H **Carlos V** pl de Vega 36 ☎206544
rm24 **A**

H **Lar** Cardenal Benlloch 1 ☎204840
rm10 **A**

H **Martha** Gl Mola 18 ☎202040 rm13 **A**

H **Moderno** Queipo Llano 2 ☎207642
rm28 **A**

H **Norte y Londres** pl A Martínez 10
☎200545 rm58 **A**

H **Ortega** Madrid 1 ☎203471 rm15 **A**

CABRERÀ (LA) Madrid (☎91) Map**19**A1
★★ **Mavi** ctra de Madrid-Irún 58
☎8688000 rm43 **A**

CÁCERES Cáceres (☎927) Map**24**C4

H **Ara** Juan XXIII 3 ☎223958 rm62 **A**

H **Iberia** Gl Franco 2 ☎212480 rm41 **A**

H **Metropol** Obispo Segura Sáez 3
☎225650 rm29 **A**

H **Naranjos** Alfonso IX 12 ☎214343
rm18 **A**

CADAQUÉS Gerona (☎972) Map**22**D3

H **S'Aguarda** Portal de la Fuente
☎258082 rm17 Apr–Sep **A**

H **Cristina** La Riera ☎258138 rm20
May–Sep **A**

H **Port Lligat** Port Lligat ☎258162 rm31
Mar–Oct **A**

CÁDIZ Cádiz (☎956) Map**24**C1

H **Bahía** Marques de Comillas 6
☎222307 rm15 **A**

H **Canarias** Santo Cristo 4 ☎212267
rm38 **A**

H **Imares** San Francisco 9 ☎212257
rm37 **A**

H **Roma** av Carranza 11 & 12 ☎211672
rm82 **A**

H **San Francisco** Valenzuela I
☎212373 rm35 **A**

H **San Remo** Paseo Marítimo ☎232202
rm34 **A**

CALAFELL Tarragona (☎977) Map**22**C2

H **Alondra** Gl Sanjurjo 79 ☎662350
rm105 May–Oct **A**

H **Salome** Monturiol 23 ☎662200 rm45
Jun–Sep **A**

H **Solimar** av San Juan de Dios 106
☎662250 rm45 15May–Sep **A**

CALATAYUD Zaragoza (☎976) Map**19**B1/2

H **Bambola** ctra Madrid-Barcelona
☎881573 rm9 Mar–Nov **A**

H **Calatayud** García Olaya 17 ☎881323
rm63 **B**

H **Marivella** ctra Madrid ☎881237
rm22 **A**

CALDAS DE MONTBUY Barcelona (☎93)
Map**22**C3

H **Balneário Termas Victoria**
Barcelona 12 ☎28 rm91 **A**

H **Farell** Montaña el Farel ☎8650650
rm36 **A**

CALDAS DE REYES Pontevedra (☎986)
Map**17**B3

H **Balneario Acuña** Herreria ☎10 rm21
Jul–Sep **B**

H **Panama** Travesía de Sagasta ☎281
rm14 **A**

Spain

CALELLA DE LA COSTA Barcelona (☎93)
Map**22**D3
- H **Altamar** Iglesia 330 ☎8990683 rm64
  15Jun–Sep**A**
- H **Balmes** Balmes ☎8990581 rm140
  Apr–Oct **A**
- H **Calella Park** Jubara 257 ☎8990318
  rm51 Apr–Oct **A**
- H **Fragata** Paseo de las Rocas
  ☎8990354 rm63 May–Sep **A**
- H **Garbi** Paseo de las Rocas ☎8990858
  rm92 11May–Oct **A**
- H **Olympic-Vistasol** Zona Riera Faro
  ☎8990907 rm371 Jun–Sep **A**
- H **Presidnt** Zona Valdenguli rm280
  May–Oct **A**
- H **Victoria** Zona Riera Faro rm280
  May–Oct **A**
- H **Volga** Jubara 350 ☎8990741 rm181
  May–Oct **A**

CALELLA DE PALAFRUGELL see
PALAFRUGELL

CALPE Alicante (☎965) Map**26**D3
- H **Paradero Ifach** Explanada del
  Puerto 50☎1 rm29 **B**
- H **Porto Calpe** Partida Peñon de Ifach
  ☎830354 rm60 **A**
- H **Rocinante** Partida Estación 10 rm28 **A**

CAMBRILS Tarragona (☎977) Map**22**C2
- H **Augustus** ctra Salou-Cambrils
  ☎381154 rm243 Apr–Oct **A**
- H **Centurión Playa** ctra de Salou
  ☎361450 rm233 Jun–Aug **B**
- H **César Augustus** ctra Salou-Cambrils
  ☎381808 rm120 May–Sep **A**
- H **Monica** Trav Rambla Jaime 1
  ☎360116 rm56 Apr–Sep **A**

CAMPELLO Alicante(☎965) Map**26**C2
- H **Costa Azul** av Gobernador
  Aramburu 103 ☎652250 rm45 **A**

CANET DE MAR Barcelona (☎93) Map**22**D3
- H **Ancora y Corona** ctra Madrid Francia
  ☎3940788 rm28 **A**
- H **Carlos** P San Telmo ☎3940257 rm83
  15Apr–15Oct **A**
- H **Rocatel** ctra Nacional II ☎3940350
  rm40 May–Sep **A**

CANFRANC Huesca (☎974) Map**20**C3
- H **Ara** Fernando el Católico 1 ☎373028
  rm31 **A**
- H **Villa Anayet** J.Antonio 8 ☎373146
  rm59 Jun–Sep **A**

CANGAS DE ONIS Oviedo (☎985)
Map**18**D4
- H **Eladia** av Covadonga 12 ☎848000
  rm24 **A**
- H **Piloña** De San Pelayo 19 ☎848088
  rm18 **A**
- H **Ventura** ctra Covadonga ☎848200
  rm16 **A**

CARBALLINO Orense (☎988) Map**17**B3
- H **Rogelia** pl Hnos Prieto 14 ☎270291
  rm26 **A**

CARBALLO La Coruña Map**17**B4
- H **Rio** Prol Desiderio Varela 3 ☎853
  rm12 **A**

CARTAGENA Murcia (☎968) Map**26**C2
- H **Alfonso XIII** Paseo Alfonso XIII 30
  ☎520000 rm239 **A**
- H **Cartagenera** Jara 32 ☎502500
  rm46 **A**
- H **Mediterráneo** Puertas de Mercia 11
  ☎507400 rm46 **B**

CASTELLDEFELS Barcelona (☎93)
Map**22**C3
- H **Colibri** Paseo Maritimo 138
  ☎3652450 rm67 Apr–Oct **B**
- H **Elivira** c 22 de la Pineda 13 & 15
  ☎3651550 rm31**A**
- H **Miramar** Los Baños 2 ☎3651212
  rm20 **A**
- H **Naranjos** via Triunfal 380 ☎3650984
  rm15 **A**
- H **Rialto** Pasco Maritimo 70 ☎3652942
  rm14 May–Sep **A**
- H **Suiza** Paseo Maritimo 114 ☎3651999
  rm18 **A**

CASTELL DE FERRO Granada (☎958)
Map**25**A1
- H **Mar y Sol** ctra de Almería ☎46 rm15
  15Mar–15Oct **A**
- H **Messón Castell** ctra de Almería ☎8
  rm59 Apr–Sep **A**
- H **Paredes** ctra Málaga Almería ☎19
  rm27 **A**

CASTELLÓN DE LA PLANA Castellón
(☎964) Map**21**B1
- H **Amat** Temprado 15 & 17 ☎220600
  rm25 **A**
- H **Brisamar** av Buenavista 26 ☎222922
  rm12 **A**
- H **Doña Lola** Lucena 3 ☎214011
  rm24 **A**
- H **Gabiska** Gral Sanjurjo 2 ☎211944
  rm35 **B**
- H **Myrian** Obispo Salinas 1 ☎222100
  rm24 **B**

CASTRO URDIALES Santander (☎944)
Map**19**A3/4
- H **Arenillas** ctra Irun-La Coruña rm15 **A**
- H **Miramar** La Playa ☎860200 rm33 **B**
- H **Royal** Jardines 3 ☎861548 rm16 **A**
- H **Vista Alegre** Barrio Brazomar ctra
  ☎860150 rm20 **A**

CAZORLA Jaén Map**25**A2
- H **Cazorla** pl del Generalísimo 4 ☎104
  rm22 **A**

CERVERA Lérida (☎973) Map**22**C3
- H **Canciller** Paseo de Balmes ☎53080
  rm40 **A**

CHIPIONA Cádiz (☎956) Map**24**C1
- H **Chipiona** Gómez Ulla 16 ☎370200
  rm40 Jun–15Oct **A**
- H **Currican** av Gral Primo de Rivera
  ☎371100 rm46 Apr–Sep **B**
- H **Del Sur** Playa Ntra Sra de Regla
  ☎370350 rm54 **B**
- H **Gran Capitán** Fray Baldomero 7
  ☎370929 rm14 Apr–Sep **A**
- H **Paquito** Isaac Peral 4 ☎370056 rm22
  15Jun–15Sep **A**

Spain

CIUDAD REAL Ciudad Real (☎926)
Map**25**A3
  H **Castillos** av del Rey Santo 6
    ☎213640 rm132 **B**

CIUDAD RODRIGO Salamanca (☎923)
Map**18**C1
  H **Cruce** av Portugal 4 ☎460450 rm30 **A**

COMARRUGA Tarragona (☎977) Map**22**C2
  H **Brisamar** Buenaventura Trillas
    ☎661700 rm102 Apr–Oct **A**
  H **Casa Marti** Vilafranca 15 ☎661750
    rm106 15Apr–15Oct **B**
  H **Gallo Negro** Santiago Rusiñol
    ☎661804 rm30 Apr–Oct **A**

COMILLAS Santander (☎942) Map**19**A4
  H **Colasa** A López ☎13 rm13 **A**
  H **Josein** ctra General ☎306 rm14
    Jun–Oct **B**
  H **Paraiso** Plaza ☎36 rm36 **B**
  H **San Pedro** J Antonio 3 ☎50 rm37
    10Jun–23Sep **A**

CÓRDOBA Córdoba (☎957) Map**24**D2
  H **Andalucía** J Zorrilla 3 ☎221855
    rm40 **A**
  H **Avenida** av del Generalisimo 28
    ☎223900 rm35 **A**
  H **Colón** Alhaken II 4 ☎226223 rm40 **A**
  H **Granada** av de América 21 ☎221864
    rm27 **A**
  H **Niza Sur** av Cadiz 60 ☎296311
    rm24 **A**
  H **Riviera** pl de Aladreros 7 ☎221825
    rm29 **A**
  H **Selu** E. Dato 7 ☎223865 rm105 **A**
  H **Serrano** Pérez Galdós 4 ☎226298
    rm40 **A**
  ★★ **Marisa** Cardenal Herrero ☎226317
    rm16 **A**

CORUÑA (LA) (Corunna) La Coruña
(☎981) Map**17**B4
  H **Brisa** Paseo de Ronda 2 ☎269650
    rm16 **A**
  H **Corunñamar** Paseo de Ronda
    ☎261327 rm21 **A**
  H **Lagos** Polígono Residencial de Elviña
    ☎286299 rm35 15Jun–15Sep **A**
  H **Marineda** Rosalía de Castro 13 & 15
    ☎224700 rm71 **A**
  H **Maycar** San Andres 175 ☎225600
    rm50 **A**
  H **Orensana** Olmas 14 ☎224005
    rm26 **A**
  H **Rivas** av Fernández Latorre 45
    ☎239546 rm70 **B**
  H **Santa Catalina** Trav Santa Catalina 1
    ☎226609 rm32 **A**
  H **Venecia** pl de Lugo 22 ☎222420
    rm19 **A**

CUENCA Cuenca (☎966) Map**25**B4
  H **Avenida** av J Antonio 39 ☎214343
    rm33 **A**
  H **Castilla** D Jiménez 4 ☎212292
    rm15 **A**
  H **Cortés** Ramón & Cajal 49 ☎220400
    rm52 **A**
  H **Xucar** Cervantes 15 ☎214042 rm28 **A**

CULLERA Valencia (☎963) Map**26**D3
  H **Bolendam** av Cabañal 17 ☎1520661
    rm39 **B**
  H **Carabela** Cabanal 5 ☎1520292
    rm14 **A**
  H **Escala** Marqués de la Romana 4
    rm20 **A**
  H **Mongrell** Rellano S Antonio 2
    ☎1521524 rm35 **B**
  H **Safi** Faro de Cullera Ptda del Dosel
    ☎1520577 rm31 **A**

DENIA Alicante (☎965) Map**26**D3
  H **Costa Blanca** Pintor Llorens 3
    ☎780336 rm53 **A**
  H **Rotas** Partida les Rotes 47 ☎780323
    rm23 Apr–Sep **A**
  H **Villa Amor** Partida las Marinas
    ☎781436 rm20 Apr–Sep **A**

DEVA Guipuzcoa (☎943) Map**19**B3
  H **Egaña** Arenal 2 ☎601040 rm21
    Jun–Sep **A**
  H **Monreal** Lersundi 30 ☎601244 rm26
    15Mar–15Oct **A**
  H **Playa** J J Azpeitia 16 ☎601156 rm36
    Jul–15Sep **A**
  ★★ **Miramar** J-J Aztiria 36 ☎601144
    rm60 **A**

EJEA DE LOS CABALLEROS Zaragoza
(☎976) Map**20**C2
  H **Cinco Villas** Gl Franco 12 ☎540300
    rm30 **B**

ELCHE Alicante (☎965) Map**26**C2
  H **Cartagena** Gl Goded 12 ☎461550
    rm34 **B**
  H **Don Jaime** av de Primo de Rivera 7
    ☎453840 rm64 **A**
  H **Enrique** Canónigo Torres 8 ☎451577
    rm23 **A**

ELDA Alicante (☎965) Map**26**C2
  H **Elda** av de Chapi 4 ☎380556 rm37 **A**
  H **Sandallo** Gl Mola 19 ☎380102
    rm18 **A**

ESCALA (LA) Gerona (☎972) Map**22**D3
  H **Casa Nieves** Caídos por la Patria 27
    ☎770100 rm25 Jun–Sep **A**
  H **Dels Pins** ctra Closa del Llop
    ☎310395 rm42 15May–15Sep **A**
  H **Miryam** Rond a Padro ☎770287
    rm10 **A**
  H **Podyum** Rond a del Padro 1
    ☎770652 rm12 Jun–Sep **A**
  H **Rallye** av Maria ☎770245 rm16
    May–Sep **A**
  H **Riomar** San Martín ☎770362 rm26
    May–Sep **A**

ESTARTIT Gerona (☎972) Map**22**D3
  H **Bell Aire** Rocamaura 6 ☎758162
    rm78 **B**
  H **Club de Campo Torre Grau**
    Descampado ☎758160 rm10 **A**
  H **Flamingo** Iglesia ☎758327 rm100
    May–Sep **A**
  H **Garbi** Paseo del Mar ☎758151 rm42
    Jun–Sep **A**
  H **Miramar** av de Roma 7 ☎758628
    rm61 Jun–Oct **A**

Spain

H **Rambla** Paseo del Puerto 2 ☎758538
rm15 Apr–Sep **A**

ESTEPONA Málaga (☎952) Map**24**C1

H **Caracas** av San Lorenzo 50 ☎800800
rm27 **B**

H **Dobar** Queipo de Llano 117 ☎800600
rm39 **A**

★ **Buenavista** Gl-Franco 119 ☎800137
rm37 **A**

FERROL DEL CAUDILLO (EL) La Coruña
(☎981) Map**17**B4

H **Aloya** Pardo bajo 28 ☎351231
rm15 **A**

H **Ryal** Galiano 43 ☎358044 rm40 **A**

FIGUERAS Gerona (☎972) Map**22**D3

H **París** Rambla de Sara Jorda 10
☎500800 rm36 **A**

H **Pirineos** Rda Barcelona I ☎500312
rm53 **B**

H **Ronda** ctra de la Junquera ☎503911
rm36 **A**

FRAGA Huesca (☎974) Map**21**B3

H **Casanova** av del Generalisimo 80
☎470050 rm56 **A**

H **Sorolla** ctra Madrid Barcelona 437 ☎8
rm36 **A**

FUENGIROLA Málaga (☎952) Map**24**D1

H **Agur** Tostón 4 ☎462780 rm33 **A**

H **El Cid** av del Ejército ☎862148
rm46 **A**

H **Italia** Italia 1 ☎461213 rm28 **A**

H **Molinos** Hernán Cortés ☎461016
rm9 2Mar–14Oct **A**

H **Torreblanca** ctra N340 Cádiz Málaga
☎462540 rm198 Apr–Oct **B**

FUENTERRABÍA Guipúzcoa (☎943)
Map**19**B3

H **Alvarez Quintero** Hnos. Alvarez
Quintero 7 ☎642299 rm14 Jun–Sep **A**

H **Concha** Javier Ugarte ☎641600 rm53
Jun–Sep **A**

H **Franco** Javier Ugarte 7 ☎141743
rm32 Jun–Sep **A**

H **Jáurequi** San Pedro 31 ☎641400
rm48 **A**

★★ **Guadalupe** Ciudad de Peñíscola
☎641650 rm35 May–Sep **A**

GANDÍA Valencia (☎963) Map**26**D3

H **Gandía Playa** Asturias ☎2841300
rm90 May–Oct **B**

H **Europa** Levante 12 ☎2840750
rm23 **A**

H **Mavi** Legazpi ☎2840020 rm30
Apr–Oct **A**

H **Rexy** Mayor 48 ☎2871151 rm 33 **A**

H **Vicmar** Pío XI 55 ☎2873143 rm40 **A**

GERONA Gerona (☎972) Map**22**D3

H **Condal** J. Maragall 10 ☎204462
rm44 **A**

H **Inmortal Gerona** ctra Bar Barcelona
31 ☎207900 rm76 **B**

H **Reyma** Subida Rey Don Martin 15
☎200228 rm18 **A**

GIJÓN Oviedo (☎985) Map**18**D4

H **Asturias** pl Mayor 12 ☎350600
rm113 **B**

H **Castilla** Corrida 50 ☎346200 rm34 **A**

H **Covadonga** 18 de Julio 10 rm8 **A**

H **París** Marqués de Casa Valdes 65
rm10 **A**

GRANADA Granada (☎958) Map**25**A1

H **Anacapri** J. Costa 7 ☎225562 rm32 **A**

H **Casablanca** Frailes 3 ☎257600
rm63 **A**

H **Faisanes** Gran Capitán 1 ☎234500
rm36 **A**

H **Manuel de Falla** Antequeruela Baja 4
☎227545 rm14 Mar–Oct **A**

H **Monte carlo** J. Antonio 44 ☎257900
rm63 **A**

H **Rallye** Carrero Blanco 97 ☎272800
rm44**B**

H **Sierra Nevada** ctra Madrid 79
☎232146 rm19**A**

H **Universal** Recogidas 16 ☎223410
rm55**A**

★★ **Inglaterra** Cetti Merien 4 ☎221558
rm50**A**

★ **America** Real Alhambra 53 ☎227471
rm13 Mar–10Nov**A**

GRANOLLERS Barcelona (☎93) Map**22**D3

H **Del Valles** ctra de Masnou ☎8703762
rm30**A**

GUADALAJARA Guadalajara (☎911)
Map**19**A1

H **España** Teniente Figueroa 3
☎211303 rm33**A**

★ **Reloj** Dr Mayoral 11 ☎211525 rm20**A**

GUADALUPE Cáceres (☎927) Map**24**D4

★★ **Parador Nacional de Zurbaran**
Marques de la Romano 10 ☎367075
rm20**A**

GUARDAMAR DEL SEGURA Alicante
(☎965) Map**26**C2

H **Delta** Torrevieja 43 ☎728712 rm14
15May–Oct**A**

H **Europa** Jacinto Benavente 1
☎729055 rm14 Apr–Sep**A**

H **Oasis** Torrevieja ☎145 rm44
Mar–Nov**A**

H **Meridional** Urb Dunas de Guardamar
☎728340 rm11**A**

HOSPITALET DEL INFANTE Tarragona
(☎977) Map**22**C2

H **Del Infante** Gl Molá 22 ☎823000
rm42 Apr–Oct**A**

M **Vandellos** ctra Nal 340 ☎823286
rm11**A**

HUELVA Huelva (☎954) Map**23**B2

H **Andalucía** Váquez López 26
☎216967 rm24**A**

H **Costa de la Luz** J. María Anmo 8
☎215808 rm35**A**

H **Granada** Gl Mola 11 ☎215308 rm66**A**

H **San Miguel** Santa Maria 6 ☎215189
rm10**A**

HUESCA Huesca (☎974) Map**20**C2

H **Mirasol** Ramón y Cajal 67 ☎223760
rm13**A**

H **Montearagon** ctra Tarragona-S.
Sebastian ☎222350 rm27**A**

H **Penqueñin** Berenguer 4 ☎212363
rm46**A**

IRÚN Guipúzoca (☎943) Map**19**B3
- H **Lara** Paseo de Colon 73 ☎612203 rm19A
- H **Machinventa** Paseo de Colon 21 ☎615059 rm6A
- H **Terminus** Estación del Norte ☎611149 rm19B
- ★★ **Lizaso** Martires de Guadalupe 5 ☎611600 rm20A

JACA Huesca (☎974) Map**20**C3
- H **Conde de Aznar** Gl Franco ☎361050 rm23B
- H **Mur** Santa Orosia 1 ☎360100 rm74A
- H **Pradas** Obispo 12 ☎361150 rm39B

JAÉN Jaén (☎953) Map**25**A2
- H **Europa** pl de Belén 1 ☎222700 rm36B
- H **Reyes Católicos** av de Granada 1 ☎222250 rm23A
- H **Yuca** ctra Nal Bailen-Motril ☎221950
- ★★ **Rey Fernando** pl Coca de la Piñera 7 ☎211840 rm36A

JATIVA Valencia (☎96) Map**26**C3
- H **Murta** Del Nuevo de Alineamiento 13 ☎2883240 rm21A
- H **Vernisa** Acadwmico Maravall ☎2882544 rm39A

JAVEA Alicante Map**26**D3
- H **Lluca** Partida Lluca de Benitachell ☎790379 rm4A
- H **Miramar** Aduanas del Mar 15 ☎790100 rm26A
- H **Plata** Playa de Montañas 83 ☎54 rm34A
- H **Villa Naranjos** ctra Montañar rm147A

JEREZ DE LA FRONTERA Cádiz (☎956) Map**24**C1
- H **Avila** 18 de Julio 3 ☎331662 rm17A
- H **Coloso** P. Alonso 13 ☎349008 rm25A
- H **Garaje Centro** Doña Blanca 10 ☎332450 rm23A
- H **Joma** Dr. J.C. Durán 22 ☎349689 rm39A
- H **Mica** J.C. Durán 7 ☎340700 rm38A

JUNQUERA (LA) Gerona (☎972) Map**22**D4
- H **Frontera** ctra Nacional II ☎540050 rm28A
- H **Goya** ctra Nacional II ☎540077 rm35 Apr-15OctA
- H **Junquera** ctra Nacional II ☎540100 rm28A
- ★★ **Mercé Park** ctra N II (4 km S) ☎502704 rm48A

LALÍN Pontevedra (☎986) Map**17**B3
- H **Palacio** Mate mático Rodriguez 10 ☎780000 rm32A

LAREDO Santander (☎942) Map**19**A4
- H **Florida** av Gl Mola ☎605150 rm65 Closed Jul-14Sep A
- H **Montecristo** Calvo Sotelo 2 ☎605700 rm23 Apr-15Sep A
- H **Ramona** Gl Mola 4 ☎605336 rm15 Apr-Sep A
- H **Rosi** Marqués de Valdecilla ☎605839 rm24 Apr-Sep A

- ★ **Ramona** av J-Antonio 4 ☎605336 rm28 (A15) Closed Nov A

LECUMBERRI Navarra (☎948) Map**19**B3
- ★★ **Ayestaran** ctra 64 ☎504127 rm120 (A94) A

LEDESMA Salamanca (☎923) Map**18**C2
- H **Balneario de Ledesma** ctra de Salamanca ☎18 rm152 Jun-Sep A

LEÓN León (☎987) Map**18**D3
- H **Carmina** independencia 29 ☎214800 rm31 A
- H **Don Suero** Suero de Quiñones 15 ☎2300600 rm50 A
- H **París** Generalísimo 20 ☎238600 rm78 A
- H **Reina** Puerta de la Reina 2 ☎215266 A
- H **Reino de León** M. Sarmiento 10 ☎216105 rm32 A

LEQUEITIO Vizcaya (☎94) Map**19**B3
- H **Beltia** Pascual - Aboroa 25 ☎6851150 rm33 Apr-Sep A

LÉRIDA Lerida (☎973) Map**21**B3
- H **Agramunt** pl de España 20 ☎242850 rm40 A
- H **Bimba** ctra Zaragoza ☎221843 rm29 A
- H **Ilerda** ctra Barcelona ☎200750 rm67 A
- H **Jamaica** ctra de Zaragoza ☎221540 rm24 A
- H **Ramón Berenguer IV** pl Ramón Berenguer IV 3 ☎237345 rm60 A

LLANES Oviedo (☎985) Map**18**D4
- H **México** av de México ☎401057 rm20 Jul-Sep A
- ★★ **Penablanca** Pidal 1 ☎400166 rm30 15Jun-15Sep A

LLANSÁ Gerona (☎972) Map**22**D3
- H **Goleta** Pintor Torroella 12 ☎254125 rm40 Jun-Sep A
- H **Grifeu** ctra de Port Bou ☎380050 rm33 15May-Sep A
- H **Grimar** ctra de Port Bou ☎380167 rm38 Apr-Oct A

At **Puerto de Llansá** (1.5km NE)
- ★★ **Berna** ☎380150 rm45 15May-15Sep A

LLORET DE MAR Gerona (☎972) Map**22**D3
- H **Acacias** av de las Acacias ☎364150 rm43 May-Oct A
- H **Capri** 2 de Febrero ☎364562 rm155 May-Sep A
- H **Copacabana** av Mistral ☎364416 rm162 May-Sep A
- H **Don Quijote** av América ☎365860 rm374 Apr-Oct A
- H **Eugenia** ctra Hostalrich Tossa ☎364400 Apr-Oct A
- H **Mercedes** av Mistral ☎364312 rm88 Apr-Oct A
- H **Olimpic-Lloret** Angel Can Tabola ☎365820 Jun-Sep A
- ★★ **Excelsior** ps M-J Verdaguer 16 ☎364137 rm45 Apr-Oct A
- ★★ **Fanals** ctra de Barcelona ☎364112 rm84 Etr-Oct A

Spain

★★ **Santa Rosa** Senia del Barral
☎364362 rm132 Apr–Nov **A**

LOGROÑO Logroña (☎941) Map**19**B3
H **Animas** Marqués de Vallejo 8
☎211003 rm28 **A**
H **El Cortijo** ctra del Cortijo ☎225050
rm40 **A**
H **Isasa** Dr Castroviejo 13 ☎221850
rm32 **A**
H **Numantina** Sagasta 4 ☎220404
rm17 **A**
H **París** J Antonio 4 ☎211508 rm51 **A**
★★ **Gran** Gl-Vara de Rey 5 ☎212100
rm83 **A**

LORCA Murcia (☎968) Map**25**B2
H **Alameda** Museo Valiente 8 ☎469511
rm43 **B**
H **Alberca** pl J Moreno 1 ☎468850
rm21 **A**

LUARCA Oviedo (☎985) Map**18**C4
H **Gayoso** El Parque ☎640054 rm26 **A**
H **Rico** pl del Parque ☎640129 rm14 **A**

LUCENA Cordoba (☎957) Map**24**D2
H **Baltanas** av J Solis ☎500524 rm32 **A**

LUCENO DEL CID Castellon (☎964)
Map**26**D4
H **Prat** Balneario ☎25 rm63 Jun–Sep **A**

LUGO Lugo (☎982) Map**17**B4
H **Gerdiz** Río Neira 25 ☎221700 rm23 **A**
H **Miño** Tolda de Castilla 2 ☎220150
rm50 **B**
H **Parames** J Antonio 28 ☎211346
rm20 **A**
H **Rivera** Gl Sanjurjo 94 ☎221037
rm13 **A**
H **San Roque** Comandante Manso 9
☎222708 rm18 **A**
H **Seoane** Ronda de Castilla 2 ☎211145
rm25 **A**

MADRID Madrid (☎91) Map**19**A1
H **Asturias** Carrera de San Jeronimo 9
☎2218240 rm141 **B**
H **Baltimore** Bravo Murillo 160
☎2348000 rm24 **B**
H **Bristol** av de J Antonio 40 ☎2224720
rm195 **A**
H **Compostela** Muñoz Torrero 7
☎231670 rm25 **A**
H **Europa** Carmen 4 ☎2212900 rm51 **A**
H **Mediodia** pl del Emperador Carlos V 8
☎2273060 rm157 **A**
H **Monaco** Barbieri 5 ☎2224630 rm28 **A**
H **Nuria** Fuencarral 52 ☎2319208
rm57 **A**
H **Ramón de la Cruz** D Ramón de la
Cruz 94 ☎4017200 rm99 **B**
H **Santander** Echegarary 1 ☎2212873
rm38 **A**

MÁLAGA Málaga (☎952) Map**24**D1
H **Astoria** av Comandante Benitez 3
☎224500 rm16 **A**
H **Avenida** av Generalisimo 1 ☎217729
rm23 **A**
H **Carambolo** Marín Garcia 7 ☎226704
rm25 **A**

H **Del Sur** Trinidad Grund 13 ☎224803
rm37 **A**
H **Larios Cuatro** Marqués de Larios 4
☎211531 rm39 **A**
H **Lynda Mar** Canales 6 ☎317200
rm30 **A**
H **Olletas** Cuba 1 & 3 ☎252004 rm66 **A**
H **Roma** Molina Larios 8 ☎210453
rm33 **A**
H **Solarium** A Pérez 2 ☎222306 rm32 **A**
H **Venecia** av Generalisimo 5 ☎213636
rm40 **A**

MANRESA Barcelona (☎93) Map**22**C3
H **Santo Domingo** av del Caudillo 22
☎8721600 rm43 **A**

MANZANARES Ciudad Real (☎926)
Map**25**A3
H **Manzanares Antigua** Antigua C
Madrid-Cadiz ☎610804 rm23 **A**
★★ **Albergue Nacional** (2km S)
☎610400 rm42 **A**

MARBELLA Málaga (☎952) Map**24**D1
H **Alfil** av R Soriano 19 ☎772350 rm56 **A**
H **Baviera** Camino del Calvario 2
☎772950 rm41 **A**
H **Cortijo Blanco** ctra Cádiz-Málaga
☎811440 rm119 **A**
H **Finlandia** Finlandia ☎823086 rm11 **A**
H **Fonda** pl del Santo Cristo 15
☎824348 rm17 **A**
H **Lima** av A. Belón 2 ☎770500 rm64 **B**
H **Nagueles** ctra Cádiz Málaga
☎771650 rm17 Apr–Oct **A**
H **Pinomar II** ctra Cádiz-Málaga
☎831306 rm101 May–Oct **A**
H **Ranchotel** ctra Cádiz-Málaga
☎831175 rm41 **A**
H **Ric-Mar** ctra Cádiz-Málaga ☎831058
rm54 Apr–Oct **A**

MENDINACELI Soria (☎975) Map**19**B1
H **Nico** ctra Nacional ☎37 rm22 **B**

MEDINA DEL CAMPO Valladolid (☎983)
Map**18**D2
H **Mota** Fernando el Catolico 4
☎800450 rm40 **A**

MEDINA DE RIOSECO Valladolid Map**18**D2
H **Almirantes** San Francisco 2 ☎290
rm31 **B**

MERIDA Badajoz (☎924) Map**24**C3
M **Lomas** ctra Madrid-Lisboa rm35 **A**
H **Texas** ctra Madrid ☎302940 rm40 **A**

MIJAS Málaga (☎952) Map**24**D1
H **Club Costa del Sol** ctra Cádiz-Málaga
☎462947 rm76 Apr–Oct **A**

MIRANDA DE EBRO Burgos (☎947)
Map**19**A3
H **Achuri** av Generalisimo 86 ☎310040
rm31 **A**

MOJÁCAR Almeria (☎951) Map**25**B1
H **Continental** Playa el Palmeral ☎225
rm22 **A**
H **Mojacar** Mirador de la Puntica ☎38
rm60 Apr–Sep **A**

Spain

H **Provenzal** Playa del Descargador
☎112000 rm11 **A**
H **Tioedy** Playa Mojacar ☎48 rm31
Apr–Oct **A**

MONDARIZ-BALNEARIO Pontevedra
Map**17**B3
H **América** R Peinador ☎104 rm31
Jun–Oct **A**
H **Avelino** R Peinador ☎102 rm45
Jun–Sep **A**
H **Balneario Roma** Constitución ☎108
rm16 Jun–Sep **A**
H **Balneario Villa Flora** Calvo Sotelo
☎107 rm21 Jun–Sep **A**

MORELLA Castellón (☎964) Map**21**B2
H **Cardenal Ram** Cuesta Suñer 2 ☎90
rm19 **A**
H **Elías** Colomar 7 ☎160092 rm17 **A**

MOTO DEL CUERVO Cuenca (☎966)
Map**25**B4
H **Mesón de Don Quijote** F Costi 2
☎502 rm36 **B**

MURCIA Murcia (☎968) Map**26**C2
H **Fontoria** Madre de Dios 4 ☎217789
rm127 **B**
H **Hispanoi** Trapería 8 ☎214561
rm49 **A**
H **Majesti** Sand Pedro 5 ☎214741
rm68 **A**
H **Rincón de Pepe** Apóstoles 34
☎212239 rm122 **B**
I **Transportista Murciano**
ctra Beniasan ☎210412 rm31 **A**

MURGUIA Avala (☎945) Map**19**B3
H **Zuya** Domingo Sauto ☎430027
rm15 **A**

NÁJERA Logroño (☎941) Map**19**B3
H **San Fernando** Paseo A Martín
Gamero 1 ☎360700 rm40 **A**

NAVA Oviedo (☎985) Map**18**D4
H **Nava** ctr General ☎716864 rm16 **A**

NAVACERRADA Madrid (☎91) Map**18**D1
H **Postas** c Madrid Segovia ☎8560250
rm21 **B**

NAVALCARNERO Madrid (☎91) Map**18**D1
H **Labrador** ctra Extremadura rm31 **A**
H **Noria** ctra Navalcarnero Cadalso de
las Vidrio ☎8110005 rm20 **A**
H **Vegas** ctra de Extremadura
☎8110400 rm26 **A**

NAVALMORAL DE LA MATA Cáceres
(☎927) Map**24**D4
H **Almanzor** J Antonio 43 ☎530600
rm36 **A**
H **Bamba** ctra Madrid-Lisboa ☎530850
rm33 **A**
H **Brazilia** ctra Madrid-Lisboa ☎530750
rm 43 **A**

NERJA Málaga (☎952) Map**25**A1
H **Cala-Bella** Puerta del Mar 10
☎520103 rm9 **A**

OLMEDO Valladolid (☎983) Map**18**D2
H **Piedras Blancas** ctra Adanero Gijón
☎600100 rm24 **A**

ORENSE Orense (☎988) Map**17**B3
H **Padre Feijoo** Calvo Sotelo 1
☎223100 rm53 **B**
H **Riomar** Accesos Puente Novisimo 15
☎220700 rm33 **A**

ORIHUELA Alicante (☎965) Map**26**C2
H **Astoria** Molino de Cox ☎302543
rm18 **A**

OROPESA Castellón (☎964) Map**21**B2
H **Ancla** Camino Morro Gros 8
☎310238 rm26 Apr–Sep **A**
H **Caribe** Paseo Maritimo ☎310075
rm21 Apr–Sep **A**
H **Europea** ctra del Faro rm12 **A**
H **Oropesa Sol** ctra del Faro 97
☎310150 rm50 Mar–Oct **A**
H **Playa** Playa de Morra de Gros
☎310235 rm40 Apr–Sep **A**
H **Sancho Panza** ctra Valencia-
Barcelona ☎310494 rm15 **A**
H **Zapata** ctra del Faro 92 ☎310425
rm42 15Jun–15Sep **A**

OVIEDO Oviedo (☎985) Map**18**C4
H **Asturias** Uría 16 ☎214695 rm19 **A**
H **Barbon** Covadonga 7 ☎225293
rm40 **B**
H **Fruela** Fruela 2 ☎218278 rm33 **A**
H **México** Uría 25 ☎240404 rm25 **A**
H **Tropical** 19 de Julio 8 ☎218779
rm44 **A**
★★ **Principado** San Francisco 8
☎217792 rm100 **B**

PALAFRUGELL Gerona (☎972) Map**22**D3
H **Costa Brava** San Sebastián 10
☎300558 rm32 Apr–Oct **A**

At **Calella de Palafrugeli** (5km SE)
★★ **Mediterraneo** Playa Banõs ☎300150
rm38 May–Sep **A**

PALAMÓS Gerona (☎972) Map**22**D3
H **Ancora Urbanización la Fosca**
☎315486 rm28 **A**
H **Garbi** Pagés Ortiz 67 ☎314292 rm26
Jun–Sep **A**
H **Nauta** av del Generalisimo 40
☎314833 rm33 **A**
H **Xamary** av J. Antonio 70 ☎314270
rm36 **A**
★★ **Marina** av de Generalismo 48
☎314250 rm62 **A**
★★ **San Juan** c Mayor de San Juan 30
☎314208 rm31 Apr–Sep **A**

PALENCIA Palencia (☎988) Map**18**D2
H **Monclus** Menendez Pelayo 3
☎723850 rm40 **A**

PAMPLONA Navarra (☎948) Map**19**B3
H **Eslava** pl Virgen de la O. 7 ☎222270
rm28 **A**
H **Europa** Espoz & Mina 11 ☎221800
rm31 **A**
H **Perla** pl del Castillo 1 ☎211903
rm67 **A**
★★ **Yoldi** av San Ignacio 11 ☎224800
rm50 **A**
★ **Valerio** av de Zaragoza 5 ☎245035
rm16 **A**

PANCORBO Burgos (☎947) Map**19**A3

Spain

H **Pancorbo** ctra Madrid Irún ☎320266 rm39 **A**

PEÑISCOLA Castellón (☎964) Map**21**B2
H **Marina** J Antonio 42 ☎480890 rm20 Apr–Sep
H **Prado** ctra a Benicarlo ☎480289 rm25 Apr–Sep **A**
H **Rio Mar** Primo de Rivera ☎480745 rm8 **A**
H **Tio Pepe** J Antonio 32 ☎440 rm10 **A**

PERELLO (EL) Valencia (☎96) Map**26**D3
H **Antina** Buenavista 20 ☎1770000 rm45 Jun–Oct **A**

PIEDRAHÍTA Avila (☎918) Map**18**C1
H **Piedrahita** Extramuros ☎461 rm45 **A**

PINEDA DE MAR Barcelona (☎93) Map**22**D3
H **Koppers** Iglesia 76 rm161 Jun–Oct **A**
H **Mar Azul** N S de Montserrat ☎46 rm29 May–Oct **A**
★★ **Taurus Park** ps Maritimo ☎7623350 rm417 May–Oct **B**

PLAYA DE ARO Gerona (☎972) Map**22**D3
H **Acapulco** Mediterráneo ☎817162 rm45 May–Oct **A**
H **Bellamar** ctra Palamós ☎817550 rm20 May–Sep **A**
H **Claramar** Pinar de Mar ☎817158 rm36 May–15Oct **A**
H **Costa Brava** Punta D En Ramis ☎817308 rm46 Apr–Sep **A**
H **Planamar** av de la Paz 173 ☎817092 rm86 May–Oct **A**
H **Xaloc** Afueras ☎817300 rm41 May–Sep **A**
★★ **Japet** ctra de Palamos ☎817366 rm48 **A**

PONFERRADA León (☎987) Map**18**C3
H **Conde Silva** ctra Madrid-La Coruña 2 ☎410407 rm60 **A**
H **Lisboa** Jardines 5 ☎411350 rm16 **A**
★★ **Madrid** J-Antonio 50 ☎411550 rm54 **A**

PONS Lérida (☎973) Map**22**C3
H **Pedra Negra** ctra Lérida-Puigcerda ☎460100 rm19 **A**

PONTEVEDRA Pontevedra (☎986) Map**17**A3
H **Universo** Benito Corbal 30 ☎854100 rm59 **B**

PORRIÑO Pontevedra (☎986) Map**17**A3
H **Azul** Ramires ☎330032 rm19 **A**
H **Brasil** Atios ☎330442 rm14 **A**
H **Internacional** A. Palacios ☎330262 rm32 **B**
H **Louro** av Buenos Aires 6 ☎330021 rm6 **A**

PORT-BOU Gerona (☎972) Map**22**D4
H **Bahía** Cerbere 1 ☎310996 rm24 May–Oct **A**
H **Comodoro** Méndez Nuñez 1 ☎390187 rm16 May–Sep **A**
★ **Costa Brava** J-Antonio 26 ☎390003 rm34 Jun–Sep **A**

POTES Santander (☎942) Map**18**D3
H **Coriscao** La Serna ☎730458 rm11 **A**
H **María Eugenia** Dr Encinas 12 ☎730154 rm12 Jun–Sep **A**
H **Picos de Europa** San Roque ☎730005 rm28 15Mar–15Oct **A**
H **Picos de Veldecoro** Roscabado ☎730026 rm24 **A**

PUERTO DE LLANSÁ see **LLANSÁ**

PUERTO DE MAZARRÓN Murcia (☎968) Map**26**C2
H **Durán** Playa de la Isla ☎594050 rm30 Apr–Oct **A**
H **Rosamar** San Juan 5 ☎590450 rm26 **A**

PUERTO DE NAVACERRADA Madrid (☎91) Map**18**D1
H **Corzo** ctra la Granja ☎8520900 rm9 **A**
H **Pasadoiro** Puerto de Navacerrada ctra de la Granja ☎2015 rm36 **A**

PUERTO DE SANTA MARÍA (EL) Cadiz (☎956) Map**24**C1
H **Campomar** Valdelagrana Parcela 18 ☎863542 rm16 **A**
H **San Nicolás** San Bartolome 25 ☎863029 rm18 **A**

PUERTO LAPICE Ciudad Real (☎926) Map**25**A3
H **El Aprisco** Carretera Madrid Cádiz, km 134 ☎576150 rm17 **A**
★★ **Puerto** ctra Madrid-Cadiz ☎576000 rm37 **A**

PUIGCERDÁ Gerona (☎972) Map**22**C4
H **Del Prado** Ctra deLlivia s/n ☎880400 rm30 **A**
H **Europa** Plaza Cabrinety 16 ☎880100 rm15 **A**
H **Tixaire** Escuelas Pias 5 ☎880126 rm44 **A**
★★ **Maria Victoria** Florenza 9 ☎880300 rm50 **A**
★★ **Martinez** ctra de Luvia ☎880250 rm15 **A**

QUINTANA DEL PUENTE Palencia Map**18**D2
H **San Cristóbal** Ctra Burgos-Portugal km54 ☎23 rm34 **A**
H **Suco** c National 620, km54 ☎6 rm10 **A**

QUINTANAR DE LA ORDEN Toledo Map**25**B4
H **Castellano** Ctra Valencia 70 ☎10 rm27 **A**
H **Santa Marta** Ctra Valencia km54 ☎152 rm19 **A**

REINOSA Santander (☎942) Map**19**A3
H **La Corza Blanca** Brañavieja ☎751099 rm44 **A**
H **Vejo** Avda Cantabria 15 ☎751700 rm71 **A**

REQUENA Valencia (☎96) Map**26**C3
H **Sol** Ctra Nat III km281 ☎2300050 rm40 **A**

REUS Tarragona (☎977) Map**22**C2
H **De Francia** Vicaria 8 ☎304240 rm39 **B**

Spain

H **Gaudi** Arrabal Robuster 49 ☎305545 rm73 **B**

H **Olle** Paseo de Prim 45 ☎311245 rm32 **A**

H **Simonet** Arrabal de Sta Ana18 ☎302131 rm57 **A**

RIAZA Segovia Map**19**A2

H **La Trucha** Avda Dr Tapia ☎71 rm31 **A**

RIBADAVIA Orense (☎988) Map**17**B3

H **Avia** José Antonio 36 ☎471000 rm27 **A**

RIBADEO Lugo (☎982) Map**18**C4

H **Ferrocarrilano** San Roque 17 ☎110600 rm26 **A**

H **Ribanova** San Roque 8y10 ☎110625 rm36 **A**

H **Riberas del Eo** Muelle de Porcillón ☎110300 rm5 Mar–Oct **A**

★★ **Eo** av de Asturnias 5 ☎110750 rm24 Apr–Sep **A**

RIBADESELLA Oviedo (☎985) Map**18**D4

H **Marina** Generalisimo 28 ☎860050 rm44 **B**

H **La Playa** La Playa 42 ☎860100 rm12 Apr–30Oct **B**

H **Sueve** Sanjurjo ☎860369 rm11 **A**

RIBAS DE FRESER Gerona (☎972) Map**22**C/D3

H **Cataluña Park** Mauri 9 ☎727198 rm22 Jul–Sep **B**

H **Fanet** General Urrutia 24 ☎3 rm27 Jun–Sep **A**

RONDA Málaga (☎952) map**24**C1

H **El Hondon** ctra de Ronda Jerez Sevilla km103 ☎872560 rm17 Jun–Sep **A**

H **Polo** Mariano Souviron 9 ☎872447 rm33 **B**

H **Royal** Virgen de la Paz 52 ☎871141 rm25 **A**

ROSAS Gerona (☎972) Map**22**D3

H **Berganti** Canyelles ☎257159 rm18 May–Sep **A**

H **Carabela** Av Caudillo 10 ☎256288 rm36 May–Sep **A**

H **Ciudadela** Av Tarragona s/n ☎257009 rm36 May–Sep **A**

H **Gallet** Madrid ☎256191 rm47 May–Sep **A**

H **Grecs** Paraje de los Griegos ☎256162 rm54 May–Sep **A**

H **Mariam Platja** Playa ☎256108 rm101 Apr–Oct **B**

H **Marina** José Antonio 1 ☎256278 rm53 **A**

H **Maritim** Benavente s/n ☎256390 rm105 Apr–Oct **A**

H **Victoria** Av Comercial s/n ☎256201 rm221 Apr–15Oct **A**

ROTA Cádiz (☎956) Map**24**C1

H **Buenos Aires** Santa Maria del Mar 1 ☎810201 rm21 **A**

H **Nuestra Sra del Rosario** Capitán Cortes 25 ☎810604 rm31 **A**

H **Playa de la Luz** Arroyo Hondo sn ☎810500 rm285 **A**

RÚA (LA) Orense (☎988) Map**18**C3

H **Espada** ctra Orense Ponferrada ☎310075 rm38 **A**

SABADELL Barcelona (☎93) Map**22**C3

H **Creu Alta** Marti Trias 2 ☎2966858 rm104 **B**

H **Urpi** Avda Ejército Espaxol 38 ☎2960500 rm59 **A**

SABÍNANIGO Huesca (☎974) Map**21**B4

H **Alpino** General Franco 58 ☎480725 rm18 **A**

H **Mi Casa** Av del Ejercito 32 ☎480375 rm72 **A**

★★ **Pardina** ☎480975 rm64 **A**

SALAMANCA Salamanca (☎923) map**18**C2

H **Aragón** Av Federico Anaya 1 ☎233129 rm20 **A**

H **Carabela** Pl de España 3 ☎212290 rm10 **A**

H **Ceylan** Pl del Peso 5 ☎212603 rm32 **B**

H **Condal** Plaza de los Hermanos Jerez 2 ☎218400 rm70 **B**

H **Emperatriz** Compañia 4 ☎219200 rm23 **B**

H **Laguna** Consuelo 13 ☎215382 rm13 **A**

H **Lorenzo** ctra de Bejar 1 ☎214306 rm22 **A**

H **Mindanao** Av del Libano 2 ☎233795 rm30 **A**

H **Universal** Rúa Mayor 13y15 ☎212006 rm42 **A**

SALER (EL) Valencia (☎963) Map**26**C/D3

H **Patilla II** Pinares 10 ☎3671558 rm28 **B**

SALOU Tarragona (☎977) Map**22**C2

H **Ancora** Urb Porta del Mer ☎380848 rm252 May–Sep **A**

H **Cala Font** c 222 ☎380454 rm318 Jun–Sep **B**

H **Calaviña** ctra Tarragona Salou km10 ☎380150 rm70 May–Oct **B**

H **Europa Park** Av Principe de Andorra ☎381400 rm325 Apr–Oct **A**

H **Donaire Park** Playa del Reco ☎381066 rm337 May–Sep **A**

H **Monaco** Barcelona 6 ☎380154 rm45 Apr–Oct **A**

H **President** Barcelona 5 ☎380285 rm60 May–Oct **B**

H **La Torre** ctra Tarragona-Salou ☎380250 rm26 Jun–Sep **A**

★★ **Planas** pl Bonet 2 ☎380108 rm100 Apr–Sep **A**

SAN CARLOS DE LA RÁPITA Tarragona (☎997) Map**21**B2

H **Miami** Av Generalisimo 37 ☎740551 rm22 **A**

H **Playa Suizo** ctra Valencia Balcelona km161 rm24 15Mar–15Sep **A**

SAN FELIÚ DE GUIXOLS Gerona (☎972) Map**22**D3

H **Avenida** Gerona, 12 ☎320800 rm28 Jun–Sep **A**

Spain

H **Cruañas** Rambla Vidal 15 ☎320508 rm20 May–Oct **A**

H **Gesoria** Campmany 3 ☎320350 rm34 20Jun–15Sep **A**

H **Mediterráneo** Penitencia 8 ☎320750 rm40 Jun–Sep **A**

H **Montserrat** José Antonio 3 ☎320604 rm10 Jun–20Sep **A**

H **Regente** Cruz 5 ☎320806 rm36 Jun–Sep **A**

H **Regina** Maragall 1 ☎320050 rm53 May–Oct **A**

★★ **Noies** Rambla J-Antonio 10 ☎320400 rm50 (A10) May–Sep **A**

★★ **Turist** San Ramón 39 ☎320841 rm23 (A9) Apr–Oct **A**

SAN FERNANDO Cádiz (☎956) Map**24**C1

H **Las Salinas** Constructora Naval 13 ☎883840 rm12 **A**

H **Salymar** pl del Ejercito 32 ☎883440 rm41 **B**

SANGENJO Pontevedra (☎986) Map**17**A3

H **Asturiana** Gondar-Sangenjo ☎743006 rm17 Jul–Sep **A**

H **Cervantes** Progreso 29 ☎720700 rm18 Jun–Sep **B**

H **Maricielo** Avda del Generalisimo 22 ☎720050 rm29 May–Sep **B**

H **Playa** av del Generalisimo ☎720015 rm23 Jun–Sep **A**

H **Silgar** Progreso 32 ☎720029 rm36 Jul–Sep **A**

H **Terraza** Progreso ☎720013 rm50 15Jun–15Sep **B**

SAN JUAN DE ALICANTE Alicante (☎965) Map**26**C2

M **Abril** ctra Murcia Valencia km 90 ☎653408 rm48 **B**

H **Santa Faz** ctra Alicante Valencia ☎651006 rm44 **A**

SANLUCAR DE BARRAMEDA Cádiz (☎956) Map**24**C1

H **Guadalquivir** Calzada del Ejército ☎360742 rm81 Apr–Sep **B**

H **Rio** Santo Domingo 27 ☎361581 rm20 **A**

SAN PEDRO DE ALCAÑTARA Málaga (☎952) Map**24**D1

H **Alcántara** Marqués del Duero 82 ☎812142 rm62 **A**

H **Alcotan** c Cadiz-Malaga km 179 ☎811548 rm84 Apr–Oct **A**

H **El Pueblo Andaluz** Cádiz Málaga km 179 ☎811642 rm179 **A**

SAN POL DE MAR Barcelona (☎93) Map**22**D3

H **Costa** José Antonio 32 ☎8905250 rm17 Jun–8Sep **A**

H **L'Hostalet III** Santa Clara ☎8905375 rm20 **A**

SAN ROQUE Cádiz (☎956) Map**24**C1

H **Bernardo** c Nal 340 km 134 ☎792132 rm8 **A**

M **San Roque** ctra Cádiz Málaga km 124 ☎780100 rm37 **A**

SAN SEBASTIÁN Guipuzcoa (☎943) Map**19**B3

H **Alameda** Alameda de Calvo Sotelo 23 ☎411284 rm30 15Mar–15Oct **A**

H **Buena Vista** Barrio de Igueldo ☎210600 rm14 **B**

H **Codina** Auda Zumalacárregui 21 ☎212200 rm80 **A**

H **Isla** Miraconcha 17 ☎417685 rm23 Apr–Oct **A**

◆ **Lasa** Vergara 15 ☎412386 rm24 **A**

H **Leku-Eder** Barrio de Igueldo ☎210107 rm11 May–Oct **A**

H **Terminus** Auda de Francia ☎410366 rm20 **A**

H **Txomin** Infanta Beatriz 14 ☎210705 rm12 **B**

★★ **Niza** Zubieta 56 ☎426663 rm41 **B**

★ **Juaristi** Sanchez Toca 1 ☎467533 rm20 15Apr–15Oct **A**

SANTANDER Santander (☎942) Map**19**A4

H **Alisas** Nicolás Salmeron 3 ☎222750 rm40 **A**

H **Carlos III** av Reina Victoria 135 ☎271616 rm20 Apr–Oct **A**

H **Carmen** San Fernanda 48 ☎230190 rm13 **A**

H **Cisneros** Cisneros 8 ☎221613 rm8 Jun–Oct **A**

H **Ignacia** General Mola 5 ☎222400 rm78 **A**

H **Isabel II** Isabel II 10 ☎210550 rm23 **A**

H **Liebana** Nicolás Salmeron 9 ☎223250 rm28 **A**

H **Mexicana** Juan Herrera 3 ☎222350 rm31 **A**

H **Rocamar** Auda de los Castros 41 ☎277268 May–Oct **A**

SANTA POLA Alicante (☎965) Map**26**C2

H **Picola** Alicante 66 ☎411044 rm23 **A**

H **Rocas Blancas** Ctra Alicante-Cartagena km 17 ☎413394 rm90 **B**

SANTIAGO DE COMPOSTELA La Coruña (☎981) Map**17**B4

H **España** Rúa Nueva 40 ☎581200 rm31 **A**

H **Fornos** Hórreo 7 ☎595130 rm14 **A**

H **Gelmirez** General Franco 92 ☎591100 rm138 **B**

H **Maria Mediadora** República el Salvador 16 ☎592822 rm56 15Jul–Sep **A**

H **México** Republica Argentina 33 ☎598000 rm57 **A**

H **Universal** pl Galicia ☎592250 rm52 **A**

SANTIAGO DE LA RIBERA Murcia (☎968) Map**26**C2

H **Don Juan** av Ntr Sra de Loreto ☎571043 rm43 Jul–Sep **A**

H **Lido** Conde Campillo 1 ☎570700 rm32 **A**

H **Manida** Muñoz 11 ☎570011 rm27 15Apr–15 Jan **A**

H **Ribera** Explanada de Barnuevo 10 ☎570200 rm38 15Mar–15Oct **A**

Spain

SANTILLANA DEL MAR Santander (☎942) Map**19**A4
- H **Trabuco** av San Javier ☎570044 rm18 **A**

SANTILLANA DEL MAR Santander (☎942) Map**19**A4
- H **Emperador** av Le Dorat 12 ☎818033 rm3 **A**
- H **Altamira** Canton 1 ☎818025 rm27 Apr–Oct **A**

SANTO DOMINGO DE LA CALZEDA Logroño (☎941) Map**19**A3
- H **Santa Teresita** General Mola 2 ☎340700 rm78 **A**

SANTOÑA Santander (☎942) Map**19**A4
- H **Juan de La Cosa** Nueva Beria ☎660100 rm30 Jul–15Sep **A**

SAN VICENTE DE LA BARQUERA Santander (☎942) Map**18**D4
- H **Luzon** ctra Santander Oviedo ☎710050 rm39 **A**
- H **Miramar** La Barquera ☎710076 rm15 **A**

SEGOVIA Segovia (☎911) Map**18**D1
- H **Acueducto** P Claret 10 ☎424800 rm77 **B**
- H **Casas** Cronista Lecea11 ☎412107 rm20 **A**
- H **Victoria** pl Franco 5 ☎412194 rm31 **A**

SEO DE URGEL Lérida (☎973) Map**22**C4
- H **Cadi** Duque de Seo de Urgel 4 ☎350150 rm42 **A**
- H **Mundial** San Odón ☎350000 rm85 **A**
- H **Nice** av del Generalisimo 4 ☎351221 rm26 **A**
- ★ **Avenida** av Gl-Franco 18 ☎350104 rm39 **A**

SEVILLA (Seville) Sevilla (☎954) Map**24**C2
- H **Avenida** Marqués de Parada 28 ☎220688 rm6 **A**
- H **Corregidor** Morgado 17 ☎218722 rm69 **B**
- H **Ducal** Pl de la Encarnacion 19 ☎215107 rm51 **A**
- H **Duque** Trajano 15 ☎228930 rm34 **A**
- H **Internacional** Aguilas 15 ☎213207 rm27 **A**
- H **Londres** San Pedro Martir 1 ☎212896 rm22 **A**
- H **Málaga** O'Donell 9 ☎216122 rm12 **A**
- H **Murillo** Lope de Rueda 7 ☎216095 rm61 **A**
- H **Paris** San Pablo 27 ☎222860 rm20 **A**
- H **Sevilla** Daoiz 5 ☎220853 rm30 **B**

SILS Gerona (☎972) Map**22**D3
- H **Chez-Mira** ctra Nat II, km707 ☎30 rm18 **A**
- H **Touring** ctra Nat II, km707 ☎20 rm12 **A**

SITGES Barcelona (☎93) Map**22**C2/3
- H **Bahia** Parelladas 27 ☎8940012 rm37 15 Apr–15 Oct **A**
- H **Caramelles** Francisco Guma 12 ☎8941962 rm28 May–Oct **A**
- H **Don Pancho** San José 2 ☎8941662 rm85 15May–Sep **A**
- H **Globos** Ntr Sra de Montserrat ☎8941412 rm22 May–Sep **A**
- H **Londres** Juan Maragall 3 ☎8941850 rm20 Apr–Oct **A**
- H **Sitges** San Guadencio 5 ☎8940072 rm52 May–Oct **A**
- H **Veracruz** Avda Sofia ☎8941526 rm26 May–Oct **A**
- ★★ **Luna Playa** Puerto Alegre 51 ☎894430 rm12 **A**
- ★★ **Sitges** San Gaudencio 5 ☎8940072 rm52 May–Oct **A**
- ★ **Romantic** San Isidro 23 ☎8940643 rm55 May–Oct **A**

SOLARES (MEDIO CUDEYO) Santander Map**19**A4
- H **Balneario Fuencaliente** av Calvo Sotelo ☎27 rm51 Jul–Sep **A**

SORIA Soria (☎975) Map**19**B2
- H **Cadosa** ctra Zaragoza – Zamora km146 ☎211502 rm12 **A**
- H **Florida** Nicolás Rabal 9 ☎212746 rm35 **A**
- H **Las Heras** Ramónycajal 4 ☎213346 rm24 **A**
- H **Viena** García Solier 5 ☎222109 rm24 **A**

SORT Lérida (☎973) Map**22**C4
- H **Pessets ii** ctra a Seo de Urgels ☎109 rm80 **A**

SOTILLO DE LA ADRADA Ávila (☎918) Map**18**D1
- H **Nuria** Ctra de Casillas 5 ☎8661000 rm21 **A**

SUANCES-PLAYA Santander (☎942) Map**19**A4
- H **Acacio** Avda Acacio Gutierrez ☎810026 rm54 Jul–Sep **A**
- H **El Caserio** El Faro 1 ☎810587 rm9 **A**
- H **El Vivero** La Playa ☎810075 rm8 **A**

TAFALLA Navarra (☎948) Map**19**B3
- H **Morase** ps Marqués de Vadillo 13 ☎821700 rm24 **A**
- H **Navarra** Blas Morte 7 ☎820908 rm40 **A**
- H **De Tudela** ctra de Zaragoza ☎820558 rm18 **A**

TALAVERA DE LA REINA Toledo (☎925) Map**24**D4
- H **Del Rio** Prado 16 ☎802350 rm30 **A**
- H **Perales** av Dio XII ☎803900 rm39 **A**
- ★★ **Auto-Estacian** av Toledo 1 ☎800300 rm40 **A**
- ★★ **Talavera** av G-Ruiz 1 ☎800200 rm80 **A**

TARANCÓN Cuenca (☎996) Map**25**B4
- H **Polo** Francisco Ruiz Jarabo 39 ☎110500 rm31 **A**
- H **Sur** ctra Madrid-Valencia km81 ☎110600 rm33 **A**

TARAZONA Zaragoza (☎976) Map**19**B2
- H **Brujas de Becquer** ctra Nacional 122 km44 ☎640404 rm60 **A**

TARIFA Cádiz (☎956) Map**24**C1

Spain

H **Hosteria Tarifa** ctra Cádiz Málaga ☎684076 rm14 Apr–Oct **A**

☆☆ **Balcon de España** ☎684326 rm38 Apr–Oct **A**

★★ **Dos Mares** ☎684117 rm19 Apr–Oct **A**

TARRAGONA Tarragona (☎977) Map**22**C2

H **Anterman** Via Augusta 221 ☎203615 rm6 Apr–Oct **A**

H **Canada** ctra de Valencia km213 ☎211035 rm32 **A**

H **Minguell** ctra Valencia km274 ☎210108 rm28 **A**

H **Torreon** via Augusta ☎207856 rm15 Apr–Oct **A**

★★ **Astari** via Augusta 97 ☎203840 rm83 Apr–Oct **A**

TÁRREGA Lérida (☎973) Map**22**C3

H **Aleix** Plaza del Carmen 11 ☎310100 rm42 **A**

TERUEL Teruel (☎974) Map**26**C4

H **Goya** Tomás Nogués 4 ☎601450 rm24 **A**

H **Oriente** Av de Sagunto 5 ☎601550 rm29 **A**

TOJA (LA) Pontevedra (☎986) Map**17**A3

H **Balneario** Isla de la Toja ☎305 rm43 Jun–15Sep **A**

TOLEDO Toledo (☎925) Map**25**A4

H **Almazara** ctra Piedrabuena 47 ☎223866 rm21 Apr–Oct **A**

H **Imperio** Cadenas 7 ☎221650 rm19 **A**

H **Labrador** Juan Labrador 16 ☎222620 rm41 **A**

H **Line** Sant Justa 9 ☎223350 rm19 **A**

H **Maravilla** Barrio Rey 5 ☎223300 rm20 **A**

H **Miraltajo** ctra de Madrid 1 ☎223650 rm12 **A**

TORO Zamora (☎988) Map**18**C2

H **Juan II** pl del Espolon 1 ☎690300 rm42 **B**

TORREBLANCA Málaga (☎952) Map**21**B2

H **Cortés** ctra Valencia Barcelona km100 ☎420102 rm31 **A**

H **Sol** ctra Valencia Barma km101 ☎420302 rm20 **A**

TORRE DEL MAR Málaga (☎952) Map**24**D1

H **Myrian** av del Generalisimo 15 ☎540150 rm38 **A**

H **Villa Las Yucas** ctra de Almería ☎150 rm33 **A**

TORREDEMBARRA Tarragona (☎977) Map**22**C2

H **Lider** Paseo Miramar 10 ☎640050 rm66 20May–25Sep **A**

H **Morros** Pérez Galdos 8 ☎640225 rm52 **A**

H **Torredembarra** ctra Nat 340 km294 ☎640032 rm12 **A**

TORRELAVEGA Santander (☎942) Map**19**A4

H **Cantabria** Pasaje de Saro 1 ☎883188 rm10 **A**

H **La Gloria** Alcalde del Rio ☎883023 rm15 **A**

H **Regio** José Maria de Pereda 34 ☎881505 rm24 **A**

H **Saja** Alcalde del Rio ☎892750 rm45 **B**

TORREMOLINOS Málaga (☎952) map**24**D1

H **Atta Vista** pl del Mercade ☎387600 rm106 **A**

H **Amaragua** Los Nidos ☎384633 rm198 **B**

H **Copenhague** av de los Manantiales ☎380711 rm21 **A**

H **Flamingo** av Imperial ☎383855 rm289 **A**

H **Lloyd** av Montemar 74 ☎380922 rm96 **A**

H **Plata** Pasaje Pizarro 1 ☎380111 rm39 **A**

H **Pozo** Casablanca 2 ☎380622 rm31 **A**

H **Sol y Sol** av Montemar ctra Nat 340 Cádiz-Málaga ☎382545 rm44 **A**

H **Venus** La Cordera ☎383188 rm100 **A**

★★ **Panorama** c Mercedes 14 ☎386277 rm53 **A**

TORREVIEJA Alicante (☎965) Map**26**C2

H **Barceló** av Alfredo Nobel 8 ☎850606 rm36 **A**

H **Berlin** Torre del Moro ☎711537 rm32 **A**

H **Mazu** Sevilla 24 ☎711250 rm39 **A**

TORRIJOS Toledo (☎925) Map**25**A4

H **El Mesón Ruta del Alcázor** Ca Toledo-Avila km28 ☎760400 rm29 **A**

TORTOSA Tarragona (☎977) Map**21**B2

H **Berenguer IV** Cervantes 23 ☎440816 rm24 **A**

TOSSA DE MAR Gerona (☎972) Map**22**D3

H **Albor** av Costa Brava ☎340204 rm59 May–Sep **A**

H **Avenida** av de la Palma ☎340162 rm57 Apr–20Oct **A**

H **Canaima** av de la Palma ☎340266 rm17 May–Sep **A**

H **Estoril** Carretera de San Feliu ☎340070 rm32 Jun–Sep **A**

H **Gallo Atrevido** Monte Villa Romana ☎340169 rm13 Apr–Oct **A**

H **Mar Blau** av Costa Brava 12 ☎340282 rm67 Jun–Sep **A**

H **Neptuno** Flechas Ezules 32 ☎340143 rm49 May–Sep **A**

H **Soms Park** Urbanización Mas Con Font ☎341080 rm88 May–Sep **A**

★★ **Corisco** J-Antonio 8 ☎340174 rm28 Mar–Oct **A**

★★ **Villa Romana** ☎340258 rm28 (A10) Mar–Sep **A**

TREMP Lerida (☎973) Map**22**C3

H **La Canonja** pl de la Cruz 9 ☎650200 rm31 **A**

H **Siglo XX** pl Cruz 32 ☎650000 rm56 **A**

TRUJILLO Cáceres (☎927) Map**24**C4

H **Cigueñas** ctra Madrid-Lisboa km 243 ☎320640 rm34 **A**

TUDELA Navarra (☎948) Map**19**B2

H **Navarra** Blas Morte 7 ☎820908 rm40 **A**

H **Remigio** Gaztambide 4 ☎820850 rm45 A

H **Santamaria** Frauca 22 ☎821200 rm56 A

★★ **Morase** ☎821700 rm26 A

★ **Tudela** ctra de Zaragoza ☎820558 rm16 A

TÚY Pontevedra (☎986) Map**17**A3

H **Parador National San Telmo** av de Portugal ☎298 rm16 B

UNION (LA) Murcia (☎968) Map**26**C2

H **Sierra Mar** Salto 1 ☎560825 rm40 A

VALDEPEÑAS Ciudad Real (☎926) Map**25**A3

H **Cervantes** Seis de Junio 46 ☎311442 rm42 A

H **Guerra** av Estudiantes 30 ☎311791 rm7 A

H **Juma** ctra Madrid Cádiz km 200 ☎311440 rm20 A

H **Tu Casa** ctra Madrid Cádiz km 200 ☎311548 rm19 A

VALENCIA Valencia (☎963) Map**26**C3

H **Bisbal** Pie de la Cruz II ☎3317084 rm21 A

H **Bristol** Abadia San Martin 3 ☎3224895 rm40 Closed 1–14 Jan B

H **Castillo Benisano** Rubén Vela 23 ☎3344049 rm10 A

H **Chicote** Playa Levante 34 ☎3716151 rm20 A

H **Europa** Ribera 4 ☎3220589 rm81 A

H **Florida** Padilla 4 ☎3213035 rm49 A

H **Lauria Roma** Roger de Lauria 4 ☎3223490 rm69 A

H **Norte** Ntra Sra de Gracia 8 ☎3213140 rm38 A

H **Oriente** pl del Caudillo 9 ☎3212278 rm13 A

H **Valencia** En Llops 5 ☎3222989 rm47 A

★★ **Bristol** Abadia de San Martin 3 ☎3224895 rm40 15Jan–Nov A

VALLADOLID Valladolid (☎983) Map**18**D2

H **Conde Rio** ctra Burgos-Portugal km 120 ☎273886 rm19 A

H **Enara** pl de España 5 ☎220480 rm26 A

H **Imperial** peso 4 ☎229898 rm90 A

H **Inglaterra** Maria de Molina 2 ☎222219 rm47 A

VERÍN Orense (☎988) Map**17**B3

H **Aurora** Luis Espada 37 ☎410025 rm40 A

H **Dos Naciones** Luis Espada 38 ☎410100 rm25 A

VICH Barcelona (☎93) Map**22**D3

H **Ausa** pl de Caudillo 4 rm24 A

★★ **Cólon** ps J-Antonio 1 ☎8891917 rm38 A

VIELLA Lérida (☎973) Map**22**C4

H **Arán** av de José Antonio 1 ☎26 rm44 A

H **Beravista** ctra Guasach ☎30 rm29 A

H **Delavall** General Mola 36 ☎237 rm28 A

H **Internacional** Gereralisimo 9 ☎9 rm54 A

H **Serrano** San Nicolás 2 ☎6 rm27 A

H **Turrull** General Sanjurjo 11 ☎36 A

VIGO Pontevedra (☎986) Map**17**A3

H **Almirante** Queipo de Llano 13 ☎223907 rm31 A

H **Arias** Lepanto 6 ☎223403 rm24 A

H **Cendon** Travesia de Isabel II 3 & 5 ☎211361 rm34 A

H **Estoril** Lepanto 12 ☎215628 rm48 A

H **Nilo** Marqués de Valladares 26 ☎213519 rm52 B

H **Panton** Leparto 18 ☎224270 rm38 A

VILLANUEVA Y GELTRÚ Barcelona (☎93) Map**22**C2

H **César** Ferrer di 9 ☎8030704 rm38 A

H **Universo Park** Antonio Ferrer Pi, 35 ☎8930450 rm43 Jun–Sep A

★ **Solvi 70** ps Ferrer Pl 1 ☎8933243 rm29 A

VILLARCAYO Burgos (☎947) Map**19**A3

H **La Rubia** Alemania 3 ☎7 rm27 A

H **Margarita** Nuxo Rasura ☎15 rm27 A

VINAROZ Castellón (☎946) Map**21**B2

H **Barralarga** ctra N. 340 ☎450258 rm7 A

H **Europa II** ctra Valencia Barcelona, km143 ☎451258 rm60 B

H **Miramar** ps Generalisimo 12 ☎451400 rm16 A

M **Versailles** San Ramon II ☎450700 rm9 A

★★ **Roca** ctra Valencia-Barcelona ☎450350 rm36 A

VITÓRIA Avala (☎973) Map**19**B3

H **Desiderio** Colegio San Prudencio 2 ☎251700 Closed 24 Dec–14 Jan A

H **Florida** Manuel Iradier 33 ☎260675 rm15 A

H **Francia** Dato 39 ☎231100 rm29 A

H **Paramo** General Alava 17 ☎230450 rm24 A

H **Savoy** Prudencio Maria de Verástegui 4 ☎258113 rm25 A

VIVERO Lugo (☎982) Map**17**B4

H **Ego** Aguadoce a Faro ☎560987 rm22 A

H **Serra** Antonio Bas 2 ☎560374 rm7 A

H **Tebar** Nicolás Cora 70 ☎560100 rm27 A

ZAFRA Badajoz (☎924) Map**24**C3

H **Huerta Honda** av López Asma ☎550800 rm50 A

ZAMORA Zamora (☎988) Map**18**C2

H **Estación** Estación de la RENFE ☎521350 rm13 A

H **La Farola** pl de Martin Alverez 2 ☎513676 rm13 A

H **San Francisco** José Antonio 5 ☎511296 rm8 A

H **Sayagues** pl Puentica 2 ☎513934 rm30 A

ZARAGOZA Zaragoza (☎976) Map**20**C2

H **Bilbaino** Escuelas Pias 21 ☎229283 rm45 A

Spain

H **Burdeos** San Lorenza 28 ☎293697 rm17 **A**
H **Cataluña** Cosa 94 ☎216938 rm51 **A**
H **Gran Via** Calva Sotelo38 ☎229213 rm31 **A**
H **Lafuente** Valenzuela 7 ☎224806 rm65 **A**
H **Maza** pl de España 7 ☎229355 rm41 **A**
H **Patria** Hermanos Ibarra 8 ☎224955 rm41 **A**
H **Sol** Molino 2 ☎221940 rm60 **A**
★ **Conde Blanco** Predicadores 84 ☎238600 rm84 **A**
★★ **Cisne** ctra Madrid ☎332000 rm61 **A**

ZARAUZ Guipúzcoa (☎943) Map**19**B3
H **Duque** Vizonde Zolina 25 ☎851100 rm19 **A**
H **Otamendi** pl de España ☎841227 rm11 Jun–Sep **A**
H **Paris** ctra Bilbao – San Sebastián 17 ☎830500 rm28 Apr–Sep **A**

Andorra

ANDORRA LA VELLA Map**22**C4
H **Cassany** av Meritxell 28 ☎20636 rm50 **A**
H **Consul** pl Rebes 5 ☎20196 rm56 16Feb–14Jan **A**
H **Florida** Llacuna 11 ☎20105 rm37 **A**

★★ **Mirador** c de la Vall ☎20920 rm30 **A**
★★ **Pyrenees** ☎20508 rm81 **A**

ARINSAL Map**22**C4
H **Pobladó** ☎35122 rm40 Closed 1–20Oct **B**
H **Solana** ☎35127 rm 40 16Nov–14Oct **B**

ENCAMP Map**22**C4
H **Paris** ☎31325 rm43 Closed 15–30Nov **A**
H **Univers** ☎31005 rm41 Closed Oct **A**

ESCALDES (LES) Map**22**C4
H **Pubilla** av Fiter i Rossell ☎20981 rm30 Closed 15–30Nov **A**
H **Andorrá** av Carlemany 34 ☎20831 rm35 **B**
★★ **Pla** ☎21432 rm32 Jun–Aug **A**

PAS DE LA CASA Map**22**C4
H **Refugi dels Isards** ☎51155 rm39 **B**

SANT JULIÀ DE LÒRIÁ Map**22**C4
H **Barcelona** (1km N) ☎41177 Mar–Oct rm50 **B**
★★ **Sardana** pl Major 2 rm25 (A4) 15Mar–Sep **A**

SERRAT (EL) Map**22**C4
H **Serrat** ☎35296 rm20 11Feb–9Jan **B**

SOLDEU Map**22**C4
H **Tarter** ☎51165 rm36 Closed Nov **B**

SWITZERLAND
AND LIECHTENSTEIN

Switzerland

The gazetteer which follows contains details of hotels and pensions which provide accommodation for a maximum of £6 per person per night at sometime during the year. The prices have been banded as follows: **A** under £5 per person per night, and **B** between £5 and £6 per person per night. It also contains some establishments (*Berghouses*) situated at high altitudes and accessible only by mountain railway or funicular, which mainly provide overnight accommodation. Owing to the high cost of living throughout the country, our list is comparatively short, and it has not been possible to include many of the larger cities, but wherever possible alternatives in the neighbourhood have been included.

Abbreviations:
pl   place, Platz
pza   piazza

r   rue
rte   route
Str   Strasse

ALTDORF Uri (☎044) Map**11**B1
  H **Bahnof** ☎21032 bed40 **B**

ARBON Thurgau (☎071) Map**12**C2
  ★ **Frohsinn** ☎461046 rm7
  11Oct–9Sep **B**

AROLLA Valais (☎027) Map**28**C4
  H **Aiguille de la Tza** ☎831406 bed35
  Dec–Sep **A**
  H **Glacier** ☎831218 bed35 **A**
  H **Pigne d'Arolla** ☎831165 bed20 **A**
  H **Poste** ☎831164 bed25 **A**

BÄCHLI St-Gallen (☎071) Map**12**C2
  H **Frohheim** ☎561160 bed30 **B**

BADEN Aargau (☎056) Map**11**B2
  H **Adler** Badstr 18 ☎225766 bed70 **B**

BALERNA Ticino (☎091) Map**29**A4
  H **Bellevista** ☎432798 bed35 **B**

BEATENBERG Bern (☎036) Map**11**B1
  ♦ **Berghaus Niederhorn** ☎411197
  bed8 Closed Nov (*Access by funicular only*) **B**
  ♦ **Favorita** ☎411204 bed15 **B**

BECKENRIED Nidwalden (☎041) Map**11**B1
  ★ **Sonne** ☎641205 rm25 **B**

BERN (BERNE) Bern (☎031) Map**11**B1
  H **National** Hirschengraben 24
  ☎251988 bed42 **B**

BOUDRY Neuchâtel (☎038) Map**11**A1
  H **Lion d'Or** av du Collége 2 ☎421016
  bed13 **B**

BOURG-ST-PIERRE Valais (☎026)
Map**28**C4
  ♦ **Pension du Valsorey** ☎49176
  bed22 **A**
  ♦ **Auberge du Vieux Moulin** ☎49103
  bed25 **A**

BUCHS St-Gallen (☎085) Map**12**C1/2
  H **Bären** Bahnhafstr 15 ☎61166
  bed18 **B**

CHAMPÉRY Valais (☎025) Map**28**C4
  H **Berra** ☎84168 bed30 Closed Nov **B**
  ♦ **Pension Buffet de la Gare** ☎84329
  bed18 **A**

CHARMEY Fribourg (☎029) Map**11**B1
  ♦ **Auberge du Chêne** ☎71134 bed8 **B**

CHATEAU D'OEX Vaud (☎029) Map**11**B1
  H **Printanière** ☎46113 bed18
  Closed Nov **B**

COL DES MOSSES Vaud (☎025) Map**11**A1
  H **Col des Mosses** ☎67192 bed22 **B**
  H **Chaussy** ☎67147 bed10 **B**

COLOMBIER Neuchâtel (☎038) Map**11**A1
  H **Couronne** ☎413281 bed41 **B**

CORNOL Bern (☎066) Map**11**B2
  H **Union des Peuples** ☎722224 bed6 **A**

ERNEN Valais (☎028) Map**11**B1
  H **Alpenblick** ☎711537 bed30 **A**

ESCHOLZMATT Luzern (☎041) Map**11**B1
  H **Rössli** ☎771241 bed20 **A**

EUSEIGNE Valais (☎027) Map**28**C4
  H **Pyramides** ☎811249 bed20 **A**

EVOLÈNE Valais (☎027) Map**28**C4
  ♦ **Pension Bellevue** ☎831139 bed20 **A**
  ★ **Enolene** ☎831202 rm45 **B**

FERPÈCLE Valais (☎027) Map**28**C4
  H **Col d'Herens** ☎831154 bed25
  Jun–Sep **A**

FIESCH Valais (☎028) Map**11**B1
  H **Alpes** ☎81506 bed27 **A**

FILZBACH Glarus (☎058) Map**12**C1
  ★ **Seeblick** ☎321455 rm10 **B**

FINHAUT Valais (☎026) Map**28**C4
  H **Alpes** ☎47117 bed25 **B**
  H **Beau-Séjour** ☎47101 bed50
  Apr–Sep, Dec & Jan **B**

GENÈVE (Geneva) Genève (☎022)
Map**28**C4
  ♦ **Clos Voltaire** r de Lyon 45 *bis*
  ☎447014 bed60 **B**

GERLAFINGEN Solothurn (☎065)
Map**11**B1/2
  H **Gerlafingerhof** ☎352424 bed20 **B**

GLETSCH Valais (☎028) Map**11**B1
  H **Blauhaus** ☎82515 bed50
  Jun–Sep **A**

GRÄCHEN Valais (☎028) Map**28**D4
  H **Allalin** ☎561293 bed20 **A**
  ♦ **Pension Ausblick** ☎561187 bed20
  Closed May & Nov **A**

GROSSHÖCHSTETTEN Bern (☎031)
Map**11**B1
  ♦ **Landgasthof Sternen** ☎910111
  bed14 **B**

GUTTANNEN Bern (☎036) Map**11**B1
  ★ **Baren** ☎731261 rm24 **B**

Switzerland

HAUDÈRES (LES) Valais (☏027) Map**28**C4
- H **Edelweiss** ☏831107 bed38 **B**
- H **Gai-Logis** ☏831413 bed16
  Closed Nov **A**
- H **Georges** ☏831137 bed12 **A**

HEITENFRIED Fribourg (☏037) Map**11**B1
- H **Sternen** ☏351116 bed20 **B**

HILDISRIEDEN Luzern (☏041) Map**11**B1
- H **Roter Löwen** ☏991888 bed10 **B**

ILANZ Graubünden (☏086) Map**12**C1
- H **Casutt** ☏21131 bed25 **B**

INNERTKIRCHEN Bern (☏036) Map**11**B1
- H **Alpenrose** ☏711151 bed50 **B**
- H **Tännler** ☏711116 bed12 **B**

INTERLAKEN Bern (036) Map**11**B1
- ★★ **Marti** Brünigster ☏222602 rm25
  Etr-mid Oct **B**
- ★ **Goldener Anker** Marktgasse 57
  rm18 **B**

KIENTAL Bern (☏033) Map**11**B1
- H **Alpenruhe** ☏761135 bed12
  Apr-Oct **A**
- ◆ **Pension Erika** ☏761240 bed22 **B**

KIPPEL Valais (☏028) Map**11**B1
- H **Lötschberg** ☏491309 bed14 **B**

KLOSTERS Graubunden (☏083) Map**12**C1
- H **Surval** ☏41121 bed30
  Closed May & Nov **B**

KRATTIGEN BEI SPIEZ Bern (☏033)
Map**11**B1
- ★ **Seeblick** ☏542969 rm20 **B**

KÜSSNACHT AM RIGI Schwyz (☏041)
Map**11**B1
- H **Adler** ☏811025 bed20 **B**

LAUTERBRUNNEN Bern (☏036) Map**11**B1
- H **Edelweiss** ☏551368 bed20 **B**

LIDDES Valais (☏026) Map**28**C4
- ◆ **Auberge des Alpes** ☏41380 bed12 **A**

LIECHENSTEIN follows **SWITZERLAND**

LOCARNO Ticino (☏093) Map**28**D4
- ◆ **Millefiori** pza Castello 1b ☏313433
  bed26 Mar-Oct **B**
- H **Pestalozzi** via A Cisen 7 ☏314308
  bed30 Closed Nov **B**

At **Muralto**
- H **Gottardo** via Gottardo 18 ☏334454
  bed70 **B**
- H **Miralago** ☏336032 bed18 **B**

LUNGERN AM SEE Obwalden (☏041)
Map**11**B1
- ★ **Rossli** ☏691171 rm17 **A**

LUZERN (Lucerne) Luzern (☏041)
Map**11**B1
- H **Bären** Pfistergasse 8 ☏221063
  bed40 **B**
- H **Einhorn** Hertensteinstr ☏220595
  bed24 Apr-Sep **B**
- H **Gambrinus** Mühlenpl 12 ☏221791
  bed50 **B**
- H **Villa Maria** Haldenstr 36 ☏312119
  bed20 **B**
- H **Weisses Kreuz** Furrengasse 19
  ☏236023 bed25 **B**

At **Rothenburg**
- ◆ **Gasthaus Bären** ☏531188 bed5 **A**

MARÉCOTTES (LES) Valais (☏026)
Map**28**C4
- H **Joli-Mont** ☏81470 bed60
  Jun-Sep & Dec-Apr **A**

MARTIGNY Valais (☏026) Map**28**C4
- ◆ **Hostellerie de Genève** ☏23141
  bed22 **B**
- H **Trois Couronnes** ☏22515 bed27 **B**
- H **Vieux Stand** ☏21506 bed40 **B**

MEIRINGEN Bern (☏036) Map**11**B1
- H **Adler** ☏711032 bed30 **B**
- H **Rössli** Bahnhofstr ☏711621 bed20 **B**
- H **Sherpa** ☏713121 bed60 **B**

MONTREUX Vaud (☏021) Map**11**A1
- H **Gambetta** pl Gambetta, Clarens
  ☏612978 bed55 **B**

MURALTO see **LOCARNO**

NEUCHÂTEL Neuchâtel (☏038) Map**11**A1
- H **Fleur-de-Lys** r du Bassin 10
  ☏243030 bed22 **B**

NEU ST-JOHANN St-Hallen (☏074)
Map**12**C2
- H **Schäfli** ☏41010 bed20 **B**

OBERBALMBERG Solothurn (☏065)
Map**11**B2
- H **Kurhaus** ☏771905 bed50
  Closed Nov **B**

OBERHOFEN Bern (☏033) Map**11**B1
- ◆ **Pension Rebleuten** ☏431308
  bed13 **B**

ORSIÈRES Valais (☏026) Map**28**C4
- H **Alpes** ☏41101 bed30 **A**

OVRONNAZ Valais (☏027) Map**28**C4
- ◆ **Auberge au Vieux Valais** ☏862163
  bed11 **B**

PORRTENTRUY Bern (☏066) Map**11**A2
- H **Belvédère** rte de Bure 61 ☏662561
  bed10 **B**
- H **Gare** pl de la Gare 45 ☏661398
  bed20 **B**
- H **Suisse** r des Annonciades 7 ☏661184
  bed20 **B**

RARON Valais (☏028) Map**11**B1
- ☆ **Simplonblick** ☏441274 rm19 **B**

RHEINFELDEN Aargau (☏061) Map**11**B2
- H **Goldener Adler** ☏875332 bed30 **B**

RIETBAD St-Gallen (☏074) Map**12**C2
- H **Kurhaus** ☏41222 bed75 **B**

ROLLE Vaud (☏021) Map**11**A1
- ◆ **Auberge de Bugnaux** ☏751682
  bed4 Closed Jan **A**

RORSCHACH St-Gallen (☏071) Map**12**C2
- H **Löwen** ☏413898 bed12 **A**

ROTHENBURG see **LUZERN (Lucerne)**

Switzerland

ROTHWALD Valais (☎028) Map**11**B1
  H **Taferna** ☎235060 bed22
    Closed May & Nov **B**

SAAS-ALMAGELL Valais (☎028) Map**28**D4
  H **Mattmerkblick** ☎572275 bed60 **A**
  H **Monte-Moro** ☎571012 bed45 **A**
  H **Spycher** ☎572494 bed22 **A**

SAAS-GRUND Valais (☎028) Map**28**D4
  H **Primavera** ☎581788 bed60 **A**
  H **Rodania** ☎572423 bed50 **A**

ST-LUC Valais (☎027) Map**28**D4
  H **Favre** ☎651128 bed35 **A**

ST-MAURICE Valais (☎025) Map**28**C4
  H **Alpes** ☎36223 bed25 **A**
  H **Gare** ☎36360 bed28 **A**

SARGANS St-Gallen (☎085) Map**12**C1
  ★★ **Post** ☎21214 rm15 **A**

SARNEN Obwalden (☎041) Map**11**B1
  H **Mühle** ☎661336 bed40 **B**

SAXON Valais (☎026) Map**28**C4
  H **Gare** ☎62878 bed6 **A**

SIERRE (Siders) Valais (☎027) Map**28**C4
  ♦ **Auberge des Collines** ☎551248
    bed25 **A**
  ♦ **Auberge du Nord** ☎551242 bed10 **A**

SIMPLON-DORF Valais (☎028) Map**28**D4
  ★ **Poste** ☎291121 rm30 (A15) **B**

TRAVERS Neuchâtel (☎038) Map**11**A1
  ★ **Cret** ☎631178 rm6 Closed Feb **B**

UNTERBÄCH Valais (☎028) Map**28**D4
  H **Zenhäusern** ☎441157 bed18 **A**

VERNAYAZ Valais (☎026) Map**28**C4
  ★ **Victoria** ☎81416 rm12 **A**

VILLARS-SUR-OLLON Vaud (☎025)
Map**28**C4
  H **Col de Bretaye** ☎32194 bed 20
    Closed May & Oct **A**
  H **Lac de Bretaye** ☎32192 bed20
    Jun–Sep & Dec–Apr **B**

YVERDON Vaud (☎024) Map**11**A1
  H **Ange** Clendy 25 ☎212585 bed30 **B**
  H **Gare** ☎311508 bed21 **B**

ZERNEZ Graubünden (☎082) Map**12**C1
  H **Sport** ☎81135 bed43 **B**

ZIZERS Graubünden (☎081) Map**12**C1
  H **Johannesstift** ☎511404 bed50 **B**

Liechtenstein (Principality of)

SCHAAN (☎075) Map**12**C2
  ★★ **Linde** Lindenpl ☎21704 rm25 **B**

YUGOSLAVIA

Yugoslavia

This gazetteer predominantly contains hotels. The majority of them provide accommodation for £6 per person per night at sometime during the year, and, wherever possible, most of the popular mainland areas have been included. Prices have been banded as follows: **A** under £5 per person per night, and **B** between £5 and £6 per person per night.

Private homes An attractive alternative to the accommodation listed below is available in most Yugoslav resorts. Under a special scheme, over 200,000 beds have been made available for visitors who can stay with Yugoslav families in their own homes. In some households meals are also provided and this offers the tourist the chance not only to save money, but also to meet the local people and have a direct contact with the Yugoslav way of life, their food and their culture.

To book this kind of accommodation, or just to find out more, you should apply to the Tourist Association or tourist office of the town you are in. In larger resorts travel agencies can offer a booking service as well, and you will find the rooms graded according to comfort into a number of categories. Prices are very reasonable and out of season considerable discounts are offered.

The province names are as follows:
Crna Gora – *Montenegro*
Hrvatska – *Croatia*
Jadranska Obla – *Dalmatia*
Slovenija – *Slovenia*
Srbija – *Serbia*.

ALEKSINAC Srbija (☎018) Map**38**C2
 M **Morava** ☎72222 beds220 **A**
 M **Ražanj** ☎89234 beds101 **A**

BAŠKA see **KRK (ISLAND OF)**

BAŠKA VODA Jadranska Obla Map**36**C1
 H **Horizont** ☎87428 beds403 **A**

BEOGRAD (Belgrade) Srbija (☎011) Map**37**B3
 H **Astorija** ☎645422 beds140 **A**
 H **Balkan** ☎325032 beds140 **A**

BIOGRAD NA MORU Jadranska Obla (☎057) Map**35**B2
 H **Crvena Luka** ☎83106 beds467 May–Oct **A**

BJELOVAR Hrvatska (☎043) Map**36**C3
 H **Zvijezda** ☎21136 beds31 **A**

BOHINJ Slovenija Map**13**B1
 H **Bellevue** ☎76331 beds49 **A**
 H **Kompas-Stane Zagar** ☎76471 beds170 **A**

BRELA Jadranska Obla Map**36**C1
 H **Brela** ☎87440 beds62 Apr–Oct **A**
 H **Soline** ☎87440 beds44 Apr–Oct **A**

ČAJNIČE Bosnia and Herzegovina Map**37**B2
 ♦ **Orijent-Pension Twist** ☎85169 beds68 **A**

CAVTAT Jardranska Obla Map**39**B3
 H **Adriatic** ☎88006 beds87 Apr–Dec **A**
 H **Epidaurus** ☎88144 beds382 Apr–Dec **A**

 H **Supetar-Garni** ☎88279 beds76 15Apr–Oct **A**

CELJE Slovenija (☎063) Map**35**B4
 H **Europa** ☎22018 beds60 **A**
 H **Merx** ☎21917 beds66 **B**
 H **Ojstrica** ☎22966 beds18 **A**

CRIKVENICA Jadranska Obla (☎051) Map**35**B3
 H **Ad Turres- Pavilions "B"** ☎831428 beds539 **A**
 H **Esplanade** ☎831124 beds155 Apr–Oct **A**
 H **International** ☎831324 beds86 **A**
 H **Mediteran** ☎831082 beds150 **A**
 H **Miramare** ☎831232 beds180 Apr–Oct **A**
 H **Zagreb** ☎831386 beds132 Apr–Oct **A**

ČRAN NA KORŠKEM Slovenija Map**35**B4
 H **Planinka** ☎89814 beds55 **A**

ČRNOMELJ Hrvatska Map**35**B3
 H **Lahinja** ☎76141 beds42 **A**

CUPRIJA Srbija (☎035) Map**38**C2
 M **Ravanica** ☎62242 beds33 **A**
 H **Ravno** ☎61314 beds42 **A**

DELNICE Hrvatska Map**35**B3
 H **Petehovac Planinarski Dom** ☎811078 beds42 **A**
 ♦ **Pension Lavǎcki Dom** ☎811077 beds30 **A**
 ♦ **Pension Risnjak** ☎811184 beds28 **A**

Yugoslavia

DOBRNA Slovenija Map**35**B4
    H **Zdravilišjki Dom** ☎778000
    beds145 **A**

DRAVOGRAD Slovenija Map**14**C1
    H **Košenjak** ☎83076 beds26 **A**

DRVENIK Hrvatska Map**39**A4
    ◆ **Pension Ribar** ☎77290 beds22
    Apr–Oct **A**

DUBROVNIK Jadranska Obla (☎050)
Map**39**B3/4
    H **Bellevue** ☎26076 beds104
    Apr–Oct **A**
    H **Gruž** ☎24777 beds78 **A**
    H **Stadion** ☎23449 beds170 Apr–Oct **A**
    H **Villa Dubrovnik** ☎22933 beds106
    Apr–Oct **A**

DUGA RESA Hratska (☎047) Map**35**B3
    H **Roganac** ☎78357 beds16 **A**

FLIP-JAKOV Jadranska Obla Map**35**B2
    H **Mayica** ☎85605 beds150 May–Oct **A**

FOČA Bosnia and Herzegovina Map**37**B2
    H **Zelengora** ☎72036 beds165 **A**

GORNJA RADGONA Slovenija Map**14**D1
    H **Grozd** ☎74030 beds54 **A**

IDRIJA Slovenija (☎065) Map**35**A3
    H **Nanos** ☎71084 beds40 **A**

ILIRSKA BISTRICA Slovenija Map**35**A3
    H **Lovec** ☎81047 beds42 **A**

JABLANAC Hrvatska Map**35**B2
    H **Jablanac** ☎883053 beds52
    Jun–Sep **A**
    H **Zavratnica** beds16 Jun–Sep **A**

JAJCE Bosnia and Herzegovina (☎070)
Map**36**C2
    ◆ **Pension Sport** ☎21067 beds108 **A**
    H **Turist** ☎21068 beds95 **A**

JURJEVO Hrvatska Map**35**B2
    H **Istra** ☎883027 beds38 **A**

KAMNIK Slovenija Map**35**B4
    H **Planinka** ☎831451 beds41 **A**

KARLOVAC Hrvatska Map**35**B3
    H **Central** ☎23694 beds68 **A**
    H **Korana** ☎26911 beds155 **A**
    H **Mrežnica** ☎31372 beds35 **A**
    H **Park** ☎26717 beds33 **A**

KORČULA (ISLAND OF) Jardranska Obla
Map**39**A4
    H **Korčula** ☎81078 beds40 **A**
    H **Park** ☎81004 beds400 **A**

KRAGUJEVAC Srbija Map**38**C2
    H **Dubrovnik** ☎60137 beds64 **A**

KRALJEVICA Hrvatska Map**35**B3
    H **Almis** ☎801312 beds27 **A**
    H **Riviera** ☎801403 beds102 **A**

KRANJ Slovenija Map**35**A4
    H **Jelen** ☎21466 beds82 **A**

KRANJSKA GORA Slovenija Map**13**B1
    H **Alpe Adria** ☎88584 beds56 **A**
    H **Erika** ☎88475 **A**
    H **Razor** ☎88428 beds33 **A**
    H **Slavec** ☎88421 beds92 **A**

At **Podkoren** (2.5km W)
    H **Vitranc** ☎88518 beds30 **A**

KRIŽEVCI Hrvatska (☎043) Map**36**C4
    H **Plan Dom Kalnik** ☎749003 beds28 **A**

KRK (ISLAND OF) Hrvatska (☎051)
Map**35**B2
    H **Dražica** ☎851022 beds320 **A**

At **Baska** (17km SE)
    H **Velebit** ☎856824 beds56 May–Oct **A**

KRŠKO Hrvatska (☎068) Map**35**B3
    H **Scremlč** ☎71005 beds160 **A**

LEŠČE Hrvatska Map**35**B3
    H **Toplice** ☎79304 beds52 **A**

LJUBLJANA Slovenija Map**35**B3
    H **Bellevue** ☎313133 beds41 **A**

MAGLAJ Bosnia and Herzegovina Map**36**D2
    H **Galeb** ☎81231 beds65 **A**

MAKARSKA Jadranska Obla (☎058)
Map**36**C1
    H **Beograd** ☎77238 beds80 Apr–Oct **A**
    M **Kuk** ☎77378 beds34 Apr–Oct **A**
    H **Makarska** ☎77244 beds64
    Apr–Oct **A**
    H **Osejava** ☎77236 beds76 Apr–Oct **A**
    H **Park** ☎77613 beds123 Apr–Oct **A**

MARIBOR Slovenija (☎062) Map**14**C/D1
    H **Orel** ☎26171 beds228 **A**
    H **Zamorec** ☎22513 beds54 **A**

METLIKA Hrvatska Map**35**B3
    H **Bela Krajina** ☎77123 beds52 **A**

MODRIČA Bosnia and Herzegovina
Map**37**A3
    M **Majna** ☎88194 beds49 **A**

MOŠČENIČKA DRAGA Slovenija Map**35**A3
    H **Biser** ☎737538 beds34
    May–24Sep **A**
    H **Rubin** ☎737538 beds54
    May–24Sep **A**

MURSKA SOBOTA Slovenija (☎069)
Map**14**D1
    ◆ **Čarda** beds10 **A**
    H **Zvezda** ☎22510 beds59 **A**

NOVIGRAD Jadranska Obla Map**35**B2
    H **Laguna** ☎74050 beds448 Apr–Oct **A**
    H **Emonia** ☎74140 beds80 Apr–Oct **A**

NOVO MESTO Slovenija Map**35**B3
    H **Kandija** ☎22410 beds53 **A**
    H **Metropol** ☎21447 beds146 **A**

NOVSKA Hrvatska Map**36**C3
    H **Slovonija** ☎71090 beds50 **A**

OPATIJA Hrvatska (☎051) Map**35**A3
    H **Adriatic** ☎711311 beds608
    4Jan–Oct **A**
    H **Jeanette** ☎711849 beds106
    May–Oct **A**

Yugoslavia

H **Paris Garni** ☎711911 beds180
May–Oct **A**
H **Residenz** ☎711204 beds80
May–Oct **A**

ORASJE Bosnia and Herzegovina Map**37**A3
M **Ataše** ☎72176 beds17 **A**

PAG (ISLAND OF) Hrvatska (☎051)
Map**35**B2
H **Bellevue** ☎891122 beds302
Apr–Oct **A**

PAZIN Jadranska Obla (☎053) Map**35**A3
M **Lovac** ☎22024 beds54 **A**

PEČ Srbija (☎039) Map**40**D4
M **Dardania** ☎21612 beds32 **A**
H **Korzo** ☎22423 beds70 **A**
H **Metohija** ☎22424 beds152 **A**

PETROVAC NA MORU Crna Gora Map**40**C3
H **Castellastua** ☎85199 beds354
Apr–Oct **A**
H **Palas** ☎85128 beds34 Apr–Oct **A**
H **Petrovac** ☎85110 beds86
Apr–Sep **A**

PIRAN Jadranska Obla Map**30**D4
H **Piran** ☎73651 beds116 Apr–15Oct **A**
H **Punta** ☎73951 beds136
Apr–15Oct **A**

PODGORA Jadranska Map**39**A4
H **Aurora** ☎77812 beds280 Apr–Oct **A**
H **Mediteran** ☎77812 beds248
Apr–Oct **A**
H **Podgorka** ☎77221 beds31
Apr–Oct **A**
H **Primordia** ☎77342 beds72
Apr–Oct **A**
H **Salines** ☎77897 beds300 **A**

PODKOREN see **KRANJSKA GORA**

POLJANA PRI PREVALJAH Slovenija
Map**14**C1
H **Poljana** ☎85175 beds17 **A**

POREČ Jadranska Obla (☎053) Map**30**D4
H **Diamant** ☎86682 beds509 **A**
H **Riviera** ☎86024 beds162 **A**

POSTOJNA Slovenija (☎067) Map**35**A3
H **Jama** ☎21172 beds134 **A**
M **Proteus** ☎21250 beds418 **A**
H **Šport** ☎21150 beds126 **A**

PREDEJANE Srbija Map**38**D1
M **Camping Predejane** ☎71620
beds150 **A**

PRNJAVOR Bosnia and Herzegovina
Map**36**D3
H **Nacional** ☎86325 beds60 **A**

PULA Hrvatska (☎052) Map**35**A2
H **Brioni** ☎23888 beds432 **A**
H **Park** ☎22342 beds254 **A**
H **Ribarska Koliba** ☎22658 beds218
Apr–Oct **A**
H **Splendid** ☎23390 beds324 **A**
H **Stoja** ☎23395 beds56 Apr–Oct **A**
H **Zlatne Stijene** ☎22811 beds748 **A**

RAB (ISLAND OF) Hrvatska (☎051)
Map**35**B2

H **Beograd** ☎871224 beds94
Apr–Oct **A**
H **Istra** ☎871133 beds192 **A**
H **Slavija** ☎871115 beds42 Apr–Oct **A**

RABAC Hrvatska (☎053) Map**35**A2
H **Apolo** ☎83222 beds110 May–Oct **A**
H **Fortuna** ☎83091 beds133
May–Oct **A**
H **Istra** ☎83243 beds75 May–Oct **A**
H **Marina** ☎83211 beds132 May–Oct **A**
H **Mimosa** ☎83024 beds292 **A**
H **St Andrea** ☎83252 beds586
May–Oct **A**

RADLJE OB DRAVI Slovenija Map**124**C1
H **Kozjak** ☎87016 beds30 **A**

RADOVLJICA Slovenija Map**35**A4
H **Grajski Dvor** ☎75585 beds142 **A**

RAKOVICA Bosnia and Herzegovina
Map**35**B2
H **Rakovica** ☎77832 beds25 **A**

RIJEKA Hrvatska (☎951) Map**35**B3
H **Kontinental** ☎42495 beds88 **A**
H **Neboder** ☎42075 beds93 **A**
H **Park** ☎41155 beds71 **A**

ROVINJ Jadranska Obla (☎052) Map**30**D3
H **Eden** ☎81402 beds622 May–Oct **B**
H **Lone** ☎81070 beds325 May–Oct **A**
H **Park** ☎81122 beds314 May–Oct **A**
H **Rovinj** ☎81408 beds150 **A**

SARAJEVO Bosnia and Herzegovina
(☎071) Map**37**A2
H **Central** ☎33566 beds65 **A**
H **National** ☎33000 beds132 **A**
H **Zagreb** ☎36680 beds72 **A**

SEMIC Hrvatska Map**35**B3
H **Smuk** ☎78342 beds16 **A**

SENJ Hrvatska (☎051) Map**35**B2
H **Nehaj** ☎881285 beds93 **A**
H **Velebit** ☎881310 beds33 **A**

SEŽANA Slovenija (☎067) Map**35**A3
H **Tabor** ☎73381 beds86 **A**
H **Triglav** ☎73361 beds120 **A**

SLANO Jadranska Obla Map**39**B4
H **Admiral** ☎87202 beds400 **A**
H **Rely** ☎87267 beds18 **A**

SLAVONSKI BROD Hrvatska Map**36**D3
H **Brod** ☎231885 beds72 **A**
H **Park** ☎231901 beds91 **A**
M **Vinogorje** ☎231118 beds77 **A**

SLOVENJ GRADEC Slovenija Map**35**B4
H **Korotan** ☎84039 beds52 **A**

SLUNJ Hrvatska (☎047) Map**35**B3
H **Park** ☎77140 beds30 **A**
H **Slunjčica** ☎77103 beds80 **A**

SPLIT Jadranska Obla (☎058) Map**36**C1
H **Central** ☎48242 beds76 **A**
H **Lav** ☎48288 beds666 **A**

STARI DOJRAN Crna Gora Map**41**B3
H **Dojran** ☎77324 beds52 **A**

STARIGRAD Jadranska Obla (☎058)
Map**35**B2
H **Alan** ☎79036 beds410 May–Oct **A**

STON Jadranska Obla Map**39**B4
  H **Adriatic** ☎84020 beds57 Jan–Oct **A**

SVETOZAREVO Srbija (☎035) Map**38**C2
  H **Palas** ☎21716 beds65 **A**

TIJESNO Jadranska Obla Map**35**B1
  H **Borovnik** ☎78065 beds162
    Jun–Sep **A**

TRAVNIK Bosnia and Herzegovina
Map**36**D2
  H **Orijent** ☎81240 beds122**A**

TROGIR Jadranska Obla (☎058) Map**36**C1
  H **Jardran** ☎73407 beds310
    May–Oct **A**
  M **Trogir** ☎73424 beds124 **A**

ULCINJ Crna Gora (☎085) Map**40**C3
  H **Bellevue-Borik** ☎84244 beds700
    Apr–Oct **A**
  H **Galeb** ☎84222 beds280 **A**
  H **Mediteran** ☎84108 beds480
    Apr–Oct **A**

  H **Olympic** ☎84026 beds240
    Apr–Oct **A**
  M **Sas** beds33 Apr–Oct **A**

UMAG Jadranska Obla Map**30**D4
  H **Kristal** ☎72307 beds186 **A**

VALJEVO Srbija (☎014) Map**37**B2
  H **Beli Narcis** ☎21140 beds126 **A**

VISEGRAD Bosnia and Herzegovina
Map**37**B2
  H **Visegrad** ☎81224 beds50 **A**

VODICE Jadranska Obla Map**36**C1
  H **Olympia** ☎83166 beds534 **A**

VRHNIKA Slovenija Map**35**A3
  H **Mantova** ☎70370 beds54 **A**

ZADAR Jadranska Obla (☎057) Map**35**B2
  H **Kolovare** ☎33022 beds450 **A**
  H **Zagreb** ☎24266 beds140 **A**

DOCUMENTS REQUIRED

As well as a current passport a tourist temporarily importing a motor vehicle should carry either an International Driving Permit or a valid national driving licence, the registration document of the car or an International Certificate for Motor Vehicles, and evidence of insurance. The proper international distinguishing sign should be affixed to the rear of the vehicle. The appropriate papers must be carried at all times and secured against loss.

British Driving Licence

Provided you are over 18 years of age you may drive in all the countries covered by this guide on a valid British driving licence (not a provisional) for a limited period and provided you are a bona fide tourist without any residential qualifications in the country you are visiting. In Austria you will need an IDP if you hold an Irish driving licence. In Spain an IDP is necessary if you hold only a British driving licence. A translation of the British driving licence is required for Italy (available from the AA).

International Driving Permit

The IDP is an internationally recognised document which enables the holder to drive a motor vehicle without local formality for a limited period in a country in which he is a visitor. Its full validity is one year from the date of its issue and it is not renewable. Its issue is necessary for some countries who do not accept the visitor's national driving licence. The Permit, for which a charge is made, is issued by the AA to an applicant who holds a valid British (or Irish) driving licence and who is over 18 years old. It cannot be issued to the holder of a provisional licence nor can it be issued to the holder of a foreign licence who must make his application in the country where his driving licence was issued.

Registration document

This must show that the vehicle is registered in the name of the importer. Clearly this would not be the case if the car is hired or borrowed in which case it is better to carry an International Certificate for Motor Vehicles, together with a letter signed by the registered owner authorising the importer to have the use of the vehicle.

International Certificate for Motor Vehicles

This is a general licence which, when used in conjunction with the recognised international distinguishing sign, makes it unnecessary to register the vehicle in the country to be visited. It is valid for one year from the date of its issue and it is not renewable. The Certificate, for which a charge is made, is issued by the AA for some countries who do not accept foreign registration papers or to avoid complication if the vehicle is not registered in the importer's name.

Insurance

With the exception of Portugal, (where it is likely to be during 1979) motor insurance is compulsory by law in all the countries covered in this guide, but you are strongly advised to ensure that you are adequately covered for all countries in which you will travel. It is best to seek the advice of your insurance company regarding the extent of cover and full terms of your existing policy. Not all insurers will be willing to offer cover in the countries that you intend to visit and it may be necessary to seek a new, special policy for the trip from another company. Should you have any difficulty AA Insurance Services will be pleased to help you.

International Green Card of Insurance

This is recognised in most countries as evidence that you are covered to the minimum extent demanded by law and the AA recommends its use. It will be issued by your own insurers but since its provisions are an extension to an existing policy, an additional premium will be charged. It will name all the countries for which it is valid and should be specially endorsed for a caravan or trailer if one is to be towed. The document will not be accepted until you have signed it.

If your cover is inadequate temporary policies may be effected at all frontiers (with the exception of Austria) but this is a most expensive way of covering yourself.

Green Cards and the EEC

In accordance with an EEC Directive, the production and inspection of Green Cards at the frontiers of EEC countries is no longer a legal requirement and the principle has been accepted by other European countries who are not members of the EEC. The EEC countries concerned are Belgium, Denmark, France, West Germany, Great Britain, Republic of Ireland, Luxembourg, and the Netherlands. The non-EEC countries also subscribing to the Directive are Austria, Czechoslovakia, the German Democratic Republic, Finland, Hungary, Norway, Sweden and Switzerland. Italy, although a member of the EEC, prefers tourists to be able to produce a Green Card if required. You are advised to consult your insurer regarding this matter.

The fact that Green Cards will not be inspected does not remove the necessity of having insurance cover as required by law in the countries concerned. All private car policies issued by British Insurance companies should now provide cover for the minimum legal requirements in the countries mentioned. This does not mean that the full extent of your cover at home is automatically extended, however, and in some circumstances you may find yourself without adequate cover. You are therefore strongly advised to contact your insurers in good time prior to any trip abroad to ensure that the cover you have is satisfactory,

The fact that Green Cards are not legally required in EEC countries or those listed above, and that they may not be inspected at the frontiers of those countries, does not mean that they have been abolished altogether. They will still be required for other countries in Europe (eg Spain) and for such countries as Turkey, Israel, Morocco and Tunisia. In addition, they may prove more effectively than an Insurance Certificate that the minimum insurance requirements operative in the country visited have been met. They are internationally recognised by police and other authorities and may save a great deal of inconvenience in the case of an accident.

Spain – Extra insurance is recommended in the form of a Bail Bond.

International Distinguishing Sign

An International Distinguishing Sign (nationality plate) of the approved pattern (oval with black letters on a white background) and size (GB at least 6.9in by 4.5in) must be displayed on a vertical or near vertical surface at the rear of your vehicle (and caravan or trailer if you are towing one). In Europe checks are made to ensure that a vehicle's nationality plate is in order. In some countries fines are imposed for failing to display a nationality plate, or for not displaying the correct nationality plate. Up to two (British or Irish) are issued free to anyone who takes out AA 5-Star Service.

Carnet de Passages en Douane

This is a valuable document which enables a motorist to import temporarily certain vehicles into another country without having to deposit duty. The cost of this document, which can be issued by the AA, depends on the number of countries to be visited which require a *Carnet de Passages en Douane*. Generally the document is not required for motor vehicles temporarily imported into European countries for periods not exceeding six months by bona fide tourists. Any other category of person should refer to the AA to ascertain if a Carnet can be issued.

Belgium a Carnet is required for towed pleasure craft over 18ft (5.5 metres) long, motor boats, and outboard motors without boats.

France a Carnet is required for outboard engines exceeding 92cc (5cv as applied to marine engines) with or without boats.

Luxembourg a Carnet is required for all towed pleasure craft.

If you are issued with a *Carnet de Passages en Douane,* you must ensure that it is properly discharged as you cross each frontier in order to avoid inconvenience and expense, possibly including payment of Customs charges, at a later date.

AA 5-Star Service

If you're motoring on the Continent of Europe, many miles from home, it makes sense to know that should the worst happen, be it breakdown, accident or illness of one of your party, you have the strength of AA 5-Star Service behind you.

Over the years hundreds of thousands of motorists have been grateful for the peace of mind this unique blend of service, personal travel insurance and emergency credit brings.

AA 5-Star Service is now available to all motorists although AA members enjoy certain additional benefits. Details are available from the Automobile Association, Overseas Motoring Services, FREEPOST, Halesowen, W Midlands B63 3BT.

MEDICAL TREATMENT

For your health abroad

The National Health Service is available in the UK only and medical expenses incurred overseas cannot be reimbursed by the UK Government. However, there are reciprocal health agreements with some countries. You are strongly advised to take out comprehensive and adequate insurance cover before leaving the UK, such as that offered by Personal Security under *AA 5-Star Service.*

Within EEC countries, some UK residents will be entitled to medical treatment for sickness or accidents abroad on the same basis as nationals of the country they are visiting. This is a result of EEC Social Security Regulations, but all the member countries have differing legislations and benefits will vary.

Not everyone is covered, so for further information concerning the EEC regulations you should obtain the leaflet SA28 from the Department of Health & Social Security. This explains who is covered and what steps should be taken to obtain cover. You will have to obtain the certificate of entitlement to treatment – Form E111 – before you leave the country. This should be done 3 to 4 weeks before departure.

Yugoslavia

In Yugoslavia, nationals of the United Kingdom may, in an emergency, obtain medical treatment under the Yugoslav Social Insurance Medical Scheme on the same terms as the nationals of that country by producing a British passport which was issued in the United Kingdom. A small charge is made for each medicine prescribed. The services available include general medical, dental and hospital.

Doctor's letter

It is wise for those with specific conditions or taking specific prescriptions to carry a letter from their doctor, preferably translated into the languages of the countries to be visited, detailing the complaint and treatment. This will prove invaluable in the event of an emergency and Customs officials would more readily understand the need to carry drugs or appliances, if these were specified. Wise also, in both this country and abroad, is to carry a note of the blood groups of the members in your party.

Medicalert

A useful service to those who have medical problems where misleading symptoms can lead to dangerous misdiagnosis in the event of an accident is given by Medicalert.

Members wear a metal emblem with the name Medicalert and the phone number of the Emergency Service engraved on the side. On the reverse the immediate medical problems of the wearer are noted, for example 'Allergic to Penicillin', 'Taking Anti-coagulants', 'Wearing Contact Lenses', 'Under Steroid Treatment', 'Diabetes', etc. For those with epilepsy, haemophaelia, diabetes, allergies and many other conditions it offers a vital insurance against damaging treatment in the event of any accident which renders the patient unconscious for any length of time. The price is £4.86 which includes life membership. Their address is: The Medic-Alert Foundation, 9 Hanover Street, London W1, *tel* 01-499 2261.

Vaccinations

There are no endemic diseases prevalent in Europe and certificates of vaccination are not normally required from Europeans. However, with local outbreaks, such as with smallpox here in Britain last year, requirements can change, often overnight. To be absolutely certain you have met all the entry requirements for the countries you plan to visit, you should check well in advance with the National Tourist Office concerned (for addresses see p222).

Buying medicines abroad

Chemists' sundries, including drugs and medicines, are usually very expensive abroad. Aspirins, for example, can cost as much as six times as much as here. Wherever possible, the best advice is to take all that you feel you will need, as it is inadvisable to treat a particular complaint with a local medicine of similar name – the dosage or mixtures can vary.

NATIONAL TOURIST OFFICES

Andorra

Sindicat d'Iniciativa de les Valls d'Andorra, 63 Westover Road, London SW18 2RF. 01–874 4806

Benelux

Belgian National Tourist Office, 66 Haymarket, London SW1Y 4RB. 01–930 9618

Luxembourg National Trade and Tourist Office, 66 Haymarket, London SW1Y 4RF. 01–930 8906

Netherlands National Tourist Office, 2nd Floor, Savory and Moore House, 143 New Bond Street, London W1Y0QS. 01–499 9367

Denmark

Danish Tourist Board, Sceptre House, 169–173 Regent Street, London W1R 8PY. 01–734 2637 (entrance in New Burlington Street)

France

French Government Tourist Office, 178 Piccadily, London W1V 0AL. 01–491 7622

Germany

German National Tourist Office, 61 Conduit Street, London W1R 0EN. 01–734 2600

Italy & San Marino

Italian State Tourist Department (ENIT), 201 Regent Street, London W1R 8AY. 01–439 2311

Portugal

Portuguese National Tourist Office, New Bond Street House, 1–5 New Bond Street, London W1Y 9PE. 01–493 3873

Spain

Spanish National Tourist Office, Metro House, 57 St James' Street, London SW1. 01–499 0901

Switzerland & Liechtenstein

Swiss National Tourist Office, Swiss Centre, 1 New Coventry Street, London W1V 3HG. 01–734 1921

Yugoslavia

Yugoslav National Tourist Office, 143 Regent Street, London W1R 8AE 01–734 5243/01–439 0399

Preparing your vehicle for a holiday abroad

We know as well as anyone how expensive mechanical repairs and replacement parts can be abroad. A vast number of the breakdowns we have dealt with have occurred simply because people did not take enough trouble to prepare their cars before setting off. Remember that a holiday abroad is not just another day trip, but often involves many miles of hard driving over roads completely new to you, perhaps without the facilities you have come to take for granted in this country. Many people think that it can never happen to them – it can and will if the car is not properly prepared or if it is overloaded.

We recommend that a major service be carried out shortly before your holiday or tour abroad. In addition it is advisable to have a general check of the car to see that there are no other visible or audible defects. It is impracticable for us to provide you with an itemised check list in view of the differences that exist between the various makes and types of car but using the manufacturer's handbook for your particular car, it should be possible to ensure that no obvious faults are missed. If AA members would like a thorough check of their car made by one of the AA's experienced engineers, any Service Centre can arrange this at a few days' notice. Our engineer will then submit a written report complete with a list of the repairs required. There is a fee for this service; for more detailed information please ask for our leaflet *Tech 8*. The following tips should prove useful:

Tyres

Inspect your tyres carefully; if you think they are likely to be more than three-quarters worn before you get back, it is better to replace them before you start out. If you notice uneven wear, scuffed treads, or damaged walls, expert advice should be sought on whether the tyres are suitable for further use. In some European countries, drivers can be fined if tyres are badly worn.

When checking tyre pressures, remember that if the car is heavily loaded the recommended pressures may have to be raised a few pounds per square inch above normal. This should also be done for high-speed driving. Check the recommendations in your handbook. Don't check the pressure immediately after a run, as the tyres will still be hot and pressure will have increased quite a lot, even after a short trip. Don't forget about your spare. Many unfortunates know how embarassing it is to have a blowout miles from anywhere, only to find that the spare, which they last pumped up a year ago, is flat!

Tubeless tyres

In some countries, tubeless tyres are not in general use. It is a good idea to take an inner tube of the correct size and type so that this can be fitted if all else fails. When the tube is inserted it is advisable to put this wheel on the rear axle, in case a blowout should occur. Moderate speeds only should be used until the tyre has been properly repaired.

Warm-climate touring

In hot weather and at high altitudes, excessive heat in the engine compartment can cause carburation problems. It is advisable, if you are towing a caravan, to consult the manufacturers about the limitations of the cooling system, and the operating temperature of the gearbox fluid if automatic transmission is fitted.

Cold-weather touring

If you are planning a winter tour in Europe make sure that you fit a high-temperature (winter) thermostat and make sure that the strength of your anti-freeze mixture is correct for the low temperatures likely to be encountered.

If you are likely to be passing through snow-bound regions, it is important to remember that for many resorts and passes the authorities insist on wheel chains, spiked or studded tyres, or snow tyres. In some countries, such as Austria and Germany, however, the use of spiked or studded tyres is banned.

Note: The above comments do not apply where severe winter conditions prevail. It is doubtful whether the cost of preparing a car, normally used in the UK, would be justified for a short period. However, the AA's Technical Services Department will be pleased to advise on specific enquiries.

Brakes

The brakes are one of the really vital parts of the car and yet they are very often neglected. Like other mechanical parts, brakes become worn with use and unless they are regularly checked and maintained, worn linings and pads, or hydraulic fluid from faulty cylinders or perished hoses could prove lethal.

If you are about to start a long overseas trip and the brake linings of your vehicle are more than half worn, it is in your interests – and other people's – to change them before you leave. It is also advisable to have your brake fluid changed if it is more than two years old. Fluid that has absorbed moisture can lead to brake failure in arduous conditions, such as descending long mountain passes.

Engine and mechanical

Consult your vehicle handbook for servicing intervals. Unless the engine oil has been changed recently, drain and refill with fresh oil and fit a new filter. Deal with any significant leaks by tightening up loose nuts and bolts and renewing faulty joints or seals.

If you suspect that there is anything wrong with the engine, however insignificant it may seem, it should be dealt with straight away. Even if everything seems in order, don't neglect such commonsense precautions as checking valve clearances, sparking plugs, and contact breaker points, and make sure that the distributor cap is sound. The fan belt should be checked for fraying and slackness. If any of the items mentioned previously are showing signs of wear you should replace them.

Any obvious mechanical defects should be attended to at once. Look particularly for play in steering connections and wheel bearings and where applicable, ensure that they are adequately greased. A car that has covered a high mileage will have absorbed a certain amount of dirt into the fuel system and as breakdowns are often caused by dirt, it is essential that all filters (petrol and air) should be cleaned.

The cooling system should be checked for leaks and any perished hoses or suspect parts replaced.

Electrical

Don't begin a journey without first making a check of the electrics. This applies particularly if the car is not so new and perhaps a light or a switch is not working. Any malfunction can very easily go unnoticed until the battery is run flat or even a fire occurs, so it is very important to trace any small fault.

Check that all the connections are sound and that the wiring is in good condition. Should any problems arise with the charging system, it is essential to obtain the services of a qualified auto-electrician.

Lighting adjustments (see also p228)

Left dipping headlights are not permitted. However, there are several adaptors which can be used, but owing to the variety both of bulbs and headlamps, manufacturers should be consulted for the best method of adapting either of these for use abroad. In France, yellow headlights are used.

Remember to have the lamps set to compensate for the load being carried.

Spares

The problem of what spares to carry is a difficult one; it depends on how long you are likely to be away. It is possible to hire an AA Spares Kit; full information about this service is available from any AA Service Centre.

In addition to the items contained in the spares kit, the following would also prove useful:

a pair of windscreen wiper blades;   a torch;
a length of electrical cable;   a fire extinguisher;
an inner tube of the correct type;   a tow rope;
a roll of insulating or adhesive tape.

It is compulsory in some countries to carry a set of spare bulbs. Remember that when ordering spare parts for dispatch abroad you must be able to identify them as clearly as possible and by the manufacturer's part numbers if known. When ordering spares, always quote the engine and chassis numbers of your car.

General

Make sure that you have clear all-round vision. See that your seat belts are securely mounted and not damaged, and remember that in most European countries their use is compulsory (see p231)

If you are carrying skis, remember that they should point to the rear. You must be sure that your vehicle complies with the regulations concerning dimensions for all the countries you intend to pass through (see page 228). This is particularly necessary if you are towing a trailer of any sort. If you are planning to tow a caravan, you will find advice and information in the AA's guide, *Camping and Caravanning in Europe.*

MOTORING REGULATIONS

Motoring laws in Europe are just as wide and complicated as those in the UK but they should cause little difficulty to the average British motorist who is usually well trained. He should, however, take more care and extend greater courtesy than he would normally do at home, and bear in mind the essentials of good motoring – avoiding any behaviour likely to obstruct traffic, to endanger persons or cause damage to property. It is also important to remember that when travelling in a country the tourist is subject to the laws of that country.

Road signs are mainly international and should be familiar to the British motorist but in every country there are a few exceptions. He should particularly watch for signs indicating crossings and speed limits. Probably the most unusual aspect of motoring abroad to the British motorist is the universal and firm rule of giving priority to traffic coming from the right and unless this rule is varied by signs, it must be strictly observed.

Accidents

International regulations are similar to those in the UK; the following recommendations are usually advisable.

If you are involved in an accident you must stop. A warning triangle should be placed on the road at a suitable distance to warn following traffic of the obstruction. The use of hazard warning lights in no way affects the regulations governing the use of warning triangles. Medical assistance should be obtained for persons injured in the accident. If the accident necessitates calling the police, leave the vehicle in the position in which it comes to rest; should it seriously obstruct other traffic, mark the position of the vehicle on the road and get the details confirmed by independent witnesses before moving it.

The accident must be reported to the police if it is required by law, if the accident has caused death or bodily injury, or if an unoccupied vehicle or property has been damaged and there is no one present to represent the interests of the party suffering damage. Notify your insurance company by letter if possible, within 24 hours of the accident; see the conditions of your policy. If a third party is injured, the insurance company or bureau, whose address is given on the back of your Green Card or frontier insurance certificate, should be notified; the company or bureau will, if necessary, pay compensation to the injured party.

Make sure that all essential particulars are noted, especially details concerning third parties, and co-operate with Police or other officials taking on-the-spot notes by supplying your name address or other personal details as required. It is also a good idea to take photographs of the scene endeavouring to get good shots of other vehicles involved, their registration plates and any background which might help later enquiries. This record may be useful when completing the insurance company's accident form.

If you are not involved in the accident but feel your assistance as a witness or in any other useful capacity would be helpful then stop and park your car carefully well away from the scene. If all the help necessary is at the scene then do not stop out of curiosity nor park your car at the site.

First Aid

Expert assistance should be summoned immediately. Unless you have a knowledge of first aid you should be extremely cautious about attending anyone injured in an accident. The following notes may be useful.

Bleeding and wounds To stop bleeding apply pressure to the sides of the wound. Cleanse around and away from the wound, taking care not to disturb any blood clot. Apply and maintain pressure to the bleeding part with dressing, cover with pad, and bandage firmly.

Broken bones Fractures should be moved as little as possible. Support the injured part at once.

Exhaled air resuscitation Lay patient on his back. Tilt the head and chin away from the chest to clear airway, making sure that it is not obstructed by the tongue or foreign matter. Open your mouth and take a deep breath. Pinch the casualty's nostrils together, then seal your lips around the mouth. Blow into his lungs until the chest rises, then remove your mouth and watch the chest deflate. Repeat giving the first four inflations as rapidly as possible. Lung inflation can also be carried out through the nose. The casualty's mouth should be sealed with the thumb holding the lower jaw.

Fainting Lay patient down and raise lower limbs, EXCEPT IN CASE OF FRACTURE. Loosen tight clothing about neck, waist, and chest, and ensure fresh air.

First-aid kit It is always advisable to carry a first-aid kit.

Shock Loosen any tight clothing, wrap the casualty in a blanket or coat and lay him down at absolute rest.

Alterations to vehicles

If a vehicle constructionally satisfies the law in its country of registration then it should be acceptable in any country into which it has been temporarily imported. Thus no changes should be necessary but there are regulations in some countries which, in the interests of courtesy or safety, should be observed.

Caravan and luggage trailers

Carry a list of contents, as this may be required at a frontier. A towed vehicle should be readily identifiable by a plate in an accessible position showing the name of the maker of the vehicle and his production or serial number.

Common Law claims

In Spain particularly, and to a lesser extent in some other countries, Common Law ie claims to be made against other parties following, for example, a road accident (not to be confused with claims made under the benefits of AA 5-Star Service) are frequently not recoverable in full. Claims for vehicle hiring charges are invariably reduced, and, in certain cases, may not be admissible at all.

If an accident occurs in Spain and your vehicle is repaired in the United Kingdom you are generally only entitled to recover, subject to liability, an amount equal to the cost of repairing the vehicle in Spain which is usually considerably less than the UK cost. AA members may contact the Association's Legal Services, Head Office, for advice on such matters.

Crash helmets

All riders of motorcycles, irrespective of the capacity of their machine, should wear crash helmets.

Dimension and weight restrictions

For an ordinary private car a height limit of 4 metres and a width limit of 2.5 metres is generally imposed. Apart from a laden weight limit imposed on commercial vehicles, every vehicle, private or commercial, has an individual weight limit. See *Overloading* page 229. See also *Major Road Tunnels*, page 241, as some dimensions are restricted by the shape of the tunnels.
If you have any doubts consult the AA.

Drinking and driving

There is only one safe rule – if you drink, don't drive. The laws are strict and penalties severe.

Hazard warning lights

Although four flashing indicators are allowed in the countries covered in this Guide, they in no way affect the regulations governing the use of warning triangles (see p232).

Level crossings

Practically all level crossings are indicated by international signs. Most guarded ones are the lifting barrier type, sometimes with bells or flashing lights to give warning of an approaching train.

Lights

For driving abroad, lights must be so adjusted that they do not dip to the left. The easiest way to achieve this is to use an adapter.

Dipped headlights should be used in conditions of fog, snowfall, heavy rain and when passing through a tunnel, irrespective of its length and its lighting (although this rule may be varied in particular cases. See *Major Road Tunnels*, p241). In some countries police will wait at the end of a tunnel, checking this requirement.

Headlight flashing is generally used as a warning of approach or a passing sign at night. In other circumstances it is accepted as a sign of annoyance or irritation and should be used with caution lest it be misunderstood.

Minibus

A minibus, equipped to carry more than 8 passengers (in addition to the driver) is classed as a commercial passenger-carrying vehicle, and, as such, attracts special regulations including the keeping of a special log recording the driver's hours and a minimum age for driving such vehicles. *It is also a legal requirement that all such vehicles be fitted with a Tachograph.* If you plan to tour in EEC countries with a vehicle in the category described you should contact the local Traffic Area Office of the Department of Transport or, if in Northern Ireland, The Ministry of Development, Belfast, well in advance of your departure.

Mountain passes

Always engage a low gear before either ascending or descending steep gradients, keep well to the right side of the road and avoid cutting corners. Avoid excessive use of brakes. If the engine overheats, pull off the road, making sure you do not cause an obstruction, leave the engine idling, and put the heater controls, including the fan, into the maximum heat position. Under no circumstances remove the radiator cap until the engine has cooled down. Do not fill the coolant system of a hot engine with cold water.

Always engage a lower gear before taking a hair-pin bend, give priority to vehicles ascending and remember that as your altitude increases so your engine power decreases. Priority must always be given to postal coaches travelling in either direction. Their route is usually signposted.

Overloading

This can create safety risks, and in most countries committing such an offence can involve on-the-spot fines. It would also be a great inconvenience if your car was stopped because of overloading – you would not be allowed to proceed until the load had been reduced.

The maximum loaded weight, and its distribution between front and rear axles is decided by the vehicle manufacturer and if your owner's handbook does not give these facts you should seek the advice of the manufacturer direct. There is a public weighbridge in all districts and when the car is fully loaded (not forgetting the passengers, of course) use this to check that the vehicle is within the limits.

When loading a vehicle care should be taken that lights, reflectors, or number plates are not masked or that the drivers view is in no way impaired. All luggage loaded on a roof rack must be tightly secured and should not upset the stability of the vehicle. Any projections beyond the front, rear, or sides of a vehicle must be clearly marked where their projection might not be noticed by other drivers.

Overtaking

When overtaking on roads with two lanes or more in each direction, always signal your intention in good time, and after the manoeuvre, signal and return to the inside lane. Do not remain in any other lane.

Always overtake on the left and use your horn as a warning to the driver of the vehicle being overtaken (except in areas where the use of the horn is prohibited). Do not overtake whilst being overtaken or when a vehicle behind is preparing to overtake. Do not overtake at level crossings, at intersections, the crest of a hill or at pedestrian crossings. When being overtaken keep well to the right and reduce speed if necessary – never increase speed.

Parking

Parking is a problem everywhere in Europe and the police are extremely strict with offenders. Heavy fines are inflicted as well as the towing away of unaccompanied offending cars. This can cause inconvenience and heavy charges are imposed for the recovery of impounded vehicles. You should acquaint yourself with local parking regulations and endeavour to understand all relative signs. As a rule always park on the right-hand side of the road or at an authorised place. As far as possible park off the main carriageway but not on cycle tracks, pedestrian verges, railway lines or tram tracks.

Passengers

It is an offence in all countries to carry more passengers in a car than the vehicle is constructed to seat, but some have regulations as to how the passengers shall be seated. In Austria, Belgium, Finland, Germany (West), Netherlands, Spain and Switzerland it is illegal for children under the age of 12 years (in France and Luxembourg under 10, Hungary 6) to travel in the front seats of a vehicle.

For passenger carrying vehicles constructed and equipped to carry more than 8 passengers in addition to the driver there are special regulations (see *Minibus* p228)

Police fines

Often called 'on-the-spot' fines, police fines can be imposed in one form or another in most countries in Europe by policemen, for minor traffic offences. They are sometimes paid in cash to the policeman and sometimes at a post office against a 'ticket' issued by the policeman. Once paid they cannot be recovered. Such fines are intended to keep minor motoring offences out of courts thus reducing administrative costs to the advantage of the motorist and the police. Nevertheless such fines are very high and punitive. If the motorist disputes the charge he can opt to go before a court but this, in the case of a tourist, can lead to delays, inconvenience and extra expense. Further, as a measure of guarantee or surety, particularly in more serious cases, the policeman is often authorised to demand a sum of money to cover anticipated fines and costs. If the depositing of cash is refused then the police officer can confiscate property to cover any deposits considered necessary. In most cases it is more straightforward to accept the fine but a receipt should always be obtained. Should AA members feel they require assistance in any matter involving local police they should appeal to the Legal Department of the national motoring organisation.

Priority

The general rule is to give way to traffic entering a junction from the right which is sometimes varied at roundabouts. This is the one aspect of European driving which may cause the British driver the most confusion because his whole training and experience makes it unnatural. Road signs indicate priority or loss of priority and tourists are well advised to make sure that they understand such signs.

Great care should be taken at intersections and tourists should never rely on receiving the right of way, particularly in small towns and villages where local traffic, often slow moving such as farm tractors, etc will assume right of way regardless of oncoming traffic.

Always give way to public service and military vehicles. Blind or disabled people, funerals and marching columns must always be allowed right of way.

Vehicles such as buses and coaches carrying large numbers of passengers will expect and should be allowed priority.

See also *Roundabouts*, below.

Road signs

Most road signs through Europe are internationally-agreed and the majority would be familiar to the British motorist. Watch also for road markings – do not cross a solid white or yellow line marked on the road centre.

Roundabouts

Priority at roundabouts is given to vehicles entering the roundabout unless signposted to the contrary. This is a complete reversal to the

United Kingdom rule, and particular care should be exercised when manoeuvring while circulating in an anti-clockwise direction on a roundabout. It is advisable to keep to the outside lane on a roundabout if possible, to make your exit easier.

Rule of the Road

In all European countries, drive on the right and overtake on the left.

Seat belts

All countries in this guide require visitors to wear seat belts, with the exceptions of Italy, Switzerland and Yugoslavia where their use is recommended. If your car is fitted with belts then in the interest of safety, wear them, otherwise you may run the risk of a police fine.

Signals

Signals of a driver's intentions must be given clearly, within a reasonable distance, and in good time. In built-up areas, the general rule is not to use horns unless safety demands it; in many large towns and resorts, as well as in areas indicated by the international sign, the use of the horn is totally prohibited.

Speed limits

It is important to observe speed limits at all times. Offenders may be fined and driving licences impounded on the spot, thus causing great inconvenience and possible expense. The chart (on page 252) gives limits for private cars and are standard legal limits, which may be varied by road signs and where these are displayed the lower limit should be accepted. At certain seasons limits may also be temporarily varied and information would be available at the frontier. It can be an offence to travel without good reason at so slow a speed as to obstruct traffic flow.

Temporary importation

A motor vehicle, caravan, boat, or any other type of trailer is subject to strict control on entering a country and attracts Customs duty and a variety of taxes, but much depends upon the circumstances and the period of the import and also upon the status of the importer. A person entering a country in which he has no residence, with a private vehicle for holiday or recreation purposes and intending to export the vehicle within a short period enjoys special privileges and the normal formalities are reduced to an absolute minimum in the interests of tourism. Importers of any type of commercial vehicle or one to be used to support commercial enterprises do not have the same tolerance.

A person entering a country with a motor vehicle for a period of generally more than three months or to take up residence, employment, or with the intention of disposing of the vehicle should seek advice concerning his position well in advance of his departure. Any AA Service Centre will be pleased to help.

A temporarily imported vehicle should not:
i   be left in the country after the importer has left;
ii   be put at the disposal of a resident of the country;
iii be retained in the country longer than the permitted period;
iv   be lent, sold, hired, given away, exchanged or otherwise disposed of.

A bona fide tourist will generally be allowed to import anything considered in use or in keeping with his status, but such articles, where not consumable, must be exported when the importer leaves the country. In the case of some portable items of high value, *eg* a portable television set, the Customs may make a note in the importer's passport and in his own interest he should ensure the entry is cancelled when exporting the item.

Traffic lights

In principal cities and towns traffic lights operate in a way similar to those in the United Kingdom, although they are sometimes suspended overhead. The density of the light may be so poor that lights could be missed. There is usually only one set on the right-hand side of the road some distance before the road junction, and if you stop too close to the corner the lights will not be visible. Watch out for 'filter' lights which will enable you to turn right at a junction against the main lights. If you wish to go straight ahead do not enter a lane leading to 'filter' lights otherwise you may obstruct traffic wishing to turn right.

Trams

Trams take priority over other vehicles. Always give way to passengers boarding and alighting. Never position a vehicle so that it impedes the free passage of a tram. Trams must be overtaken on the right except in one-way streets.

Tyres

If the tyres on your car conform to British regulations then they would be acceptable abroad – but if you are found with tyres not up to standard then you face a fine and the possibility of being held until the tyres are changed.

Amongst other things, the British regulations state that tyres must display a clearly visible tread and pattern with a tread of at least one millimetre throughout the entire breadth and around the whole circumference.

Warning triangles

In all countries in this book the use of a warning triangle is compulsory, except for two-wheeled vehicles. It should be placed on the road behind a stopped vehicle to warn traffic approaching from the rear of an obstruction ahead. They should be used when a vehicle has stopped for any reason – not only breakdowns.

The triangle should be placed in such a position as to be clearly visible up to 100m (109yds) by day and by night, about 2 feet from the edge of the road but not in such a position as to present a danger to on-coming traffic. It should be set about 30m (33yds) behind the obstruction but this distance should be increased up to 100m (109yds) on motorways.

Hazard warning lights should not be used in place of a triangle but may complement it in use.

Warning triangles can be purchased from the AA.

PASSES AND TUNNELS

Principal mountain passes

It is best not to attempt to cross mountain passes at night, and daily schedules should make allowances for the comparatively slow speeds inevitable in mountainous areas.

Gravel surfaces (such as grit and stone chips) vary considerably; they are dusty when dry, slippery when wet. Where known to exist, this type of surface has been noted. Road repairs can be carried out only during the summer, and may interrupt traffic. Precipitous sides are rarely, if ever, totally unguarded; on the older roads stone pillars are placed at close intervals. Gradient figures take the mean on hairpin bends, and may be steeper on the insides of the curves, particularly on the older roads.

Before attempting late evening or early morning journeys across frontier passes, check the times of opening of the Customs offices. A number of offices close at night eg the Timmelsjoch border crossing is closed between 20.00 and 07.00hrs.

Caravans

Passes suitable for caravans are shown. Those shown to be *negotiable by caravans* are best used only by experienced drivers driving cars with ample power. The remainder are probably best avoided. A correct power-to-load ratio is always essential.

Conditions in winter

Winter conditions are given in italics in the last column. *UO* means usually open although a severe fall of snow may temporarily obstruct the road for 24–48 hours, and wheel chains are often necessary; *OC* means occasionally closed between the dates stated and *UC* usually closed between the dates stated. Dates for opening and closing the passes are approximate only. Warning notices are usually posted at the foot of a pass if it is closed, or if chains or snow tyres should or must be used.

Wheel chains may be needed early and late in the season, and between short spells (a few hours) of obstruction. At these times conditions are usually more difficult for caravans.

In fair weather, wheel chains, or snow tyres are only necessary on the higher passes, but in severe weather you will probably need them (as a rough guide) at altitudes exceeding 2,000ft.

Pass and height	From To	Distances from summit and max gradient		Min width of road	Conditions
*Albula 7,595ft Switzerland (Map 12C1)	Tiefencastel (2,821ft) La Punt (5,546ft)	31km 9km	1 in 10 1 in 10	12ft	*UC Nov–late May.* An inferior alternative to the Julier; tar and gravel; fine scenery. Alternative rail tunnel.
Allos 7,382ft France (Map 28C2)	Barcelonnette (3,740ft) Colmars (4,085ft)	20km 24km	1 in 10 1 in 12	13ft	*UC early Nov–late May.* Very winding, narrow, partially unguarded but not difficult otherwise; passing bays on southern slope, good surface.
Aprica 3,875ft Italy (Map 29 A4)	Tresenda (1,220ft) Edolo (2,264ft)	14km 15km	1 in 11 1 in 16	13ft	*UO.* Fine scenery; good surface, well graded; *suitable for caravans.*

Pass and height	From To	Distances from summit and max gradient	Min width of road	Conditions
Aravis 4,915ft France *(Map 28 C4)*	La Clusaz (3,412ft) Flumet (3,008ft)	8km 1 in 11 12km 1 in 11	13ft	*OC Dec–late Mar.* Outstanding scenery, and a fairly easy road.
Arlberg 5,912ft Austria *(Map 12 C1/2)*	Bludenz (1,905ft) Landeck (2,677ft)	33km 1 in 8 35km 1 in 7½	20ft	*OC Nov–Apr.* Modern road; short steep stretch from west, easing towards the summit; heavy traffic; *negotiable by caravans;* parallel new road tunnel opened Dec 1978.
Aubisque 5,610ft France *(Map 20 C3)*	Eaux Bonnes (2,461ft) Argelès-Gazost (1,519ft)	11km 1 in 10 32km 1 in 10	11ft	*UC early Nov–June.* A very winding road; continuous but easy ascent; the descent incorporates the Col de Soulor (4,757ft); 8km of very narrow, rough, unguarded road, with a steep drop.
Ballon d'Alsace 3,865ft France *(Map 11 A2)*	Giromagny (1,830ft) St-Maurice-Sur-Moselle (1,800ft)	17km 1 in 9 9km 1 in 9	13ft	*OC Dec–Mar.* A fairly straightforward ascent and descent, but numerous bends; *negotiable by caravans.*
Bayard 4,094ft France *(Map 28 C3)*	Chauffayer (2,988ft) Gap (2,382ft)	18km 1 in 12 8km 1 in 7	20ft	*UO.* Part of the Route Napoléon. Fairly easy, steepest on the southern side; *negotiable by caravans* from north or south.
***Bernina** 7,644ft Switzerland *(Map 12 C1)*	Pontresina (5,915ft) Poschiavo (3,317ft)	15.5km 1 in 10 17km 1 in 8	16ft	*OC Nov–late Apr.* During the day, but closed at night. A good road on both sides; *negotiable by caravans.*
Bonaigua 6,797ft Spain *(Map 22 C4)*	Viella (3,150ft) Esterri del Aneu (3,185ft)	23km 1 in 12 16km 1 in 12	14ft	*UC Nov–Apr.* A sinuous and narrow road with many hairpin bends and some precipitous drops; the alternative route to Lèrida through the Viella tunnel is open in winter.
Bracco 2,018ft Italy *(Map 29 A2)*	Riva Trigoso (141ft) Borghetto di Vara (318ft)	15km 1 in 7 18km 1 in 7	16ft	*UO.* A two-lane road with continuous bends; passing usually difficult; *negotiable by caravans;* alternative toll motorway available.
Brenner 4,495ft Austria-Italy *(Map 13 A1)*	Innsbruck (1,885ft) Vipiteno 3,115ft	39km 1 in 12 14.5km 1 in 7	20ft	*UO.* Parallel toll motorway open; heavy traffic may delay at Customs; *suitable for caravans;* Resia Pass and Felbertauern Tunnel possible alternatives.
***Brünig** 3,304ft Switzerland *(Map 11 B1)*	Brienzwiler Station (1,886ft) Giswil (1,601ft)	6km 1 in 12 13km 1 in 12	20ft	*UO.* An easy but winding road; heavy traffic at weekends; *suitable for caravans.*
Bussang 2,365ft France *(Map 11 A2)*	Thann (1,115ft) St-Maurice-sur-Moselle (1,800ft)	22km 1 in 10 8km 1 in 14	13ft	*UO.* A very easy road over the Vosges; beautiful scenery; *suitable for caravans.*
Campolongo 6,152ft Italy *(Map 13 A1)*	Corvara (5,145ft) Arabba (5,253ft)	6km 1 in 8 4km 1 in 8	16ft	*OC Jan–Mar.* A winding but easy ascent; long level stretch on summit followed by easy descent good surface; *suitable for caravans.*
Cayolle 7,631ft France *(Map 28 C2)*	Barcelonnette (3,740ft) Guillaumes (2,687ft)	32km 1 in 10 33km 1 in 10	13ft	*UC early Nov–May.* Narrow and winding road with blind bends.

*Permitted maximum width of vehicles 7ft 6in

Pass and height	From To	Distances from summit and max gradient	Min width of road	Conditions
Costalunga (Karer) 5,752ft Italy *(Map 13 A1)*	Cardano (925ft) Pozza (4,232ftft)	23km 1 in 8 10km 1 in 7	16ft	*UO*. A good well-engineered road; *caravans prohibited.*
Croix-Haute 3,858ft France *(Map 27 B3)*	Monestier-de Clermont (2,776ft) Aspres-sur-Buëch (2,497ft)	36km 1 in 14 28km 1 in 14	18ft	*UO*. Well-engineered; several hairpin bends on the north side; *suitable for caravans.*
Envalira 7,897ft Andorra *(Map 22 C4)*	Pas de la Casa (6,851ft) Andorra (3,375ft)	6km 1 in 12 30km 1 in 10	20ft	*OC Nov–Apr*. A good two-lane road with wide bends on ascent and descent; fine views; *negotiable by caravans.*
Falzarego 6,945ft Italy *(Map 13 A1)*	Cortina d'Ampezzo (3,958ft) Andraz (4,622ft)	17km 1 in 12 9km 1 in 12	16ft	*OC Jan–May*. Well-engineered; bitumen surface; many hairpin bends on both sides; *negotiable by caravans.*
Faucille 4,331ft France *(Map 10 D1)*	Gex (1,985ft) Morez (2,247ft)	11km 1 in 10 28km 1 in 12	13ft	*UO*. Fairly wide, winding road across the Jura mountains; *negotiable by caravans;* but it is probably better to follow La Cure–St-Cergue–Nyon.
Fern 3,969ft Austria *(Map 12 D2)*	Nassereith (2,742ft) Lermoos (3,244ft)	9km 1 in 10 10km 1 in 10	20ft	*UO*. An easy pass but slippery when wet; *suitable for caravans.*
***Flüela** 7,818ft Switzerland *(Map 12 C1)*	Davos-Dorf (5,174ft) Susch (4,659ft)	13km 1 in 10 13km 1 in 8	16ft	*OC Nov–May*. Tolls levied in winter to pay for snow clearance (Nov16–May 15): 5 Swiss Francs per car. Easy ascent from Davos; some acute hairpin bends on the eastern side; bitumen surface; *negotiable by caravans.*
*†**Forclaz** 5,010ft Switzerland– France *(Map 28 C4)*	Martigny (1,562ft) Argentière (4,111ft)	13km 1 in 12 19km 1 in 12	16ft	*UO Forclaz; Montets OC Nov–early Apr*. A good road over the pass and to the frontier; in France narrow and rough over Col des Montets (4,793ft); *negotiable by caravans.*
Fugazze 3,802ft Italy *(Map 29 B4)*	Rovereto (660ft) Valli del Pasubio (1,148ft)	27km 1 in 8 12km 1 in 8	10ft	*UO*. Bitumen surface; several hairpin bends, narrow on northern side.
***Furka** 7,972ft Switzerland *(Map 11 B1)*	Gletsch (5,777ft) Realp (5,066ft)	10km 1 in 10 13km 1 in 10	13ft	*UC late Oct–Jun*. A well-graded modern road, but with narrow sections and several sharp hairpin bends on both ascent and descent. Fine views of the Rhône Glacier.
Galibier 8,385ft France *(Map 28 C3)*	Lautaret Pass (6,751ft) St-Michel-de Maurienne (2,336ft)	7km 1 in 14 34km 1 in 8	10ft	*UC Oct–May*. Mainly wide, well-surfaced but unguarded. Ten hairpin bends on descent then 5km narrow and rough. Rise over the Col du Télégraphe (5,249ft), then eleven more hairpin bends. Tunnel under Galibier summit caved in; new, longer road over summit rises to 8,678ft).
Gardena (Grödner-Joch) 5,959ft Italy *(Map 13 A1)*	Val Gardena (6,109ft) Corvara (5,145ft)	6km 1 in 8 10km 1 in 8	16ft	*OC Nov–late May*. A well-engineered road, very winding on descent.

*Permitted maximum width of vehicles 7ft 6in
†Permitted maximum width of vehicles 8ft 2½in

Pass and height	From To	Distances from summit and max gradient		Min width of road	Conditions
Gavia 8,604ft Italy *(Map 12 D1)*	Bormio (4,019ft) Ponte di Legno (4,140ft)	25km 16km	1 in 5½ 1 in 5½	10ft	*UC early Nov–late Jun.* Steep and narrow but with frequent passing bays; many hairpin bends and a gravel surface; not for the faint-hearted; *extra care necessary.*
Gerlos 5,341ft Austria *(Map 13 A2)*	Zell am Ziller (1,886ft) Wald (2,890ft)	29km 15km	1 in 12 1 in 11	14ft	*UO.* Hairpin ascent out of Zell to modern toll road, the old, steep, narrow, and winding route with passing bays and 1-in-7 gradient is not recommended, but is *negotiable with care.*
†**Grand St Bernard** 8,114ft Switzerland– Italy *(Map 28 C4)*	Martigny (1,562ft) Aosta (1,913ft)	44km 33km	1 in 9 1 in 9	13ft	*UC late Oct– late May.* Modern road to entrance of road tunnel (usually open); then narrow but bitumen surface over summit to frontier; also good in Italy; *suitable for caravans,* using tunnel. Pass road closed to vehicles towing trailers.
*****Grimsel** 7,100ft Switzerland *(Map 11 B1)*	Innertkirchen (2,067ft) Gletsch (5,777ft)	25km 6km	1 in 10 1 in 10	16ft	*UC late Oct–Jun.* A fairly easy, modern road, but heavy traffic at weekends. A long ascent, finally hairpin bends; then a terraced descent with six hairpins into the Rhône valley.
Grossglockner 8,212ft Austria *(Map 13 B2)*	Bruck an der Glocknerstrasse (2,480ft) Heiligenblut (4,268ft)	33km 15km	1 in 8 1 in 8	16ft	*UC late Oct– early May.* Numerous well-engineered hairpin bends; moderate but very long ascents; toll road; very fine scenery; heavy tourist traffic; *negotiable preferably from south to north by caravans.*
Hochtannberg 5,510ft Austria *(Map 12 C2)*	Schröcken (4,163ft) Warth (near Lech) (4,921ft)	6km 4km	1 in 7 1 in 11	13ft	*OC Jan–Mar.* A reconstructed modern road.
Ibañeta (Roncesvalles) 3,468ft France–Spain *(Map 20 C3)*	St-Jean-Pied- de-Port (584ft) Pamplona (1,380ft)	26km 53km	1 in 10 1 in 10	13ft	*UO.* A slow and winding, scenic route; *negotiable by caravans.*
Iseran 9,088ft France *(Map 28 C4)*	Bourg-St-Maurice (2,756ft) Lanslebourg (4,587ft)	49km 33km	1 in 12 1 in 9	13ft	*UC mid Oct–late Jun.* The second highest pass in the Alps. Well-graded with reasonable bends, average surface; several unlit tunnels on northern approach.
Izoard 7,743ft France *(Map 28 C3)*	Guillestre (3,248ft) Briançon (4,396ft)	32km 20km	1 in 8 1 in 10	16ft	*UC late Oct–mid Jun.* A fairly easy but winding road with many hairpin bends.
*****Jaun** 4,948ft Switzerland *(Map 11 B1)*	Broc (2,378ft) Reidenbach (2,759ft)	25km 8km	1 in 10 1 in 10	13ft	*UO.* A modernised but generally narrow road; some poor sections on ascent, and several hairpin bends on descent; *negotiable by caravans.*
*****Julier** 7,493ft Switzerland *(Map 12 C1)*	Tiefencastel (2,821ft) Silvaplana (5,958ft)	36km 7km	1 in 10 1 in 7½	13ft	*UO.* Well-engineered road approached from Chur by Lenzerheide Pass (5,098ft); *suitable for caravans.*
Katschberg 5,384ft Austria *(Map 13 B2)*	Spittal (1,818ft) St Michael (3,504ft)	35km 6km	1 in 5½ 1 in 6	20ft	*UO.* Steep though not particularly difficult; parallel to motorway, including tunnel, no open; *negotiable by light caravans,* using tunnel.

*Permitted maximum width of vehicles 7ft 6in
†Permitted maximum width of vehicles 8ft 2½in

Pass and height	From To	Distances from summit and max gradient	Min width of road	Conditions
*Klausen 6,404ft Switzerland (Map 12 C1)	Altdorf (1,512ft) Linthal (2,165ft)	25km 1 in 11 23km 1 in 11	16ft	*UC early Nov–late May.* Easy in spite of a number of sharp bends; *no through route for caravans as they are prohibited on part of road in Canton of Glarus.*
Larche (della Maddalena) 6,545ft France–Italy (Map 28 C3)	Condamine (4,291ft) Vinadio (2,986ft)	19km 1 in 12 32km 1 in 12	10ft	*OC Nov–Mar.* An easy, well-graded road; narrow and rough on ascent, wider with better surface on descent; *suitable for caravans.*
Lautaret 6,752ft France (Map 28 C3)	Le Bourg-d'Oisans (2,359ft) Briançon (4,396ft)	38km 1 in 8 28km 1 in 10	14ft	*OC Dec–Apr* during the day, but *closed between 19.00–07.00hrs Nov–Apr.* Modern, evenly graded, but winding, and unguarded in places; very fine scenery; *suitable for caravans.*
Loibl (Ljubelj) 3,500ft Austria–Yugoslavia (Map 14 C1)	Unterloibl (1,699ft) Kranj (1,263ft)	10km 1 in 5½ 29km 1 in 8	20ft	*UO.* Steep rise and fall over Little Loibl Pass to tunnel under summit; from south to north just *negotiable by experienced drivers with light caravans.* The old road over the summit is closed to through traffic.
* Lukmanier (Lucomagno) 6,289ft Switzerland (Map 12 C1)	Olivone (2,945ft) Disentis (3,772ft)	18km 1 in 11 22km 1 in 11	16ft	*UC early Nov–early June* Rebuilt, modern road; *suitable for caravans.*
† Maloja 5,960ft Switzerland (Map 12 C1)	Silvaplana (5,958ft) Chiavenna (1,083ft)	11km level 32km 1 in 11	13ft	*UO.* Escarpment facing south; fairly easy but many hairpin bends on descent; *negotiable by caravans, possibly difficult on ascent.*
Mauria 4,258ft Italy (Map 13 B1)	Lozzo Cadore (2,470ft) Ampezzo (1,837ft)	14km 1 in 14 31km 1 in 14	16ft	*UO.* A well-designed road with easy, winding ascent and descent; *suitable for caravans.*
Mendola 4,475ft Italy (Map 12 D1)	Appiano (1,365ft) Sarnonico (3,208ft)	15km 1 in 8 8km 1 in 10	16ft	*UO.* A fairly straightforward, but winding road; well guarded; *suitable for caravans.*
Mont Cenis 6,834ft France-Italy (Map 28 C3)	Lanslebourg (4,587ft) Susa (1,624ft)	11km 1 in 10 28km 1 in 8	16ft	*UC Nov–May.* Approach by industrial valley. An easy, broad highway but with poor surface in places; *suitable for caravans;* alternative rail tunnel.
Monte Croce di Comélico (Kreuzberg) 5,368ft Italy (Map 13A/B1)	San Candido (3,847ft) Santo Stefano di Cadore (2,978ft)	15km 1 in 12 22km 1 in 12	16ft	*UO.* A winding road with moderate gradients; beautiful scenery; *suitable for caravans.*
Montgenèvre 6,100ft France-Italy (Map 28 C3)	Briançon (4,396ft) Cesana Torinese (4,429ft)	11km 1 in 14 8km 1 in 11	16ft	*UO.* An easy, modern road; *suitable for caravans.*
Monte Giovo (Jaufen) 6,869ft Italy (Map 12 D1)	Merano (1,063ft) Vipiteno (3,115ft)	41km 1 in 8 19km 1 in 11	13ft	*UC Nov–early May.* Many well-engineered hairpin bends; *caravans prohibited.*
* Mosses 4,740ft Switzerland (Map 11 A1)	Aigle (1,378ft) Château-d'Oex (3,153ft)	18km 1 in 12 15km 1 in 12	13ft	*UO.* A modern road; *suitable for caravans.*

*Permitted maximum width of vehicles 7ft 6in
†Permitted maximum width of vehicles 8ft 2½in

Pass and height	From To	Distances from summit and max gradient	Min width of road	Conditions
Nassfeld (Pramollo) 5,092ft Austria-Italy *(Map 13 B1)*	Tröpolach (1,972ft) Pontebba (1,841ft)	10km 1 in 5 12km 1 in 10	13ft	*UO.* An alternative to the Plöcken Pass, which is often closed for long periods during the winter. The Austrian section is mostly narrow and winding, with tight, blind bends; the winding descent in Italy has been improved.
Nufenen 8,130ft Switzerland *(Map 11 B1)*	Ulrichen (4,416ft) Airolo (3,745ft)	13km 1 in 10 24km 1 in 10	13ft	*UC mid Oct–mid Jun.* The approach roads are narrow. with tight bends, but the road over the pass is good; *negotiable by light caravans* (limit 1.5 tons).
***Oberalp** 6,709ft Switzerland *(Map 12 C1)*	Andermatt (4,737ft) Disentis (3,772ft)	10km 1 in 10 22km 1 in 10	16ft	*UC early Nov–mid May.* A much improved and widened road with a modern surface; many hairpin bends but long level stretch on summit; *negotiable by caravans.*
***Ofen (Fuorn)** 7.070ft Switzerland *(Map 12 C/D1)*	Zernez (4,836ft) Santa Maria im Münstertal (4,547ft)	22km 1 in 10 14km 1 in 8	12ft	*UO.* Good fairly easy road through the Swiss National Park; *suitable for caravans.*
Petit St Bernard 7,178ft France-Italy *(Map 28 C4)*	Bourg-St-Maurice (2,756ft) Pré-St-Didier (3,335ft)	31km 1 in 20 23km 1 in 12	16ft	*UC late Oct–Jun.* Outstanding scenery; a fairly easy approach but poor surface and unguarded broken edges near the summit; good on the descent in Italy; *negotiable by light caravans.*
Peyresourde 5,128ft France *(Map 20 D3)*	Arreau (2,310ft) Luchon (2,067ft)	18km 1 in 10 14km 1 in 10	13ft	*UO.* Somewhat narrow with several hairpin bends, though not difficult.
***Pillon** 5,070ft Switzerland *(Map 11 B1)*	Le Sépey (3,212ft) Gsteig (2,911ft)	14km 1 in 11 7km 1 in 11	13ft	*UO.* A comparatively easy modern road; *suitable for caravans.*
Plöcken (Monte Croce-Carnico) 4,468ft Austria-Italy *(Map 13 B1)*	Kötschach (2,316ft) Paluzza (1,968ft)	14km 1 in 7 16km 1 in 14	16ft	*OC Dec–Apr.* Nassfeld Pass possible alternative. A modern road with long reconstructed sections; heavy traffic at summer weekends; delay likely at the frontier; *negotiable by caravans;* to avoid congestion caravans are prohibited at summer weekends.
Pordoi 7,346ft Italy *(Map 13 A1)*	Arabba (5,253ft) Canazei (4,806ft)	9km 1 in 10 12km 1 in 10	16ft	*OC Nov–May.* An excellent modern road with numerous hairpin bends; *negotiable by caravans.*
Port 4,098ft France *(Map 22 C4)*	Tarascon (1,555ft) Massat (2,133ft)	18km 1 in 10 13km 1 in 10	14ft	*OC Nov–Apr.* A fairly easy road but narrow on some bends; *negotiable by caravans.*
Portet-d'Aspet 3,507ft France *(Map 22 C4)*	Audressein (1,625ft) Fronsac (1,548ft)	19km 1 in 7 38km 1 in 7	11ft	*UO.* Approached from the west by the easy Col des Ares (2,611ft) and Col de Buret (1,975ft); well-engineered road, but calls for particular care on hairpin bends, rather narrow.
Pötschen 3,221ft Austria *(Map 13 B2)*	Bad Ischl (1,535ft) Bad Aussee (2,133ft)	17km 1 in 11 8km 1 in 11	23ft	*UO.* A modern road; *suitable for caravans.*

*Permitted maximum width of vehicles 7ft 6in

Pass and height	From To	Distances from summit and max gradient		Min width of road	Conditions
Pourtalet 5,879ft France-Spain *(Map 20 C3)*	Eaux-Chaudes (2,152ft) Biescas (2,821ft)	23km 34km	1 in 10 1 in 10	11ft	*UC late Oct–early Jun.* A fairly easy, unguarded road, but narrow in places; poor but being rebuilt on Spanish side.
Puymorens 6,281ft France *(Map 22 C4)*	Ax-les-Thermes (2,362ft) Bourg-Madame (3,707ft)	29km 27km	1 in 10 1 in 10	18ft	*OC Nov–Apr.* A generally easy modern tarmac road, but narrow, winding, and with a poor surface in places; not suitable for night driving; *suitable for caravans.* Alternative rail service available between Ax-les-Thermes and La Tour-de-Carol.
Quillane 5,623ft France *(Map 22 C4)*	Quillan (955ft) Mont-Louis (5,135ft)	63km 5km	1 in 12 1 in 12	16ft	*OC Nov–Mar.* An easy, straightforward ascent and descent; *suitable for caravans.*
Radstädter-Tauern 5,702ft Austria *(Map 13 B2)*	Radstadt (2,808ft) St-Michael (3,504ft)	21km 26km	1 in 6 1 in 7	16ft	*UO.* Northern ascent steep but not difficult otherwise; parallel toll motorway including tunnel now open; *negotiable by light caravans, using tunnel,*
Resia (Reschen-Scheideck) 4,954ft Italy–Austria *(Map 12 D1)*	Spondigna (2,903ft) Prutz (2,841ft)	30km 35km	1 in 10 1 in 10	20ft	*UO.* A good straightforward alternative to the Brenner; *suitable for caravans.*
Restefond (La Bonette) 9,193ft France *(Map 28 C2/3)*	Jausiers (near Barcelonnette) (3,986ft) St-Etienne-de-Tinée (3,766ft)	23km 27km	1 in 9 1 in 9	10ft	*UC early Oct–early Jun.* The highest pass in the Alps. completed in 1962. Narrow, rough, unguarded ascent with many blind bends, and nine hairpins. Descent easier; winding with twelve hairpin bends.
Rolle 6,463ft Italy *(Map 13 A1)*	Predazzo (3,337ft) Mezzano (2,126ft)	21km 25km	1 in 11 1 in 14	16ft	*OC Nov–Mar.* Very beautiful scenery; bitumen surface; a well-engineered road; *negotiable by caravans.*
Rombo (see **Timmelsjoch**)					
Route des Crêtes 4,210ft France *(Map 11 A/B2)*	St-Dié (1,125ft) Cernay (902ft)	— —	1 in 8 1 in 8	13ft	*UC Nov–Apr.* A renowned scenic route crossing seven ridges, with the highest point at Hôtel du Grand Ballon.
†St Gotthard 6,860ft Switzerland *(Map 11 B1)*	Göschenen (3,704ft) Airolo (3,745ft)	19km 15km	1 in 10 1 in 10	20ft	*UC mid Oct–early Jun.* Modern, fairly easy; a new road avoids top twenty-five hairpin bends of the famous terraced descent of thirty-seven bends. Heavy traffic; *negotiable by caravans* (max height vehicles 11ft 9in). Alternative rail tunnel.
*San Bernardino 6,778ft Switzerland *(Map 12 C1)*	Mesocco (2,549ft) Hinterrhein (5,328ft)	22km 8km	1 in 10 1 in 10	13ft	*UC Nov–mid Jun.* Easy, modern roads on northern and southern approaches to tunnel; narrow and winding over summit; via tunnel *suitable for caravans.*
Seeberg (Jezersko) 3,990ft Austria–Yugoslavia *(Map 14 C1)*	Eisenkappel (1,821ft) Kranj (1,263ft)	14km 33km	1 in 8 1 in 10	16ft	*UO.* An alternative to the steeper Loibl and Wurzen passes; moderate climb with winding, hairpin ascent and descent.

*Permitted maximum width of vehicles 7ft 6in
†Permitted maximum width of vehicles 8ft 2½in

Pass and height	From To	Distances from summit and max gradient		Min width of road	Conditions
Sella 7,264ft Italy *(Map 13 A1)*	Plan (5,269ft) Canazei (4,806ft)	9km 9km	1 in 9 1 in 9	16ft	*OC Nov–May.* A finely engineered, winding road; exceptional views of the Dolomites.
Semmering 3,215ft Austria *(Map 14 D2)*	Mürzzuschlag im Mürztal (2,205ft) Gloggnitz (1,427ft)	13km 16km	1 in 16 1 in 16	20ft	*UO.* A fine, well-engineered highway; *suitable for caravans.*
Sestriere 6,660ft Italy *(Map 28 C3)*	Cesana Torinese (4,429ft) Pinerolo (1,234ft)	12km 55km	1 in 10 1 in 10	16ft	*UO.* Mostly bitumen surface; *negotiable by caravans;*
Silvretta (Bielerhöhe) 6,666ft Austria *(Map 12 C1)*	Partenen (3,451ft) Galtür (5,195ft)	15km 10km	1 in 9 1 in 9	16ft	*UC late Oct–early Jun.* For the most part reconstructed; thirty-two easy hairpin bends on western ascent; eastern side more straightforward. Toll road; *caravans prohibited.*
†**Simplon** 6,578ft Switzerland– Italy *(Map 28 D4)*	Brig (2,231ft) Dormodóssola (919ft)	22km 41km	1 in 9 1 in 11	23ft	*OC Nov–Apr.* An easy, reconstructed modern road, but 13 miles long, continuous ascent to summit; *suitable for caravans.* Alternative rail tunnel.
Somport 5,350ft France–Spain *(Map 20 C3)*	Bedous (1,365ft) Jaca (2,687ft)	31km 30km	1 in 10 1 in 10	12ft	*UO.* A favoured, old established route; generally easy, but in parts narrow and unguarded; fairly good-surfaced road; *suitable for caravans.*
*****Splügen** 6,930ft Switzerland– Italy *(Map 12 C1)*	Splügen (4,790ft) Chiavenna (1,083ft)	9km 30km	1 in 9 1 in 7½	10ft	*UC Oct–early June.* Mostly narrow and winding, with many hairpin bends, and not well guarded; care also required at many tunnels and galleries.
††**Stelvio** 9,080ft Italy *(Map 12 D1)*	Bormio (4,019ft) Spondigna (2,903ft)	22km 28km	1 in 8 1 in 8	13ft	*UC Oct–Jun.* The third highest pass in the Alps; the number of acute hairpin bends, all well-engineered, is exceptional – from forty to fifty on either side; the surface is good, the traffic heavy. Hairpin bends are too acute for long vehicles.
†**Susten** 7,300ft Switzerland *(Map 11 B1)*	Innertkirchen (2,067ft) Wassen (3,018ft)	28km 19km	1 in 11 1 in 11	20ft	*UC Nov–Jun.* A very scenic route and a good example of modern road engineering; easy gradients and turns; heavy traffic at weekends; *negotiable by caravans.*
Tenda (Tende) 4,331ft Italy–France *(Map 28 C2)*	Borgo S Dalmazzo (2,103ft) La Giandola (1,059ft)	24km 29km	1 in 11 1 in 11	18ft	*UO.* Well guarded, modern road with several hairpin bends; road tunnel at summit; *suitable for caravans; but prohibited during the winter.*
Thurn 4,177ft Austria *(Map 13 A2)*	Kitzbühel (2,502ft) Mittersill (2,588ft)	19km 11km	1 in 12 1 in 16	16ft	*UO.* A good road with narrow stretches; northern approach rebuilt; *suitable for caravans.*
Timmelsjoch (Rombo) 8,232ft Austria–Italy *(Map 12 D1)*	Obergurgl (6,322ft) Moso (3,304ft)	14km 23km	1 in 7 1 in 8	12ft	*UC mid Oct–late June.* Roadworks on Italian side still in progress. The pass is open to private cars (without trailers) only as some tunnels on the Italian side are too narrow for larger vehicles; toll road.
Tonale 6,181ft Italy *(Map 12 D1)*	Edolo (2,264ft) Dimaro (2,513ft)	30km 27km	1 in 14 1 in 8	16ft	*OC Jan–Apr.* A relatively easy road; *suitable for caravans.*

*Permitted maximum width of vehicles 7ft 6in
†Permitted maximum width of vehicles 8ft 2½in
††Maximum length of vehicle 30ft

Pass and height	From To	Distances from summit and max gradient		Min width of road	Conditions
Tosas 5,905ft Spain *(Map 22 C4)*	Puigcerdá (3,708ft) Ribas de Freser (3,018ft)	25km 25km	1 in 10 1 in 10	16ft	*UO.* Now a fairly straightforward, but continuously winding two-lane road with many sharp bends; some unguarded edges; *negotiable by caravans.*
Tourmalet 6,936ft France *(Map 21 B4)*	Luz (2,333ft) Ste-Marie-de-Campan (2,811ft)	19km 16km	1 in 8 1 in 8	14ft	*UC Oct – late Jun.* The highest of the French Pyrenees routes; the approaches are good though winding and exacting over summit; sufficiently guarded.
Tre Croci 5,935ft Italy *(Map 13 A1)*	Cortina d'Ampezzo (3,983ft) Pelos (2,427ft)	7km 48km	1 in 9 1 in 9	16ft	*UO.* An easy pass; very fine scenery; *suitable for caravans.*
Turracher Höhe 5,784ft Austria *(Map 13 B1)*	Predlitz (3,024ft) Reichenau (3,281ft)	20km 8km	1 in 5½ 1 in 4½	13ft	*UO.* Formerly one of the steepest mountain roads in Austria, now much improved; steep, fairly straightforward ascent, followed by a very steep descent; good surface and mainly two-lane width; fine scenery.
***Umbrail** 8,205ft Switzerland-Italy *(Map 12 D1)*	Santa Maria im Münstertal (4,547ft) Bormio (4,019ft)	13km 19km	1 in 11 1 in 11	14ft	*UC early Nov – mid May.* Highest of the Swiss passes; narrow; mostly gravel-surfaced with thirty-four hairpin bends but not too difficult.
Vars 6,919ft France *(Map 28 C3)*	St-Paul-sur-Ubaye (4,823ft) Guillestre (3,248ft)	8km 20km	1 in 10 1 in 10	16ft	*OC late Nov – late Apr.* Easy winding ascent with seven hairpin bends; gradual winding descent with another seven hairpin bends; good surface; *negotiable by caravans.*
Wurzen (Koren) 3,520ft Austria–Yugoslavia *(Map 13 B1)*	Riegersdorf (1,752ft) Kranjska Gora (2,657ft)	7km 6km	1 in 5½ 1 in 5½	13ft	*UO.* A steep two-lane road which otherwise is not particularly difficult; *caravans prohibited.*
Zirler Berg 3,310ft Austria *(Map 12 D2)*	Seefeld (3,870ft) Zirl (2,041ft)	7km 5km	1 in 7 1 in 6¼	20ft	*UO.* An escarpment facing south, part of the route from Garmisch to Innsbruck; a good modern road but heavy tourist traffic and a long steep descent, with one hairpin bend, into the Inn Valley. Steepest section from the hairpin bend down to Zirl.

Permitted maximum width of vehicles 7ft 6in

MAJOR ROAD TUNNELS

In addition to the nine road tunnels below, more are being planned. The Fréjus road tunnel between France and Italy (12.7km long) and the St Gotthard road tunnel in Switzerland (16.3km long) may now not open until 1980.

Pyrenees *France–Spain*

This new trans-Pyrenean tunnel is now open.

The tunnel is 3km long, and runs nearly 6,000ft above sea level between Aragnouet and Bielsa. *It is probable that there will be a toll.*

Grand St Bernard *Switzerland–Italy*

The tunnel is over 6,000ft above sea level; although there are covered approaches, wheel chains may be needed to reach it in winter. The Customs, passport control, and toll offices are at the entrance. The tunnel is 5.9km long. The permitted maximum dimensions of vehicles are: height 4m (13ft 1in), width 2.5m (8ft 2½in). The minimum speed is 40kph and the maximum 80kph. Do not stop or overtake. There are breakdown bays with telephones on either side. *Tolls payable.*

Mont Blanc *Chamonix (France)–Courmayeur (Italy)*

The tunnel is over 4,000ft above sea level. It is 11.6km long. Customs and passport control are at the Italian end. The permitted maximum dimensions of vehicles are: height 4.15m; length 18m; width 2.5m. Total weight 35 metric tons; axle weight 13 metric tons. The minimum speed is 50kph and the maximum 80kph. Do not stop or overtake. Keep 100m between vehicles. Turn side and rear lights on, but not head-lights. There are breakdown bays with telephones. *Tolls payable.*

San Bernardino *Switzerland*

This tunnel is over 5,000ft above sea level. It is 6.6km long, 4.8m high, and the carriageway is 7m wide.
Do not stop or overtake in the tunnel. Keep 100m between vehicles. Switch on side and rear lights, but not headlights. There are breakdown bays with telephones. *No tolls are charged.*

Arlberg *Austria*

This new tunnel (opened Dec 1978) is 14km (8¾ miles)long and runs at about 4,000ft above sea level, to the south of, and parallel to the Arlberg pass. *Tolls payable.*

Felbertauern *Austria*

This tunnel is over 5,000ft above sea level; it runs between Mittersill and Matrei, west of and parallel to the Grossglockner Pass.
The tunnel is 5.2km long, 4.5m high, and the two-lane carriageway is 7m wide. From November to April wheel chains are usually needed on the approach to the tunnel. *Tolls payable.*

Gleinalm *Austria*

This new tunnel (opened August 1978) is 8.3km (5 miles) long and runs between St Michael and Friesach, near Graz. The tunnel forms part of the A9 Pyhrn autobahn which will in due course run from Linz, via Graz, to Yugoslavia. *Tolls payable.*

Katschberg *Austria*

This tunnel is 3,642ft above sea level, and forms an important part of the Tauern autobahn between Salzburg and Carinthia. The tunnel is 5.4km long, 4.50m high, and the two-lane carriageway is 7.50m wide. *Tolls payable.*

Radstädter Tauern *Austria*

This tunnel is 4,396ft above sea level. It is 6.4km long, and runs east of and parallel to the Tauern railway tunnel. With the Katschberg Tunnel (see above) it forms an important part of the Tauern autobahn between Salzburg and Carinthia. *Tolls payable.*

METRIC EQUIVALENTS

Kilometres		Miles
1.61	1	0.62
3.22	2	1.24
4.83	3	1.86
6.44	4	2.49
8.05	5	3.11
9.66	6	3.73
11.26	7	4.35
12.87	8	4.97
14.48	9	5.59

Metres		Feet
0.30	1	3.28
0.61	2	6.56
0.91	3	9.84
1.22	4	13.12
1.52	5	16.40
1.83	6	19.68
2.13	7	22.97
2.44	8	26.25
2.74	9	29.53

Metres		Yards
0.91	1	1.09
1.83	2	2.19
2.74	3	3.28
3.66	4	4.37
4.57	5	5.47
5.49	6	6.56

Metres		Yards
6.40	7	7.66
7.31	8	8.75
8.23	9	9.85

Kilograms		Pounds
0.45	1	2.20
0.91	2	4.41
1.36	3	6.61
1.81	4	8.82
2.27	5	11.02
2.72	6	13.23
3.17	7	15.43
3.63	8	17.64
4.08	9	19.84

Litres		Gallons
4.55	1	0.22
9.09	2	0.44
13.64	3	0.66
18.18	4	0.88
22.73	5	1.10
27.28	6	1.32
31.82	7	1.54
36.37	8	1.76
40.91	9	1.98

Litres		Pints
0.57	1	1.76
1.14	2	3.52
1.70	3	5.28
2.27	4	7.04
2.84	5	8.80
3.41	6	10.56
3.98	7	12.32
4.55	8	14.08
5.11	9	15.85

Kilograms per sq cm		Pounds per sq in
0.07	1	14.22
0.14	2	28.45
0.21	3	42.67
0.28	4	56.89
0.35	5	71.12
0.42	6	85.34
0.49	7	99.56
0.56	8	113.79
0.63	9	128.01
0.70	10	142.23
1.41	20	284.47
2.11	30	426.71
2.81	40	568.94
3.51	50	711.18
4.22	60	853.41
4.92	70	995.65
5.62	80	1137.88
6.33	90	1280.12

Conversion formulae

If you have a calculator, it is far easier to find metric equivalents by multiplying by the appropriate number.

To convert	Multiply by		
Inches to centimetres	2.540	Gallons to litres	4.546
Centimetres to inches	0.3937	Litres to gallons	0.22
Feet to metres	0.3048	Pints to litres	0.57
Metres to feet	3.281	Litres to pints	1.76
Yards to metres	0.9144	Ounces to grams	28.35
Metres to yards	1.094	Grams to ounces	0.03527
Miles to kilometres	1.609	Pounds to grams	453.6
Kilometres to miles	0.6214	Grams to pounds	0.002205
Kilograms/sq cm to lbs/sq in	14.223	Pounds to kilograms	0.4536
Lbs/sq in to kilograms/sq cm	0.07	Kilograms to pounds	2.205

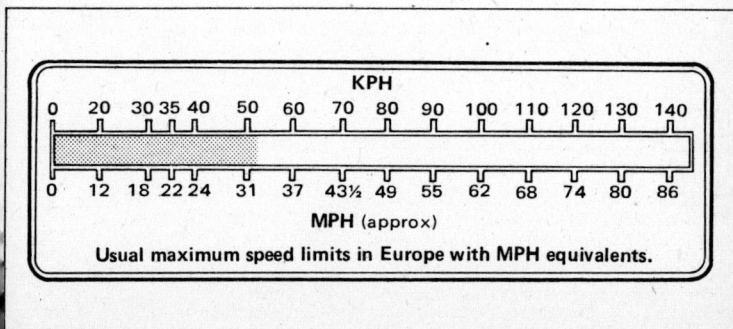

KPH

0	20	30	35	40	50	60	70	80	90	100	110	120	130	140

0	12	18	22	24	31	37	43½	49	55	62	68	74	80	86

MPH (approx)

Usual maximum speed limits in Europe with MPH equivalents.

USEFUL WORDS

This is not meant to be a comprehensive vocabulary and has been compiled specifically for the non-linguist. The AA publication *Car Components Guide* written in twelve languages will also prove useful.

English	French	German	Italian	Spanish
Greetings				
Good morning (afternoon), Sir	Bonjour, monsieur	Guten Morgen, (Guten Tag) Herr X	Buon giorno, Signore	Buenos dias señor
Good evening, Madam	Bonsoir, madame	Guten Abend, Frau X	Buona sera, Signora	Buenas noches, señora
Good-bye, Miss X	Au revoir, mademoiselle	Auf Wiedersehen, Fräulein X	Arrivederci, Signorina	Hasta la vista, Señorita
Excuse me	Excusez-moi	Entschuldigen Sie	Mi scusi	Dispénseme Vd
Please	S'il vous plaît	Bitte	Prego	Por favor
Thank you	Merci	Danke	Grazie	Gracias
Yes. No	Oui. Non	Ja. Nein	Si. No	Si. No
Speaking the language				
Do you speak . . . ?	Parlez-vous . . . ?	Sprechen Sie . . . ?	Parla . . . ?	¿Habla Vd . . . ?
I speak . . .	Je parle . . .	Ich spreche . . .	Io parlo . . .	Yo hablo . . .
I do not speak . . .	Je ne parle pas . . .	Ich spreche nicht . . .	Io non parlo . . .	Yo no hablo . . .
French	français	französisch	francese	francés
English	anglais	englisch	inglese	inglés
Spanish	espagnol	spanisch	spagnolo	español
Portuguese	portugais	portugiesisch	portoghese	portugués
German	allemand	deutsch	tedesco	aleman
Italian	italien	italienisch	italiano	italiano
Dutch	hollandais	holländisch	olandese	holandés
Danish	danois	dänisch	danese	danés
Do you understand . . . ?	Comprenez-vous . . . ?	Verstehen Sie . . . ?	Capisce . . . ?	Comprende Vd . . . ?
I do not understand . . .	Je ne comprends pas . . .	Ich verstehe nicht . . .	Non capisco . . . ?	No comprendo .
Speak slowly	Parlez lentement	Sprechen Sie langsam	Parli adagio	Hable Vd despacio
Could you repeat it?	Répétez	Wiederholen Sie	Ripeta	Repita
At the bank				
Where is a Bureau de Change?	Où se trouve le bureau de change?	Wo ist eine Wechselstube?	Dove si trova un ufficio cambi?	¿Dónde hay una oficina de cambio?
Can I change some Pounds Sterling?	Puis-je changer ces livres?	Kann ich diese Pfund Sterling wechseln?	Posso cambiare delle sterline?	¿Puedo cambiar unas Libras?
Can I cash this cheque here?	Puis-je encaisser ce chèque ici?	Kann ich diesen Scheck einlösen?	Posso riscuotere questo cheque?	¿Puedo cobrar este cheque aquí?
I have a Eurocard/ bankcard	J'ai une Euro-carte/une carte bancaire	Ich habe eine Eurokarte/ Scheckkarte	Ho una Eurocard/ cartolina di banca	Tengo Eurocheque tarjeta de crédito
At the hotel				
Where is the Hotel . . . ?	Où se trouve l'Hôtel . . . ?	Wo ist das Hotel . . . ?	Dov'è l'Albergo . . . ?	¿Dónde esta el Hotel . . . ?
Where is a telephone?	Où se trouve un téléphone?	Wo ist ein Telephon?	Dov'è c'è un telefono?	¿Dónde hay un teléfono?
Have you a room, two rooms . . . ?	Avez-vous une chambre, deux chambres . . . ?	Haben sie ein Zimmer, zwei Zimmer . . . ?	Avete una camera, due camere . . . ?	¿Tiene una habitación, dos habitaciones . .

& PHRASES

Dutch	Portuguese	Danish	Serbo-Croat
Goeden morgen (goeden middag), Meneer	Bom dia	God morgen (god dag), Hr.	Dobar dan, gospodine
Goedenavond, mevrouw	Boa tarde, minha senhora	God aften, Frue	Dobro veče gospodo
Tot ziens, juffrouw	Adeus	Farvel, Frøken	Dovedenja, gospodice
Neemt u mij niet kwaliijk	Desculpe	Undskyld	Izvinite
Alstublieft	Faz favor	Vær så venlig at . . .	Molim
Dank u wel	Obrigado	Tak	Hvala
Ja. Nee	Sim. Não	Ja. Nej	Da. Ne

Dutch	Portuguese	Danish	Serbo-Croat
Spreekt u . . . ?	Fala . . . ?	Taler De . . . ?	Govorite li . . . ?
Ik spreek . . .	Falo . . .	Jeg taler . . .	Govorim . . .
Ik spreek geen . . .	Não falo . . .	Jeg taler ikke . . .	Ne govorim . . .
Frans	francês	fransk	Francuski
Engels	inglês	engelsk	engleski
Spaans	espanhol	spansk	španski
Portugees	português	portugisisk	portugalski
Duits	alemão	tysk	nemački
Italiaans	italiano	italiensk	talijanski
Nederlands	holandês	hollandsk	holandski
Deens	dinamarquês	dansk	danski
Verstaat u . . . ?	Compreende . . . ?	Forstår De . . . ?	Razumete li . . . ?
Ik versta geen . . .	Não compreendo . . .	Jeg forstår ikke . . .	Ne razumen . . .
Spreek langzaam	Fale lentamente se faz favor	Tal lengsomt	Govorite lagano
Kunt u dat herhalen	Repita, se faz favor	Vil De gentage?	Ponovite

Dutch	Portuguese	Danish	Serbo-Croat
Waar is een wisselkantoor?	Onde é um Bureau de Change?	Hvor et der et vekselkontor?	Gde je menjačnica?
Kan ik Engelse ponden wisselen?	Posso cambiar livras esterlinas?	Kan jeg veksle nogle pund sterling?	Mogu li razmeniti funte sterling?
Kan ik deze cheque hier verzilveren?	Posso descontar este cheque aqui?	Kan jeg indløse denne check her?	Mogu li unovčiti ovaj ček ovde?
Ik heb een Eurokaart/ bankkaard	Tenho uma Eurocard/carta bancária	Jeg har et Eurokort/ bankkort	Imam Eurocard/ bankovnu karticu

Dutch	Portuguese	Danish	Serbo-Croat
Waar is Hotel . . . ?	Onde é o Hotel . . . ?	Hvor er Hotel . . . ?	Gde je Hotel . . . ?
Waar is een telefoon?	Onde é um telefono?	Hvor er der en telefon?	Gde je telefon?
Heeft u een kamer, twee kamers . . . ?	Tem uma camara, duas camaras . . . ?	Har De et værelse, to værelser . . . ?	Imate li sobu, dve sobe . . . ?

English	French	German	Italian	Spanish
. . . for one night, for two nights . . . ?	. . . pour une nuit, pour deux nuits . . . ?	. . . für eine Nacht, für zwei Nächte . . . ?	. . . per una notte, per due notti . . . ?	. . . para una noche, para dos noches . . . ?
. . . for one person, two persons . . . ?	. . . pour une personne, pour deux personnes . . . ?	. . . für eine Person, für zwei Personen . . . ?	. . . per una persona, per due persone . . . ?	. . . para una persona, para dos personas . . . ?
. . . with a single bed, double bed, two beds . . . ?	. . . à un lit, à un grand lit, à deux lits . . . ?	. . . mit einem Einzelbett, mit einem Doppelbett, mit zwei Betten . . . ?	. . . con un letto per una persona, matrimoniale, due letti . . . ?	con cama sencilla, cama doble, dos camas . . . ?
. . . with bath, shower, WC?	. . . avec bain, douche, WC?	. . . mit Bad, Dusche, Toilette?	. . con bagno, doccia, WC?	. . . con baño, ducha, water?
No vacancies	complet	Voll	Completo	No hay habitaciones
May I see the room, please?	Puis-je regarder la chambre s'il vous plaît?	Kann ich das Zimmer besichtigen, bitte?	Posso vedere la camera, per favore?	¿Puedo ver las habitaciones, por favor?

At the shops

English	French	German	Italian	Spanish
How much?	Combien? *	Wieviel?	Quanto?	¿Cuánto cuesta?
Yes, that's fine (meaning, 'Yes, I'll have it . . .')	Oui, je l'achête	Ja, das möchte ich	Va bene	Si, està bien
Too dear	Trop cher	Zu teuer	Troppo caro	Demasiado caro

Telling the time

English	French	German	Italian	Spanish
Yesterday	Hier	Gestern	Ieri	Ayer
Tonight	Cette nuit	Heute Nacht	Questa notte	Esta noche
This morning	Ce matin	Heute Morgen	Questa mattina	Esta mañana
Today	Aujourd'hui	Heute	Oggi	Hoy
This afternoon	Cet après-midi	Heute Nachmittag	Questo pomeriggio	Esta tarde
At noon	A midi	Um Mittag	A mezzogiorno	A mediodïa
At midnight	A minuit	Um Mitternacht	A mezzanotte	A medianoche
This evening	Ce soir	Heute Abend	Questa sera	Esta noche
Tomorrow	Demain	Morgen	Domani	Mañana
The day after tomorrow	Après-demain	Übermorgen	Dopo domani	Pasado mañana
Early. Late	Tôt. Tard	Früh. Spät	Presto. Tardi	Temprano. Tarde
At once	Tout de suite	Sofort	Subìto	En seguida
Minute (in time)	Minute	Minute	Minuto	Minuto
Hour	Heure	Stunde	Ora	Hora
What time is it?	Quelle heure est-il?	Wieviel Uhr ist es?	Che ore sono?	¿Qué hora es?

Dining out

English	French	German	Italian	Spanish
Can we eat here?	Peut-on manger ici?	Kann man hier essen?	Possiamo mangiare qui?	¿Se puede comer aqui?
Have you a table for 2 (3, 4, 5, 6)?	Avez-vous une table pour deux (trois, quatre cinq, six)?	Haben sie einen Tisch für zwei (drei, vier, fünf, sechs)?	Avete una tavola per due (tre, quattro, cinque, sei)?	¿Tiene una mesa para dos (tres cuatro, cinco, seis)?
What time is . . .	A quelle heure est . . .	Um wieviel Uhr servieren Sie (gibt es)?	A che ora é . . . ?	¿A qué hora se sirve . . . ?
breakfast	le petit déjeuner	das Frühstück	la prima colazione	el desayuno
lunch	le déjeuner	das Mittagessen	la colazione	el almuerzo
dinner	le dîner	das Abendessen	il pranzo	la comida
How much is the meal?	Quel est le prix du repas?	Was kostet die Mahlzeit?	Qual è il prezzo del pasto?	¿Cuánto cuesta el cubierto?
Show me the menu	Montrez-moi le menu	Zeigen Sie mir das Menü	Mi faccia vedere la lista delle vivande	Muéstreme el menú
Give me the wine list	Donnez-moi la carte des vins	Geben Sie mir die Weinkarte	Mi dia la lista dei vini	Déz Vd la lista de vinos

Something to eat

English	French	German	Italian	Spanish
I should like . . .	Je voudrais . . .	Ich möchte . . .	Vorrei . . .	Yo quería . . .
We would like . . .	Nous voudrions . . .	Wir möchten . . .	Vorremmo . . .	Queremos . . .

Dutch	Portuguese	Danish	Serbo-Croat
. . . voor één nacht, voor twee nachten . . . ?	. . . para uma noite, para duas noites . . . ?	. . . for en nat, for to nætter . . . ?	. . . za jadnu noć, za dve noći . . . ?
. . . voor één persoon, voor twee personen . . . ?	. . . para uma pessoa, para duas pessoas . . . ?	. . . til en person, til to personer . . . ?	. . . za jednu osobu, za dve osobe . . . ?
. . . met een éénpersoonsbed, dubbel bed, twee bedden . . . ?	. . . com uma cama para uma só pessoa, cama de casal, duas camas . . . ?	. . . med enkeltseng, dobbeltseng, to senge . . . ?	. . . sa jednim krevetom, duplim krevetom, dva kreveta . . . ?
. . . met bad, douche, toilet?	. . . com banho, com chuveiro, WC?	. . . med bad, brusebad, WC?	. . . sa kupatilom, tušem, toaletom?
Vol	Completo	Ingen ledige værelser	Nema mesta
Kan ik de kamer alstublieft zien?	Posso ver a cámara, faz favor?	Må jeg se værelset?	Mogu li videti sobu?
Hoeveel?	Quanto?	Hvad koster det?	Koliko?
Ja, dat is goed	Sim, muito bem	Ja, jeg vil gerne have det	Da, uzeću to
Te duur	Muito caro	For dyrt	Preskupo
Gisteren	Ontem	I går	Juče
Vannacht	Esta noite	I nat, i aften	Noćas
Vanmorgen	Esta manhã	Til morgen	Jutros
Vandaag	Hoje	I dag	Danas
Vanmiddag	Esta tarde	I eftermiddag	Danas popodne
Om twaalf uur	Ao meio-dia	Til middag	U podne
Om middernacht	À meia-noite	Ved midnat	U ponoć
Vanavond	Esta noite	I aften	Večeras
Morgen	Amanhã	I morgen	Sutra
Overmorgen	Depois de amanhã	I overmorgen	Prekosutra
Vroeg. Laat	Cedo. Tarde	Tidligt. Sent	Rano. Kasno
Dadelijk	Imediatamente	Med det samme	Odmah
Minuut	Minuto	Minut	Minuta
Uur	Hora	Time	Sat, čas
Hoe laat is het?	Que horas são?	Hvad er klokken?	Koliko je sati?
Kunnen we hier eten?	Podemos comer aqui?	Kan vi spise her?	Možemo li dobiti jelo ovde?
Heeft u een tafel voor twee (drie, vier, vijf, zes)?	Tem uma mesa para dois (três, quatro, cinco, seis)?	Har De et bord til to (tre, fire, fem, secks)?	Imate li sto za dve (tri, četiri, pet šest) osobe?
Hoe laat is . . . ?	A que horas é . . . ?	Hvornår er der . . . ?	U koliko sati je . . .
het ontbijt	o pequeno almoço	morgenmad	doručak
de lunch	o almoço	frokost	ručak
het avondeten	o jantar	middag	večera
Hoeveel kost de maaltijd?	Qual é o preço da refeição?	Hvad koster måltidet?	Koja je cena obeda?
Kan ik het menu zien?	Mostre-me a ementa	Vis mig menu-kortet	Pokažite mi jelovnik
Kan ik de wijnkaart zien?	Dê-me a carta dos vinhos	Giv mig vinkortet	Dajte mi vinsku kartu
Ik zou graag . . .	Eu queria . . .	Jeg vil gerne have	Želeo bih . . .
Wij zouden graag . . .	Desejaríamos . . .	Jeg vil gerne have . . .	Želeli bi . . .

English	French	German	Italian	Spanish
some soup	de la soupe	Suppe	della zuppa, della minestra	Sopa
some fish	du poisson	Fisch	del pesce	pescado
some meat	de la viande	Fleisch	della carne	carne
a chop or a cutlet	une côtelette	ein Kotelett	una cotoletta	una chuleta
some veal	du veau	Kalbfleisch	del vitello	ternera
some beef	du bœuf	Rindfleisch	del manzo	vaca
some lamb	du mouton	Hammelfleisch, Schaffleisch	dell' agnello	cordero
some pork	du porc	Schweinefleisch	del maiale	cerdo
some ham	du jambon	Schinken	del prosciutto	jamón
some chicken	du poulet	Huhn	del pollo	pollo
some beefsteak	du bifteck	Beefsteak	una bistecca	bistek ...
... underdone,	... saignant	... blutig (englisch)	... al sangue	... poco pasado
... well done	... bien cuit	... durch gebraten, gar	... ben cotta	... bien pasado
... medium done	... à point	... halbenglisch	... cotta a puntino	... a punto
some bread	du pain	Brot	del pane	pan
some butter	du beurre	Butter	del burro	mantequilla
Rice	du riz	Reis	del riso	arroz
some eggs	des œufs	Eier	della uova	huevos
an omelette	une omelette	eine Omelette	una frittata	una tortilla
a salad	une salade	Salat	una in-salata	ensalada
some vegetables	des légumes	Gemüse	dei legumi	legumbres
some potatoes	des pommes de terre	Kartoffeln	delle patate	patatas
Cabbage	du chou	Kohl	cavolo	coles
Cauliflower	du chou-fleur	Blumenkohl	cavolfiori	coliflores
Green peas	des petits pois	Grüne Erbsen	dei pisellini	guisantes
Beans	des haricots	Bohnen	dei fagiuoli	habichuelas, judías
(with) no garlic please	(avec) sans ail, s'il vous plait	(mit) ohne Knoblauch bitte	per favore (con) senza aglio	por favor (con) sin ajo
Cheeses	Fromages	Käse	Formaggio	Queso
Fruits	Fruits	Früchte	Frutta	Frutas
Biscuits	Biscuits	Biskuits, Kekse	Biscotti	Bizcochos
Tart	Tarte	Torte	Torta	Tarta
Pastries	Pâtisseries	Feines Gebäck	Pasticceria	Pastelería
Jam	De la confiture	Konfitüre	Della marmellata	mermelada
Ice creams	Glaces	Eis	Gelato	Helados

Something to drink

English	French	German	Italian	Spanish
A bottle	Une bouteille	Eine Flasche	Una bottiglia	Una botella
Half a bottle	Une demi-bouteille	Eine halbe Flasche	Una mezza bottiglia	Media botella
Water	De l'eau	Wasser ...	Dell'acqua	Agua
Iced water	... glacée	eisgehühltes Wasser	... ghiacciata	...helada
Hot water	... chaude	warmes Wasser	... calda	... caliente
White wine	Du vin blanc	Weisswein	Del vino bianco	Vino blanco
Red wine	Du vin rouge	Rotwein	Del vino rosso	Vino tinto
Rosé wine	Du vin rosé	Wein Rosé	Vino rosato	Vino rosado
Lemonade	De la citronnade	Limonade	Una limonata	Limonada
Beer	De la bière	Bier	Della birra	Cerveza
Mineral water	De l'eau minérale	Mineralwasser	Dell'acqua minerale	Agua mineral
Liqueurs	Des liqueurs	Liköre	Dei liquori	Licores
Coffee	Du café	Kaffee	Del caffè	Café
Tea	Du thé	Tee	Del tè	Té
Milk	Du lait	Milch	Del latte	Leche
Sugar	Du sucre	Zucker	Dello zucchero	Azúcar
Chocolate	Du chocolat	Schokolade	Della cioccolata	Chocolate
Cream	De la crême	Sahne	Della panna	Crema

The finale

English	French	German	Italian	Spanish
Waiter! the bill	Garçon! l'addition	Kellner! die Rechnung	Cameriere! Il conto	¡Camarero! la cuenta
Are tips included	Pourboire compris?	Ist das Trinkgeld inbegriffen?	Mancia compresa?	¿Está incluída la propina?
Service included	Service compris	Bedienung inbegriffen	Servizio compreso	Servicio incluído

248

Dutch	Portuguese	Danish	Serbo-Croat
willen/soep	sopa	. . . suppe	corbu
vis	peixe	fisk	ribu
vlees	carne	kød	meso
karbonade	uma costeleta	en kotelet	kotlet
kalfsvlees	vitela	kalvekød	teletinu
rundvlees	vaca	oksekød	govedinu
schapevlees	carneiro	fårekød	jagnjetinu
varkensvlees	porco	svinekød	svinjetinu
ham	presunto	skinke	sunku
kip	frango	kylling	piletinu
biefstuk	bife	engelsk bøf	biftek
. . . niet gaar/ rood van binnen	em sangue	rød	krvav
. . . goed doorgebakken/ gaar	bem passado	gennemstegt	dobropečen
. . . half gaar	passado	mellem	srednje pečen
brood	pão	noget brød	hleb
boter	manteiga	noget smør	maslac puter
rijst	arroz	ris	pirinač
eieren	ovos	nogle æg	jaja
een omelet	uma omelette	en omelet	omlet
een salade/sla	uma salada	en salat	salata
groenten	legumes	nogle grønsager	povrće
aardappelen	batatas	nogle kartofler	krompir
Kool	couve	kål	kupus
Bloemkool	couve-flor	blomkål	karfiol
Doperwtjes	ervilhas	grønærter	mladi grašak
boontjes	feijão	bønner	pasulj
(met) zonder knoflook alstublieft	(com) dem alho se faz favor	(med) uden hvidløg, tak	sa češnjakom (sa belim lukom bez belog luka)
Kaas	Queijos	Ost	Sir
Fruit	Frutas	Frugt	Voće
Beschuit, crackers	Biscoitos	Biscuits	Biskviti, keksi
taartje	Torta	Tærte	Torta
Gebak	Pastelaria	Kager	Kolači, pecivo
Jam	Compota	Syltetøj	Marmelada, džem
Ijs	Gelados	Is	Sladoled

Dutch	Portuguese	Danish	Serbo-Croat
Een fles	Uma garrafa	En flaske	Boca, flaša
Een halve fles	Uma meia-garrafa	En halv flaske	Pola boce, Flaše
Water	Agua	Vand	Voda
Ijswater	. . . gelada	Isvand	. . . ledena, hladna
Heet water	quente	varmt vand	topla
Witte wijn	Vinho branco	Hvidvin	Belo vino
Rode wijn	Vinho tinto	Rødvin	Crno vino
Rosé	Vinho rosado	Rosévin	Ružicu vino
Seven-up	Limonada	Lemonade	Limunada
Bier	Cerveja	Øl	Pivo
Mineraal water	Água mineral	Apollinaris	Mineralna voda
Likeurs	Licores	Likør	Likeri
Koffie	Café	Kaffe	Kafa
Thee	Chá	Te	Čaj
Melk	Leite	Mælk	Mleko
Suiker	Açúcar	Sukker	Šećer
Chocolademelk	Chocolate	Chokolade	Čokolada
Room	Natas	Fløde	Slag

Dutch	Portuguese	Danish	Serbo-Croat
Ober! de rekening	Faz favor! a conta	Tjener! regningen	Konobar! platiti
Is een fooi inbegrepen?	a gorjeta está incluída?	Er det med betjening?	Da li je servis uključen?
Inclusief bediening	Serviço incluido	Betjening inkluderet	Servis uračunat

English	French	German	Italian	Spanish
At the garage				
Fill up the tank, please . . .	Faites le plein s'il vous plaît . . .	Füllen Sie den Tank bitte . . .	Mi faccia il pieno . . .	Sirvase llenar el depósito . . .
with petrol	d'essence	mit Benzin	di benzina	de gasolina
with oil	d'huile	mit Öl	d'olio	de aceite
Give me five, ten, twenty, thirty litres of petrol	Mettez-moi cinq dix, vingt, trente litres d'essence	Geben Sie mir fünf, zehn, zwanzig, dreissig Liter Benzin	Mi metta cinque, dieci, venti, trenta litri di benzina	Póngame cinco diez veinte, treinta litros de gasolina
My car won't start	Ma voiture ne démarre pas	Mein Wagen fährt nicht an	La mia automobile non si mette in moto	Mi coche no arranca
Please check the oil, the water, the tyre pressures	Veuillez vérifier le niveau d'huile, le niveau d'eau, la pression des pneus	Bitte kontrollieren Sie den Ölstand, den Wasserstand, den Reifendruck	Si prega di controllare l'olio, l'acqua, la pressione delle gomme	Por favor, compruebe aceite, agua, presión de las ruedas
Have you got this bulb, windscreen wiper?	Avez-vous une telle ampoule, un tel essuie-glace?	Haben Sie eine solche Birne, einen solchen Scheibenwischer?	Avete questa lampadina, questo tergicristallo?	¿Tiene este tipo de bombilla, limpiapara-brisas
Can you mend . . .	Pouvez-vous réparer . . .	Können Sie . . .	Potete riparare . . .	¿Puede reglar . .
. . . my car?	. . . ma voiture?	. . . meinen Wagen . . .	. . . la mia mecchina?	. . . el coche?
. . . my engine?	. . . le moteur?	. . . den Motor . . .	. . . ol mio motere?	. . . el motor?
. . . the clutch?	. . . l'embrayage?	. . . die Kupplung . . .	. . . l'innesto?	. . . el embrague?
. . . the ignition?	. . . l'allumage?	. . .die Zündung. . .	. . . l'accensione?	. . . el encendido
. . . the radiator (hose)?	. . . le radiateur (durite)?	. . . den Kühler (Schlauch) . . .	. . . il radiatore (manicotto)?	. . . el (tubo de goma del) radiador?
. . . the brakes?	. . . les freins?	. . .die Bremsen . . .	. . . i freni?	. . . los frenos?
. . . the electrical system?	. . . le systéme éléctrique?	. . . die elektrische Austrüstung . . .	. . . l'impianto elettrico?	. . . el equipo electico?
. . . this tyre?	. . . ce pneu?	. . . diesen Reifen . . . . . . reparieren?	. . . questa gomma?	. . . este neumático?
How long will it take?	Pour quand sera-t-elle prête?	Bis wann?	Quanto tempo ci vorrà?	¿Cuando estará listo?
How much will it cost?	Combien coûtera-t-elle?	Wieviel kostet sie?	Quanto costerà?	¿Cuánto costará
I wish to hire a car	Je désire louer une automobile . . .	Ich möchte ein Auto . . . mieten	Vorrei noleggiarc una automobile	Deseo alquilar un automóvil

Dutch	Portuguese	Danish	Serbo-Croat
Vul de tank ... ... alstublieft	Encha o depósito	Vær så venlig at fylde tanken op	Napunite, molim vas
... met benzine ...	de gasolina	med benzin	benzin
... met olie ...	de óleo	med olie	ulje
Kan ik vijf, tien, twintig, dertig liter benzine hebben?	meta, cinco, dez, vente, trinta litros de gasolina	Vær så venlig at give mig fem, ti, tyve, tredive liter benzin	Sipajte mi pet, deset, dvadeset, trideset, litara benzina
Mijn wagen start niet	O meu carro não arranca	Min bil vil ikke starte	Moja kola ne mogu da upale
Kijkt u alstublieft de olie, het water, de wieldruk na	Queira verificar o aciete, a agua, a pressão dos pneus	Vil De kontrollere oliestanden, vandet, dæktrykket?	Molim proverite ulje, vodu, pritisak u gumama
Heeft u deze lamp, ruitenwisser?	Tem o Senhor esta lámpara, este limpador de parabrisas?	Har De såden en pære, vinduesvisker?	Imate li ovu sijalicu, brisač?
Kunt u ...	Pode o Senhor concerter ...	Kan De reparere ...	Možete li opraviti ...
... mijn auto ...	... o meu carro?	... min bil?	... moja kola?
... de motor ...	... o meu motor?	... motoren?	... motor?
... de koppeling ...	... a embriagem?	... koblingen?	... kvačilo?
... de ontsteking ...	... a ignição?	... tændigen?	... starter/ paljenje?
... de radiator (slang) ...	... o radiador (a mangueira do radiador)?	... køleren (kølerslangen)?	... hladnjak (crevo)?
... de remmen ...	... os freios?	... bremserne?	... kočnice?
... het elektrisch systeem ...	... a instalação electrica?	... det elektriske system?	... električni system?
... deze band ... ... repareren?	... este pneu?	... dette dæk?	... ovu gumu?
Hoe lang duurt het?	Quanto tempo levará?	Hvor længe vil det tage?	Koliko dugo će trajati?
Hoeveel kost dat?	quanto custa a reparação?	Hvor meget vil det koste?	koliko ćé stajati opravka?
Ik wil een auto huren	Quero alugar um automóvel	Jeg vil gerne leje en bil	Hteo bih da unajmin jedna

	Speed limits in KPH (MPH)				Warning triangle X=use compulsory	Seat belts	Petrol (see also p56)				
	In built-up areas	Outside built-up areas	Motorways	With trailer			Currency	Per litre at pump Super	Octane	Per litre at pump Regular	Octane
Austria	50 (31)	100 (62)	130 (80)	100 (62)	X	X	Schilling	7	96/99	6.60	87/92
Belgium	60 (37)	90 (56)	120 (74)	–	X	X	Franc	15.80	98	15.42	92/94
Denmark	60 (37)	90 (56)	110 (68)	70 (43)	X	X	Krone	2.73	97/99	2.65	93
France	60 (37)	90 (56)	130 (80)	–	X	X	Franc	2.68	98	2.48	90
Germany	50 (31)	100 (62)	130 (80)	80 (49)	X	X	Mark	0.91/1.00	97/99	0.84/0.96	91/92
Italy 601-900cc / 901-1300cc / over 1300cc	50 (31)	90 (56) / 100 (62) / 110 (68)	110 (68) / 130 (80) / 140 (87)	–	X	Wearing recommended	Lire	*500	96/100	*485	84/86
Luxembourg	60 (37)	90 (56)	120 (74)	–	X	X	Franc	12.66	97/99	12.20	90/92
Netherlands	50 (31)	80 (49)	100 (62)	80 (49)	X	X	Florin	1.09	98	1.05	96
Portugal	60 (37)	90 (56)	120 (74)	70 (43)	X	X	Escudos	26.00	98	23.00	85
Spain	60 (37)	90 (56)	100 (62)	70 (43)	X	X	Pesetas	37/40	96/98	31.00	90
Switzerland	60 (37)	100 (62)	130 (80)	80 (49)	X	Wearing recommended	Franc	0.99/1.05	98/99	0.95/1.01	90/92
Yugoslavia	60 (37)	80 (49)	–	80 (49)	Use recommended	Wearing recommended	Dinar	*7.00	98	*6.70	86/88

*Subject to coupon reduction – see p56

Limits may be varied by signs in which case the lower limit must be observed

INDEX

Accommodation report form (confidential) 1979/80

To:	The Automobile Association, Publications Research Unit, Fanum House, Basingstoke, Hants RG21 2EA.

Town	
Country	
Hotel	
Location	
Date	
Food	
Rooms	
Service	
Sanitary arrangements	
Value for money	
Name (block letters)	
Address (block letters)	
Tel no.	
Membership number	
for office use only	acknowledged recorded
General remarks overleaf	

Accommodation report form (confidential)

General remarks

_____

_____

_____

_____

_____

_____

_____

_____

_____

_____

_____

_____

_____

_____

_____

_____

_____

_____

_____

_____

_____

_____

_____

We welcome comments on any establishments you may have stayed in. If there is insufficient room on this report form please continue on a separate sheet, using this form as a guide.